NEURAL NETWORKS FOR KNOWLEDGE REPRESENTATION AND INFERENCE

NEURAL NETWORKS FOR KNOWLEDGE REPRESENTATION AND INFERENCE

Edited by

DANIEL S. LEVINE

MANUEL APARICIO IV

The University of Texas at Arlington

Psychology Press
Taylor & Francis Group

New York London

First Published by
Lawrence Erlbaum Associates, Inc., Publishers
10 Industrial Avenue
Mahwah, New Jersey 07430

Transferred to Digital Printing 2009 by Psychology Press
270 Madison Ave, New York NY 10016
27 Church Road, Hove, East Sussex, BN3 2FA

Library of Congress Cataloging-in-Publication Data

Neural networks for knowledge representation and inference / Daniel S.
  Levine and Manuel Aparicio IV, editors.
      p.   cm.
  Includes bibliographical references and index.
  ISBN 0-8058-1158-3. -- ISBN 0-8058-1159-1 (pbk.)
    1. Neural networks (Computer science) 2. Knowledge representation
  (Information theory)   I. Levine, Daniel S. II. Aparicio, Manuel.
  QA76.87.N4845 1993
  006.3--dc20   93-25277
                                        CIP

Publisher's Note
The publisher has gone to great lengths to ensure the quality of this reprint
but points out that some imperfections in the original may be apparent.

Contents

SECTION III. APPLICATIONS OF CONNECTIONIST REPRESENTATION

Preface

This book is the second of a series of books based on conferences sponsored by the Metroplex Institute for Neural Dynamics (M.I.N.D.), an interdisciplinary organization of Dallas-Fort Worth area neural network professionals in both academia and industry. M.I.N.D. has a nearly annual conference on some topic within neural networks. The topics are chosen

(1) to have broad interest both to those interested in designing machines to perform intelligent functions and those interested in studying how these functions are actually performed by living organisms.

(2) to generate discussion of basic and controversial issues in the study of mind.

Thus far, the topics have been as follows:

May, 1988 — Motivation, Emotion, and Goal Direction in Neural Networks
June, 1989 — Neural Networks for Adaptive Sensory-motor Control
October, 1990 — Neural Networks for Knowledge Representation and Inference
February, 1992 — Optimality in Biological and Artificial Networks?

A book based on the May, 1988 conference, with the same title, was published by Lawrence Erlbaum Associates, Inc., in 1992. This book is based on the October, 1990 conference.

Specifically, the topic of this conference was chosen because it is at the interface of neural network theory and artificial intelligence. A controversy exists in the artificial intelligence and cognitive science communities concerning the role of neural network (often called connectionist, or parallel distributed processing) approaches. The great enthusiasm generated by the resurgence of connectionism, partly due to the impact of the two-volume book of Rumelhart and McClelland (1986), led in turn to a "backlash" in which the ability of connectionist models to account for reasoning, inference, and linguistic capabilities was challenged (*e.g.*, Fodor & Pylyshyn, 1988; Pinker & Prince, 1988).

In fact, there is active response to this "backlash" from researchers in a variety of disciplines, including computer science, neurobiology, psychology, and neural network theory among many others. Many of those who spoke at the M.I.N.D.-sponsored conference are among the most innovative workers in these areas. The discussion that followed the presentations was remarkable for the convergence of insights and the absence of arbitrary jargon boundaries across different disciplines. Other recent collections of articles on the general theme of using connectionist models to mimic symbolic processes have been published elsewhere, notably Barnden and Pollack (1991) and Hinton (1991).

The speakers and poster presenters at the conference included all the authors of chapters in this book, except for Pratt Mounfield, and several others. Additional presentations were given by Warren Bean, Texas Instruments, Inc.; Claude Cruz, Plexus Systems, Inc.; Robert Dawes, Martingale Research Corporation; Nilendu Jani, University of Texas at Arlington; Janet Metcalfe, Dartmouth College; Lynn Peterson, University of Texas at Arlington; Jordan Pollack, Ohio State University; Lokendra Shastri, University of Pennsylvania, and David Sudbeck, NCR, Inc. These speakers made strong contributions to the dialogue; they were unfortunately unable to contribute chapters to the book directly, but their influence is felt in the points raised by the chapter authors.

As the presentations were organized into book chapters, they fell naturally into four sections. These sections, and the authors in them, are as follows:

Neurons and Symbols: Toward a Reconciliation —
Manuel Aparicio, International Business Machines, Inc.; and Daniel Levine, University of Texas at Arlington
John Barnden, New Mexico State University
Samuel Leven, Radford University and For a New Social Science
Bruce MacLennan, University of Tennessee

Architectures for Knowledge Representation —
Arun Jagota, State University of New York at Buffalo
Pratt Mounfield, Louisiana State University; Ljubomir Grujić, University of Belgrade; Suresh Guddanti, Louisiana State University
Gadi Pinkas, Washington University (St. Louis)
Thomas Jackson, British Aerospace, and James Austin, University of York

Applications of Connectionist Representation —
Ron Sun, Honeywell Corporation
Wullianallur Raghupathi, California State University, Chico; Daniel Levine, Raju Bapi, and Lawrence Schkade, University of Texas at Arlington
Richard Golden, University of Texas at Dallas; David Rumelhart, Stanford University; Joseph Strickland and Alice Ting, University of Texas at Dallas
James Anderson, Kathryn Spoehr, and David Bennett, Brown University

Biological Foundations of Knowledge —
George Mobus, University of North Texas
Karl Pribram, Radford University
William Hudspeth, Radford University
Jean-Paul Banquet, Boston University and CNRS Paris; Saad El Ouardirhi and Antoine Spinakis, Université Pierre et Marie Curie; Mark Smith and Wilfried Günther, Nervenklinik Bamberg

The first section discusses the philosophical issues regarding the debate between advocates of connectionist paradigms and those of symbolic paradigms from artificial intelligence, and some possible ways to reconcile the ensuing differences. The second section shows some neural network architectures for performing various operations of mathematical logic and abstract reasoning. The third section shows variants on these types of networks that are applied in a variety of spheres, including reasoning from a geographic database, legal decision making, story comprehension, and performing arithmetic reasoning. The fourth and final section discusses knowledge representation processes in living organisms, including evidence from experimental psychology, behavioral neurobiology, and electroencephalographic responses to sensory stimuli.

In addition to the speakers and chapter authors, we acknowledge the contributions made to this volume by several other individuals and organizations. International Business Machines, Inc., generously provided us with the conference facilities at their laboratories in Westlake, Texas, along with refreshments, other conference amenities, and considerable assistance with conference planning and organization. The other members of the Metroplex Institute for Neural Dynamics lent us considerable financial and organizational support, especially Warren Bean, Alice O'Toole, Wesley Elsberry. In addition, Robert Dawes gave a general tutorial presentation on neural networks that provided an enthusiastic beginning for the conference. We are also grateful to Texas Instruments, Inc., for additional corporate support and co-sponsorship of the conference.

We owe a debt of thanks to the staff of Lawrence Erlbaum Associates, Inc., particularly to Judi Amsel and Amy Pierce, our editors at different stages; Kathleen Dolan, our editorial assistant; and Arthur Lizza, our production editor for the camera-ready copy. Judi in particular promoted this book as a natural sequel to the book on Motivation and Emotion with which she had previously been involved.

Finally, we thank our wives, Lorraine Levine and Jacquelyn Renée Aparicio, for their patience and support. Their intuitive understanding of and proximity to our editorial efforts made them in effect co-creators with us.

Daniel S. Levine
Arlington, TX

Manuel Aparicio IV
Arlington, TX

References for Preface

Barnden, J. A., & Pollack, J. B. (Eds.) (1991). *Advances in Connectionist and Neural Computation Theory 1, High-level Connectionist Models.* Norwood, NJ: Ablex Publishing Corporation.

Fodor, J. A., & Pylyshyn, Z. W. (1988). Connectionism and cognitive architecture: A critical analysis. *Cognition* **28**, 3-71.

Hinton, G. E. (Ed.) (1991). *Connectionist Symbol Processing.* Cambridge, MA: MIT Press.

Pinker, S., & Prince, A. (1988). On language and connectionism: Analysis of a parallel distributed processing model of language acquisition. *Cognition* **28**, 73-193.

Rumelhart, D. E., & McClelland, J. J. (Eds.) (1986). *Parallel Distributed Processing.* Cambridge, MA: MIT Press.

List of Contributors

James Anderson, Department of Cognitive and Linguistic Sciences, Box 1978, Brown University, Providence, RI 02912. (anderson@browncog.bitnet)

Manuel Aparicio, IV, International Business Machines Corporation, Internal Zip 030440, 5 West Kirkwood Boulevard, Roanoke, TX 76299-0001. (aparici@dalhqic.ibm.vnet.com)

James Austin, Advanced Computer Architecture Group, Dept of Computer Science, University of York, York, Y01 5DD, England.

Jean Paul Banquet, LENA — CNRS, Hôpital de la Salpêtriere, 47 Boulevard de l'Hôpital, 75651 Paris, Cédex 13, France. Also: Center for Adaptive Systems, Boston University, 111 Cummington Street, Boston, MA 02215. (banquet@cns.bu.edu)

Raju S. Bapi, Department of Mathematics, University of Texas at Arlington, 411 S. Nedderman Drive, Arlington, TX 76019-0408. (b645zih@utarlg.uta.edu)

John Barnden, Computing Research Laboratory and Computer Science Department, New Mexico State University, Box 30001/3CRL, Las Cruces, NM 88003-0001. (jbarnden@nmsu.edu)

David J. Bennett, Department of Cognitive and Linguistic Sciences, Box 1978, Brown University, Providence, RI 02912.

Saad El Ouardirhi, Université Pierre et Marie Curie, 4 Place Jussieu, 75006 Paris, France. Future: 18 cité CIL Aviation, Rabat, Morocco.

Richard Golden, University of Texas at Dallas, School of Human Development GR41, Box 830688, Richardson, Texas, 75083-0688. (golden@utdallas.edu)

Ljubomir T. Grujić, Faculty of Mechanical Engineering, University of Belgrade, P.O. Box 174, 11000 Belgrade, Serbia, Yugoslavia.

Suresh Guddanti, Department of Mechanical Engineering, Louisiana State University, Baton Rouge, LA 70803-6413.

Wilfried Günther, Psychiatric University Hospital ldI, D-800, Munich 2, Germany.

William J. Hudspeth, 415-B Sanford Street, Radford, VA 24141.

Thomas Jackson, Systems Computing, British Aerospace MAL, England.
Also: Department of Computer Science, University of York, York, Y01 5DD, England.
(tom@minster.york.ac.uk)

Arun Jagota, Department of Computer Science, State University of New York at Buffalo,
Buffalo, NY 14260. (jagota@cs.buffalo.edu) After August 15, 1993: Department of Mathematical
Sciences, Memphis State University, Memphis, Tennessee 38152.

Samuel J. Leven, For a New Social Science, 4681 Leitner Drive West, Coral Springs, FL 33067.

Daniel S. Levine, Department of Mathematics, University of Texas at Arlington, 411 S.
Nedderman Drive, Arlington, TX 76019-0408. (b344dsl@utarlg.uta.edu)

Bruce McLennan, Department of Computer Science, University of Tennessee, 107 Ayres Hall,
Knoxville, TN 37996-1301. (mclennan@cs.utk.edu)

George E. Mobus, Department of Computer Science, University of North Texas, Denton, TX
76203-3886. (mobus@ponder.csci.unt.edu)

W. Pratt Mounfield, Jr., M & M Technologies, Inc., P.O. Box 211544, Columbia, SC
29221-6455. Previously at Department of Mechanical Engineering, Louisiana State University,
Baton Rouge, LA 70803-6413. (memoun@lsuvax.sncc.lsu.edu)

Gadi Pinkas, Computer Science Department, Campus Box 1045, Washington University, St.
Louis, MO 63130. (pinkas@cics.wustl.edu)

Karl H. Pribram, Director, Center for Brain Research and Informational Sciences, Radford
University, Radford, VA 24142. (kpribram@ruacad.ac.runet.edu)

Wullianallur "RP" Raghupathi, Department of Accounting and Management Sciences,
California State University, Chico, CA 95929-0011. (rpraghupathi@oavax.csuchico.edu)

David E. Rumelhart, Psychology Department, Jordan Hall, Stanford University, Stanford, CA
94305. (der@psych.stanford.edu)

Lawrence L. Schkade, Department of Information Systems and Management Sciences,
University of Texas at Arlington, Arlington, TX 76019-0437.

Mark J. Smith, LENA — CNRS, Hôpital de la Salpêtriere, 47 Boulevard de l'Hôpital, 75651
Paris, Cédex 13, France.

Antoine Spinakis, Université Pierre et Marie Curie, 4 Place Jussieu, 75006 Paris, France.

Kathryn T. Spoehr, Department of Cognitive and Linguistic Sciences, Box 1978, Brown University, Providence, RI 02912.

Joseph Strickland, University of Texas at Dallas, School of Human Development GR41, Box 830688, Richardson, Texas, 75083-0688.

Ron Sun, Department of Computer Science, University of Alabama, Tuscaloosa, AL 35487. (rsun@athos.cs.ua.edu)

Alice Ting, University of Texas at Dallas, School of Human Development GR41, Box 830688, Richardson, Texas, 75083-0688.

I

NEURONS AND SYMBOLS: TOWARD A RECONCILIATION

1

Why are Neural Networks Relevant to Higher Cognitive Function?

Manuel Aparicio IV
International Business Machines, Inc.

Daniel S. Levine
University of Texas at Arlington

> What is a man, that he may know a number; and a number, that a man may know it?
>
> Warren S. McCulloch, *Embodiments of Mind*

The rapid rise in popularity and productivity of artificial neural networks has been due mainly to the success of these networks in performing relatively low-level functions. These functions include, for example, perception, segmentation, and classification of patterns. In the light of this success, there have been questions raised in the artificial intelligence and cognitive science communities as to whether the types of connections and algorithms used in these networks are also relevant to the understanding of higher-level functions such as concept formation, reasoning, and inference (Chandrasekharan, Goel, & Allemang, 1988; Fodor & Pylyshyn, 1988).

We take the view that there is a continuum rather than a sharp split between the two general classes of functions. Understanding of how they are both performed in the brain is still at an early stage, but there appear to be common organizing principles to both even if they involve different brain regions. We now examine some of the historical roots of the connectionist movement. Our inquiry shows how current connectionist architectures for knowledge representation in fact bring us back to some of these roots.

1. HISTORICAL INTRODUCTION

In the 1940s and early 1950s, the "cybernetic revolution" captured the imaginations of many talented researchers. A movement led by John von Neumann, Warren McCulloch, Norbert Wiener, and others was based on exploring the analogies between brains and the newly developed computers, both digital and analog. In particular, the von Neumann architecture (which is used for symbolic processing systems in artificial intelligence) was heavily influenced by the work of McCulloch and Pitts (1943). The artificial neurons of McCulloch and Pitts, which could be designed to reproduce an arbitrary logical function, introduced the concepts of all-or-none activity, linear threshold logic, and inhibitory reset. These components could be used in the design of logic circuits and memories.

These intellectual pioneers drew on current ideas in a wide variety of disciplines, and did not make the types of distinctions that later became popular. Subsequently, a split occurred between those that were interested in modeling cognitive functions as performed by biological organisms and those that were interested in designing machines to perform such functions regardless of biological realism. At the time, this split was justified by the complexity of the issues and the lack of sophistication of both the available technology and the available neurobiological knowledge. However, the long-term effects have been, until recently, to foster acrimony between intellectual camps that has led to hasty and erroneous conclusions by one camp about the value of ideas from another. Even in less acrimonious form, the simple separation of disciplines has perpetuated weaknesses in each of the different approaches. To encourage the current reconciliation of connectionist and symbolic outlooks, we need to understand better how the earlier split occurred.

The birth of artificial intelligence (AI) as a definable discipline was marked by the Dartmouth Conference of 1956. Had John von Neumann, an avid proponent of neurobiological inspiration for computer design, not been terminally ill and therefore had attended this conference, its flavor might have been radically different. The conference was dominated by logicians, such as John McCarthy, and notable for the absence of anyone involved in neurobiology. In fact, Marvin Minsky, as a fresh Ph.D., was one of the few to represent the "neural" viewpoint at the conference; perhaps in part because of influence from the emphasis of the conference, a generation of his subsequent work was largely divorced from biological constraints.

For the next twenty to thirty years, AI followed the model of the Dartmouth Conference in not being genuinely interdisciplinary, expect for a smattering of influence from cognitive psychology and from linguistics. There were many early successes of symbolic programs in a variety of narrow areas (e.g., three-dimensional solid recognition, checkers-playing, and logical theorem-proving), many of them designed to perform specific tasks rather than to be a basis for an overall theory. These early successes led to a collective confidence that the same AI techniques would ultimately yield results in larger areas like machine vision, automatic translation, and voice recognition, a confidence that proved unjustified.

After more than thirty years, the main tangible benefit of these approaches to AI has been the development of expert systems that still perform a relatively narrow class of problems efficiently. We now review the many arguments about the limitations of AI and why these methods have begun to fail in more complex problems. We should keep in mind that the computer metaphor of mind is just one of a long series of comparisons with current state-of-the-art technology (previously, the hydraulic pump, the steam engine, the telephone system, and so on).

2. LIMITATIONS OF THE SYMBOLIC APPROACH

2.1. THE LANGUAGE OF THOUGHT

Fodor and Pylyshyn (1988) presented the now notorious argument that the "connectionist framework" is incapable of systematically representing constitutive relations between concepts. This incapability of connectionism is in contrast to the "Classical approach", which we take to mean traditional AI and symbolistic Cognitive Science. The Fodor and Pylyshyn paper amounts to a paradigmatic challenge for neural networks to prove they are better than the Classical approach, but in a battle of paradigms, the Classical approach does not have much territory to stand on in the first place as any General Theory of the Mind.

The goal of explaining intelligence has always been secondary to AI, being relatively unconcerned about the label "false intelligence." Through the 1950s and 60s, "neural muddling" produced good models of respiration, cardiac control, and reflexive function, but was unsuccessful in the complex cognitive tasks of interest to AI. In contrast, AI adopted the tactic of assuming the inconsequence of lower order structure to higher level functions, and focused attention on demonstrations of function. Again, AI's primary goal was not to understand intelligence as much as to make machines more useful (Gevarter, 1984; Winston, 1977).

In 1956, intelligent functions were already demonstrated. Even those functions considered most lofty (mathematical and logical) were demonstrated by LOGIC THEORIST. This immediately generated a crusade to discover the holy grail of AI, the General Learning Mechanism. The idea was to find an analytical engine, a powerful general process, that could solve almost any problem by using logic to generate deductions toward a final solution. From LOGIC THEORIST, Newell and Simon (1963) developed General Problem Solver (GPS). GPS used means-ends analysis to reduce the difference between the current and goal states. GPS also established the hypothesis of the problem space — a set of states representing all possible situations, and operators for transforming one state into another. While this approach is intuitively appealing and was successfully applied to a number of games, real world complexity overwhelmed these endeavors.

After several decades and the bridling of earlier naivete toward profitable goals, AI has made limited strides in robotics and expert systems, but there should be little if any remaining pretense for these traditional techniques to hold themselves as a science of the mind. Let us begin with that aspect of mind which is closest to the Classical approach — language. Fodor and Pylyshyn's arguments are weakened by the inadequacies of the Classical approach to understanding even this most symbolic aspect of cognitive activity, particularly its semantic aspects. Chomsky (1964) developed his theory of deep structures to explain underlying syntactic relations within sentences. He was aware, though, that his theory did not explain how the deep structures were influenced by learned aspects of meaning. Moreover, natural language is not like logic or mathematics; it doesn't have the regularity that Chomsky's model assumed.

A recent review article by Pinker (1991) suggests that language is both rule-driven and associative. Both rule-based and associative theories, he asserts, are partially correct, each for different aspects of the tasks of language generation and understanding. Furthermore, Pinker suggests that neither of these theories appears to tap the real computational power of the brain, which seems to be much more heterogeneous with more sophisticated properties than either or both of these theories can explain. While Pinker is not himself a connectionist and has been critical of PDP models of language (Pinker & Prince, 1988), we are in agreement with him about the basic requirements for more realistic models of language.

Fodor and Pylyshyn do not directly hold that the Classical approach is linguistic and include the usual caveat that a cognitive life is available to those that cannot hear or speak language as it is spoken, and they try to stay away from the Language of Thought hypothesis (Whorf, 1965). Nevertheless, the fundamental position of the Classical Approach is that thought is linguistic - that thought requires labeling or tokenizing into symbols and manipulating such symbols according to a logical engine or syntax. The usual caveat notwithstanding, the idea that thought is essentially symbolic originates from the Language of Thought hypothesis (Fodor, 1975) and the primacy of logic in human thought. The study of symbolic computation and formal languages has historically been intertwined with the notions of human language and thought, and these roots are still telling. For instance, Turing's definition of computing arose from his conceptions of human memory and control processes that were popular in the psychological and linguistic sciences of that time.

However, the psychological science of the 1930s should not continue to hold sway, and we should be looking for much deeper representations of thought. The basic notion of control is legitimate, but such manipulation may or may not be linguistic/symbolic. Cognitive "atoms" are more likely to be perceptual and motor, and as such do not always yield to linguistic structures. In this regard, language is neither primary or secondary; it is both. A feedback exists between language and concepts (Lakoff & Johnson, 1980). The way we structure our thoughts leads to categorizations reflected in our use of language. These linguistic categories then in turn influence the organization of our thoughts and perceptions. Whorf (1965) carried this idea too far, by asserting that language IS thought. As an example, he discussed the fact that the Eskimo language contains words for many more kinds of snow than does English, and that the Eskimos really perceived these kinds of snow as different, which we do not. We believe this is an exaggeration, because categories, while influenced by words, are initially self-organized from raw perceptions. For instance, our perceptions of color are determined more by physiological than by lexical structure; cross-cultural studies bearing on this point are reviewed by Gardner (1987, p. 345). Hence the distinction between, say, red and orange along a natural continuum is an arbitrary one, contrary to the strict Whorfian hypothesis.

As expressed in previous accounts of AI's limitations (Denning, 1986; Sutherland, 1986), we should not accept our current predilections about intelligence given by analytical philosophers and mathematicians who have an inordinate reverence of logic and procedure. The ancestry of such thinking is traceable to the ancient Greeks' hierarchy of human activity, in which philosophy and mathematics ranked as the higher and more difficult of cognitive activities.

In contrast to this hierarchy, theorem proving and game playing have been easily engineered, but we still have difficulty building systems for real-world expertise, understanding language, and cleaning house. Not only do lower order functions such as vision and motor control need a different computational framework (different from logic and symbol), but higher order thought processes must be understood as evolving from this common framework. There is no doubt that logical and sequential processes are important components for such functions as planning, but they are only component functions in a larger mechanics not essentially logical. We should emphasize experiential knowledge and interaction and develop architectures best suited for extraction of knowledge from the environment. This approach (see also Levine & Leven, 1992) is in contrast to that of Pylyshyn (1984), who defines cognitive science as excluding learning, development, and mood.

2.2. KNOWLEDGE ACQUISITION

The source of knowledge acquisition comes from the perceptual and motor components of knowledge. Specifically, it arises from the real world stimulation of sensors and from the feedback derived from the consequences of real world motor actions. We believe that these natural sources of knowledge can provide guides for the design of artificial knowledge acquisition systems that cannot be provided by collections of purely abstract symbols as primitives.

The distinction between rule-based and natural knowledge spawns a distinction between causality as typically defined in artificial intelligence and in experimental psychology. The former relates to abstract, logical implication. The latter relates to the temporal predictiveness of sensory and motor events as in Pavlovian or instrumental conditioning (Levine & Leven, 1992, chapters 1-5). Mobus (chapter 13, in this volume) discusses temporal causality in sensory-motor systems as a prototype for if-then relationships. Such temporal representations are one part of the dynamics of a system which includes both associative and nonassociative properties. While inferential reasoning is quite different from learning a conditioned reflex, we believe that the two types of processes contain many similar underlying structures at the "atomic" levels, and toward the unifying goals of science, we should ask how such cognitive processes evolved from primitive, subconscious mechanisms.

Fodor and Pylyshyn (1988) argue that connectionism (for them, mostly, the three-layer standard back propagation architecture) does not lead naturally to the learning of logical functions such as AND. They argue that PDP configurations can be designed to learn the relationship, say, between the concepts "John," "Mary," and "John and Mary," but can be designed just as easily to learn any other relationship that is less symmetric and less logically based.

However, future neural networks that are more biologically inspired need not be formed by arbitrary design. They should be constructed from better principles of how we know, not what we know. This is the basic philosophy of connectionism, but stronger ties to actual biology are still lacking (see below).

Part of the inadequacy of this type of neural network relates to the fact there is homogeneity of structure within each layer and complete connectivity between layers. A review of neural network theory (e.g., Levine, 1991) shows that connectionist models frequently have biases, and many of them have a greater richness of subnetworks with definable structures. Complete connectivity is not the usual rule. In actual brains, many of these structures are hard-wired as well as learned. The topology of brain regions and pathways, and the modulatory properties of specific transmitter substances, control and constrain what can be learned. Current developments in connectionist architectures include incorporation of many of the known inhomogeneities of the brain.

Hence, the biases of the brain, and therefore of realistic neural networks, are not arbitrary. However, these biases are not necessarily logical. Neural design principles which generate adaptive behavior in a nonstationary environment can in fact sometimes lead to logically inconsistent belief structures (e.g., Tversky and Kahneman, 1974, 1981). This may provide a way to understand the problem of intuition, which has been a difficulty for traditional AI theorists.

In contrast, Pinkas (chapter 7, this volume) demonstrated a general equivalency between propositional logic and symmetrical networks. Thus, connectionism does have links to systematic structures as defined by Fodor and Pylyshyn, but the logic formalism is found to have weaker expressiveness. For one, the network representation allows a penalty logic, a metric for unreliability/certainty of belief. A parallel movement within AI itself is the development of modal logic, fuzzy logic, and various other kinds of non-binary logics (see Sun, 1991). This, too, is a constructive step toward reconciliation between the symbolicist and connectionist camps.

Anderson, Spoehr, and Bennett (chapter 12, this volume) explored how to model learning arithmetic in a way that is fairly similar to actual human learning processes. They noticed that while mathematical knowledge itself is abstract, the characteristic way it is learned involves creating visual or kinesthetic constructs as analogs of the more abstract concepts. This kind of analogy is, if anything, more pronounced in expert mathematicians than in novices. The result was a neural network that makes more mistakes than some symbolic processing systems, but makes the same type of mistakes that we are likely to make, and thereby approaches our type of broad, intuitive conceptual understanding. Such cognitive understanding is generally considered the more valuable type of human cognitive skill, although less accurate than the mechanized control needed for arithmetic computing. In very skilled mathematicians, however, detailed emotional imagery about numbers can combine with great precision. For example, Alexander Craig Aitken, a calculating prodigy who became a professor at Edinburgh, sometimes "told of results that 'came up from the murk,' and would say of a particular number that it 'feels prime,' as indeed it was" (Ball & Coxeter, 1987, p. 387).

2.3. IDEALISM

The symbolistic approach to cognitive processes is enduring because it bears a superficial resemblance to how we think that we think. But GPS shows that superficial resemblance can obfuscate more essential differences. GPS and symbolic manipulation have historical and continued allegiance to logical problem solving. Cognitive exploration is within a problem space, and procedures such as subgoaling can divide the problem space into smaller subspaces.

However, monotonic progression of subgoaling can lead to even harder solution of subspaces. Hofstadter (1980) gives an example of a dog wanting a bone on the other side of a fence. One subgoal of going up to the fence may be easily solved, but this leaves the difficult job of now getting over the fence. A less monotonic solution would be to move away from the bone - to the gate at the end of the fence, and then proceed to the bone. The point is that there are different ways to represent the problem and problem distances, and how a problem is solved (indeed if it is to be solved at all) depends on how it is mentally represented.

Hofstadter also makes a most provocative suggestion for overcoming this problem - turn the method of problem reduction back on itself, opening up a search of spaces for the problem space. He then dismisses the suggestion as theoretically appealing but perhaps too complex and unrealistic. This rejection is quite reasonable from the perspective of the classical approach and AI techniques, but a similar speculation is not dismissed within the realm of neuroscience.

There appear to be great evolutionary differences between species in cognitive search abilities, but this very "search of search spaces" that Hofstadter evades appears to be precisely what humans and other primates do routinely. The searching of reptiles is based largely on olfaction, which can be seen as analogous to a simple gradient descent method. In non-primate mammals, this is supplemented by the formation within the hippocampus of cognitive maps based on previous searches (Eichenbaum & Buckingham, 1991; O'Keefe & Nadel, 1978). It is noteworthy that the hippocampus is part of the limbic system, which is adjacent to the olfactory cortex and was formerly called the rhinencephalon ("nose brain") because it was thought, by its location, to serve only the sense of smell. Even in human abstract thought, the smell analogy remains powerful; we say "this idea stinks."

Teyler and DiScenna (1986) proposed that in mammals, the hippocampal cognitive maps are a way-station to switches in the representations of concepts at the cortical level. Levine, Parks, and Prueitt (1993) review a wide range of literature on the frontal cortex and rule formation in primates, both monkeys and humans. They note that frontal lesions interfere with the ability to learn and be guided by behavioral rules on a variety of levels, based on reinforcement. These rules can be as diverse as: classify objects on the basis of a particular feature; move toward whichever object is most novel; go back and forth between two objects on successive trials, and so on. This diversity, including abstract and temporal properties, and the ability to variably focus on such properties indicates the power of hippocampal control.

It appears that the brain can project a search space and then search within that space. Rewards and frustrations not only determine the course of the primary search but also determine the projection of the search-space itself. This is a very complex cognitive control, which has arguably evolved from the same structures used for motor search of real-world space. As such, we expect the same properties and primitives to reappear across different levels of cognition.

In contrast to real systems, the application of the classic approach to robotics has had limited success, like expert systems, working only for highly circumscribed problems and environments. A growing dissatisfaction with traditional robotics is leading to a new approach more closely allied with the elements of neurobiology and psychophysics (Brooks, 1991). Brooks stresses the central ideas of this new approach as "situatedness" and "embodiment"; the system's dynamics are founded on direct experience of and feedback from the external world - not abstract, symbolic descriptions. A robotic agent can interact with the world without symbolic labeling of objects in the interaction. The agent (or the observer) may discuss the objects, beliefs, plans, and goals of behavior, but this linguistic exercise is secondary to the agent's dynamics.

Robotic activity serves as a better metaphor (better than GPS) for the activities of nervous systems, which experience real world extension rather than logical extension. Roughly defined, subgoaling is an important property of intelligence, but the brain's representations whereby subgoals and even the search space itself are created and discarded does not appear to be approachable by the power of logic and symbols. Furthermore, real-world problems tend to have unknown, fuzzy, fragmented, unordered, and contradictory borders. The precision of logic and symbol is ill-founded on these real-world problems. We wish our connectionist models to go beyond the sensory roots of our processes, but we should not abandon these roots.

2.4. IMPLEMENTATION MATTERS

The symbolic descriptions of cognition might be pragmatic to a certain degree (some academic understanding or specific application to engineering), but we should prefer models which have a lower ratio of system complexity compared to how much they can explain and how much they can do.

Two approaches may be functionally equivalent, but other aspects also matter such as cost, performance, esthetic appeal, and simplicity. In the needs of engineering as well as science, the ratio of simplicity to power matters supremely; simplicity can provide an implementation that is faster, cheaper, and so on; power can provide robustness, easy conversion to new problems, and so on. AI has been counted as too slow and too specific, and even its greatest models have been criticized as mere demonstrations, otherwise being too complicated and difficult to understand. Fodor and Pylyshyn try to argue that the success of NNs to model the Classical approach is simply implementational; however, the decades of argument against the weaknesses of AI suggest that "mere implementation" matters.

Using Ajjanagadde and Shastri's (1991) model as an example, the mere implementation of rule-based systems by connectionism allows performance to be very fast - the time to infer is independent of the size of the rule set. Whether or not this is a property of human brains is controversial (Smith, Langston, & Nisbett, 1992). Nevertheless, this is an illustration that connectionist implementations of rules often work very well and are likely to be useful in engineering applications.

Sun (chapter 9, this volume) seeks to add the good properties of connectionism to more traditional approaches. To be an alternative to AI, connectionism must represent rules better than rules. If connectionism can outperform Classical approaches, the pragmatics would indicate that abstract arguments about implementation are superficial and irrelevant.

There has been much Talmudic hair splitting over the definitions of "representation" and "implementation". All models include extraneous details, but only the builder of a model can determine where the line between representation and implementation should be drawn. The Classical Approach has determined to exclude biological implementations as mere implementation. Limiting their scope of interest is fine, but an onus must be placed on any one-level approach to provide a breadth of explanation across more than that single level — in this case cognitive functions, which the Classical approach does not provide in any case. Compositionality is not the only property of cognitive systems, and connectionism has done much better to explain and provide such essential phenomena as content accessibility and flexibility.

Although more diverse in their modeling intentions, connectionist modelers generally intend that the neuron-like details are part of the model - they are not irrelevant. These models hope not only to provide a functional breath surpassing the Classical approach, they also hope to understand and use the structural constraints that might be used in real systems. Embracing this larger domain is a more difficult task (models are more falsifiable), and as such, a measure of bridging several disciplines can be used to judge the goodness of competing models. A good theory has "striking formal simplicity" (Hempel, 1966) relative to the breadth of its application. Goodness is a matter of both the number of basic assumptions or concepts used as well as the wealth of phenomena addressed. To a deeper degree than AI's belief in heuristics, connectionism has a fundamental belief in searching for simplicity, assuming that simple structures give rise to emergent functional properties (as in Rosenblatt's genotypic approach and Grossberg's method of minimal anatomies). The structure largely defines the model as a bridge between the disciplines of psychology and neurobiology.

The Classical approach has always had a weak understanding of model validation. Traditional AI believed in "sufficiency analysis" for its relationship to psychology; if an algorithm met the functional requirements, it was deemed to be a good model of psychology. However, psychology itself has been very concerned with sufficient but overly complex models, especially when now given the power of the computer. Loftus (1985) speculated on what might have happened if Kepler had a computer. Kepler could have easily added more epicycles to the sky rather than the spend 40 years that eventually gave us the beautiful simplicity of the ellipse. This argument was directed at cognitive models that merely fit the data using highly abstract concepts. Sufficiently complex models only restate complex behavior, they do not explain it as required for the development of a psychological science. For example, there has been extensive psychological and neural evidence for humans forming mental images (e.g., Farah, 1989; Kosslyn, 1980). Most logical accounts to date of these phenomena have been rather clumsy and make no connection with the neurobiological findings. A preliminary connectionist model of one such phenomenon, mental rotation, has been proposed by Tani and Fujita (1992).

Jenkins (1981) has even considered that Cognitive Science, in search of a Theory of Mind, is impossible from the techniques of task or functional analysis. Again, functional correctness can be achieved by an infinite variety of models - some of which might be elegant, and some of which might be Rube Goldberg devices. Second and more importantly, a Universal Turing machine like the human brain can "configure" itself to different machine levels and types as required for different tasks. The art of experimental cognitive psychologists is to construct an experimental situation such that the behavior of the subject matches that of the psychologist's favorite theory. In some situations, the cognitive machinery is parallel; in other situations, it is serial. Ask a friendly Universal machine to perform some trivial task, and it will. But as Jenkins suggests, the "models" constructed to explain the external behavior might have little or nothing at all to do with the nature of the mind. Such models characterize the task at hand; if the task is important in practice (such as skilled typing or medical diagnosis), then the model of the task is important. However, such functional analysis is too limited to probe the underlying capacity of the human universal machine. A model using symbols and logic control might be important as the analysis of an important task, but the model of a task (even a rather generic task) is not a full model of the mind.

Arguments that the Classical approach has selected the appropriate "level of analysis" - regarding lower levels as irrelevant - does not recognize the dangers of losing a biological touchstone in the verification of cognitive models. An infinite number of symbolic constructions can provide the same function, but many would be completely unrealistic contraptions, of no good use to the advancement of science and of a cost prohibitive to application.

Connectionist models assume more than surface function. They are at least within the rubric of neural structure, and are attempting to move closer and closer to biological significance.

By including neural predictions with behavioral ones, they are more disconfirmable as scientific models. Otherwise, cognitive science assures us that the mind is parallel (and serial), discrete (and continuous), gradual (and catastrophic). In all of science, we can't ask twenty questions of nature and get a straight answer. This problem as discussed is fundamental within cognitive science; all theories of mind have been disconfirmed by the experiments of competing theorists. But as cognitive models align with connectionism, neural and psychological modeling will become more unified into a larger theoretical system. Larger systems have more touchstones toward finding truth, and have an onus toward finding unifying, simplifying constructs. Making clear ties with known physiology guards against the development of sufficiently complex models to explain data. Parameters with no physical significance have no experimental verifiability and, therefore, the parameter values can be arbitrarily adjusted to produce results.

The Classical approach and AI have always overpretended its importance to psychology. Even Hull's system of inferred postulates, which was intrinsically developed from within the discipline of psychology, has very little enduring value. Some basic concepts of drive, attention, and such endure but are now more firmly rooted in empirical physiology, as evidenced in the current neural network modeling of these phenomena. Likewise, the concepts of subgoaling, labeling, searching, backtracking and such will endure but will be better founded in a dynamics that is more powerful that symbol mechanics. Like Freudian and earlier hydraulic models of psychological forces, many ill-founded notions will retain their metaphorical appeal, but will have no scientific substance in how cognition actually works.

Even when an abstract construct is naively compelling, its validation must also include its simplicity. Consider the hopes of the General Problem Solver (GPS), which has been under development by Newell since shortly after the birth of AI. The ideas of problem decomposition and subgoaling are reasonable, but on the other hand, it was founded on the hopes of pure logic. As such it is typical of AI systems as a collection of complicated procedures and bookkeeping. For instance, SOAR - the current best embodiment of GPS — has a process called "identifier variablization" (Laird, Rosenbloom, Newell, 1985). If we remove such esoteric nomenclature (Kurzweil (1985) accused AI of using terminology that is vague — vagueness being its primary purpose), this process amounts to generalization. Within connectionism, the property of generalization isn't viewed as an algorithmic process as much as an intrinsic property of the structural system. In a Hopfield net, for instance, this is one of the emergent properties given by an elegantly simple system. Identifier variablization in SOAR and content addressability in Hopfield nets both provide the same function — generalization — but one is more natural by reason of simplicity and emergence. These are the properties that science uses in evaluating truth by reason of beauty.

Sun (chapter 9, this volume) also points out that in spite of this attempt at generalization, SOAR is very brittle. Because AI's idealism starts with the symbol rather than sensors, it does not have access to the subsymbolic structure from which concepts are built. Sun shows how AI's brittleness is caused by this lack of subsymbolic structure. MacLennan (chapter 4, this volume) takes this requirement of subsymbolic processing to its extreme, arguing that a continuous symbol system allows decomposition of any object to an arbitrary degree. Robustness is provided by recursive decomposition and by the continuity of small changes leading to small effects. Furthermore, a continuous system does not presuppose any particular decomposition; there are many possible segmentations and magnifications depending on the task.

Even von Neumann suggested that "the language of the brain [is] not the language of mathematics" (von Neumann, 1958, p. 80). He did not mean to indict the entire field of descriptive and analytical tools which we use to describe nature. The context of this statement instead suggests that formal logic is not the language of the brain.

A continuous system is more in line with the non-digital representation of neural mechanisms and the fact that all real-world problems begin with inaccuracy and uncertainty. In vision for instance, edges may be hidden or may be missing because of lighting. Such objects could be labeled, or symbolized, but this adds an unfounded accuracy. Von Neumann reasoned early that the brain cannot pass around large symbolic structures and that neural computation must be more statistical than logical. Even though we now understand some means by which symbolic activity might take place, it would be naive to think that the cognitive machinery was not intricately embedded in the neural substrate.

Grossberg and Mingolla (1985) stated that all visual contours are illusory, even those that happen to conform to existing contours in real world. In the same vein, Edelman (1989) said that we don't "process information," but rather we construct our own reality.

We admit that discrete, symbolic activity can take place within neural structures, but because the precision of language and logic appears to be a special skill, our quest should be focused on how the discrete emerges from the continuous (see MacLennan, chapter 4, this volume). Even more towards a reunification of connectionism and the Classical approach, we should follow MacLennan's suggestion of a discrete-continuous duality.

Paradigmatic arguments against other paradigms are always overzealous, and we are simply making a plea for the Classical approach to be symbiotic with connectionism. Scientific integrity implies the joining of various disciplines into a unified view of nature. Connectionism is desirable in attempting to extend the functional study of cognitive science into the functional/structural study of neural science. Great progress has been made at the lower levels of behavioral analysis; in sensory and motor systems, many perceptual phenomena and action patterns have been explained. As well, excellent attacks are being made at the interface of neuropharmacology and psychological mood. Reaching a similar understanding for higher level cognitive functions is of course more difficult but is no less desired or needed as a matter of scientific progress. But the challenge to explain compositionality is well-taken, and should drive connectionism to become a better paradigm than it currently is.

3. PROBLEMS WITH MANY CONNECTIONIST APPROACHES

Paradigmatic attacks from other approaches are not to blame for the inability of neural networks to embody the capabilities of symbolic systems. The reemergence of neurocomputing since the early 1980s has gone far beyond the efforts of the 1950s and 1960s. Many applications have established its utility, and the recent advances in neuroscience allow for deeper influence of biology on computer science than was ever before possible. However, one basic error similar to that of Minsky and Papert's "Perceptrons" (1969), responsible for the temporary disappearance of neural networks, is still being recommitted: many commentators view the body of neural network theory as a monolithic architecture, the Multilayer Perceptron (MLP), in its most simplistic form. For instance, many complexity analyses of neural learning (Blum & Rivest, 1992; Judd, 1991) assume a simple sort of MLP — most notably, a fixed architecture over the course of learning. Such analyses are essentially correct; MLPs have poor scaling properties, are notoriously slow to learn, are sensitive to initial conditions, and require "black arts" for proper network configuration. On the other hand, MLPs do not characterize the full breath and power of current, let alone potential future, connectionism, nor of real systems.

The rebirth of connectionism is to be applauded, but the same architectures that were involved in this rebirth continue to have such overwhelming influence even while we continue to confront their fundamental weaknesses. A large part of connectionist work revolves around the application of back-propagation to one or another industrial application or psychological behavior — or on the theoretical side, to some characterization or incremental performance improvement. At the same time, a large number of workers express dissatisfaction with back-prop's weaknesses and the relative stagnation of the neural network field.

The connectionist community itself can be held partly to blame for this stagnation; we hope that connectionism will advance itself toward greater discernment among, and improvement on, current models. We believe that more realism is required before quantum improvements in the speed, capacity, and control of neural networks can be made.

3.1. WEAK TIES TO NEUROSCIENCE

Aside from assuming a monolithic architecture, the second error similar to Minsky and Papert's attack on the Perceptron, is to again underestimate what neurocomputing will become with the further symbiosis of neuroscience. Even within the neural network community itself, real neurons are vastly underestimated. As the most glaring instance, the very reemergence of neurocomputing included the notion that individual neurons are computationally weak. Neuronal signalling is still characterized as slow and imprecise, and the neuron is presented as a simple summator and thresholding device.

This simplification is fine for didactic purposes, but it seems that even mature researchers in the field believe that such simplifications are true — or that such simplifications are wholly adequate for a computational model of the neuron. Just as the Classical approach rejects the entire study of biology as irrelevant to cognitive computation, a large part of connectionism regards the slight inclusion of a neural rubric to be computationally sufficient; the rest of the biological detail is irrelevant, serving to support the neuron's metabolism for example.

While it is assumed that the weak computational power of the neuron is saved only by parallelism and distributed representation (Rumelhart & McClelland, 1986), parallelism itself cannot overcome the fundamental problems of combinatoric complexity, and there are still many problems, such as real-world stereopsis, which are solved by neurological systems, but for which we have no adequate, parameter-free model of computation.

In all neural models of stereopsis, for example, we must first know the properties of the visual field (isoplanar, curvilinear, etc.) so that we can set the right parameters for the model to compute depth and contour. Marr was never satisfied with his own model of stereopsis (Marr & Poggio, 1979), and more recent attempts such as applying back-prop to this problem (Hinton & Becker, 1990) simply repeat all the problems of back-prop (slow convergence, black arts for correct parameter settings) which then only performs within a curvilinear visual field.

Aside from repeating Marr and Poggio's demonstration of competitive processes, Hinton and Becker provide no advancement in the understanding of stereopsis itself nor of the neural circuitry that actually underlies this computation. As argued against the Classical approach, the mere demonstration of function is trivial, if not irrelevant.

Stereopsis is also modeled by Grossberg (1987) using a connectionist model based on competition within subnetworks of feature detectors, and modifiable resonant feedback between different subnetworks. While that type of network also lacks biologically realistic detail at the neuronal level, it is a more promising approach because it incorporates architectural principles that tie together functionally significant subsystems. These sorts of principles, based in mathematical theories, are discussed further in ensuing sections.

3.2. MONOTONIC FUNCTIONS

Defining a weak neuron is as troublesome as defining a weak "atom" as in the Classical approach. Both lead to additional complexity beyond the atom in order to compensate for the loss of primitive power. A little more detail at the appropriate level can greatly simplify the subsequent, higher levels.

The simplified neuron model is a case in point. For example, the sigmoid function is the most commonly used activation function. As given by the more elementary textb,ooks, such a monotonic activation function ensures that an excitatory change of input will lead to an excitatory effect, and an inhibitory change of input will lead to an inhibitory effect. Such monotonic activation is prototypical for sensory transduction neurons, which need to compress the range of physical input intensities while preserving the ordinality of weak to strong. Its simplicity is didactic, but the sigmoid function should not be used as a general model of neuron-to-neuron transmission. A more general model of post-sensory processing should include the reversal potential, the point at which further presynaptic excitation will produce postsynaptic inhibition (or vice versa). This is a rarely used but classic principle of neural science (Kandel & Schwartz, 1985). Its discussion has recently been reinjected into the neurocomputing literature (Davenport, Jakobsson, & Gerber, 1991), in hopes of replacing the standard monotonic functions more commonly in use.

Instead of including this further realism, connectionism has its own form of sufficiency analysis; the sigmoidal function has been proved to be universal, and configurations of many sigmoids have been demonstrated as sufficient for nonlinearities such as the exclusive-or problem. Beyond such proofs and demonstrations, a better representation of the neuron can be more efficient. Reversal potentials act to bound and reverse the activation function between a lower, negative reversal and higher, positive reversal. Given a reversal potential, an excitatory change of input can have either an excitatory or inhibitory effect (and the same for an inhibitory change of input). Reversal potentials simply make the direction of postsynaptic change caused by one presynaptic input to be interactive with other presynaptic inputs, meaning that a nonlinearity such as the exclusive-or can be computed by a single patch of membrane — a single activation function — rather than by a network of less powerful "neurons." We can consider the standard MLP using sigmoid functions to be a weaker machine, capable of emulating a more powerful formulation but at a greater cost.

The inclusion of the reversal potential at the implementation level leads to a fundamentally different representation at the functional level. Such a convolutional activation function allows the formation of non-local, Fourier neighborhoods in the input vector space. Vectors that are not linearly separable can be defined as equivalent within some periodic function. Within these higher order neighborhoods, periodic vectors can be separated. While convolutional functions have been too summarily dismissed (Lee & Kil, 1991; Stinchcombe & White, 1989), they are effectively included in Tattersall's (1990) use of Fourier functions and Szu's (1992) use of wavelets.

Given the poor learning speeds of our learning architectures and shallow capacities of our memory architectures, we sorely need at least to investigate other representations such as convolution. Computational and neurobiological theory has held a long debate between matrix versus Fourier representations. Recent findings about 40Hz brain activity as possibly underlying variable binding has refueled the debate, but interest in the Fourier domain has a long history. In conversation with McCulloch before his death, one of us (Daniel Levine) asked him for advice to a young scientist, "What do you hold is the preferred mathematics for neural networks?" McCulloch's reply was to read Minorsky's book "Nonlinear Oscillations." Karl Pribram (see chapter 14, this volume), who has long argued for the inclusion of Fourier representations, thought that McCulloch was a secret holographer. Within this volume, several chapters move toward convolutional representations (see the chapters by MacLennan, Pribram, and Hudspeth).

3.3. FUZZY METAPHOR

To advance a more realistic model of the neuron, the neural metaphor must also be further resolved. Models such as the MLP regard the unit as a "node", without committing to whether such a node represents a neuron or a membrane compartment. The position is that within the PDP rubric, this detail doesn't matter to the computation. However, we are still very ignorant within neurocomputing and could use further guidance from biology, because these mushy definitions can be confusing and even misleading. For instance, the definition of a node does not differentiate itself as either a membrane transfer for a single dendritic compartment or as a threshold function for an entire neuron of such compartments. We suspect that there are profound functional differences between dendritic network of graded, semi-local compartment functions (including a reversal potential) and the all-or-none decision made by a single axon hillock which follows. Better specification of the neural metaphor will then lead to better specification of connectivity between nodes. In contrast to arbitrary fan-in and fan-out in a global neural network, the structure of a dendritic tree is more fan-in than fan-out, and demonstrates the segmentation of inputs onto various portions of the tree.

We also argue that computing logic functions in a network of neurons is at the wrong level of neural metaphor. Shepherd and Brayton (1987) have shown how mere patches of dendritic membrane can compute logic functions. It might be argued that whether logic functions are computed by membrane "nodes" or "neuron" nodes is irrelevant to the computation itself, but focus on the axon hillock's threshold function as the neuron's activation function has the insidious effect of maintaining monotonic functions (thresholds and sigmoids) as universal activation functions. The mismetaphor maintains its status as probably what the biology is doing, and this notion, as irrelevant detail, hinders the introduction of membrane compartment models and the reversal potential discussed above.

Furthermore, the mushy metaphor is misleading in the context of whether connectivity should be static or dynamic. If we are using real systems as a touchstone for our insights and progress, then dynamic connectivity must be rejected if the creation and destruction of neurons is considered. Any requirement that neurons are born during the course of learning will simply make biologists laugh and further consider the irrelevance of neural modeling to their discipline. On the other hand, conformational change within the dendritic tree is at least possible, although controversial. Szu has been advocating the design of neurons as dynamic tree structures during learning (perhaps by microtubule control; Hameroff, 1990; Szu, 1989).

In fact, there is a lot of connectionist modeling already that is dynamic (see Levine, 1991, Chapters 5-7). There are many other works with this approach to dynamic structure (Carpenter, Grossberg, & Reynolds, 1991; Jokinen, 1991; Mota Tenorio, 1990; Sankar & Mammone, 1991; to name only a few), including decision tree learning. Many other schemes try to determine the number of required hidden units in a MLP (Hirose, Yamashita, & Hijiya, 1991; Lee & Kil, 1991). Also, and in contrast to his own strong assumption of a fixed architecture, Judd (1990) reports of Valiant's interest in dynamic architectures as some hope for machine learning. This is an important area of study for improving the state-of-the-art, and the selection of guiding metaphors will either help or hinder the cross-disciplinary flow of ideas about conformational change - whether structural or not.

3.4. GRADUALIST LEARNING THEORY

Additionally, basic concepts from the psychology of learning and memory are not well appreciated. It is true that the PDP approach is essentially behavioristic, emphasizing contiguity and repetition. The focus on repetition reinforces the intuitive (and not entirely false) notion that learning is a gradual process which follows the sigmoidal learning curve. On the other hand, many aspects of discrimination and concept learning - the very staples of neurocomputing - are better explained by the alternative theory, known as noncontinuity theory or hypothesis testing (Crowder, 1976; Hulse, Egeth, & Deese, 1980). In simple discrimination experiments, the sigmoidal learning curve might be a statistical artifact of running many subjects, where each subject makes hypotheses until finding and testing the correct discriminant on one of the trials. Thereafter, the subject responds correctly, but instead of a step function, the experiment-wise learning curve is gradual because each subject learns the correct answer on different trials.

Even where learning within a subject appears to be gradual, the best current theory on discrimination learning and associative memory tasks is that the subject learns some quantum aspect of the problem on each trial; a complex problem is learned gradually by micro-hypothesis testing and the accumulation of these quanta. Each hypothesis is formed instantly and several hypotheses can be simultaneously entertained.

Such instant learning is in contrast to the slow learning times of MLPs but is closer to the instant loading of vectors into a memory. However, connectionist memory architectures such as Hopfield networks (Hopfield, 1982) are also based on a simplistic model of the neuron, which we believe leads to their very shallow capacities. Whereas current associative memories have a memory capacity that is some fraction of the number of nodes, we should hope that more realistic models will be able to store arbitrarily more memories than nodes. While a sigmoidal activation function can make only a single linear separations, more sophisticated functions (as required by reversal potentials) should allow more complex separations, and therefore, should give better compression of memories per node.

The gradual-quantized (*i.e.*, continuous-discrete) dichotomy can be partly resolved by noting that in continuous dynamical systems of differential equations (cf. Hirsch & Smale, 1974), small changes in one or more parameters can lead to sudden changes in the system's long-term behavior. This does not contradict the fact that the system's behavior is robust within a certain range of parameters, but merely states that there are critical ranges at which transitions take place. This insight is at the root of a wide range of psychological phenomena, from the generation and rejection of hypotheses discussed above to the stages of development outlined by Piaget (1952) to switches in decision preference with motivational context changes.

3.5. IMPRECISION

This leads to the more controversial aspects of the goals of neural modeling. Real neural systems behave suboptimally in a large number of circumstances; we are poor at arithmetic, awful at probability estimations, we are forgetful, illogical, and the list goes on. One approach is to say that we are not capable of better performance because we have not needed to be in the course of evolution.

Our memories are not perfect, but this imperfection is often adaptive. During acquisition, we maintain a host of perceptual filters in order to eliminate the irrelevant; even once our memories are in storage, we actively forget some memories and consolidate others.

Adaptive system behavior can arise from elements with weak processing power. Conversely, there can be complex processing at the lower levels combined with maladaptive system behavior; examples in human neurology include idiot savantism and uncontrollable eidetic memory. The most effective neural network models of the future will combine powerful processing by individual elements with structures for adaptive control of the system as a whole.

The precision of the computer and the symbolicist approach itself was founded on the McCulloch-Pitts model of the neuron. It is clear that such a neuron model can "do" numbers. The precision of number has been lost in the stochastic approach of more recent neural modeling. Since the Perceptron, neural modeling has been aligned more with statistical rather than logical methods. Number and logic existed in early models, but we have not returned yet to these early roots. Current neural network theory remains the same, but there are many exceptions, some of which are represented in this volume. Jagota (chapter 5, this volume) for example moves away from statistical structures. He presents how neural networks are related to general discrete representations such as graphs, sets, and such. It is important to note the exactness of these representations.

Pinkas' work (chapter 7, this volume) also acts as a bridge, developing a language for both symbol and connection. Pinkas also shows how structures are manipulated, thereby including discrete knowledge and control within the neural approach. Pinkas further suggests the fruits of collaboration between approaches. Monotonic systems are plagued by intractable complexity, and simple shifts toward parallelism or analog codes do not relieve the fundamental scaling problems. If there is a solution to the combinatoric complexity problems of computer science, new formalisms beyond logic and set theory might be required, at least to provoke new ideas about enumeration, and connectionism may be the source of these formalisms.

3.6. LACK OF CONTROL

The problems of understanding rule formation, spatiotemporal sequence generation and processing, and planning have been historically difficult for neural network research. These issues have been beyond the capacity of simple multilayer perceptrons and other simple neural networks, but have been the object of much recent modeling (e.g., Dapi & Levine, 1990; Bradski, Carpenter, & Grossberg, 1992; Dehaene, Changeux, & Nadal, 1987; Wang & Arbib, 1990; Zipser, 1990). These sequencing and control problems are the ones that connectionist networks must solve in order to contribute to the traditional pursuits of artificial intelligence such as language skills and general problem solving.

It is by now commonplace in neuroscience and network modeling that day-to-day biological processes are not driven by logic as much as by instinctive and emotional processes that arose in response to evolutionary pressures. Logic can be seen as a corrective for human thought, one that becomes more necessary with greater environmental complexity. An example of this is variable binding (e.g., Ajjanagadde & Shastri, 1991) whereby associations can be formed among linguistic or conceptual "atoms" apart from their overall contexts. This issue has been studied in a neural network by Grossberg (1975), who noted for example that if one eats roast turkey with one's lover, associations form between turkey and hunger satisfaction and between lover and sexual satisfaction but not vice versa. Touretzky and Hinton (1986) studied in a connectionist framework the emergence of sequential thought from variable binding, which had previously been suggested in a non-connectionist framework by Newell (1980).

These studies serve to reinforce the notion that dichotomies such as sequential versus parallel and automatic versus controlled are superficial, and can be resolved readily within dynamic connectionist architectures. Several chapters in this volume investigate such syntheses. For example, Banquet (chapter 16, this volume) has studied their biological bases in recordings of evoked potentials (ERP's), that is, gross cortical electrical patterns in response to stimuli that are either novel or significant to the organism. Banquet found both automatic and controlled components to ERP's; even within the same cognitive task, the automatic and controlled elements are intricately connected. Also, there are differences in ERP response to more and less probable stimuli. This suggests that studying the capacity for inference can be enhanced by placing inference along a continuum with psychological processes that are not strictly logical, such as expectation, anticipation, and priming.

Jackson and Austin (chapter 8, this volume) present a computational model that shows how hierarchical associative mechanisms can be used to represent high level concepts and that combines these parallel associative mechanisms with several sequential control concepts such as the paging of frames for contextual control, hypothesis generation and testing, and an implicit form of backtracking during memory search. Jackson starts with basic pattern matching, but the control mechanisms introduce focus of attention, which allows variable resolution and interpretation of input vectors, in contrast to the Classical approach's requirement of consistent atoms and their interpretation.

In a similar vein, Mounfield (chapter 5, this volume) illustrates how networks of the Hopfield type can be used for inference about the truth of falsity of logical statements given a set of logical primitives. His system can be used for a connectionist implementation of truth maintenance. Golden, Rumelhart, Strickland, and Ting (chapter 11, this volume) apply the ideas of truth maintenance and temporal causality to a connectionist model of story comprehension. Within their dynamical system model one can see analogs of such artificial intelligence concepts as counterfactual reasoning, production systems, and scripts. The biological basis for some of these processes is explored further by Pribram (chapter 14, this volume). Pribram's account of episodes, defined roughly as the periods of time between orienting responses, and narratives includes a controller, an executive processor that is identified with the frontal cortex. This macroscopic account is synthesized with an elaborate theory of subneuronal dendritic computation.

Adaptive control of cognitive processes cannot be done by a single network with homogeneous structure. Rather it depends on a variety of interacting subnetworks, each with definable functions; the work of Banquet, Pribram, and others hints at some tentative identifications between subsystems and brain regions. We now explore approaches toward isolating important subfunctions and combining them into the larger functions needed for a wide variety of tasks.

4. RECONCILIATION AND UNIFYING PRINCIPLES

Neural networks of the simplest variety are weak in providing such mechanics, but the basic principles of subnetwork organization (e.g., associative learning, error-correcting learning, lateral inhibition) that have been successful in modeling sensory categorization are now starting to be used in different combinations to model concept formation, context switching, and planning (aside from contributions to this volume see Cohen, Dunbar, & McClelland, 1990; Dehaene & Changeux, 1989, 1991; Grossberg, Carpenter, & Reynolds, 1991; Levine & Prueitt, 1989; Ogmen & Prakash, 1992). Neuroscience still lacks a complete and general theory, but nothing fundamentally exists in the way and modern neuroscience is heavily founded on the establishment of common principles across various systems. (See Grossberg, 1988; Hestenes, 1992; and Levine, 1989 for discussions of these various principles.)

These principles beg for further use and exploration, particularly in regard to understanding cognition. For instance, biological systems are replete with opponent processes, such as the biceps-triceps opposition for motor control of the arm. Noncontraction of the biceps does not imply contraction of the triceps. Assuming a binary simplification, there are four possible actions — to contract, to extend, to relax, or to flex — and so two bits of output information are required.

We can easily understand this real motor system and how two outputs express more control of a single articulation, but we tend to ignore how such architectures found in the lower parts of the nervous system can have important corollaries for higher cognitive functions. We tend to think of cognitive processing in terms of decision theory, requiring one bit for specifying a yes-no decision. "Separability" is typically defined as a single-bit decision problem, but in so doing, both rule-based and connectionist classification systems have no idea whether a "yes" decision is founded on an actual instance from memory or whether the case is included by reason of generalization (or whether a "no" is founded on a actual instance or excluded by generalized discrimination).

The cognitive function of spell-checking should be comparable in principle to 2-bit decision requirements of arm movement. The opposite of certain knowledge that a word is spelled correctly is the certain knowledge of not knowing if it is spelled correctly. It might also be known that the word is spelled incorrectly, but as follows, this requires an additional bit of knowledge. Two separate neurons, labeled CORRECT and INCORRECT, are required for the four possibilities: 1) neuron CORRECT fires - the word is known to be spelled correctly, 2) neuron INCORRECT fires - the word is known to be spelled incorrectly, 3) neither neuron fires - the word's correctness is not known, or 4) both neurons fire - the word is ambivalent, both correct and incorrect (archaic, British, etc).

Our human memories are not perfect, but we do have meta-knowledge about our knowing, which necessitates more informatic control than simple separability. We can both know and know-that-we-know; or we can not-know and know-that-we-not-know. We easily both know our name and know that we know our name. At another extreme, we could be asked, "What is the seventh largest mountain on the earth?" Many of us would probably say, "I am not sure" and feel confident that any guess would be an inference. A few of us know such facts and would express adamant confidence on the matter.

Even in apparently straightforward classification problems, a real expert maintains a valuable separation of knowledge from inference. An unknown bird very similar to a robin might be discovered, except that it is green with red stripes. Even though it is obviously a bird — and is even prototypical in so many regards — the examiner can both classify it as a bird (an inference) while still knowing that this is not a known bird from memory (a fact). In contrast to this ability, both rule-based knowledge and common connectionist classification models confound memory and inference, and some workers such as Barnden (see chapter 2, this volume) argue that constructs such as generalization cannot be manipulated because they are all immanent in the connection weights. Barnden reconciles connectionism with other branches of AI, such as analogy-based and case-based reasoning in which single cases are sufficient for reasoning and in which generalization and exception are explicit constructs that can be manipulated. Leven (chapter 3, this volume) also argues for the separability and control of distinct constructs. For instance, classification and categorization architectures presuppose the structure of knowledge in overly rigid terms. Leven suggests that real systems do not maintain preexisting categories; that instead, categories are formed dynamically to meet the nature of various problems.

Rather than logic, set, and decision theory, fundamental principles from neural systems are required for more flexible systems. On the other hand, connectionism must reconcile with other branches of AI to gain more explicit constructs and their controls. However, we believe this reconciliation and additional power will emerge from further exploration of connectionism, particularly by also integrating the various approaches within connectionism itself. Spell-checking for instance is not typically regarded as a decision problem in the way presented above. Knowing that a word is spelled incorrectly, we might then need to reference the word's correct spelling, probably by content-addressability. This leads us to suggest that any real function is not well provided by any single algorithm, by a single, separate decision architecture or memory architecture. Instead of asking, "Are neural networks like the brain?", we should ask "Which neural networks have some component in the brain?", and "How are such networks concatenated into powerful complexes such as the brain?"

Finally, we suggest that such concatenation of models will yield a better understanding of how constituent structures are maintained in neural systems. Consider a simple system that combines both heteroassociative and autoassociative mechanics, such as feedforward mapping and content-addressability, respectively. Assume two binary inputs, A and B, to two sensory units, which internally represent the existence of each input. These two sensory units are then connected to an output unit with a threshold of 2, with both connection weights equal to 1. Presentation of the (1,1) vector to the two input units then activates the output. Both inputs are required for the output unit to fire, so we would label this function as an AND. Fodor and Pylyshyn argue that such networks do not display constituent structure because the output unit (representing the AND function) can be on without the constituents (A and B) necessarily having been on. This is true but myopic; the simple addition of autoassociative mechanics can provide the required structure. Because of the weights between each sensory unit and the output unit, the state of the sensory units can be coupled to the output unit. If the output unit is on, a recurrent autoassociative, "relaxation" mechanism can determine from the positive weights and the threshold of 2 that both sensory units must be turned on. Representations of A and B are required given the existence of the A AND B relationship. Given the same weights but a lower threshold of 1, such commonly used relaxation techniques guarantee that EITHER the A OR the B sensory unit must be on whenever the output unit is on. Given such a threshold, the output neuron represents the OR function.

Any statement of the form, "Such and such kind of network can't do so and so ...," is typically oversimplistic and attacks a straw man. Minsky and Papert committed such an error against the Perceptron, and current efforts appear to undermine connectionism again. However, this time a strong body of both camps appear to be working toward common understandings. This is to be applauded, and in spite of philosophical arguments, inevitable consequences will prevail.

5. CONCLUSION

The overriding conclusion is that both connectionist and symbolic approaches have their strengths and drawbacks. Therefore, asking twenty questions of Nature to discern which is "correct" is fruitless. Instead, the object of our endeavors should be to build the largest and simplest framework for explaining cognitive dualities. How can the same brain be both serial and parallel? How can the same architecture be both distributed and localist? How is learning both gradual and quantal? How are common principles of neural computing used both for perceptual and conceptual functions? Bridging such dualities will test the true power of any Theory of Mind, and including the additional constraints of neural principles will serve as a further test. Some of the chapters in this volume are particularly illustrative of possible bridges; for example, Banquet (chapter 16) synthesizes automatic and controlled processes, and MacLennan (chapter 4) synthesizes discrete and continuous processes.

The human brain is an existence proof that such dualities exist within one machine. It refutes the statement, common in professional folklore, that neural networks mostly do pattern recognition and categorization, rather than higher-level tasks such as reasoning and inference. Humans often do the latter, albeit fitfully. Reason and inference are hard, but not impossible or extra-biological. Connectionist models are in fact making great strides toward capturing this type of process, even if these models are not yet biologically realistic (e.g., Carpenter et al., 1991; Fu, 1989; Hestenes, 1992; Kosko, 1987; Thagard, 1989; Touretzky & Hinton, 1986). Fodor and Pylyshyn's (1988) strongest statement, "Connectionists ... are committed to mental representation that don't have combinatorial structure" (p. 45) is thus refuted by a large body of recent work. In fact, several of these models make some tentative suggestions for how hypothesis testing can occur.

Cognitive science was founded on the "levels of analysis" argument. The idea that one mental event causes another suggested a separate science of thought as the study of mental causality. However, such academic levels are arbitrary. While there is a rough hierarchical organization to the brain, it is replete with feedback (or in the terms of Edelman, 1989, "reentrant connections") from "higher" to "lower" levels. The organization of the nervous system, like that of other biological systems, is influenced by myriad constraints arising from physical mechanics, magnetic fields, and so on, in which biology, chemistry, and physics demonstrate cause-and-effect across levels. We cannot deny a mental level, but its study must be integrated with that of other levels with which it shares a natural continuum.

As well, it is one thing to say *theoretically* that the computational description of mind can be done separately from the brain. However, we do not actually have such a complete description. Hence, in a practical sense, neurobiological study is an important part of the search for algorithms to emulate cognitive processes. We can both invent such algorithms (via models) and discover them. We cannot argue that biology is weak at such and such, so don't study it. For example, while arithmetic in one sense doesn't come naturally to us (see Anderson et al., chapter 12 in this volume), our ability to learn it is unlimited. In this vein, we must remember that the foundations of computer science have strong roots in neural modeling, particularly through the influence of the McCulloch-Pitts neuron on von Neumann. Here was a model of the neuron that in fact did logic and numerical operations, although not through learning. The resurgence of neurocomputing has somewhat lost touch with these roots, and it is time to return to them, except with half a century's extra knowledge of cognitive and neural science. We should find what other machines are available to us. If we can understand biology, in principle we can mimic it mechanically.

The quote that begins this chapter is the response of McCulloch to one of his mentors, Professor Rufus Jones from Haverford College, when asked what he would like to do with his life (cf. McCulloch, 1965). Professor Jones replied, "Thee will be busy as long as thee lives, Warren." Such interdisciplinary interest is obviously the more difficult path to follow, but such breadth is absolutely required if we are to fulfill the dreams of the founders of cognitive science.

REFERENCES

Ajjanagadde, V., & Shastri, L. (1991). Rules and variables in neural nets. *Neural Computation* 3, 121-134.

Ball, W. W. R., & Coxeter, H. S. M. (1987). *Mathematical Recreations and Essays*. New York: Dover.

Bapi, R. S., & Levine, D. S. (1990). Networks modeling the involvement of the frontal lobes in learning and performance of flexible movement sequences. *Proceedings of the Twelfth Annual Conference of the Cognitive Science Society* (pp. 915-922). Hillsdale, NJ: Lawrence Erlbaum Associates.

Blum, A. L., & Rivest, R. L. (1992). Training a 3-node neural network is NP-complete. *Neural Networks* 5, 117-127.

Bradski, G., Carpenter, G. A., & Grossberg, S. (1992). Working memory networks for learning temporal order with application to three-dimensional object recognition. *Neural Computation* 4, 270-286.

Brooks, R. A. (1991). New approaches to robotics. *Science* 253, 530-535.

Carpenter, G. A., Grossberg, S., & Reynolds, J. H. (1991). ARTMAP: Supervised real-time learning and classification of nonstationary data by a self-organizing neural network. *Neural Networks* 4, 565-588.

Chandrasekharan, B., Goel, A., & Allemang, D. (1988, July). Connectionism and information processing abstractions. *AI Magazine*, pp. 24-34.

Chomsky, N. (1964). *Syntactic Structures*. The Hague: Mouton.

Cohen, J. D., Dunbar, K., & McClelland, J. L. (1990). A parallel distributed processing model of the Stroop effect. *Psychological Review* 97, 332-361.

Crowder, R. G. (1976). *Principles of Learning and Memory*. Hillsdale, NJ: Lawrence Erlbaum Associates.

Davenport, R., Jakobsson, E., & Gerber, B. (1991). Possible dual effects of synapses that are putatively purely excitatory or purely inhibitory: Bases in stability theory and implications for neural network behavior. *Biological Cybernetics* 65, 47-53.

Dehaene, S., & Changeux, J.-P. (1989). A simple model of prefrontal cortex function in delayed response tasks. *Journal of Cognitive Neuroscience* 1, 244-261.

Dehaene, S., & Changeux, J.-P. (1991). The Wisconsin Card Sorting Test: Theoretical analysis and modeling in a neuronal network. *Cerebral Cortex* 1, 62-79.

Dehaene, S., Changeux, J.-P., & Nadal, J. P. (1987). Neural networks that learn temporal sequences by selection. *Proceedings of the National Academy of Sciences, USA* 84, 2727-2731.

Denning, P. J. (1986). The science of computing: Expert systems. *American Scientist* 74, 18-20.

Edelman, G. M. (1989) The Remembered Present. New York: Basic Books.

Eichenbaum, H., & Buckingham, J. (1991). Studies on hippocampal processing: Experiment, theory, and model. In M. Gabriel and J. Moore (Eds.), *Learning and Computational Neuroscience: Foundations of Adaptive Networks* (pp. 171-231). Cambridge, MA: MIT Press.

Farah, M. (1989). The neural basis of mental imagery. *Trends in NeuroSciences* 12, 395-399.

Fodor, J. A. (1975). *The Language of Thought*. New York: Crowell.

Fodor, J. A., & Pylyshyn, Z. W. (1988). Connectionism and cognitive architecture: A critical analysis. *Cognition* 28, 3-71.

Fu, L.-M. (1989). Integration of neural heuristics into knowledge-based inference. *Connection Science* 1, 327-342.

Gardner, H. (1987). *The Mind's New Science: A History of the Cognitive Revolution*. New York: Basic Books.

Gevarter, W. B. (1984).   Overview of artificial intelligence and robotics, Vol. 1, Artificial Intelligence, Part-A, The core ingredients. National Technical Information Service, PB84-178037.

Grossberg, S. (1975).   A neural model of attention, reinforcement, and discrimination learning. *International Review of Neurobiology* **18**, 263-327.

Grossberg, S. (1987).   Cortical dynamics of three-dimensional form, color, and brightness perception, II Binocular theory. *Perception and Psychophysics* **41**, 117-158.

Grossberg, S. (1988). *Neural Networks and Natural Intelligence.* Cambridge, MA: MIT Press.

Grossberg, S., & Mingolla, E. (1985).   Neural dynamics of form perception: boundary completion, illusory figures, and neon color spreading. *Psychological Review* **92**, 173-211.

Hameroff, S. (1991).   Microtubule automata: Sub-neural information processing in biological neural networks. *Theoretical Aspects of Neurocomputing, Selected Papers from Symposium on Neural Networks and Neurocomputing,* 3-12.

Hempel, C. G. (1966). *Philosophy of Natural Science.* Englewood Cliffs, NJ: Prentice-Hall.

Hestenes, D. (1992).   A neural network theory of manic-depressive illness. In D. S. Levine & S. J. Leven (Eds.), *Motivation, Emotion, and Goal Direction in Neural Networks* (pp. 209-257). Hillsdale, NJ: Lawrence Erlbaum Associates.

Hinton, G. E., & Becker, S. (1990).   An unsupervised learning procedure that discovers surfaces in random-dot stereograms. *Proceedings of the International Joint Conference on Neural Networks,* January, 1990 (Vol. 1, pp. 218-222). Hillsdale, NJ: Lawrence Erlbaum Associates.

Hirose, Y., Yamashita, K., & Hijiya, S. (1991).   Back-propagation algorithm which varies the number of hidden units. *Neural Networks* **4**, 61-66.

Hirsch, M. W., & Smale, S. (1974). *Differential Equations, Dynamical Systems, and Linear Algebra.* New York: Academic Press.

Hofstadter, D. R. (1980). *Godel, Escher, Bach: An Eternal Golden Braid.* New York: Vintage Books.

Hopfield, J. J. (1982).   Neural networks and physical systems with emergent collective computational abilities. *Proceedings of the National Academy of Sciences* **79**, 2554-2558.

Hulse, S. H., Egeth, H., & Deese, J. (1980). *The Psychology of Learning.* New York: McGraw-Hill.

Jenkins, J. J. (1981).   Can we have a fruitful cognitive psychology? In H. E. Howe, Jr., and J. H. Flowers (Eds.), *Cognitive Processes: Nebraska Symposium on Motivation* (pp. 211-238). Lincoln, NE: University of Nebraska Press.

Jokinen, P. A. (1991).   A nonlinear network model for continuous learning. *Neurocomputing* **3**, 157-176.

Judd, J. S. (1991). *Neural Network Design and the Complexity of Learning.* Cambridge, MA: MIT Press.

Kandel, E. R., & Schwartz, J. H. (Eds.) (1985). *Principles of Neural Science.* New York: Elsevier.

Kosko, B. (1987).   Adaptive inference in fuzzy knowledge networks. *IEEE First International Conference on Neural Networks* (Volume II, pp. 759-766). San Diego: IEEE/ICNN.

Kosslyn, S. M. (1980). *Image and Mind.* Cambridge, MA: Harvard University Press.

Kurzweil, R. (1985). What is artificial intelligence anyway? *American Scientist* **73**, 258-264.

Laird, J. E., Rosenbloom, P. S., & Newell, A. (1985). Chunking in SOAR: The anatomy of a general learning mechanism. Tech. Rep. No. CMU-CS-85-154, Carnegie-Mellon University.

Lakoff, G., & Johnson, M. (1980). *Metaphors We Live By*. Chicago: University of Chicago Press.

Lee, S., & Kil, R. M. (1991). A Gaussian potential function network with hierarchically self-organizing learning. *Neural Networks* **4**, 207-224.

Levine, D. S. (1983). Neural population modeling and psychology: A review. *Mathematical Biosciences* **66**, 1-86.

Levine, D. S. (1989). Neural network principles for theoretical psychology. *Behavior Research Methods, Instruments, and Computers* **21**, 213-224.

Levine, D. S. (1991). *Introduction to Neural and Cognitive Modeling*. Hillsdale, NJ: Lawrence Erlbaum Associates.

Levine, D. S., & Leven, S. J. (Eds.) (1992). *Motivation, Emotion, and Goal Direction in Neural Networks*. Hillsdale, NJ: Lawrence Erlbaum Associates.

Levine, D. S., Parks, R. W., & Prueitt, P. S. (1993). Methodological and theoretical issues in neural network models of frontal cognitive function. *To appear in International Journal of Neuroscience*.

Levine, D. S., & Prueitt, P. S. (1989). Modeling some effects of frontal lobe damage: Novelty and perseveration. *Neural Networks* **2**, 103-116.

Loftus, G. (1985). Johannes Kepler's computer simulation of the universe: Some remarks about theory in psychology. *Behavior Research Methods, Instruments, and Computers* **17**, 149-156.

Marr, D., & Poggio, T. (1979). A computational theory of human stereo vision. *Proceedings of the Royal Society of London, Series B* **204**, 301-328.

McCulloch, W. S. (1965). *Embodiments of Mind*. Cambridge, MA: MIT Press.

McCulloch, W. S., & Pitts, W. (1943). A logical calculus of the ideas immanent in nervous activity. *Bulletin of Mathematical Biophysics* **5**, 115-133.

Minsky, M., & Papert, S. (1969). *An Introduction to Computational Geometry*. Cambridge, MA: MIT Press.

Mota Tenorio, M. F. (1990). Topology synthesis networks: Self organization of structure and weight adjustment as a learning paradigm. *Parallel Computing* **14**, 363-380.

Newell, A. (1980). HARPY, production systems, and human cognition. In R. Cole (Ed.), *Perception and Production of Fluent Speech* (pp. 289-295). Hillsdale, NJ: Lawrence Erlbaum Associates.

Newell, A., & Simon, H. A. (1963). GPS: A program that simulates human thought. In E. A. Feigenbaum & J. Feldman (Eds.), *Computers and Thought* (pp. 279-293). New York: McGraw-Hill.

O'Keefe, J., & Nadel, L. (1978). *The Hippocampus as a Cognitive Map*. Oxford: Oxford University Press.

Piaget, J. (1952). *The Origin of Intelligence in Children*, translated by M. Cook. New York: International University Press.

Pinker, S. (1991). Rules of language. *Science* **253**, 530-535.

Pinker, S., & Prince, A. (1988). On language and connectionism: Analysis of a parallel distributed processing model of language acquisition. *Cognition* **28**, 73-194.

Pylyshyn, Z. W. (1984). *Computation and Cognition: Toward a Foundation for Cognitive Science*. Cambridge, MA: MIT Press.

Rumelhart, D. E., & McClelland, J. L. (Eds.) (1986). *Parallel Distributed Processing*, Vol. I. Cambridge, MA: MIT Press.

Sankar, A., & Mammone, R. J. (1991). Combining neural networks and decision trees. SPIE Vol. 1469, *Applications of Artificial Neural Networks II*.

Shepherd, G. M., & Brayton, R. K. (1987). Logic operations are properties of computer-simulated interactions between excitable dendritic spines. *Neuroscience* **21**, 151-165.

Smith, E. E., Langston, C., & Nisbett, R. E. (1992). The case for rules in reasoning. *Cognitive Science* **16**, 1-40.

Stinchcombe, M., & White, H. (1989). Universal approximation using feedforward networks with non-sigmoid hidden layer activation functions. *International Joint Conference on Neural Networks, Washington, DC*, Vol. I, 613-617.

Sun, R. (1991). Integrating rules and connectionism for robust reasoning: A connectionist architecture with dual representation. Unpublished doctoral dissertation, Brandeis University.

Sutherland, J. W. (1986). Assessing the artificial intelligence contribution to decision technology. *IEEE Transactions on Systems, Man, and Cybernetics* **SMC-16**, 3-20.

Szu, H. H. (1989). A dynamic reconfigurable neural network. *Journal of Neural Network Computing*, special report.

Szu, H. H. (1992, February). Why do we study neural networks on VLSI chips and why are wavelets more natural for brain-style computing? Paper presented at MIND conference on Optimality in Biological and Artificial Networks?, Richardson, TX.

Tani, J., & Fujita, M. (1992). Coupling of memory search and mental rotation by a nonequilibrium dynamics neural network. *IEICE Transactions on the Fundamentals of Electronic Communication and Computer Science (Japan)* **E75-A**, 578-585.

Tattersall, G. D. (1990). Optimal rule induction in neural networks. *International Neural Network Conference, Paris*, Vol. II, 788.

Teyler, T. J., & DiScenna, P. (1986). The hippocampal memory indexing theory. *Behavioral Neuroscience* **100**, 147-154.

Thagard, P. (1989). Explanatory coherence. *The Behavioral and Brain Sciences* **12**, 435-502.

Touretzky, D. S., & Hinton, G. E. (1986). A distributed connectionist production system. Technical Report CMU-CS-86-172, Carnegie-Mellon University.

Tversky, A., & Kahneman, D. (1974). Judgment under uncertainty: Heuristics and biases. *Science* **185**, 1124-1131.

Tversky, A., & Kahneman, D. (1981). The framing of decisions and the rationality of choice. *Science* **211**, 453-458.

von Neumann, J. (1958). *The Computer and the Brain*. New Haven: Yale University Press.

Wang, D., & Arbib, M. A. (1990). Complex temporal sequence learning based on short-term memory. *Proceedings of the IEEE* **78**, 1536-1543.

Whorf, B. L. (1965). *Language, Thought, and Reality: Selected Writings*. Cambridge, MA: MIT Press.

Winston, P. H. (1977). *Artificial Intelligence*. Reading, MA: Addison-Wesley.

Zipser, D. (1990).   Short term active memory: A recurrent network model of the neural mechanism.   Tech. Rep. No. 9003, Department of Cognitive Science, University of California, San Diego.

2

On Using Analogy to Reconcile Connections and Symbols

John A. Barnden
New Mexico State University

How do we gain both the standard advantages of connectionism and those of symbolic systems, without adopting hybrid symbolic/connectionist systems? Fully connectionist systems that support analogy-based reasoning are proposed as an answer, at least in the realm of high-level cognitive processing. This domain includes commonsense reasoning and the semantic/pragmatic aspects of natural language processing. The proposed type of system, purely by being analogy-based, gains forms of graceful degradation, representation completion, similarity-based generalization, learning, rule-emergence and exception-emergence. The system therefore gains advantages commonly associated with connectionism, although the precise forms of the benefits are different. At the same time, through being fully connectionist, the system also gains the traditional connectionist variants of those advantages, as well as gaining further advantages not provided by analogy-based reasoning per se. And, because the system is in part an implementation of a form of symbolic processing, it preserves the flexible handling of complex, temporary structures that are well supported in traditional artificial intelligence and which are essential for high-level cognitive processing. This chapter is in part a reaction against the excessive polarization of the connectionism/symbolicism debate. This polarization is seen as resulting from over-simplified, monolithic views both of what symbolic processing encompasses and of the nature of the benefits that connectionism provides.

1. INTRODUCTION

Connectionists and symbolicists each tend to look at their own camp through rose-colored spectacles, and at that of their opponents through darkly tinted ones. Such is the effect of polarization. In particular, each camp tends to take a simplistic view of the opportunities provided by the other. But the use of less highly colored spectacles reveals a more complex scenario. My purpose in this chapter is to argue that there is an untrodden road towards the possible future reconciliation of connectionism and symbolicism[1], adhering to the best part of each camp, circumventing the worst of each, and yet not involving the common idea of hybrid systems.

The term "hybrid" (within the confines of the connectionist/symbolicist debate) is often left unclarified, and misunderstanding sometimes arises as a result. By a hybrid system I mean one that has both connectionist aspects and symbolicist ones, where the latter has no stated implementation in connectionist terms. There are several things to emphasize here. First, I use the word "aspect" to avoid the implication that a hybrid system need have two different types of *module*, namely connectionist and symbolicist. On the contrary, a system might be hybrid in a much more intimately integrated way, by being, say, a network which operates much as a connectionist net does but in which the signals passed on connections are more complex than single real numbers. Secondly, the crucial feature of the definition is the lack of a stated connectionist implementation of the symbolicist aspects. Consider an *implementational-connectionist* system — one that can be accurately described at a high level as manipulating symbolic structures in a conventional symbolic manner, but where these structures and manipulations are fully cashed out in terms of connectionism (using for instance the implementational capabilities of the tensor-based approach of Smolensky (1990), the signature-based approach of Lange and Dyer (1989), the time-phase-based techniques of Ajjanagadde and Shastri (Ajjanagadde, 1990; Shastri & Ajjanagadde, 1989), or the techniques of Barnden (1988a, 1988b, 1989, 1991; Barnden & Srinivas, 1991). I do *not* cast such a system as hybrid, even though it has a symbolicist aspect — namely its nature under the high-level, symbolicist description — simply because that aspect is indeed given a connectionist implementation. Finally, I do not require that in a hybrid system the symbolicist aspects *cannot* be given a connectionist implementation. I merely require that no such implementation shall have been stated by the author of the system to be part of the system as such. If this makes hybridness partly a matter of viewpoint, so be it.

Hybridness so defined is probably more complex a notion than it is usually taken to be, but I believe it to be the notion implicitly intended in the literature.

I mentioned a road towards reconciliation that does not involve hybrid systems. This is not because I think hybrid systems are undesirable in themselves. I have several motivations for steering clear of hybridness. One is simply that it is theoretically interesting and methodologically useful to see how far connectionism can be pushed without resorting to system aspects with no defined connectionist implementation. Another is that the branch of connectionism aimed at illuminating biological neural networks must ultimately deal with *fully* connectionist systems. Finally, I argued elsewhere (Barnden & Srinivas, 1992) that, from the point of view of engineering capable cognitive systems, irrespective of any pretence at psychological or biological plausibility, there are technical advantages to having fully connectionist systems as opposed to hybrid ones. However, I stress that there are perfectly valid reasons for wanting to go hybrid.

---

[1] I use the term "symbolicism" rather than the easier and more common word "symbolism," since the latter already has perfectly good meaning of its own.

After all, the technical advantages just alluded to may be irrelevant to a particular project. The researcher might have no eye on neural inspiration. The researcher might also have no interest in seeing how far connectionism can be pushed.

The road towards reconciliation that I propose is that of devising fully connectionist systems that, at a high level of description, can be viewed as doing *analogy-based reasoning* (henceforth ABR). I clarify later on what I mean by this, and also clarify why it is that typical connectionist systems are not to be viewed as doing ABR in any standard sense, even though they do a sort of *similarity*-based processing. The significance of ABR is as follows: Attacks on symbolicism by connectionists are usually presented in very brief, simplistic terms, and seem to be directed at simple (and usually unclarified) forms of rule-based processing. Hence, one hears of the rigidity of symbolic processing, the lack of graceful degradation, and so forth. I review later the nature of the claimed deficiencies, and indeed agreeing that there is some pragmatic validity to the claims. Now, one possible reaction would be to argue that sufficiently elaborate rule-based systems could indeed achieve non-rigidity, graceful degradation, and so on (Pinker & Prince, 1988, pp. 130-136, 153ff.; Smolensky 1988a). However, I go a big step beyond, or over, this: I argue that ABR, normally left unstressed by either side in the connectionist/symbolicist debate, *intrinsically* and without contrivance avoids many of the deficiencies of rule-based reasoning. It does so even in its conventional, purely-symbolic forms. However, it can be made even more advantageous by being realized in fully connectionist systems. Furthermore, this realization can be made partly by means of already-known techniques of implementational connectionism (as defined above), so that the resulting connectionist system *also* evades that notorious bug-bear of connectionism, the difficulty of getting standard connectionist techniques to cope with complex processing of complex structures of information.

A word on such structures and manipulations: The overarching motivation behind the advocated approach is the design of systems capable of what can be summarized as *high-level cognitive processing* — which includes, notably, commonsense reasoning and (at least) the semantic and pragmatic aspects of natural language processing. Therefore, I am concerned with systems that can indeed cope with the sorts of complex, temporary packages of information that arise in the course of reasoning and natural language processing. For instance, the interpretation of a sentence is one such package. Intermediate results of some train of reasoning form another such package. (These packages take the form of lists, trees, graphs and so on in symbolicist systems.) Incidentally, it probably needs emphasizing that under "reasoning" I include multiple forms of non-sound reasoning, such as abduction, induction, and various forms of default and plausible reasoning, not just sound deduction.

A common argument against the use of implementational connectionism is that it just inherits the deficiencies of traditional symbolicist processing, whereas it is felt that much of the point of connectionism is to avoid those deficiencies. So, the overall train of thought on the connectionist side of the symbolicist/connectionist debate appears to be as follows.

(a) Symbolicist systems are undesirable (because of rigidity, etc.).

(b) Implementational-connectionist systems are undesirable for reasons inherited from (a).

(c) So, we had better use non-implementational connectionism in the new wave of cognitive systems, which ...

(d) ... should not have anything that smacks very closely of conventional symbolic structures.

However, a central point of this chapter is that step (d) is a rank non sequitur. The unstated assumption in the argument is that the class of systems that use anything like conventional symbolic structures is exhausted by the class of symbolicist systems that are the target of implementational connectionism under the common understanding of that term. On the contrary, what I claim is that connectionistically realized ABR systems use conventional symbolicist structures but nevertheless avoid the deficiencies implicitly complained about in (a) and (b).

Another strong theme in this chapter is that, not only has the connectionist view of the symbolicist realm been made simplistic through polarization of issues, but the connectionist view of its own strong points, such as graceful degradation and similarity-based generalization, has also been simplistic. The impression one gets from much of the connectionist literature is that there is one unitary thing called graceful degradation, one unitary thing called similarity-based generalization, and so on, and that connectionism achieves them. However, I point out that there are several varieties of graceful degradation (etc.), and that it is by no means clear that the particular variety that connectionism achieves is actually the most, or the only, desirable form. In particular, I argue that ABR achieves its own useful forms of graceful degradation, etc. These forms are not necessarily readily achievable in standard connectionist systems. I do not seek to adjudicate between the various forms, because in fact the advocated style of system ends up having both.

The course of the argument is fairly tortuous, because of the need to address several different types of advantage:

(1) commonly claimed advantages of standard connectionist systems, such as graceful degradation and similarity-based generalization;

(2) commonly claimed advantages of symbolicist systems (such as easy support of systematicity and structure-sensitivity: Fodor & Pylyshyn, 1988);

(3) variants of the advantages in (1) that are also obtainable in ABR systems even when in conventional symbolicist clothes;

(4) those advantages of standard connectionism that are *not* achievable by purely symbolic ABR.

We also have the complication of having to observe the distinction between implementational and non-implementational forms of connectionism. Recall that in implementational connectionism the system is an implementation of symbolic processing.

Accordingly, the chapter proceeds as follows. It first reviews (1), the advantages usually attributed to (non-implementational) connectionism. It then reviews (2), the disadvantages of such systems, or to put it another way, the advantages of symbolicist systems.   It then summarizes the nature of ABR. The chapter then addresses (3), showing how symbolic ABR systems can achieve benefits parallel to *some* of the advantages in (1).   Next, the chapter summarizes (4) and makes clear the (complex) state of play up to that point. The last major task of the chapter is to outline the particular style of system that is being advocated, namely a class of connectionistically realized ABR systems.

Although I am developing a particular system in this class, the chapter is not concerned with detailing it. (See instead Barnden & Srinivas, 1992, for the detail of a preliminary version.) Also, I should emphasize that the purpose of the chapter is to point at a promising avenue of research, not to prove that this avenue can in fact be successfully followed. I believe it can be, but there remain several research issues to be worked through. Some of these are mentioned in the concluding section.

2. STANDARD CONNECTIONIST ADVANTAGES

Here I review some advantages that standard connectionist systems are often claimed to have. They are listed in the lefthand column of Table 2.1. For the sake of argument I uncritically assume that these claims are justified. There seems little doubt that they are at least partially justified.

STANDARD CONNECTIONIST	TRADITIONAL AI	ANALOGY-BASED
graceful degradation	*no*	*yes*
representation completion	*no*	*yes*
similarity-based generalization	*no*	*yes*
learning	*yes*	*yes*
emergent rules	*no*	*yes*
emergent exceptions	*no*	*yes*
content-based access	*no*	*no*
holistic structure processing	*no*	*no*
soft-constraint satisfaction	*no*	*no*
no	complex temp info structures	*yes*

Table 2.1. Advantages of various types of system.

A system is said to exhibit *graceful degradation* when it can tolerate significant corruption of its inputs and/or its internal workings and still give reasonable performance. We can therefore distinguish between graceful degradation *with respect to input corruption* and graceful degradation *with respect to system corruption*. Connectionist systems, especially distributed ones, often exhibit one or both types.

First we consider graceful degradation with respect to input corruption. Suppose a significant proportion of the elements of an input vector have been corrupted. Let I be the uncorrupted vector. It is then typically the case that the system can still perform roughly as it would have done with the correct input vector, I. (There are natural exceptions to this, as when the corruption takes the vector near an uncorrupted vector that correctly leads to performance markedly different from the response to I.) Also, in some types of network, if the input vector units are not clamped one can let the internal influences between units massage the input vector into one closer to what the system expects. As for graceful degradation with respect to system corruption, a significant proportion of the weights can often be corrupted without drastically affecting the performance of the network. This scenario also covers the case of deleting nodes, because this can usually be viewed as setting the weights on the nodes' connections to zero. These types of graceful degradation are more readily found in distributed than in localist networks, since in the former variety any individual unit or connection is much less important than it is in a localist network.

It is worth reviewing some reasons why it is fair to say that traditional AI systems tend not to degrade gracefully. For definiteness, I consider a straightforward rule-based system. A small corruption of an input data structure is likely to make it fail to match the precise form expected by the rules which would have operated on the uncorrupted data structure. (See also Holyoak, 1991, p. 313, on this point.) For instance, if a rule R expects to see a list whose first element is a symbol A (which is not a variable), and A in the actual input has been replaced by a different non-variable symbol B, then the rule will typically no longer be triggered. This is the case even if there is no other rule that matches the input more closely than R does. (Of course, if A or B were a variable, the way would be open for one to be bound to the other. But atomic elements that are not variables are required to match exactly.) Also, corruptions that take the form of deletions of items, rather than a replacement of items by incorrect ones, also typically cause large changes in the performance of the system. For instance, either drastically too few rules may be triggered, or new rules that lead to run-time errors might be triggered. As for lack of graceful degradation with respect to system corruption, damage to some component of a rule in a rule-based system can have large effects on how the system operates. The corruption might even have the effect of making the system break down, giving a run-time hard error of some sort, rather than merely giving a wrong answer. In sum, it is plausible to say that some prototypical types of traditional AI system suffer from a lack of both varieties of graceful degradation.

In a connectionist system, we often find a *representation completion* or *pattern-completion* property. This can take two basic forms. An incomplete pattern of activation on an input bank of units can lead to a known completion of the pattern appearing on an output bank. Or, an incomplete pattern on some bank of units can lead to a known completion appearing on that same bank. What it means to say that a pattern is incomplete varies somewhat with the specific nature of the system, but an incomplete pattern typically consists either of a pattern (of values of any sort) in which some elements have been replaced by occurrences of a special *don't-care* value (which is typically 0 if the possible values are -1, 0, and 1), or of a pattern of 0s and 1s in which some elements have been replaced by 0s (or values that are randomly 0 or 1). A known completion of an incomplete pattern P is a pattern on which the system has been in some sense completion of an incomplete pattern P is a pattern on which the system has been in some sense trained and from which P could be derived by suitable replacements of the sort just described. Clearly, the pattern completion property of (many) connectionist systems can be seen as just a special case of graceful degradation with respect to input corruption. Therefore, it was implicitly subsumed by the discussion in the previous subsection.

Connectionist systems are also widely noted for their capability for *automatic similarity-based generalization*. This property is closely related to, if not essentially identical to, the property of graceful degradation with respect to input corruption. Previously unseen inputs that are sufficiently similar to inputs on which the system has been trained lead to behavior that is usefully similar to that elicited by the training inputs.

A strongly related property of standard connectionist systems is their ability to *learn* generalizations or category prototypes by virtue of exposure to instances of the generalizations or categories. These generalizations or prototypes are implicit in the weights, that is, implicit in the way the system operates. They are not themselves items that can be used as input to reasoning processes within the network. I return to this important but often overlooked point later on. Notice that learning, in a wide variety of forms, is widely studied in traditional AI. Perhaps, however, it is fair to say that certain types of learning are more intrinsically and wholeheartedly supported by connectionism.

It has been claimed that connectionism provides a framework in which a system can have *merely-emergent rule-like behavior*. Such a system can be described (approximately, at least) as following rules, without actually operating by means of the interpretation of explicit rules (Rumelhart & McClelland, 1986; Smolensky, 1988a, 1988b). One potential benefit of emergence is that the system's actual operation can be more subtle and more sensitive to nuances of the situation than would be (practically) possible by means of explicit rule interpretation.

As an aspect of emergent rule-like behavior, one can point also to *merely-emergent exceptions*. A connectionist system need not explicitly note or work out that something is an exception. For instance, in the past-tense model of Rumelhart and McClelland (1986), rules and exceptions to them develop without the system ever having to become aware of the *fact that* irregularities are exceptions to the regularities. On the other hand, a traditional AI learning system that developed its own rules during training would be likely to have to construct rules dedicated to particular irregularities or sets of irregularities. To that extent it would have to observe the fact that regularities are being violated, and reason about that fact. To be fair, however, it is by no means clear that the merely-emergent quality of exceptions in connectionist systems is actually an advantage. Presumably it is dubbed an advantage because it represents a saving of work, and a saving in the mechanism that would otherwise be needed for noting and reasoning about exceptions. (And it would seem that such a mechanism would be difficult to build using traditional connectionist tools.) However, there is a case for the hypothesis that it is *desirable* for systems to notice and reason about exceptions. After all, we do. And don't we want connectionist systems eventually to be able to answer questions like "How does one form past tenses of verbs in English?" Surely we want learning systems to be able, at least sometimes, to output descriptions of their generalizations and the exceptions to them, not just act in accordance with them. (I argue this point more fully in Barnden (1992) for the case of generalizations, but do not consider exceptions there.) In sum, the fact that rules and exceptions in connectionist systems can be merely emergent is not an unalloyed advantage.

It is important to realize that rule-based systems in AI are by no means forced to have any awareness of exceptions, or special mechanisms for them, while performing (as opposed to learning). Consider a rule-based system equipped with a specificity rule for conflict resolution. This means, roughly, that if two rules apply to a situation, but one has a more specific condition part, then that one will be chosen in preference to the other, other things being equal. For instance, if one rule is *if X is a bird then X flies* and the other is *if X is a penguin then X does not fly*, then the specificity heuristic will give preference to the latter (assuming the system knows that penguins are a particular type of bird). Here there is no difference in basic form between the rule encoding the subregularity concerning penguins and the generalization concerning birds, nor are these rules applied in different ways, nor do they enter into conflict resolution in different ways. Really, the only feature of the system that comes close to being a special mechanism for exceptions is the specificity-preference mechanism itself. However, even this is not *dedicated* to exception-handling, since the rule preferred by specificity need not encode an exception anyway. For instance, the more specific rule in our example could have been *if X is a roadrunner then X eats snakes*, which merely provides extra, not exceptional, information. The real purpose of the specificity heuristic is to focus on more special information, of which exceptional information is just one special case.

At the same time, the system does have the ability to work out, when necessary, what are its generalizations and exceptions, by meta-reasoning about its own rules. A standard connectionist system does not have the corresponding luxury of being able to reason efficiently *about* the knowledge that is encoded in its own weights (as opposed to *using* that knowledge to transform activation patterns passing through the net). This is because a standard connectionist system cannot, in general, efficiently convert its own pattern of weights into a pattern of activation values. Since activation patterns are what are directly processed by the system, it follows that it cannot reason efficiently about its own weight-encoded knowledge. With very specialized subnetworks, such as those used for the long-term memory of ART 3 (Carpenter & Grossberg, 1990), it is indeed possible for some subpatterns of weights to lead directly to a corresponding activity pattern which can be subjected to whatever processing is desired. However, most connectionist systems do not have subnetworks of this form.

Connectionism has an intrinsic capability for efficient *content-based access* (or: *associative access*) to long-term memory, in two different senses. First, given that a standard connectionist system's long-term memory is its weight matrix, and that specific situations that the system has encountered have left their mark on that matrix, the manipulation of an input vector by the network can be thought of as the bringing to bear of relevant long-term memories on that vector. Secondly, a hetero-associating connectionist network can be thought of as outputting activity patterns encoding long-term memories that are in some specific sense relevant to the input vector. Content-based access is not so easily provided in symbolic systems, as implemented on conventional computers, although some extent of content-based access can indeed be provided by the hashing technique (see, e.g., Standish, 1980), by tailor-made indexing schemes, and by associative computer memories (see, e.g., Hwang & Briggs, 1984).

Some connectionist systems have demonstrated an ability to perform *holistic structure-sensitive processing*. In this style of processing, encodings of whole complex information structures (*e.g.*, trees) are manipulated in structure-sensitive ways but without decomposition. That is, the processing does not involve working out the encodings of the parts of the whole structures from the encodings of the wholes. The systems of Chalmers (1990) and Blank, Meeden, and Marshall (1992) are able to holistically manipulate activation patterns that are encodings of sentences or propositions, where the manipulations must be sensitive to the sentence/proposition syntax. These systems rely on encodings that appear on the middle layers of Recursive Auto-Associative Memories or RAAMs (Pollack, 1988, 1990). These encodings are a form of reduced representation (Hinton, 1988, 1990). Reduced-representation techniques provide a way of compressing several part encodings of some size into a vector of the same size that encodes the whole structure. This then allows the possibility of recursion; the new vector can itself be compressed together with several companions into a further vector.

A large number of connectionist systems are cast as performing efficient, parallel *soft-constraint satisfaction*, whereby, broadly put, some hypotheses compete and cooperate with each other, gradually influencing each other's levels of confidence until a stable (though not necessarily totally consistent) set of hypotheses is found. It is also sometimes claimed that connectionism provides a ready means for combining the influence of very different sorts of hypothesis, because all communication is in the lingua franca of activation levels. However, this point is suspect, since it makes the assumption that activation levels have a completely uniform interpretation as confidence levels. It is by no means clear, however, that activation levels need always encode confidence levels; and even when they do, one has to add the assumption that the activation-level to confidence level function is uniform (up to a constant scale factor) across different connections coming into any given node. Further, symbolic data structures can, when necessary, act as a lingua franca, so it is unclear why a contrast to symbolic systems is claimed. The advantages that connectionism does have are softness of the constraints and the ability to deal with a large number of constraints simultaneously.

3. SOME STANDARD CONNECTIONIST DISADVANTAGES

Here we look briefly at certain pertinent disadvantages of standard connectionist techniques. The issues have been discussed more extensively elsewhere (Barnden 1984; Barnden & Pollack, 1991; Dyer, 1991; Norman, 1986; Pinker & Prince, 1988).

The difficulties arise as soon as one seeks to use connectionism to deal with the sorts of quickly constructed and often temporary bodies of information that need to be dealt with in traditional AI tasks, such as natural language understanding and commonsense reasoning. For instance, in understanding the sentence "Susan gets angry whenever Tom talks about going to Tibet," the system must in some way represent the content of the sentence. But this may involve bringing together concepts that have never before been brought together. Moreover: the bringing together, though often complex, needs to be done rapidly; the representation should not be required to attain the status of a long-term memory (unless one were to adopt the surprising thesis that all incoming information goes into long-term memory); and the representation should be of a form that supports reasonably efficient inferencing, the products of which are themselves representations of the same ilk. For instance, one possibly useful inference is that Susan probably does not want Tom to go to Tibet. Furthermore, the representation has no fixed "shape" or size; for instance, items of widely varying complexity could replace "Tibet" in the example. For instance, the speaker could have used the description, "any country that isn't a parliamentary democracy." Another difficulty is the multiple-instantiations problem: allowing a system to support several temporary concept-combinations of a similar type simultaneously, such as several propositions that all state causation relationships between events.

Furthermore, Fodor and Pylyshyn (1988) remarked that cognition requires qualities of *systematicity* and *structure-sensitivity*. Even Fodor and Pylyshyn's critics (e.g., Chalmers, 1990; Smolensky, 1988a) agree with that requirement, even though they may disagree about what the qualities amount to and how they are to be assured. The variable-binding problem is one form of the systematicity problem, and is still widely recognized to be a stumbling-block for connectionism despite the growing number of approaches to it (for instance in: Ajjanagadde, 1990; Barnden, 1988b, 1989, 1991; Lange & Dyer, 1989; Smolensky, 1990; Touretzky, 1986, 1990).

Standard connectionist techniques do not readily support the just noted arbitrariness, temporariness, rapidity of construction, inferentiability, and widely varying complexity of the combinations of concepts required by natural language understanding, and the systematicity and structure sensitivity of the required processing of such combinations. It is beyond the scope of the present chapter to justify why the techniques are deficient in these regards. Indeed, the justification is by no means simple, partly because of the slipperiness of the very notion of connectionism, and few authors trouble to provide a general justification. Some of the basic sources of difficulty are that: standard connectionism does not allow rapid changes in network topology; even if such changes are allowed, there is great difficulty in using newly-created subnetworks in inferencing; the use of binding nodes to establish temporary pathways without topology changes has drawbacks; any close analogue of pointers is repudiated by standard connectionism, which at the same time, curiously, has not sought close analogues of the other computer data-structuring primitives, namely sequential allocation and associative addressing[2]; and it is desirable to allow a given information structure to appear in a multiplicity of alternative positions in the overall network.

Of connectionist work using standard techniques, the holistic-processing work mentioned in Section 2 comes the closest to achieving the requirements I have alluded to in this section. However, it is still a long way from demonstrating that the requirements can be fully met, and is also a long way from matching the capabilities of implementational-connectionist techniques such as those in Ajjanagadde (1990), Barnden (1988b, 1989, 1991), Lange and Dyer (1989), Smolensky (1990) and Touretzky (1986, 1990). As I remark more fully in Barnden (1992), the performance of the systems even on the actual experiments performed leaves something to be desired, and these experiments only scratch the tip of the iceberg of the types of structures and manipulations that need to be accounted for. In particular, there is a major problem involved in accounting for *embedded reasoning*, such as inferring that if (i) X believes P and (ii) X believes Q follows from P, then (iii) X is likely to believe Q, without decomposing the reduced representations for (i) and (ii) into parts.

---

[2] Close analogues to these are, however, provided in the Relative-Position Encoding and Pattern-Similarity Association techniques (Barnden 1988a, 1988b, 1991a; Barnden & Srinivas, in press).

4. ANALOGY-BASED REASONING

Analogy-based reasoning (ABR) is the process of reasoning about one situation, problem or domain — the *target* — by transferring information from one or more other already-known situations, problems, or domains — the *retrieved sources* — that are perceived to be similar to the target. Different ABR systems in the literature vary significantly in their overall organization and detailed processing, but the following account summarizes a common view of analogy, which is the one adopted in this chapter. A much fuller account of ABR can be found in Kedar-Cabelli (1988), Hall (1989) and Vosniadou and Ortony (1989).

In ABR, the sources are retrieved from a *long-term memory of sources*, or *source memory* for short. Apart from the retrieval phase, at least two other phases are commonly identified: *mapping* and *transfer*. In the mapping phase the system establishes some detailed mapping from items (objects, properties, relationships, ...) in the source(s) to items in the target. In the transfer phase the system expands the target by the addition of transformed items from the source(s). The source items are transformed by the mapping that was established. For instance, if the mapping maps *John* and *Mary* in a source to *Susan* and *David* respectively in the target, and maps *loves* in the source to *likes* in the target, then the effect of transferring the proposition *John loves Mary* would be to add *Susan likes David* to the target. (The transferred items are source items that are not themselves mapped by the mapping that was set up.)

Further phases are often identified: notably the *evaluation* of transferred information (which may be inconsistent with what is known about the target, or with what later comes to be known), and a *learning* phase when transferred information has been given a positive evaluation. The learning can consist of adding the expanded target to source memory, or can consist of creating a generalization that fits the expanded target and the source(s), and then putting that generalization into source memory.

ABR has been studied in AI for some considerable time, as is apparent from the reviews of Kedar-Cabelli (1988) and Hall (1989). In spite of this, the area is still only a minority interest, and ABR systems can fairly be said to be "non-traditional" or "non-classical" AI systems. In recent years, *case-based reasoning* (Kolodner, Simpson, & Sycara-Cyranski, 1985; Riesbeck & Schank, 1989; Schank, 1982) has become another intensively studied but minority interest. CBR is essentially the same as ABR, but there is much more of a tendency to use sources that come from the same conceptual domain as the target, whereas much or most of the effort on ABR has concentrated in source(s) from a different conceptual domain. Thus, to transfer knowledge about water flow to a heat flow situation (Falkenhainer, Forbus, & Gentner, 1989) would be typical for ABR but atypical for CBR, while to transfer knowledge about one industrial conflict case to another such would be typical for CBR (Sycara, 1989) but atypical for ABR. However, these boundaries can be crossed. To take just two instances, Sycara and Navinchandra (1991) use transfers more like the water/heat one in a system that is said to do CBR, while Cook (1991) gives as an example of ABR the derivation of programs from other similar ones.

There are certainly differences in outlook, motivation and methodology between ABR and CBR researchers. For instance, CBR work tends to be more intensively directed at practical applications. Perhaps as a result of this, it has paid more attention to the algorithmic details of "efficiently retrieving relevant sources (called *cases* in the CBR area) than has ABR work, which has been more focused on mapping and the later stages.

ABR and CBR are also strongly related, if not essentially identical, to *memory-based reasoning* (MBR) (Stanfill & Waltz, 1986). Perhaps it is fair to say that the MBR field uses simpler notions of mapping and transfer than are typical in ABR and CBR. Henceforth, we will keep to the term ABR when talking about the reasoning itself, and will take this term to cover also the styles of reasoning dubbed as CBR or MBR in the literature. However, I will use "XBR literature" and "XBR field" to mean the literature and field that explicitly refers to XBR as opposed to some YBR.

It seems to be generally accepted that in ABR the sources are *explicit* individuals, separately encoded in memory. That is, ABR does not encompass styles of reasoning that do depend indirectly on similarities to past cases but where memory has no record of those cases as individuals. For instance, a reasoning system that relies on generalizations or prototypes *distilled from* examples that it has encountered, and does not make direct, explicit appeal to those examples themselves, does not count as an ABR system. (This comment applies equally well to symbolic inductive learning systems as to standard connectionist learning systems.) The matter is really one of degree; the more that a system makes direct appeal to individual examples and the more that the long-term memory consists of separate memories of individual examples, the more we are inclined to say that the system does ABR.

A sidelight on this restriction of the nature of ABR is that ABR can, when necessary, make inferences about a target on the basis of a single source, where, moreover, that source may well encode a situation encountered only once[3]. Indeed, that is the usual case studied in the ABR literature. The CBR and MBR literatures are, by contrast, often concerned with using several or many sources to illuminate a single target, but the systems concerned are still able to use single sources. However, in a standard connectionist learning system, trained with a large number of examples, no single example has much effect on the generalizations encoded in the weights (unless the example is presented to the system on a sizable proportion of the training events).

The ABR paradigm allows the degree or goodness of match between the target and a source to influence the degree of confidence with which information is transferred from the source. That is, transferred information is only ever tentative, ABR being a form of merely plausible reasoning. The worse the match between source and target, the less the confidence that should be attached to the transfers. Also, I allow the tentativeness of a transfer from a source to be influenced by the degree of confirmation from other sources. Thus, if another source fails to generate the same transfer, or generates a transfer that is inconsistent with it, then the transfer should be more tentative than it would otherwise be. In the same vein, there is a case for attaching more confidence to conclusions transferred from generalizations/prototypes than those transferred from individual examples, except when the examples match the target better.

---

[3] This is not to say that the system has actually encountered the situations encoded in its sources. Often the sources are constructed by hand, and we are merely to imagine that the system has encountered them.

5. NON-1-1 MAPPINGS IN ANALOGY

ABR work has concentrated to a considerable extent on 1-1 mappings. This is especially so within the psychology literature (K.J. Holyoak, personal communication, October 15, 1991). Systems are typically limited to making a mapped item in the source correspond to at most one item in the target, and making an item in the target correspond to at most one item in the source. For instance, the Structure Mapping Engine (Falkenhainer et al., 1989) throws out non-1-1 mappings during the construction of global maps, although it seems that the underlying theory (Gentner, 1983) appears not to be committed to 1-1-ness, and in later work Falkenhainer (1990) allows non-1-1 maps (although it would appear that in this work the *roles* in target and source map one to one). However, in this chapter it is important to allow non-1-1 mappings. In the present section I argue that non-1-1-ness is desirable, although allowing that 1-1-ness can still be adopted as a default or first preference.

First, however, we should note that some types of non-1-1-ness can be dressed up as 1-1-ness, in the sense that target and/or source can contain explicit representations of groups of items. By making a group-denoting item in one of the two structures correspond to an ordinary item or a group item in the other structure, we can get the effect of a (restricted type of) many-one, one-many, or many-many mapping of ordinary items. This technique is used to good effect in the Copycat system (Hofstadter & Mitchell, 1988; Mitchell & Hofstadter, 1990a, 1990b). The method is at its most powerful when groups can be dynamically determined (as in Copycat) rather than being pre-encoded in targets or sources, since the particular grouping required may depend on the target/source pair in question.

A more liberal approach to non-1-1-ness is to be found in the ACME system (Holyoak & Thagard, 1989; see also Holyoak, 1991). This system prefers 1-1 mappings, but allows deviations when there is sufficient pressure to do so from the way that items hang together in source and target[4].

Indeed, it is not very difficult to see that it is a mistake to make 1-1-ness a hard and fast requirement, and that the group technique is not always a good avenue of escape. The general point is that two purposes in one situation might be served by the same entity, but those purposes might be served by separate entities in another, analogous situation. For instance, Falkenhainer (1990) points out that the handle of an ordinary ceramic cup serves both to protect the hand from heat and to provide something to grasp, whereas in a polystyrene cup these purposes are served by different aspects of the cup, namely the styrofoam material and the conical shape, respectively. The two sorts of cup are nevertheless analogous. (This example is adapted from the work of Kedar-Cabelli, 1988.)

This example may, unfortunately, be ill-conceived. It rests on distinguishing two aspects of the body of a cup — its shape and material — while refraining from similarly analyzing the handle. After all, one could equally well say that it is the shape and rigidity of the handle that

---

[4] The fact that ACME establishes mappings by a connectionist process is irrelevant to the present discussion, but will be taken up below.

provide graspability, while heat-protection is provided by the relatively non-conducting nature of the material together with separation from the body of the cup. A fairer example, still based on cups, would be to say that the body of a polystyrene cup serves both to insulate the hand from heat and to hold the liquid, whereas in an ordinary cup these purposes are served by the handle and the body respectively. In this formulation, there is greater parity of analysis.

Let us consider a different example. Suppose a target case T says that *Mary's dog bit John*, and a source case S says that *Susan's dog bit Susan* and that *the dog had been badly trained*. (See Table 2.2. Note that in this and following tables I use English expressions to stand for formal representations that would be used in reality. This is for ease of exposition and to avoid commitment to any specific representational scheme.) There is no reason in general why S should not be used to generate the analogical inference that the dog in T had been badly trained. However, this requires that the occurrence of *Susan* in *Susan's dog* be mapped to *Mary*, whereas it requires the occurrence of *Susan* as the recipient of the bite in S to be mapped to *John*. Susan is therefore being mapped to more than one thing. (T and S can be interchanged, in which case we get a many-to-one mapping as opposed to a one-to-many mapping.)

One might complain that 1-1-ness could be held on to by refusing to match the two ownership relationships with each other, thereby effectively viewing T as merely saying that *some dog or other* bit John and S as merely saying that *some badly trained dog or other* bit Susan. However, this suggestion has no apparent motivation other than that of maintaining 1-1-ness, and can therefore hardly be used as an argument against the thesis that non-1-1-ness can be useful. Also, there seems to be no uncontrived way to use the group technique in this example.

TARGET	SOURCE
Mary's dog bit John.	*Susan's dog bit Susan.*
	Susan's dog was badly trained.

Table 2.2. Non-1-1 mapping.

Moreover, the suggestion fails to capture the point that the presence of the ownership relationships strengthens the match between T and S even though these relationships do not perfectly cohere with the rest of the match. One could cope with *this* objection by treating T as if it said that some *owned* dog bit John and similarly treating S as if it said that some badly--trained, *owned* dog bit Susan (Table 2.3). Again, however, the only motivation for proceeding in this way would seem to be the desire to preserve 1-1-ness.

TARGET   SOURCE

Some owned dog bit John.   *Some owned dog, d, bit Susan.*
                                d was badly trained.

Table 2.3. Non-1-1 mapping.

Another foreseeable but mistaken riposte to the dog example goes like this. There might be something special in a dog's biting *its owner*. Therefore, it is wrong to seek to use S to derive conclusions about T, since in the latter the dog bites someone other than its owner. However, the possible feeling that there might be something special in a dog's biting its owner is based on extra information *we* might, actually, have about dogs. As we have not yet commented on how *this* information might appear in our hypothetical ABR system, it is unfair to criticize that system for not paying attention to the information. Suppose, in fact, that the system also had source structures in which dogs bit people other than their owners and in which the dogs are *not* stated to be badly trained. Then these sources will match our T — and in fact might do so more strongly than our old S did because now there is no violation of 1-1-ness. However, the lack of any analogical inference from these sources to the effect that Mary's dog is badly trained should serve to swamp the presence of such an inference constructed on the basis of the old S. Implicitly, therefore, the system would have an inkling that the old S is somehow special.

In sum, although there is a tendency in the analogy field to restrict mappings to be 1-1, ABR should, in fact, allow departures from it, and certain major systems do already.

6. PARALLELS TO SOME CONNECTIONIST ADVANTAGES

Here I show that ABR can achieve variants of some the advantages associated with connectionist systems. These advantages were reviewed in Section 2 and listed in Table 2.1. I believe that an awareness of the advantages underlies much of the work on analogy, although they are rarely argued for in explicit detail.

6.1. GRACEFUL DEGRADATION

ABR systems are much less susceptible than traditional AI systems are to system and input corruptions, under suitable natural assumptions. To take a simple example of input-corruption first, suppose that the system observes John kissing Mary, and therefore constructs a target case T, consisting of the single proposition *John kissed Mary*. Suppose that T analogically matches a certain source case S, and causes S to be retrieved from memory. Let S be a case saying that *David kissed Susan, Susan slapped David*, and that the kissing caused the slapping (Table 2.4). Structures *T* and *S* therefore match to some moderate degree, and the tentative conclusions that Mary slapped John and that the kissing caused the slapping can be added to *T*. Now suppose that *T* had been corrupted during construction, so that its single proposition had been *John kissed ?????* where *?????* was some corrupted symbol, perhaps one previously unknown to the system. Then the analogical retrieval, matching and transfer could have proceeded just as before, except that the constructed tentative conclusions would have said that *?????* slapped John and that the kissing caused the slapping. Such a modification is a simple example of graceful degradation.

TARGET	SOURCE
John kissed Mary.	*David kissed Susan.*
	Susan slapped David.
	The kissing caused the slapping.

Table 2.4. Input-corruption in ABR.

For a more complex example, suppose now that the uncorrupted *T* says that *John kissed Mary* and *Mary disliked John*, and *S* says that *David kissed Susan, Susan disliked David, Susan slapped David*, and that the kissing and dislike, in combination, caused the slapping. (See Table 2.5.) Much as before, the tentative conclusion that the John/Mary kissing-and-dislike caused Mary to slap John is added to *T*. Now suppose *T* had been corrupted, only this time the corruption took the form of the omission of the whole proposition that Mary disliked John. Then we would still have obtained a match with *S*, and the same tentative conclusion (augmented now with the proposition that Mary disliked John) would still have been produced. However, the match would have been less good than with the uncorrupted *T*, since fewer propositions are being matched. Therefore, the conclusion would have been more tentative: but that effect is, precisely, a desirably graceful sort of degradation.

These simple examples show that it is possible for significant corruptions to a target case *T* to stand a good chance of only altering the analogical inferencing to a graceful extent. The essential point here is that ABR is specifically designed to tolerate large deviations of target case from source case, so that further deviations caused by input corruption may well not cause any harm.

Consider now the following more complex example. Suppose *S* and the uncorrupted *T* are as in Table 2.5, but that the corruption merely causes the *John kissed Mary* proposition to be changed to *John kissed ?????*. The proposition that *Mary disliked John* is preserved unharmed. (See Table 2.6.) We have a problem now with the idea that corrupted *T* matches *S*. Without the corruption, *Susan* in *S* can be coherently mapped to *Mary* in *T*, as can be seen from

Table 2.5. But with the corruption, the most complete mapping would be to map the occurrence of *Susan* in *Susan disliked David* to *Mary* but to map the occurrence of *Susan* in *David kissed Susan* to *?????*. This is a difficulty if one insists on 1-1 mappings. However, we argued earlier that a hard 1-1 constraint is unwarranted. In our example, we may therefore map *Susan* both to *?????* and Mary.

TARGET   SOURCE

John kissed Mary.   *David kissed Susan.*
Mary disliked John.   *Susan disliked David.*
                                Susan slapped David.
                                The kissing and dislike caused the slapping.

Table 2.5. Input-corruption in ABR.

This then raises the issue of how to treat the *Susan* in transferring the source proposition that *Susan slapped David*. Should the analogical inference be that *Mary slapped John*, or that *????? slapped John*, or what? My current suggestion is that both these propositions should be tentatively proposed as conclusions. As a variant of this, they could be joined together as a disjunction. But whatever choice is made on this issue, the behavior is a graceful degradation from the behavior in the uncorrupted case.

CORRUPTED TARGET   SOURCE

John kissed ?????.   *David kissed Susan.*
Mary disliked John.   *Susan disliked David.*
                                Susan slapped David.
                                The kissing and dislike caused the slapping.

Table 2.6. Input-corruption in ABR.

I turn now to the other variety of graceful degradation, concerned with system corruption. Once again, there is a sense in which ABR inherently provides such gracefulness. This is especially so if an analogical inference becomes the less tentative the greater the number of sources that support the inference. For instance, in our kissing/slapping examples, there might be several or many sources in which a kissing caused the appropriate slapping. Then the loss or corruption of some significant proportion of this set of sources would not, by itself, demolish the conclusion that Mary slapped John, but merely make it more tentative. Of course, if there were other source structures in which the kissee did *not* slap the kisser then the mentioned source corruption might reduce the number of slap sources to a level lower than the number of non-slap sources. In this case the slapping conclusion might, at best, be posted merely as an improbable possibility rather than as something that is probable. But this is not wrong behavior on the part of the system, and is analogous to what happens in a connectionist system where one corrupts weights to such an extent that other weights, mediating distinctly different behavior, begin to take over.

Even if the system is using only one source to derive analogical inferences for a target, considerable corruption can be gracefully tolerated. The observations to be made are similar to those we made for target corruption. Suppose T says once again that John kissed Mary and Mary disliked John, and S says that David kissed Susan, Susan disliked David, and that consequently Susan slapped David. (See Table 2.5.) Suppose now that S is corrupted. We proceed to consider various forms of corruption.

If the corruption is to replace all occurrences of *Susan* in S by the same symbol *?????*, then clearly no harm is done at all, because the corrupted S maps just as well as the uncorrupted one to T. If the corruption is the loss of the proposition that Susan disliked David, then again not much harm is done, except that the degree of match may be reduced since less of T would now match into S. On the other hand, if the proposition that Susan slapped David, together with the causation of it, is lost, then of course there is no information to transfer into the target. In this case, degradation is not graceful: but no one claims even for connectionist systems that the system should degrade gracefully with respect to *all* possible corruption! Indeed, we might suspect that the amounts of corruption that our ABR system *can* gracefully tolerate are already much more radical than any connectionist reasoning system has ever been shown to exhibit.

Consider now what happens when some but not all occurrences of *Susan*, say, in S are corrupted. The easiest case is when only the occurrence in *Susan slapped David* is corrupted, to become a symbol *?????*. (See Table 2.7.) This does not affect the degree to which T matches S[5]. On the other hand, suppose only the occurrence of *Susan* in *Susan disliked David* is replaced by *?????*. We then have the situation depicted in Table 2.8, which is the mirror image of the situation in Table 2.6. Therefore, we have the need for a many-to-one mapping: both *?????* and *Susan* map to *Mary*. But this is an easier matter than the one-to-many effect we considered earlier. In the present situation, the resultant *Susan slapped David* gets mapped with no trouble

---

[5] At least, it does not under simpler ways of assessing the strength of a match. If one were to take into account the strength with which the mapped source propositions were linked to other, non-mapped propositions, then the match in Table 2.5 might be stronger than that in Table 2.7.

to *Mary slapped John*. The only degradation is an increase of the tentativeness of this analogical inference, since the goodness of match between S and T has been reduced somewhat[6].

TARGET   SOURCE

John kissed Mary.   *David kissed Susan.*
Mary disliked John.   *Susan disliked David.*
                                ????? slapped David.
                                The kissing and dislike caused the slapping.

Table 2.7. System-corruption in ABR.

   Altogether, therefore, it is reasonable to suggest that ABR (especially when liberalized to allow non-1-1 mappings) exhibits useful forms of graceful degradation. Notice that I have not argued that ABR can achieve the *same* forms of graceful degradation as connectionism can. But that does not put ABR at a disadvantage with respect to connectionism, because, conversely, it has not been established that connectionism (other than that of a strict "implementational" variety) can achieve the forms of graceful degradation that ABR can. Nor has it been shown what sorts of graceful degradation are actually most useful in practice.

TARGET   SOURCE

John kissed Mary.   *David kissed Susan.*
Mary disliked John.   *????? disliked David.*
                                Susan slapped David.
                                The kissing and dislike caused the slapping.

Table 2.8. System-corruption in ABR.

---

[6] Speculatively, we could contemplate the possibility of using the match of T and S to repair S. Since the system now knows that the roles of *?????* and Susan in a situation can possibly be combined, and S provides no constraint on the nature of the individual denoted by *?????* or on how it relates to other entities, the system might tentatively conclude that *?????* is a corrupted symbol, and could be replaced by *Susan*.

6.2. AN ISSUE OF LEVELS

In discussing graceful degradation, we have considered ABR (and rule-based reasoning, in section 2) only at the level of symbols and propositions. Should we look at it instead at the level of bit-strings and so forth in a computer implementation? In that case, corruptions could take forms that are not readily translatable into the types of corruption we considered earlier. The whole low-level integrity of a high-level data structure such as a proposition might be compromised by a small corruption at the implementational level, leading perhaps to seriously-corrupted analogical inferences or even run-time crashes of the system. Also, a small corruption of the addressing machinery or logic circuitry could have disastrous high-level effects. Therefore, ABR implemented on a (conventional) computer has the same lack of graceful degradation that any system implemented on such a computer has[7]. However, this carries with it the implication that it is not *ABR* as such that lacks graceful degradation. Rather, conventional computer implementations lack it. I believe this distinction of the level at which one might analyze graceful degradation has seriously confused discussions of the relative merits of symbolicist computing and connectionism.

One can either view connectionist systems as *low-level computational architectures*, on a par level-wise with computer hardware, or as *high-level virtual machines* on a par level-wise with rule-based systems, ABR systems, and so on. In the former case, one can say that connectionist systems degrade more gracefully than conventional computer architectures do, and more gracefully than systems *implemented on these architectures* do. However, if one views connectionist systems as high-level virtual architectures, one should be comparing their graceful degradation properties with those of rule-based systems, ABR systems, or what have you, without bringing in a specific style of implementation. We should not forget that a connectionist system in the high-level, virtual machine view can itself be implemented on a conventional computer, without in any way impugning its status as a connectionist system. But, of course, under such an implementation the connectionist system itself inherits the lack of graceful degradation of the conventional computer.

What has not been considered here is ABR systems implemented in some connectionist framework *qua* low-level computational architecture. Such a scheme could avoid the lack of graceful degradation of conventional computers and could gain forms of graceful degradation for which connectionism is noted. A scheme of this sort will be proposed later on in this chapter.

6.3. REPRESENTATION COMPLETION

It is clear that ABR systems do have a representation-completion property. Suppose a source case S in memory contains propositions P_1 to P_n, and the system is presented with a target

---

[7] In the case of computers, graceful degradation with respect to system corruption is usually referred to as fault-tolerance. Under the heading of conventional computers I am excluding fault-tolerant ones, for simplicity of discussion.

structure T consisting of just some non-empty proper subset of this set of propositions. Then, T will match S to a degree dependent on the size of that subset. The ordinary process of transferring information from source to target will then complete T to form a copy of S. The tentativeness of the completion can be made to depend on the goodness of the match.

It should also be clear from the discussion of graceful degradation that ABR can easily complete target structures in which some symbols have been replaced by variables, say, where completion now means the binding of the variables to corresponding items in the source. Note, however, that different occurrences of a symbol might be replaced by different variables, so that we may have the one-to-many mapping issue to cope with again.

6.4. AUTOMATIC SIMILARITY-BASED GENERALIZATION

In section 2 I characterized the property of automatic similarity-based generalization, in connectionist systems, as holding when previously unseen inputs that are sufficiently similar to inputs on which the system has been trained lead to behavior that is usefully similar to that elicited by the training inputs. Of course, this is exactly the quality on which ABR is founded, if for "training inputs" one reads source structures in the system's memory.

It is difficult to compare the similarity-based generalization obtained in ABR systems with that obtained in connectionism, since the two paradigms have largely been applied to different sorts of problems. In particular, few connectionist systems can cope with the complex structures of information used in typical ABR systems. However, the recent work on holistic processing of reduced descriptions, mentioned in sections 2 and 3, is a promising step. It appears that the similarity relationships between the reduced descriptions correlate to a useful extent with the structural similarity relationships of the encoded structures.

In comparing the connectionist and ABR paradigms on the point of generalization, we should consider whether or not systems actually construct representations that directly encode the generalizations. One could say that the weights in a trained connectionist system that exhibits similarity-based generalization are an explicit (though usually fairly inscrutable) representation of the learned generalizations. Note, however, that such a system does *not* create explicit representations of generalizations, if by a representation we mean an activity pattern. In other words, the generalizations are not themselves data that can be manipulated or reasoned over by the system itself. I argue in Barnden (1992) that connectionists do need to consider the construction of activity patterns that encode generalizations, rather than always focusing on the use of weights to represent generalizations.

The situation is rather different in ABR. It is possible for an ABR system to construct new memory items that are generalizations over collections of source structures (see, e.g., Kolodner & Simpson, 1989). A source structure that says *X kissed Y and Y disliked X, causing Y to slap X*, where X and Y are variables, might be constructed if memory contained several structures of that form, for specific substitutions for X and Y, and memory contained at most a few structures that contradicted the generalization. The generalizations can be used in analogical inference much as ordinary source structures are (although such use begins to look less different from more standard forms of inference, such as rule-based inference). Furthermore, they can be subject to various types of manipulation in their own right. Since they would be the correlate of connectionist activity patterns that encoded trained generalizations, ABR is in a position to go beyond what connectionism considers. Certainly, a very pure form of ABR would lack the explicit generalizations. Moreover, it would not even have a correlate of the connectionist encoding of generalizations in weights. But there is little reason to insist on such purity.

6.5. OTHER OBSERVATIONS

Here I make some observations about qualities that are often associated with connectionist systems but over which connectionism hardly has a monopoly. The first of these qualities is the ability to learn. Connectionism provides an interesting, simple approach to learning, but ABR also provides a simple approach — the continual addition of source structures in memory. (There are also other possible types of learning, such as the storage of analogical mappings between sources, the creation of explicit generalizations, and the refinement of the indexing scheme, to name just three.) The accumulation will gradually alter the pattern of analogical inferencing done by the system. The alterations may sometimes merely be adjustments in the tentativeness levels assigned to analogical inferences, but may also be more far-reaching. In a population of sources that contribute analogical inferences to a target T, different sources can conflict — some could suggest that Mary slapped John, some could suggest that she did not. As the numerical balance of such sources changes, the system could flip from preferring one of the conclusions to preferring the other.

ABR systems can exhibit merely-emergent rule-like behavior. Suppose a target structure T contains the single proposition that *John kissed Mary*, and that a source structure S says that David kissed Susan, causing Susan to slap David. The system can use S to add tentative analogical inferences to T, to the effect that John's kissing Mary caused her to slap him. This effect has nothing specifically to do with the fact that T involves John and Mary in particular — the process would have worked just as well for Peter and Sally instead. With such targets, therefore, the system can be construed by an outside observer as executing a rule of the form *If X kisses Y then the kissing causes Y to slap X*. Nevertheless, there has been no interpretation of an explicit rule. (Except, that is, in the sense that the processes of source/target mapping, transfer, and so on might themselves be performed by explicit rule interpretation — but this is as uninteresting for our present concerns as pointing out that each node in a connectionist network can be thought of as a rule). Certainly, S is not to be construed as being such a rule. This point becomes clearer if we consider that the same S could be used with a target T that says that Mary slapped John. The tentative analogical inference would be that John kissed Mary, and this caused the slap. In this case the system appears to be following the rule *If Y slaps X then the slapping is caused by X kissing Y*.

ABR systems can take explicit note of exceptions, while also being able to exhibit merely emergent ones. If there are sources in which a meek kissee does not slap the kisser, then the meekness will strengthen the match to a T which says that John kissed Mary and Mary was meek. As a result, the conclusion that Mary slapped John, coming from sources that lack the meekness, can be blocked or at least made more suspect. The system need not have noted during source accumulation that the meekness-containing sources are exceptional with respect to other sources (although the system could do this, and it might well be a desirable thing to do).

7. CONNECTIONIST ADVANTAGES NOT PARALLELED

I am not claiming that ABR intrinsically provides parallels of all the connectionist advantages reviewed in section 2 and listed in Table 2.1. In particular, there is nothing in traditional ABR that directly corresponds to efficient, parallel soft-constraint satisfaction or holistic structure-sensitive processing

ABR has a need for efficient, content-based access to long-term memory items (source structures) that stand a good chance of being relevant to a given target structure through being somewhat similar to it. But it does not of itself provide any particular mechanism for achieving the access, although, of course, particular ABR systems have included specific mechanisms. Much of the literature on analogy sidesteps the issue of how to achieve efficient source retrieval, as it concentrates on the post-retrieval stages. The case-based reasoning and memory-based reasoning literature has been much more sensitive to the issue.

Earlier we discussed the formation of explicit generalizations in ABR systems. What we did not dwell on there was the mechanism by which such generalizations are formed. ABR of itself has nothing in particular to say about the details of this process (much as it is silent on the details of how efficient source access is to be achieved). On the other hand, connectionist learning systems are adept at distilling the general essence(s) of a large number of training examples. This is not to say that this ability is just what is needed for ABR; as we noticed in sections 2 and 6, the generalizations learned by connectionist systems are immanent in the weights, and are not themselves data structures that can be manipulated by the system. Also, connectionist learning from examples is usually on the basis of very many examples, whereas in ABR it is reasonable to contemplate generalization once there are just a few compatible examples. The point is merely that ABR does not intrinsically provide a mechanism for distilling generalizations from examples, whereas connectionism does.

8. INTERIM SUMMARY

We have seen that ABR and standard connectionism supply some "shared" benefits, for want of a better term. More strictly, there are benefits, such as graceful degradation, which appear in one form in ABR and in another in connectionism. Also, each paradigm has benefits not shared with the other. ABR preserves the traditional-AI facility with encoding and manipulating complex structures of information. On the other hand, the previous section summarized benefits that connectionism provides but ABR does not. In a little more detail, we have seen the following.

(1) Connectionist systems are commonly proposed as an alternative to traditional symbolic AI systems, on the grounds that they can exhibit graceful degradation, representation completion, automatic similarity-based generalization, certain forms of learning (based on automatic development of generalizations, implicit in the weights), efficient content-based long-term memory access, holistic structure-sensitive processing, parallel soft-constraint satisfaction, emergent rule-like behavior, and emergent exceptions. To oversimplify matters somewhat, traditional symbolic AI systems do not have these emergent capabilities. Neither

do standard implementational-connectionist systems, confined as they are to implementing traditional symbolic AI techniques.

(2) On the other hand, non-implementational connectionist systems have well-known difficulties in representing and manipulating complex, short-term structures of information, in the service, for instance, of commonsense reasoning and pragmatic reasoning in natural language understanding.

(3) Symbolic ABR systems do achieve forms of graceful degradation, representation completion, automatic similarity-based generalization, learning, emergent rule-like behavior, and emergent exceptions.

ABR does not necessarily achieve the *same* forms as are obtained in connectionism, but the converse is also true, and in any case the ABR forms of the benefits are highly desirable in their own right.

Points (2) and (3) together justify the claim that it is a non-sequitur to jump from (1) to the proposition that cognitive science should now concentrate on (standard) connectionism in order to escape the deficiencies of traditional AI techniques. At least, it is a non-sequitur unless it can be shown that ABR cannot be extended or implemented in such a way as to expand the list in (3) to match that in (1). The rest of the paper is devoted to suggesting that this expansion can be performed.

9. CONNECTIONIST ANALOGY-BASED REASONING

We have seen that ABR as such gives us advantages *parallel* to many of those normally associated with connectionism. *I suggest that as a way of getting the actual connectionist versions of those shared advantages as well, and moreover getting the connectionist advantages not yet accounted for, we develop fully connectionist systems that at a high level can be viewed as doing ABR.*

This view of the system could be exact or approximate. In the former case, we could develop a connectionist system that strictly implemented a standard symbolic ABR system. Under an approximate view, on the other hand, the system might be subsymbolic (Smolensky, 1988a, 1988b) at a low level of description and only approximately be describable as doing mappings and transfers between target structures and source structures of any conventional sort.

Both views are worth investigating, but the first is more within the abilities of well-developed, currently available tools. I outline here one broad strategy that comes, roughly, under the first view. It does so only roughly because it has crucial aspects that take it away from being mere implementational connectionism. Tools from standard, *non*-implementational connectionism are proposed for various aspects of the system, such as the long-term memory indexing/retrieval mechanism.

A point of terminology: It is fair to say that the phrase "implementational connectionism" conveys to most people only the connectionist implementation of *standard* symbolic AI mechanisms. These exclude ABR, which is still not "standard." Therefore, in advocating the connectionist implementation of symbolic ABR, I am advocating *non-standard* implementational connectionism. Nevertheless, I suggest that individual targets and retrieved sources be implemented using the tools of standard implementational connectionism. It is the overall system that exhibits non-standard implementational connectionism.

I have designed and partially implemented a specific system developed on the strategy to be outlined. The system is variously called ABR Conposit or CDR Conposit, and is descended from the connectionist *rule*-based Conposit system (Barnden, 1988b, 1989, 1990, 1991). A preliminary design of ABR-Conposit is presented in some detail in Barnden and Srinivas (1992). Instead of detailing that specific design, however, the purpose of the present chapter is to concentrate on the broad strategy, though with occasional mention of the specific case of ABR-Conposit in order to make the points more precise. We look at

· the nature of targets and retrieved sources

· target-source mapping and transfer

· sources as stored in long-term memory, and their retrieval.

Then we look at a form of high-level parallelism in ABR and at the introduction of a form of connectionist learning.

9.1. WORKING MEMORY

There are one or more working memories each of which can contain a set of propositions at any time. In particular, a working memory can contain a set of propositions that together constitute a target structure, a retrieved source structure, or a target structure together with a retrieved source structure. The last possibility is so as to enable the mapping and transfer processes to be described later.

A working memory is a connectionist subnetwork, and the set of propositions it contains is implemented as the overall activation pattern across that whole subnetwork. Further, the activation pattern is divided up into separate portions for the different propositions. This does not necessarily mean that there is a fixed partitioning into submemories (buffers) that are each capable of holding one proposition[8]. The assumption that the activation pattern is partitioned into subpatterns implementing different propositions is not strictly necessary for my goals, but simplifies the following account, and accords with ABR-Conposit. Fig. 2.1 is an impressionistic sketch of a single working memory. The motive for having multiple working memories is to support multiple strands of ABR proceeding in parallel. This matter is taken up later on.

---

[8] Indeed, in (ABR-)Conposit the working memory is an array of register-like subnetworks, and bunches of contiguous registers are dynamically recruited when propositions are created. There is no division into buffers above the grain-size of registers themselves.

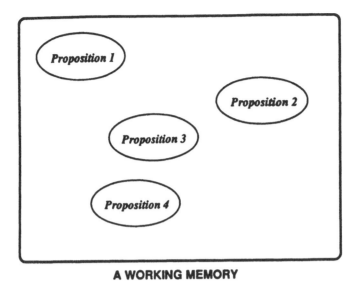

A WORKING MEMORY

Fig. 2.1. Temporary positioning of propositions in a working memory.

There are various detailed forms that a working memory of the proposed type might make. I mention just three. First, some extension of the RAAM-based approach (Pollack, 1988, 1990) could be used. Separate propositions would be implemented as activation patterns that are reduced descriptions. This approach is attractive, although I point out in Barnden (1992) that there are unstudied problems that need to be resolved if the method is to be useful in practice. Second, some extension of the tensor-product approach (Smolensky, 1990) to complex-structure representation could be used. Third, and this is the method used in ABR-Conposit, the representational techniques developed for the working memory of the rule-based Conposit could be used with little modification. They allow great flexibility and expressiveness. In particular, they conveniently allow the nesting of structures to any depth (within the overall resource bounds of working memory), the joining of propositions by connectives, and so on[9].

---

[9] The structuring primitives used in the Conposit work are called *relative-position encoding* and *pattern-similarity association*. They are subjected to a general discussion in Barnden and Srinivas (1991). Since they are non-standard even from the point of view of implementational connectionism, we have here another sense in which the approach of this chapter can involve *non-standard* implementational connectionism.

9.2. SOURCE-TO-TARGET MAPPING AND TRANSFER

In a given working memory, we require a mechanism for comparing the set of propositions making up the retrieved source with those making up the target, in the hope that a fair proportion of the target propositions can be viewed as mapped versions of source propositions. Notice carefully that the following features make the problem quite difficult.

(a) Even in a strong analogy, *some* target propositions can be left out of the final mapping.

(b) Even in a strong analogy, *many* source propositions can be left out of the final mapping, since, for one thing, they may be irrelevant to the target.

(c) When a target proposition and a source proposition are deemed to correspond to each other, their parts can nevertheless differ greatly. *John loves Mary* can match *David loves Susan.*

All in all, (a) to (c) conspire to ensure that, even when the target and source are quite similar to each other *qua* proposition sets, the overall activation patterns for the source and target can differ greatly from each other *qua* activation vectors. This abolishes any possibility of just doing a straightforward comparison of the overall patterns.

The hybrid symbolic/connectionist ACME system of Holyoak and Thagard (1989) does find mappings between sources and targets, but does so by first dynamically constructing a connectionist network whose nodes stand for the set of match hypotheses, or possible correspondences between items in the target and items in the source. Links stand for constraints between the match hypotheses. This scenario is crucially different from ours, where there is a *fixed* network and the encodings of the source and target are activation patterns over that network.

Structural matching is the goal of the system of Bienenstock and von der Malsburg (1987). However, the primitive parts of the structures being compared are encoded as individual nodes, whereas in our case the primitive parts are activation subpatterns that could appear in many different alternative positions.

Barnden and Srinivas (1992) describe a way of doing source/target mapping in an ABR-Conposit working memory. It rests on a process that sequences through the propositions of the target, trying to find propositions in the source that match it. To facilitate this search, a fast heuristic method is used that relies on a form of *hashing* (see, e.g. Standish, 1980). The activation pattern for a proposition contains a subpattern that is the result of applying a hashing transformation to the rest of the pattern. That is, the subpattern is a hash key for the proposition. The transformation is such that similar propositions have similar hash keys. Also, the hash keys are reminiscent of reduced-descriptions, especially those recently proposed by Plate (1991). For each target proposition, the hash key is broadcast throughout the working memory, and source propositions with similar hash keys announce themselves in a certain way.

The major problem with this technique is that it must be greatly complicated to take account of feature (c) (non-identity of corresponding parts of source and target). The process described in Barnden and Srinivas (1992) rests on replacing constants by variables, and then relying on the fact that the subpatterns implementing variables are all similar to each other. However, this leads to a very cumbersome overall process. Recently, we started to investigate a process, still using the hash keys, that avoids the replacing of constants by variables. The process is broadly similar to that used in ACME. In ACME, for each possible correspondence between a source item (proposition or object) and a target item, a special node is created that stands for the hypothesis that that correspondence is indeed wanted. Such a match-hypothesis node is connected by excitatory links to the nodes for the two items in question. Nodes for mutually in-compatible match-hypotheses are connected by mutually inhibitory links, while mutually compatible ones are connected by mutually excitatory links. These links support a parallel constraint-satisfaction process that eventually settles on a reasonable mapping between the target and source.

In the new ABR-Conposit technique, we rely on conceptually similar match hypotheses, but they are encoded as dynamically created, proposition-like activation subpatterns in the working memory. The constraint-satisfaction process rests on the broadcasting of hash keys, and other pieces of information, by the various subpatterns in working memory. (This avoids an ACME-like dynamic creation of connections to carry the constraint-satisfaction process.) As shown in Fig. 2.2, the broadcasting is done through a central module attached to the working memory and called the working memory's *parallel distributor*. Hence, the broadcasts done by different subpatterns must be serialized[10]. This slows the process down, with respect to ACME, but since we are not talking about very large sets of propositions and match hypotheses[11], the slow-down is not very damaging. Note also that within each individual broadcast the message does go to all the destinations in parallel.

The approach to the transfer of information from source to target is to add to the target the mapped versions of all source propositions not involved in the discovered mapping. Now, the designation of a particular proposition in a working memory as being in the target or as being in the source is done by a simple marking technique. Hence, if all (source-item, target-item) correspondences happened to be identities (e.g., Mary in source corresponded to Mary in target, and so forth), then all that would be needed for transfer would be to mark all source propositions not involved in the mapping as being in the target (as well). In the general case, however, a prior act is to replace source items by the target items they map to[12]. The resulting state is tantamount to the case of identity mappings.

---

[10] The serialization is done by a variant of the temporal-winner-take-all technique (Barnden, Srinivas, & Dharmavaratha, 1990).

[11] The initial creation of match hypotheses is constrained. It is not the case that there is a hypothesis for every possible (target-item, source-item) pair.

[12] Notice that the source in its long-term memory form, from which the source in working memory was retrieved, is not affected by this replacement.

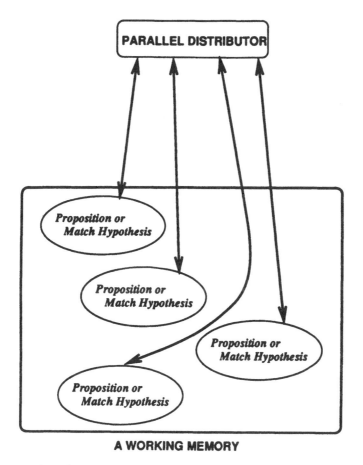

Fig. 2.2. The arrows show the communication pathways supporting the broadcasting used in the constraint satisfaction process for matching.

This transfer process is crude in two senses. It ignores the possible irrelevance of transferred propositions, and it ignores the possibility that transferred propositions may contradict information that is in the target or is inferable from it. However, these problems are general ones for ABR, not the result of our specific implementational strategy. I envisage curing direct contradictions within an expanded target by further pieces of ABR. That is, if propositions *P* and *not-P* are both in a target, this may cause the retrieval of a source that contains contradictory propositions *Q* and *not-Q* and that recommends some action to be taken.

9.3. LONG-TERM SOURCE MEMORY AND RETRIEVAL

Sources in long-term memory are not stored as activation patterns. Instead, they are stored in weight settings. Therefore, conversion processes are required for the retrieval of sources into working memories for the purpose of mapping/transfer to a particular target and creation of source memories from the contents of working memories.

Barnden and Srinivas (1992) specify a long-term storage method for ABR-Conposit that is time-efficient and easily implemented. To oversimplify, each source is represented by a single unit s. This unit is connected to each unit u in a certain working memory that acts as storage/retrieval buffer. The weight on the connection directly encodes the strength of activation which that unit u would have if the source were to appear in the working memory. Simple circuitry allows the conversion of these weights into a pattern of activation over the working memory, and the conversion of a pattern over working memory into suitable weight settings. (We assume that weights can be changed rapidly.)

The drawback of this method, which has been implemented in a partial simulation of ABR-Conposit, is the large number of units u and the consequent large number of connections (of the order of 10^5) into any given s. Although these connections work entirely in parallel so that there is no time penalty, and there is no reason in principle why connectionist systems should not have this extent of connectivity, it is of interest to see whether it can be avoided. I recently began to investigate the possibility of storing reduced descriptions of a source as a whole and of each proposition within it. These reduced descriptions would be the same as those used within working memories for the purposes of the target/source mapping process described earlier. The reduced descriptions for a particular source would each be stored in connection weights of some single unit s. The different s units used for the source would be connected together, largely in order to facilitate the LTM indexing scheme to be described in a moment.

A technical obstacle to this new scheme is that the reduced descriptions currently used within ABR-Conposit's working memories are not decodable. That is, a proposition activation pattern cannot be reconstructed from the reduced description alone. This is acceptable for within-working-memory processing, because the full propositions are there anyway. However, reconstructibility is needed for long-term memory purposes. In order to move to reconstructible reduced descriptions, we might consider recent proposals such as those of Pollack (1990) or Plate (1991). However, I wish to avoid the lengthy training process needed for Pollack reduced descriptions to be developed. This is because whenever a new proposition is created in a working memory (e.g., because of transfer from a source), it must have a reduced description created for it rapidly. An approach such as that of Plate appears more suitable, since the reduction/expansion mechanism is hand-designed, obviating any need for learning. (However, the reconstruction process is noisy, so a clean-up process is needed, and relies on an explicit memory of all the structures for which the system has created reduced descriptions.) We are investigating the possibility of adapting the Plate scheme, and variants of it that use reduction functions other than his circular convolution, for use in the ABR-Conposit working memories and long-term memory. One possibility is to have the reduction function be fixed in advance, but to have the system learn the inverse (i.e., decoding) function.

The use of reconstructible reduced descriptions does not remove the need for non-reduced representations inside working memories. Despite the partial success of attempts to do structure-sensitive manipulations holistically on reduced descriptions, I argue in Barnden (1992) that there are major obstacles to overcome.

As for the question of indexing into long-term memory, the reduced descriptions are used for this purpose as well (in both of the long-term memory schemes mentioned). Suppose it is desired to subject a target structure T to analogical inferencing. Structure T is put into one of the storage/retrieval buffer working memories mentioned above. Its reduced descriptions are then broadcast throughout LTM, essentially by a conventional, parallel, spreading-activation process. LTM units s whose connection weights match the broadcast reduced descriptions gain activation as a result. Activated LTM units for sources then compete in a winner-take-all fashion to load their sources into the storage/retrieval buffer[13]. The loading is done in such a way that the winning source does not overwrite T, but rather goes in together with T. The process, in the form needed for the first LTM storage method mentioned, has been implemented in the ABR-Conposit simulation.

The indexing process ensures that if a stored source contains propositions identical to some in the target T, it will become highly activated. However, we do not wish to activate only those sources, but also ones which match target propositions only under some mapping. For this purpose, the individual symbols (implemented as connectionist activation patterns) in the target are also broadcast, and there are units s in LTM for all the symbols. These units are connected to the proposition and source s units that involve those symbols. Therefore, proposition and source units that, say, merely use some of the same predicate symbols as the target T will be somewhat activated. This allows *John loves Mary* to lead to activation of sources containing *David loves Susan*.

It appears that the use of reduced descriptions for source retrieval in ABR systems may be a novel idea. It makes the retrieval process content-based (associative), and solves the problem noted primarily in the CBR literature of needing to have a mechanism that allows LTM access by indices that reflect the complex informational structure in targets. (By contrast, much of the analogy literature ignores the computational problem of efficiently retrieving relevant sources.) Of course, the technique has a very strong relationship to the use of hashing in ordinary computer programs to achieve efficient memory access into large sets of data. One departure from ordinary hashing is that we do not require exact matches between broadcast reduced descriptions and the ones stored in LTM. To some extent, similarities between reduced descriptions reflect meaningful similarities in the represented propositions or sources.

The question of when new sources should be created and stored into long-term memory is an outstanding issue. The current approach in ABR-Conposit is to store as an LTM source any target as expanded by analogical inferencing that is reasonably non-tentative.

---

[13] In ABR-Conposit this is done by temporal-winner-take-all, after conversion of activation differences into signal timing differences, rather than by a conventional winner-take-all mechanism.

Although the long-term memory as described here is localist with respect to symbols, propositions and sources, there appears to be no reason in principle why a distributed version with the same or better functionality should not be constructed. I see the current localist approach as possibly being merely a staging post on the way to a future distributed version.

9.4. PARALLEL PROCESSING IN MULTIPLE WORKING MEMORIES

A way in which the strategy pushes beyond standard symbolic ABR is that it involves parallel processing in multiple working memories. The primary point of this is to allow different mapping/transfer processes to proceed in parallel. For instance, when analogical inferencing is to be done on a target T, T is typically loaded into several storage/retrieval buffers, not just one. The chances are that different sources are retrieved into these different buffers. After copying of the buffer contents into other working memories, mapping/transfer using these different sources can proceed in parallel. The resulting expanded targets have differing degrees of confidence attached to them. These degrees control the strength with which the expanded targets compete by a winner-take-all mechanism to be loaded into storage/buffer working memories, leading to further retrieval and analogical inferencing.

9.5. A TYPE OF CONNECTIONIST LEARNING

The strategy leaves open the possibility of various types of standard connectionist learning. I sketch here just one possibility (although it has not yet been implemented in ABR-Conposit). Suppose target cases involving *friends* repeatedly cause successful analogical inferencing from sources involving *dogs* instead. As a result of the second approach to LTM that was outlined earlier, it will be the case that both the friend-symbol node and the dog-symbol node in LTM will be highly activated on these occasions. It is not difficult to devise a mechanism that ensures that connection paths joining these two units are strengthened on each occasion. By this means, the strength with which dog-mentioning sources are retrieved as a result of friend-mentioning targets — and vice versa — will increase, thus gradually making it more and more likely that dog sources will be retrieved for friend targets, and vice versa. Remember that retrieval is competitive, and other types of source may be in the running.

9.6. SUMMARY: ACHIEVING VARIOUS ADVANTAGES

The broad strategy outlined clearly achieves the advantages of symbolic ABR, such as ABR's own forms of graceful degradation, representation completion, automatic similarity-based generalization (implicit in mapping/transfer), learning by creating explicit generalizations of (few) exemplars, one-shot learning of new sources, merely-emergent rule-like behavior, and merely-emergent exceptions. The strategy also preserves the normal symbolic-processing flexibility and facility with the encoding and manipulation of complex structures of information. The structures of information in targets and sources can be just as complex as those in more standard sorts of symbolic AI system.

At the same time, the strategy leaves room for *standard* connectionist forms of some of the benefits just listed: graceful degradation, representation completion, automatic similarity-based generalization, and automatic development of representations. We take these in order.

Connectionist-style graceful degradation with respect to system corruption is obtained to some extent in the embodiment of the strategy in ABR-Conposit in its current design. This is because of the multiplicity of working memories and because propositions do not have to occupy fixed positions in working memories   (In ABR-Conposit, portions of a working memory are dynamically recruited when propositions are introduced.) Thus, corruptions to part or whole of a working memory is not fatal as long as the use of that part, or the whole working memory, can be avoided, although proper exploitation of this possibility would require some capability, not yet devised, for the system to detect such faults. A more thorough-going type of graceful degradation with respect to system corruption could be obtained by adopting a wholly or partially distributed implementation of propositions within working memories, and a distributed form of LTM. The registers making up ABR-Conposit's working memories are already partially distributed in quality, by virtue of the fact that the symbol in a register is an activation pattern. There are other pieces of register state that are encoded in a localist way, but it is probably quite easy to replace the localist encoding by a distributed one.

For connectionist-style graceful degradation with respect to input corruption, note that the target/source mapping process and the LTM indexing process rest on activation-pattern similarity, the patterns in question being either reduced descriptions or symbol patterns. Hence, minor corruptions of these patterns during processing can be tolerated. Further, the creation of reduced descriptions from the activation patterns in the non-reduced structures serves to attenuate corruptions in those patterns.

As for connectionist-style representation completion, we saw earlier that pattern completion in typical connectionist systems was just a form of graceful degradation with respect to input corruption.

If symbols denoting similar things were similar as activation patterns, then the LTM indexing scheme would display a standard connectionist form of automatic similarity-based generalization. Also, consider the dog/friend association-forming mentioned above, transposed now to a distributed framework. Suppose the distributed pattern for dog is quite similar to that for cat. Then the associational dog/friend learning will automatically look like associational cat/friend learning, albeit with lower intensity.

Although the symbol activation-patterns in ABR-Conposit as it stands are completely arbitrary, they could be automatically developed by modules outside the reasoning system itself. For instance, the symbol for dog might itself be a reduced description derived from large representations elsewhere, based on perceptual input for instance. Of course, if existing symbols are modified once long-term memories involving those symbols have been formed, we would be faced with the task of modifying those long-term memories. Although this might be a cumbersome process, it should be observed that current systems that evolve their own representations (e.g., Lee, Flowers, & Dyer, 1989; Pollack, 1990) also need a fairly cumbersome moving-target learning mechanism to ensure that mutual consistency of representations is maintained.

In Section 7 we saw that ABR does not intrinsically provide mechanisms for paralleling the connectionist advantages of efficient soft-constraint satisfaction or efficient content-based access to memories. However, we saw that the adopted connectionist indexing method in the advocated strategy does provide content-based memory access. Also, the advocated method for target/source matching rests on a soft-constraint satisfaction process implemented in parallel connectionist circuitry (although the overall degree of parallelism is less than what is customary in connectionism). It is still true that there is no soft constraint satisfaction process operating over, for instance, the tentative propositions transferred from sources to targets. (Such a process could actually be added, but I have not yet investigated the possibility.) But this is hardly a deficiency compared to standard connectionism, which does not have the ability to cope in any serious way with multiple, dynamically-created, complex propositions in the first place, let alone apply a constraint satisfaction process to them.

The advocated strategy does parallel some connectionist systems in getting a lot of mileage out of reduced descriptions. However, the strategy does not rest on the type of holistic inferencing over reduced descriptions that was mentioned in sections 2 and 3. The importance of this lack is not clear at present, partly because the work on holistic inferencing is itself at a very preliminary stage and it is by no means clear that it will bear mature fruit.

10. CONCLUSION

I argued that the connectionist realization of ABR is a promising route to achieving advantages normally associated with connectionism while not losing advantages associated with traditional AI. The argument has been conducted on the initial assumption that it is interesting to seek fully connectionist as opposed to hybrid systems. The reasoning has been somewhat complex, for several reasons: traditional AI is not quite as guilty of the charges leveled at it as is commonly assumed; there is the split between implementational and non-implementational connectionism; ABR, even when purely symbolic, provides advantages such as graceful degradation, but in different varieties from those provided by standard connectionism; the standard varieties themselves reappear when we couch ABR within connectionism; and it is by no means clear whether the connectionist varieties are more desirable than the ABR varieties of the "shared advantages" or not. On the way, in section 6.2, we saw the importance of being clear about the levels of description applied to two types of systems when they are being compared.

Despite this complexity, one salient feature of my stance is the simple point that it is a non sequitur to claim that, because traditional AI has certain troublesome disadvantages, what we must do is uncritically adopt (standard) connectionism. In other words, I am trying, in one particular way, to counter the polarization and consequent over-simplification of issues that has occurred between these two camps.

Smolensky (1988a) recommends getting hardness, when it is needed at all, out of softness: that is, letting apparently hard-edged rule-based processing emerge from soft, subsymbolic processing. Softness is graceful degradation, fluidity of processing, and so on; hardness is the rigidity and definiteness usually associated with symbolic structures and processing. My own strategy can be viewed, to a degree, as an attempt to get softness out of hardness. This is because the softness immanent in ABR, even in its ordinary symbolic varieties, rests on the hardness of individual targets and sources. (However, when the ABR is implemented in connectionism using the outlined strategy, further types of softness are added, in the form of the approximate, heuristic matching based on reduced descriptions, the retrieval process also based on reduced descriptions, and forms of connectionist learning such as that suggested in section 9.) Smolensky (1988a) recognizes that softness can be obtained from hardness when the latter is complex enough. My claim is that the degree of complexity in the type of system I am advocating, while high, is not frightening; and that in any case subsymbolic systems are going to have to have an as yet unknown, but high, degree of complexity when scaled up to be fuller models of cognition.

I do not claim to have yet demonstrated that the outlined strategy will actually work as expected, or that all the standard connectionist benefits can ultimately be provided or paralleled. Technical difficulties remain, for instance, in doing target/source mapping and transfer efficiently and adequately, and in indexing and retrieving sources efficiently and adequately. I claim merely to have provided a reasonable basis for thinking that the strategy will be successful, and, furthermore, could be so in the relatively near future. Certainly, there is at least as much — I would say considerably more — reason to hope that the strategy is a good one for developing high-level cognitive models as there is to hope that either standard AI or standard connectionism is.

ACKNOWLEDGMENTS

I benefitted from discussions with Tom Eskridge, Heather Pfeiffer, and K. Srinivas, and I am grateful to them for assistance with system development.

REFERENCES

Ajjanagadde, V. (1990). Reasoning with function symbols in a connectionist system. *Proceedings of the Twelfth Annual Conference of the Cognitive Science Society* (pp. 285-292). Hillsdale, NJ: Lawrence Erlbaum Associates.

Barnden, J. A. (1984). On short-term information processing in connectionist theories. *Cognition and Brain Theory* 7, 25-59.

Barnden, J. A. (1988a). The right of free association: Relative-position encoding for connectionist data structures. *Proceedings of the Tenth Annual Conference of the Cognitive Science Society* (pp. 503-509). Hillsdale, NJ: Lawrence Erlbaum Associates.

Barnden, J. A. (1988b). Conposit, a neural net system for high-level symbolic processing: Overview of research and description of register-machine level. *Memoranda in Computer and Cognitive Science*, No. MCCS-88-145, Computing Research Laboratory, New Mexico State University, Las Cruces, NM.

Barnden, J. A. (1989, August). Neural-net implementation of complex symbol-processing in a mental model approach to syllogistic reasoning. *Proceedings of the 11th International Joint Conference on Artificial Intelligence* (pp. 568-573). San Mateo, CA: Morgan Kaufmann.

Barnden, J. A. (1990). Syllogistic mental models: exercising some connectionist representation and control methods. *Memoranda in Computer and Cognitive Science*, No. MCCS-90-204, Computing Research Laboratory, New Mexico State University, Las Cruces, NM.

Barnden, J. A. (1991). Encoding complex symbolic data structures with some unusual connectionist techniques. In J. A. Barnden & J. B. Pollack (Eds), *Advances in Connectionist and Neural Computation Theory, Vol. 1: High Level Connectionist Models* (pp. 188-240). Norwood, NJ.: Ablex.

Barnden, J. A. (1992). Connectionism, generalization and propositional attitudes: A catalogue of challenging issues. In J. Dinsmore (Ed.), *The Symbolic and Connectionist Paradigms: Closing the Gap* (pp. 149-178). Hillsdale, NJ: Lawrence Erlbaum Associates.

Barnden, J. A., & Pollack, J. B. (1991). Introduction: problems for high-level connectionism. In J. A. Barnden & J. B. Pollack (Eds.), *Advances in Connectionist and Neural Computation Theory, Vol. 1: High Level Connectionist Models* (pp. 1-16). Norwood, NJ: Ablex.

Barnden, J. A., & Srinivas, K. (1991). Encoding techniques for complex information structures in connectionist systems. *Connection Science* 3, 263-309.

Barnden, J. A., & Srinivas, K. (1992). Overcoming rule-based rigidity and connectionist limitations through massively-parallel case-based reasoning. *International Journal of Man-Machine Studies* 36, 221-246.

Barnden, J. A., Srinivas, K., & Dharmavaratha, D. (1990, May). Winner-take-all networks: time-based versus activation-based mechanisms for various selection goals. Proceedings of the IEEE International Symposium on Circuits and Systems, New Orleans (pp. 215-218).

Bienenstock, E., & von der Malsburg, C. (1987). A neural network for invariant pattern recognition. *Europhysics Letters* 4, 121-126.

Blank, D. S., Meeden, L. A., & Marshall, J. B. (1992). Symbolic manipulations via subsymbolic computations. In J. Dinsmore (Ed.), *The Symbolic and Connectionist Paradigms: Closing the Gap* (pp. 113-148). Hillsdale, NJ: Lawrence Erlbaum Associates.

Carpenter, G. A., & Grossberg, S. (1990). ART 3: Hierarchical search using chemical transmitters in self-organizing pattern recognition architecture. *Neural Networks*, 3, 129-152.

Chalmers, D. J. (1990). Syntactic transformations on distributed representations. *Connection Science*, 2, 53-62.

Cook, D. J. (1991). The base selection task in analogical planning. *Proceedings of the Twelfth International Joint Conference on Artificial Intelligence* (pp. 790-794). San Mateo, CA: Morgan Kaufmann.

Dyer, M. G. (1991). Symbolic NeuroEngineering and natural language processing: a multilevel research approach. In J. A. Barnden & J. B. Pollack (Eds.), *Advances in Connectionist and Neural Computation Theory, Vol. 1: High Level Connectionist Models* (pp. 32-86). Norwood, NJ: Ablex.

Falkenhainer, B. (1990). Analogical interpretation in context. *Proceedings of the Twelfth Annual Conference of the Cognitive Science Society* (pp. 69-76). Hillsdale, NJ: Lawrence Erlbaum Associates.

Falkenhainer, B., Forbus, K. D., & Gentner, D. (1989). The Structure-Mapping Engine: Algorithm and examples. *Artificial Intelligence* 41, 1-63.

Fodor, J. A., & Pylyshyn, Z. W. (1988). Connectionism and cognitive architecture: a critical analysis. In S. Pinker & J. Mehler (Eds.), *Connections and Symbols* (pp. 3-71). Cambridge, MA: MIT Press, and Amsterdam: Elsevier. (Reprinted from *Cognition*, **28**, 1988.)

Gentner, D. (1983). Structure-mapping: A theoretical framework for analogy. *Cognitive Science*, 7, 95-119.

Hall, R. P. (1989). Computational approaches to analogical reasoning. *Artificial Intelligence*, 39, 39-120.

Hinton, G. E. (1988).   Representing part-whole hierarchies in connectionist networks. *Proceedings of the Tenth Annual Conference of the Cognitive Science Society* (pp. 48-54). Hillsdale, NJ: Lawrence Erlbaum Associates.

Hinton, G. E. (1990). Mapping part-whole hierarchies into connectionist networks. *Artificial Intelligence* **46**, 47-75.

Hofstadter, D. R., & Mitchell, M. (1988). Conceptual slippage and analogy-making: a report on the Copycat project. *Proceedings of the Tenth Annual Conference of the Cognitive Science Society* (pp. 601-607). Hillsdale, NJ: Lawrence Erlbaum Associates.

Holyoak, K. J. (1991). Symbolic connectionism: towards third-generation theories of expertise. In K. A. Ericsson & J. Smith (Eds), *Toward a General Theory of Expertise* (pp. 301-335). Cambridge, UK: Cambridge University Press.

Holyoak, K. J., & Thagard, P. (1989). Analogical mapping by constraint satisfaction. Cognitive Science 13, 295-355.

Hwang, K., & Briggs, F. A. (1984). *Computer architecture and parallel processing*. New York: McGraw-Hill.

Kedar-Cabelli, S. (1988). Analogy — from a unified perspective. In D. H. Helman (Ed.), *Analogical Reasoning* (pp. 65-103). Dordrecht: Kluwer.

Kolodner, J. L., & Simpson, R. L. (1989). The MEDIATOR: Analysis of an early case-based problem solver. *Cognitive Science* 13, 507-549.

Kolodner, J. L., Simpson, R. L., & Sycara-Cyranski, K. (1985). A process model of case-based reasoning in problem solving. *Proceedings of the Ninth International Joint Conference On Artificial Intelligence* (pp. 284-290). San Mateo, CA: Morgan Kaufmann.

Lange, T. E., & Dyer, M. G. (1989). High-level inferencing in a connectionist network. *Connection Science* 1, 181-217.

Lee, G., Flowers, M., & Dyer, M. G. (1989). A symbolic/connectionist script applier mechanism. *Proceedings of the Eleventh Annual Conference of the Cognitive Science Society* (pp. 714-721). Hillsdale, NJ: Lawrence Erlbaum Associates.

Mitchell, M., & Hofstadter, D. R. (1990a). The right concept at the right time: How concepts emerge as relevant in response to context-dependent pressures. *Proceedings of the Twelfth Annual Conference of the Cognitive Science Society* (pp. 174 181). Hillsdale, NJ: Lawrence Erlbaum Associates.

Mitchell, M., & Hofstadter, D. R. (1990b). The emergence of understanding in a computer model of concepts and analogy-making. *Physica D* **42**, 322-334.

Norman, D. A. (1986). Reflections on cognition and parallel distributed processing. In J. L. McClelland & D. E. Rumelhart (Eds.), *Parallel Distributed Processing* (Vol. 2, pp. 531-546). Cambridge, MA: MIT Press.

Pinker, S., & Prince, A. (1988).   On language and connectionism: analysis of a parallel
    distributed processing model of language acquisition. In S. Pinker & J. Mehler (Eds.),
    Connections and Symbols (pp. 73-194). Cambridge, MA: MIT Press, and Amsterdam:
    Elsevier. (Reprinted from *Cognition*, **28**, 1988.)

Plate, T. (1991).   Holographic reduced representations. Technical Report CRG-TR-91-1,
    Department of Computer Science, University of Toronto, Canada.

Pollack, J. B. (1988). Recursive auto-associative memory: devising compositional distributed
    representations. In *Proceedings of the Tenth Annual Conference of the Cognitive Science
    Society* (pp.33-39). Hillsdale, NJ: Lawrence Erlbaum Associates.

Pollack, J. B. (1990). Recursive distributed representations. *Artificial Intelligence*, 46, 77-105.

Riesbeck, C. K., & Schank, R. C. (1989). *Inside case-based reasoning*. Hillsdale, NJ: Lawrence
    Erlbaum Associates.

Rumelhart, D. E., & McClelland, J. L. (1986). On learning the past tenses of English verbs. In
    J. L. McClelland & D. E. Rumelhart (Eds.), *Parallel Distributed Processing* (Vol. 2, pp.
    216-271). Cambridge, MA: MIT Press.

Schank, R. C. (1982). *Dynamic memory: a theory of reminding and learning in computers and
    people*. New York: Cambridge University Press.

Shastri, L., & Ajjanagadde, V. (1989). A connectionist system for rule-based reasoning with
    multi-place predicates and variables. Technical Report MS-CIS-8905, Computer and
    Information Science Department, University of Pennsylvania, Philadelphia, PA.

Smolensky, P. (1988a). The constituent structure of connectionist mental states: a reply to Fodor
    and Pylyshyn. In T. Horgan & J. Tienson (Eds), *Connectionism and the Philosophy of
    Mind*, Supplement to Vol. XXVI of *The Southern Journal of Philosophy* (pp. 137-161).

Smolensky, P. (1988b). On the proper treatment of connectionism. *Behavioral and Brain
    Sciences* **11**, 1-74.

Smolensky, P. (1990). Tensor product variable binding and the representation of symbolic
    structures in connectionist systems. *Artificial Intelligence*, **46**, 159-216.

Standish, T. A. (1980). *Data Structure Techniques*. Reading, MA: Addison-Wesley.

Stanfill, C., & Waltz, D. (1986). Toward memory-based reasoning. *Communications of the
    ACM* **29**, 1213-1228.

Sycara, K. P. (1989). Argumentation: Planning other agents' plans. *Proceedings of the Eleventh
    International Joint Conference on Artificial Intelligence* (pp. 517-523). San Mateo, CA:
    Morgan Kaufmann.

Sycara, K. P., & Navinchandra, D. (1991). Index transformation techniques for facilitating
    creative use of multiple cases. *Proceedings of the Twelfth International Joint Conference
    on Artificial Intelligence* (pp. 347-352). San Mateo, CA: Morgan Kaufmann.

Touretzky, D. S. (1986). BoltzCONS: Reconciling connectionism with the recursive nature of
    stacks and trees. *Proceedings of the Eighth Annual Conference of the Cognitive Science
    Society*. Hillsdale, NJ: Lawrence Erlbaum Associates.

Touretzky, D. S. (1990). BoltzCONS: Dynamic symbol structures in a connectionist network.
    Artificial Intelligence, **46**, 5-46.

Vosniadou, S., & Ortony, A. (Eds). (1989). *Similarity and Analogical Reasoning*. Cambridge,
    UK: Cambridge University Press.

3

Semiotics, Meaning, and Discursive Neural Networks

Samuel J. Leven
Radford University and For a New Social Science

Knowledge representation is too complicated to be well-served by the traditional semantic approach (e.g., Katz, 1972; Winston, 1977). The problems encountered by Rumelhart and McClelland (1986), as pointed out by Fodor and Pylyshyn (1988), are endemic to the model employed. Eco (1976, 1984) and others have urged that we see all systematically-generated information as parts of a "science of signs", semiotics. The three-faceted semiotic structure embraces information from the genetic level to language — and production. Semiotics fits modern neurolinguistic approaches (e.g., Dingwall, 1980) and neurophysiological theorizing (Arnold, 1984; Black *et al.*, 1988; Posner & Keele, 1968). It also enables us to employ "holographic models" (Pribram, 1971) — and to extend our models to higher level processes (Leven, 1987a, 1987b; Levine, 1986). Ultimately, both internal and interpersonal interactions are discursive.

> And this is what I have been trying to do...: identify and mathematize the relevant abstract patterns... in a scientific study of meaning and information. In terms of this definition, what is presented here is mathematics. It just does not look like it (yet).
>
> Keith Devlin, *Logic and Information*, p. 294.

1. INTRODUCTION

Recent challenges to neural network modeling of complex behavior, notably Fodor and Pylyshyn (1988), provided painful reminders of how primitive our capacity to comprehend — and render — human performance is. The problem of representing the most elementary visual illusions produces quite differently motivated answers (e.g., Grossberg, 1980; Rumelhart & McClelland, 1986, Ch. 14). It becomes clear that there are *fundamental differences in underlying models of neural process* implicit in these carefully implemented models. Some, like the PDP School, are concerned with problems of "framing" and "dynamic schemata" that are inherited from classical logic and artificial intelligence. Others, like Grossberg and his school, seek to replicate physiological data with techniques as closely emulating the underlying "wiring" as possible.

What is evident, both from the cogent criticisms of Fodor and Pylyshyn and from the internal disagreement on underlying models, is the failure of the discipline to *specify a common logic*. This lack of comity may not be the result of philosophical or personal differences. The neural science fraternity may not have failed classical logic. Instead, it may be the opposite: *Classical logic cannot respond to complex problems of coding, learning, and representation* (Devlin, 1991).

We suggest, below, that *semiotics* (as practiced by Peirce, Morris, and Eco) presents an effective model of basic and elaborate mental process (see Fig. 3.1).[1] Semiotics, as a theory of the nature of signs and the structure of thought, illuminates many puzzling aspects of brain performance. We shall suggest, briefly, some biological support for such an approach and offer fragmentary evidence of its usefulness.

Briefly, semiotics finds that all systems of interpretation and representation (from DNA genetic structures to our body of knowledge) are built in three parts. The three elements are the object itself, the logical categories it can be placed in, and its sense to its observer. These three can be contrasted to, for example, common models of semantic networks, which represent information as systematically related data. We shall find that the semantic net paradigm fits within the structure of semiotics — allowing us to find the important (but limited) place imposed categories have in the composition of thought processes.

Finally, we explore a few implications of such a modular — *and distributed* — structure. We show that componentiality need not be as restrictive as some (e.g., Changeux, 1986) have feared — yet, it can yield results explaining ordered behaviors (e.g., learned helplessness) and otherwise discontinuous phenomena (e.g., visual illusions).

2. SIGNS, SEMANTICS, AND SEMIOTICS

Peirce (1965-1966) proposed a thorough-going revision of logic based on the insight that *meaning had been obscured* by classical logic. He suggested that all systematically generated information presents itself in embedded sets of three characteristic ways. *Firstness*, he held, derives from the immediate quality of being and is constituted of basic perceptions, instinctive reactions, and homomorphic mappings. *Secondness* is the process of relating (contrast, similarity); it is evidenced in competitive systems, indexical inference (classical logic), and "perceptual judgments." *Thirdness* is intuitive mapping, broad categorization, based in abstraction which serves to reduce complexities (usually to first or second level representation).

---

[1] While we discuss these matters *briefly*, we refer a serious reader to Eco (1976) for a thorough introduction to semiotics. For a gloss of Peirce's work (a none-too-simple task), see Hookway (1985). Note, too, that Karl Pribram suggested the use of both linguistics and Peircean semiotics as ways of exploring perceptual and memory process (e.g., Pribram, 1979).

A. PEIRCE TRILOGIES
  i. Icons - indexes - symbols as representation
  i. Aspects (elements) of the sign:
    1. the sign itself (sign-aspect)
      -- Qualisign (sensory quality)
      -- Sinsign (individual reality -- context)
      -- Legisign (general type -- category)
    2. the sign relating to its object (object-aspect)
      -- Icon (sign that resembles its object)
      -- Index (sign like a pointer, symptom)
      -- Symbol (interpreted as sign abstractly, a
      flag)
    3. the sign relating to its interpretant (int.-
    aspect)
      -- Rhema (like "term" -- not true or false)
      -- Dicent (a sign translatable into
      proposition)
      -- Argument (rationally necessary sign)
  ii. Classes of interpretants
    1. Immediate (as the sign represents it, initial
    sense)
    2. Dynamic (reaction the sign provokes)
    3. Final (meaning if fully evaluated,
    dispassionately)
  iii. Categories: always reducible to threes
    1. Firstness: immediate "quality of feeling"
      -- Homomorphisms; aesthetics; brute reaction
      -- perceptions
    2. Secondness: relation -- "contrast or similarity"
      -- Competitive systems (dyads); ethics
      -- perceptual judgments; indexical inference
    3. Thirdness: relation by classes or qualities
      -- Intuitive, broad mappings; reflexive
      -- Category which unites other two; TRUE logic
      -- Generality; continuity; abstraction
      -- Hypostatic abstraction reduces complexity

B. MORRIS' IMPULSE-GUIDED TRILOGY
  i. Taxonomy of "motivation" (absent reward)
    1. Orientation: impulse-controlled perception
      -- Modality-restricted: not received by producer
      -- Impulse-related: keyed to receiver's state
      -- Situation-contingent: context
      -- Function-dependent: acted on only IN CONTEXT
    2. Manipulation: obtaining/producing desired object
    3. Consummation: satisfaction (or distraction)
  ii. Action and Value Theory: Control and Satisfaction
    1. Orientation produces DETACHMENT
      -- Environmental data tends to overwhelm
      -- Try to avoid domination by/of environment
    2. Manipulation leads to DOMINANCE
      -- Satisfy impulse to act
      -- Extend sphere of influence
    3. Consummation produces DEPENDENCE; submits to object

Fig. 3.1. Some elements of Peirce-Morris Semiotic Theory.

Signs, Peirce taught, embrace virtually all we experience. One follower has developed *zoosemiotics* to consider animal-to-man and animal-to-animal communication — and even considered DNA as a sign system.[2] Yet, all signs are similar in pattern.

At base, there is the sign itself[3], the way it is experienced by the senses, its place in the context of surrounding signs, and its general category. The next "layer" involves the relation the sign bears to its object: The sign as *Icon* (one-to-one representation), as *Index* (pointer to a category), and as *Symbol* (meaning-laden abstraction, like a flag). Finally, the sign relates to its receiver like a "given" term, a proposition-maker, and an absolute "truth".

Interpreters encounter signs in three ways, as well. Their responses can be *immediate* (taking the initial sense of the sign), *dynamic* (reacting as anticipated to the sign), and *final* (making "sense" of the complexities of the sign). These relate directly to the ways in which the interpreter thinks about all signs.

Problem solving is easily mapped to the same categories. *Induction* is performing stereotyped knowledge-mapping processes. *Deduction* is distinguishing among alternatives, step-by-step, as in an expert system or traditional semantic net. *Abduction* is the mapping of sensory and instinctive processes onto previously unsuccessful deductive processes, performed in a relaxed state.

Modern writers, led by Eco, have extended Peirce's work (see Fig. 3.2).[4] Their most cogent suggestion (made most clearly by Eco, 1984) is that human knowledge is stored in multi-layered, multi-dimensional *encyclopedias*. He contrasts this notion of knowledge structured by syntactic, semantic, and semiotic criteria (a trichotomy) with what is fully available — a set of indexical (two-dimensional) tree structures. These indexical structures are usually portrayed as *semantic networks* (Sowa, 1983; Winston, 1977); yet, they are based on flat contrasts and simplified categories. What is missed in these narrow structures is *context*, the many different senses a term can take (e.g., the comments of Eco, 1985, on colors and cultures).

Morris (1946) applied semiotics in social interaction. Based on drive-reduction models, he suggested a trichotomy of motivation that tied attention (*orientation*) to strict pattern-matching context cues. Interaction is, inevitably, a move toward dominance (*manipulation*). Finally, the resultant goal is drive-reduction (*consummation*). This system is represented in a new network model that emulates an economic bargaining case (Leven, 1989; Leven & Elsberry, 1990). It represents the first *discursive* system.

The message of the move from simple semantic structures to semiotic nets is at the center of sensory, affective, and cultural influences on perception, learning, recalling, and communicat-

---

[2] See the work of Thomas Sebeok, which is best discussed in Sebeok and Umiker-Sebeok (1986), Ch. 24.

[3] Figure 3.1 represents an abbreviated model of Peirce's classes of signification and meaning. There, we include the names he attached to the many elements of his typology.

[4] For clues to the many directions semiotics has taken, see Bailey, Matejka, and Steiner (1978) and Sebeok and Umiker-Sebeok (1986). As this work reflects, not all semioticians share Peirce's vision.

ing. Even the "dynamic schemata" suggested by Schank (1982) and supported by Rumelhart and McClelland (1986, Ch. 14) do not contain the *sense* of experience Ogden and Richards (1924) underlined. The project of representing knowledge in its many dimensions, left us by Peirce, is resisted because it is formidable — it is much simpler to implement a syntax simulation.

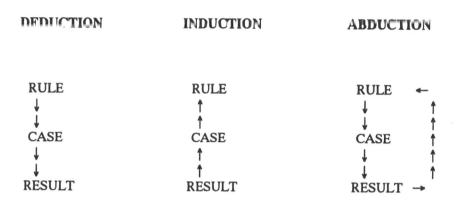

Fig. 3.2. Peirce's (and Eco's) Inferential Schemes. (Reprinted from Eco (1984), p. 40, by permission of the University of Indiana Press.)

Joining in the struggle against oversimplification are Barwise and Perry (1983) who emphasize that linguistic meaning is a relation between an utterance situation, a described situation, and background (resource) situations. Meaning, then, is not simply extracted from statements deductively; it is contingent on context. In these situations, $A \Rightarrow C$ does not suggest $A + B \Rightarrow C$ universally. It is the context that distinguishes meanings; what makes sense under some circumstances does not under others (Engdahl, 1988). This notion has been codified as *pragmatic logics*, which recognize logical contingency (Bell, 1991): Buying a *New York Post* was a perfectly safe and normal behavior, until labor strife resulted in bombings of dealers who carried it. The act of a normal reader, in one setting, quite rapidly became the stunt of a fool.

3. THE TRIUNE BRAIN AND MEMORY

Modern neurophysiology supports Peirce's work. Levine (1986) has pointed to MacLean's (1970, 1990) "triune brain" hypothesis as a useful tool in network modeling. MacLean proposed that the embedded brain structures inherited from "lower" animals (reptilian and limbic) continue to play central functions in knowledge acquisition, storage, and retrieval — and even "compete" with the neocortex for "control".

MacLean's work may rest on questionable biological principles (Pribram, personal communication), although support for many of his hypotheses continues to be found by researchers (Gabriel, Sparenberg, & Stolar, 1987). Brain history may not be laid out conveniently for such hypotheses. But, while the model MacLean has proposed is faulty, what it suggests may not be: *Levine may be right, regardless.*

Recent neurochemical research has made Levine's suggestion plausible. Martinez, Weinberger, & Schultheis (1988) identified an enkephalin-controlling enzymatic mechanism that is sensitive to learning and probably controls behavior, partly from *outside the blood-brain barrier* (as a peripherally-generated process). Black et al. (1988) found neurochemical changes that produce hundreds of different states — and Gazzaniga (1988) suggests that these are likely to be learned and recallable states. These are supportive of Mishkin's (1982) advocacy of thalamically based "flash-bulb" memory states.

Perhaps even more significant is work reported by Nottebohm's (1989) group. They observed that male birds performed elegant and complex songs during the spring mating season, forgot their songs after mating season, then learned new ones the next season. During the mating period, of course, the song each learned was remembered accurately. But, as soon as the season ended, it was completely forgotten.

Nottebohm has tied the mating song process (learning, recalling, and forgetting) *directly to the increased presence of male hormone* (testosterone). In controlled experiments, he was able to engender song learning and singing in *females* exposed to appropriate neural quantities of testosterone. He was able to force males to forget their songs by reducing the hormone's level. And he was able to sustain the learned song's presence by forcing continuing high testosterone amounts after mating season. He found that the level of testosterone *enabled learning and maintenance of songs* — its decline erased memory and learning capacity.

Work by Nottebohm has confirmed the hypotheses of Black and Martinez et al.. Neurotransmitters serve as representational media. It is important to recognize one quality of neurochemical processes which is easy to ignore in a digitally oriented age; quantities of neuromodulators are brain-wide mixes, *analog* quantities which vary continuously. Thus, the number of chemically representable states far exceeds the count of neurally effective substances.

Our approach combines these neurochemically induced states with other peripheral feedback. Arnold (1984) described motor system memory as the product of interaction between periphery and motor centers. Much of this processing is nearly automatic, as it derives from systematic training over long periods. Lieberman's (1985) work in language centers is suggestive that some apparently high-order functions are partly stored routines in motor centers.

Further, clinical evidence is strongly suggestive of the role of physicochemical state as a memory "key." Substance abuse specialists cite numerous cases in which alcoholic pianists learn and perform pieces in drug-induced states — but cannot perform or recall the music once sobriety returns (K. Sees, San Francisco VA Medical Staff, personal communication). This *state-dependent* memory tends to be especially unyielding to cognitive — and affective — therapy techniques for recall. Return of the state is the requirement.

Meanwhile, Arnold (1984) and Bear (1979) supported Zajonc's (1980) assertion of "affective memory" with neurophysiological data. Panksepp (1986 et seq.) has found supportive neurochemical results supporting control of evaluation and recall by limbic function. Further, Heath (1986) has emphasized the fundamental role of affect in recalling events; hippocampal and other limbic systems "cue" lateral geniculate nucleus in recalling visually significant experience.

For our model of categorical or "semantic" memory, we need go no further than Norman and Rumelhart (1970). The process of recognition consists, they assert, of checking incoming data against a "dictionary" based in a content-addressable memory. These *indexical* recall processes require greater recognition time as the complexity or ambiguity of data increases.

Many writers, including Arnold (1984) and Pribram (1984), questioned the proposition that learning and memory can be considered a single-modality process. Work from Posner and Keele (1969) on has demonstrated the global nature of recognizing complex data; our models must drive us toward this complexity.

We can think of learning and memory processes as a dynamical system, filled with feedback effects from physiological (motoric) state to logical (neocortical) storage and retrieval, feeding forward to affective (limbic) conditions.[5] This matches, in "wiring", the model introduced by Leventhal (1984) (see Fig. 3.3).

These results suggest a typology of memory function which supports Peirce's concepts. Flash-bulb and "instinctive" memories seem dependent on physiological state (arousal, long-term stress) and on environmental icons (simple signs). Matches might have to be quite close (we don't panic at the sound of a car horn 150° behind us; when it is 180°, we are quite prepared to jump without further examination). These are highly stereotyped processes — fitting to *immediate, first* responses. These may be tied to "procedural memory" models like that of Tulving (1983).

A second class of memory suggests itself. "Semantic" and "frame" memories (Schank, 1982; Tulving, 1985) are plainly demonstrable. We may tie these to Peirce's *iconic, dynamic* sense. This process is described by Norman and Rumelhart's "dictionary", composed of logical language (or semantic) trees which are massively inter-connected.

Peirce's *Thirdness* has received support from an unlikely source, Roger Schank (1988). Organization of memory and cognition (Leven, 1987a) should be considered a third mapping (Tulving's "episodic" memory), based on the "feel of events" (e.g., Foa & Kozak, 1986). This third mapping, as Peirce sensed, enables us to reflect the *generalized affective experience* which enables scientists to make discoveries. And, this same vehicle operates in ordinary problem solving situations — as Tikhomirov (1983) established. The neurophysiology of language has proved supportive to the view that both functional and memorial processes can be parsed in a Peirce-like manner. Dingwall (1980) substantiated a model of a three-part basis for human communication, based in reflexive (striatal), affective (limbic), and cognitive (neocortical) systems (see Fig. 3.4). And Lieberman (1985) has stressed how central a role the speech center's historic motor control task has played in syntactic ability; the routine nature of motor control has led to the routine nature of syntax. He has also recognized the evolutionary role of limbic cortex as central to expressive capacity (Lieberman, 1984).

Vaina (1984), in fact, suggested a similar model. She asserts that three "modules of representation" can distinguish among symbols: a category module (hierarchical/dyadic), a

---

[5] Pribram (1980) uses a similar threefold typology for "central processing": image processing (sensory-motor), episodic processing (fronto-limbic), and information processing (posterior). Image processing, he argues, *is* distributed processing. Information processing is differentiating between alternatives. Episodic processing is finding familiarity or novelty. The last, he claims, dominates neural function, directing attentional resources. Thus, brain processes are critically context-dependent.

functional module (relational), and a descriptive module (surface appearance). Elements in her "threads" can be held commonly by many recalled objects, yielding (in effect) a multidimensional network. In fact, Leven (1987b) suggested such a framework.

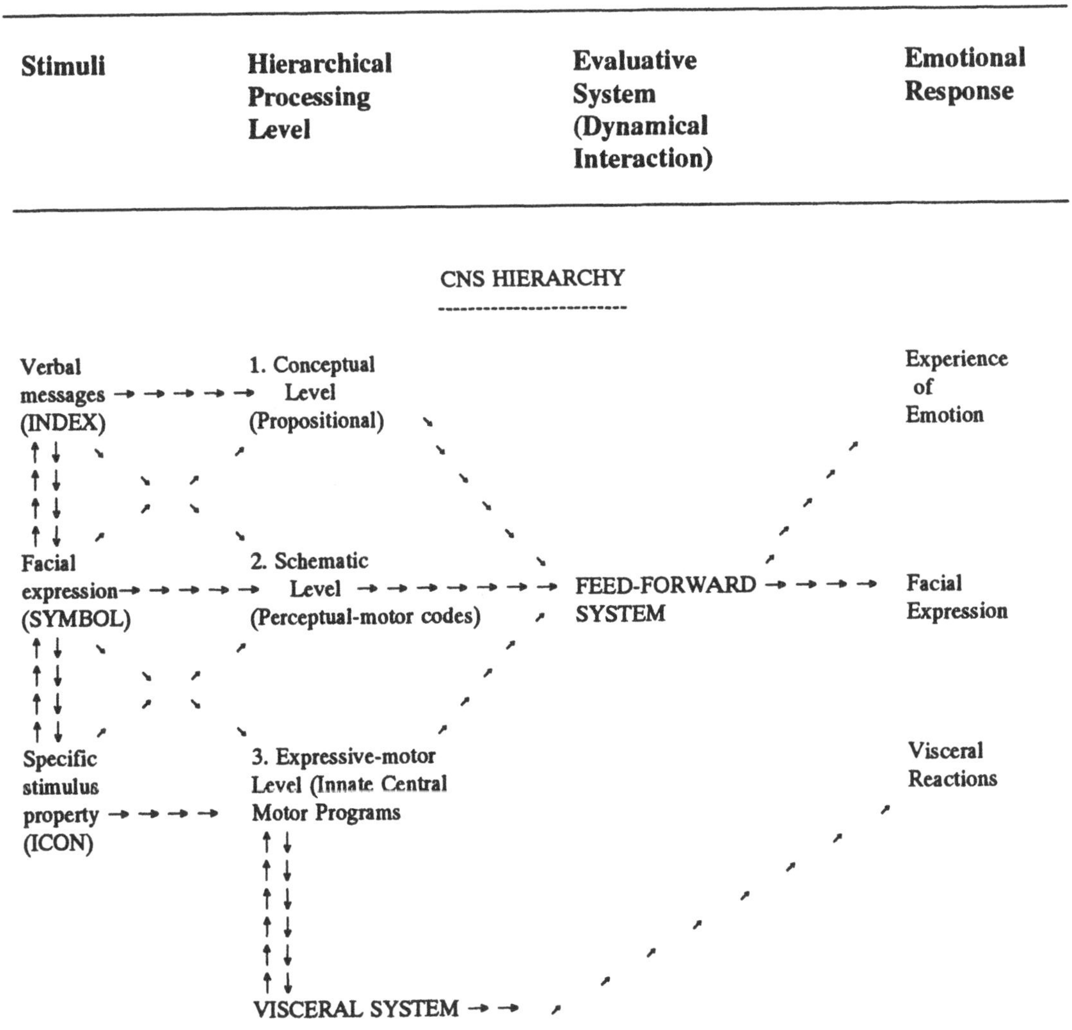

Stimuli	**Hierarchical Processing Level**	**Evaluative System (Dynamical Interaction)**	**Emotional Response**

CNS HIERARCHY

Verbal messages → → → → → (INDEX)   1. Conceptual Level (Propositional)   Experience of Emotion

↑↓ ↑↓ ↑↓ ↑↓

Facial expression → → → → → (SYMBOL)   2. Schematic Level → → → → → → → (Perceptual-motor codes)   FEED-FORWARD SYSTEM → → → →   Facial Expression

↑↓ ↑↓ ↑↓ ↑↓

Specific stimulus property → → → → (ICON)   3. Expressive-motor Level (Innate Central Motor Programs

↑↓ ↑↓ ↑↓ ↑↓ ↑↓ ↑↓

Visceral Reactions

VISCERAL SYSTEM → →

Fig. 3.3. Scheme for CNS hierarchy due to Leventhal (1984). (Modified from Leventhal, 1984, p. 274, with permission of Lawrence Erlbaum Associates.)

And Newell and his collaborators sought to use such a framework in their SOAR model of knowledge processing and representation. Analogizing their work to Tulving's, they write, "the SOAR architecture supports and constrains the representation, storage, retrieval, use, and acquisition of three pervasive forms of knowledge: procedural, episodic, and declarative ..." (Rosenbloom, Newell, & Laird, 1991, p. 108).

Finally, Pribram's (1984) "Colonic" approach can be reconciled with these preceding three-part models. Pribram proposed that processing is performed in *four* ways: viscerally ("labile-stabile"), homeostatically ("epicritic-protocritic"), affectively (effective-affective), and esthetically ("ethical-esthetic"). Pribram emphasized the role of forebrain function in all "dimensions" — and that they were highly interactive. *Seeing neural process as a system*, filled with recursive, cooperative processing, reconciles these two models. The notion we have offered (Leven, 1987a) considers visceral and homeostatic representations to be a single category. The unity we suggest is, partly, a logical one: the two are reflective of lower-level propagational functions. And, in fact, the *ensemble* of peripheral signals and neurochemical processes, at this basic level seems to fit well the Firstness that Peirce suggested.

Reflexive system (STRIATAL)	Affective System (LIMBIC)	Cognitive System (NEOCORTICAL)
PRIMARY SIGN BEHAVIOR (Global crying)	VISCERAL SIGN COMPLEXES (Differentiated crying) SOMATOVISCERAL SIGN SCHEMATA (Cooing) SOMATOVISCERAL SIGN LEARNING (Tracking affective states of the communicator) VOLITIONAL SIGNAL COMMUNICATION (Babbling)	PROPOSITIONAL COMMUNICATION STAGES: GESTURAL NAMING HOLOPHRASTIC TWO-WORD TELEGRAPHIC LANGUAGE

Fig. 3.4. Speech development. (Reprinted from Dingwall (1980), p. 68, by permission of the Indiana University Press.)

4. TRIUNE INFORMATION PROCESSING

We briefly pose a question for this "new" framework. We take an example the PDP group considers: the Necker Cube visual illusion (Rumelhart & McClelland, 1986, Ch. 14). We explain some anthropological findings that *not everybody detects the illusion*. Next, and even more briefly, we outline an explanation for the "learned helplessness" phenomenon (e.g., Seligman, 1975) that resists a modern neurophysiological model.

Rumelhart and McClelland (1988) suggest that "a simple constraint satisfaction model can capture [the] exactly two good interpretations of a Necker cube" (p. 58). Yet, research with African tribesmen shows that there is a third interpretation: The Necker cube presents no illusion *and is not even box-like* (Leven, 1987a). Those unaccustomed to "modern" geometric forms find the figure a mass of jumbled lines. In fact, "civilized" men can detect that a visual "trick" is present *if it is explained* (e.g., Wertheimer, 1982).

The PDP version attaches a weight to each vertex, then forces nearby units to be mutually excitatory. Vertices, then, are the primitives to which the eyes attend. In fact, a detailed map of retinal images is maintained in visual cortex in a center-surround light-dark contrast enhancement framework. Many cells have unique feature-sensitivity (including lines, edges, and space), leaving higher visual cortex the task of "painting" a picture from many features (Kandel & Schwartz, 1981, Ch. 20). The combinatorial task is conditioned, heavily, by training in the physical environment (Shevelev, 1983) and social training (Kosslyn, 1988, p. 269).

Instead of resolving the cube figure at a very low level of processing then, the perceptual task is several layers removed from the sensors. It responds to preprocessing, categorization, environmental cues, and social knowledge.

Many templates are offered to explain the primitives, based on expectations derived from previous interaction with "original" and "modern" geometric forms. A person, then, interprets the object as he has *prepared*.

Following Grossberg (1987), we suggest that much of the data is "masked" in preprocessing; we tend to find what we seek. This preprocessing is based, of course, on environmental demands, physiological and affective state, and prior cognitions. The data are then interpreted, based on the "priority" attached (Levine & Prueitt, 1989); this determines the number of categories attempted and the number of cues considered.

In a state of high arousal, the illusion may not be present — the perceiver may not attend to the stimulus at all. Shevelev (1983) suggested that enough serotonin can even "wipe out" visual memory and often retards recognition. Equally significant is the report of Nottebohm (1989): The routine-oriented (procedural) learning Wise (1987) called "Variable Action Pattern" processing can be facilitated or denigrated by neurotransmitter levels. Visual routines that are socially mediated, such as forms with implicit depth (Rosch & Mervis, 1975), can be disrupted by system-wide stresses. Leven (1988) modeled such arousal-based neurochemistry as providing "site-binding", blocking potential inhibition and leading to "sensory overload."

Casual perusal, in a relaxed state, should lead to adoption of one of the alternative illusions for a trained viewer. The Gestaltists emphasize that a viewer recognizes the duality far more often *when it is pointed out*. But Kosslyn (1988) suggests that economy requires that one version out-compete the other in most environments. A classic on center-off surround architecture is implicit in Kosslyn's discussion.

Only when many attentional resources are available can the illusion be experienced — and when the viewer is *interested*. A sufficiently motivated viewer employs semantic resources to evaluate the primitives. Then, by *varying vigilance*, he is able to induce first one version, next the other. We should expect that one suitable model for this process includes Adaptive Resonance architecture (see Grossberg, 1987).

Those not exposed to modern geometry are puzzled, however, by the Western fascination with visual illusions. Untrained to "see" the reversals, they fail to find the *implicit dimensionality* that the illusions require. Lacking the semantic categories that seeing complex surfaces brings (and possibly lacking the trained retinal neurons), they see straight lines overlaid, as Rosch and Mervis (1975) found.

Hence, the model introduced by the PDP writers is *culture-bound*. We can be trained to see many visual illusions — but the recognition of novel mismatches (e.g., the cube reversing depth) is a higher brain function which requires more complex modeling (Leven & Levine, 1987).

The importance of the case Rumelhart and McClelland raise is that mathematical elegance should not be the benchmark by which models of brain function are judged — instead, we ought to focus on the phenomena themselves (Pribram, personal communication). We offer an abbreviated description of a more suitable model — in hope of clarifying our view.

Many elements of current conditions must be introduced to specify the cause of many conditions. The "frame problem" that concerns PDP is central here; how is much information masked, some repressed, and some distorted? Only a *dynamical frame*, including semantic, affective, and lower-level states, can capture a sufficient picture of person and environment.

In fact, other leading writers on structures of information and knowledge have taken a similar perspective. As Nicolis (1991, pp. 191-193) writes, "the social milieu plays the role of the collective macroparameter ... which ... determines the 'frame' ..." Nicolis distinguishes three levels. Syntactic communication corresponds to classical "Shannonian" information, he asserts. Semantic communication deals with correspondences among sets of objects and symbols-attractors; Nicolis associates this process with cognitive psychology. Finally, the pragmatic level, for Nicolis, corresponds to the emergence of meaning and value through the mapping of psychological patterns and conceptual categories. He suggests that, at this pragmatic level, the communicants wage a *game*.

We begin by recognizing that two observers must be postulated in the Necker Cube case: a naive subject and a trained one. As in John (1980, pp. 97-101), we envision memory to constitute an *ensemble* of waves generated by trained cells.[6] This ensemble (or, as John prefers, ensemble of ensembles) represents an interpretive network for input patterns. It can be tied to motivational, affective, and cognitive processes.

In fact, Eco (1985) and Rosch and Mervis (1975) maintain that our ways of *seeing* the world (interpreting presented visual cues) are central to our world view. The structure we impose of implied depth in images reflects both the assumption of straightness and corners (not so prevalent in the bush) and the *assertion of order*. Rosch's primitives were undisturbed by an object whose lines met at angles — they *did not expect to see a cube*. As Kosslyn (1988) would explain it, the "primitives" lacked the specific *categorical relations* encoding for "depth-seeking" that is employed by Western viewers. In order to develop specific models of objects, we need

---

[6] See also Bohm's (1983, pp. 181-183) description of information: "ensembles of elements ... can nevertheless be distinguished ... in which the members of each ensemble are related through the force of an overall necessity ... [In] general, only one of these ensembles will unfold at a time ... We call this an *intrinsically implicate order*."

first to obtain a representation in "local coordinate system" for multi-part objects. These are lower-level, "bottom-up" processes which precede hypothesis formation (Kosslyn, 1988, pp. 256-259). Only then can we evaluate ("top-down") properties objects matching the feed-forward description should have.

In other words, *first we obtain a basic representation; then we evaluate it* using established, "logical" categories. So, when the Western viewer constructs from the Necker Cube image an object possessing depth, he or she does so at a low processing level, very close to actual retinal input. This apparently "precognitive" stage is fully trained from environmental cues and experience.[7]

Contrast the low-level processing performed by "primitives" in the Necker Cube case to the processing taking place in Western subjects. Kosslyn's (1988, p. 266) steps to image processing include:

2. The preprocessing subsystem and pattern activation subsystem are used whenever one "inspects" the image for a shape.
3. The categorical relations encoding subsystems are used [to interpret] a spatial relation
...
4. Whenever the imaged object includes more than one part, one of the two [higher category] lookup systems is used [usually] the categorical property lookup subsystem ...
9. [When] the imaged object must be transformed ..., the pattern shifting subsystem is used.

These higher level functions are primarily temporal and parietal; they connect to higher cortical functions (for category matching) and, as John tells us, to an astonishing variety of other structures whose mission is not primarily visual interpretation.

How can Peirce be helpful to us? Peirce (1965-1966) defines the trichotomy of experience as *quality, fact*, and *thought*. The appearance of an object without interpretation, the basic stimulation we experience and interpret[8], is a quality. The cube, as it was presented to the "primitives", was a mass of lines. It did not specifically present edges and lines as cues. Instead, it was a product of firstness, a sign made by experimenters which took on a quality ("picture-ness") when presented. Qualities, Peirce tells us, are "mere potentialities" — we *frame* them as we choose, as a separate operation.

Fact, according to Peirce, is construed from experience. It is the ordering of perception as effort to stabilize the world we encounter, hold it against contradiction. In other words, facts are *excluding* — they rule out competing sense data and explanations. It is this categorizing function that the cube illusion defies: neither explanation (of depth) can be excluded. It is a

---

[7] See Shevelev's (1983) work on low-level visual memory.

[8] Peirce (1955) writes: "It is not anything which is dependent, whether in the form of sense or in that of thought ... That quality is dependent upon sense is the great error ... A quality is a mere abstract potentiality; and the error ... lies in holding that the potential ... is nothing but what makes the actual to be" (p. 85).

framing activity, cognitive in practice. As in any indexing activity, categories are systematically grouped.

What is being categorized? Edges, lines, and excluded space. To a person not trained to open cereal boxes, for whom street corners are irrelevant and tic-tac-toe squares meaningless, these apparently self-evident qualities are strange and lack explanatory power. *Corners are not part of his or her experience.*

As we learned from John (1980) and Pribram (e.g., 1979), the process of visual interpretation is not instinctive or reflexive — it is *interpretive.* It involves higher order cognitive structures. Peirce makes their point clearer, by imposing the contexts of indexing by category and selecting through conflict.

The third quality, thought or mediation, offers the insight the cube problem demands. For the conflict of categorization by edges can be resonant (Grossberg, 1980) and unresolvable. Or, the "sophisticated" subject who perceives the conflicting indexing can recognize that the illusion is based on the *inadequacy of categorization schemata* "modern" viewers employ. The reversibility of the cube is a higher order masking problem, presumably directed by action of temporal cortex.[9] This higher order control is the vehicle by which context can make choices meaningful. The reversing quality of the cube suggests that the conflict of stable categories implied by accessing indexes of sets of cues is as useless to the "modern" in this case as it would be to the "primitive."

Also suggested by the need to access higher mental functions in resolving category conflicts is the critical role of *motivation* as an attentional guide (ignoring conflicting cues) and as a means of accessing greater resources (to understand the conflict). This part of Thirdness, the "connective tissue" between quality and fact, calls us to Wertheimer's (1982) reminder:

> In real thinking processes, items often do not remain rigidly identical; and as a matter of fact, precisely their change, their improvement is required.... For statements, etc., have a direction in their context. It is here that a basic feature of traditional logic comes to the fore: its disregard of the intense directedness of live thought processes as they improve a given situation. (p. 259)

What emerges from this discussion is the notion that *no perceptual or learning process operates independent of context — and no response is possible in its absence.* The illusion as icon has no meaning without context; untrained viewers simply do not recognize it. The illusion as index is accessible as a paradox — each "version" of the cube "fights" and sometimes "wins." Without the context that neurophysiology offers, it remains irreducible, lacking meaning

---

[9] Pribram (1971) writes: "the inferior temporal cortex influences visual processes not so much because it *receives* visual information *from* the primary cortex, but because it *operates* through corticofugal connections *on* visual processes occurring *in* subcortical structures ... [The] connections exist whereby the so-called association cortex can exert control over input. That this control intimately involves motor mechanisms fits with the neurobehavioral evidence that the temporal cortex plays a role when *active* choices have to be made" (pp. 318-321).

or significance (a trick). Only when icon and index are connected by the symbol, the sense, of the problem can understanding take place.

In fact, recent experimental animal work by Gabriel et al. (1987) reinforces Peirce's instinct. Simple pattern recognition and motor responses are "stored" in cerebellar areas once learned. But, in order to *learn* the responses, contextual cues must be supplied by limbic areas. And, while under certain circumstances the trained responses can be educed in the absence of part of the limbic system, Gabriel's group finds that contextual keys supplied by limbic cortex are critical to effective performance.

Even routine motor tasks require us to recall our sense of the environment. And even higher order "logical" tasks may utilize contextual keys; Gabriel et al. (1987) speculate that chess masters may use *different spatial representations* of the board to encode the many complex strings of moves they can choose. Here, context could induce — as it does in trained viewers of the cube illusion — an appropriate *indexing schema* to order the many hierarchies of possible moves.

5. LESSONS FOR NEURAL NETWORK THEORY

So, what is the significance of Peirce's model and the supporting scientific evidence for neural network models?

First, they take some of the air out of assertions by writers like Fodor and Pylyshyn (1988) that the models are not supported by classical logic (or that, somehow, any model that does not conform is inferior). Classical logic, built on the two-dimensional tree model, cannot capture subtleties of meaning — and, more important — *it does not embrace the process of gaining insight.* Such a method, then, would be flawed for the implementation of expert systems of any kind and could not expect to seek the "feel" of events that a semiotic net might reach.

Second, there is more to be gained by emulating sensory and motor processes than has been thought. If the process of solving physics problems, for example, requires that we "feel" the forces involved, then a model that learns complex visual or pattern recognition may also, eventually, help us analyze the Three Body Problem. In fact, some forms of knowledge — and understanding — may not be accessible in any other way (Eich, 1989).

Third, consider Peirce's notion that *layers of signs* exist, each composed of the three co-equal representations: first, a one-to-one mapping (like early retinal images), second, a dualistic and hierarchical ordering (like the categories we match images trace to), and third, a meaning-laden and intuitive rendering (like the unconventional way we understand a visual illusion). These, we have asserted (Leven, 1987a, 1987b), match *instinctive, semantic,* and *affective* mappings.

Fourth, if human decision making is heavily dependent on instinctive and affective responses, then models emulating choice behavior must integrate these into the most modest fuzzy decision machines. Thus, suggestions like Pearl's (1988) that "realistic" decision models can be built from "Bayesian" networks are inappropriate at best. On the other hand, this evidence may provide grounds for hope that higher-level processes may be measurable (in part, at least) and, hence, emulable (Gabriel *et al.*, 1987; Leven, 1989).

Fifth, if we are to use the brain as a model for the development of computing environments, we ought to reconsider the notion that systems be regulated on traditional message-passing and ACTOR models. The *state of the machine environment* should be a critical criterion in determining the operation of the machine (as it is in humans). New processes and loads should be treated as "novel events" and recalled; a machine could be trained to "sense" the introduction of a virus by unusual demands on resources and redundant use of limited algorithms. In fact, a machine could be wired to accept the state of "learned helplessness" (Leven, 1989, 1993) and gradually withdraw access to its "abusers".

Sixth, if the nature of knowledge is largely social, as work by Barwise and Perry (1983), Eco (1984), and Winograd and Flores (1987) suggests, then cultural and social frames ought to be specified. Only by comprehending the expectations, values, and fears of actors can we hope to specify what they see and know.

Finally, if "cooperative" memory models, like Pribram's (1971, 1991), are to be implemented, this evidence of mixed memory models should prove useful. Leven (1987b, 1988) has offered a very tentative proposal.

ACKNOWLEDGMENTS

Special thanks are due to Dan Levine and Karl Pribram for their help and encouragement. All errors, though, are the author's.

REFERENCES

Arnold, M. (1984). *Memory and the Brain.* Hillsdale, NJ: Lawrence Erlbaum Associates.

Bailey, K., Matejka, L., & Steiner, B. (1978). *The Sign: Semiotics Around the World.* Ann Arbor, MI: University of Michigan Press.

Barwise, J., & Perry, J. (1983). *Situations and Attitudes.* Cambridge, MA: MIT Press.

Bear, D. M. (1979). The temporal lobes: An approach to the study of organic behavioral changes. In M. Gazzaniga (Ed.), *Neuropsychology* (pp. 75-95). New York: Plenum.

Bell, J. (1991). Pragmatic logics. In J. Allen, R. Fikes, & E. Sandewall (Eds.), *Principles of Knowledge Representation* (pp. 50-60). San Mateo, CA: Morgan Kaufmann.

Black, I., Adler, J., Dreyfus, C., Friedman, W., LaGamma, E., & Roach, A. (1988). Experience and the biochemistry of information storage in the nervous system. In M. Gazzaniga (Ed.), *Perspectives in Memory Research* (pp. 3-22). Cambridge, MA: MIT Press.

Bohm, D. (1983). *Wholeness and the Implicate Order.* London: Routledge and Kegan Paul.

Changeux, J. P. (1986). *Neuronal Man.* New York: Oxford University Press.

Devlin, K. (1991). *Logic and Information.* New York: Cambridge University Press.

Dingwall, J. (1980). Human communicative behavior: A biological model. In I. Rauch & G. Carr (Eds.), *The Signifying Animal* (pp. 51-86). Bloomington, IN: Indiana University Press.

Eco, U. (1976). *A Theory of Semiotics.* Bloomington, IN: Indiana University Press.

Eco, U. (1984). *Semiotics and the Philosophy of Language.* Bloomington, IN: Indiana University Press.

Eco, U. (1985). How culture conditions the colours we see. In M. Blonsky (Ed.), *The Signs* (pp. 157-175). Baltimore: Johns Hopkins University Press.

Eich, E. (1989). Theoretical issues in state dependent memory. In H. Roediger, III, & F. Craik (Eds.), *Varieties of Memory* (pp. 331-354). Hillsdale, NJ: Lawrence Erlbaum Associates.

Engdahl, E. (1988). Relational interpretation. In R. Kempson (Ed.), *Mental Representations* (pp. 63-82). New York: Cambridge University Press.

Foa, E., & Kozak, M. (1986). *Emotional processing of fear: Exposure to corrective information. Psychological Bulletin* **99**, 20-35.

Fodor, J. A., & Pylyshyn, Z. W. (1988). Connectionism and cognitive architecture: a critical analysis. In S. Pinker & J. Mehler (Eds.), *Connections and Symbols* (pp. 3-71). Cambridge, MA: MIT Press.

Gabriel, M., Sparenberg, S., & Stolar, N. (1987). A reply from neurobiologists. In J. LeDoux & W. Hirst (Eds.), *Mind and Brain* (pp. 270-272). New York: Cambridge University Press.

Gazzaniga, M. (Ed.) (1988). *Perspectives in Memory Research.* Cambridge, MA: MIT Press.

Grossberg, S. (1980). How does a brain build a cognitive code? *Psychological Review* **87**, 1-51.

Grossberg, S. (Ed.) (1987). *The Adaptive Brain, Vols. I and II.* New York: Elsevier.

Heath, R. (1986). The neural substrate for emotion. In R. Plutchik & H. Kellerman (Eds.), *Biological foundations of emotion* (pp. 3-36). New York: Academic Press.

Hookway, C. (1985). *Peirce.* London: Routledge and Kegan Paul.

John, E. R. (1980). A neurophysiological model of purposive behavior. In R. Thompson, L. Hicks, & V. Shvyrkov (Eds.). *Neural Mechanisms of Goal-Directed Behavior and Learning* (pp. 93-115). New York: Academic Press.

Kandel, E. R., & Schwartz, J. H. (1981). *Principles of Neural Science.* Amsterdam: Elsevier North Holland.

Katz, J. (1972). *Semantic Theory.* New York: Harper.

Kosslyn, S. M. (1988). Imagery in learning. In Gazzaniga, M. (ed.), *Perspectives in Memory Research* (pp. 245-274). Cambridge, MA: MIT Press.

Leven, S. J. (1987a). Choice and neural process. Unpublished doctoral dissertation, University of Texas at Arlington.

Leven, S. J. (1987b, October). S.A.M.: a triune extension to the A.R.T. model. Paper presented at the Conference on Networks in Brain and Computer Architecture, Denton, TX.

Leven, S. J. (1988, May). Memory, learned helplessness, and the dynamics of hope. Paper presented at Workshop on Motivation, Goal Direction, and Emotion, Dallas.

Leven, S. J. (1992). Learned helplessness, memory, and the dynamics of hope, in D. S. Levine & S. J. Leven (Eds.), *Motivation, Emotion, and Goal Direction in Neural Networks* (pp. 259-299). Hillsdale, NJ: Lawrence Erlbaum Associates.

Leven, S. J. (1989, April). OPEC as a game: Toward realistic models in bargaining. Paper presented at Southwest Social Science Association Meeting, Little Rock.

Leven, S. J., & Elsberry, W. R. (1990). Interactions among embedded extensive networks under uncertainty. *Proceedings of the International Joint Conference on Neural Networks* (Vol. III, pp. 739-746). San Diego: IEEE.

Leven, S. J., & Levine, D. S. (1987). Effects of reinforcement on knowledge retrieval and evaluation. *IEEE First International Conference on Neural Networks* (Volume II, pp. 269-277). San Diego: IEEE/ICNN.

Leventhal, H. (1984). A perceptual motor theory of emotion. In K. Scherer, & P. Ekman (Eds.), *Approaches to Emotion* (pp. 271-292). Hillsdale, NJ: Lawrence Erlbaum Associates.

Levine, D. S. (1986). A neural network theory of frontal lobe function. *Proceedings of the Eighth Annual Conference of the Cognitive Science Society* (pp. 716-727). Hillsdale, NJ: Lawrence Erlbaum Associates.

Levine, D. S. & Prueitt, P. S. (1989). Modeling aspects of frontal lobe damage: novelty and perseveration. *Neural Networks* **2**, 103 116.

Lieberman, P. (1984). *The Biology and Evolution of Language.* Cambridge, MA: Harvard University Press.

Lieberman, P. (1985). On the evolution of human syntactic ability: its pre-adaptive bases — motor control and speech. *Journal of Human Evolution* **14**, 657-668.

MacLean, P. D. (1970). The triune brain, emotion, and scientific bias. In F. Schmitt (Ed.), *The Neurosciences Second Study Program* (pp. 336-349). New York: Rockefeller University Press.

Martinez, J., Jr., Weinberger, S., & Schultheis, G. (1988). Enkephalins in learning and memory: A review of evidence for a site of action outside the blood-brain barrier. *Behavioral and Neural Biology* **49**, 192-221.

Mishkin, M. (1982). A memory system in the monkey. *Philosophical Transactions of the Royal Society of London, Series B* **298**, 85-95.

Morris, C. (1946). *Signs, Language, and Behavior.* Chicago: University of Chicago Press.

Nicolis, J. (1991). *Chaos and Information Processing.* New York: World Scientific.

Norman, D. A., & Rumelhart, D. E. (1970). A system for perception and memory. In D. Norman (Ed.), *Models of Human Memory* (pp. 21-64). New York: Academic Press.

Nottebohm, F. (1989). From bird song to neurogenesis. *Scientific American*, February 1989, 74-79.

Ogden, C., & Richards, I. A. (1924). *The Meaning of Meaning.* London: Kegan Paul.

Panksepp, J. (1986). The anatomy of emotions. In R. Plutchik & H. Kellerman (Eds.), *Biological foundations of emotion* (pp. 91-124). New York: Academic Press.

Pearl, J. (1988). *Probabilistic Reasoning in Intelligent Systems.* San Mateo, CA: Morgan Kaufmann.

Peirce, C. S. (1965-1966). *Collected Papers.* Cambridge, MA: Harvard University Press.

Posner, M., & Keele, S. (1968). On the genesis of abstract ideas. *Journal of Experimental Psychology* **77**, 353-363.

Pribram, K. H. (1971). *Languages of the Brain.* Englewood Cliffs, NJ: Prentice-Hall.

Pribram, K. H. (1979). Journal of Biological and Social Structures.

Pribram, K. H. (1980). Image, information, and episodic models of central processing. In R. Thompson, L. Hicks, & V. Shvyrkov (Eds.). *Neural Mechanisms of Goal-Directed Behavior and Learning* (pp. 319-340). New York: Academic Press.

Pribram, K. H. (1984). Emotion: A neurobehavioral analysis. In K. Scherer & P. Ekman (Eds.), *Approaches to Emotion* (pp. 13-39). Hillsdale, NJ: Lawrence Erlbaum Associates.

Pribram, K. H. (1991). *Brain and Perception: Holonomy and Structure in Figural Processing.* Hillsdale, NJ: Lawrence Erlbaum Associates.

Rosch, E., & Mervis, C. (1975). Family resemblances: Studies in the internal structure of categories. *Cognitive Psychology* **7**, 573-605.

Rosenbloom, P. S., Newell, A., & Laird, J. E. (1991). Toward the knowledge level in SOAR: The role of the architecture in the use of knowledge. In Van Lehn, K., ed. *Architectures for Intelligence* (pp. 75-112). Hillsdale, NJ: Lawrence Erlbaum Associates.

Rumelhart, D. E., & McClelland, J. L., Eds. (1986). *Parallel Distributed Processing*, Vols. 1 and 2. Cambridge, MA: MIT Press.

Rumelhart, D. E., & McClelland, J. L. (1988). *Explorations in Parallel Distributed Processing*. Cambridge, MA: MIT Press.

Schank, R. C. (1982). *Dynamic Memory*. New York: Cambridge University Press.

Schank, R. C. (1988). Creativity. New York: MacMillan.

Sebeok, T., & Umiker-Sebeok (1986). *The Semiotic Sphere*. New York: Plenum.

Seligman, M. (1975). *Helplessness*. New York: W. H. Freeman.

Shevelev, I. A. (1983). Adaptivity and dynamic properties of visual cortex neurons. In E. Asratyan & P. Simonov (Eds.), *The Learning Brain* (pp. 76-96). Moscow: MIR.

Sowa, J. (1983). *Conceptual Structures*. Cambridge, MA: MIT Press.

Tikhomirov, O. (1983). Informal heuristic principles of motivation and emotion in human problem solving. In R. Groner, M. Groner, & W. Bischof (Eds.), Methods of Heuristics (pp. 153-170). Hillsdale, NJ: Lawrence Erlbaum Associates.

Tulving, E. (1983). *Elements of Episodic Memory*. New York: Oxford University Press.

Tulving, E. (1985). How many memory systems are there? *American Psychologist* **40**, 385-398.

Vaina, L. (1984). Toward a computational theory of semantic memory. In L. Vaina & J. Hintikka (Eds.), *Cognitive Constraints on Communication* (pp. 97-113). Dordrecht/Boston: Reidel.

Wertheimer, M. (1982). *Productive Thinking*. Chicago: University of Chicago Press.

Winograd, T., & Flores, F. (1987). *Understanding Computers and Cognition: A New Foundation for Design*. Norwood, NJ: Ablex.

Winston, P. H. (1977). *Artificial Intelligence*. Reading, MA: Addison-Wesley.

Wise, S. (1987). *Higher Brain Functions*. New York: Wiley.

Zajonc, R. (1980). Feeling and thinking: Preferences need no inferences. *American Psychologist* **35**, 151-175.

4

Continuous Symbol Systems: The Logic of Connectionism

Bruce MacLennan
University of Tennessee, Knoxville

Our present knowledge of human perception leaves no doubt as to the general form of any theory which is to do justice to such knowledge: a theory of perception must be a *field theory*. By this we mean that neural functions and processes with which the perceptual facts are associated in each case are located in a continuous medium; and that the events in one part of this medium influence the events in other regions in a way that depends directly on the properties of both in their relation to each other.

W. Köhler, *Dynamics in Psychology*

Nothing is more practical than a good theory.

Kurt Lewin, in A. J. Marrow, *The Practical Theorist: the Life and Work of Kurt Lewin*

The disadvantage of regarding things in separate parts is that when one begins to cut up and analyze, each one tries to be exhaustive. The disadvantage of trying to be exhaustive is that it is consciously (mechanically) exhaustive ... Only one who can imagine the formless in the formed can arrive at the truth.

Chuang-tzu (Soshi)

> Symbolic representation of qualitative entities is doomed to its rightful place of minor importance in a world where flowers and beautiful women abound.
>
> Albert Einstein, *Hyperbolic Aesthetic*

It has been long assumed that knowledge and thought are most naturally represented as *discrete symbol systems* (calculi). Thus a major contribution of connectionism is that it provides an alternative model of knowledge and cognition that avoids many of the limitations of the traditional approach. But what idea serves for connectionism the same unifying role that the idea of a calculus served for the traditional theories? We claim it is the idea of a *continuous symbol system*. This chapter presents a preliminary formulation of continuous symbol systems and indicates how they may aid the understanding and development of connectionist theories. It begins with a brief phenomenological analysis of the discrete and continuous; the aim of this analysis is to directly contrast the two kinds of symbol systems and identify their distinguishing characteristics. Next, based on the phenomenological analysis and on other observations of existing continuous symbol systems and connectionist models, I sketch a mathematical characterization of these systems. Finally the chapter turns to some applications of the theory and to its implications for knowledge representation and the theory of computation in a connectionist context. Specific problems addressed include decomposition of connectionist spaces, representation of recursive structures, properties of connectionist categories, and decidability in continuous formal systems.

1. NEED FOR A THEORY OF CONTINUOUS SYMBOL SYSTEMS

1.1 HUMAN SYMBOLIC COGNITION

It is now widely recognized that human symbolic cognition, by which we mean the use of language, logic, and explicit reasoning, is much more flexible than symbolic AI systems. If an expert system has too few rules, then it exhibits *brittle* behavior, failing in catastrophic ways when faced with novel situations or minor exceptions to the rules. On the other hand, trying to anticipate all the situations and exceptions that may occur leads to a proliferation of rules and an exponential explosion in the machine resources required. Human cognition does not have these limitations. When people reason explicitly, their use of categories is sensitive to the context of the problem, and their inferential processes are generated from and constrained by relevance to the situation. This seems to be a natural result of the implementation of these processes, rather than a result of special context rules or relevance rules. Human language use has similar characteristics: it is flexible, context-sensitive, and controlled by relevance. Further, flexibility and "softness" is the natural state of both reason and language; ''hard'' logic and precise language use are skills that are not easily acquired, and they are special tools used by the expert when they are called for, but not otherwise. How can we achieve similar flexibility in connectionist symbol processing?

It is not sufficient to replace categories with hard boundaries by categories with fuzzy boundaries (as is done in fuzzy set theory). Although fuzzy categories do eliminate some sources of brittleness, they do not address the complex processes by which categories may be sensitive to the global context. To achieve the flexibility of human cognition and true context-sensitive symbol use, a more radical reinterpretation of symbolic processing is necessary. We must see context-sensitive holistic processes as the normal mode of operation, and see context-free discrete symbol manipulation as a specialized modification of this norm.[1]

These observations have practical implications, for they mean human-like flexibility and competence are unlikely to result from a simple hybrid of neural network technology and expert systems technology. Wherever it appears in a hybrid system, discrete, formal, context-free symbol manipulation will be a source of brittleness and other forms of unskillful behavior (see also Sun, chapter 9, this volume). If we want implementations of symbolic cognition that exhibit the flexibility and competence of people's, then they must be built on a foundation that is fundamentally continuous, holistic, and context-sensitive.

1.2. EMERGENCE OF THE DISCRETE

Human symbolic cognition is built upon a *subsymbolic substrate*, which is continuous in its principles of operation, and is the ultimate source of the flexibility of human symbol use. To see this, observe that the basic neural processes are best described as continuous, since information is represented by continuous quantities such as spiking frequency and membrane potential. Most neurons seem to operate as low precision analog devices. Furthermore, the large number of neurons found in the brains of the higher animals implies that functional areas can often be viewed as *spatially* continuous. That is, we can view such an area as a continuum of neurons, rather than as a large number of discrete neurons. This view is even more appropriate if, as some suggest, the basic computational unit is not the neuron, but the synapse (Shepherd, 1978). Thus the basic neural processes are both temporally and spatially continuous. This is important from a theoretical perspective, because it means that powerful mathematical tools may be brought to bear on the problem of mental representation.

In addition, many of the most basic cognitive processes, such as perception, association, sensory-motor coordination, and judgement of similarity, are by their nature continuous. We share these faculties with the lower animals, and we observe that they show the same flexibility in their use as we do. Discreteness is most apparent when we come to higher cognitive processes, such as language use and explicit reason, but these faculties partake of the flexibility of the underlying continuous processes.[2]

---

[1] We use the term "holistic" in spite of some of its unfortunate connotations; it is the only term that correctly denotes systems whose structures are misrepresented by being analyzed into independent parts.

[2] Nalimov (1981, Ch. 8) uses continuous *semantic fields* as a basis for discrete language and thought. Lakoff (1988) discusses the grounding of linguistic structures in continuous sensory-motor processes, and the relation between cognitive linguistics and connectionism.

These considerations suggest that a critical research goal is to understand the processes by which discrete and approximately discrete symbols can emerge from continuous processes. Of course this is an inversion of the usual situation in computer science and even logic, where discrete symbols are taken as given, and continuous quantities are approximated by discrete structures. We must understand how the discrete structures found in logic and language can emerge from continuous representations and processes.

1.3. GOALS

Our goal is to develop a theoretical framework for connectionist knowledge representation that fills a role analogous to the theory of formal systems in symbolic knowledge representation. The properties we expect of this theory include formality, idealization, qualitative inference, and elucidation of the emergence of the discrete from the continuous. I discuss each in turn.

First observe that "formal" is used in two distinct but related ways. In the first case, *form* is contrasted with *meaning*, or equivalently, syntax with semantics. In this sense a system is formal if its inferential processes depend only on the "shapes" of symbols, not on their meanings. Therefore, we distinguish *formal systems*, which are purely syntactic, from *symbol systems*, in which the symbols have meanings; a symbol system is a formal system together with an *interpretation* or a *semantics*, which assigns the meanings.

In the second case *form* is contrasted with *matter* (as in Plato), and *formal* means that the system's information processing capacities depend only on abstract relationships rather than on their material embodiment. It is in this sense that computer programs are formal, since they define the same computations whether they are implemented electronically or in some other way. It is this kind of formality that allows calculi (discrete formal systems) to be implemented in any medium that is sufficiently close to the discrete ideal. Analogously, we expect a theory of *continuous formal systems* to be independent of material embodiment and to depend only on idealized properties of continuous media.

Both notions of formality are important for connectionist theories of knowledge representation. First, by their being purely syntactic we are confident that our definitions of cognitive processes do not appeal to homunculi.[3] Second, by their being abstract we know that our theories have captured the essential characteristics of cognition, as opposed to the accidents of its biological or electronic implementation. The syntactic kind of formality ensures that the theory is self-contained; the abstract kind ensures that it contains no more than is necessary.

It will be worthwhile to say a few words about "idealization." The familiar theory of discrete formal systems makes a number of *idealizing assumptions* (detailed below, Section 2.2), which are only approximately realized in physical implementations. An example of an idealizing assumption is that there are only two atomic symbols, "0" and "1", and that there is nothing "between" them. In reality these symbols might be represented by two voltage levels between which there is a continuum of levels. However, many implementations are a good approximation to the ideal, and this is the reason that discrete formal systems provide a useful theoretical

---

[3] This approach in effect reduces semantics to syntax, which seems necessary to understanding the mechanisms of cognition. This contentious issue cannot be addressed further here.

framework for understanding digital computers. We expect an analogous situation in the theory of continuous formal systems. We make certain idealizing assumptions, such as that all functions are continuous, and the success of our theory depends on the extent to which these assumptions approximate well the physical embodiments of connectionist knowledge representation. For example, we assume that there is always an analog value between two given analog values, even though in some implementations analog values might be represented by electric charge, which is quantized.

Connectionist models are typically continuous nonlinear dynamical systems with very large numbers of variables. Analytic prediction of the behavior of these systems is usually impossible, so it is often necessary to resort to simulation. However, such systems may be very sensitive to inaccuracies of the simulation. These considerations suggest that we need qualitative tools for understanding connectionist models, since qualitative prediction may be possible even when detailed quantitative analysis is not. For example, the existence of a Lyapunov function allows us to predict that the system will approach an asymptotically stable equilibrium, even though we may not be able to describe its exact trajectory. More generally, we expect the theory of continuous formal systems to be a *topological* theory rather than a *numerical* theory.

As argued above, a central problem of connectionist knowledge representation is the emergence of symbolic cognitive processes from subsymbolic processes. Therefore, a principal goal of the theory of continuous formal systems is that it should elucidate the relation between continuous and discrete knowledge representation, and in particular should show how continuous connectionist systems can approximate idealized discrete cognition. Some preliminary results are found in Section 5.2.

2. PHENOMENOLOGICAL ANALYSIS

2.1. INTRODUCTION

All mathematical theories are *idealizing*; that is, they select out certain properties in their domain and ignore the remainder so that they permit rigorous reasoning about the phenomena that depend on the selected properties. A mathematical theory is useful to the extent that it selects properties that are relevant to central phenomena of the domain, and to the extent that it ignores those that are peripheral. Unfortunately, when we are investigating a new domain of phenomena, it may not be obvious which phenomena are central and which are peripheral; as a result idealization is problematic. In these cases a *phenomenological analysis* may help to identify the central phenomena and relevant properties.

This is the basic procedure we follow: First we identify a domain of interest, such as connectionist systems or continuous symbol systems. The domain cannot be defined, because the identification of characteristic properties is the very problem to be solved; instead the domain must be *indicated*, largely through examples. Once the domain has been grasped we look for *invariances*, properties that hold always or for the most part. These invariances are the elements around which a mathematical theory can be constructed.

Since this kind of phenomenological analysis will be unfamiliar to many readers, we illustrate it first for the familiar *discrete* symbol systems (calculi), before applying it to the less familiar *continuous* symbol systems (image systems). This twofold analysis also brings into the foreground the similarities and differences between the two kinds of systems.

2.2. DISCRETE SYMBOL SYSTEMS

2.2.1. INDICATION OF THE DOMAIN

As discussed above, our phenomenological analysis begins by indicating the domain of phenomena to be analyzed. In this case we are aided by the fact that (discrete) formal systems, digital systems and calculi are all recognized categories. Therefore, the identification of invariances can begin with an analysis of the *reasons* that people find these to be useful categories; these are the *pragmatic* invariances. First, however, we indicate the domain by asking, "What sorts of things are *seen as* calculi (discrete symbol systems)?"

The most familiar and characteristic example of a discrete symbol system is *written language*, and in this example we can see many of the invariances of such systems. First, discrete symbols have a hierarchical constituent structure: sentences composed of words, and words of letters. Second, the lowest level components, the letters, are considered *atomic* (indivisible), and these atomic components (*tokens*) belong to a finite number of *types*. Finally, sentences are *finite* assemblages of tokens obeying a *finite* number of syntactic rules.

Real written natural language is more complicated than implied here; for example real languages may not be characterized by a finite number of syntactic rules. Thus, although they are the main inspiration for discrete symbol systems, written languages may not be the best examples. Closer to the ideal are artificial languages such as the formulas of algebra and symbolic logic. Here the syntactic rules are finite and explicit, as are the rules for calculating with the symbols.

Less obvious but equally familiar examples of discrete symbol systems are board games, such as checkers, chess, and go. Again, there is a finite set of rules defining the allowable configurations of tokens, and there are explicit rules defining the allowable "moves" (manipulations of the tokens).

The most complex and sophisticated discrete symbol systems are found in computer science, especially in artificial intelligence, where powerful knowledge representation languages permit the mechanization of some inferential processes (Fig. 4.1). The limitations of these systems has been a major motivation for the exploration of connectionist alternatives to conventional knowledge representation (Dreyfus, 1979; MacLennan, 1988a).

2.2.2. PRAGMATIC INVARIANCES

Having indicated the domain of calculi (discrete symbol systems), we can begin the phenomenological analysis. Our goal is to find out *why* calculi are what they are. To discover this we must first ask how the phenomena *seen as* calculi are perceived. In this way we investigate why is it important to people to recognize some phenomena as calculi. This will form a basis for identifying the other invariances of this domain.

The first characteristic of calculi is that they are *definite*. Ideally, we know exactly what we have got: what letter or symbol, what grammatical relation, what piece (white king, black rook), what board position, and so forth. Second, calculi are *reliable*. Errors, so long as they are not too large, do not affect the use of the calculus. For example, in transmitting binary information, there can be considerable variation in the signal representing a 1, and it can still be decoded correctly, so long as it doesn't change so much that it looks more like a 0. Similarly, we can tolerate noise or other degradation in the form or position of printed symbols so long as it isn't so much as to make one symbol or spatial relation look like another. In general, all observers agree on the types of the tokens and the syntax of the formulas. Third, the discrete symbols are *reproducible*. Repeated reproduction does not result in cumulative error; the syntax of structures is not changed by copying.

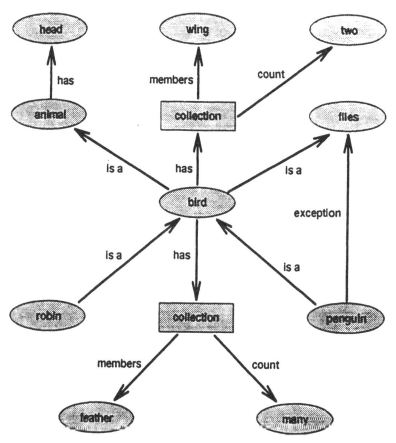

Fig. 4.1. Example of a semantic net. Knowledge is represented by a set of atomic tokens connected by atomic relations. English-language labels make the nodes and links comprehensible to people, but are irrelevant to computer processing. In other words, *bird* and *has* could as well be *p0061* and *r0035*.

Most of the characteristics of calculi result from their being *finitely specifiable*. That is, against an appropriate background of assumptions, we can completely describe a calculus, its syntax, semantics and rules of calculation, in a finite number of words. (Think of formal logic, board games and computer programs.)

These pragmatic invariances of calculi account for much of the success of digital computers and other digital technologies (such as digital audio). For some applications, however, other properties are more important, and it is in these applications that connectionist approaches are most promising.

(a)   (b)

Fig. 4.2. Discrete types are determined against a background of assumptions about what constitutes significant and insignificant variation in the tokens. For example, features of tokens that are assumed to be irrelevant to determining the type of the token might include not only size and font, but also marks considered "noise." These assumptions are usually unstated (i.e., in the background).

2.2.3. SYNTACTIC INVARIANCES

Next I outline the background assumptions we routinely make about the syntax of discrete formal systems. By making these assumptions explicit we are better able to see the possibilities of other kinds of formal systems. A syntactic type is one that can be determined by perception (for natural systems) or by a simple mechanism (for artificial systems). For example, we may think of recognition of letters by a person, or recognition of bits by an electronic device. Types depend on the form or "shape" of tokens, not on their meaning, but, as Fig. 4.2 illustrates, certain aspects of the shape are considered significant to a calculus while others (such as size or font) are not, and this set of assumptions varies from calculus to calculus. For mathematical purposes, "A" and "*A*" might be considered different types; for other purposes they would be insignificant variants of a single type.   Further, we always assume for calculi that tokens can be correctly classified — an idealizing assumption that of course ignores the difficulties of real-world pattern classification. We also assume that a calculus has a *finite* number of (atomic) syntactic types. This is implied by the condition that a calculus be finitely specified, since an infinite set of types could be finitely specified only by giving some general rule for their generation, in which case they are not atomic, but defined in terms of some more primitive types.

Finally, we assume that in a calculus the tokens can be unambiguously separated from the background, that is, that we always know whether or not a token is actually present (Fig. 4.3). This again is an idealization, since in real-world symbol processing the separation of signal from noise may be a difficult problem.

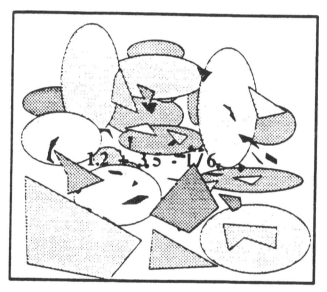

Fig. 4.3. Discrete formal systems assume that it can be unambiguously determined whether or not a token is present, that is, it is assumed that a token can always be separated from the background. This *idealizing assumption* ignores the complexities of real-world signal detection. In this case, is the second number 35 or 3.5? Is there a decimal point after the 6? Is the symbol before the slash "1", "i", or "l"? Is the second operator a minus sign or an equal sign?

We have considered the assumed properties of the atomic tokens and types of calculi; now we turn to the relations by which they are assembled into composite symbol structures.

A *syntactic relation* is one that can also be detected by a simple perceptual or mechanical process. (Thus, types are single-place perceptual predicates, whereas relations are multiplace perceptual predicates.) Once again, this classification process is assumed to be perfect, so we can always determine whether or not a relation holds (Fig. 4.4). Also, in a given calculus some characteristics are considered significant to the relationships (e.g., vertical displacement) while others are not (e.g., horizontal displacement; see Fig. 4.4).

Fig. 4.4. Discrete relations. Certain features of the arrangement are considered relevant to syntactic relations, other are not. For example, (a) one symbol being to the right of another may be significant, but the actual distance may not be. (b) Analogously, one symbol being a superscript of another is what is significant here.

Finite specifiability again dictates that there be a finite number of syntactic relationships (otherwise they are not primitive and can be specified in terms of more basic relations). The formation rules of most calculi can be applied recursively to build up composite formulas of arbitrary size, but the resulting formulas are required to be finite in size (number of tokens). Thus the formation rules can be applied only a finite number of times.

Most calculi are not static, that is, in addition to defining a set of symbolic structures, they define syntactic processes (*rules of calculation*) by which these structures are transformed. Finite specifiability determines many of the properties of processes. First, the number of rules is assumed to be finite. Second, the rules are assumed to be applied in discrete steps, so that in a finite amount of time only a finite number of rules may be applied. Further, the rules must be syntactic (*formal*), which means that determining the applicability of a rule depends only on the types of the tokens and their syntactic relations. Finally, application of a rule generates only a finite number of tokens and produces or changes only a finite number of relations. Thus rules are finite in their effects.

A very important property of calculi may be called *syntactic independence*: the actual syntactic types and relations used are arbitrary; they can be replaced by others with the same formal properties. This is the basis of digital computation, in which physical properties (charge, current, magnetic flux) replace other, sometimes abstract, properties (being an 'A', being immediately to the left of, etc.).

2.2.4. SEMANTIC INVARIANCES

Two assumptions are typically made about the semantics of discrete symbol systems. First, the operation of a calculus is *formal* or *syntactic*, that is, it is independent of any meaning that may be attached to the formulas. As far as calculation is concerned, the symbols have no meaning. Second, the semantics are *compositional*. That is, formulas are interpreted — given a meaning — recursively, by attaching meaning to the atomic types and to the syntactic rules of composition. Composite formulas are thus interpreted implicitly and there is a regular (finitely specifiable) relation between formulas and their meanings.

2.2.5. IDEALIZATION

Finally, it is important to observe that real (physical) discrete symbol systems are only approximations to this ideal (although often quite good approximations). For example, types may be confused ('O' vs. '0', '1' vs. 'l'). Manuscripts and even digital signals do get corrupted. Signal is sometimes taken for noise, and vice versa. In the theoretical characterization of discrete symbol systems we ignore this practical fuzziness and intrusion of the continuous into the idealized world of the discrete.

2.3. CONTINUOUS SYMBOL SYSTEMS

2.3.1. INDICATION OF THE DOMAIN

Now that we have had some practice with phenomenological analysis in a familiar domain, we turn to *continuous* symbol systems, which have been investigated much less.

Spoken language provides the most familiar example of a continuous symbol system. Here we find significance conveyed by continuously variable and continuously varying parameters, including loudness, pitch, tone, tempo and rhythm.[4] The nonspoken components of everyday communication, such as body language, are also examples, and they remind us of gestural languages such as American Sign Language (ASL). Another informative example is the language of musical conducting: it clearly has a grammar, yet its communicative efficacy depends on continuous variation in a number of dimensions. Indeed, we can see that music and visual arts derive much of their communicative power from continuous variation (Arnheim, 1971; Goodman, 1966, 1968; Nalimov, 1981).

Of course all these continuous languages also have discrete elements, but the important point here is that they have a significant admixture of the continuous that is treated as a valuable *representational resource*, rather than as an interfering source of noise and error.

Many familiar devices are controlled through continuous symbol systems: musical instruments, of course, but also automobiles and aircraft, cameras and stereos. The steering wheel and brake both make significant use of continuous variation: how much to turn and how quickly to stop. The piano keyboard may seem to be a clear case of a discrete symbol system,

---

[4] Ihde (1986, Ch. 1) provides an insightful analysis of the phenomenology of voice, including the contrast between the continuous and the discrete as exemplified by speech and writing.

but it permits continuous variation in both the time and intensity of impact.[5] We observe also that many devices, including stereos and lights, are controlled by rheostats.[6] Finally, the mouse and high-resolution screens have made even our interaction with computers more continuous. Continuous symbol systems are a ubiquitous and natural aspect of our interaction with the world.

Finally, we mention briefly the most obvious examples of continuous symbol systems. Analog recording devices (both audio and video) provide examples of analog representational systems with limited computational ability. Analog computers are better examples of continuous information processing. Of course, analog computers have been out of favor for several decades, and analog audio and video equipment seem headed that way. There are good technological reasons for this move away from analog technology, and some of them have already been mentioned (Section 2.2); nevertheless, analog representational and computational systems have their own advantages, to which we now turn.

2.3.2. PRAGMATIC INVARIANCES

In performing a phenomenological analysis of continuous symbol systems, we face the problem that they have not been generally recognized or studied *as a class*. (Indeed that is a principal goal of this chapter.) Therefore we cannot *analyze* the class of continuous symbol systems, asking why certain things are seen as continuous symbol systems, because in fact they generally *aren't* so seen. Instead, we must take a *synthetic* approach, identifying common reasons for the use of continuous symbol systems, and thereby *creating* a category of continuous symbol systems. By way of analogy, we are not here trying to explain why some figure stands out from the background. Rather we are pointing out features of the background, with the intent that the set of features become figural. Once I've pointed out the face in the clouds, then you can see it too.

What then are the reasons for using continuous symbol systems? First, they are *flexible*. This means that, in the simplest terms, there is always another choice between too much and too little, there is always an opportunity for adjustment. Aristotle recognized the utility of such flexibility to biological systems in his doctrine of the "relative mean" (*Nichomachean Ethics* II. vi. 4-17): there is a "right amount," between excess and deficiency, that is appropriate for a given organism at a given time. In other words, optimal operating points are in principle achievable by continuous variation between excess and deficiency.

A second invariance of continuous symbol systems is that they are *robust*. Small errors (noise or malfunctions) generally lead to small effects; such systems degrade gracefully. The general absence of this property from discrete systems is in fact the root of the "software crisis"

---

[5] A commonplace of piano instruction is to stress *legato* playing, thus making the sound more continuous (e.g., Lhevinne, 1972, p. 37-39). Conversely, violinists are encouraged to stress articulation. "Play the piano as though it were a violin, and the violin as though it were a piano" expresses the necessity of balancing the discrete and continuous.

[6] Apparently reflecting the view that "if it's digital it must be better," some stereos now have digital volume controls that have a discrete set of positions. It is often observed that the volume one wants is between the allowed positions.

that plagues digital computer programming. In traditional engineering disciplines design is simplified by approximation, since continuity permits low-level effects to be ignored. Software engineering does not have this characteristic, since even one incorrect bit can lead to the catastrophic failure of a software system. In discrete symbol systems we typically have no bound on the effects of even the smallest changes.[7]

Third, because continuous structures can change gradually over time, they can be more easily made *adaptive*. In contrast, for a discrete symbol system to adapt, it is necessary to add or delete rules, which results in abrupt behavioral changes. A discrete symbol system cannot change its behavior gradually, but adaptability is common in continuous symbol systems.

Finally, we note that continuous symbol systems may have significant advantages in the time-critical situations often faced by animals and machines. For example, a continuous process converging to an asymptotically stable equilibrium permits the use of preliminary results, if they are needed before convergence occurs. Here we use a partial result when the "correct" answer cannot be obtained in time. Continuity also permits extrapolating to likely future states, thus allowing limited anticipation, which can improve the efficiency of future computations.

Continuous symbol systems no doubt have other pragmatic invariances, but the ones listed above will serve to contrast them with discrete symbol systems.

2.3.3. SYNTACTIC INVARIANCES

There is nothing in the definition of the word "symbol" that requires symbols to be discrete; for example, we find "symbol" defined as "something that represents something else by association, resemblance, or convention; especially, a material object used to represent something invisible" (Morris, 1981, *s.v.* symbol). That is why we have spoken of *discrete* symbol systems versus *continuous* symbol systems.[8] Nevertheless, the word connotes discreteness and atomicity, a tendency reinforced by terms such as "symbolic AI." Therefore we prefer to speak of *images* rather than continuous symbols; this is consistent with the term's use in cognitive science, as well as in common usage[9]:

---

[7] Of course specific discrete systems can be designed that are insensitive to fixed errors; an example is an error-correcting code.

[8] We have previously suggested *simulacrum* as a term for the continuous analog of the discrete *calculus*, that is, for what is here called a *continuous symbol system* (MacLennan, in press).

[9] A comprehensive terminology is sadly lacking. C. S. Peirce did pioneering work in this area, but his terms are not widely known, and would be confusing in this context. What we are calling a *symbol* seems to correspond to Peirce's *icon*, which has subtypes which he calls *images*, *diagrams*, and *metaphors* (Buchler, 1955, pp. 99-107; Peirce, 1931-1958, Vol. 2, pp. 274-304).

A reproduction of the appearance of someone or something ...A mental picture of something not real or present ... represe/ntation to the mind by speech or writing. (Morris, 1981, s.v. image).

The images of a continuous formal system are drawn from one or more *image spaces* or *continua*.

The *syntax* of continuous symbol systems is concerned with the formal properties of images, which can be described by continuous formal systems. The *semantics* of continuous symbol systems is concerned with the representative properties of images.

Semantics is considered in the next section; in this section we identify some of the syntactic invariances of continuous symbol systems. These are the properties that we want to capture in our theory of continuous *formal* systems. Thus we begin our investigation with the formal or syntactic properties of *uninterpreted* images. In the course of identifying invariances it will be helpful to look back at the examples we have collected of continuous symbol systems (Section 2.3.1). However, to convince ourselves that they are genuine invariances, we must use the procedure of *phenomenological variation*, that is, exploring the range of systems (phenomena) in the indicated domain (Ihde, 1977). Unfortunately, space limitations force us to leave this process to the reader's imagination.

Our examples of continuous symbol systems show that similarity of images is a matter of degree. Further, the flexibility of continuous symbol systems results from the fact that for any two images there is always a third image that is closer to either of the first two. For linear (one-dimensional) continua we may say that there is always an image between any two other images.

It is often convenient to assume that similarity is measured by a metric, but this is not always the case, and the choice of metric may be problematic. For example, the L_2 (Euclidean) metric is often used to measure the distance between images, but this is more through habit and mathematical convenience than principled choice. An L_p metric ($p > 2$) would accord greater significance to differences between the images, with L_∞ (maximum deviation) being the extreme case; conversely, L_1 tends to devalue differences. For another example, it is not obvious how differences in orientation or size should be combined with differences in color.

Processes in discrete formal systems are sensitive to the *types* of the tokens, and analogously we expect continuous formal systems to be sensitive to the *forms* of images, that is, to their syntactic type or category. The nature of these syntactic categories is different from those in discrete formal systems, since the pragmatic invariances of robustness and adaptability both imply that infinitesimal changes of an image not result in discontinuous changes of behavior. Therefore, category membership must vary continuously with changes in the images, which means that all syntactic categories must be in some way *fuzzy* (See also Section 5.2).

Next we consider the syntactic relationships that may obtain in continuous formal systems. Discrete formulas are constructed from atomic parts. In continuous systems, in contrast, the images are usually given as wholes, and their division into parts is problematic. This is illustrated in Fig. 4.5. What are the "parts" of the image of the frog? Since this image is represented as a bit map, the obvious answer is that the elementary parts are the pixels illustrated in the upper-right corner. This might be appropriate for some purposes, but for others a different decomposition would be more appropriate; we illustrate analyses into anatomical "parts," elementary splines, elementary polygons, and a stick-figure representation. There is no unique decomposition, as there would be for a formula in an (unambiguous) discrete formal system. Furthermore, in many cases there is no natural end to the analysis. For example, the anatomical analysis can be continued to arbitrarily smaller parts of the image.

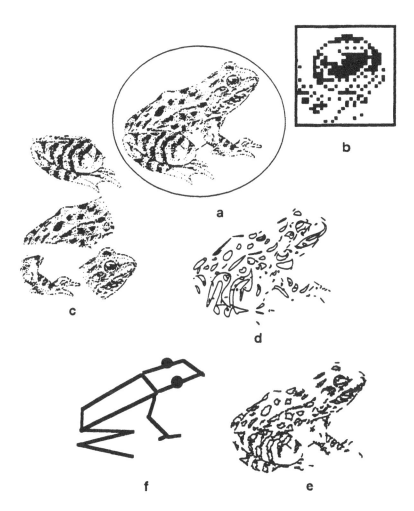

Fig. 4.5. Decomposition of images. Images do not have a unique decomposition into elementary "parts." The kind and degree of decomposition depends on the purpose to which it will be put. (a) The original image. Example decompositions: (b) pixels (only the eye is shown); (c) anatomical components; (d) elementary splines (of thresholded image); (e) elementary polygons (of thresholded image); (f) stick-figure analysis.

Finally we turn to computation in continuous formal systems. The adaptability and time-criticality invariances suggest that processes in continuous formal systems be assumed to progress continuously in time. Thus we take images to be transformed continuously (although we often use discrete-time approximations). See Fig. 4.6. Also note that there may be a number of paths by which one image may be reached from another by a process of continuous transformation.

The foregoing are the syntactic invariances that we attempt to capture in a mathematical theory of continuous formal systems.

2.3.4. SEMANTIC INVARIANCES

We expect the semantics of continuous symbol systems to be an interesting topic of study, for corresponding to the *compositionality* of discrete semantics we have the *continuity* of continuous semantics; in other words, the pragmatic invariances all require a continuous function mapping images onto their interpretations (meanings). One implication of this requirement is that although continuous symbol systems may be completely formal, they are nevertheless not completely independent of their interpretations. This is familiar from the idea of analog computing: there must be some *analogy* between the symbol (image) and what it represents.

2.3.5. IDEALIZATION

As for discrete symbol systems, our characterization of continuous symbol systems is idealized. Apparently continuous processes may in fact be discrete (e.g., accumulation of charge in terms of electrons); images may be composed of discrete parts (atoms, electrons, silver grains); processes may progress in tiny finite steps. In perception there are "just noticeable differences." These all may be viewed as incursions of the discrete into the continuous. In both the discrete and continuous case, the relevant questions are: Which model is most useful? Which idealization does less violence to the phenomena?

3. POSTULATES OF CONTINUOUS SYMBOL SYSTEMS

Based on the foregoing phenomenological analysis we can now propose a candidate set of properties possessed by any continuous symbol system. In later sections we explore particular classes of such systems that have properties in addition to those enumerated here.

We begin with the syntax of continuous symbol systems. We have seen that in discrete symbol systems tokens are either of the same type or they are not, whereas in continuous symbol systems similarity is a matter of degree. It is generally unproblematic to assume that this degree of similarity is quantifiable and that the quantification has the properties of a *metric*, that is, a measure of distance, which is a binary function ρ from a space X to the real numbers, $\rho : X \times X \rightarrow \mathbf{R}$ that satisfies these identities:

$\rho(x,x) = 0$ Self-identity,
$\rho(x,y) = \rho(y,x)$ Symmetry,
$\rho(x,y) + \rho(y,z) \geq \rho(x,z)$ Triangle Inequality.

Therefore, unless stated otherwise, we assume that an image space is a metric space.[10]

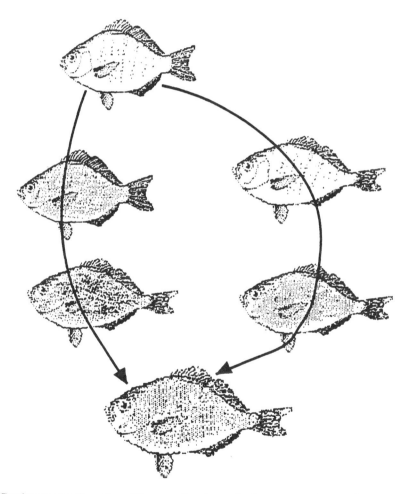

Fig. 4.6. Continuous transformation of images. Any image in the space can be transformed into any other by one or more processes of continuous transformation.

---

[10] Section 4.1.4 considers cases in which this assumption may be too strong.

The second syntactic invariance we address is that any image in the space may be continuously transformed into any other, which is expressed mathematically as follows. Let a, b $\in$ X be any two images in the space. We require that there be a continuous, one-to-one function P: $\mathbb{R}$ → X such that for some t_o, $t_f \in \mathbb{R}$ (think of them as times) we have $P(t_o)$ = a and $P(t_f)$=b. The function P represents a continuous transformation of a into b. Without loss of generality we require t_o=0 and t_f=1. In topological terms P is a *path* or *arc* from a to b, and since we require there to be a path between any two images, the space is *path-connected* (*arcwise-connected*).[11]

Another invariance of continuous symbol systems is that for any two images a,b we can always find a third c closer to either (but not necessarily to both); that is, we can pick a c such that $\rho(a,c) < \rho(a,b)$ and we can pick a c′ such that $\rho(b,c') < \rho(a,b)$. However, we do not have to postulate this property, since it follows from image spaces being path connected: For example, since c=P(t) → b as t → 1, c will eventually be in an arbitrarily small neighborhood of b, and thus can be made as close as we like to b.

A path-connected space is also connected in the more general sense, that is, it is not a union of separated sets. There is good evidence that image spaces are connected metric spaces, including:

1. A nontrivial[12] connected metric space has at least the cardinality of the real numbers (Hausdorff, 1937/1957, p. 175).
2. In topology a *continuum* is defined to be a closed connected metric space (Hausdorff, 1937/1957, p. 173).[13]
3. A finite or countable set is totally disconnected; therefore discrete symbol systems are totally disconnected (Hausdorff, 1937/1957, p. 175).

On the other hand, we believe that image spaces must satisfy the stronger condition of being *path*-connected, since otherwise images would not necessarily be reachable by a *finite* process of continuous transformation.

The foregoing considerations lead us to propose:

Postulate 1. *Image spaces are path-connected metric spaces.*

Next we turn to a complex of properties that is at the heart of the continuity of image spaces: completeness and separability. A space is *complete* if all its Cauchy sequences have

---

[11] More carefully, P is a homeomorphism because [0,1] is compact and X is Hausdorff (since all metric spaces are Hausdorff). Therefore P is a homeomorphism between [0,1] and P[0,1], which makes it a path (Moore, 1964, pp. 68, 71, 161).

[12] Here "nontrivial" means that it has more than one point.

[13] Sometimes a continuum is defined as a nontrivial compact connected space; the issue of compactness is addressed later.

limits in the space. A space is *separable* if it has a countable dense subset, roughly, if all its images can be approximated by sequences of images with rational coordinates. The phenomenological analysis does not seem to require either property, and one can imagine image spaces that don't satisfy one or the other (for example, a disk missing its central point is not complete). Nevertheless, we tentatively assume both properties, because they are mathematically important and because most image spaces satisfy them. In particular, if a metric space is *compact* (perhaps the closest analog to the finiteness and definiteness of discrete formal systems), then it is both separable and complete.[14] Therefore:

Postulate 2. *Image spaces are separable and complete.*

Next we characterize mathematically the syntactic categories and syntactic relations of continuous symbol systems. From our phenomenological analysis (Section 2.3.3) we know that formal properties must vary continuously with changes in the images. Thus we propose:

Postulate 3. *Maps on image spaces are continuous.*

We take this to be the case for the syntactic maps on which formal relations depend, but also for semantic maps between image spaces and their domains of interpretation (which thus must be continua).[15]

Finally, our phenomenological analysis has shown that processes in continuous formal systems proceed continuously in time, and that infinitesimal changes in the state image do not result in behavioral discontinuities. This is formalized as follows.

In mathematical terms, a *process* is a continuous function $p: X \times \mathbf{R} \to X$ satisfying $p(s,0) = s$ and $p[p(s,t_1),t_2] = p(s,t_1 + t_2)$ (the group property). Here X is the *state space* of the process and $p(s,t)$ is the state of the process time t after starting in state s. In addition, we allow the possibility that some processes are defined over only an interval of time, bounded or unbounded. For a fixed s, the function $m(t) = p(s,t)$ is called a *motion* and defines a *continuous curve* (Moore, 1964, p. 156). A *trajectory* is the set of images produced by a motion over an interval I of time, $m[I]$.

Given these definitions we propose:

---

[14] Indeed, many mathematicians define a continuum to be a nontrivial connected *compact* metric space.

[15] One consequence of this semantic rule is that exact interpretations of continuous symbol systems are inherently continuous; discrete interpretations can only be approximated. The situation is analogous for discrete symbol systems, the interpretations of which are inherently discrete, and for which continuous interpretations can only be approximated. We take this to be the import of the Löwenheim-Skolem Theorem, which states that any formal system (with a countable number of symbols) has a countable model. Therefore, any axiomatization of the real continuum cannot exclude countable, discrete interpretations (the Löwenheim-Skolem Paradox).

Postulate 4. *A process in a continuous formal system is a continuous function of time and process state.*

We take these postulates to be satisfied by any continuous symbol system. In the remainder of this chapter we present a number of conclusions that can be drawn from these postulates as well as additional results for more specific classes of continuous symbol systems.

4. CONNECTIONIST SPACES

4.1. TOPOLOGY

Although we have identified path-connected metric spaces with the general class of connectionist spaces, many of the latter have additional useful structure. Therefore, in this section we consider several important classes of connectionist spaces.

4.1.1. FINITE-DIMENSIONAL EUCLIDEAN SPACES

One common class of connectionist spaces is the class of continua that was the historically first to be recognized: finite-dimensional Euclidean spaces, E^n. This is the natural choice when images are defined by a few real parameters (Fig. 4.7) and it has been the mathematical context of most neural network theory.

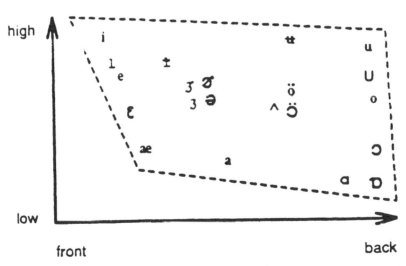

Fig. 4.7. Continuous space of low dimension. The diagram shows the approximate location of the tongue when articulating the indicated vowels.

4.1.2. HILBERT SPACES

The use of finite-dimensional Euclidean spaces is less obvious when the number of dimensions is very large. Consider auditory images represented by instantaneous power spectra (Fig. 4.8). We can, of course, view these as members of a finite-dimensional space E^n, but in the case of human auditory images $n \approx 20,000$ (Shepherd, 1988, p. 315). The situation is even worse for visual images (Fig. 4.9), where $n \approx 1.3 \times 10^8$ (the number of receptors; even the number of ganglion cells $\approx 10^6$) (McFarland, 1987, p. 588). Although from a mathematical standpoint $n = 1.3 \times 10^8$ is just as finite as $n = 2$, there are practical differences. At very least, it seems more natural to think of these images as continuous functions; their discreteness in fact is a physical detail that can often be ignored, like the discreteness of fluids in hydrodynamics.

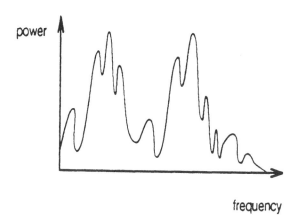

Fig. 4.8. Continuous space of high or infinite dimension. The diagram represents the instantaneous power spectrum of a sound. Even though the number of dimensions may be finite, it is so large that the image is most usefully considered a continuous function (infinite-dimensional).

For this reason we suggest that many connectionist spaces are best treated as *infinite*-dimensional Euclidean spaces, in other words, Hilbert spaces (see also Pribram, chapter 14, this volume).[16] Certainly they already provide the context for much of the theoretical work in vision, signal processing and image analysis, but in neural network research, finite dimensional vectors are still the norm. We have argued elsewhere that the most interesting neural networks — those with a *large* number of neurons — are best treated as having an *infinite* number of neurons (MacLennan, 1987a, 1987b, 1988b, 1989a, 1989b, 1990). Such an approach abstracts

---

[16] To be precise: The set of infinite-dimensional vectors of finite length is a Hilbert space, namely l_2.

away from the details of the neural fabric, which works well as long as the number of neurons is large enough.[17]

Fig. 4.9. Continuous space of very high dimension. A visual image such as this may have a dimension of 10^6 or even 10^8. It is much more reasonable to consider it a continuous function (infinite dimensional).

Another argument for Hilbert spaces is that they are — mathematically — where the continuous meets the discrete. The reason is the Riesz-Fischer Theorem, which is certainly one of the most profound in mathematics: L_2 is isomorphic and isometric to l_2, the set of square-integrable functions is isomorphic and isometric to the set of square-summable sequences of reals. This is the basis for expansions of functions as infinite series, including the Fourier. In particular, this shows how a discontinuous function, such as a step function, can emerge from a superposition of continuous functions, such as sinusoids. Thus we may hope that Hilbert spaces may provide a mathematical context for understanding the emergence of discrete (or nearly discrete) symbols from the subsymbolic continuum. Further evidence of the relevance of Hilbert spaces to the relation between continuous and discrete representations can be found in MacLennan (1991).[18]

---

[17] Pribram (1991; chapter 14, this volume) has also argued for the use of Hilbert spaces as a framework in which to define the "neural wave equation."

[18] Indeed, the central importance of Hilbert spaces is shown by a theorem of Urysohn's which states that any metric space with a countable base is homeomorphic to some subset of the Hilbert

4.1.3. METRIC SPACES

Even with a low-dimensional space like that in Fig. 4.7, there is little reason to suppose that the Euclidean metric is always appropriate. For example, it is quite possible that perceptual similarity is more sensitive to high/low position than to front/back position, or vice versa. Further, this sensitivity difference might vary over the space. In other words, there is no guarantee that the equal-similarity contours around a sound are the circles that are defined by the Euclidean metric; they could be ellipses or even less regular curves. Thus, connectionist spaces need not be *isotropic* (the same in all directions). Isotropy is even less likely when we consider higher dimensional spaces such those indicated in Figs. 8 and 9, since similarity is unlikely to be equally sensitive to differences throughout the function's domain.

One simple improvement is to attach a weight function to the Euclidean metric. This allows differing sensitivities across the image, so that, for example, visual similarity may depend more on the centers of images than their peripheries, and auditory similarity may depend more on the midband (if that is what we want).

Since the provision of a fixed weight function still restricts the set of possible metrics more than we would like, a still more general notion of distance if often useful. In fact, we often do not know or care how the similarity of images depends on their microfeatures. In this case it is better to assume only that some quantifiable measure of distance holds among the images, that is, that they belong to a *metric space*. However, as we saw before (Section 3) it is also necessary to assume that the space is path-connected.

4.1.4. SEMIMETRIC SPACES

In some cases even a metric space may imply too much structure; certainly the triangle inequality (see Section 3) is problematic for some cognitive images. Fortunately, some results are obtainable even for *semimetric spaces*, which have a distance measure that need not satisfy the triangle inequality (MacLennan, 1988a). Nevertheless, in this chapter we assume that all connectionist spaces are metric spaces.

4.1.5. FINITE DECOMPOSITION OF SPACES

We saw (Section 2) that discrete and continuous formal systems differ in what is taken as *unproblematic givens*. In a discrete system, the atomic components are given, and these are assembled into more complex formulas through the use of syntactic relationships. If these relations are unambiguous, as is usually the case, then any formula can be decomposed in a unique way into its atomic components. On the other hand, in continuous formal systems, whole images are usually the unproblematic givens. Further, it is normal that there are many competing decompositions into lower-level images, and the appropriate decomposition often depends on the

---

pace E^∞ (Nemytskii & Stepanov, 1989, p. 324). Note however that the homemorphism need not preserve the metric.

use to which it will be put. Finally, there is often no "bottom" to the decomposition; that is, there is no natural notion of atomic components.

It is important to realize that this problem is not just theoretical; it pervades empirical investigations into the "representational primitives" of sensory and motor systems. This is apparent in early vision research, where there is ongoing debate about whether images in the visual cortex have as elementary components oriented edges, wavelets, radial basis functions, two-dimensional Gabor functions, three-dimensional Gabor functions, and so on. (MacLennan, 1991a). Sometimes it is not even obvious what the representational alternatives are, and techniques such as *multidimensional scaling* have been used in an attempt to find *possible* decompositions of a space into subspaces (Shepard, 1980). The continuous formal system viewpoint suggests that in some cases images may be processed holistically, that is, without decomposition, and in other cases by simultaneously using several incompatible decompositions.

Before discussing the mathematical decomposition of continua, it is necessary to say a few words about the suggestive but misleading terms *analytic* and *synthetic*. Perhaps because of their association with analytic and synthetic cognitive styles (e.g., Churchland, 1986, p. 199; Gregory, 1987, p. 744; Vernon, 1962, pp. 221-224), there is a natural tendency to consider discrete systems analytic and continuous systems synthetic. Unfortunately, there is another perspective on these terms that would use them in exactly the opposite way, for we have seen that discrete formulas are usually seen as being built up — synthesized — from atomic components, and continuous images are seen as being decomposed — analyzed — into simpler images. From this viewpoint, discrete systems are synthetic and continuous systems analytic.

Perhaps we can understand this paradox as follows. Since in a discrete symbol system the decomposition of a formula into its constituents is generally unproblematic, it it natural for discrete processes to be defined in terms of processes operating on the constituents, which is consistent with one definition of *analytic*: "Reasoning from a perception of the parts and interrelationships of a subject" (Morris, 1981, *s.v.* analytic). In other words, the process operates on the *analysis*, the separation of the whole into its constituents (Morris, 1981, *s.v.* analysis). Conversely, since in continuous systems decomposition is often problematic, it is natural for these processes to operate directly on the *synthesis*, the coherent whole resulting from a combination of elements (Morris, 1981, *s.vv.* synthetic, synthesis). Although this is perhaps the explanation of the paradoxical use of these terms, for the sake of clarity I avoid them whenever possible.

In the simplest case a set of images can be expressed as a Cartesian product of two or more other sets of images, $X = Y \times Z$. We have an example of this in Fig. 4.7, which shows the decomposition of the set of vowel sounds into the sets of front/back position and high/low position. In general, such decompositions are not obvious, and may require extensive experiments for their discovery.

Decomposition of a space involves more than simply expressing its set of images as a Cartesian product of other sets of images, for we must also show how the topology of the composite space results from the topologies of the constituent spaces. For example, in Fig. 4.7 we need to know how similarity or distance between vowels relates to similarity or distance in each of the two dimensions of tongue position. We cannot assume the obvious Euclidean relationship, $\rho^2[(x_1,x_2), (y_1,y_2)] = \rho_1^2(x_1,y_1) + \rho_2^2(x_2,y_2)$. At very least, the component distances might have different weights,

$$\rho^2[(x_1,x_2),\ (y_1,y_2)] = w_1\rho_1^2(x_1,y_1) + w_2\rho_2^2(x_2,y_2).$$

Further, the decomposition need not even be Euclidean (l_2), for we could have a different l_p ($p \neq 2$) decomposition rule:

$$\rho^p[(x_1,x_2),\ (y_1,y_2)] = w_1\rho_1^p(x_1,y_1) + w_2\rho_2^p(x_2,y_2),$$

or even an l_∞ decomposition:

$$\rho[(x_1,x_2),\ (y_1,y_2)] = \max[w_1\rho_1(x_1,y_1),\ w_2\rho_2(x_2,y_2)].$$

No doubt more complex decompositions may also occur, and for some metric spaces there may be *no* practical decomposition.

It is also possible that we might find that a *different* choice of axes effects a better decomposition of the metric (which is the point of multidimensional scaling and many other statistical techniques). Fig. 4.10 shows a case in which an alternative decomposition is more consistent with the equal-similarity contours around a set of points in vowel space.

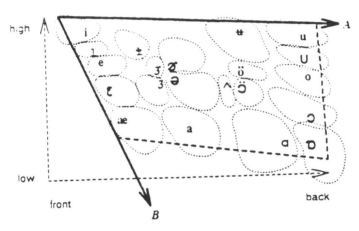

Fig. 4.10. Alternate decomposition of a low dimensional space. The diagram indicates how a different set of axes might better decompose the two-dimensional metric (indicated by equal-distance contours). (Contours are for the sake of the example and do not represent the actual range of the vowels.)

4.3. RECURSIVE DECOMPOSITION OF SPACES

Recursive structures, which allow finite but unlimited nesting, such as trees, have been a mainstay of the analysis of linguistic structures since at least the time of Chomsky. The very flexibility of recursive structures has brought with it a problem: actual linguistic performance does have its limits, whereas the theory demands no limits. This has led to a central dogma, the *competence/performance distinction*, that is, our theoretical (but never observed) linguistic competence is distinguished from our actual linguistic performance. Linguists in the Chomskian tradition have tended to concentrate on the *ideal* — competence, and have mostly ignored the *real* — performance.

In contrast, from its beginnings connectionism has taken performance into account; witness the "100 step rule." Thus we may hope that connectionism will provide a model of recursive nesting that effects a better reconciliation between competence and performance. This may follow from the theory of continuous formal systems, as I indicate below.

Consider a simple example, a space X of binary trees. We must have a construction operation $\oplus: X \times X \to X$ that joins two binary trees x, y $\in$ X into a larger tree x $\oplus$ y $\in$ X. Conversely, we also need operations to extract the left and right subtrees of a composite tree, **left**(x $\oplus$ y) =x, **right**(x $\oplus$ y) = y. Finally, we require the operations $\oplus$, **left** and **right** to all be continuous, since that is an axiom of continuous formal system theory. This means that there is a *homeomorphism* (one-to-one, continuous map) between the space X of binary trees and its possible decompositions: the space L of *leaves* and the space X $\times$ X of pairs of trees. Thus

$$X \approx L \sqcup X \times X,$$

where $\approx$ represents homeomorphism and $\sqcup$ represents disjoint union.

With this background, we can now address the question of the *continuous* recursive decomposition of a space. Our first result is that this is *impossible for finite-dimensional Euclidean spaces*, since Brouwer's theorem of the Invariance of Dimensionality shows that Euclidean spaces E^m and E^n are not homeomorphic if m$\neq$n (Hausdorff, 1937/1957, p. 232); indeed even subsets of these spaces cannot be homeomorphic (provided the subset of the higher dimensional space has interior points). In other words, finite-dimensional Euclidean spaces are characterized by their dimension. Therefore $E^n \times E^n \approx E^{2n}$ and is not homeomorphic to any subspace of E^n. Thus arbitrary trees or sequences cannot be represented continuously in finite-dimensional Euclidean spaces; we must turn to richer spaces.

We have already seen that images are often conveniently represented as continuous functions, which belong to *infinite*-dimensional Euclidean spaces, so they are the next candidates we consider.

We also observe that many infinite spaces are homeomorphic to two or more disjoint subspaces of themselves. For example, the unit interval [0,1] is homeomorphic to the one-third intervals [0,1/3] and [2/3,1] as well as to many others. The unit square $[0,1]^2$ can also be embedded in itself in many different ways. Self-embeddable spaces such as these suggest one mechanism for the continuous recursive composition and decomposition of spaces.

Suppose images are represented by continuous functions f : $\Omega \to$ Y in some function space $\Phi(\Omega)$. Most of the domains Ω in which we are interested can be homeomorphically embedded in themselves in two or more different ways, so suppose h : $\Omega \to$ h[Ω], h$'$: $\Omega \to$ h$'$[Ω] are homeomorphisms such that h[Ω] and h$'$[Ω] are separated subsets of Ω. We now define the construction of f and g, f $\oplus$ g, to be any continuous c : $\Omega \to$ Y such that f = c $\circ$ h and g = c $\circ$ h$'$, where $\circ$ indicates composition. The selection operations are simply **left**(c) = c $\circ$ h and **right**(c) = c $\circ$ h$'$.

To make these ideas clearer we present a concrete example, binary trees of one-dimensional images represented as continuous functions over [0,1]. Let Ω = [0,1]; there are homeomorphisms h, h′ such that h[[0,1]] = [0,1/3] and h′[[0,1]] = [2/3,1], namely h(x) = x/3, h′(x) = (2 + x)/3. For the construction x $\oplus$ y we take any continuous interpolation between x(1/3) and y(2/3); see Fig. 4.11. Clearly the same kind of construction could be used for images over the unit square. In this case we can map [0,1] × [0,1] into [0,1/3] × [0,1] and [2/3,1] × [0,1].

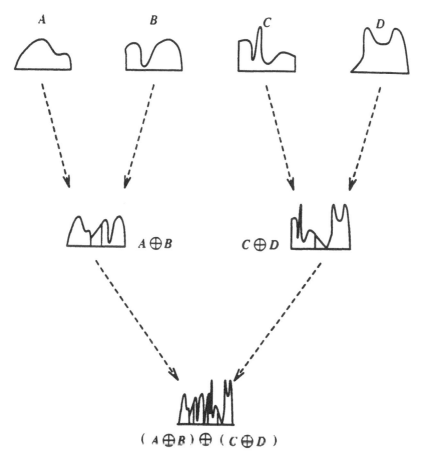

Fig. 4.11. Recursive structure represented by functions over self-similar spaces. For the sake of example, we assume that the domain of all the functions is the interval [0,1], which is homeomorphic to disjoint subintervals of itself, such as [0,1/2−ε] and [1/2+ε,1]. Two functions A, B are combined by contraction, making [0,1/2−ε] the domain of A and [1/2+ε,1] that of B. Continuity is preserved by interpolation between A(1/2−ε) and B(1/2+ε). Depth of recursive nesting is limited only by the ability of the underlying medium to sustain higher gradients.

We consider now an alternative representation of continuous recursive spaces that makes use of the properties of Hilbert spaces. Suppose $f, g \in L_2(\Omega)$. Then we can represent them by generalized Fourier series: $f = \Sigma c_k e_k$, $g = \Sigma d_k e_k$, where $\{e_k\}$ is any orthonormal basis for $L_2(\Omega)$. Next represent the construction of f and g by the interleaved series: $f \oplus g = \Sigma\; c_k e_{2k} + d_k e_{2k+1}$ (Fig. 4.12). This operation is a homeomorphism; indeed, it is linear (versus bilinear) on $L_2(\Omega) \times L_2(\Omega)$, and even an isometry, since $|f \oplus g|^2 = |f|^2 + |g|^2$. Clearly the component selector functions **left** and **right** are easily defined.

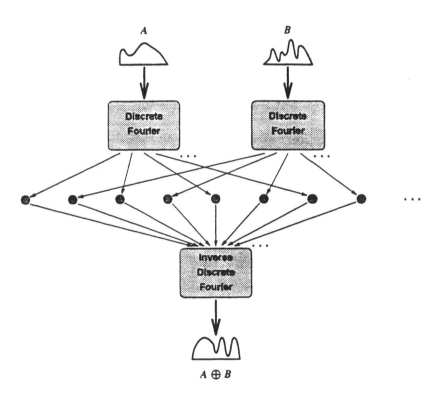

Fig. 4.12. Recursive nesting in function spaces. Suppose $c_0, c_1, c_2, \ldots$ are the Fourier coefficients of A and $d_0, d_1, d_2 \ldots$ are the Fourier coefficients of B. Then the pair (A,B) is represented by the function whose coefficients are $c_0, d_0, c_1, d_1, c_2, d_2, \ldots$, the interleaved coefficients of A and B. Recursive nesting is limited only by the ability of the underlying medium to sustain higher frequencies. (Waveforms shown are merely schematic.)

We make several observation about the continuous recursive representations that we have defined. First, we can construct binary trees to an arbitrary (finite) depth, since if x, y and z are in the space X, then so are x ⊕ y, (x ⊕ y) ⊕ z, and so on. Similarly, if x ∈ X, then we can select its right and left components, **left**(x), **right**(x), *regardless of whether it resulted from a construction*. In this representation there are no atomic symbols (leaves); we can always "go deeper" in our analysis. This potentially bottomless recursive decomposition seems to agree with the properties of continuous images revealed by our phenomenological analysis. We also observe that a temporal sequence of images x_t can be recursively folded into a sequence s by the formula $s_{t+1} = x_t ⊕ s_t$, which defines a right branching binary tree.

In both of the representations we have defined, successive composition pushes deeper information (for trees) or earlier information (for sequences) into higher frequency bands. Ideally, this doesn't matter; from a mathematical standpoint all bands are equally recoverable. Practically, however, physical media will not sustain arbitrarily high frequencies; also noise tends to be high frequency. Thus from a practical standpoint, components that are deeper or more in the past are progressively less recoverable. This seems to be a natural model of the competence/performance distinction, since noise and physical properties of the media limit performance to less than its theoretical competence. For example, arbitrarily large trees or sequences could be represented in the ideal continuous neural tissue. But real neural tissue, being composed of discrete neurons, places an upper limit on representable spatial frequency, and so on the size of trees or sequences.

5. CONNECTIONIST MAPS

5.1. MATHEMATICAL PROPERTIES

Nonrecurrent neural networks implement a map between two spaces. For example, associative memories, filters, pattern classifiers and feature extractors can often be implemented without recurrent connections. The only restriction we have postulated on such maps is that they be mathematically continuous, and for this we can take whatever definition of continuity is most appropriate to the spaces being mapped. For example, if they are metric spaces, then f: S → T is continuous at a point x if and only if for all ε > 0 there exists a δ > 0 such that $\rho_T[f(x), f(y)]$ < ε whenever $\rho_S(x,y)$ < δ. If the spaces are Euclidean, then we can use the Euclidean metric. If the spaces are not metric, then continuity must be defined in terms of open sets. Next we consider the consequences of this postulate.

5.2. CATEGORIZATION

5.2.1. EXACT CATEGORIZATION IMPOSSIBLE

Suppose we wish to divide a continuum S into two disjoint, mutually exclusive categories, A and non-A. Thus, for every image x ∈ S we want a continuous map f: S → {0, 1} such that

$f(x) = 1$ if x is in category A and $f(x) = 0$ if it is not.[19] We may take this as a precise statement of the problem of exact categorization (Fig. 4.13).

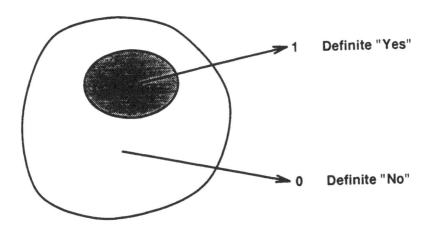

Fig. 4.13. Requirements for exact classification in a continuous symbol system. We require a *continuous* function that is 1 on the category and 0 on the complement of the category. This is impossible in a continuum.

Our first important result from the theory of continuous formal systems is that *exact categorization is impossible*. This is because it is easy to show that a space is connected if and only if it cannot be continuously mapped to a nontrivial discrete space (i.e., a space with more than one point) (Moore, 1964, p. 66). That is, a continuum cannot be discretized by a continuous map. Therefore we have:

Theorem 1 (Exact Categorization). A continuous formal system cannot perform exact classification.

Notice that this result is quite robust, since it follows from only two assumptions: connectionist spaces are connected, and connectionist maps are continuous.

---

[19] The use of 0 and 1 is not important; any discrete space with two elements would do.

5.2.2. CONNECTIONIST CATEGORIZATION

Given that exact categorization is impossible, we must consider the kinds of categorization possible to connectionist systems. We find that various topological separation axioms correspond to various kinds of categorization; we consider several examples.

It is easy to show that for each open set in a metric space, there is a real-valued continuous function that is positive just on the set (Hausdorff, 1937/1957, p. 129). Notice, however, that the boundary is fuzzy; hard thresholds are not possible (Fig. 4.14). As images approach the boundary, the categorization must leave the certain values (say ±1) and approach uncertainty, 0. We can, of course, in principle make the uncertain area as small as we like, but the Exact Categorization Theorem says that we can never decrease it to zero.

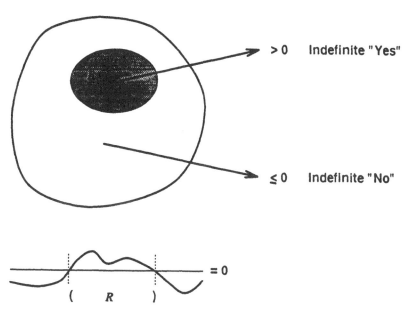

Fig. 4.14. One form of classification permitted in continuous formal systems. We are permitted a function that is positive on the category (an open region) and nonpositive on its complement, but it must be continuous, so it will be arbitrarily close to zero near the boundary.

In a *normal* topological space (such as a metric space) Urysohn's Lemma forms a basis for categorization (Moore, 1964, p. 122): For a pair of nonempty disjoint closed subsets of the space, there is a continuous map into [0,1] that is 1 on one subset and 0 on the other (Fig. 4.15). This captures the idea of two categories being mutually exclusive, but preserves their essential fuzziness. That is, we can have "definitely A" and "definitely B" provided the remainder of the space is indefinite (varies between the two). (There must be a remainder, since otherwise the space would be the union of separated sets, and hence disconnected.)

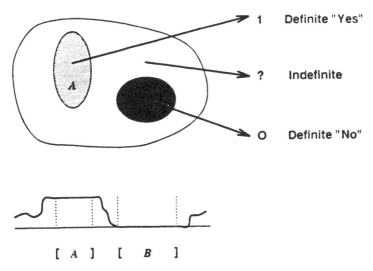

Fig. 4.15. Classification by Urysohn's Lemma. We are permitted a closed region on which the classification is definitely "yes," and a closed region on which it is definitely "no," but there must be a nonempty region between the two where the classification is indefinite.

In *completely regular* spaces (such as metric spaces) we have the following categorization theorem (Moore, 1964, p. 132): For each point in the space and each neighborhood of the point, there is a continuous map into [0,1] that is 1 at the point and 0 outside the neighborhood (Fig. 4.16). This too gives a kind of category to which some points definitely do not belong; however the category itself is defined relative to the point as exemplar. We have a sense of an image being "too far away" from the exemplar.

6. CONNECTIONIST PROCESSES

6.1. DECIDABILITY

When we consider a new notion of computation, such as is provided by continuous formal systems, the question immediately arises of whether they are subject to the same undecidability results as are discrete formal systems.[20]

---

[20] Two other extensions of computation into the continuous realm are Blum (1989), Blum, Shub, and Smale (1988), and Stannett (1990). Their notions of decidability are somewhat different from ours.

However, before the question of decidability can even be addressed, we must ask what constitutes a decision in the context of continuous formal systems. Intuitively, making a decision is reaching a definite state that will not be later left (Fig. 4.17). (More accurately, the decision is required to be stable only as long as the context is stable. That is, reasoning is monotonic in an unchanging context, but a change of context may destabilize the decision.) In mathematical terms, *a continuous decision is an asymptotically stable equilibrium*: it remains as long as the context and initial conditions are fixed.[21] Then, determining if an image is decidable is accomplished by determining whether it is in the basin of attraction of some equilibrium. Conversely, an image is undecidable if it is outside all basins of attraction (Fig. 4.18).

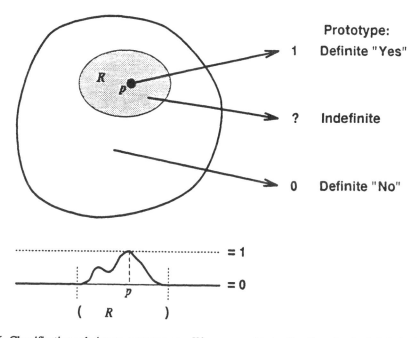

Fig. 4.16. Classification relative to a prototype. We are permitted a function that is definitely "yes" for the prototype, and definitely "no" for images sufficiently far from the prototype, but it must vary continuously between these extremes.

---

[21] For some purposes a mere stable equilibrium can be considered a decision: in effect the system has settled into a set of possible results.

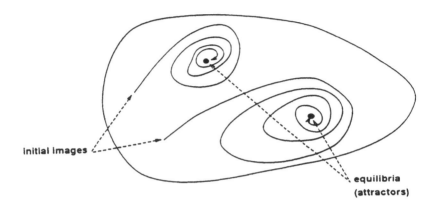

Fig. 4.17. Decisions. In a continuous formal system a "decision" is an asymptotically stable equilibrium, a state which once approached will not be left.

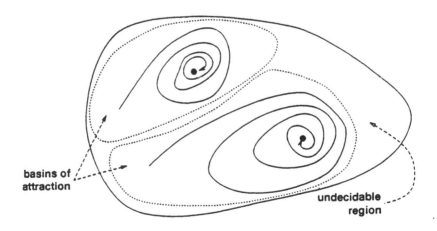

Fig. 4.18. Decision basins. A "decision basin" is the basin of attraction of an asymptotically stable equilibrium. An *undecidable image* is one that is outside of all decision basins.

Suppose we have a stable state with a corresponding basin of attraction D. Call an image undecidable if it is outside this basin. Thus D represents the decidable images. Obviously we can define a function that is 1 on D and 0 on X-D. Thus, if we do not restrict ourselves to continuous formal systems and use instead our familiar discrete logic, then we can easily talk about the decidable and undecidable images. It is a sharp distinction: D vs. X-D.

On the other hand, from *within* a continuous formal systems, in order to categorize an image as decidable or undecidable, we need a continuous decision function $d \rightarrow \{0, 1\}$ such that $d[D] = \{1\}$ and $d[X-D] = \{0\}$. But this is impossible for continua; it is just the exact categorization problem. As we saw, continuous categories are always fuzzy, and this includes the category "decidable." Notice, however, that this "undecidability result" comes from the fact that *in a continuous formal system it is impossible to ask a yes-or-no question*. Thus, from the perspective of continuous logic, *the decidability question is not even well-formed*.

What kinds of question *can* we ask a continuous formal system to decide? Here is one example. We can define a "definitely undecidable" set $U \subset X-D$ (proper subset). If D and U are disjoint closed sets, then we can define a continuous f such that $f[D] = \{1\}$ and $f[U] = \{0\}$, but there will remain a fuzzy region $X-D-U$ between D and U.[22]

These decidability results have nowhere near the significance of the classical results of Gödel and Turing, but they do illustrate the fact that continuous formal systems bring with themselves an entirely new way of *asking* these questions. We hope that the future will bring deeper insights into decidability in both discrete and continuous formal systems.

7. CONCLUSIONS

We have argued that connectionist knowledge representation requires a theory of continuous symbol systems analogous to the theory of discrete symbol systems, which informs our understanding of traditional ("symbolic") knowledge representation. A phenomenological analysis exposed the differences between the two kinds of symbol systems, and revealed invariances that are important to capture in the mathematics. Based on this analysis we tentatively concluded that continuous symbol systems are characterized by path-connected metric spaces which are separable and complete, and by continuous maps and processes over those spaces.

Next we considered a number of connectionist spaces and concluded that many are profitably treated as Hilbert spaces. Problems associated with the decomposition of image spaces were addressed, including especially the possibility of recursive decomposition, which was shown to require function spaces (such as Hilbert spaces).

We found that the continuity of connectionist maps precludes exact classification, but does permit other kinds of classification that are more robust and less likely to lead to brittleness. Finally I argued that in the context of continuous formal systems, decisions are equivalent to attractors and that an image is decidable when it is in a basin of attraction. We discovered that yes-or-no decidability questions cannot be formulated in continuous symbol systems, and

---

[22] This construction presumes that the space is normal, for example, a metric space.

therefore that a theory of continuous decidability must take a different form from that for discrete systems.

A few words about future research. I do not see much need for a lot of additional work trying to establish which mathematical structure is the "right" formalization of continuous symbol systems. Sometimes Hilbert spaces will be the best model, and other times connected metric spaces or finite-dimensional Euclidean spaces will be the best. This is analogous to discrete symbol systems, which are sometimes assumed to be deterministic and other times nondeterministic, sometimes assumed to have a finite number of types, other times a denumerably infinite number, and so forth. However, I do anticipate significant research in other areas, including continuous knowledge representation and an expanded theory of computability and decidability.

REFERENCES

Arnheim, R. (1971). *Visual Thinking*. Berkeley, CA: University of California Press.

Blum, L. (1989). Lectures on a theory of computation and complexity over the reals (or an arbitrary ring) (Report No. TR-89-065). Berkeley, CA: International Computer Science Institute.

Blum, L., Shub, M., & Smale, S. (1988). On a theory of computation and complexity over the real numbers: NP completeness, recursive functions and universal machines. *The Bulletin of the American Mathematical Society* 21, 1-46.

Buchler, J. (Ed.) (1955). *Philosophical Writings of Peirce*. New York: Dover.

Churchland, P. S. (1986). *Neurophilosophy: Toward a Unified Science of the Mind-Brain*. Cambridge, MA: MIT Press.

Dreyfus, H. L. (1979). *What Computers Can't Do: The Limits of Artificial Intelligence* (rev. ed.). New York: Harper & Row.

Goodman, N. (1966). *The Structure of Appearance* (2nd ed.). Indianapolis: Bobbs-Merrill.

Goodman, N. (1968). *Languages of Art: An Approach to a Theory of Symbols*. Indianapolis: Bobbs-Merrill.

Gregory, R. L. (Ed.) (1987). *The Oxford Companion to the Mind*. Oxford, UK: Oxford University Press.

Hausdorff, F. (1937/1957). *Set Theory* (J. R. Aumann et al., Trans.). New York: Chelsea.

Ihde, D. (1977). *Experimental Phenomenology: An Introduction*. New York: Capricorn Books, G. P. Putnam's Sons.

Ihde, D. (1986). *Consequences of Phenomenology*. Albany, NY: State University of New York Press.

Lakoff, G. (1988). A suggestion for a linguistics with connectionist foundations. In D. Touretzky, G. Hinton and T. Sejnowski (Eds.), *Proceedings of the 1988 Connectionist Models Summer School* (pp. 301-314). San Mateo, CA: Morgan Kaufmann Publishers.

Lhevinne, J. (1972). *Basic Principles of Pianoforte Playing*. New York: Dover.

MacLennan, B. J. (1987a). Technology-independent design of neurocomputers: The universal field computer. In M. Caudill & C. Butler (Eds.), *Proceedings, IEEE First International Conference on Neural Networks* (Vol. 3, pp. 39-49). New York: Institute of Electrical and Electronic Engineers.

MacLennan, B. J. (1987b). *Field computation and nonpropositional knowledge* (Report No. NPS52-87-040). Monterey, CA: Naval Postgraduate School, Computer Science Department.

MacLennan, B. J. (1988a). Logic for the new AI. In J. H. Fetzer (Ed.), *Aspects of Artificial Intelligence* (pp. 163-192). Dordrecht, Holland: Kluwer Academic Publishers.

MacLennan, B. J. (1988b). Field computation: A model of massively parallel computation in electronic, optical, molecular and biological systems. Extended abstract in *Proceedings of AAAI Spring Symposium. Parallel Models of Intelligence: How Can Slow Components Think So Fast?* (pp. 180-183). Stanford, CA: American Association for Artificial Intelligence.

MacLennan, B. J. (1989a). *Continuous computation: Taking massive parallelism seriously* (Report No. CS-89-83). Knoxville, TN: University of Tennessee, Department of Computer Science. Also, poster presentation, *Los Alamos National Laboratory Center for Nonlinear Studies 9th Annual International Conference: Emergent Computation*. Los Alamos, NM.

MacLennan, B. J. (1989b). Outline of a theory of massively parallel analog computation. Abstract in *Proceedings, IEEE/INNS International Joint Conference on Neural Networks* (Vol 2, p. 596). New York: Institute of Electrical and Electronic Engineers. For full text see Report No. CS-89-84, Knoxville, TN: University of Tennessee, Department of Computer Science.

MacLennan, B. J. (1990). *Field computation: A theoretical framework for massively parallel analog computation, parts I-IV* (Report No. CS-90-100). Knoxville, TN: University of Tennessee, Department of Computer Science.

MacLennan, B. J. (1991). *Gabor representations of spatiotemporal visual images* (Report No. CS-91-144). Knoxville, TN: University of Tennessee, Computer Science Department. Also submitted for publication.

MacLennan, B. J. (in press). Characteristics of connectionist knowledge representation. To appear in *Information Sciences*.

McFarland, D. (Ed.). (1987). *The Oxford Companion to Animal Behavior*. Oxford, UK: Oxford University Press.

Moore, T. O. (1964). *Elementary General Topology*. Englewood Cliffs, NJ: Prentice-Hall.

Morris, W. (Ed.) (1981). *The American Heritage Dictionary of the English Language*. Boston: Houghton Mifflin Company.

Nalimov, V. V. (1981). *In the Labyrinths of Language: A Mathematician's Journey* (R. O. Colodny, Ed.). Philadelphia: ISI Press.

Nemytskii, V. V., & Stepanov, V. V. (1989). *Qualitative Theory of Differential Equations*. New York: Dover.

Peirce, C. S. (1931-1958). *Collected Papers of Charles Sanders Peirce*, ed. by C. Hartshorne, P. Weiss, & A. Burks. Cambridge, MA: Harvard University Press.

Pribram, K. H. (1991). *Brain and Perception: Holonomy and Structure in Figural Processing*. Hillsdale, NJ: Lawrence Erlbaum Associates.

Shepard, R. N. (1980). Multidimensional scaling, tree-fitting, and clustering. *Science* **210**, 390-398.

Shepherd, G. M. (1978). Microcircuits in the nervous system. *Scientific American* **238**, 92-103.

Shepherd, G. M. (1988). *Neurobiology* (2nd ed.). New York: Oxford University Press.

Stannett, M. (1990). X-machines and the halting problem: Building a super-Turing machine. *Formal Aspects of Computing* **2**, 331-341.

Vernon, M. D. (1962). *The Psychology of Perception*. Baltimore: Penguin Books.

II

ARCHITECTURES FOR KNOWLEDGE REPRESENTATION

5

Representing Discrete Structures in a Hopfield-Style Network

Arun Jagota
State University of New York at Buffalo

We have developed a variant (essentially a special case) of the discrete Hopfield network, which we call Hopfield-Style Network (HSN). The stable states of HSN are the maximal cliques of an underlying graph. We exploit this graph-theoretic characterization to represent — as associative memories — several discrete structures in HSN. All representable structures are stored in HSN via its associative memory storage rule. We describe representations of sets (with PDP schemata Üas example), relations (with PDP "Jets and Sharks" as example), multi-relations (with word-dictionaries as example), graphs (with PDP schemata and binary relations as examples), Boolean formulae, and *-free regular expressions (with restaurant script as example). We also discuss robustness of these representations. Our main result is that several different kinds of discrete structures are representable — in distributed fashion — in HSN — a simple Hopfield-type energy-minimizing (constraint-satisfaction) parallel-distributed network. For knowledge representation and retrieval, we have extended the scope of representations possible in Hopfield networks, while retaining (and improving upon) the good features of such networks: (1) spontaneous constraint-satisfaction and (2) retrieval of stored schemata from noisy and incomplete information.

1. INTRODUCTION

Knowledge representation (KR) is a key issue in artificial intelligence (AI). As compared with traditional KR systems, neural networks (connectionist models) provide *novel* (e.g., distributed) means of representing knowledge, in "natural" analogies with the brain. For them to have serious applications in AI however, novelty and brain-analogies alone are insufficient — efficient representability of a variety of knowledge that AI systems deal with is also required.

Knowledge representation issues using neural networks have been much studied. For a good overview see Zeidenberg (1990, Chapter 4). One model that has received considerable attention is the PDP schemata model of Rumelhart, Smolensky, McClelland, and Hinton (1986). Their approach is *distributed* — schemata are stored *implicitly* as collections of micro-features, one network unit per micro-feature. Units (micro-features) can appear in multiple schemata. This model is essentially a Hopfield constraint-satisfaction network (Hopfield, 1982). The stored knowledge is retrieved by Hopfield energy-minimizing (relaxation) computations. Implicit schemata and error-correcting associative retrieval emerge spontaneously as collective properties of the units and the weights. This is the main significance of their work, and also that of the Hopfield network.

Whereas the above properties are attractive, the PDP/Hopfield approach to AI has in practice[1] been limited to representing non-recursive finite structures. In AI, recursive structures (e.g., trees) are frequently needed. Jordan Pollack observed that this representational inadequacy is a common feature of most connectionist models to date. He suggests a connectionist architecture (Pollack, 1989) which forms recursive distributed representations, as a solution to this problem.

In this chapter we take the (opposite) bottom-up approach. Rather than attempting to find a connectionist model to represent structures (perhaps difficult to represent in connectionist models) that might be required for certain AI tasks, we start with a simple connectionist model and explore what it *can* represent.[2] Our simple structure is a Hopfield-Style Network (HSN), a variant (essentially a special-case) of the Hopfield network, that we proposed recently (Jagota, 1990a). As with the Hopfield network, structures are "representable" in HSN exactly as stable states. In contrast to the Hopfield network, the stable states of HSN are characterised simply and exactly — as exactly the *maximal cliques* of an underlying graph. This has allowed us to theoretically ascertain what HSN can represent. Generally, any discrete structure is representable if it can be transformed to a graph so that the maximal cliques of the latter represent the desired information. Here we specifically describe how HSN can represent *sets, relations, "multi-relations", graphs, Boolean formulae, and *-free regular expressions*. For all the above structures except sets and graphs[3], HSN provides "perfect" *stable storage* — *any* collection (up to order of 2^N) memories can be stored *stably* in a network of 2N units. Spurious memories do develop however, but have a graph-theoretic interpretation. The stable storage properties of HSN are near-optimal in space and time. Due to spurious memories, however, what scales poorly is not the complexity, but the functional performance. Nevertheless, we think that this near-optimal space and time complexity is of importance to knowledge representation in AI.

---

[1] In principle the recurrent nature of such networks should hold promise for representing recursive structures also.

[2] It seems to us that both top-down and bottom-up researches must happen for the state of a field to advance.

[3] The concept of stable storage is not applicable to graphs.

We illustrate applications of the above representable structures to knowledge representation in AI. For example, PDP-style schemata are represented in HSN as *graphs*. Constraints are represented by *edges* and schemata emerge as maximal cliques. Schemata can also be represented explicitly, in which case the *set* representation is used. Since HSN is a Hopfield-type Network, the PDP approach and ours are very similar at the macro-level. As with theirs, our representations are distributed, and associative retrieval is a natural emergent property. The theory of HSN provides additional support, however. The schemata (stable states) are characterised exactly. It is easier to see if a schema will be stored *stably* and if *spurious* schemata will emerge. Thus the application of HSN to PDP-style schemata is likely to scale better because storage properties are easier to ascertain, both analytically, and by inspection. In Section 3.4.1, we compare the PDP approach and ours in more detail.

We should mention that this idea of representing knowledge in maximal cliques dates back to at least the early 1970s — in the guise of graph theoretical cluster techniques. Augustson and Minker (1970) discuss how thesauri can be represented as maximal cliques. The terms used to index documents are represented by the vertices. An edge between two vertices denotes a positive association between terms. A maximal clique denotes a maximal set of terms which are pairwise positively associated. The emergence of maximal cliques from pairwise positive associations is termed "clustering."

Our work goes further in the sense that it relates stable states of a Hopfield-type network to maximal cliques. Another way to say this is that the Hopfield-Style Network serves as a natural implementation vehicle/computation model for these (e.g., thesaurus) applications based on graph clustering techniques. Retrieval of the stored information is a spontaneous computational ability of the network's error-correcting dynamics (see below).

Finally, the main advantage of HSN is not just in its representational power, but in its spontaneous error-correcting (noise-removing + pattern-completing) ability — via energy-minimizing dynamics — on a represented structure. In this chapter, we do not discuss such abilities of HSN at all. These (dynamical) issues have been discussed extensively elsewhere (Jagota, 1990a). In this chapter, it will be understood implicitly that the error-correcting abilities of HSN can be applied to any structure that can be represented in it.

All examples in this chapter have been tested on an HSN simulator[4].

2. HOPFIELD-STYLE NETWORK (HSN)

HSN is a fully-connected N-unit binary Hopfield network with self-weights $w_{ii} = 0$, and off-diagonal (symmetric) weights $w_{ij} \in \{\rho\} \cup (0,1]$, for fixed $\rho < 0$. Unit activation states are binary ($S_i \in \{0,1\}$). The HSN energy function is

$$E = -\frac{1}{2}\sum_{i,j} w_{ij} S_i S_j - \sum_i w_0 S_i$$

---

[4] This simulator is available in the public domain and has been used extensively. For details, contact the author by e-mail or otherwise.

which differs from that of the Hopfield (1982) net energy function only in the second term, which, for positive but sufficiently small w_0, prevents $\bar{0}$ from being a stable state, while not affecting other stable states. In this chapter, choosing $w_0 = 1$ suffices, although in general, a smaller value is required. Except for the above-mentioned use, this term can be ignored.

We find it useful to characterise an HSN weight matrix by an *undirected* graph $G_N = (V,E)$, where V is the set of (indices of) units, and (i,j) is an edge in G_N if and only if $w_{ij} > 0$. That is, G_N has edges exactly for the positive weights in W. In a graph G, a subset V' of its vertices is called a *clique*, iff there is an edge between every pair of vertices in V'. A clique is *maximal* if no proper superset of it is also a clique. For notational convenience, we represent a network state-of-the-units vector $\bar{S}$ by the set $\{\, i \mid S_i = 1 \,\}$. We have the following theorem from Jagota (1990a).

Theorem 1. For $\rho < -N$, the network stable states are *exactly* the maximal cliques of G_N.

That is, a set of ON units (equivalently, its $\{0,1\}^N$ network state vector) is a network stable state if and only if $w_{ij} > 0$ for all pairs of units in this set and this set is maximal for this property. The exact values of the positive w_{ij} are irrelevant. Fig. 5.1 shows the graph G_N underlying a network whose stable states, for $\rho < -5$ are, by Theorem 1:

$$\{\, a\ c\ e\,\} \quad \{\, a\ b\ d\,\} \quad \{\, a\ b\ c\,\}$$

the maximal cliques in G_N. Replacing all the off-diagonal 0 entries in the adjacency matrix of G_N by ρ gives us the weight matrix of the network.

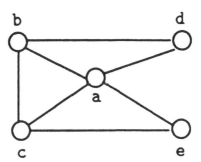

Fig. 5.1. G_n after training.

2.1. STORAGE RULE

We now describe a storage rule that constructs a binary-weights special case of HSN in which $w_{ij} \in \{\rho,1\}$. As we shall see in the next section, all representable structures can be stored in HSN via application of this storage rule. This storage rule is on-line (each "memory" is stored immediately after its first presentation).

Initially, for all $i \neq j$: $w_{ij} = \rho$, where $\rho < -2N$

A set $S \subseteq V(G_N)$ is stored by

$$w_{ij}(t+1) := \begin{cases} 1 & \text{if } i \text{ and } j \in S \\ w_{ij}(t) & \text{otherwise} \end{cases} \tag{2}$$

3. REPRESENTING DISCRETE STRUCTURES

We now show one by one how the various structures that we referred to earlier are represented in HSN. A collection of sets is stored by applying the HSN storage rule to each set. Every other structure is first represented as a set of sets, which is then stored via the storage rule as above. Relations or multi-relations are represented as sets of sets. Graphs are represented by their sets of edges (binary vertex sets). Boolean formulae and *-free regular expressions are transformed to graphs.

3.1. STORING SETS

We illustrate the storage of sets in a simplified version of the PDP schema example (Rumelhart et al., 1986). The set of 8 micro-features is:

{ceiling, walls, fridge, stove, tub, toilet, bed, dresser}

Consider the following sets, each representing a room, to be stored.

{ceiling,walls,fridge,stove}
{ceiling,walls,tub,toilet}
{ceiling,walls,bed,dresser}

The storage rule is applied to store each set. The graph G_N formed after storage is shown in Fig. 5.2. By inspection and simulation we found the following. All the sets are represented as maximal cliques of G_N. That tells us that all the stored sets are stable states. Moreover, there are no additional maximal cliques. That tells us that there are no spurious stable states.

In general, stable storage is not guaranteed for an arbitrary collection of sets. However, stable storage is guaranteed for arbitrary relations (binary vectors as special case) and sets can always be encoded as such. The spurious memory problem is not solved however for any discrete structure. There is no systematic prevention of these, except in special cases.

3.2. STORING RELATIONS

An n-ary relation $R \subseteq D_1 \times D_2 \times ... \times D_n$ is stored as follows. First, the domain name (D_i) is explicitly encoded in every symbol (element) it contains. This has the advantage of forcing all symbols to be distinct, as well as allowing a symbol's domain to be identified from its name. Tuples are then stored as sets of the symbols they contain. We have the following result from (Jagota, 1990a).

Theorem 2. Any relation R can be stored stably in HSN.

That is, every tuple in R is guaranteed to remain a distinct stable state.

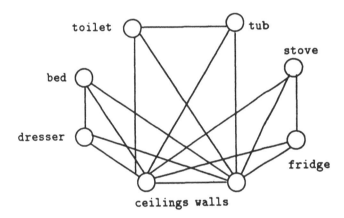

Fig. 5.2. PDP rooms example.

We illustrate the storage of relations on a simplified version of another PDP example — the Jets and Sharks example illustrating interactive activation and competition (McClelland & Rumelhart, 1988; McClelland, Rumelhart, & Hinton, 1986). In our terminology,

$$R \subseteq \text{Name} \times \text{Gang} \times \text{Age} \times \text{Occupation}$$

and the set of tuples in R is

Name	Gang	Age	Occupation
Art	Jets	40s	Pusher
Al	Jets	30s	Burglar
Phil	Sharks	30s	Pusher

with the domain sets

```
Name      = { Art, Al, Phil }
Gang      = { Jets, Sharks }
Age       = { 30s, 40s }
Occupation = { Pusher, Burglar }
```

After including domain names, the set denoting the first tuple is as follows.

{ Name=Art   Gang=Jets   Age=40s   Occupation=Pusher }

The sets formed as above are stored in HSN. Fig. 5.3 shows G_N formed after storage. The set of units is the set of all symbols, the number of which is, counting by domain:

$$3 + 2 + 2 + 2 = 9.$$

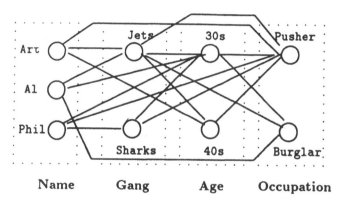

Fig. 5.3. PDP Jets and Sharks example.

By inspection and simulation we have checked that all stored tuples are stable and it can be readily seen why this must necessarily be so. Our simulation also indicated an additional spurious stable state: { **Jets 30s Pusher** }. Although, as above, spurious memories may develop, one nice property of our representation, exhibited by the above example, is that no spurious memory can contain an element from the domain Name, because Name is the key field. We do not prove this here, but this fact is easy to see from Fig. 5.3. This provides an easy test for whether a stable state is spurious or not. It also has important consequences for information retrieval. We do not discuss this here, but basically, retrieving by Name is guaranteed to always give non-spurious results. Simulation confirms this on the above example.

3.3. STORING MULTI-RELATIONS

Multi-relations are a generalization of a relation in which variable length tuples of the following kind are allowed. They can also be considered as the union of relations of different length from 1 to n, as shown below.

Definition 1. Let $A_i = D_1 \times D_2 \ldots \times D_i$ and $A = \bigcup_{i=1}^{n} A_i$. Then any subset, MR, of A is called an *n-ary multi-relation* on $D_1 \times D_2 \ldots \times D_n$.

Multi-relations can be naturally and efficiently represented in HSN, with the following guarantee (Jagota, 1990a).

Theorem 3. Any multi-relation MR can be stored stably in HSN.

That is, every tuple in MR is guaranteed to remain a distinct stable state. Finite languages on Σ^*, that is, bounded-length (n) sequences on the fixed alphabet Σ are special cases of multi-relations. This has practical significance for storing finite languages (e.g., collections of English words) naturally, efficiently, and with guarantee of stable storage. That is, no stored word will be forgotten.

For storage purposes, the representation of a multi-relation as a collection of sets is an extension of that of a relation. First, the domain name (D_i) is explicitly encoded in every symbol (element) it contains. A set is associated with each tuple and contains the symbols in the tuple. The main difference is that the length of a tuple is also explicitly included as an element in its associated set. This is a *crucial* part of the representation and necessary for guaranteeing stable storage in HSN. The collection of these sets is then stored in HSN via its storage rule.

We illustrate the storage of multi-relations on a collection of English word spellings. The words are:

a, do, car, cat, dot

The domains for their multi-relation representation are

$$D1 = \{ a,c,d \} \quad D2 = \{ a,o \} \quad D3 = \{ r,t \}$$

where D_i is the set of letters that occurs at position i. The multi-relation is then

$$\{ (a), (d,o), (c,a,r), (c,a,t), (d,o,t) \}$$

For simplicity, we append the position i to a symbol in domain D_i. This serves the purpose of domain identification. The sets associated with the above tuples are then

$$\{ a1,1 \} \{ d1,o2,2 \} \{ c1,a2,r3,3 \} \{ c1,a2,t3,3 \} \{ d1,o2,t3,3 \}$$

Fig. 5.4 shows G_N formed after storage of these sets. The set of units is the set of all symbols, plus n "length" units. The total number in this example is 10.

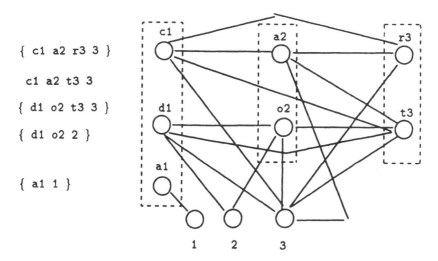

{ c1 a2 r3 3 }

c1 a2 t3 3

{ d1 o2 t3 3 }

{ d1 o2 2 }

{ a1 1 }

Fig. 5.4. G_a after storing words: a, do, car, cat, dot.

By inspection and simulation we confirmed, consistent with Theorem 3, that all stored sets (representing words) are stable. It is a bit harder to see why it must necessarily be so. One might note that the role of "length" units is to prevent words (e.g., *cat*) that are subsets of other stored ones (e.g., catamaran) from becoming unstable. Spurious memories may develop in general, but in this example, by inspection and simulation we have checked that there are none.

3.4. STORING GRAPHS

Any *simple undirected* graph G can be stored in HSN, by storing the binary vertex set associated with each edge in G, via the HSN storage rule. By Theorem 1, the maximal cliques of G are the stable states, which can denote representations that emerge implicitly. This point becomes clearer as we discuss specifics in the next subsections.

3.4.1. PDP-STYLE SCHEMATA

In the work of Rumelhart et al. (1986), schemata are stored implicitly in a Hopfield-type constraint-satisfying (energy-minimizing) network by using weights to represent the constraints. Each weight w_{ij} represents a constraint between a specific pair of micro-features, represented by units i and j. The weight w_{ij} is set by a Bayesian analysis of the probability that unit i should be ON given that unit j is ON and vice versa. A bias term is also associated with each unit. Once the weights are set, schemata emerge implicitly as local maxima of the associated energy function.

Here we describe how PDP-style schemata can be stored in HSN. Although *real-valued* constraints between pairs of micro-features can also be captured in the positive weights $w_{ij} \in$ (0,1] of HSN, for simplicity, we consider only Boolean constraints. This is also done to draw attention to the fact that for such constraints, binary-weights HSN suffices, and that storage can be accomplished via the (binary-weights) storage rule of Equation (2) (Section 2.1). The (Boolean) constraints are represented by a constraint graph on the units. An edge in the graph means the two associated micro-features are (symmetrically) compatible, an absence of an edge means that they are not. A constraint graph is then stored in HSN and the schemata emerge implicitly as its maximal cliques (stable states by Theorem 1). That is, the schemata are the maximal sets of all-pairs compatible micro-features.

This process is analogous to the PDP approach, in its limit. In binary-weights HSN, w_{ij} are in $\{\rho,1\}$. Applying the storage rule to store an edge is equivalent to setting a particular w_{ij} to 1 if units *i* and *j* are *compatible*, setting it to ρ otherwise. Once the weights have been set, the schemata emerge implicitly as local minima of the associated energy function, that is, as the maximal cliques of the constraint graph. We think that the advantages of our approach over the PDP one are that the weights are *binary* and the schemata that emerge have an exact characterisation (maximal all-pairs compatible sets). A minor advantage is that no biases are needed. Ours is amongst the simplest models in which rich sets of well-characterised schemata can emerge implicitly.

We illustrate the emergence of schemata on the PDP example of rooms of Section 3.1 and Fig. 5.2. Consider the following pairs of compatible micro-features.

{ceiling,walls},	{ceiling,dresser},	{ceiling,bed},	{ceiling,toilet},
{ceiling,tub},	{ceiling,stove},	{ceiling,fridge}	
{walls,dresser},	{walls,bed},	{walls,toilet},	{walls,tub},
{walls,stove},	{walls,fridge}		
{dresser,bed},	{toilet,tub},	{stove,fridge}	

The storage rule is applied to store each compatible pair. The graph G_N formed after storage is the same as before (Fig. 5.2). The schemata that emerge are the maximal cliques of G_N. They are the same as the ones explicitly stored in Section 3.1, and implicitly represent different rooms.

3.4.2. BINARY RELATIONS AND EMERGENT REPRESENTATIONS

Any symmetric binary relation $R \subseteq A \times A$ can be represented by a graph G_R whose vertex set is A. R can be stored in HSN by storing G_R. We now ascertain what representations emerge as stable states, and how they relate to R.

For sufficiently negative ρ, the stable states are maximal cliques of G_R. Due to this, there is a one-to-one correspondence between stable states and sets $S \subseteq A$ characterized by the following property P_1 of R:

S is maximal set such that, for all $x \neq y \in S$: $R(x,y)$	If $|S| > 1$
For $x \in S$: $R(x,x)$ and $\neg \exists y \neq x \in A$: $R(x,y)$	If $|S| = 1$

That is, either S is a maximal set of at least two elements such that all pairs of its elements are related by R or S is a set of one element related (by R) to itself and not related (by R) to any other element of A. The second case requires that R have the following property, which we call *iso-reflexivity*.

Every x in A that is not related (by R) to any other element in A must be related to itself.

It is required for consistency, ensuring that every *isolated* vertex in G_R — a maximal clique of G_R (hence stable state) — is also a maximal set in R with property P_1. Without iso-reflexivity, isolated vertices in G_R need not satisfy property P_1. Clearly reflexive relations are also *iso-reflexive*. In summary, a binary relation R to be stored in HSN with the property P_1 represented as stable states must be symmetric and iso-reflexive.

For ρ negative but sufficiently close to 0, we have shown that the following lemma holds (Jagota, 1990a).

Lemma 1. There is a one-to-one correspondence between the set of stable states and the set of all unions of connected components of G_R.

Due to this, there is a one-to-one correspondence between stable states and the sets S satisfying the following property P_2 of R:

P_2: S is a union of **maximal** sets $S_i \subseteq A$, each S_i having the following property:
$\forall x,y \in S_i$: there is a path from x to y of the form: $R(x,t_1) \wedge R(x,t_2) \wedge ... \wedge R(t_k,y)$ where t_1, t_2, ..., $t_k \in S_i$.
Special Case: If x is not related to any other element in A, then $R(x,x)$ is such a path.

That is, P_2 is a union of path closures of R. Note that path closures — connected components of G_R — are disjoint. The second part of P_2 is required for consistency. Here also, it requires R to be iso-reflexive. This will ensure that every *isolated* vertex in G_R — a connected component of G_R (hence stable state) — is also a set in R with property P_2. Without iso-reflexivity, isolated vertices in G_R need not satisfy property P_2.

If R is transitive, as well as being symmetric and iso-reflexive, then R is an equivalence relation. The connected components of G_R are the equivalence classes (transitive closures) of R. By Lemma 1, there is a one-to-one correspondence between the set of stable states and the set of all unions of equivalence classes (transitive closures) of G_R. Some of the stable states represent exactly the transitive closures of R, and the network can be used to compute them. Another property of these emergent implicit representations of transitive closures and their unions as stable states is that G_R need contain only the minimal number of edges — the rest are inferred by transitivity (see Fig. 5.6).

Example — Iso-reflexive, symmetric relation

Consider a relation *friends* and assume that it is symmetric and iso-reflexive. That is, if B is a friend of C then C is a friend of B and if B has no other friend, then B is one's own friend. Let

A = { george henry jim jack john jeff }

and the binary pairs of friends be

{george,henry}, {jim,jack}, {jim,george}, {john,henry}, {jim,henry}.

$G_{friends}$ after storage is shown in Fig. 5.5. From Fig. 5.5, the Theorem 1 stable states (maximal cliques of $G_{friends}$ are

{george,henry,jim}, {john,henry}, {jack,jim}

the maximal sets of people who are "friends" with all others in their set.

Example — Reflexive, symmetric, and transitive relation

Consider a relation *can-fly-to* and assume that it is reflexive, symmetric, and transitive. That is: (1) we can-fly-to from B to itself, (2) if we can-fly-to from B to C then we can-fly-to from C to B, and (3) if we can-fly-to from B to C and from C to D then also from B to D. Let

A = { atlanta, buffalo, dallas, la, nyc }

and the binary pairs of (direct) can-fly-to's be

{atlanta,buffalo}, {buffalo,dallas}, {la,nyc}.

$G_{can-fly-to}$ after storage is shown in Fig. 5.6. From Fig. 5.6, the Lemma 1 stable states (unions of connected components of $G_{can-fly-to}$) are

{la,nyc}, {atlanta,buffalo,dallas}, {atlanta,buffalo,dallas,la,nyc}, that is, all different unions of the transitive closures of can-fly-to.

3.5. REPRESENTING BOOLEAN FORMULAE

We have shown (Jagota, 1990b) that Boolean formulae can be represented in HSN. This aspect of our work is closely related to that of Pinkas (chapter 7, this volume), who shows that propositional logic can be represented in symmetric neural networks (Hopfield nets) in general. He provides a simple constructive way of transforming well-formed formulae (WFF) to quadratic energy functions, and establishes the equivalence between truth-assignments to these WFFs and energy-minima of these functions. His transformations are quite compact and appear to require only low-precision weights. For formulae in conjunctive normal form, the number of units required seems only linear in the number of variables n. The connectivity is also sparse, although it is unclear how this can be exploited in an implementation. His scheme also provides a constant-time evaluation on a given value-assignment. By comparison, our method requires roughly km + 2n units to store a formula in conjunctive normal form, where n is the number of variables, m the number of clauses, and k the average number of literals in a clause. This number can be much larger than that of Pinkas's scheme.

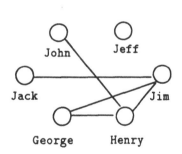

Fig. 5.5. Symmetric and iso-reflexive relation.

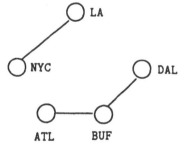

Fig. 5.6. Equivalence relation.

For the example of Fig. 5.7, Pinkas's scheme requires 3 units, whereas ours requires 10. Our network is also fully-connected. Finally, evaluating a given value-assignment takes a linear (in number of units) number of cycles.

All these advantages of Pinkas's scheme over ours do not, however, negate the main motivation for our work, namely, to demonstrate that Boolean formulae are one additional discrete structure that can be represented in HSN — a simple network of binary weights. Our goal was not to find an optimal Hopfield-type network for representing Boolean formulae, rather to study what else HSN — which has unique representational properties for certain structures like relations, multi-relations) — can represent.

We now discuss details of our representation. A Boolean formula Φ in conjunctive normal form (CNF) is stored as follows. Φ is first transformed to a graph G_Φ via the standard transformation used to prove that the *maximum clique* problem is NP-complete. This transformation is described in Jagota (1990b). For a more accessible description, see Garey and Johnson (1979, pp. 54-56). It describes a transformation that is very similar and is used to prove that the *vertex cover* problem is NP-complete. G_Φ can then be stored in HSN as any graph is. HSN has stable states to represent different ways of satisfying Φ. Such stable states encode the values of the variables in satisfying assignments, as well as which variables satisfy which clauses. The following lemma (Jagota, 1990b) shows that stable states also have sufficient information for *easy* testing of whether a particular value assignment to its variables satisfies Φ.

Let SU denote the set of vertices (see example and Fig. 5.7) representing a truth-value assignment to Φ. Let Φ have n variables and m clauses.

Lemma 2. U satisfies Φ **if and only if** the size of **every** maximal clique that is a superset of SU is equal to n + m.

We illustrate the representation of Boolean formulae and the above issues using the following example. Consider the following variables

is-heavy, is-quick, is-short

and the following CNF formula to represent *football-player-test*

(is-heavy V ~is-short) AND (~is-heavy V is-quick)

where the clauses could be interpreted as

dominance-criterion, speed-criterion

After the transformation, the graph G_Φ is very dense. For that reason, Fig. 5.7 shows $G_\Phi{}^c$, its complement graph. G_Φ can be obtained from $G_\Phi{}^c$ by complementing the edge set. Alternately, the HSN stable states can be read as the maximal independent sets[5] of the $G_\Phi{}^c$ in Fig. 5.7.[6] Some of the stable states of Fig. 5.7 that represent different ways of satisfying Φ are listed below.

{ is-heavy is-quick is-short dominance[1] speed[2] }
{ ~is-heavy is-quick ~is-short dominance[2] speed[2] }
{ ~is-heavy is-quick ~is-short dominance[2] speed[1] }

---

[5] Maximal sets of vertices with no edges

[6] Maximal cliques in a graph G are maximal independent sets in its complement G^c.

We note that the second and third of these correspond to the same value assignment. They represent different ways of satisfying the formula with the same value assignment. Consistent with Lemma 2, we also note that the size of these stable states is $5 = n + m$. Some other stable states which represent value assignments that do not satisfy Φ are listed below.

> { is-heavy ~is-quick ~is-short dominance[1] }
> [is-heavy is-quick ~is-short dominance[2] }

These are the only stable states which contain the value assignment: { is-heavy ~is-quick ~is-short }, and the size of both of them is less than 5=n + m, so this assignment does not satisfy Φ.

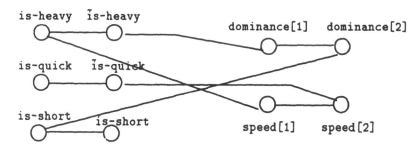

Fig. 5.7. G_{sc} for CNF formula: (is heavy ∨ ~is short) AND (~is heavy ∨ is quick).

3.6. REPRESENTING *-FREE REGULAR EXPRESSIONS

A *-free regular expression α is stored as follows. α is first transformed to a graph G_α via a novel transformation described in Jagota (1990b). G_α can be stored in HSN via the storage rule. The strings in α are represented by maximal cliques of G_α (hence stable states). The following theorem (Jagota, 1990b), in analogy with Theorems 2 and 3 (stable storage results), shows that the transformation is *stable*, that is, every string in α is guaranteed to be represented.

Theorem 4. Our transformation of any *-free regular expression α to a graph G_α has the property that for every string in α there is a distinct maximal clique in G_α.

The transformation will be illustrated via the following example.

> **Restaurant script as a *-free regular expression**

We illustrate the representation of *-free regular expressions in HSN via the following example of a partial restaurant script, represented as a *-free regular expression.

{(([make-reservation U join-friend-there].[drive U take-train.take-bus]) U make-reservation.drive-together}.get-table

Sub-expressions in this script represent (complex) actions, the 'U' operator denotes a choice on two actions, and the '.' operator denotes a sequencing on two actions. Primitive actions are the atomic sub-expressions. Compound sub-expressions (complex actions) can be parenthesized. Different style parentheses are used only for illustrative purposes. The above script encodes the knowledge that we must *first* make a reservation unless a friend is waiting there, and then drive, or take a train followed by a bus, to reach there. Alternately, if we plan to go as a group, then we must first make a reservation and then drive together. And so on ... .

Fig. 5.8 shows G_α after transformation. We note that legal strings (legal sequences of actions in the script) are represented as maximal cliques of G_α. For example, the following maximal clique

{ make-reservation1 take-train2 take-bus3 get-table4 4 }

represents the legal sequence it denotes. The ordering is encoded explicitly in the elements of the unordered maximal clique set. The second symbol '4' in the set represents the length of the sequence. The length of a sequence is always represented explicitly, as this guarantees that all stored sequences remain stable states (Jagota, 1990b). For this script example, we confirmed by inspection and simulation that indeed all the legal sequences are represented as stable states, and there are no additional spurious stable states. In more complex examples, however, spurious sequences (spurious stable states) could also develop.

4. ROBUSTNESS OF REPRESENTATIONS

So far we have explored which structures can be represented in HSN. In this section we examine the robustness of HSN to the representations it provides. We illustrate our main points on representations for schemata, although our arguments apply equally well to other structures. A network is *robust* if "damage" to a small number of the weights does not cause changes in the stable states (e.g., stored schemata). HSN requires stable states to be maximal cliques. This has been important and the basis for all our representational properties. An undesirable consequence of this, however, is that HSN is not robust at all. We sketch a possible way in which HSN can exhibit some robustness, at the expense of losing the simple characterisation of stable states as maximal cliques.

We illustrate the non-robustness of HSN as follows. Consider a binary-weights HSN ($w_{ij} \in \{\rho,1\}$). The only errors we consider are those in weights of the form: $w_{ij} = \rho$ when it should really be 1.

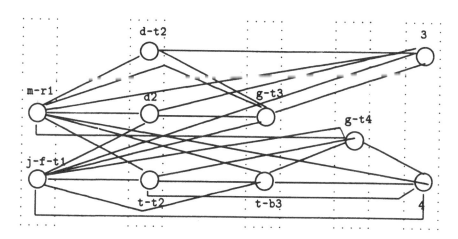

Fig. 5.8. G_t after transformation of the restaurant script regular expression: $\{([m\text{-}r \cup j\text{-}f\text{-}t].[d \cup t\text{-}t.t\text{-}b])\cup$ m-r.d-t}.g-t.

Such a weight error might result from damage, expressed by the change: $w_{ij} = 1 \to \rho$. Here, a reasonable interpretation is that $w_{ij} = \rho$ is the "default" state of a weight, $w_{ij} = 1$ carries information, and damage is the process of causing a weight to revert back to its default state, thereby causing the stored information to be lost. This view is also consistent with the initial weight state (corresponding to "zero information") of the network being: for all $i \neq j$: $w_{ij} = \rho$.

Alternately, such a weight error could also result when the associated pair of micro-features is compatible, but we lack knowledge of this fact. As a consequence, the weight remains ρ but it really should be 1. We say that a network is robust to incomplete knowledge if the correct schemata emerge even when *some* of the compatible pairs are missing in the training set. In our case, robustness to damage is identical to robustness to incomplete knowledge. The weight state of the network is the same whether a weight is damaged, or whether information about the weight was unavailable in the first place.

For $\rho < -N$, the stable states of HSN are the maximal cliques of the underlying graph G_N. This means that a single weight error can cause a desired schemata to not be a stable state. That is, HSN is not robust at all. The PDP schemata model, however, appears to be much more robust, because the stable states do not have to satisfy requirements as strict as those of HSN. However, we are unaware of formal analyses of the robustness of the PDP model, whereas such analyses appear relatively easier for HSN.

We show that some amount of robustness is possible by controlling ρ. Briefly, for $\rho << 0$, the stable states have tight constraints (maximal cliques) whereas for ρ that is smaller in magnitude, the stable states need only meet the constraints weakly. The following lemma (Jagota, 1990b) presents this necessary condition in a formal sense. Let

$$uniform\text{-}density(V') = \min_{v \in V'} \frac{d_{G_N[V']}(v)}{e_{G_N[V']}(v)}$$

for a vertex set $V' \subseteq V(G_N)$, where $d_{G_N[V']}$ is the degree of vertex v in $G_{N[V']}$, the subgraph of G_N induced by V', and $e_{G_N[V']}$ is the *co-degree* of v in the same subgraph, that is, the number of vertices in $G_{N[V']}$ that v is *not* adjacent to. Then uniform-density(V') indicates the minimum degree/co-degree ratio which is in some sense, the degree of looseness of constraints that can be tolerated.

Lemma 3. A necessary condition for S to be a network stable state is that

$$uniform\text{-}density(S) \geq |\rho| \qquad (3).$$

Lemma 3 represents the precise relationship between ρ and the degree that constraints must be satisfied. When ρ is large, the stable states require constraints to be satisfied tightly (maximal cliques at the extreme). When ρ is small, the network stable states only require the constraints to be satisfied loosely.

Lemma 3 offers a prescription for setting ρ to attempt to achieve robustness. Generally, the larger the required robustness (in terms of number of edges to which damage can be tolerated), the smaller the magnitude of ρ that is required. However, whereas theorem 1 characterises stable states exactly (as maximal cliques), Lemma 3 provides only a necessary condition. We have shown (Jagota, 1990b), via counter-examples, that the condition of Lemma 3 is not a sufficient condition. We discuss other possible problems with this scheme, following the example below.

We illustrate the above ideas on the PDP-style rooms schemata example of Section 3.4.1, on the graph G_N of Fig. 5.2. We assume that the edge: {ceiling,walls} has been "damaged", or alternately, was missing from the training set in the first place. For $\rho < -N$, this damage affects all three stored schemata, splitting each into two. The new stable states are:

{bed,dresser,ceiling}   {bed,dresser,walls}
{tub,toilet,ceiling}   {tub,toilet,walls}
{stove,fridge,ceiling}   {stove,fridge,wall}

We would like to try to choose a ρ for which the deletion (damage) of this edge does not affect the stable states. This requires, from Lemma 3, that we must pick that ρ which satisfies uniform-density(V') $\geq |\rho|$ for every stable state (schema) V' that previously contained the edge: {ceiling,walls}. Fortunately, all stable states contained this edge, and all were of size 4. So the uniform-density of all stable states, when this edge is deleted, is $\frac{2}{1}$. This gives a necessary condition for the stable states to not be affected by this damage as: $\rho \in [-2,0)$. We found, via simulation on our first attempt, that setting $\rho = -1.8$ preserved the stable states. The network had exactly the three original stable states of Section 3.1, representing bedroom, bathroom, and kitchen respectively. We then "restored" the edge: {ceiling,walls} and found that the stable states remained unchanged, for this $\rho = -1.8$. This illustrates the robustness.

In more complex situations, it is unlikely that robustness such as illustrated above can be systematically achieved. Given a collection of desired schemata, there is no guarantee that there even exists a ρ for which HSN can at least preserve, after damage, the stable states for at least all the schemata, let alone preclude the development of additional spurious ones, due to the choice of ρ. Nevertheless, the architecture of HSN does hold the promise of more systematic exploration of robustness issues in the future.

5. CONCLUSION

We showed how a variety of discrete structures (sets, relations, multi-relations, graphs, Boolean formulae, *-free regular expressions) are representable in a Hopfield-Style network (HSN) that we proposed earlier. We illustrated, via examples, the applications of these various structures represented in HSN to knowledge representation in Artificial Intelligence. Some applications include PDP-style schemata, relational databases, and scripts. We compared and contrasted our technique of representing PDP-style schemata with the PDP approach. Although both approaches are similar at the macro-level — schemata emerge as stable states of an energy function — our approach has the advantage of exact characterisation, in simple terms, of the schemata that emerge. We pointed out that our approach, however, lacks robustness, but sketched a means for a partial remedy to the problem. We compared our technique of representing Boolean formulae with the approach of Pinkas.

We think that the ability of HSN to represent a variety of discrete structures establishes HSN as a practical neural network-based computing device. Especially in conjunction with energy-minimizing dynamics on HSN that can be used for error-correcting (noise-removing + pattern-completing) retrieval on any kind of represented structure.

REFERENCES

Augustson, G., & Minker, J. (1970). An analysis of some graph theoretical cluster techniques. *Journal of the Association for Computing Machinery* 17, 571-588.

Garey, M. R., & Johnson, D. S. (1979). *Computers and Intractability - A Guide to the Theory of NP-Completeness*. New York: W. H. Freeman & Company.

Hopfield, J. J. (1982). Neural networks and physical systems with emergent computational properties. *Proceedings of the National Academy of Sciences of the U.S.A.* 79, 2554-2558.

Jagota, A. (1990a). A new Hopfield-style network for content-addressable memories. Technical Report 90-02, Department of Computer Science, State University of New York At Buffalo.

Jagota, A. (1990b). The Hopfield-style network as a maximal-clique graph machine. Technical Report 90-25, Department of Computer Science, State University of New York At Buffalo.

McClelland, J. L., Rumelhart, D. E., & Hinton, G. E. (1986). The appeal of parallel distributed processing. In D. E. Rumelhart & J. L. McClelland (Eds.), *Parallel Distributed Processing* (Vol. 1, pp. 3-44). Cambridge, MA: MIT Press.

McClelland, J. L., & Rumelhart, D. E. (1988). Interactive activation and competition. In J. L. McClelland & D. E. Rumelhart (Eds.), *Explorations in Parallel Distributed Processing* (pp. 11-47). Cambridge, MA: MIT Press.

Pollack, J. B. (1989). Implications of recursive distributed representations. In D. S. Touretzky (Ed.), *Advances in Neural Information Processing Systems 1* (pp. 527-536). San Mateo, CA: Morgan Kaufmann.

Rumelhart, D. E., Smolensky, P., McClelland, J. L., & Hinton, G. E. (1986). Schemata and sequential thought processes in PDP models. In D. E. Rumelhart & J. L. McClelland (Eds.), *Parallel Distributed Processing* (Vol. 2, pp. 7-57). Cambridge, MA: MIT Press.

Zeidenberg, M. (1990). *Neural Networks in Artificial Intelligence*. New York: Ellis Horwood.

6

Modeling and Stability Analysis of a Truth Maintenance System Neural Network

William Pratt Mounfield, Jr.
Louisiana State University

Ljubomir T. Grujić
University of Belgrade

Suresh Guddanti
Louisiana State University

Artificial intelligence expert systems problems are shown to be solved by the novel use of a new neural network formulation, the Boolean neural network. Following the Truth Maintenance System form of knowledge representation, known facts are represented by neurons and the interconnections among the neurons form the actual knowledge base. The network finds valid solutions (equilibrium points) representing a consistent set of facts provided such a solution exits. The hardware implementation of such a network operates asynchronously with the use of simple discrete components and converges to (possibly non-zero) equilibrium points provided these points exist. In order to prove the stability of such candidate equilibrium points, the asynchronous Boolean logic system is mathematically transformed to a synchronous algebraic set of dynamic equations which retain the original candidate equilibrium points. These equilibrium points are translated to the origin to use a Lyapunov stability criterion for discrete systems. Examples are shown which model different knowledge bases, and steps are also given to analyze the stability of such knowledge bases.

1. INTRODUCTION

One application of neural networks is expert systems. Conventional computer oriented expert systems (Winston, 1984) are programs that make use of knowledge and inference procedures to solve problems that require human intelligence. An expert provides facts and rules to the expert system, and the expert system then provides its expertise in solving the problem for the user. The manner in which the rules and facts are stored and "expertly" operated on is through a knowledge base and an inference engine. The knowledge base consists of rules relating various facts presented to a system. Inferencing is arriving at a conclusion, which follows from the given facts and the rules. For example, assume that a knowledge base contains the following rules regarding automobile diagnostics for a car that will not start:

(1) If ENGINE CRANKS *and* SPARK PLUGS FIRE
   then FUEL SYSTEM IS FAULTY
(2) If BATTERY IS LOW
   then ALTERNATOR IS BAD *or* BATTERY IS BAD.
(3) If SPARK PLUGS DO NOT FIRE
   then BATTERY IS LOW *or* IGNITION COIL IS FAULTY
(4) If ENGINE DOES NOT CRANK
   then BATTERY IS LOW

Note that the words in uppercase are facts and the *if-then* statements are the rules that link the facts. The part before *then* is called the antecedent and the part after *then* is called consequence. These rules may be stored in a tree format so that they are easily searched. Given a fact that the engine is not cranking, the inferencing program searches through the rule tree among the antecedent parts of the rules and finds a match with Rule #4. Rule #4 indicates LOW BATTERY is a probable cause. The inferencing program then searches for LOW BATTERY among the antecedents and finds a match with Rule #2. There are two consequences for Rule #2 namely BAD ALTERNATOR, BAD BATTERY. The inferencing program then branches out and tries to find either of the two consequences in the antecedent part of the rules but (here) finds no match. The inferencing program therefore arrives at two possibilities for the cause, namely a bad alternator or a bad battery. In practice, the knowledge data base may be very large and may require complex search techniques.

2. NEURONS AND NETWORKS

A neural network is a set of computational units whose interconnections are analogous to the interconnection between biological neurons (Hopfield & Tank, 1986; Tank & Hopfield, 1986). Many models which resemble the interconnections of a biological neuron have been classified as neural networks. Each computational unit has an output and some inputs. Each input of the neuron is usually connected to at least one output of another unit (neuron). In some cases one input of the neuron may be connected to its own output, this is termed self or direct feedback (Caudill, 1987). In electronic implementations of neural networks, the interconnections are through amplifiers with gains ranging over $W_{ij} \in [0,+\infty)$. The gains of these amplifiers are generally referred to as weights.

A neuron in an artificial network is said to be triggered or "fired" when its output goes (logically) high. If the neuron has a complementary output, then this output would simultaneously go (logically) low. The inputs can be of two types, (1) excitatory and (2) inhibitory. Excitatory inputs have a positive effect in triggering a neuron in contrast to the inhibitory inputs. A neuron gets triggered when the sum of all the weighted inputs exceed the threshold of that neuron. The thresholding function is referred to as the activation function. The activation function is typically a sigmoid curve.

Various learning schemes like Hebbian Learning, Delta Learning Rule (Caudill, 1988a), and Back Propagation Learning (Caudill, 1988b), are used to determine the interconnection weights W_{ij}. The interconnections in a neural network may be symmetric or asymmetric. The interconnections are symmetric if $W_{ij} = W_{ji}$. If all neurons in a neural network update their states simultaneously, the network is synchronous. Symmetric synchronous neural networks have the tendency to limit cycle, that is, the network outputs a sequence of states and then repeats a particular sequence of states (Martland, 1987). If the updating is randomly sequential, that is, one neuron at a time is updated, or several, but not all neurons are updated at a time the neural network is asynchronous. Based on the nature of the states of a neuron, neural networks are further classified into discrete-space or continuous networks. The states of the neurons X^k, $k \in 0,1,2,...,+\infty$ where $X^k = [x^k_1, x^k_2, ... x^k_N]$ for the k-th step in time in a discrete-space network (which may be implemented with digital logic circuits) are generally $X^k \in [-1,1]$ or sometimes $X^k \in [0,1]$. Digital logic neural networks (Vidal, Pemberton, & Goodwin, 1987) have the same advantage over analog neural networks as digital circuits have over analog circuits via immunity to noise in small voltage ranges. The network model presented in this chapter is of the discrete-space type using simple digital logic circuits, where the only valid states of a neuron are $X^k \in [0,1]$.

3. EXISTING NEURON-LIKE NETWORKS FOR INFERENCING

Many hardware implementations of inferencing reported in the literature make use of a hybrid architecture involving an external computer. Some implementations for example store rules in ROM (Read Only Memory). Cleary (1987) describes a VLSI chip in which the communication between neurons is multiplexed. The VLSI chip is accessed by a host computer and performs the mathematical operations or thresholds. One suggested application of this VLSI chip is for rule-based reasoning as used in expert systems. In this system one unit (neuron) is assigned to each rule, fact, and conclusion present in the expert system. A rule is said to fire if each of its preconditions is true, programmed by setting the threshold equal to the number of preconditions. This threshold operation is similar to the logical AND function with the number of inputs equal to the number of preconditions. A conclusion is considered *true* if there is any rule that fires which makes the conclusion true. Simple *true/false* reasoning is possible in this system.

An approach taken by Green and Michalson (1987) uses a network similar to an inference net. The nodes consist of summing junctions for their weighted inputs and each has a particular activation level. The node gives a Boolean result based on the inputs. This network is called an Evidence Flow Graph (EFG). The graph shows the links between the input hypothesis and Knowledge Source Procedures (KSPs). This technique lacks specific mapping procedures to map decision processes into an EFG.

Another inference net approach was taken by Venkatasubramanian (1985) who designed a parallel network expert system for inexact reasoning. He used a parallel network of binary, threshold units. The solution was obtained by a probabilistic search through the solution space using the simulated annealing algorithm (Kirkpatrick, Gelatt, & Vecchi, 1983). The simulated annealing algorithm is a probabilistic technique in which the system is excited so that the current state is capable of escaping from a local minimum, and then left to settle down at a new local minimum. Venkatasubramanian's architecture had three levels of nodes (1) input data nodes which were clamped either in the on state or the off state depending on the observed characteristics of the model (which happened to be a process control problem), (2) the intermediate level nodes which were driven by the nodes at the same level along with the data supplied by the input nodes, and (3) the answer nodes which represented the decision reached by the system. The number of levels for the class of intermediate nodes depend on the problem. Knowledge was represented by the weighted interconnections between the nodes. The weights were initially assigned randomly, and were then refined by comparing the outputs with the real world data. There is no mention of any hardware implementation or explicit rule formulation.

Kemke (1987) provides mathematical definitions of neurons in neurobiological terms. She shows the similarities of the models of human neuron operations occurring in neural networks. If the appropriate parameters are selected, human neurons could behave as flip-flops and logical functions such as AND, OR and NOT. McNaughton and Papert (1971) had written earlier on the appearance of neurons as a type of flip-flop. Other neurons, in particular optical implementations, have been referred to for their use in expert systems (Eichmann & Caulfield, 1985; McAulay, 1987; Warde & Kottas, 1986).

4. THE NEED FOR TRUTH MAINTENANCE SYSTEMS

Since an expert system contains a rule database and an inference engine, as more and more rules are added, there is a possibility of having conflicts between the most recent rules and the existing rules in the database. This could lead to faulty inferences. A Truth Maintenance System (TMS) (Doyle, 1979) has been offered as a valuable tool in maintaining the consistency in the database. In order to demonstrate the concept of facts and consistent truth values, consider a system of facts

FACT #1: (A) = CLOUDY SKY
FACT #2: (B) = RAIN
FACT #3: (A→B) = CLOUDY SKY implies RAIN
FACT #4: (⅂A) = Not CLOUDY SKY.

In the above system there are four facts. If we assign truth values (a truth value can be True (T) or False (F)) to each fact in the following order: T F T F then by looking at the facts we can conclude by using our own logical reasoning that these truth values T F T F are not consistent among each other with respect to the rules defined above. This conclusion can be arrived at by the following. It is trivial that the first (T) and fourth (F) truth values are consistent with each other. The first truth value (T) tells us the SKY is CLOUDY. Since Fact #3 is assigned True we can conclude that it will rain. However, the second truth value (F) indicates NO RAIN. Therefore, we have an inconsistency or contradiction in the set of truth values T F T F. Although this is a very simple example with only four facts, one can see that the reasoning chain is complex. Since the actual number of possible combinations of truth values are 2^N for N number of facts, the total number of combinations of the truth values in the above example is 16. For a large problem with thousands of facts, the total number of combinations of truth values becomes tremendously large. For such a large problem, one can imagine how long it would take to find out even one set of consistent truth values. A Truth Maintenance System provides a methodology to maintain consistency for such a set of truth values.

Consider a system containing a finite number of facts. The facts are interrelated by rules. In a Truth Maintenance System the rules are lists of truth values which make a particular fact true. A fact can have two truth values — *true* or *false*. Each rule may use the truth values of some or all of the remaining facts. The truth value for any fact may be "justified" if at least one rule associated with that fact is satisfied. If the truth values of all facts are justified, then the truth values are said to be consistent. A TMS algorithm solves for a consistent set of truth values for a set of facts stored in a knowledge base. State-of-the-art TMS algorithms makes use of a recursive labelling algorithm (Doyle, 1979) involving list manipulations. Such an algorithm is well suited for implementations in LISP. However, for systems with large knowledge bases, the software based recursive labeling algorithm could be prohibitively time consuming.

5. TMS AS AN EXPERT SYSTEM

A Truth Maintenance System Neural Network (TMSNN), which is described in the next section, can also be adapted as an expert system. Consider a system containing a finite number of facts. In a TMS, the rules are lists of truth values associated with these facts. Using the concept of justification and consistency from above, for a set of four (4) facts only one or two or possibly none of the combinations (depending on the rules) may be consistent out of the 16 possible combinations of the truth values. In this set of four facts (section 4) to see if a Fact 1, and a Fact 2 imply a Fact 3, Fact 3 (the goal node) is clamped to a *false* state while the nodes for Fact 1 and Fact 2 are clamped *true*. If the system arrives at a consistent solution, then the implication of the goal is *false*. The inference of the goal would be *true* only if the system does not reach a consistent solution, that is, it keeps oscillating. Thus to make inferences, one only has to clamp the appropriate truth values. By clamping a truth value for a particular node, the node is not allowed to be updated. It is said to be locked. A convenient form of representing the rules lists the facts which are *true* in one group called the **TLIST** and facts which are *false* in a second group called **FLIST**. This representation scheme is shown in Table 6.1 for the CLOUDY SKY/RAIN example of four facts.

6. A TMS AND EXPERT SYSTEM NEURAL NETWORK

In all the literature reviewed so far, except for McNaughton & Papert (1971) none of the implementations make use of the flip-flop model of neuron. The basis of the network described in this work is a combination of the flip-flop model of neurons, feedback of the outputs of the neurons, and the TMS representation method of facts. The TMSNN defined in this work and others (Guddanti, Mounfield, & Grujić, 1991; Mounfield & Guddanti, 1990) stands out as unique based on its capability to maintain consistency among all the facts in the database. At the same time, the TMSNN allows for inferences to be made in the manner of the previous section. A neural network model is then proposed which generates consistent truth values for a given set of facts and rules. The TMSNN is based on the representation given by Doyle (1979).

No.	Fact	Justifications	
		TLIST	FLIST
1	A	{} {}	{4} {3}
2	B	{1 3} {3}	{} {4}
3	A→B	{2} {} {4}	{} {1} {}
4	˥A	{3} {}	{2} {1}

Table 6.1. Facts and justifications for the CLOUDY SKY/RAIN example with four facts.

This TMSNN embodies (1) fact representation, (2) knowledge representation, and (3) a labelling or inferencing process. A specific implementation architecture for the problem of Table 6.1 is shown in Fig. 6.1. There is only one layer of neurons which act as both the input and output neurons. This one layer is interconnected based on relationships between the facts.

The proposed logic solving neural network is a discrete, asymmetric asynchronous system. The TMSNN model is different from the Hopfield model of Hopfield & Tank (1986) conceptually as well as architecturally. This Hopfield model arrives at solutions (patterns) which were stored in the network in terms of the interconnection weights. The known solutions are used to teach the Hopfield network to determine the interconnection weights via a storage scheme. Once the interconnection weights are determined, the network will converge to one of the stored patterns closest to the given input arbitrary pattern. This type of memory access system is known as associative memory. However, in the TMSNN the interconnections are fixed by the user based on rules and the solutions are not known a priori. The fixed connections are similar to the constraint satisfaction problem in Tank & Hopfield (1986). However, the TMSNN is asymmetric, as compared to the symmetric network of Tank & Hopfield.

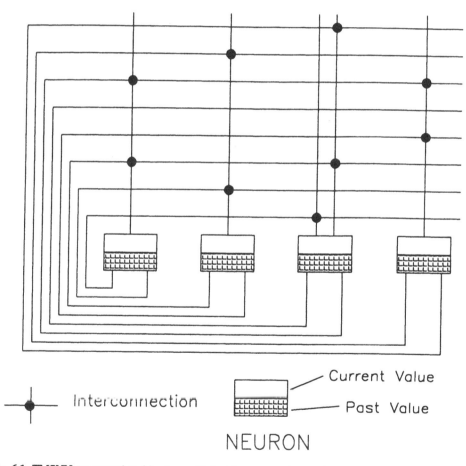

Fig. 6.1. TMSNN conceptual architecture with fact interconnections and past and current states.

6.1. FACT REPRESENTATION

Each neuron I,J,K,L in Fig. 6.1 represents a fact in the knowledge data base. In Fig. 6.1, each neuron is depicted by partitioned boxes. The upper half of each box represents the input or current state of that neuron, while the lower half of each box represents the output or immediate past state. The input states of all neurons are volatile; that is, their states are determined by the instantaneous outputs of the knowledge base. The output states store the input state value that was present during updating or triggering. The input and output states of a neuron can be either 0 or 1. For simplicity in the wiring, the inhibitory inputs are realized by having complementary (inverted) neuron outputs in addition to the regular neuron output. The combined output states of all these neurons form the output of the system. The inputs to these neurons come from the knowledge base as explained below. The outputs of these neurons are fed back to the knowledge base. The feedback channels enable the knowledge base to process the output state and feed the result back to the neuron inputs. Thus, at any instant, the neuron input state represents the current state X^k while the output state represents the past state X^{k-1}. When the neuron is updated or triggered, the state at the input gets transferred to the output. That is, the past state becomes current. The interconnections are explained in the next section.

6.2. KNOWLEDGE REPRESENTATION

Knowledge is represented in the knowledge base in the form of rules. These rules are supplied from the real world by the user. The rules are represented in the justification format shown by Doyle (1979). A justification for a particular fact is a set of truth values of the remaining facts in the database. The truth values in a justification are the necessary and sufficient conditions to make the fact *true*. It should be noted that a justification does not contain a truth value of the same fact, there is no self feedback present in the system.

A justification contains the truth values of a number of facts. Facts are identified by node numbers. In order to identify the facts as well as their truth values, the justification is split up into two lists, namely the TLIST and the FLIST. The TLIST contains the node numbers of the facts which are *true* while the FLIST contains the node numbers of the facts which are *false*.

The justification can be understood by considering the example from Table 6.1. There is a total of four facts and each fact is identified by node numbers ranging from 1 to 4. Take for example node 1 which represents the fact A. If NOT A is *false* then it can be trivially concluded that A is *true*. Hence node 4 is placed in the FLIST. The TLIST is empty in this justification. Node 3 represents the fact A implies B which is logically equivalent to NOT A OR B. Thus, if node 3 is *false* then it is certain that NOT A is *false*. Which means that A is certainly *true*. Therefore node 3 is also placed in the FLIST. Negation of node 3 alone is sufficient to make node 1 *true*, therefore a second justification list is created with node 3 in the FLIST. Thus, to make node 1 *true*, any one of its two justifications need to be satisfied. Now Consider fact B. It is necessary that node 3 should be *true* to make node 2 *true*, but this condition alone is not sufficient. In addition, Node 1 should also be made *true* to make node 2 *true*. Therefore, one justification for node 2 consists of node 1 and 3 in the TLIST. On similar grounds one can show that it is necessary and sufficient that node 3 be *true* and node 4 be *false* to make node 2 *true*.

The mapping of the justifications into interconnections is straight forward. Each justification list contributes a column of interconnections. If a fact has three justifications, then there would be three columns of interconnections corresponding to that neuron. The rows contain the neuron output states. Since each neuron has a normal output as well as a complimentary output, there are then $2N$ rows. The complimentary outputs would represent the FLIST while the regular outputs would represent the TLIST. The node numbers in the justification list indicate locations of the interconnections. If the node number is in the TLIST then the interconnection is formed on the normal output row of that neuron. In the example shown, there are two columns of interconnections corresponding to the two justifications for the first node. In the first column, the interconnection is made at the first row from the bottom, since it corresponds to the complimentary output of the first neuron. This is the mechanism of transformation of node 4 in the FLIST into an interconnection.

6.3. LABELLING PROCESS

As explained earlier, the knowledge base has access to the (past) truth values of all the neurons. The TMSNN processes these past truth values in parallel and computes the current truth value from the inputs to each neuron. Each neuron, therefore, has at any instant its current state as well as its past state. The (current) input state of a particular neuron is consistent with the (past) output states of all the other neurons. A valid labelling requires consistency between *all* the (current) input states of *all* neurons. If the (current) input and (past) output states are identical for each of the other neurons, then the (current) input states of a particular neuron would be consistent with the (current) input state of the neurons. In general, one can conclude that if the (current) input state of every neuron is identical to its (past) output state, then the current states of all the neurons constitute a valid labelling or a consistent solution. It is trivial to observe that the (past) input state of all neurons would also constitute a consistent solution. If the (past) input states are consistent, the knowledge base will not observe any conflict and therefore, its result (the current state) will not change.

The update mechanism, which consists of a pair of switches associated with each neuron, has two important functions. First, this will enable an update of only one neuron at a time, thereby making the updates asynchronous. Second, it updates a neuron only if it detects a difference in the input state and output state of a neuron. Therefore, the potential energy which drives the system from one state to another is a function of the difference between the input state and output state of the neurons. Even if one neuron has a different input and output state, the update sequence occurs. As long as there is conflict among the past states, the system will keep searching for a consistent labelling.

6.4. HARDWARE IMPLEMENTATION

An integrated circuit (IC) design of the network using CMOS IC's is shown in Fig. 6.2 (Guddanti & Mounfield, 1993). The network consists of interconnected AND gates (point 1 in Fig. 6.2), and OR gates (point 2 in Fig. 6.2). Each column of interconnections corresponding to a particular neuron represents an AND gate. The AND gates ensure that all nodes in a particular justification satisfy the required conditions. The outputs of all AND gates of a particular neuron are connected to an OR gate. The OR gates provide an output when a justification becomes *true*. The output of each AND gate is connected to one of the inputs of the OR gate. The output of each OR gate is connected to the neuron input. Thus, the current state of each neuron is represented by the output of an OR gate.

The outputs of each neuron are connected to the inputs of the other AND gates through latches or flip-flops (point 3 in Fig. 6.2). The latches store the past state of the network. There is no self feedback for individual neurons. Some outputs of the neurons are inverted before they connect with other neurons. These inverted outputs are derived from the complimentary outputs of the latches. Unconnected inputs of the AND gates are set to logic level 1 by means of pull up resistors. The unconnected inputs of the OR gates are held at logic level 0 by grounding them. The state of the network at any instant is given by the binary logic level pattern and consists of 1s and 0s. The interconnection between each neuron is defined by the interrelationship between the stored facts (point 8 in Fig. 6.2). The network is said to be stable when there is no change in state between each cycle. Each cycle consists of an update sequence which transfers the current state to the past state. This sequence is a function of the update sequence hierarchy; in the network of Fig. 6.2, the hierarchy is {1,2,3,4}.

The truth values of facts are represented by the discrete logic levels of '1' and '0'. A logic '1' corresponds to a *true* value while '0' corresponds to a *false* value. At power-up the network stabilizes with random initial set of truth states at the output of each OR gate. Since the latches at power-up are not activated the network remains inactive. The updating process is then initiated sequentially starting from the first neuron. Note that any update sequence may be used. The update of a neuron takes place when one of the flip-flops is clocked with one pulse. At this stage, the neuron logic state (current state) at the D input of the flip-flop is transferred to the Q output (past state) and its complement $\bar{Q}$. As soon as this update takes place, the new value will alter the current states of the remaining neurons, depending on the interconnections. After the propagation delay which is of the order of nanoseconds (CMOS Data Book, 1981), all neuron inputs stabilize to the appropriate new logic states.

Clock pulses are supplied by an oscillator at point 10 (Fig. 6.2). The updating procedure is minimal, in the sense that clock pulses for updating are not sent to those neurons which have identical current and past states. This is achieved for each neuron by means of a pair of switches (points 5 and 6 in Fig. 6.2) controlled by an XOR gate (point 4 in Fig. 6.2) which monitors the past and current state of that neuron. The switches associated with a given neuron direct the clock pulses to the other neurons or to itself, depending on the past and current states of the neuron in question. The switching arrangement allows only one neuron to be updated at a time. If stability is reached then the clock pulses start appearing at point 17 (Fig. 6.2). Clamping of truth values of '0' or '1' is achieved by using the RESET and SET inputs of the flip-flop.

With the neural network model of TMS the computation time is reduced by a large factor when compared with a software implementation of the conventional labelling algorithm on a traditional computer. The reduction in computation time can be attributed to the massively parallel computation process which takes place in a neural network. To our knowledge, there is no such model reported in the literature which uses the concept of TMS in arriving at consistent truth values.

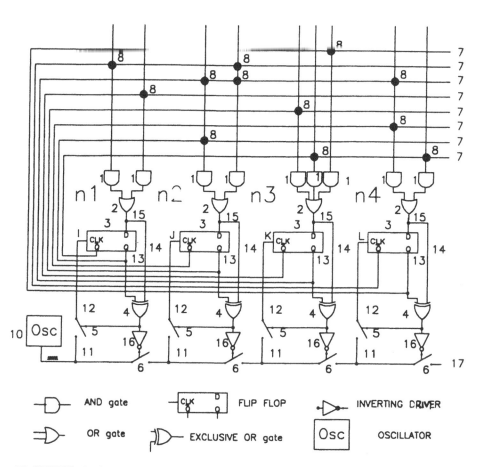

Fig. 6.2. TMSNN circuit constructed from simple gates for justification logic and flip-flops for memory.

7. TMS EXAMPLE PROBLEMS

7.1. FOUR LOGICAL FACTS

Consider a case consisting of four different formulas (S. Kundu, personal communication, 1989) as shown in Table 6.1. The interconnection information is stored in the network by using the justifications from column 3. Node 1 is represented by neuron 1, Node 2 by neuron 2, that is, node n by neuron n. Each justification list corresponds to the inputs of one AND gate. If the node number appears in the TLIST of the justification then the Q output corresponding to that neuron is used. If the node number appears in the FLIST of the justification then the NOT ($\bar{Q}$) output is used. For example, node 1, has two justifications, therefore two AND gates will be used. The complete interconnection for the problem in Table 6.1 is shown in Fig. 6.2.

7.2. EXPERIMENTAL RESULTS OF FOUR LOGICAL FACTS

An experimental setup was constructed of CMOS IC's with the interconnections shown in Fig. 6.2. LED's were used to indicate the output states of individual neurons. Table 6.2. shows that the solutions were exactly the same as those obtained by the an exhaustive search of the solution space (2^N, N=4 possibilities). The clock frequency was slowed down to about 1 Hz, so that one could visually see the updates taking place. With no clamping, each time the circuit was switched on, the network began with a random set of truth values for the past states of each neuron, and subsequently arrived at one of the stable states. The solution was observed almost instantaneously when the clock was stepped up to 1 Mhz.

Conventional	Solution Space Search	TMS Neural Network Experimental
TTTF	TTTF	TTTF
FFTT	FFTT	FFTT
TFFF	TFFF	

Table 6.2. Comparison of stable solution for four facts from different solution methods.

7.3. KUNDU'S SIX LOGICAL FACTS

Another example using 6 logical facts is shown in Table 6.3 (S. Kundu, personal communication, 1989). This problem has three valid states. The network converged at one of these equilibrium points when presented with different initial conditions. The three equilibrium points are also shown in Table 6.3 and they agree with the results of a conventional TMS solutions.

7.4. DOYLE'S SIX LOGICAL FACTS

An example problem presented by Doyle (1979) was also tried using the TMSNN. The justifications and the correct solutions are given in Table 6.4. Note that Doyle had shown only one of the two solutions given in Table 6.4.

Node	Formula	Justifications	
1	A	{}	{4}
		{}	{3,2}
2	B v C	{1,3}	{}
		{3}	{4}
3	A → B v C	{1,2}	{}
		{}	{1}
		{4}	{}
4	⌐ A	{3}	{2}
		{}	{1}
5	A v C	Sw	{4}
		{6}	{2}
6	⌐ A → B	{1}	{2}
		{1,2}	{4,5}

Stable solutions to 6 facts case
TFFFTT TTTFTF FFTTFF

Table 6.3. Kundu's example using six logical facts with three valid solutions by TMS methods.

7.5. EIGHT QUEENS PROBLEM

A well known problem of constraint satisfaction which can be modified as a TMS problem, is the Eight Queens problem (Cleary, 1987). As many as eight queens are to be placed on an 8x8 checkerboard so that they cannot attack one another vertically, horizontally, or diagonally. Only one queen per row or column comprises a consistent solution. There are a possible (8x8)!/(8x8-8)! = 1.784630 x10^{14} choices for the positions of the queens. The order of the neurons is {1,1}, {1,2}, {1,3} ..., {8,8} numbered from 1 to 64 consecutively. The TMS TLIST and FLIST in Table 6.5 are given for several example positions on the checkerboard matrix. Since the initial conditions of this problem significantly affect the outcome, two different initial conditions solutions are shown in Figs. 3 and 4. Fig. 6.3 contains the solution of eight queens with an initial condition of {6,4}= 1 (*true*). The second example (Fig. 6.4) starts from the initial condition {1,4}= 1 (*true*).

Node	Justifications	
1	{3}	{}
2	{}	{1}
3	{1}	{}
4	{2}	{}
	{3}	{}
5	{}	{}
6	{3,5}	{}
Stable solutions to Doyle's 6 fact case		
FTFTTF TFTTTT		

Table 6.4. Doyle's example of six logical facts and their stable solutions by TMS methods.

8. ITERATION PROCESS OF TMSNN

The TMSNN as defined from the previous sections is a sequential updating network for a particular update order (hierarchy). The system produces an output state based on an input state. The new output is fed back into the system to produce another output state. This process is repeated until the output state becomes equal to the input state. The operation of the TMSNN can therefore be thought of as a discrete iterative process. Robert (1976) further defined this process by visualizing a Boolean iterative network as an iteration graph. The iteration graph of the TMSNN for Table 6.1 will be shown in the subsequent sections.

Fact No.	Fact	TLIST	FLIST
1	11	{}	{ 12,13,14,15,16,17,18, 21,31,41,51,61,71,81, 22,33,44,55,66,77,88 }
...	...	...	...
20 Row, Col # 3,4	34	{}	{ 31,32,33,35,36,37,38, 14,24,44,54,64,74,84, 12,23,45,56,67,78, 16,25,43,52,61 }
...	...	...	...
64	...	...	...

Table 6.5. Eight Queens facts and justifications posed as a TMS problem.

An iterative process can be mathematically described as given in

$$X^{k+1} = F(X^k), \ k = 0,1,... \tag{1}$$

where $X \in \Re^n$ and $F \in \Re^n$ and whose components are given by

$$\begin{aligned}
X_1^{k+1} &= f_1(x_1^k, x_2^k,..., x_n^k) \\
X_2^{k+1} &= f_2(x_1^k, x_2^k,..., x_n^k)
\end{aligned}$$

$$\begin{aligned}
&\cdot \\
&\cdot \\
&\cdot
\end{aligned} \tag{2.}$$

$$X_n^{k+1} = f_n(x_1^k, x_2^k,..., x_n^k)$$

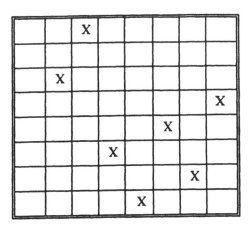

Fig. 6.3. An eight queens solution to the Eight Queens problem posed as a TMS problem.

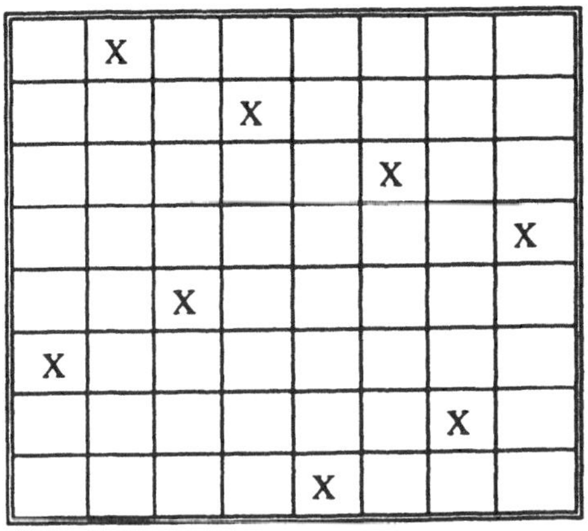

Fig. 6.4. A seven queens solution to the Eight Queens problem posed as a TMS problem.

Since X is an n-dimensional vector, the above operation constitutes a synchronous update mechanism. This is because the output states of all neurons are computed simultaneously based on the current input state. However, in the TMSNN, only one neuron is allowed to compute the output and feed the result to all other neurons. Thus for modelling purposes, an operator is necessary that will map the sequential update to a synchronous update. This mapping will allow the expression of the asynchronous network in the synchronous format (2). One such candidate is the Gauss-Seidel operator.

The iteration graph for the TMS synchronous update mode is shown in Fig. 6.5 for the sequence if the network did not operate asynchronously. The graph consists of segments connecting the input state code for X (column 1 of Table 6.6) and output state code (column 4) as calculated in Table 6.6. Note that there are two graphs that are cyclic. Starting from an initial state 2, 15, or 6 the system cycles between states 6 and 15. Starting from an initial state of 9, 12, 13, or 10, the system cycles between 10 and 13. For all other initial states except, 8 and 14 the system reaches a fixed point namely, 3. The other two fixed points 8 and 14 are isolated fixed points. The fixed points (3, 8, and 14) are defined as stable states and are highlighted in Table 6.6.

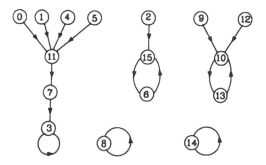

Fig. 6.5. Iteration graph for synchronous model (F(x)) from Table 6.6 sequences.

Fig. 6.6 shows the iteration graph for the equivalent asynchronous update model. Note the absence of cyclic states. For all possible initial states, the system reaches one of the three stable states. The stable states in both synchronous as well as asynchronous cases are identical. This is true for all cases in which stable states exist.

The above iteration graph for the asynchronous model was for an update sequence of {1,2,3,4}. A different update sequence gives the same three stable states namely 3, 8, and 14. However, the iteration graph might be different. For example, in Fig. 6.6 for an update sequence of {1,2,3,4} and an initial state of 1, the network trajectory is 1 → 11 → 3. With an initial state of 9, the network trajectory is 9 → 11 → 3. If the update sequence is changed to {4,3,2,1} the network trajectories for the initial state of 1 is 1 → 3, and for the initial state 9, the network trajectory is 9 → 8.

9. STABILITY OF TMS NETWORK

This stability of neural networks has previously been addressed from the continuous time viewpoint (Tank & Hopfield, 1986). The network formulation above to solve Truth Maintenance

System (Mounfield & Guddanti, 1991) did not, however, match these solutions, because of the asymmetry of our connections leading possibly to cyclic behavior. As stated above, the TMSNN operates on a set of facts and the rules relating these facts. If one or more valid relationships exists between the facts based on the given rules, the TMSNN converges to one of those relationships. The relationships may be expressed in terms of the truth values *true* and *false* or 1 and 0, thus this TMS network is a Boolean network. The implementation of the TMS neural network for N facts operates in the n-dimensional discrete Boolean state space. Stability analysis of such a system was not found in the literature. These next sections describes a method to transform an asynchronous n-dimensional Boolean network to synchronous n-dimensional discrete space. The new description of the system is used to test the Lyapunov stability (LaSalle, 1976; Hahn, 1963) of the network for multiple equilibrium states.

INPUT		Synchronous O/P		Asynchronous O/P	
Code	x	F(x)	Code	G(x)	Code
0	0 0 0 0	1 0 1 1	11	1 0 0 0	8
1	0 0 0 1	1 0 1 1	11	1 0 1 1	11
2	0 0 1 0	1 1 1 1	15	1 1 1 0	14
3	0 0 1 1	0 0 1 1	3	0 0 1 1	3
4	0 1 0 0	1 0 1 1	11	1 0 0 0	8
5	0 1 0 1	1 0 1 1	11	1 0 1 1	11
6	0 1 1 0	1 1 1 1	15	1 1 1 0	14
7	0 1 1 1	0 0 1 1	3	0 0 1 1	3
8	1 0 0 0	1 0 0 0	8	1 0 0 0	8
9	1 0 0 1	1 0 1 0	10	1 0 1 1	11
10	1 0 1 0	1 1 0 1	13	1 1 1 0	14
11	1 0 1 1	0 1 1 1	7	0 0 1 1	3
12	1 1 0 0	1 0 1 0	10	1 0 0 0	8
13	1 1 0 1	1 0 1 0	10	1 0 1 1	11
14	1 1 1 0	1 1 1 0	14	1 1 1 0	14
15	1 1 1 1	0 1 1 0	6	0 0 1 1	3

Table 6.6. Comparison of iteration graph sequences for TMS formulation of CLOUDY SKY/RAIN problem with four facts and synchronous and asynchronous updating.

There are three known equilibrium points for the TMS from Table 6.1. Proof of the existence of these equilibrium points was sought by classical stability theory. Since no stability analysis method was found for such a network, a mathematical transformation was necessary to use Lyapunov's stability criterion.

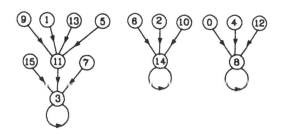

Fig. 6.6. Iteration sequence using asynchronous model (G(x), update sequence {1,2,3,4}) from Table 6.6 sequences.

The TMSNN in Fig. 6.2 operates in a sequential asynchronous update mode. Most mathematical models of neural networks use the synchronous update mechanism for convenience. In actual practice, however, no hardware "asynchronous" system is truly synchronous due to propagation delays. In simulation runs of the TMSNN with synchronous updates, the network went into limit cycles even though consistent solutions existed (see Section 7). In asynchronous update mode, the network was never observed to enter into a limit cycle. The asynchronous update mechanism is therefore presumed to play a significant role in the convergence of the system.

10. SYNCHRONOUS TRANSFORMATION OF AN ASYNCHRONOUS SYSTEM

The mathematical model of a synchronous update mechanism is a difference equation in state space form. The Gauss-Seidel operator (Robert, 1976) maps an asynchronous update mechanism into a synchronous update model as shown in (3). Note that $f_i(x)$ denotes the result of the ith neuron at the ith update and $g_i(x)$ denotes the output of the ith neuron after a synchronous update.

$$g_1(x_1,...,x_n) = f_1(x_1,...,x_n)$$
$$g_2(x_1,...,x_n) = f_2(g_1(x),...,x_n)$$

$$\cdot$$
$$\cdot \qquad\qquad\qquad\qquad\qquad\qquad\qquad (3)$$
$$\cdot$$

$$g_n(x_1,...,x_n) = f_n(g_1(x),g_2(x),...,g_{n-1}(x))$$

where $x=(x_1...x_n)$, $x_i \in [0,1]$, $i=1,2,...,n$.

This "synchronous" model incorporates a *specific* update sequence. The mapping is done in two steps: (1) the Boolean equations for the Boolean value of each neuron is realized in terms of the other neuron values, then (2), the Gauss-Seidel operator is applied to force sequential updating. The mapping for the network in Fig. 6.2 is for the update sequence {1,2,3,4}. Note that in the Boolean logic equations (4) below the OR operator is represented by addition, the AND operator by multiplication, and the summation 1 + 1 is equal to 1.

$$
\begin{aligned}
f_1(x) &= \bar{x}_3 + \bar{x}_4 \\
f_2(x) &= x_1 x_3 + x_3 \bar{x}_4 \\
f_3(x) &= x_2 + \bar{x}_1 + x_4 \\
f_4(x) &= x_3 \bar{x}_2 + \bar{x}_1 .
\end{aligned}
\tag{4}
$$

After applying the Gauss-Seidel operator and simplifying the Boolean expressions, we obtain the following system of equations:

$$
\begin{aligned}
g_1(x) &= \bar{x}_3 + \bar{x}_4 \\
g_2(x) &= x_3 \bar{x}_4 \\
g_3(x) &= x_3 + x_4 \\
g_4(x) &= x_4 .
\end{aligned}
\tag{5}.
$$

The system (5) must be transformed into purely algebraic terms using the following equations in order to apply the Lyapunov stability criteria:

[NOT] $\bar{a} \rightarrow 1- a$ (6).
[OR] $a + b + c \rightarrow a + b + c - ab - bc - ac + abc$
[AND] $ab \rightarrow ab$.

11. APPLICATION OF LYAPUNOV STABILITY CRITERIA

The TMSNN can also be classified as a force-free stationary system. The system (5) with the algebraic equivalents of (6) may be expressed in the vector difference form:

$$
X^{k+1} = \Phi[X^k],
\tag{7}
$$

where Φ is a nonlinear function dependent on the state vector and k, the iteration number. The system (7) generates solutions reaching an equilibrium state. Each equilibrium state satisfies the following:

$$
X_e = \Phi[X_e]
\tag{8}.
$$

The description in equations (7) and (8) is identical to the description of classical systems (Hahn, 1963; LaSalle, 1976), except that the TMSNN has multiple, non-zero equilibrium states. Thus the assumption of uniqueness of the solution is dropped. The system equations (7) must be mapped so as to translate the equilibrium point(s) to zero. Using Lindorff (1965) or Michel, Farrell, and Sun (1989) the translation of the equilibrium from (7) to the transformed coordinate Y is:

$$Y = X - X_e \qquad (9a)$$
$$X = Y + X_e \qquad (9b)$$

so that

$$X^k = Y^k + X_e \qquad (9c)$$

and

$$X^{k+1} = Y^{k+1} + X_e. \qquad (9d)$$

Substituting (9) into (7) forms the new system equation:

$$Y^{k+1} = \Phi[Y^k + X_e] - X_e \qquad (10),$$

which has an equilibrium at $Y_e = 0$.

12. TEST OF EQUILIBRIUM POINTS

The algebraic system equation for the network shown in Fig. 6.2 in algebraic form or vector difference form (7) is as follows:

$$
\begin{aligned}
x_1^{k+1} &= 1 - x_3^k x_4^k \\
x_2^{k+1} &= x_3^k (1 - x_4^k) \\
x_3^{k+1} &= x_3^k + x_4^k (1 - x_3^k) \\
x_4^{k+1} &= x_4^k
\end{aligned}
\qquad (11)
$$

or compactly $X^{k+1} = \Phi(X^k)$. The equilibrium points are at $X_{e1} = [0\ 0\ 1\ 1]^T$, $X_{e2} = [1\ 0\ 0\ 0]^T$, and $X_{e3} = [1\ 1\ 1\ 0]^T$.

The system in equation (11) is defined via total valued variables x_j, $j=1,...,4$. For the stability analysis of an equilibrium state X_{ek}, $k \in \{1,2,3\}$, it is more convenient to translate the origin to that equilibrium state by using (9). The new network description (12) is expressed in terms of the state deviation variables $y_j = x_j - x_{ej}$, $j=1,...,4$, which are the entries of the state deviation vector Y (9a). The following equations result from (9b) and (11) after simple calculations:

$$
\begin{aligned}
y_1^{k+1} &= 1 - x_{e1} - (y_3^k + x_{e3})(y_4^k + x_{e4}) \\
y_2^{k+1} &= -x_{e2} + (y_3^k + x_{e3})(1 - y_4^k - x_{e4}) \\
y_3^{k+1} &= y_3^k + (y_4^k + x_{e4})(1 - y_3^k - x_{e3}) \\
y_4^{k+1} &= y_4^k
\end{aligned}
\tag{12a}.
$$

For a specific equilibrium state the form of (12a) is more compact as shown in what follows:

$$
\underline{X}_{e1} = [0\ 0\ 1\ 1]^T:
$$
$$
\begin{aligned}
y_1^{k+1} &= -y_3^k - y_4^k - y_3^k y_4^k \\
y_2^{k+1} &= -y_4^k - y_3^k y_4^k \\
y_3^{k+1} &= -y_3^k y_4^k \\
y_4^{k+1} &= y_4^k
\end{aligned}
$$

$$
\underline{X}_{e2} = [1\ 0\ 0\ 0]^T:
$$
$$
\begin{aligned}
y_1^{k+1} &= -y_3^k y_4^k, \\
y_2^{k+1} &= y_3^k - y_3^k y_4^k, \\
y_3^{k+1} &= y_3^k + y_4^k - y_3^k y_4^k, \\
y_4^{k+1} &= y_4^k.
\end{aligned}
$$

$$
\underline{X}_{e3} = [1\ 1\ 1\ 0]^T:
$$
$$
\begin{aligned}
y_1^{k+1} &= -y_4^k - y_3^k y_4^k, \\
y_2^{k+1} &= y_3^k + y_4^k - y_3^k y_4^k, \\
y_3^{k+1} &= -y_3^k - y_3^k y_4^k, \\
y_4^{k+1} &= y_4^k.
\end{aligned}
$$

The preceding equations show that $Y=0$ is the unique equilibrium state of (12a) for X_{ek}, $\forall k=1,2,3$. Let h_j, $j=1,...,4$, be defined by the next equations formed from the right-hand side of (12a):

$$
\begin{aligned}
h_1(Y) &= 1 - x_{e1} - (y_3 + x_{e3})(y_4 + x_{e4}) \\
h_2(Y) &= -x_{e2} + (y_3 + x_{e3})(1 - y_4 - x_{e4}) \\
h_3(Y) &= y_3 + (y_4 + x_{e4})(1 - y_3 - x_{e3}), \\
h_4(Y) &= y_4
\end{aligned}
\tag{12b}.
$$

Now, the equations (12b) can be set in the scalar form

$$
y_j^{k+1} = h_j(Y^k), \quad j=1,...,4
\tag{13},
$$

or in the vector form

$$
Y^{k+1} = h(Y^k)
\tag{14}
$$

where $h = [h_1\ h_2\ h_3\ h_4]^T$.

We may generalize (14) by accepting $Y=[y_1 \; y_2 ... y_n]^T$ and $h=[h_1 \; h_2 ... h_n]^T$, which will be assumed in the subsequent analysis. Notice that $Y=0$ is considered as the unique equilibrium state of (14), that is $h(Y)=0$ holds if and only if $Y=0$.

Every entry y_j is a trinary valued variable, $y_j \in \{-1, 0, 1\}$, $j=1,2,...,n$. Hence, the state space of (14) is a finite set $\mathcal{Y}$:

$$Y=\{\mathcal{Y}: \; Y=[y_1 \; y_2 ... y_n]^T, \; y_j \in \{-1, 0, 1\}, \; j=1,2,...,n\} \tag{15}.$$

The state space $\mathcal{Y}$ of (14) has 3^n different states. Evidently, $\mathcal{Y} \subset \mathfrak{R}^n$.

13. STABILITY CRITERION

In what follows we use the classical definition and properties of stability. In fact, the discrete-valued discontinuous nature of y_j's, h_j's, and hence, of the system described by equation (14), requires a subtle stability analysis. It will be carried out via the Lyapunov method that will be broadened to the stability analysis of (14) as follows. We shall use the notion of a radially increasing function $v: \mathfrak{R}^n \rightarrow \mathfrak{R}$ by referring to Grujić, Martynyuk, and Ribbens-Pavella (1987).

<u>Definition 1.</u> A function $v: \mathfrak{R}^n \rightarrow \mathfrak{R}$ is *radially increasing (on $\mathfrak{R}^n$)* if and only if $v(\lambda_1 Y) < v(\lambda_2 Y)$, $\forall \lambda_j \in]0,+\infty[$, $j=1,2$, $\lambda_1 < \lambda_2$, $\forall (Y \neq 0) \in \mathfrak{R}^n$. If $v(\lambda_1 Y)$ is the magnitude (length) of the n-dimensional vector Y, then a scalar multiple of the individual components of Y by λ_2, where $\lambda_2 > \lambda_1$, would produce a larger magnitude (length) of this new vector (λY). In fact the function $v(\lambda Y)$ is increasing for every $\lambda_2 > \lambda_1$, since this particular function example produces a magnitude of a vector without regard of the vector direction. If a function has this property, it is said to be radially increasing. Several more examples are shown below.

<u>Example 1.</u> Let $v_1(Y)= 1^T|Y|$, $1=[1...1]^T \in \mathfrak{R}^n$ and $|Y|=[|y_1| \; |y_2|...|y_n|]^T$. Then, $v_1(\lambda_j Y)= \lambda_j 1^T|Y|= \lambda_j v_1(Y)$, $j=1,2$. Since $\lambda_j \in]0,+\infty[$, $j=1,2$ and $v_1(Y)>0$, $\forall (Y \neq 0) \in \mathfrak{R}^n$, then $v_1(\lambda_1 Y) < v_1(\lambda_2 Y)$, $\lambda_1 < \lambda_2$, $\forall (Y \neq 0) \in \mathfrak{R}^n$. Hence, v_1 is radially increasing.

<u>Example 2.</u> Let $v_2(Y)= Y^T H Y$ with positive definite symmetric matrix $H \in \mathfrak{R}^{n \times n}$. Now, $v_2(\lambda_j Y)= \lambda_j^2 Y^T H Y= \lambda_j^2 v_2(Y)$, $j=1,2$. Since $v_2(Y)> 0$, $\forall (Y \neq 0) \in \mathfrak{R}^n$ then for $\lambda_j \in]0,+\infty[$, $j=1,2$, $v_2(\lambda_1 Y) < v_2(\lambda_2 Y)$, $\lambda_1 < \lambda_2$, $\forall (Y \neq 0) \in \mathfrak{R}^n$. The function v_2 is also radially increasing.

Notice that both v_1 and v_2 as defined are positive definite in the whole, that is

(i) $v_j(Y) \in C(\mathfrak{R}^n)$, $j=1,2$,
(ii) $v_j(Y)= 0$ if and only if $Y=0$, $j=1,2$,
(iii) $v_j(Y)> 0$, $\forall (Y \neq 0) \in \mathfrak{R}^n$, $j=1,2$.

In the sequel we shall use the first forward difference $\Delta v(Y)$ of the function v along a motion of the system (14), which is defined by:

$$\Delta v(Y)= v[h(Y)] - v(Y) \tag{16}.$$

Let v_ζ be the largest connected neighborhood of $Y=0$ on which $v(Y)<\zeta$, that is, for a radially increasing function v, $v(Y)<\zeta$ if and only if $Y\in v_\zeta$. The boundary and closure of v_ζ are denoted by ∂v_ζ and $\bar{v}_\zeta$, respectively. If a function v is radially increasing then

$$\partial v_\zeta=\{Y:v(Y)=\zeta\} \text{ and } \bar{v}_\zeta=\{Y:v(Y)\leq\zeta\}.$$

The radially increasing property of v is important for the stability analysis of (14) because of the system's digital-valued discontinuous nature. Let $|.|$ be the Euclidean norm, $\bar{\beta}_\zeta = \{Y:|Y|\leq\zeta\}$ and $[\bar{\beta}_\zeta\cap\mathcal{Y}]\backslash\{0\}= \{Y:(Y\in\bar{\beta}_\zeta), (Y\in\mathcal{Y}) \text{ and } Y\neq0\}$.

Theorem 1. In order for $Y=0$ of the digital discrete-time system (14) to be stable it is sufficient that there exists a function $v:\mathfrak{R}^n\to\mathfrak{R}$ and a positive number ζ such that

(i) v is radially increasing in the whole and positive definite in the whole,

(ii)   if $\zeta=\min(|Y|:Y\in\partial v_\zeta)$ then $[\bar{\beta}_\zeta\cap\mathcal{Y}]\backslash\{0\}$ is non-empty,

(iii) $\Delta v(Y)\leq0, \forall Y\in v_\zeta$.

Proof. Let $\varepsilon\in[0,+\infty]$ be arbitrary and $\xi=\min \{v(Y):|Y|=\varepsilon\}$. Let $\tau=\min(\zeta,\xi)$ and $\delta(\varepsilon)=\max \{|Y|:Y\in\partial v\tau\}$. Hence, $\bar{\beta}_{\delta(\varepsilon)}\neq\bar{v}_\tau$ so that $Y\in\bar{\beta}_{\delta(\varepsilon)}$ implies $\Delta v(Y)\leq0$, or, $v[h(Y)]\leq v(Y)$. This result, positive definiteness in the whole and radially increasing in the whole of v imply $Y^1=h(Y)\in\bar{v}_\tau$, which together with $\bar{v}_\tau\subseteq\bar{\beta}_\varepsilon$ yield $Y^1\in\bar{\beta}_\varepsilon$. Taking now Y^1 for a new Y and repeating the procedure we prove $Y^k\in\bar{\beta}_\varepsilon$, $\forall k=1,2,...$, as soon as $Y^0\in\bar{\beta}_{\delta(\varepsilon)}$, $\forall\varepsilon\in]0,+\infty[$, which proves stability of $Y=0$ of (14).

This proof shows that $\bar{v}_\zeta$ is an estimate of the stability domain of $Y=0$ (Grujić, Martynyuk, & Ribbens-Pavella, 1987).

Theorem 2. In order for $Y=0$ of the digital discrete-time system (14) to be asymptotically stable it is sufficient that there exists a function $v:\mathfrak{R}^n\to\mathfrak{R}$ and a positive number ζ such that

(i) v is radially increasing in the whole and positive definite in the whole,

(ii)   if $\zeta=\min(|Y|:Y\in\partial v_\zeta)$ then $[\bar{\beta}_\zeta\cap\mathcal{Y}]\backslash\{0\}$ is non-empty,

(iii) $\Delta v(Y)<0, \forall(Y\neq0)\in\partial v_\zeta$.

Proof. Under the conditions of Theorem 2 all the requirements of Theorem 1 are satisfied. Hence, the equilibrium $Y=0$ of the system (14) is stable. This implies pre-compactness of the system motions relative to $\bar{v}_\zeta$. Now, the conditions (i) and (iii) imply $\lim(Y^k:k\to+\infty)=0$ as soon as $Y^0 \in \bar{v}_\zeta$, due to the Invariance Principle of LaSalle (1976). Hence, Y=0 is both attractive and asymptotically stable.

This proof verifies that $\bar{v}_\zeta$ is an estimate of both the attraction domain and asymptotic stability domain of the equilibrium Y=0 of (14) (Grujić, Martynyuk, & Ribbens-Pavella, 1987). The significance of meeting the requirements of Theorem 2 is that a systems possessing theoo qualities will return to the equilibrium condition Y=0 from anywhere within the stability domain $\bar{v}_\zeta$. It is very desirable for the stability domain to include all values of the function v that can be reached. The primary difference between Theorems 1 and 2 is that Theorem 1 allows limit cycles since $\Delta v(Y)=0$ is a possibility from some $Y \neq 0$. If this derivative were to become zero when the system was not identically zero, there would be no motion further towards the origin yet the system would be still "in motion" perhaps oscillating back and forth between two or more states with the same functional value of $v(Y)$.

14. STABILITY ANALYSIS

Using the transformed TMSNN system (14) for X_{e1} and with positive definite matrix H as follows:[1]

$$H = \begin{bmatrix} 10 & -2 & 0 & 0 \\ -2 & 20 & -15 & 20 \\ 0 & -15 & 30 & -20 \\ 0 & 20 & -20 & 40 \end{bmatrix} \tag{17},$$

$v_2(Y) = Y^T HY$ and $\Delta v_2(Y)$ (16) were evaluated over the entire space of $Y \in \mathcal{Y}$. These calculations are shown over several tables, Table 6.7 through Table 6.12. The entries in each table are arranged so that the value of $v_2(Y)$ is decreasing for each value of $|Y|^2 = k$, $k \in \{0, 1, 2, 3, 4\}$. The largest ζ in Table 6.7 is $\zeta = 40$, for the greatest value of $v_2(Y)$, that is where $\zeta = \max[v(Y):|Y|=1, Y \in \mathcal{Y}]$. The first-forward difference of the function $v_2(Y)$ was then evaluated using (16) and (17) for the same X_{e1}, these values are also shown in Tables 7-12. Note that $\Delta v_2(Y)<0$, for $|Y|=1$, $Y \in \mathcal{Y}$. The next radius of increasing $v(Y)$, for $|Y|=\sqrt{2}$, $Y \in \mathcal{Y}$ is shown in Table 6.8 and Table 6.9. Note that $\Delta v_2(Y)>0$ for several $Y \in \mathcal{Y}$. Since the conditions on $\Delta v_2(Y)<0$, or $\Delta v_2(Y) \leq 0$ did not hold, the following can be said for this system.

---

[1] The selection of a suitable positive definite matrix for nonlinear systems which fulfills our requirements of Theorems 1 and 2 is and has been the subject of much research in the last one hundred or so years. Unfortunately, there are few methods that work better that an educated guess along with trial and error. Not finding a suitable H, however, does not prove stability, that is, if once a system is shown to be stable it is stable, yet most H's produce results that do not meet Theorem 1 or Theorem 2's requirements.

$Y \in \mathcal{Y}$	$\|Y\|^2$	$v_2(Y)$	$\Delta v_2(Y)$
[0 0 0 0]	0	0	0
[0 0 0 1]	1	40	-14
[0 0 0 -1]	1	40	-14
[0 0 1 0]	.	30	-20
[0 0 -1 0]	.	30	-20
[0 1 0 0]	.	20	-20
[0 -1 0 0]	.	20	-20
[1 0 0 0]	.	10	-10
[-1 0 0 0]	1	10	-10

Table 6.7. Lyapunov function evaluation and first-forward difference for $v_2(Y)$, $|Y|^2 = 0,1$.

Let us define the set

$$E_{10} = \{Y : v_2(Y) \le 10\} = \{[1 \ 0]^T, [-1 \ 0]^T\} \tag{18}.$$

For every $Y \in E_{10}$ it follows that $\Delta v_2(Y) < 0$ for $Y \not\equiv 0$ so that the motion of every $Y \in E_{10}$ will converge to the origin $Y = 0$. However, for some other neighborhood

$$E_{20} = \{Y : v_2(Y) \le 20\} \tag{19}$$

and for every $Y \in E_{20}$ it *does not* follow that $\Delta v_2(Y) \le 0$ so that the motion of every $Y \in E_{20}$ will *not* converge to the origin $Y = 0$. In fact, such E_{20} is *not* an estimate of the attraction or asymptotic stability domain. Moreover, $\bar{v}_\zeta = \{Y : v_2(Y) \le \zeta\} = \{[1 \ 0]^T, [0]^T, [-1 \ 0]^T\}$ does not estimate the domain of asymptotic stability or the domain of stability because for $\zeta = \min\{|v| : Y \in \delta v_{\zeta=10}\}$ we get that $[\bar{\beta}_\zeta \cap \mathcal{Y}]\setminus\{0\} = \emptyset$ where $\emptyset$ is the empty set. The condition (ii) of Theorem 1 and of Theorem 2 is not satisfied. Note that since $h_4(Y) = y_4$ in (12b), there is no dynamic part to change in y_4, therefore y_4 remains constant so that for any $Y = \{Y : Y \in \mathcal{Y}, y_4 = \pm 1\}$ the corresponding motion cannot converge to the origin!

$Y \in \mathcal{Y}$	$\|Y\|^2$	$v_2(Y)$	$\Delta v_2(Y)$
[0 0 1 -1]	2	110	-58
[0 0 -1 1]	2	110	-70
[0 1 0 1]	.	100	-74
[0 -1 0 -1]	.	100	-74
[0 1 -1 0]	.	80	-70
[0 -1 1 0]	.	80	-70
[1 0 0 1]	.	50	-24
[-1 0 0 -1]	.	50	-24
[1 0 0 -1]	.	50	-24
[-1 0 0 1]	.	50	-24
[1 0 1 0]	.	40	-30
[-1 0 -1 0]	2	40	-30

Table 6.8. Lyapunov function evaluation and first-forward difference for $v_2(Y)$, $|Y|^2 = 2$, part 1 of 2.

In Table 6.12, the largest value for $v_2(Y)$, $Y \in \mathcal{Y}$, is $\zeta=214$ and $\Delta v_2(Y)=-174<0$. Thus, $\bar{v}_{\zeta=214}$ is positively invariant with respect to the system motion. Further, $Y^0 \in \bar{v}_{\zeta=214}$ implies $Y(k;Y^0) \in \bar{v}_{\zeta=214}$, $\forall k=0,1,2,3,...$, that is, belong to the state forever. Note that for $\zeta=206$, $\bar{v}_{\zeta=206}$, and from Table 6.10 for $\zeta=200$, $\bar{v}_{\zeta=200}$, are also positively invariant. The largest value for ζ where $\Delta v_2(Y) \geq 0$ is in Table 6.12 for $\zeta=74$, $\Delta v_2(Y)=+42$, hence this set is *not* positively invariant and motions in this set will move away from this set. The domain of the set $\bar{v}_{\zeta=80}=\{Y:v_2(Y)\geq\zeta=80\}$ bounds motion which means that such a set is positively invariant. The two remaining equilibrium sets X_{e2} and X_{e3} could be evaluated by these methods to determine their own particular positively invariant set for which the motion would converge to the origin.

$Y \in \mathcal{Y}$	$\|Y\|^2$	$v_2(Y)$	$\Delta v_2(Y)$
[1 0 -1 0]	2	40	-30
[-1 0 1 0]	2	40	-30
[1 -1 0 0]	.	31	-34
[-1 1 0 0]	.	31	-34
[0 0 1 1]	.	30	+86
[0 0 -1 -1]	.	30	+10
[1 1 0 0]	.	26	-26
[-1 -1 0 0]	.	26	-26
[0 1 1 0]	.	20	-10
[0 -1 -1 0]	.	20	-10
[0 1 0 -1]	.	20	+6
[0 -1 0 -1]	2	20	+6

Table 6.9. Lyapunov function evaluation and first-forward difference for $v_2(Y)$, $|Y|^2 = 2$, part 2 of 2.

15. CONCLUSION

The methods of synchronous transformation, origin shifting, and evaluation of a Lyapunov function over a minimal neighborhood comprise a general methodology to evaluate the stability of equilibrium points for any asynchronous discrete Boolean system of equations. The question of stability of the equilibrium points is of particular importance for Truth Maintenance Systems and expert systems in order to avoid unexpected results. A Lyapunov function and its first-forward difference for a particular TMSNN were investigated to find the domain of asymptotic stability. A set was found for which the motions in that set would converge to the origin. Moreover, a positively invariant set of the equilibrium was discovered and determined in this work.

$Y \in \mathcal{Y}$	$\|Y\|^2$	$v_2(Y)$	$\Delta v_2(Y)$
[0 1 -1 1]	3	200	160
[0 -1 1 -1]	3	200	-148
[1 0 1 -1]	.	120	-68
[1 0 -1 1]	.	120	-80
[-1 0 -1 1]	.	120	-80
[-1 0 1 -1]	.	120	-68
[1 -1 0 -1]	.	114	-88
[-1 1 0 1]	.	114	-88
[1 1 0 1]	.	106	-80
[-1 -1 0 -1]	.	106	-80
[1 -1 1 0]	.	94	-84
[-1 1 -1 0]	.	94	-84
[1 1 -1 0]	.	86	-76
[-1 -1 1 0]	.	86	-76
[0 1 1 -1]	.	60	-8
[0 -1 -1 1]	3	60	-20

Table 6.10. Lyapunov function evaluation and first-forward difference for $v_2(Y)$, $|Y|^2 = 3$, part 1 of 2.

REFERENCES

Caudill, M. (1987). Neural networks PRIMER Part I. *AI EXPERT*, December, 46-51.
Caudill, M. (1988a). Neural networks PRIMER Part II. *AI EXPERT*, February, 55-61.
Caudill, M. (1988b). Neural networks PRIMER Part III. *AI EXPERT*, June, 53-59.
Cleary, J. G. (1987). A simple VLSI connectionist architecture. *Proceedings of the First International Conference on Neural Networks*, Vol III, pp. 419-426. San Diego IEEE/ICNN.

$Y \in \mathcal{Y}$	$\|Y\|^2$	$v_2(Y)$	$\Delta v_2(Y)$
[0 1 1 1]	3	60	+56
[0 -1 -1 -1]	3	60	-20
[1 0 1 1]	.	40	+76
[-1 0 -1 -1]	.	40	0
[1 0 -1 -1]	.	40	0
[-1 0 1 1]	.	40	+76
[0 1 -1 -1]	.	40	0
[0 -1 1 1]	.	40	+76
[1 -1 -1 0]	.	34	-24
[-1 1 1 0]	.	34	-24
[1 -1 0 1]	.	34	-8
[-1 1 0 -1]	.	34	-8
[1 1 1 0]	.	26	-16
[-1 -1 -1 0]	.	26	-16
[1 1 0 -1]	.	26	0
[-1 -1 0 1]	3	26	0

Table 6.11. Lyapunov function evaluation and first-forward difference for $v_2(Y)$, $|Y|^2 = 3$, part 2 of 2.

CMOS databook (1981). Santa Clara, CA: National Semiconductor Corporation.

Doyle, J. (1979). A truth maintenance system. *Artificial Intelligence* **12**, 231-272.

Eichmann, G., & Caulfield, J. H. (1985). Optical learning (inference) machines. *Applied Optics* **24**, 2051-2054.

Green, P. E., & Michalson, W. R. (1987). Real time evidential reasoning and network based processing. *Proceedings of the First International Conference on Neural Networks* (Vol. II, pp. 359-365.) San Diego IEEE/ICNN.

$Y \in \mathcal{Y}$	$\|Y\|^2$	$v_2(Y)$	$\Delta v_2(Y)$
[-1 1 -1 1]	4	214	-174
[-1 -1 1 -1]	4	206	-154
[1 1 -1 1]	.	206	-166
[-1 -1 1 -1]	.	206	-154
[1 -1 -1 1]	.	74	-34
[-1 1 1 -1]	.	74	-22
[1 -1 -1 -1]	.	74	-34
[-1 1 1 1]	.	74	+42
[1 1 1 1]	.	66	+50
[-1 -1 -1 -1]	.	66	-26
[1 1 1 -1]	.	66	-14
[-1 -1 -1 -1]	.	66	-26
[1 -1 1 1]	.	54	+62
[-1 1 -1 -1]	.	54	-14
[1 1 -1 -1]	.	46	-6
[-1 -1 1 1]	4	46	+70

Table 6.12. Lyapunov function evaluation and first-forward difference for $v_2(Y)$, $|Y|^2 = 4$.

Grujić, L. T., Martynyuk, A. A., & Ribbens-Pavella, M. (1987). *Large-Scale Systems Stability Under Structural and Singular Perturbations*. Berlin: Springer Verlag.

Guddanti, S., & Mounfield, W. P. (1993). Neural Network Logic System. U.S. Patent No. 5,179,631 (January 12, 1993 issue date).

Guddanti, S., Mounfield, W. P., & Grujić, L. T. (1991). Stability of an asynchronous TMS neural network. *Proceedings of the 13th IMACS World Congress on Computational Mathematics* July 22-26, Trinity College, Dublin, Ireland, 3, 1258-1259.

Hahn, W. (1963). *Theory and Application of Liapunov's Direct Method*. Englewood Cliffs, NJ: Prentice-Hall.

Hopfield, J. J., & Tank, D. W. (1986). Computing with neural circuits: A model. *Science* **233**, 625-632.

Kemke, C. (1987). Modelling neural networks by means of networks of finite automata. *Proceedings of the First International Conference on Neural Networks* (Vol. III, pp. 23-29.) San Diego: IEEE/ICNN.

Kirkpatrick, J., Gelatt, C. D., Jr., & Vecchi, M. P. (1982). Optimization by simulated annealing. *Science* **220**, 671-680.

LaSalle, J. P. (1976). *The Stability of Dynamical Systems*. Philadelphia: Society for Industrial and Applied Mathematics.

Lindorff, D. P. (1965). *Theory of Sampled Data Systems*. New York: John Wiley & Sons.

Martland, D. (1987). Behavior of autonomous (synchronous) Boolean networks. *International Conference on Neural Networks* (Vol. II, pp. 243-250.) San Diego: IEEE/ICNN.

McAulay, A. D. (1987). Real time optical expert system. *Applied Optics* **26**, 1927-1933.

McNaughton, R., & Papert, S. (1971). *Counter-Free Automata*. Cambridge, MA: MIT Press.

Michel, A. N., Farrell, J. A., & Sun, S. F. (1989). Synthesis techniques for discrete time neural network models. *Proceedings of the 28th Conference on Decision and Control*, Tampa, Florida, December, pp. 773-778.

Mounfield, W. P., & Guddanti, S. (1991). A truth maintenance system neural network. *ASME Journal of Dynamic Systems Measurements & Control* **113**, 187-191.

Robert, F. (1976). *Discrete Iterations —A Metric Study*. Berlin: Springer-Verlag.

Tank, D. W., & Hopfield, J. J. (1986). Simple "neural" optimization networks: An A/D converter, signal decision circuit, and a linear programming circuit. *IEEE Transactions on Circuits and Systems* **CAS-33**, 533-541.

Venkatasubramanian, V. (1985). Inexact reasoning in expert systems: A stochastic parallel network approach. *IEEE Computer Society Conference on AI Applications* (Part I, Vol. 1, pp. 13-15).

Vidal, J. J., Pemberton, J. C., & Goodwin, M. (1987). Implementing neural nets with programmable logic. *International Conference on Neural Networks* (Vol. III, pp. 539-545.) San Diego: IEEE/ICNN.

Warde, C., & Kottas, J. (1986). Hybrid optical inference machines: architectural considerations. *Applied Optics* **25**, 940-994.

Winston, P. H. (1984). *Artificial Intelligence* (2nd ed.). Reading, MA: Addison-Wesley.

7

Propositional Logic, Nonmonotonic Reasoning and Symmetric Networks — On Bridging the Gap Between Symbolic and Connectionist Knowledge Representation

Gadi Pinkas
Washington University, St. Louis

This chapter discusses the relationships between propositional logic and symmetric connectionist networks. The task is two-fold: 1) to develop a framework for reasoning with inconsistency that can be implemented on connectionist networks; 2) to develop a high-level language that may be used as an intermediate level of abstraction between symbolic description and low-level connectionist implementation. The article shows how to represent arbitrary logic formulas using symmetric networks and how logic can be used as a specification language for such networks. Propositional calculus is extended by augmenting beliefs with real positive penalties. The extended logic is capable of representing nonmonotonic knowledge as well as of coping with inconsistency in the knowledge base. Every formula in the extended logic can be compiled into a network, and every network can be described by a formula of the logic. Efficient algorithms are given to translate between the two forms of knowledge representation.

1. INTRODUCTION

For many years now, philosophers and mathematicians have tried to formalize human thought using a universal language. This quest can be tracked back to the Greek philosophers and later to Herbrand, Skolem, and Gödel who developed predicate calculus along these lines. Later, after computing machines started to appear and resolution was discovered (Robinson, 1965), we started to witness a plethora of emerging logicist languages and formal reasoning processes. Indeed, since the early 1970s logicist knowledge representation has dominated Artificial Intelligence (AI) and has become a central issue.

Only since the early 1980s have AI researchers realized that the classical logic systems developed by mathematicians are far from being adequate for modeling of human reasoning. Human beings are astoundingly good at inferring useful and often reliable information from knowledge that seems mostly irrelevant, sometimes erroneous and self-contradictory. AI has realized that the analysis of such reasoning mechanisms is a major task. As a result, many nonmonotonic systems have been proposed as formal models for this kind of reasoning. Some well known examples are circumscription (McCarthy, 1980) and default logic (Reiter, 1980).

An almost standard approach in AI going back to McCarthy (1968), is to represent an agent's knowledge as a collection of formulas, which can be viewed as a knowledge base. An agent is then said to know a fact, if it is provable from the formulas in the knowledge base. The majority of existing formal AI reasoning systems are based on this logicist view; that is, the use of logic formulas and a formal proof theory in order to reason about facts or beliefs not mentioned explicitly.

The most obvious advantage of the logicist approach is that it allows a compact representation, and enables us to deduce facts that were not explicitly mentioned. Other advantages are for example the declarative form of logic and its susceptibility to rigorous analysis. Indeed, even when we use a different (and often more efficient) knowledge representation paradigm it is always beneficial to formally describe the representation's power in logic. Such formal description enables us to perform a rigorous analysis, and compare the representation we use to other approaches.

While scientists in traditional, symbolic AI were concentrating on development of powerful knowledge representation systems, connectionists were concentrating on powerful learning and adaptation mechanisms. Connectionism was criticized for lacking mechanisms like compositionality and systematicity, which are essential for high level cognitive tasks and are easy for symbolic approaches (Fodor & Pylyshyn, 1988). It is clear that we would like to have systems that have sufficient expressive power, that perform quickly (the brain suggests massive parallelism), and that are capable of learning and adjusting. As Hinton (1990) pointed out, "the ultimate goal for both scientific approaches is to find efficient learning procedures for representationally powerful systems."

Appreciating the benefits of both the connectionist paradigm and the logicist approach, this article tries to build the foundations for a bridge across the two. Dealing with foundations, it concentrates on a logical formalism that is simple and well understood — propositional logic. Then, the article extends propositional calculus, so that more complex forms of knowledge can be represented. In this chapter, I consider only propositional knowledge; however, the approach can be extended to predicate calculus with nonmonotonic abilities (Pinkas, 1991b). The task is two-fold: we would like to use networks to represent symbolic knowledge (logic), and we would like to describe the knowledge encapsulated in a network using a logic language.

One big difference between connectionist networks and symbolic knowledge representations is that symbolic systems need an interpreter to process the information expressed in the representation, and to reason with it. Connectionist networks have no such interpreter. The interpreter and the control mechanism should be included in the knowledge that is being represented. We strive therefore to find a connectionist representation that is capable of representing the information, as well as the procedural knowledge that is needed for reasoning and control.

Among the different connectionist models, I choose to consider those with symmetric matrix of weights. This family of models includes Hopfield networks (Hopfield, 1982, 1984), Boltzmann machines (Hinton & Sejnowski, 1986), harmony theory (Smolensky, 1986), mean field theory (Hinton, 1989), and other variations. The reasons for using *symmetric* connectionist networks (SCNs) are the following:

1. Symmetric networks can be characterized by energy functions. These functions make it easier to specify the networks' behavior (Feldman, 1985).
2. Symmetric networks have been used successfully to express and solve (approximate) "hard" problems (Hopfield & Tank, 1985).
3. Symmetric networks are capable of representing a large set of asymmetric networks (Pinkas, 1991b);[1] therefore they are quite powerful and we will not lose expressive power if we restrict ourselves to the symmetric case.[2]

Ideally, we would like a wide range of logical formalisms to be representable in connectionist networks; however, we will be satisfied to represent an incomplete but general class of logicist frameworks. Also, it would be beneficial if we had a formal, declarative language that is capable of describing the knowledge encapsulated in a network; such high-level, declarative language may then be used for specification and "programming" of connectionist networks.

My purpose is to show that 1) propositional logic can be represented efficiently in SCNs; 2) knowledge that is encapsulated in any SCN can be described by an extended version of propositional logic; 3) nonmonotonic knowledge can be captured naturally in SCNs and finally, 4) networks can capture both the information embedded in the logic formulas as well as the procedural knowledge used for reasoning and control (the interpreter).

---

[1] In fact, every non-oscillating network of binary threshold units is representable in SCNs.

[2] Sometimes an asymmetric form of a symmetric network will perform better; therefore, for efficiency, we may consider not to restrict ourselves to the symmetric case.

The chapter is organized as follows:[3] Section 2 introduces SCNs and the energy minimization paradigm. Section 3 shows that propositional logic can be represented in SCNs and that every SCN can be described by a propositional formula. Section 4 presents an extended version of propositional calculus (penalty logic). The extended calculus is useful for representation of nonmonotonic knowledge (like defaults and exceptions) as well as for coping with inconsistency (Rescher & Manor, 1970)[4] in the knowledge base. Section 5 shows an equivalence between symmetric networks and penalty logic, which enables one to efficiently compile a formula into a network and vice versa. Section 6 discusses related work and Section 7 provides conclusions. Formal proofs appear in Pinkas (1990a) and Pinkas (1992a).

2. THE ENERGY PARADIGM

Finding minima for quadratic functions is the essence of symmetric connectionist models used for parallel constraint satisfaction (Hinton & Sejnowski, 1986; Hopfield, 1982; Smolensky, 1986). These models are characterized by a recurrent network architecture, a symmetric matrix of weights (with zero diagonal) and a quadratic energy function that should be minimized. Each unit asynchronously computes the gradient of the function and adjusts its activation value, so that energy decreases gradually. The network eventually reaches equilibrium, settling on either a local or a global minimum. Hopfield (1982) demonstrated that certain complex optimization problems can be stated as constraints that are expressed in quadratic energy functions and approximated using these kinds of networks.

There is a direct mapping between these networks and the quadratic energy functions they minimize. Every quadratic energy function can be translated into a corresponding network and vice versa. Weighted arcs (i.e., pairwise connections) in the network correspond to weighted terms of two variables in the energy function (with opposite sign). Thresholds of units in the network correspond to single-variable terms in the function. Most of the time I do not distinguish between the function and the network that minimizes it. An example of a network and its energy function is given in Fig. 7.1.

2.1. HIGH-ORDER ENERGY FUNCTIONS

To represent arbitrary logic formulas, a network needs the power of either high-order connections or hidden units. This section defines high-order networks, and shows how to convert them into standard (pair-wise) networks by introducing new hidden units.

---

[3] Some of the material in this chapter appears in a shorter form in Pinkas (1990b) and Pinkas (1991a). Some of the figures and the examples are taken from Pinkas (1990a) and Pinkas (1992).

[4] Inconsistency may be a result of noisy, unreliable (possibly redundant) sources of knowledge.

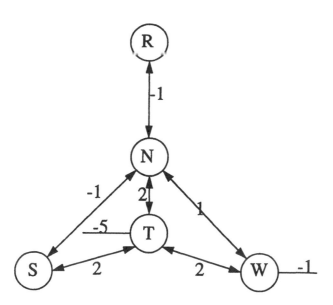

Fig. 7.1. A symmetric network that represents the function E= – 2NT – 2ST – 2WT + 5T + NS + RN – WN + W, describing the Well Formed Formula: (N∧S→W) ∧ (R→(¬N)) ∧ (N ∨ (¬ W)) as will be discussed in the next section. T is a hidden unit.

High-order connectionist networks have sigma-pi units (Rumelhart, Hinton, & McClelland, 1986) with multiplicative connections. It is a common intuition that high-order networks can better express high-order problems (Sejnowski, 1986), and can compute functions that are not computable if only second-order connections are allowed (Williams, 1986).

In particular, *symmetric* networks can be easily extended to handle high-order connections. Naturally, such networks may be viewed as minimizing high-order energy functions (Sejnowski, 1986).

A k-order energy function is a function E:$\{0,1\}^n \rightarrow \mathbf{R}$ that can be expressed as sum of products, with product terms of up to k variables. A k-order energy function is denoted by: $E^k(x_1, ..., x_n)=$

$$\sum_{1 \le i_1 < i_2 < ... < i_k \le n} w_{i_1,...,i_k} X_{i_1} ... X_{i_k} + \sum_{1 \le i_1 < ... < i_{k-1} \le n} w_{i_1,...,i_{k-1}} + ... + \sum_{1 \le i \le n} w_i X_i$$

Quadratic energy functions (or second-order functions) are special cases of the high-order case:

$$\sum_{1 \le i < j \le n} W_{ij} X_i X_j + \sum_{i \le n} W_i X_i$$

In the high-order model each node is assigned a sigma-pi unit that updates its activation value using:

$$net_i = \frac{dE}{dX_i} = \sum_{i_1 \ldots i \ldots i_k} -w_{i_1, \ldots, i, \ldots, i_k} \prod_{1 \le j \le k, i_j \neq i} X_{i_j}$$

$$a_i = F(net_i)$$

where $a_i = F(net_i)$ is the standard update rule that is unique to the model we wish to extend. In the Hopfield model, for example, $F(net_i) = 1$ if $net_i > 0$ and $F(net_i) = 0$ otherwise. A high-order network (see Fig. 7.2) is a hypergraph, where k-order terms are translated into hyper-arcs connecting k nodes. The arcs are not directed (the weight is the same for every node that is part of the arc) and the weight of an arc is determined by the weight of the corresponding term in the energy function (with an opposite sign). As in the quadratic case, there is a translation back and forth between k-order energy functions and symmetric high-order networks with k-order sigma-pi units.

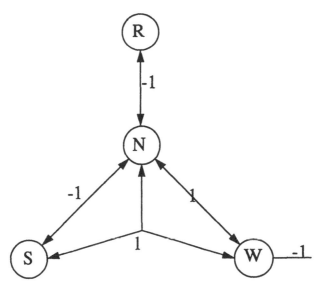

Fig. 7.2. A cubic network that represents E=-NSW+NS+RN-WN+W using sigma-pi units and a cubic hyper-arc. (It is equivalent to the network of Fig. 7.1 without hidden units).

The variables of an energy function can be arbitrarily divided into two sets: visible variables and hidden variables. The hidden variables correspond to the hidden units of the corresponding network, and the visible variables correspond to the visible units. An energy function with both hidden and visible variables is denoted usually as a function $E(\vec{x}, \vec{t})$, where $\vec{x}$ represents the visible variables and $\vec{t}$ represents the hidden variables.

An assignment of zeros and ones to the visible variables is called a visible state. The value of the hidden units is not usually of any interest to the external observer. The visible units, on the other hand, are used as inputs and outputs. The user clamps (or adds bias to) some units that act as inputs, and looks at the output units after the network has settled. The values of the visible units after an equilibrium is reached, are considered as the "answer" of the network. Later in this article, I interpret visible states as truth assignments: the visible variables are viewed as atomic propositions, "1" is interpreted as "true" and "0" is interpreted as "false".

The set of minimizing vectors projected onto the visible variables is called "the visible solutions" of the minimization problem $(\mu(E) = \{\vec{x} | (\exists \vec{t}) E(\vec{x}, \vec{t}) = \min_{\vec{y}, \vec{z}} \{E(\vec{y}, \vec{z})\}\})$. Connectionist models like Boltzmann machines, harmony theory, mean field theory, as well as other variations, may be looked as searching for a *global minimum*[5] of the corresponding energy functions. Local minima or spurious memories may exist. In general however, local minima are considered to be undesirable phenomena, and cause a degradation in the performance of the network. Local minima that are not global do not represent any meaningful knowledge.

For every network with energy function $E(\vec{x}, \vec{t})$ and with $\vec{t}$ hidden variables, define the *characteristic* function of the network to be: $Erank_E(\vec{x}) = \min_{\vec{y}} \{E(\vec{x}, \vec{y})\}$. The $Erank_E$ function defines the energy of all visible states (the energy of a visible state is the energy level obtained when the visible units are clamped with the state's values, and the hidden units are free to settle so that a minimum is reached). This $Erank_E$ function characterizes the network's behavior: it is independent of the hidden units and it is also independent of the exact topology of the original network. I use the characteristic function to show equivalence between different networks.

2.2. THE EQUIVALENCE BETWEEN HIGH-ORDER NETWORKS AND LOW-ORDER NETWORKS

Two energy functions are *strongly equivalent*, if their corresponding characteristic (Erank) functions are equal up to a constant difference; that is: $E_1 \approx E_2$ iff $Erank_{E_1} = Erank_{E_2} + c$. Networks that are strongly equivalent not only have the same set of global minima, but also have a very similar energy surface and induce the same ordering on the visible states; that is, if s_1 and s_2 are visible states then "same ordering" means that $E_1(s_1) < E_1(s_2)$ iff $E_2(s_1) < E_2(s_2)$.

---

[5] Several global minima may exist, all with the same energy level.

I now show an algorithm to convert any high-order network into a strongly equivalent low-order one with additional hidden units. In addition, any energy function with hidden variables can be converted into a strongly equivalent, (possibly) higher order network by eliminating some or all of the hidden units. These algorithms allow us to trade the computational power of sigma-pi units for additional simple units and vice versa. As a result we see that the expressive power of high-order networks is the same as that of low-order networks with hidden units.

Theorem 1. · Any k-order term $(w\prod_{i=1}^{k} x_i)$ with NEGATIVE coefficient w, can be replaced by the quadratic terms: $\sum_{i=1}^{k} 2wX_iT - (2k-1)wT$ generating a strongly equivalent energy function with one additional hidden variable T.

· Any k-order term $(w\prod_{i=1}^{k} x_i)$ with POSITIVE coefficient w, can be replaced by the terms: $w\prod_{i=1}^{k-1} x_i - (\sum_{1}^{k-1} 2wX_iT) + 2wX_kT + (2k-3)wT$ generating a strongly equivalent energy function of order k−1 with one additional hidden variable T.

EXAMPLE 2.1. The cubic function E=−NSW+NS+RN−WN+W is strongly equivalent to −2NT−2ST−2WT+5T+NS+RN−WN+W, (introducing the hidden variable T). The corresponding high-order network appears in Fig. 7.2 while the equivalent quadratic one appears in Fig. 7.1.

EXAMPLE 2.2. The following is a 4-order energy function with a 4-order term XYZU. It can be converted into a quadratic energy function using two additional hidden variables T and T'.

$$
\begin{aligned}
-XY+XYZU &\approx -XY+XYZ-2XT-2YT-2ZT+2UT+5T \\
&\approx -XY+XY-2XT'-2YT'+2ZT'+3T'-2XT-2YT-2ZT+2UT+5T \\
&= -2XT'-2YT'+2ZT'+3T'-2XT-2YT-2ZT+2UT+5T
\end{aligned}
$$

The symmetric transformation, from low-order into high-order functions by eliminating any subset of the variables, is also possible (of course we are interesting in eliminating only hidden variables). To eliminate T, bring the energy function to the form:

$$
E=E' + \text{oldterm}, \quad \text{where } \boldsymbol{oldterm} = (\sum_{j=1}^{k} w_j \prod_{i=1}^{l_j} X_{j_i})T.
$$

Consider all assignments S for the variables ($\hat{X} = x_{i_1} \cdots x_{i_l}$) in *oldterm* (not including T), such that

$$\beta_S = \sum_{j=1}^{k} w_j \prod_{i=1}^{l_j} x_{j_i} < 0.$$ Each negative β_S represents an energy state of the variables in $\hat{X}$ that pushes T to become "one" and decreases the total energy by $|\beta_S|$. States with positive β_S cause T to become zero, do not reduce the total energy, and therefore can be ignored. The only states that matter are those that reduce the energy; *that is*, β_S is negative. Let

$$L^{J_x} = \begin{cases} X_{i_j} & \text{if } S(X_{i_j}) = 1 \\ (1 - X_{i_j}) & \text{if } S(X_{i_j}) = 0 \end{cases}$$

It is the expression "X_i" or "$(1-X_i)$" depending whether the variable is assigned 1 or 0 in S. The expression $\prod_{j=1}^{l} L^{J}{}_S$ therefore determines the state S, and the expression

$$newterm = \sum_{S \text{ such that } \beta_S < 0} \beta_S \prod_{j=1}^{l} L^{J}{}_S$$

represents the disjunction of all the states that cause a reduction in the total energy. The new function E$'$ + *newterm*, is therefore equivalent to E$'$ + *oldterm* and does not include T.

With this technique, any network with hidden units can be converted into a strongly equivalent network without any such units.

EXAMPLE 2.3. Let T be the hidden variable to be eliminated, then:

$$AB+TAC-TA+2TB-T=AB+T(AC-A+2B-1)$$

The following assignments for (A,B,C) cause β to be less than zero:

$$\beta_{(0,0,0)}=-1$$
$$\beta_{(0,0,1)}=-1$$
$$\beta_{(1,0,0)}=-2$$
$$\beta_{(1,0,1)}=-1$$

The new term equals:

$-(1-A)(1-B)(1-C)-(1-A)(1-B)C-2A(1-B)(1-C)-A(1-B)C = -ABC+AB+AC-A+B-1.$

Therefore:

$$AB+TAC-TA+2TB-T \approx -ABC+2AB+AC-A+B.$$

3. PROPOSITIONAL CALCULUS AND SCNS

This section shows that every well formed formula (WFF) of propositional logic can be represented in a SCN, such that the models that satisfy the formula are exactly the global minima of the network. It also shows that in this sense, every SCN can be described by a formula of propositional logic.

3.1. SATISFIABILITY AND SATISFYING MODELS

A *well formed formula* (a WFF) is defined as an expression that combines atomic propositions (variables) and connectives $(\vee, \wedge, \neg, \rightarrow, (,))$.

A WFF can be defined recursively using the following definitions:

- if φ is an atomic proposition then φ is a WFF;
- if φ_1 and φ_2 are WFFs, so are: $\varphi_1 \vee \varphi_2)$, $(\varphi_1 \wedge \varphi_2)$, $(\varphi_1 \rightarrow \varphi_2)$, $\neg \varphi_1$ and (φ_1);
- nothing else is a WFF.

For example, $((A \vee \neg B) \rightarrow C)$ is a WFF.

The *characteristic function* is defined to be $H_\varphi : 2^a \rightarrow \{0,1\}$ such that:

$$\cdot H_{x_i}(x_1, \cdots, x_n) = x_i$$
$$\cdot H_{\neg\varphi}(x_1, \cdots, x_n) = 1 - H_\varphi(x_1, \cdots, x_n)$$
$$\cdot H_{\varphi_1 \vee \varphi_2}(x_1, \cdots, x_n) = H_{\varphi_1}(x_1, \cdots, x_n) + H_{\varphi_2}(x_1, \cdots, x_n) - H_{\varphi_1}(x_1, \cdots, x_n) \times H_{\varphi_2}(x_1, \cdots, x_N)$$
$$\cdot H_{(\varphi_1 \wedge \varphi_2)}(x_1, \cdots, x_n) = H_{\varphi_1}(x_1, \cdots, x_n) \times H_{\varphi_2}(x_1, \cdots, x_n)$$
$$\cdot H_{(\varphi_1 \rightarrow \varphi_2)}(x_1, \cdots, x_n) = H_{(\neg\varphi_1 \vee \varphi_2)}(x_1, \cdots, x_n)$$

A *model (truth assignment)* is a vector of binary values that assigns 1 ("true") or 0 ("false") to each of the atomic propositions (variables). Truth assignments are propositional models of possible worlds.

The standard definitions of satisfiability and entailment are used. The definitions are given hereby for completeness:

A model $\vec{x}$ *satisfies* a WFF φ, iff its characteristic function H_φ evaluates to "one" given the vector $\vec{x}$.

A model that satisfies a formula φ is a truth assignment that satisfies the constraints imposed by the formula. For example, given $A \vee \neg B$, the satisfying models will be those that assign 1 to A or 0 to B or both.

The *satisfiability search* problem for a WFF φ is to find an $\vec{x}$ (if one exists) such that $H_\varphi \vec{x} = 1$.

Entailment in propositional calculus is denoted by the relation $\vDash$. The knowledge ψ *entails* φ ($\psi \vDash \varphi$) iff all the models that satisfy ψ also satisfy φ (for example $(A \vee \neg B) \wedge B \vDash A$).

3.2. EQUIVALENCE BETWEEN PROPOSITIONAL FORMULAS

In order to convert a WFF efficiently into an energy function, we need an intermediate step: The WFF needs first to be transformed into an equivalent form called Conjunction of Triples Form (CTF).

The atomic propositions of a WFF can be divided into visible and hidden propositions (similarly to the division of the variables of an energy function). Atomic propositions that are of interest for a certain application are called "visible variables" and are denoted by $\vec{x}$. Additional atomic hidden propositions (denoted by $\vec{t}$) may be added without changing the set of relevant models that satisfy the WFF. The set of models that satisfy φ projected onto the visible variables is then called "the visible satisfying models" ($\{\vec{x} | (\exists \vec{t}) H_\varphi(\vec{x}, \vec{t}) = 1\}$). Two WFFs are *equivalent*, if the set of visible satisfying models of one is equal to the set of visible satisfying models of the other. The two equivalent formulas have the same truth table with respect to the visible variables and therefore the same meaning.

A WFF φ is in Conjunction of Triples Form (CTF) if $\varphi = \overset{m}{\underset{i=1}{\wedge}} \varphi_i$ and every φ_i is a sub-formula of at most three variables.[6]

If we can convert any WFF to a CTF of the same order of size, we will be able then to convert the CTF into a quadratic energy function that preserves the size. Thus, the motivation for CTF is technical only: The conversion to CTF guarantees that the generated network is of the same order of size as the original formula.

Every WFF can be converted into an equivalent WFF in CTF by adding hidden variables. Intuitively, a new hidden variable is generated for every binary connective (e.g., $\vee$, $\rightarrow$) except for the top-most one, and the binary logical operation is "named" by a new hidden variable using the connective ($\leftrightarrow$). The number of hidden variables needed is in the order of the number of binary connective in the original formula. The size of the new formula (in CTF) is therefore linear in the size of the original formula.

EXAMPLE 3.1. Converting $\varphi = (\neg ((\neg A) \wedge B) \rightarrow (\neg C \rightarrow D))$ into CTF:
From $(\neg ((\neg A) \wedge B))$ we generate: $(\neg (\neg A \wedge B) \leftrightarrow T_1)$ by adding a new hidden variable T_1,
from $(\neg C \rightarrow D)$ we generate: $((\neg C \rightarrow D) \leftrightarrow T_2)$ by adding a new hidden variable T_2,
for the top most connective ($\rightarrow$) we generate: $(T_1 \rightarrow T_2)$.
The conjunction of these sub-formulas is:

---

[6] CTF differs from the familiar Conjunctive Normal Form (CNF). The φ_i's are WFFs of up to 3 variables that may include any logical connectives and are not necessarily a disjunction of literals as in CNF. To put a bidirectional CTF clause into a CNF we would have to generate two clauses, thus $(A \leftrightarrow B)$ becomes $(\neg A \vee B) \wedge (A \vee \neg B)$.

$(\neg\,(\neg\,A\wedge\,B)\leftrightarrow T_1)\wedge((\neg\,C\rightarrow\,D)\leftrightarrow\,T_2)\wedge(T_1\rightarrow T_2)$. It is in CTF and is equivalent to φ .

The next section shows how to reduce a conjunction of triples into energy terms.

3.3. DESCRIBING WFFS USING ENERGY FUNCTIONS

Let us associate the visible variables of an energy function with the visible atomic variables of a WFF in CTF. An energy function E describes a WFF φ if the set of visible satisfying models of φ is equal to the set of visible solutions of the minimization of E.

If E describes φ then E preserves the meaning of φ by storing the satisfying models of φ as the global minima of the energy function. The set of global minima of E is exactly equal to the set of satisfying models of φ.

Assume $\varphi\,=\,\overset{m}{\underset{i=1}{\bigwedge}}\,\varphi_i$ then, the φ_is are called sub-formulas. The energy function E_φ of a WFF φ is a function $E_\varphi:\{0,1\}^n\rightarrow N$, that penalizes sub-formulas of the WFF that are not satisfied. It computes the characteristic of the negation of every sub-formula φ_i in the upper level of the WFF's conjunctive structure:

$$E_\varphi(\vec{x}) = \sum_{i=1}^{m}(H_{\neg\varphi_i}(\vec{x})) = \sum_{i=1}^{m}(1 - H_{\varphi_i}(\vec{x}))$$

If $\vec{x}$ does not satisfy φ_i then $\vec{x}$ satisfies $\neg\varphi_i$ and therefore $H_{\neg\varphi_i}(\vec{x}) = 1$. Thus, if $\vec{x}$ satisfies φ_i then $H_{\neg\varphi_i}(\vec{x}) = 0$. If all the sub-formulas are satisfied, E_φ gets the value zero; otherwise, the function computes how many sub-formulas are unsatisfied.

It is easy to see that φ is satisfied by $\vec{x}$ iff E_φ is minimized by $\vec{x}$(the global minima have a value of zero). Therefore, every satisfiable WFF φ has a function E_φ, such that E_φ describes φ.

EXAMPLE 3.2

$E_{((N\wedge S)\rightarrow W)\wedge(R\rightarrow\neg N)\wedge(N\vee\neg W)}$

$= H_{\neg((N\wedge S)\rightarrow W)} + H_{\neg(R\rightarrow(\neg N))} + H_{\neg(N\vee(\neg W))}$

$= H_{N\wedge S\wedge(\neg W)} + H_{R\wedge N} + H_{(\neg N)\wedge W}$

$= (NS(1-W)) + (RN) + ((1-N)W)$

$= -NSW+NS+RN-WN+W$

The corresponding high-order network appears in Fig. 7.2.

The cubic function that is constructed can now be converted into a quadratic energy function using the algorithm that was discussed in Section 2.2.

Theorem 2. Every WFF is described by some quadratic energy function.

The following algorithm transforms a WFF into a quadratic energy function that describes it, generating $O(length(\varphi))$ hidden variables:

· Convert φ into CTF φ' (Section 3.2).
· Convert the CTF φ' into a cubic energy function $E_{\varphi'}$ and simplify it to a sum of products form (Section 3.3)
· Convert the cubic terms in $E_{\varphi'}$} into quadratic terms. Each of the triples generates only one new variable (Section 2.2).

The algorithm generates a network whose size is linear in the number of binary connectives of the original WFF. The fan-out of a single hidden unit is bounded by a constant.

3.4. EVERY ENERGY FUNCTION DESCRIBES SOME SATISFIABLE WFF

Section 2.2 shows that we can convert any energy function to contain no hidden variables. This subsection shows that for any such function E with no hidden variables, there exists a satisfiable WFF φ such that E describes φ.

The procedure is first to find the set $\mu(E)$ of minimum energy states (the vectors that minimize E). For each such state create an n-way conjunctive formula of the variables or their negations depending whether the variable is assigned 1 or 0 in that state. Each such conjunction $\bigwedge_{i=1}^{n} L^{i}{}_{s}$

where $L^{i}{}_{s} = \begin{cases} X_i & \text{if } S(X_i) = 1 \\ (\neg X_i) & \text{if } S(X_i) = 0 \end{cases}$ represents a minimum energy state. Finally the WFF is

constructed by taking the disjunction of all the conjunctions: $\varphi = \bigvee_{s \in \mu(E)} (\bigwedge_{i=1}^{n} L^{i}{}_{s})$. The

satisfying truth assignments of φ correspond directly to the energy states of the network. The procedure is not efficient, but it does show existence of such a formula for every network.

We therefore conclude:

Theorem 3. Every energy function describes some WFF.

The conversion is done by first eliminating the hidden variables and then computing the WFF by looking at the global minima.

EXAMPLE 3.3. Let the energy function be:

$$[E(X,Y) = -XY + 1.5X]$$

Trying all instantiations:

$$E(0,0)=0$$
$$E(0,1)=0$$
$$E(1,0)=1.5$$
$$E(1,1)=0.5$$

The characteristic function of the WFF is:

$$H(0,0)=1$$
$$H(0,1)=1$$
$$H(1,0)=0$$
$$H(1,1)=0$$

The WFF that is described by E is therefore:

$$[((\neg X \wedge \neg Y) \vee (\neg X \wedge Y))\backslash]$$

3.5. DESCRIBING NETWORKS USING WFFS

The language of propositional logic could be used as a high-level specification language but it has some serious limitations:

· Propositional logic is not as compact a language as we would like it to be. Some networks are described only by a formula that is much longer than the size of the network. The algorithm to transform a network into a WFF is not an efficient one, and it may generate exponentially long WFFs.
· A propositional formula captures only the states of global minima. The logic formalism fails to capture stable states that are not global, it fails to capture the energy landscape and it fails to preserve even the order of the visible energy states (whether one state has lower energy than another).[7]
· Propositional calculus is incapable of efficiently representing nonmonotonic knowledge (like defaults and exceptions) and its proof procedure cannot cope in a useful way with inconsistency that may occur in real situations.

The above limitations motivate a search for a better language, that is capable of describing SCNs in a compact, efficient and rich way, and that is capable of representing more realistic forms of knowledge (for example: nonmonotonic, inconsistent knowledge).

---

[7] The order among the states is important when new knowledge is added or when nonmonotonic information is captured.

4. PENALTY LOGIC

Humans seem to be able to reason about the surrounding world from a noisy and incomplete knowledge and at a remarkably high speed. Research in nonmonotonic reasoning has tried to understand the basic mechanisms and the rationale behind our intuition when dealing with an incomplete description of the world.

Recent nonmonotonic (NM) systems are quite successful in capturing our intuitions about default reasoning (see for example Geffner, 1989). Most of them, however, are still plagued with intractable computational complexity, sensitivity to noise, inability to combine other sources of knowledge (like probabilities, utilities, ...) and inflexibility to develop personal intuitions and to adjust themselves to new situations. Connectionist systems may be the missing link. They can supply us with a fast, massively parallel platform; noise tolerance can emerge from their collective computation; and their ability to learn may be used to incorporate new evidence and dynamically change the knowledge base.

This section and the next one demonstrate that symmetric connectionist networks (SCNs) are natural platforms for propositional defeasible reasoning and for noisy knowledge bases.

I now extend propositional calculus so that it will be capable of expressing nonmonotonic knowledge, strength of belief, reliability of sources of knowledge, etc. In the extended calculus (called penalty-logic), we add a real positive number (penalty) to every belief. This penalty may be interpreted as a "certainty" or "likelihood" (Shortliffe, 1976), as a priority of a belief (Brewka, 1989; Lifschitz, 1985) or as a maximal entropy constraint (Goldszmidt & Pearl, 1991). Also, when the knowledge sources are unreliable, a penalty may represent a measure of reliability (Rescher & Manor, 1970). Note that some of these systems compute the penalty from less explicit information, while other systems let the user specify the penalties explicitly. I do not insist on a particular use or interpretation, since the intention is to develop a framework into which many logicist systems could be reduced.

A *Penalty Logic WFF* (PLOFF) ψ is a finite set of pairs. Each pair is composed of a real positive number, called *penalty*, and a standard propositional WFF, called *assumption* (or belief); that is, $\psi = \{<\rho_i,\varphi_i> \mid \rho_i \in \mathbb{R}^+, \varphi_i$ is a WFF, i=1...n$\}$.

EXAMPLE 4.1. The Nixon diamond can be stated as:

1000	N→R	Nixon is a Republican
1000	N→Q	Nixon is also a Quaker
10	R→¬P	Republicans tend not to be pacifist
10	Q→P	Quakers tend to be pacifist
3000	N	Nixon is the person we reason about.

An illustration of the example is shown in Fig. 7.3.

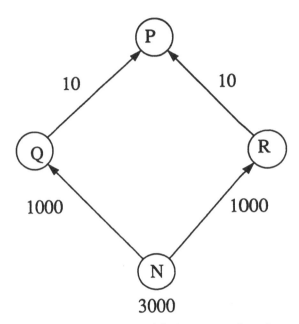

Fig. 7.3. An illustration of the Nixon diamond as an inheritance network: nodes represent atomic propositions; the numbers are the penalties.

The penalties in this example reflect the strength with which we believe each proposition. High penalty is given to strict logic rules (facts) like the one that states that Nixon is a Republican. Strict facts are not allowed to be defeated. The last fact (N) states that Nixon is the one we reason about. This fact receives the highest penalty of all since it is considered as *evidence*. The evidence is not usually part of our knowledge base and we would like to "jump" to conclusions once it is given; that is, evidence is considered a temporary but very certain fact. Lower penalties are given to "defeasible" rules (*tend to be* rules), like the one that states that Republicans tend not to be pacifist. When we know that somebody is a Republican, we tend to believe that the person is not pacifist (by default); however, this "jumping" to conclusion is blocked, if we know that the person is an exception to the rule. For example, we wouldn't like to conclude that a person is pacifist, if the person is also a Quaker, or if it was explicitly mentioned that the person is not pacifist. Clearly, we would like to conclude that Nixon is both a Republican (R) and a Quaker (Q); however, we would not like to conclude anything about the pacifism of Nixon. There is no adequate reason either to believe P or ¬ P; therefore P is considered ambiguous.

If we would like to express our belief that religious ideas are stronger than political affiliations in influencing one's pacifism, then we may increase the penalty (strength) for Q→P to 15; leaving the penalty for R→¬P unchanged (10).

EXAMPLE 4.2

1000	N→R	Nixon is a Republican
1000	N→Q	Nixon is also a Quaker
10	R→¬P	Republicans tend not to be pacifist
15	Q→P	Quakers tend to be pacifist
3000	N	Nixon is the person we reason about.

In the revised set of assumptions, there are two competing arguments. One argument supports the pacifism of Nixon while the other supports its negation. The pacifism of Nixon is not ambiguous in this case, since the argument that supports P wins (the winning argument is stronger and therefore manages to defeat the other contradicting argument (Loui, 1987).

There are many ways to interpret the penalties and the assumptions in our formalism. I give one such interpretation that I found to be convenient, useful and general.

Given a knowledge base of assumptions and penalties $\psi = \{<\rho_i,\varphi_i>\}$, ψ determines a ranking over the set of all possible models (truth assignments of n atomic propositions). This ranking reflects "normality" or "goodness" we tend to associate with possible models of the world (see Shoham, 1988). By specifying ψ we informally mean that models that satisfy many "important" assumptions are "better" than models that satisfy fewer or less important assumptions. Every two models may always be compared by looking at the assumptions (in ψ) that are violated. Two models that violate the same set of assumptions are considered to be "equally good." Even if the models violate different sets of assumptions but the sum of the penalties of both sets is the same, then the two models are "equally good." A model is more "normal" (or "better") than another model if the sum of the penalties of the violated assumptions of the first is less than the sum of the second.

This interpretation of the penalties induces a ranking function that assigns a real value (rank) to all the possible models. The ranking function that is induced is called the violation rank of ψ: The *violation-rank* of a PLOFF ψ is the function ($Vrank_\psi$) that assigns a real-valued rank to each of the truth assignments. The $Vrank_\psi$ for a truth assignment $\vec{x}$ is computed by summing the penalties for the assumptions of ψ that are violated by the assignment; *i.e.*,

$$Vrank_\psi(\vec{x}) = \sum_i \rho_i H_{\neg\varphi_i}(\vec{x}) = \sum_{\vec{x}\neg\varphi_i} \rho_i.$$

The models that minimize the function are called *preferred models*.

A PLOFF ψ *semantically entails* φ ($\psi \vDash \varphi$) iff all the preferred models of ψ also satisfy φ. In the Nixon example, the preferred models are only two: (NRQP) and (NRQ¬P). Examples of some valid conclusions are therefore N,R∧Q, and so on (since these conclusions are satisfied by all the preferred models). The pacifism of Nixon is ambiguous, since P holds in one preferred model while ¬P holds in the other.

A sound and complete proof theory was developed for penalty logic in Pinkas (1991a). This proof theory is based solely on syntactic considerations and gives another clarifying look at the reasoning process in penalty logic. Instead of ranking the models and using the "best" models for the reasoning process, we can rank consistent-subsets of the assumptions of ψ, and use the preferred ("best") consistent-subsets to perform deduction. A conclusion is made in the proof theory iff all the preferred consistent-subsets entail it.

Formally, T is called a *theory* of a PLOFF ψ iff T is a *consistent* subset (in the classical sense) of the assumptions in ψ; that is, the set of T is a subset of the assumptions in ψ and is not contradictory. The *penalty* of a theory T of ψ is the sum of the penalties of the assumptions in ψ that are not included in T; that is, $penalty_\psi(T) = \sum_{\varphi_i \in (v_\psi - T)} \rho_i$, and is called the *penalty function* of ψ. The rank that is induced by ψ on the set of theories of ψ is therefore computed by the sum of the penalties of the missing assumptions.

A *preferred* theory of ψ is a theory T that minimizes the penalty function of ψ; that is, $penalty_\psi$ (T)=$\min_S$ {penalty$_\psi$ (S) | S is a theory of ψ}.

Let $T_\psi = \{T_i\}$, the set of all preferred theories of ψ. A PLOFF ψ *entails*[8] φ ($\psi \vdash \varphi$) iff all preferred theories T_i of ψ entail (in the classical sense) φ; that is:

$$(\bigvee_{T_i \in T_\psi} T_i) \vdash \varphi$$

In the Nixon example, the set of assumptions is inconsistent (leads to a contradiction); however, there are 2^4 non-empty consistent subsets where at least one belief of ψ is missing. If we rank each of the consistent subsets by summing the penalties of the missing beliefs, we get that the preferred theories are $T_1 = \{N,N\rightarrow Q,N\rightarrow R,Q\rightarrow P\}$ and $T_2 = \{N,N\rightarrow Q,N\rightarrow R,R\rightarrow\neg P\}$. These preferred theories are ranked 10 since only one belief in ψ (of strength 10) is missing in each such theory.

Each of the two preferred theories entails the obvious conclusions (like N,Q ∧ R), but neither P nor ¬ P can be concluded, since the two preferred theories do not agree on either. The reasoning process can be intuitively understood as a competition among consistent-subsets. The subsets that win are those theories with minimal penalty. A conclusion is entailed only if all the winners conclude it independently.

Theorem 4. $\psi \models \varphi$ (using preferred models) iff $\psi \vdash \varphi$ (using preferred theories).

---

[8] Note that the deductive closure of preferred theories roughly resemble extensions (as in Reiter, 1980). The definition of entailment in penalty logic resembles therefore entailment by intersection of all extension.

5. THE EQUIVALENCE OF PENALTY LOGIC AND SCNS

This section shows that penalty logic can be represented efficiently in SCNs and that every SCN can be described efficiently by a penalty logic formula.

A PLOFF ψ is *strongly equivalent* to an energy function E iff the violation rank of ψ is equal to the characteristic function of E (up to a constant difference); that is,

$$(\forall \vec{x})(Vrank_\psi(\vec{x}) = Erank_E(\vec{x}) + c)$$

.

This notion of equivalence suggests that the two forms of knowledge representation have the same interpretation. The ranking functions that are induced by either the network or the formula are the same (up to a constant difference). If ψ is strongly equivalent to a network represented by an energy function E then:

1. The set of global minima of E is equal exactly to the set of the preferred models of φ.
2. Both knowledge representations induce the same order on the possible models; that is, s is *better* than s' iff $Erank_E(s) < Erank_E(s')$ iff $Vrank_\psi(s) < Vrank_\psi(s')$.
3. Evidence is cumulative (see Pinkas, 1991a), a property that is important for nonmonotonic systems but is out of the scope of this article.

Once we know in what sense we would like a PLOFF to describe a network, we can continue to the main results of this section.

5.1. REDUCING PENALTY LOGIC

In this section I finally show that penalty logic can be represented using symmetric networks.

Theorem 5. For every PLOFF $\psi = \{<\rho_i, \varphi_i> | i = 1 \cdots n\}$ there exists a strongly equivalent quadratic energy function $E(\vec{x}, \vec{t})$, that is, there exists a constant c such that $Vrank_\psi = Erank_E + c$.

An energy function E can be constructed from ψ using the following procedure:

1. Start with an empty set of assumptions ψ'. For every pair $<\rho_i, \varphi>$ in ψ, create a new hidden variable T_i, "name" φ_i using $T_i \leftrightarrow \varphi_i$ and add the pairs $<\beta, T_i \leftrightarrow \varphi_i>$ and $<\rho_i, T_i>$ into ψ'. The penalty β represents a real value that is large enough to force the naming constraint to be satisfied. The original penalty ρ_i causes the T_i's to compete with each other; while the high penalty β guarantees that if T_i holds (among the winners) then φ_i

also holds. ψ' is therefore strongly equivalent to ψ and the T_i's may be considered as hidden variables; that is, $Vrank_\psi = Vrank_{\psi'} + c$.

2. Construct the energy function $\sum_i \beta E_{T_i - \varphi_i} - \sum_j \rho_j T_j$, where E_φ is the function generated by the algorithm of Section 3.3.

The network that is generated can be seen as performing a search for a preferred model of ψ. According to the sound and complete proof theory, it can also be seen as searching for a preferred theory of ψ; that is, the T_i's that win the competition correspond to the assumptions in some preferred theory.

The naming of the first step, is needed only if the number of variables in an assumption φ_i is greater than three. If this is the case and we do not name φ_i, then the second step of the algorithm might generate more then one "triple." Each triple will have a penalty that will contribute to the energy function independently of the other triples and the constraint as a whole will not have the atomicity expected. Thus, the ranking function that will be generated will not be the one we wished. The high penalty used for the naming causes the system to *always* find solutions that satisfy the naming constraints (indeed, it is always possible to satisfy the naming constraints). Once we guarantee that all the naming constraints are satisfied, all we need to do is to make the T_i's compete as if they were the original assumptions. When the number of variables is less or equal to three, the way the energy function is constructed guarantees that only one triple is generated. Thus, either the constraint is satisfied as a whole (with zero penalty) or it is not satisfied (and the penalty is ρ_i); that is, the splitting of one constraint into more then one "triple," does not happen in the case of less than four variables.

In the following example the assumptions have no more then three variables, thus naming is not needed.

EXAMPLE 5.1. The Nixon diamond case of Example 4.1.

The PLOFF that is to be converted is:

$$\psi = \{<3000,N>,<1000,N \to Q>, <1000,N \to R>, <10,Q \to P>, <10, R \to \neg P>.$$

No naming is needed, so $\psi' = \psi$.
Each of the pairs is converted to an energy function:

1000	N→R	$1000(E_{\neg N \lor R}) = 1000(N-NR)$
1000	N→Q	$1000(E_{\neg N \lor Q}) = 1000(N-NQ)$
10	R→¬P	$10(E_{\neg R \lor \neg P}) = 10(RP)$
10	Q→P	$10(E_{\neg Q \lor P}) = 10(Q-QP)$
3000	N	$3000(E_N) = 3000(-N)$

Summing the energy terms together:

$$E = -1000NQ-1000NR+10RP-10QP-1000N+10Q$$

The corresponding network appears in Fig. 7.4.

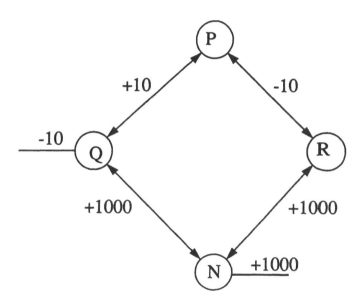

Fig. 7.4. The network that represents the Nixon Diamond example. It corresponds to the energy function: E= − 1000NQ − 1000NR + 10RP − 10QP − 1000N + 10Q.

Once we can generate a network that searches for preferred models (or preferred theories), it is possible to construct a network that will reason according to our definition of entailment. A construction of such a network is described in Pinkas (1991a).

5.2. DESCRIBING SCN AS PENALTY LOGIC FORMULAS

This section shows that it is possible to describe any network efficiently by a penalty logic formula. The motivation here is to demonstrate that penalty logic is an efficient and compact language for specifications of symmetric connectionist networks.

Theorem 6. Every energy function E is strongly equivalent to some PLOFF ψ; that is, there exists a constant c such that $Erank_E = Vrank_\psi + c$.

The following algorithm generates a strongly equivalent PLOFF from an energy function:

1. Eliminate hidden variables (if any) from the energy function, using the algorithm of Section 2.2.

2. The energy function (with no hidden variables) is now brought into a sum-of-products form and is converted into a PLOFF in the following way:

Let $E(\bar{x}) = \sum_{i=1}^{m} w_i \prod_{n=1}^{k_i} s_{i_n}$ be the energy function. The sum of products formula is converted to

a PLOFF $\psi = \{<-w_i, \bigwedge_{n=1}^{k_i} x_{i_n}> | w_i < 0\} \cup \{<w_i, \neg \bigwedge_{n=1}^{k_i} x_{i_n}> | w_i > 0\}$.

The formula that is generated is strongly equivalent to the original energy function (network). The size of the formula is in the order of the size of the original network (linear in the number of connections).

EXAMPLE 5.2. Looking at the network of Fig. 7.4, let us describe this network as a PLOFF: The energy function is:

$$E = -1000NQ - 1000NR + 10RP - 10QP - 1000N + 10Q$$

The negative terms are:

$$<1000, N \wedge Q>, <1000, N \wedge R>, <10, Q \wedge P>, <1000, N>.$$

The positive terms are:

$$<10, \neg R \vee \neg P>, <10, \neg Q>]$$

The final PLOFF is therefore:

$$<1000, N \wedge Q>, <1000, N \wedge R>, <10, Q \wedge P>, <1000, N>, <10, \neg R \vee \neg P>, <10, \neg Q>$$

Note, that as it is usually the case with reverse-compilation; the formula constructed is not very meaningful; however, it is clear that a compact description exists for every network.

6. RELATED WORK AND DISCUSSION

6.1. CONNECTIONIST APPROACHES

Derthick (1990) observed that weighted logical constraints (which he called "certainties") can be used in massively parallel architecture. Derthick translated those constraints into special energy functions and used his technique to implement a subset of the language KL-ONE. The approach described in this chapter has a lot of similarities to his system. Looking at his translation from logic to energy functions (Derthick uses different energy functions and no hidden units), there are however, several basic differences: 1) Derthick's "mundane" reasoning is based on finding a most likely single model; his system is never skeptical. The system described in this chapter is more cautious and closer in its behavior to recent symbolic nonmonotonic systems; 2) my system can be implemented with standard low-order units, using relatively well-studied architectures like Hopfield networks or Boltzmann machines. We can therefore take advantage of the hardware implementations as well as of the learning algorithms that were developed for these networks; 3) the system described has a sound and complete proof theory; 4) a two-fold symmetry between networks and formulas is shown and formally proved.

Another connectionist nonmonotonic system is Shastri (1988). It uses evidential reasoning based on maximum likelihood to reason in inheritance networks. My approach is different; I use low-level units and am not restricted to inheritance networks.[9] Shastri's system is guaranteed to work and has a linear time complexity, whereas the system described here tries to solve intractable problems and trades correctness with time; that is, a correct solution (a global minimum) is not guaranteed; however, chances to find one improves as more time is given.

This chapter shares with Barnden (1991), Hölldobler (1990) and Shastri and Ajjanagadde (1991) the implementationalist motivation (Pinker & Prince, 1988). We may look at penalty logic as one of the layers of abstraction that are needed between descriptions of high level cognitive processes and low-level neural implementations. Thus, penalty logic may be seen as a first level of abstraction, that is, it spans higher than the neural implementation (see Barnden, 1991 for a nice discussion on the multi-span approach). The above systems implement subsets of predicate calculus by either spreading activation or by rule firing. The expressive power of the above mechanisms is limited by performance and tractability considerations, and they all stress the problems of representing complex structures, syntax sensitivity and multiplace predicates. In this chapter I had no intention to attack these problems; rather, I wanted to show how to represent *any* propositional constraint and how networks can cope naturally with inconsistency. Therefore, on the surface the systems could not be compared. However, using

---

[9] The approach may be extended to handle inheritance nets by looking at the atomic propositions as predicates with free variables. Those variables are bound by the user during query time.

the foundations described in this chapter we can map[10] most of these systems into penalty logic, and then compile them into symmetric networks (possibly by sacrificing efficiency; Pinkas, 1991b). What is more important is that these techniques may be used to construct networks that represent unrestricted[11] predicate logic clauses (Pinkas, 1992b).

6.2. SYMBOLIC SYSTEMS

Satisfiability of propositional calculus is one of the most investigated problems in computer science. There is a large literature dealing with the problem, its complexity, and methods to solve it. The direction pointed in this chapter may suggest a new way to attack the problem; that is, by means of massively parallel constraint satisfaction done by connectionist networks.

Penalty logic is along the lines of work done in preferential semantics (Shoham, 1988). Specifically, it is related to systems with preferential semantics that use ranked models, like Lehmann (1989), Lehmann and Magidor (1988), and Pearl (1990). Lehmann and Magidor's results about the relationship between rational consequence relations and ranked models can be applied to our paradigm: A *consequence relation* is a binary relation between sets of WFFs (evidence) and WFFs (conclusions). A consequence relation R_ψ with respect to a knowledge base ψ is a set of pairs $R_\psi = \{<\varphi',\varphi>\}$, where, a pair $<\varphi',\varphi>$ means that given the evidence φ' (which is a set of formulas), φ is a valid conclusion that may be drawn. Lehmann and Magidor defined a *rational* consequence relation as one that satisfies certain conditions, and proved that a consequence relation is rational iff it is induced by some ranking function. As a result we may conclude a rather strong result for our system: For every rational consequence relation we can build a ranked model and implement it as a ranking function on a symmetric network. Also, once an arbitrary network is used to implement an inference engine, we may be sure that every such implementation generates a rational consequence relation.

One system of ranked models that can be reduced directly to penalty logic is that of Goldszmidt and Pearl (1991), which actually computes the penalties from a given conditional knowledge (the user does not specify any penalty) based on maximal entropy considerations. The system uses the same ranking function as the one described in this article.

Penalty logic has some similarities with systems that are based on priorities (given to beliefs). One such system (Brewka, 1989) is based on levels of reliability. Brewka's system for propositional logic can be mapped into penalty logic by selecting large enough penalties. Systems like Poole (1988) (with strict specificity) can also be implemented using our architecture, and as in Goldszmidt, Morris, & Pearl (1990), the penalties can be generated automatically.

---

[10] Only nonoscillating networks may be reduced into SCNs, therefore Shastri's system cannot be mapped.

[11] The knowledge is not restricted but the proof length is bound by the network's size.

Another system that is based on priorities is system Z^+ (Goldszmidt & Pearl, 1991) where the user does specify the penalties, but there is a "ghost" that changes them so that several nice properties hold (e.g., specificity). Penalty logic can only approximate those systems by assigning scaled penalties according to the priorities. Every conclusion that is entailed in a priority system like system Z^+, will also be entailed by the approximating penalty logic knowledge base. However, some conclusions that are ambiguous in a priority system, are drawn decisively in penalty logic. In this sense penalty logic may be considered as bolder (less cautious) than those which are based on priorities.

For example consider the "penguins and the wings" case (Goldszmidt & Pearl, 1991), where the following defaults are given: birds fly; birds have wings; penguins are birds and penguins do not fly. Many systems based on priorities (like Z^+), will not be able to conclude that penguins have wings; penalty logic will boldly conclude according to our intuition; that is, that penguins do have wings despite the fact that penguins do not fly. The reason for this intuitive deduction is that penalty logic considers the models where penguins do not fly but have wings, to be more "normal" than models where penguins do not fly and have no wings (as in Goldszmidt, Morris, & Pearl, 1990). Priority-based systems are ambiguous about this conclusion, since they don't have such preference.

As another example consider the Nixon case (Example 4.1) when we add to it: $<1000, N \rightarrow FF>$ and $<10, FF \rightarrow \neg P>$ (Nixon is also a football fan and football fans tend to be not pacifist). Most other nonmonotonic systems will still be skeptical about P (see for examples: Lehmann, 1989; Loui, 1987; Pearl, 1990; Touretzky & Hinton, 1988). Our system decides $\neg P$ since it is better to defeat the one assumption supporting P, than the two assumptions supporting $\neg P$. However, this behavior can be corrected by multiplying the penalty for $Q \rightarrow P$ by two. Further, a network with learning capabilities can adjust the penalties autonomously and thus develop its own intuition and nonmonotonic behavior.

Because we do not allow for arbitrary partial orders (Geffner, 1989; Shoham, 1988) of the models, there are other fundamental problematic examples where our system (and all systems with ranked models semantics) boldly concludes, while other systems are skeptical. These are cases where intuition tells us that skepticism is the right behavior (example in Pinkas, 1991a).

7. CONCLUSIONS

In the spirit of implementational connectionism (Pinker & Prince, 1988), our task was to start building the foundations for possible mappings between symbolic reasoning mechanisms and connectionist networks. Such foundations are based on expressing propositional logic constraints in networks and describing networks as propositional logic formulas. The power of such mapping exceeds the propositional case, and allows also for higher level paradigms (like first-order logic) to be represented (Pinkas, 1992b).

The first part of the chapter shows how to map propositional logic efficiently into symmetric networks, and how to describe networks (not very efficiently) as logic formulas. The second part of the chapter extends propositional logic into a more powerful language called penalty logic. The new logic can better express nonmonotonic knowledge, and its reasoning mechanism is built to cope with inconsistency. I showed equivalence between the problem of minimum for a symmetric network.

Penalty logic is based on assumptions augmented by penalties and an inference mechanism that is based on competing theories. The mechanism fits very naturally in the symmetric models' paradigm and can be used as a platform for nonmonotonic reasoning and inconsistency handling. Several recent nonmonotonic systems can be mapped into this paradigm and therefore suggest settings for the penalties. When the right penalties are given, penalty logic features a nonmonotonic behavior that matches our intuition. Penalties do not necessarily have to come from a syntactic analysis of a symbolic language; since those networks can learn, they can potentially adjust their ranking function and develop their own intuition. It is possible to show, though, that some intuitions cannot be expressed as ranking functions.

Revision of the knowledge base and adding evidence are efficient if we use penalty logic to describe the knowledge: adding (or deleting) a PLOFF is simply computing the energy terms of the new PLOFF and then adding (deleting) it to the background energy function. A local change to the PLOFF is translated into a local change in the network.

Several equivalent high-level languages can be used to describe SCNs: 1) quadratic energy functions; 2) high-order energy functions with no hidden units; 3) propositional logic, and finally 4) penalty logic. All these languages are expressive enough to describe any SCN, and every sentence of such languages can be translated into a SCN; however penalty logic has properties that make it more attractive than the other languages. Algorithms are given for translating between any two of the knowledge representation forms above.

ACKNOWLEDGMENTS

Thanks to Bill Ball, Jon Doyle, Hector Geffner, Sally Goldman, Dan Kimura, Stan Kwasny, Fritz Lehmann, Ron Loui and Judea Pearl for helpful discussions. This research was supported by NSF grant 22-1321 57136.

REFERENCES

Barnden, J. A. (1991). Encoding complex symbolic data structures with some unusual connectionist techniques. In J. A. Barnden and J. B. Pollack (Eds.), *Advances in Connectionist and Neural Computation Theory 1, High-level Connectionist Models* (pp. 180-240). Norwood, NJ: Ablex Publishing Corporation.

Brewka, G. (1989). Preferred sub-theories: An extended logical framework for default reasoning. *Proceedings of IJCAI*, 1043-1048.

Derthick, M. (1988). Mundane reasoning by parallel constraint satisfaction. Unpublished doctoral dissertation, Carnegie Mellon University.

Derthick, M. (1990). Mundane reasoning by parallel constraint satisfaction. *Artificial Intelligence* **46**, 107-158.

Feldman, J. A. (1985). Energy and the behavior of connectionist models. Tech. Rep. No. TR-155, University of Rochester, Computer Science Department.

Fodor, J. A., & Pylyshyn, Z. W. (1988). Connectionism and cognitive architecture: A critical analysis. *Cognition* 28, 3-71.

Geffner, H. (1989). Defeasible reasoning: Causal and conditional theories. Unpublished doctoral dissertation, UCLA.

Goldszmidt, M. E., Morris, P., & Pearl, J. (1990). A maximum entropy approach to nonmono-tonic reasoning. *Proceedings of the 8th Annual Conference of AAAI*, Vol. I, 646-652.

Goldszmidt, M., & Pearl, J. (1991). System Z^+: A formalism for reasoning with variable strength defaults. *Proceedings of the 9th Annual Conference of AAAI*, 399-404.

Hinton, G. E. (1989). Deterministic Boltzmann learning performs steepest descent in weight space. *Neural Computation* 1, 143-150.

Hinton, G. E. (1990). Preface to the special issue on connectionist symbol processing. *Artificial Intelligence* 46, 1-4.

Hinton, G. E., & Sejnowski, T. J. (1986). Learning and re-learning in Boltzmann machines. In J. L. McClelland & D. E. Rumelhart, Parallel Distributed Processing: Explorations in The Microstructure of Cognition (Vol. I, pp. 282-317). Cambridge, MA: MIT Press.

Hölldobler, S. (1990b). CHCL, a connectionist inference system for Horn logic based on connection method and using limited resources. Tech. Rep. No. TR-90-042, International Computer Science Institute TR-90-042.

Hopfield, J. J. (1982). Neural networks and physical systems with emergent collective computational abilities. *Proceedings of the National Academy of Sciences* 79, 2554-2558.

Hopfield, J. J. (1984). Neurons with graded response have collective computational properties like those of two-state neurons. *Proceedings of the National Academy of Sciences* 81, 3088-3092.

Hopfield, J. J., & Tank, D. W. (1985). "Neural" computation of decisions in optimization problems. *Biological Cybernetics* 52, 144-152.

Lehmann, D. (1989). What does a conditional knowledge base entail? *Proceedings of the International Conference on Knowledge Representation and Reasoning*, Toronto, pp. 212-222.

Lehmann, D., & Magidor, M. (1988). Rational logics and their models: A study in cumulative logic. Tech. Rep. No. TR-86-16, Leibnitz Center for Computer Science, Hebrew University, Jerusalem.

Lifschitz, V. (1985). Computing circumscription. *Proceedings of IJCAI*, 121-127.

Loui, R. P. (1987). Defeat among arguments: A system of defeasible inference. *Computational Intelligence* 3, 100-106.

McCarthy, J. (1968). Programs with commonsense. In M. Minsky (Ed.), *Semantic Information Processing* (pp. 403-418). Cambridge, MA: MIT Press.

McCarthy, J. (1980). Circumscription, a form of nonmonotonic reasoning. *Artificial Intelligence* 25, 41-72.

Pearl, J. (1990). System Z: A natural ordering of defaults with tractable applications to nonmonotonic reasoning. In M. Vardi (Ed.), *Proceedings of TARK-90*), 121-135.

Pinkas, G. (1990a). Energy minimization and the satisfiability of propositional calculus. Tech. Rep. No. WUCS-90-03, Department of Computer Science, Washington University.

Pinkas, G. (1990b). Energy minimization and the satisfiability of propositional calculus. *Neural Computation* **3**, no. 2. Also in Touretzky, D. S., Elman, J. L., Sejnowski, T. J., & Hinton, G. E. (Eds), *Proceedings of the 1990 Connectionist Models Summer School* (pp. 217-224). San Mateo, CA: Morgan Kaufmann.

Pinkas, G. (1991a). Propositional non-monotonic reasoning and inconsistency in symmetric neural networks. *Proceedings of International Joint Conference on Artificial Intelligence*, Sydney, Australia, Vol. I, pp. 282-291.

Pinkas, G. (1991b). Converting binary threshold networks into symmetric networks. Tech. Rep. No. WUCS-91-31, Computer Science Department, Washington University.

Pinkas, G. (1992a). Making connectionist networks logical. Unpublished doctoral dissertation, Washington University.

Pinkas, G. (1992b). Constructing proofs in symmetric networks. In *Advances in Neural Information Processing Systems*, (NIPS-4, pp. 217-224). San Mateo, CA: Morgan Kaufmann.

Pinker, S., & Prince, A. (1988). On language and connectionism: Analysis of a parallel distributed processing model of language acquisition. *Cognition* **28**, 73-193.

Poole, D. (1988). A logical framework for default reasoning. *Artificial Intelligence* **36**, 27-48.

Reiter, R. (1980). A logic for default reasoning. *Artificial Intelligence* **13**, 81-132.

Rescher, N. (1976). *Plausible Reasoning*. Amsterdam: Van Gorcum.

Rescher, N., & Manor, R. (1970). On inference from inconsistent premises. *Theory and Decision* **1**, 179-217.

Robinson, J. A. (1965). A machine-oriented logic based on the resolution principle. *Journal of the Association for Computing Machinery* **12**, 23-41.

Rumelhart, D. E., Hinton, G. E., & McClelland, J. L. (1986). A general framework for parallel distributed processing. In J. L. McClelland & D. E. Rumelhart (Eds.), *Parallel Distributed Processing: Explorations in The Microstructure of Cognition* (Vol. I, pp. 45-76.) Cambridge, MA: MIT Press.

Sejnowski, T. J. (1986). Higher-Order Boltzmann machines. In J. Denker (Ed.), *Neural Networks for Computing* (pp. 398-403). AIP Conference Proceedings, Vol 151. New York: American Institute of Physics.

Shastri, L. (1988). *Semantic Networks: An Evidential Formulation and its Connectionist Realization*. London: Pitman.

Shastri, L., & Ajjanagadde, V. (1991). From simple associations to systematic reasoning: A connectionist representation of rules, variables and dynamic bindings. Tech. Rep. No. MS-CIS-90-05, University of Pennsylvania.

Shoham, Y. (1988). *Reasoning about Change*. Cambridge, MA: MIT Press

Shortliffe, E. H. (1976). *Computer-based Medical Consultation, MYCIN*. New York: Elsevier.

Smolensky, P. (1986). Information processing in dynamic systems: Foundations of harmony theory. In J. L. McClelland & D. E. Rumelhart (Eds.), *Parallel Distributed Processing: Explorations in The Microstructure of Cognition* (Vol. I, pp. 194-281). Cambridge, MA: MIT Press.

Touretzky, D. S., & Hinton, G. E. (1988). A distributed connectionist production system. *Cognitive Science* **12**, 423-466.

Williams, R. J. (1986). The logic of activation functions. In J. L. McClelland & D. E. Rumelhart (Eds.), *Parallel Distributed Processing: Explorations in The Microstructure of Cognition* (Vol. I, pp. 423-443). Cambridge, MA: MIT Press.

8

The Representation of Knowledge and Rules in Hierarchical Neural Networks

Thomas Jackson
British Aerospace MAL

James Austin
University of York

Neural networks display the property of generalisation. This makes them insensitive to noise and corruption in pattern classification applications. In this chapter we discuss how this property may be exploited in neural network architectures developed for knowledge representation. We show how neural network architectures may be designed to exhibit a hierarchical data-structure suitable for knowledge representation. We also describe how structured rules might be captured within a neural architecture and processed in a manner that can accommodate uncertainty or ambiguity in a reasoning process.

1. INTRODUCTION

The work presented here describes two approaches to knowledge representation in connectionist networks. The models developed cover two different aspects of knowledge representation and so the chapter has been divided into two logical sections. The first section deals with the problem of representing reasoning processes in a connectionist architecture. Details of a rule-based processor for reasoning, that has been implemented in an associative memory, are presented. The discussion of the processor focusses on two issues, firstly how rules may be represented in a connectionist architecture, and secondly how the architecture implicitly deals with noisy, corrupt or otherwise ambiguous input that gives rise to the situation of rule conflict.

In the second section a hierarchical neural network architecture that has been developed to explore knowledge representation issues is discussed. This section is concerned with the methodology for representing high-level conceptual knowledge in a connectionist architecture. The approach adopted has been to develop a rigourous framework for structuring knowledge within a connectionist network. A symbolic representation approach has been investigated and in particular the schema model of knowledge representation has been mapped onto a connectionist architecture. This model presents a framework for representing abstract high-level knowledge as well as mechanisms for implicit reasoning and associative search processes.

Both of the methods presented make use of a connectionist associative memory which is described in Section I.

SECTION I. RULE-BASED REASONING IN AN ASSOCIATIVE MEMORY

2. THE ADAM MEMORY

The work in this chapter primarily exploits the use of the Advanced Distributed Associative Memory (ADAM) developed by Austin (1987). This memory can be viewed as an extension of the Willshaw, Buneman, and Longuet-Higgins (1969) correlation matrix memory. The network has a number of properties that make it highly suitable for use in reasoning as the following discussion shows.

The ADAM memory combines the recognised N-tuple pattern preprocess method (Bledsoe & Browning, 1959), with a two stage correlation matrix memory (see Fig. 8.1). The principal aim of the design of the memory was to allow the recall of a complete description of an input pattern containing noise. However, as well as operating as an autoassociative store, heteroassociation is also possible. Subsidiary aims in the development of the device were training and testing at high speed and simple implementation. The original design was aimed at problems in pattern recognition (Austin, 1987; Austin & Stonham, 1987). More recently, its general use as a device for reasoning on images and uncertain data has been proposed (Austin, Jackson, & Wood, 1991). As Fig. 8.1 shows, the first stage of the network consists of a preprocessing N-tuple stage. This extracts N-tuples from the input vector, passes them through a state and assignment function, f(), and represents the output as a 1 in f(N) code. The state assignment function shown implements a logical decoder which unequally identifies one of 2^N patterns on its input tuple. In this case $f(N_{max}) = 2^N$. As will be shown later, this stage is essential in the operation of the memory and for its use in uncertain reasoning applications. In general terms the N-tuple stage partially orthogonalises the input patterns, allowing a simple learning rule to be used in the subsequent stages of the network. A similar technique is used in function link networks (Pao, 1989) to reduce learning time. The sampling of the tuples from the input vector is typically random with each input element feeding only one tuple line, this raises the likelihood that the patterns will be recognised.

The second stage of the network consists of a correlation matrix, this associates the tupled input vector with a "class" vector. In this stage each input vector with a unique classification is associated with a unique binary class vector. The class vector is defined as having a random pattern of N bits set to one. This specification of the class vector ensures reliable recovery of the class during tests. Training of this memory consists of the following operation:

$\underline{X}_{pi}$ is an array of p_{max} input patterns, each i_{max} in size.
$\underline{T}_{pj}$ is an array of p_{max} patterns, each with j_{max} N-tuple states.
$\underline{C}_{ri}$ is an array of r_{max} class patterns, each i_{max} in size.
$\underline{W}_{rij}$ is the correlation matrix, consisting of i_{max} tuples, j_{max} tuple states, and r_{max} classes.

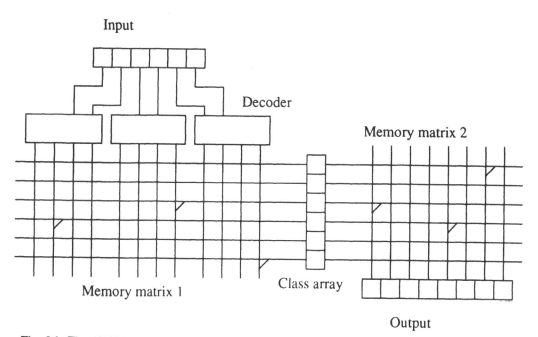

Fig. 8.1. The ADAM memory: The input vector is shown as a vector of 6 inputs feeding logical n to 2^n decoders. The memory consists of two correlation matrices, matrix 1 and matrix 2. The first associates the input to the class; the second feeds the class to the output.

The first stage of training is to tuple the image into samples of size N; this is achieved by the use of a mapping function, $M()$. Typically this mapping function selects the tuples in a random fixed order, selecting each pixel only once from the image. Each tuple is assigned a state by the state assignment function $f()$, which in this case assigns 1 of 2^N states. Each class is randomly assigned into C by the following procedure:

```
For all j
      if C_ij = 1
          For all p
              T_p = M[X_p]
              For all i
                      s = f[T_pi]
                      W_ijs = 1
              endfor
          endfor
      endif
endfor
```

Subsequent tests of the matrix consists of presentation of the input vector, fed through the N-tuple transformation and a matrix multiplication:

Training:

Select a class pattern to be trained,

$\underline{R}$ = raw class array
$\underline{X}$ = unknown pattern

```
For all r
      For all p
          T_p = M[X_p]
          For all i
                  s = f[T_pi]
                  if W_ijs = 1
                          increment R_r
          endfor
      endfor
endfor
```

The resulting raw class vector, $\underline{R}$, is then "n point thresholded" by the selection of the N highest elements of the raw class and setting these to 1, the others to zero. This operation robustly ecovers the class vector. The thresholding operation makes the memory robust to additive and lestructive noise in the input vector. Recent extensions to ADAM have allowed the class to be utomatically assigned and evenly distributed (in a pattern sense) (Brown & Austin, 1991).

The final stage of ADAM recalls the external associated image from the class pattern ecovered in the previous stage. This is achieved by the use of another correlation matrix. Training and testing the matrix is achieved in exactly the same way as in the previous memory. However, the raw vector recalled is thresholded by setting to 1 all outputs that are equal to n, where n is the number of bits set to one in the class.

The use of the class pattern is an essential factor in this network. The class pattern allows wo very large patterns to be associated in a very small memory, that is, two images of a and b n size can be stored in a memory containing only axc + cxb binary weights instead of axb pinary weights, where c is the size of the class array and c << a, b.

The class vector overcomes the problems involved in thresholding the output vector to ecover the pattern taught. The class vector in ADAM ensures that all candidate elements of b vill have a value of N, the number of bits set to one in the class. (This assumes that the class s accurately recalled during testing). If the class vector were not used and image 'a' were lirectly correlated with vector 'b' the resultant raw values of 'b' after tests could not be hresholded so simply.

The N-tuple preprocessing ensures that the input to the first correlation memory has a ixed number of bits set to 1, while preserving all the structure of the input image. If this were lot provided, the correlated matrix could easily be saturated during teaching if the input vector ontained all bits set to 1.

The use of the N-tuple preprocess also allows simple learning to be used because the nput images are partially orthogonalised and as a result the first correlation matrix need only act s a linear discriminator. It is possible that the network will not be able to store some patterns, his occurs when two patterns that are in different classes are not linearly separable. To vercome this the network can be trained with the same pattern in a slightly different position i.e., slight translation). Testing is then performed on the basis of the best of a set of tests with he input image slightly shifted on each test. Alternatively, a non-linear discriminator (multilayer letwork) can be used instead of the linear discriminator (Austin, 1988).

The networks implementation with binary weights and binary inputs mean that a simple ardware implementation is possible (Austin et al., 1991). Extensions to allow efficient mplementations for reasoning applications have also been proposed (Austin, 1992).

1. REASONING WITH ADAM

In this section we consider how associative processors, particularly ADAM, can be used o perform reasoning operations. For our purposes, we see the basic operation as being rule-ased processing. As such, any reasoning processor must be capable of performing the type of perations shown below

If (A) then B
If (A&B) then C
If (A+B) then C
If (NOT A) then D

That is, the system must be able to compute logical AND, OR (conjunction and disjunction) over a set of variables. The evaluation of preconditions must result in the assertion of a new piece of knowledge. The association between the preconditions and assertions represents "knowledge." When rules are combined in rule sets, they represent the knowledge of some domain. We show how rules may be represented in association memories and as such how "active" knowledge can be stored.

It is our belief that neural networks, such as ADAM, may be used to process uncertain information in particular uncertainty arising out of rule conflict or arising from imprecise data being presented to the system. The way we view uncertainty is in the form of uncertain rules. First, we see that rules can give uncertain outcomes, that is,

If (A) then B or C

In that if precondition A is true then the outcome is either B or C (exclusively). This can alternatively be represented as two rules.

If (A) then B
If (A) then C

In case of exclusivity between B and C, this is an example of rule conflict.

The second form of uncertainty is in the form of effects on the variables in the preconditions of rules. In the example above the variables were either true or false, this can be extended to a continuum of certainties, typically 0 represents no certainty in the variable and 1 represents total certainty in the variable. The effect that this certainty has an outcome in combination with other variables may simply be represented as a function, R(). We then can define R() in any way we like or use one of the conventional forms of reasoning. The function R() also combines the process of AND, OR and NOT (as shown in section 2.2).

We can now define

R(A,B,C) = D

as being some logical combination of the variables A, B and C, where R() implements the rule which asserts D.

2.2. USING ADAM

The ADAM memory can be used to store functions such as these with a suitable representation of the variable pre- and post-conditions, such that the application of the precondition variables causes the assertion of the post-condition variable. It is necessary to consider how the variables are represented on the inputs and outputs of the network to ensure correct operation of the memory.

The most effective representation is to replace each variable with a pattern or icon representing that variable. This is ideal for discrete variables, and allows a large number of variables to be coded using a small number of inputs. A continuous variable would need a large number of discrete variables to represent it, as is typically encountered in digital computers. As becomes clear later, for the efficient operation of the system, the icons must be well separated from each other (in a Hamming sense). In ADAM the icons consist of binary patterns containing a fixed number of bits set to one.

An iconic representation can be used to express uncertainty in a number of ways. In the present case we consider uncertainty as being expressed as a removal of parts of the icon representing the variable. Thus, when there is no confidence in the variable, the icon will be totally removed. Total confidence is represented by the complete variable being present.

We now consider how ADAM implements the rule expressed by the function R(). Any Boolean function can be broken into sum of products form, where it is expressed as a linear combination of disjunct terms (sets of AND functions combined by OR functions). For example, any rule R(A,B,C) -> D can be defined by a set of functions that compute the AND terms;

f1(A,B,C) = i
f2(A,B,C) = j
f3(A,B,C) = k,

disjunctively combined by a function,

f4(i,j,k) -> D

which linearly combines the i,j,k variables.

Inspecting ADAM, we see that the logical decoders implement the AND terms, and the first matrix stage computes the OR terms.

2.3. RULE IMPLEMENTATION AND VARIABLE BINDING

To see how ADAM can implement a rule, consider the rule

A.B.C+D -> E

We can first assign unique patterns to all the variables (which are all certain in this example).

The rule states that from either (A AND B AND C OR D) one can infer E. It is obvious that A, B, and C can be in any order to satisfy the rule. This is a major problem in neural networks, and can be seen as the variable binding problem. When expressed as a function, R(A,B,C,D)->E, the input variables must be bound to the correct locations on the input function.

This problem occurs because the typical network implementations tie the variables to particular units on the inputs of networks. as shown in Fig. 8.2.

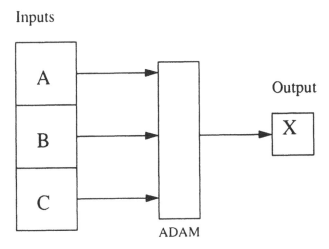

Fig. 8.2. Typical illustration of how variables are presented to a neural network. The icons A, B, and C occupy fixed, and distinct, input to the network. Thus you have the problem of binding the values (A, B, C, etc.) to the slots (the variable binding problem).

If variables are bound to spatially organised slots, the variable binding problem occurs. To overcome this, and make the network insensitive to the position of the variables, a number of alternatives are possible. First the variables could be trained in all orderings on the front of the network, this solution would be slow for large problems. Alternatively, the variables could be multiplexed onto the correct slots. This approach is effectively taken by Shastri (1985) by allowing units to be selective to particular variables by resonating to a global broadcast of the variable, literally using a frequency encoded approach. This and other multiplexing schemes are quite complex to implement. The approach taken here solves the problem by having a single slot on the input of ADAM and for all the variables that must be ANDed together, the icons for these variables are ORed together in to a single icon and placed in the slot. This combined icon, or "pseudo" variable, is a pattern that will uniquely fire that particular rule. For example, to train A.B.C + D -> E, icons for A, B, and C are ORed together and placed on the input to an ADAM memory. The output of the memory is E and the memory is trained. Then D is presented on the input to the memory and also trained to produce E. It will be clear that the patterns A.B.C together on the input will recall E on testing, as will D. More importantly, the variables A,B and C are not ordered, thus the problem of variable binding, in this example, does not exist.

The processing performed by the tuples and the first stage of ADAM is quite subtle in this application, and is vital to allow the approach above to work.

The AND function between variables (i.e., A.B.C) is performed by the N-tuple decoders as indicated above and only occurs where the N inputs to a single tuple fall between variable icons, that is, each input line of a tuple going to an element belonging to a different icon within the pseudo icon. Fig. 8.3a shows a pseudo icon produced by ANDing icons of A and B. Tuple 1 receives inputs from both A and B icons. Tuple 2 receives its inputs from just B. If tested on this pattern, both tuples would see what they did in training, and thus the pattern would be recognised. However, only tuple 1 is recognising the presence of both A and B. If B is just presented to the system, as in Fig. 8.3b, then tuple 2 still sees what it did in training, but tuple 1 no longer does. Thus only tuple 1 is recording the function A & B.

In practice, on large examples, the result of this is a "soft" response ability. For example, if the network is trained on A.B.C + D -> E, then the application of A.B.C will cause a strong E output. If just A is presented, then E will still be produced but at a much lower response. The system is indicating that some evidence is available for the belief in E. As will be shown, this is a very useful property of the system.

It will be apparent that to get a good AND function between variables, many tuples will need to "join" a number of variable icons. To achieve this the icons need to have a large number of bits set to 1. However, the more bits set per icon, the fewer icons can be joined into pseudo icons, as the input image to network would get saturated with 1s. To alleviate this, the number of tuples can be increased - to increase the chances of selecting tuples which span icons.

The examples above considered what happens in ADAM for a single rule. We now look at the processing of a network holding multiple rules. In this case, the process of "n point thresholding" the result of testing the first matrix effectively selects the best matching rule. If a set of icons present on the input exactly match a previous rule taught, then the post-condition variable for that rule will be output from the network. If the icons on the input do not exactly match any rule, then the network will output the variable of the rule with the most preconditions met, but this will be at a reduced confidence.

When two rules match the preconditions on the input, due to insufficient information, or conflict during training, the network will recall the post-conditions for both rules and output the icons for both these rules. This allows uncertainty to be exhibited.

2.4. PROCESSING WITH UNCERTAINTY

The above discussion has shown how ADAM may be used to implement a rule processing system. It has shown how rules expressed in an iconic form may be trained into the network and how rules are fired by the application of icons. Using this model, data can be mapped into an iconic form, presented to ADAM and rules fired in response. The result of these rules can be placed back into the memory space for further processing or reinterpreted for the outside world.

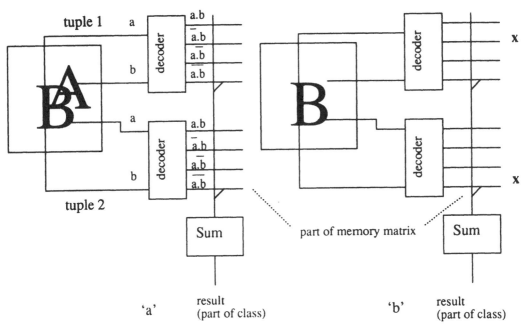

Fig. 8.3. (a) This diagram shows how an input pattern made up of icons for A and B are sampled such that tuple 1 performs a logical AND between A and B which is recorded by the appropriate weight at the output of decoder 1. Decoder 2 selects its tuple lines only from the icon B, and thus cannot compute A.B. (b) This illustrates how the decoders are activated when only icon B is present. The 'x' indicates the output line of the decoder that is activated when B is presented.

It was clearly shown how the network could respond with multiple post-conditions from data that resulted in a rule conflict. This was expressed as the icons for both the post conditions being present in the network output. Now we consider what happens when an uncertain, or conflicting output, is presented back to the input of the network, and show how initial conflict may be resolved by the application of subsequent rules.

Consider a network trained on:

i) A -> P
j) B -> Q
k) A -> T
l) P Q -> S

The net is then presented with A.B. A single resultant pseudo icon is not known for this combination of inputs, but three rules fire i,j,k above. This results in three icons being outputted, P, Q, and T. The two rules i and k are in conflict. The presence of multiple icons indicates a possible conflict. However, if the output is re-presented to the network the conflict is resolved. Only the rule (l) fires, presenting a single icon, S, on the output.

A number of important processes have taken place in this example. First, the uncertainty has been recorded (indicated by multiple icons outputted). Second, a parallel distributed search has taken place, where the variables and the rules are distributed. It is clear that the network is able to maintain conflicting states and deal with the conflicts.

In a more complex example, the initial conflicts could have resulted in further conflicts, which must be resolved with further data or through the process of search.

3. THE GENERIC ASSOCIATIVE INFORMATION PROCESSING MODEL

The current work has developed a generic architecture for supporting reasoning with ADAMs. This is shown in Fig. 8.4. The architecture consists of 3 basic parts, a memory plane, associative processors and input output processors. Each input/output processor deals with information and presents it to the memory plane in the correct form and position. As mentioned above, this representation is typically a random bit pattern. The memory plane holds a number of icons and acts as a working storage device. A number of associative memories feed from this taking input from a number of icons and producing a number of icons. Although simple, this generic model is powerful enough to represent the most complex systems, as is shown.

3.1. SUMMARY

The discussion has highlighted how rules are implemented in ADAM, but only the basic mechanisms have been described here. More remains to be investigated; for example, how is the control structure imposed, how can forward and backward reasoning be performed, how are the icons defined? All these aspects are currently being investigated.

The next section examines the problem of knowledge representation in neural networks and embeds the ADAM memory into a control structure for representation of schema knowledge.

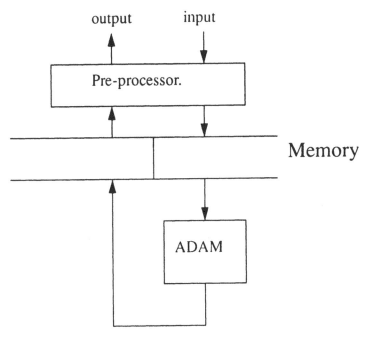

Fig. 8.4. Generic ADAM architecture for reasoning with data. The inputs come via a preprocessor which converts them to iconic form and places them into a memory surface. From the memory ADAM, memories take data and return them to the surface. Using this simple model, complex systems can be built.

SECTION II. SCHEMA KNOWLEDGE REPRESENTATION IN HIERARCHICAL NEURAL NETWORKS

4. INTRODUCTION

In the previous section we discussed the use of neural networks for handling reasoning processes. In this section we address the more general issue of knowledge representation. We are primarily concerned with the question of whether current connectionist paradigms are capable of supporting large (i.e., real world) knowledge representation tasks. There is a growing trend of using neural networks as a preprocessing technique for expert systems; delegating low-level signal processing tasks to neural networks and confining high-level symbolic processing to an expert system or similar knowledge base system. We present here a methodology whereby neural networks can be utilised for the high level processing requirements as well as the low-level ones. We make use of AI models of knowledge representation and show that these models can be implemented in connectionist architectures that are capable of representing abstract high level information. Furthermore, we propose mechanisms whereby the stored knowledge is used to direct processing in a connectionist model of perception.

We present a hierarchical connectionist model which integrates the properties of both symbolic and connectionist paradigms. The model addresses many of the failings of current connectionist implementations and specifically addresses two major limitations; the scaling of neural networks to large tasks and the structuring of knowledge within the networks. The framework for these studies is a hierarchical neural network system for 2D image analysis. Image analysis has been chosen as an area where the need for knowledge-directed reasoning is widely acknowledged (Ballard, 1982).

5. A CONNECTIONIST KNOWLEDGE-BASED MODEL

The fundamental approach that is adopted for knowledge-based reasoning is a hypothesis fire-and-test paradigm, that is, any search of the knowledge scheme will involve generating a candidate set of possible solutions (or hypotheses) and the validation of one of those hypotheses. To make hypothesis fire-and-test systems workable (that is, workable within acceptable time constraints) it is essential that efficient search mechanisms are implemented. We consider search, at the lowest level, to be a pattern matching process. Current neural network topologies are predominantly pattern recognition paradigms and so we argue that they are a natural technology for this search task. The approach uses neural based search mechanisms that are capable of guiding the search to generate a hypothesis (or set of hypotheses) constrained by the current input data. However, as well as mechanisms for search and hypothesis-generation, a fire-and-test methodology requires procedures for:

(a) Hypothesis combination (or inheritance) - such that higher level knowledge structures can inherit the results of lower level instantiated hypotheses.

(b) Hypothesis verification - to confirm the instantiation of a hypothesis in respect to all the current supportive data. This process must include an evaluation of all plausible alternative hypotheses.

We describe neural network techniques for dealing with both of these requirements that avoid the need to resort to conventional symbolic implementations. The use of a hypothesis fire-and-test model can in many situations lead to cases of combinatorial explosion of search in the knowledge space (particularly in the presence of ambiguous data). We discuss how the proposed neural network hierarchy can effectively constrain the search process - particularly in the case of uncertain data.

5.1. FEATURES OF THE SYSTEM

As we already noted, one of the most important features that we require for a hypothesis fire-and-test model is efficient search. In this context, efficient implies the minimal iterative search to generate the most appropriate hypothesis with, if possible, parallel implementation and immunity to ambiguity or noise in the data. To achieve these goals mechanisms are required to direct the search. Two cognitive features that we model to provide the necessary guidance procedures are expectation and focus-of-attention. Expectation is a top-down knowledge driven process that can provide heuristic constraints on the search process. Expectation must use knowledge of the domain as well as knowledge pertaining to the domain task, such that appropriate responses to verify a hypothesis can be made. These two levels of representation are typically referred to as declarative representation and procedural representation respectively. Focus-of-attention is a procedural response of the system to identify areas of current interest within the domain.

Knowledge-based reasoning often implies a large domain model and, by consequence, a large search space. Traditionally this has been a problematic issue for neural computing. This is because the standard connectionist paradigms have, by and large, suffered from the same limitations as many AI implementations - they do not scale well to real world representation tasks. Our approach to this problem has been to develop hierarchical neural network models which partition the search space into manageable size subsets, each of which can be adequately represented by a unique network. It also allows representation of information at increasing levels of abstraction. We present a novel architecture to support the hierarchical abstraction that avoids massive hardware requirements but supports a large virtual memory space. This is a central issue to the representation task - if we were to physically implement each of the required networks we would very quickly have an unrealisable hierarchy architecture. A minimalist physical architecture makes use of "weight paging" - that is, storing individual network weight matrices in memory and loading the weights as and when required - so that the functionality and properties of the networks can be dynamically reconfigured. The control functions for this implementation are described.

As well as investigating techniques to scale neural networks to large representation tasks we have also been considering the implementation of implicit inference mechanisms. We already hinted that pattern recognition can play a key role within cognitive activities. We use the pattern recognition properties of neural networks to model features that Minsky describes as innate to reasoning - Pattern Matching, a Clustering Theory and a Similarity Network (Minsky, 1975). We also use patterns to implement a symbol representation scheme. In the system the symbols will be patterns defined within predefined data structures. The benefit of using patterns in this manner is that a continuous representation format can be utilised throughout every level of abstraction in the hierarchy. This provides a continuous mapping from the low-level iconic data through to the high level knowledge structures. The architecture that we propose presents a consistent symbol representation at each of the levels of abstraction, and will display the necessary conditions of a symbol processing system.

6. A SCHEME REPRESENTATION METHODOLOGY

The work that is presented here describes the mapping of a schema (or frame) knowledge representation paradigm onto a neural network architecture. Other AI representation paradigms have been implemented in connectionist architectures, notably semantic networks (Shastri, 1985), production systems (Hinton & Touretzky, 1985) and fuzzy logic, however, we believe there are strong motivations for the novel use of frame representation.

Frames became an active research area during the late 1970s, influenced by Minsky's extension of the concept (Minsky, 1975). Frames are data structures that are able to represent stereotyped models of objects or concepts. This is achieved by capturing the regular features of an object/concept in a frame data structure that is composed of terminal slots. Minsky proposed that frames could model many cognitive capabilities and suggested that frames described not only the mechanisms for knowledge storage but also the means by which knowledge can direct reasoning. Minsky proposed that we do not store specific information pertaining to individual objects/concepts but rather store stereotyped models as schemata. When a frame is instantiated by a search process, the current input data or symbols are placed in the appropriate slots of that frame to create a specific instance of that object/concept. Any vacant slots can be filled by default values. We believe the most useful properties that frames display are stereotyped, feature based modelling and expectation. Expectation is generated as a consequence of any instantiated frame providing *a priori* feature information pertaining to the object/concept.

We wish to exploit these latter two properties extensively in the neural network realisation of a frame processing system. We make the important distinction, however, that our conceptualised frames are implemented with feature slots that contain patterns as the data primitives. This is far more than just an implementation issue; the use of pattern based schemas in a neural hierarchy creates implicit inference mechanisms without the need to resort to external reasoning processes.

6.1. WHY FRAMES IN A CONNECTIONIST IMPLEMENTATION?

Schemata can be made to model many dominant cognitive functions, most notably those of expectation, inheritance, generalisation and stereotype modelling. However, it is primarily the following reasons that have led us to adopt their use for neural implementation:

a) Frames rely on associative search for hypothesis cueing.
b) Frame verification is a process of pattern matching.
c) Frames rely on hierarchical inheritance structures.

In each of these requirements for frame-based reasoning processes, neural computing techniques have properties that can be exploited, and further can circumvent some of the difficulties associated with frame based processing systems.

The most obvious connectionist feature used in our implementation is associative search. Neural networks perform highly efficient distributed pattern search. This can be exploited in matching input features/symbols against frames in memory (which we shall refer to as long term memory) and because the search looks for partial pattern matches a frame in memory can be cued from any one (or more) of its terminal slots. This is the action required for generating hypotheses from low-level data driven search. It is highly probable that in many cases multiple hypotheses will be selected by a partial pattern match search - where the actual number is dependent on the number of parameters that the search was based on. This conflict is not a negative feature, because it allows the system to generate a *set* of candidate hypotheses. This fuzziness is advantageous in the early stages of processing where uncertainty and inconclusive evidence create ambiguity. A candidate set of hypotheses does not constrain the search too rigidly in the early stages of processing but generates sufficient conceptual information to initiate a cycle of schema refinement by guided search. We describe later how high level processes can support a candidate set of solutions until further high level evidence allows invalid hypotheses to be rejected. Frame validation can also benefit from neural network pattern matching properties if we generalise the role of frame validation as a search for maximal pattern match against the current input data. Similarity matching is thus implicit in the action of the associative search. Frame inheritance is the means by which data are communicated through increasing levels of abstraction in the knowledge representation scheme. The successful classification of a feature or object is used as the input to frames in the next layer of the hierarchy. This is not an implicit feature of neural computing techniques but rather one that is created by using a hierarchy of networks. The communication mechanisms are, however, simplified by the use of neural networks because a consistent data format - namely symbolic pattern strings - is maintained at each layer of the hierarchy.

The above discussion indicates the obvious features that justify the application of neural networks as the realisation of a frame system. We report on results of these studies and show that not only are the above assumptions justified but there are also many other advantages of this approach.

7. A HIERARCHICAL CONNECTIONIST ARCHITECTURE

A data flow diagram of the hierarchical connectionist structure is shown in Fig. 8.5. The networks that are employed at each layer of the hierarchy, including the feature classification input layer, are the ADAM networks described earlier. The choice of this network is by no means binding to the design philosophy - it was chosen primarily because its dynamics are well understood and because it is a one-pass learning network. For the scale of the system that is described here, this is an enormous advantage; otherwise, training times would have been prohibitive even for research investigations. Furthermore, the network displays all the necessary properties we require - namely adaptive learning, distributed representation, parallel associative search, and generalisation.

We first describe the features of the physical architecture. We explain how the hierarchy can be trained to represent data at different levels of abstraction. We then proceed with a description of the bottom-up data flow through the hierarchy and discuss how the hierarchy can be used to direct a search process.

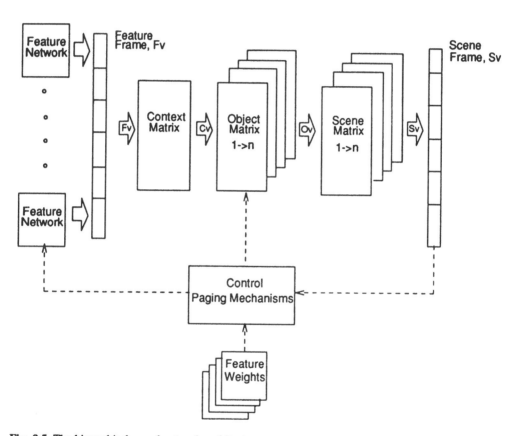

Fig. 8.5. The hierarchical neural network architecture.

7.1. THE PHYSICAL ARCHITECTURE

7.1.1. THE INPUT LAYER

The input layer to the system is a parallel layer of neural network feature detectors. The detectors are trained to classify the data primitives found in the domain (or at least those deemed to be relevant). Our application is to two-dimensional vision, and the primitives are line edges, colour, texture, size, and orientation. The detectors are trained independently to each other and independently of the rest of the hierarchy. Each of the detectors has a unique symbol set for its classification task. The length and format of the symbols (binary strings) is consistent across all the detectors in order to maintain uniformity in the data structures. The number and type of detectors required by the system is obviously application specific but the parallel implementation is easily scaled to any desired number of units.

7.1.2. THE CONTEXT LAYER

The second stage of the system is the context network. This network is trained on the data from the feature detectors which is captured in a frame structure, F_v. The context network is used to gain an overall view of the characteristics of the input data. It is trained to classify the generic type of features found in the input rather than a specific object or concept containing those features. As an example, if we could detect that the dominant features in the input domain are, say, shades of green and textures of grass, we might well deduce that we are dealing with an outdoor scene as opposed to an indoor scene. The context network is trained to recognise the global attributes of the input data and provide a classification of the generic context. The output of the network is a binary vector, C_v. An alternative network topology for this function might be a self-organising feature map, as typified by the work of Kohonen. These maps have been shown to perform well on data quantisation tasks where clustering is required (Kohonen, 1987)

The context network differs from the other networks in the hierarchy in that it is an analogue implementation of the ADAM network. The binary correlation matrix that we described previously is replaced with an analogue weight matrix. The functionality of the network is unchanged and the learning paradigm remains Hebbian based. However, the weight matrix values are now incremented by a predetermined amount on each training pass as opposed to being set to binary values. After each training pass the weight values are normalised. The recall mechanisms are unaffected and the class vector is recovered by n point thresholding. The analogue weight matrix does, however, create different generalisation properties that are exploited at this stage. By using an analogue weight matrix with incremental learning we can force the associative memory to create a higher weighting for features that are more dominant in a training phase. More simply, we can implement reinforcement learning. This ensures that the internal representations that the networks create for a context classification are actually based on global attributes. This ensures, in turn, that the classification performance of the network will be more invariant to changes in non-critical input features (for example, colour may be an attribute that is highly variant across a range of otherwise closely related features - the analogue implementation will learn to ignore the colour feature).

7.1.3. THE OBJECT LAYER

At the third layer of the hierarchy the representational abstraction is increased to the object level. At this stage the input features are classified into an object description. The object network is trained on the same input features as the context network, that is the feature frame F_v. However, the classification task is now directed at identifying specific objects on the basis of the input features. At this level of the hierarchy we envisage a classification task required to cover several hundreds of objects. For this reason the object layer is arranged as a number of parallel classification networks - each of which is trained on a subset of the classification task. This can be considered a partitioning of the pattern space at the object level. The parallel implementation has also been adopted as an attempt to overcome the scalability limitations of neural networks. In particular, we wish to avoid the degradation of generalisation performance when training networks in a high dimensional but highly overlapping classification space. We require the object layer to provide good classification performance within a category and also good performance across categories. However, if there is significant overlap between nonrelated categories this creates conflicting requirements. We also require the object classification layer to be able to indicate instances where the classification may belong to one of several categories (given the possibly incomplete input criteria). A single large network cannot combine these requirements. A layer of parallel, individual networks can, however, by providing good localised (or interclass) generalisation with the ability to represent several categories simultaneously and independently.

The parallel structure may at first appear expensive and cumbersome in terms of hardware; however, each of the parallel networks is not physically implemented, instead they are stored in virtual memory as weight matrices. When a network is required, the weights are loaded into the physical network (this is simplified by use of the ADAM network since it is a fixed topology). An analogy can be drawn with virtual memory paging techniques. The mechanisms for the paging of a network are data driven. In a bottom-up classification process each of the networks could be searched in parallel but this would be an extremely inefficient search scheme. Instead techniques have been developed to constrain the search at each level and minimise the memory paging. These are described in later sections.

7.1.4. THE SCENE LAYER

The fourth layer of the hierarchy is the scene stage. At this level the system uses a frame data structure to store related objects to represent concepts. The scene stage of the hierarchy is a two stage heteroassociative ADAM network, unlike the earlier stages which are single stage networks. The lower layers of the hierarchy are required to output a classification vector for any network input. However, the scene stage does not recall a vector but instead it recalls a complete symbol frame. The differences are described in Fig. 8.6. The output frames are stored in the second stage of the matrix during the training cycle, simultaneously with the scene input frames. The second stage of the heteroassociative matrix has been structured so that the frames can store additional information other than the features derived from the bottom-up processing chain. This extra information can be procedural information or exception handling, for example. It is facilitated by adding extra terminal slots to the frame structure that is stored in the second stage of the matrix. Thus in the first stage of the matrix, the recognition stage, only the object features are stored. In the recall matrix however, we can store any additional information relating to a concept through the extra terminal slots. This creates a mechanism whereby we can instantiate a frame purely on the basis of associative feature matching but can recall information pertaining to that frame at several different levels of abstraction.

One Stage ADAM Matrix

Two Stage ADAM Matrix

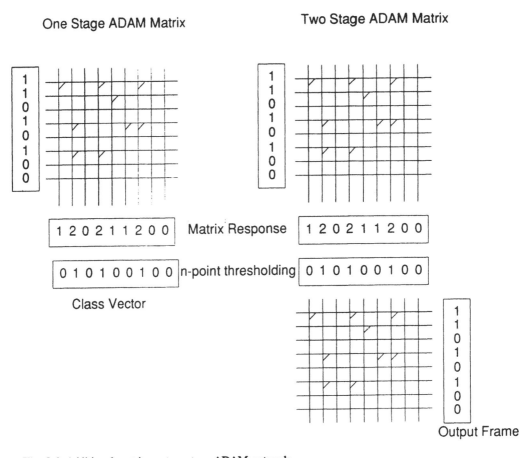

Fig. 8.6. Additional matrix on two-stage ADAM network.

The scene layer of the hierarchy is trained on the object vectors, O_v. The training mechanisms are the same as those described for the lower layers - a frame is generated to store an exemplar of a scene. The terminal slots of the frame are filled by the object vector symbols.

The terminals are filled sequentially as the objects are identified at the object layer. Once the necessary exemplar features are extracted from the input domain, the scene network can be trained with the complete frame. The scene stage of the knowledge hierarchy is arranged in a similar manner to the object layers — there are parallel layers of networks, each of which is specific to a type of scene.

7.1.5. CONTROL MECHANISMS

Fig. 8.5 also shows a control structure for paging weights. The control mechanisms are responsible for the implementation of top-down processing, namely expectation and focus-of-attention. The implementation is relatively crude — the control processor is primarily an associative look-up-table. Information contained within the high level frames is used to control the paging action of the processor. Weights are loaded into the network at two different levels. The processor can page new weight matrices into the feature detector networks in the input layer — this allows dynamic reconfiguration of the functionality of the detectors. The processor also loads weight matrices into the object matrix to "prime" the network during a directed search sequence. We currently use an ADAM network to perform the mapping of the high level data into weight paging action. We envisage, however, that more complex networks could be installed here to allow greater subtlety in the control mechanisms.

7.2. FRAME STRUCTURES

We now turn our attention to the way that data are structured within the hierarchy and in particular to the frame concept. This is most easily seen at the input layer of the system. The outputs of the feature detectors are stored in a feature frame, F_v, each network generating data appropriate to just one terminal slot of a frame, as shown in Fig. 8.7. Each feature detector has a local symbol set for its feature representation. The output of all the detectors are concatenated into a frame structure, each slot of which is a unique attribute. The benefits that are gained from the use of neural representation are generalisation and the ability to learn the frame features through training examples. The property of generalisation allows the network to cope with noisy or incomplete frames, and to a lesser degree, ambiguous information in the frame. The classification of the frame is based on a maximum similarity match over the entire contents of the frame. However, due to the fact that the frames are developed by training examples the underlying features of the data are extracted and weighted according to significance to the classification task. Attaching values to features in an expert system, via fuzzy set theory or Bayesian probabilities for example, is typically a difficult task.

7.3. BOTTOM-UP DATA-FLOW MECHANISMS

We have described the physical architecture of the system and the manner in which data can be represented at increasing layers of knowledge abstraction, from low-level features at the input to high-level concepts at the output layer. We now describe the data flow process through the hierarchy that allows bottom-up low-level feature information to instantiate high-level conceptual knowledge. We have described only three layers of abstraction for simplicity, in many cases this may not be adequate but layers can be added at any level of the abstraction as required.

7.3.1. LOW-LEVEL SEARCH

As the schematic Fig. 8.5 highlights, the hierarchy uses both parallel and serial data flow paths. However, the data flow from the context layer to the final layer is serial. It should be noted that although the data flow is serial, parallel distributed representation is used at each layer and the search mechanisms at each layer are implemented in parallel. Frame representation is fundamentally a feature-based representation paradigm - the architecture reflects this because the input stage of the system is a parallel layer of neural network feature detectors. The outputs of the detectors are stored in the frame structure, F_v, which forms the input to the context network. An associative search is activated on the contents of this frame, the result of which is a classification of the global context of the input. This is the vector, C_v, which is used, via an associative look-up-table, to select the appropriate object network (or set of object networks) in the next layer of the hierarchy. The feature frame is then reapplied as the input to the selected network and a classification of the object type will occur at this stage. The object symbol, O_v, is a pattern vector identifying the object. This process is shown in Fig. 8.8.

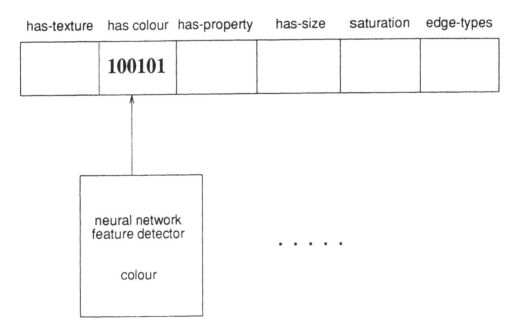

Fig. 8.7. The symbols are represented by patterns on the output of each neural feature detector (e.g., the pattern 100101 could uniquely define the colour blue.

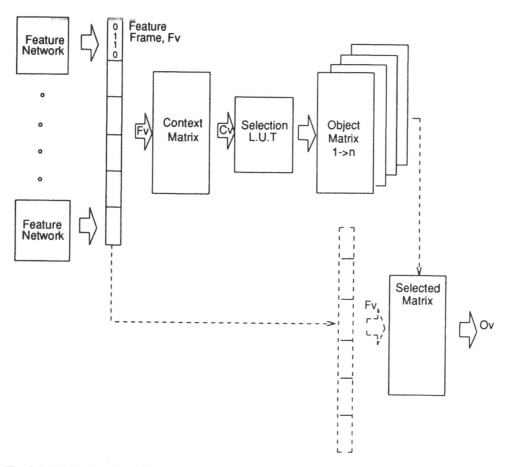

Fig. 8.8. The low-level data flow mechanisms for object classification.

At this point we begin to see how a large feature space can be partitioned into subpartitions by the hierarchy. It is not possible to train the context matrix stage to capture all the domain features and yet maintain good generalisation performance. This approach deals with the problem by using the input layer to generate only a coarse estimate of which class the object belongs to. The coarse estimate directs further search to one (or more) of the "expert" object networks. Each of the indicated object matrix networks can then be allocated highly localised classification tasks for a class of objects. This is illustrated in Fig. 8.9.

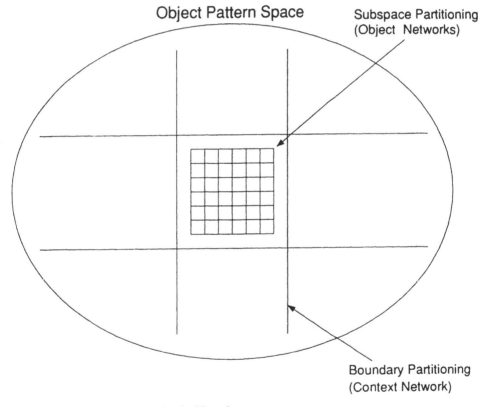

Fig. 8.9. Pattern space partitioning by the hierarchy.

There are two main benefits to this two step object classification approach. Firstly, the combined stages can be trained on a very large symbol set. The size of the symbol set is constrained only by the number of object networks that are used in the second layer. The second benefit, as described earlier, is that we can place tight bounds on the generalisation performance on between category classification. If the input information is ambiguous and a distinct classification is not possible then several networks can respond with a class to generate a candidate set of possible solutions. Also, each object network also has a localised object set to represent where class variance can be minimised. Consequently the object networks can be trained to generate unique object symbols for each object stored in the network. The ability to generate a set of distinct hypothesis solutions is of importance to the later stages of the network.

An alternative solution to that of using the intermediary representation created by the context matrix would be to search all of the object networks in parallel. However, this has the computational overhead of requiring an exhaustive search, which, given the large number of object networks, is computationally expensive. The intermediary context network approach can be viewed as providing context to guide the search, thereby constraining the number of search paths.

7.3.2. HYPOTHESIS GENERATION

The system has the facility for representing hypothesis solutions across class sets but it is also possible to generate candidate solutions within a class. This is a feature of the recall mechanisms of the ADAM network. All of the patterns trained in the ADAM network are stored against a class vector. The class response during recall of the ADAM network contains response from all patterns in the memory that are close (by Hamming distance) to the input pattern. Fig. 8.10 illustrates the recall response from a network trained using class vectors with only three bits set. We can thus recall multiple class vectors, C_v, from the associative memory which can be ranked in order of the highest degree of match. The ranking of the hypotheses into a candidate set is an implicit feature of the network and involves minimal computational overhead, merely iterative thresholding of the matrix response. The hypothesis ranking, in the simplest case, is achieved by iteratively thresholding the highest three responses to retrieve the class vectors. In each case the original class pattern is retrieved by *n-point* thresholding the components to a binary form. This simple example assumes that all class vectors are nonoverlapping. The advantage of this feature is that it does not commit the system to a unique classification decision at an early stage in the processing chain but rather to generation of a ranked candidate set of hypotheses that can be validated with a local iterative search at a later stage.

These benefits of this approach are most apparent when the system is presented with conflicting or ambiguous data. It allows the system to cope with uncertainty at the low-level data stage (which is essential for most domains and especially vision) and postpone categorical classification until higher-level knowledge or procedures can be used to influence a decision. This is achieved with computational efficiency simply by communicating the hypothesis ranking through the levels of the hierarchy until such time as sufficient information is available to validate a unique hypothesis. This may involve extra local iterative search but this search is highly constrained by the limits imposed by the ranking process.

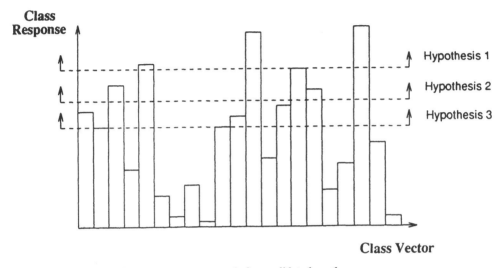

Fig. 8.10. Thresholding the class response to rank the candidate hypotheses.

8. SEARCH AT THE SCENE LEVEL

The result of processing in the lower layers of the hierarchy is the instantiation of a set (one or more) of object vectors. The search process now attempts to map the identified objects into a high-level conceptual scene frame. High-level frames are retrieved by the same mechanisms as in the object layer, namely a global search on any active output from the object networks. This is an associative search and a frame can be cued by a match of the input to any of its terminal slots. All of the scene networks are searched in parallel and the frame selection process is based on a winner-take-all voting mechanism. At the scene level of representation many features will overlap across frames. For example, if we are considering room schemas for a house, it is highly likely that an object such as a chair may be contained within many different room schemata. A search initiated by the recognition of a chair will generate a response from each of the relevant schemata (unless it is a chair specific to a single scene). In this case there is no clear winning hypothesis. The system will accept each hypothesis as equally valid at this stage, until further evidence can be acquired to refine the hypothesis selection. The initial associative search has, however, limited the scope of the search for further stages of the verification process.

The mechanisms for generating a hypothesis set are the same as those used for the object layer. The closest frame to the input data will generate the smallest Hamming distance measure. The frames can thus be ranked on the basis of a similarity measure. The multiple hypothesis representation properties of the network can, however, be viewed from a different perspective; that of relational representation. The search path technique that we are presenting can be approximated by a directed graph. In a directed graph there are typically links between concepts indicating relational associations. These links are explicit and hardwired into the graph. In an associative distributed architecture these links can be formed implicitly. Any frames in the long-term memory that share feature attributes will implicitly be evoked on each associative search. Concepts that are related at the object level can thus be retrieved simply by associative search mechanisms and need not be explicitly programmed into the system. There are, however, limitations with this perspective - primarily that the links only exist at one level of generality, namely feature similarity. This is because frames are only stored at one level of representation at the input stage of the scene networks. We have yet to investigate the use of recurrent feedback mechanisms at the scene stage but we envisage that more complex relational links can be created by such techniques.

8.1. INVARIANT REPRESENTATION

The training input to the scene matrix is a binary symbol string, collated from the output of the object networks. The frame is collated serially which means that the network is sensitive to the position of a symbol within a frame during a recall sequence. Since there is no means to predetermine that an object is going to be located in the same relative position that it was during training this implies very poor recall performance in most situations. We investigated three alternative techniques to make the networks invariant to the ordering of the input features during recall. The first is testing the inputs in all positions in the input frame. This method is highly impractical. A second option is to train the inputs at all positions within the input frame. The third option is to only allow predefined data types to fill particular terminal slots in a frame. Hence each output vector, Ov, is directed to a unique terminal according to its data type (as is the case with the input layer from the feature detectors).

Currently we have implemented the second option, training each input at all terminal positions. We are able to do this because the object vectors are very sparse and testing has shown that overlapping the inputs does not appear to effect the generalisation performance or the stability of the networks. It allows efficient recall mechanisms because no extra processing is required prior to an associative search. In due course we shall implement the third option - specific data fields - which is a truer analogy to scheme methodology. It does, however, require a mechanism to ensure that the object vectors can be classed into a type according to their data content. For example, vector symbols for the objects desk, chair, sofa can all be cast into the generic type furniture. A mechanism that we suggest but have not yet implemented is to use the first few bits of the vector as an index field to indicate the data type and appropriate terminal slot. We are currently investigating the advantages of this approach. Obvious disadvantages are the extra processing required to index the symbols, and more significantly, the difficulty of creating generic data types to cover the range of objects that will be contained with the object networks. At the input layer the range of primitives and feature types is limited by the pre-processing mechanisms applied, however, the range of objects that can be represented by these primitives is obviously orders of magnitude higher.

Related studies (Brown & Austin, 1991) have investigated the use of self-organising networks (Kohonen Feature Maps or the ART network of Grossberg, 1988) as a preprocessor on the training data to find the optimal class types for ADAM networks. The results of this technique have been very successful and it could potentially be applied to the issue of predefining optimal frame structures.

8.2. SUMMARY

In the above discussion we focused on the architecture for the hierarchy, presenting the details of the data-flow mechanisms driven from the low-level processes. We discussed the methods adopted for dealing with a large search space and the way that a frame representation can be utilised to structure knowledge within a hierarchical architecture. We discussed the mechanisms by which the low level data can initiate search and generate a candidate set of hypothesis solutions to a given set of input conditions. We now wish to discuss the mechanisms within the system that are used to refine a set of solutions to a unique solution.

9. CONTROL AND FEEDBACK MECHANISMS

So far, we have only discussed the data-flow mechanisms that direct the associative search in a bottom-up flow through the hierarchy. In the following sections we discuss the mechanisms that are responsible for controlling the knowledge-driven top-down processes, in particular expectation and focus of attention.

9.1. THE PERCEPTUAL CYCLE

The control mechanisms that we developed are motivated by the action-oriented model of perception (Arbib, 1972). This model proposes a cyclic as opposed to a linear processing chain; with high-level knowledge refining and directing the process flow; see Fig. 8.11. Minsky (1975) qualifies this search process in the following manner: "Thinking always begins with suggestive but imperfect plans and images; these are progressively replaced by better - but not usually perfect - ideas" (p. 230). The refinement stage uses a focus of attention mechanism. The mechanisms that guide the search are driven by high-level knowledge. This is generated by the concept of top-down expectation.

9.2. EXPECTATION

We described how a frame representation scheme can model conceptual expectation by creating data structures that capture the stereotypical features of a concept. Any frame selected as a hypothesis solution based on the current input conditions provides expectation by predicting which other relevant features should be located in the domain. We now discuss how we have used the representation properties to provide process control for a validation cycle.

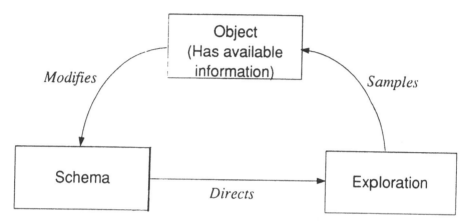

Fig. 8.11. The perceptual cycle.

9.2.1. TOP-DOWN PROCESSING

In the current implementation, the scene output frame stores two fields of information at each terminal slot. Each terminal stores an object symbol - which is a feature of the invoked scene - and a paging vector. This high-level knowledge can be used to direct further search in the lower stages of the hierarchy. The hypothesis verification process is currently implemented with relatively coarse heuristics. From the set of candidate hypotheses the frame with the highest response is selected as the most likely solution. Given that we have selected the frame on the basis of only one or two input data features, the verification process attempts to locate the other features defined in the frame. A simple heuristic to guide the search is created by ranking the features within the frame in order of relevance to the classification task. Those features that can be considered as providing the highest information content are searched for first. We mention this to highlight the advantages of forcing a rigid data structure onto the neural network output representation scheme. Consequently, to validate a hypothesis a frame provides us with information indicating which features to look for and in which order to look for them. However, this information only tells us which features to look for and it does not tell us how to look.

It is for this reason that each terminal slot contains the feature symbol plus a paging vector. The paging vector is procedural information for the control mechanisms. The paging slot contains the cueing vector, C_v, which locates the memory matrix that contains the object that is to be identified during the next phase of the search. This information is used in two ways.

Firstly, the control mechanism pages the appropriate memory matrix in the layers of the hierarchy; this constrains the available search paths. This can be thought of as priming the network for the search process and it is effected primarily to reduce computational load. Secondly, the control mechanism uses this information to load new weight matrices into the feature detector networks in the input layer. This action allows the system to redefine the functionality of the input layer. This may include options such as increasing the resolution of the feature detectors or using a specific network function to detect a particular feature. This top-down feedback could also be used to control sensors prior to the input detection layer. The control implementations that we have experimented with are relatively coarse. The mapping between the feedback from the top level and the input layers is achieved by an associative look-up table. This is not ideal but our current emphasis is on the properties of the feedforward and feedback data flow mechanisms.

9.2.2. REFINEMENT CYCLE

The feedback control primes the network to search for a specific object on the basis of high-level expectation. If an object is located, the vector, O_v, from the object network is placed into the frame structure with the previously identified objects. The frame acts as a short-term memory buffer during a verification cycle. A search is initiated at the scene stage with the updated contents of the frame, initially the search is restricted to the candidate set of hypothesis frames. If the object that was searched for is located then the candidate hypothesis frame that initiated the search will create the maximum response from the search, thus reinforcing its level of verification. In this case, the next object in the frame structure is searched for - instigating a cyclic search process until the frame is verified or classification fails. In the latter case, processing must back-track to the object level and an alternative object description is chosen from the candidate set of object vectors for the original input. In the worst case, the object is rejected and new features are searched for at the input.

If the candidate hypothesis was not reinforced on the basis of the extra information then there are two alternative causes: either the hypothesis was invalid or the object was not located. Assuming the former case, the system must refine its hypothesis selection. On the basis of the last search of the current hypothesis set it is possible that a new winning hypothesis has been identified. If so, then a cyclic search process is initiated for the new hypothesis frame. If no new winning hypothesis was identified then the contents of the frame buffer are reapplied to all of the scene networks. Given that extra object information is available the search will generate a new set of hypothesis solutions. The new set will be a union of the old set and those frames fired by the new object. A new hypothesis is selected from this revised set.

The refinement of the hypothesis set is analogous to a backward chaining process. If a hypothesis is rejected because its features cannot be instantiated then a new hypothesis is selected - in many knowledge-based system paradigms this would involve backtracking up a data-tree structure. In the distributed neural representation used here the process of backtracking is made implicit to the search process. The transition from one search tree to another is implemented by the associative search switching to a frame with a closer pattern match. As more features are retrieved from the input (cumulative evidence) support for one frame may weaken whilst another is strengthened. As these features are captured in the temporary scene frame an associative search will force the output of the system to tend toward the frame in memory with the closest match. Effectively the system is backtracking to another search tree but this is implemented as a continuous transition - avoiding a discrete trace back through the search space.

In the worst case, the transition to a new hypothesis set will merge the members of two disjoint frame sets that have no common objects. The confidence measure (based on a pattern similarity metric) for the members of the set will be equal and no winning hypothesis will be selected. The selection of a hypothesis in this case is instead based on the relevance of the current identified objects to each frame. As was described earlier, the objects are ranked in the frames in order of relevance to the concept captured by a frame. The hypothesis frame is thus selected on the basis of the how significant the located objects are to each of the frames in the set. The process of selection refinement is repeated until the network settles onto a single frame. This frame will be the one with the closest pattern match to the short-term representation held in the scene input frame.

9.2.3. EXPLICIT REPRESENTATION

A typical criticism of neural network applications is that because the internal representation within a network is fully distributed across the weight topology there is no method by which a network can be interrogated to justify the output classifications. The use of a frame representation scheme, whilst still employing a distributed internal representation, enforces an explicit representation at the output of a network. This implies that a decision a network makes is in fact open to scrutiny. In particular, at the scene level of the system, it is a trivial task to examine which features the network based the classification on. It is also possible to investigate the reasons why the system may have rejected a particular frame hypothesis. In many applications, particularly those in the financial sector, this is a highly beneficial feature.

9.2.4. IMPLICIT REASONING MECHANISMS

The search mechanisms described demonstrate two properties of the system. Firstly, a hierarchical system based purely on neural network processing can be used to achieve simple heuristic reasoning with high-level concepts. Second, the mechanisms that support the reasoning processes are implicit and based on simple computations.

The reasoning process has implemented a fire-and-test paradigm. This combines frame instantiation from low-level feature identification and cyclic refinement to match the features to a conceptual model. Frames, and therefore concepts, are accepted or rejected on the basis of whether cumulative supportive evidence can be found to match the expected features of a model. Reasoning is thus also directed by high-level conceptual knowledge within the system. Three important mechanisms are handled implicitly by the architecture - multiple hypothesis generation, similarity matching, and hypothesis selection. Hypothesis generation and similarity matching are both dealt with by using connectionist techniques to store the frame structures. In each case it is associative search and recall — inherent neural network properties — that provide the functionality. Hypothesis selection is primarily based on simple distance metrics. Despite these simple mechanisms the system implements many processes necessary for reasoning (at least in a fire-and-test paradigm) extremely efficiently.

10. CONCLUSIONS

We presented a neural based framework for the implementation of a knowledge representation system coupled with simple heuristic reasoning mechanisms. The motivation behind the architecture was to investigate the properties of distributed associative representation and recall mechanisms in a hierarchical system. We discussed how adopting a rigorous representation methodology (i.e., frames) allows a neural network based system to represent information at many levels of abstraction. The incentive for this approach was primarily one of increasing the efficiency of knowledge representation inference mechanisms. The computational mechanisms for search and recall that have been implemented are all computationally simple and efficient. The inferencing processes based on these are also simplistic but the lack of flexibility and structure compared with traditional representation paradigms are offset by the gains in processing speed for frame instantiation and validation.

As a cognitive model for knowledge representation, the model herein has many weaknesses and omissions. The most obvious is probably that the conceptual models developed by the system are purely feature-based and make no account for functional or complex relational description. On these issues the approach has nothing to contribute to areas that traditional AI implementations have long struggled with. What we do hope to achieve in the long term is a deeper understanding of the issues involved in using connectionist topologies for representing information via abstracted internal world models. We are concerned not only with the representation issues, however, but also with the methodology for exploiting connectionist network properties - associative search and recall, generalisation, and distributed representation - for implicit inferencing and reasoning processes.

The application of connectionist networks to modelling cognitive processing and knowledge representation tasks has been fiercely contested. Probably the most recent concerted criticism has been led by Fodor and Pylyshyn (1988), who argued that connectionist models have yet to contribute anything further to the understanding of cognitive reasoning mechanisms. The reasoning behind their negative viewpoint is their emphatic belief that cognitive activity can only be captured within a symbolic processing system. They infer that such a system must display the properties of semantic and syntactic structure, systematicity, and compositionality. The systematicity of a system is defined as the ability to attach semantic interpretation to any of the internal states of the system. Compositionality specifies that any symbol must maintain a consistent semantic interpretation regardless of its occurrence within any other string of symbols, that may have higher-level semantic interpretation. Although Fodor and Pylyshyn acknowledge the pattern recognition properties of connectionist architectures, they argue that none of the current connectionist models display any of the necessary properties for symbolic processing. Fodor and Pylyshyn may feel justified in many of their criticisms but they ignore some very central issues. Firstly, the models that they discuss in their critique are individual networks (in fact their discussions are limited to just one particular connectionist model) - they do not consider how systems of such networks may be combined to increase the functionality of a connectionist model. Second, because they maintain that all cognitive processing must be contained within a symbolic rule-based model they do not consider the role that connectionist-type pattern recognition could fulfill within a cognitive framework.

It is perhaps unfortunate that the symbolic and connectionist camps are settling into such mutually exclusive viewpoints because it is our opinion that both are valid and necessary paradigms. Furthermore, we hope to have shown that rather than being merely an implementation issue, as Fodor and Pylyshyn argued, the form of representation required within a connectionist model will have a major influence on the mechanisms required for a symbolic system. We make no claims for the work presented here being a cognitive model but it has been our intent to illustrate that connectionist paradigms do have potential for implementing traditional AI tasks.

REFERENCES

Arbib, M. A. (1972). *The Metaphorical Brain: An Introduction to Cybernetics as AI and Brain Theory.* New York: Wiley Interscience.

Austin, J. (1987). The design and application of associative memories for scene analysis. Unpublished doctoral dissertation, Brunel University.

Austin, J., (1988). Hybrid neural networks. *Neural Networks,* 1, Suppl. 1, 5.

Austin, J. (1992). Uncertain reasoning with RAM based neural networks. *Journal of Intelligent Systems* 2, 121-154.

Austin, J., Jackson, T., & Wood, A. (1991). Efficient implementation of massive neural networks. *In J. G. Delgado-Frias & W. R. Moore (Eds.), VLSI for Artificial Intelligence and Neural Networks* (pp. 399-409). New York: Plenum.

Austin, J., & Stonham, T. J. (1987). An associative memory for use in image recognition and occlusion analysis. *Image and Vision Computing* 5, 251-261.

Ballard, D. (1982). *Computer Vision.* Englewood Cliffs, NJ: Prentice-Hall.

Bledsoe, W. W. & Browning, I., (1959). Pattern recognition and reading by machine. *Proceedings of the International Joint Computer Conference,* pp. 255-232.

Brown, M., & Austin, J. (1991). Application of the Kohonen algorithm to the ADAM network. Tech. Rep. No. VAR-TR-YORK-, 1991-1, University of York.

Fodor, J. A., & Pylyshyn, Z. W. (1988). Connectionism and cognitive architectures: A critical analysis. *Cognition* 28, 3-71.

Grossberg, S. (1988). *Neural Networks and Natural Intelligence.* Cambridge, MA: MIT Bradford Press.

Hinton, G. E., & Touretzky, D. (1985). Symbols among the neurons: Details of a connectionist inference architecture. *Proceedings of the Ninth International Joint Conference on Artificial Intelligence,* pp. 238-243.

Kohonen, T. (1987). *Self-Organization and Associative Memory.* Berlin: Springer-Verlag.

Minsky, M. (1975). A framework for representing knowledge. In P. H. Winston (Ed.), *The Psychology Of Computer Vision* (pp. 213-280). New York: McGraw Hill.

Pao, Y.-H. (1989). *Adaptive Pattern Recognition and Neural Networks.* Reading, MA: Addison-Wesley.

Shastri, L. (1985). Evidential reasoning in semantic networks: A formal theory & its parallel implementation. Tech. Rep. No. 166, University of Rochester, Department of Computer Science.

Willshaw, D. J., Buneman, O. P., & Longuet-Higgins, H. C. (1969). Non-holographic associative memory. *Nature* **222**, 960-962.

III

APPLICATIONS OF CONNECTIONIST REPRESENTATION

9
Connectionist Models of Commonsense Reasoning

Ron Sun
University of Alabama

We investigate connectionist models of rule-based reasoning, and show that while such models usually carry out reasoning in exactly the same way as symbolic systems, they have more to offer in terms of commonsense reasoning. A connectionist architecture for commonsense reasoning, CONSYDERR, is proposed to account for commonsense reasoning patterns and to remedy the brittleness problem in traditional rule-based systems. A dual representational scheme is devised, which utilizes both localist and distributed representations and explores the synergy resulting from the interaction between the two. CONSYDERR is therefore capable of accounting for many difficult patterns in commonsense reasoning. This work shows that connectionist models of reasoning are not just "implementations" of their symbolic counterparts, but better computational models of commonsense reasoning.

1. INTRODUCTION

There is no doubt that rule-based reasoning has been the most prominent paradigm of symbolic artificial intelligence so far. Based on this paradigm, numerous AI systems for theoretical or practical purposes have been built and/or deployed. Despite various problems and objections leveled against them, they are proven to be at least partially valid models. So when connectionism came to the scene, it was natural to ask the question of how to account for this type of reasoning in connectionist models. Whether connectionist models can be a viable alternative to symbolic AI depends, to some extent, on their ability to account for rule-following behaviors and rule-based reasoning (cf. Fodor & Pylyshyn, 1988; Pinker & Prince, 1988; Touretzky & Hinton, 1985).

To account for rules in connectionist models, some approaches have been explored, and several different systems have been implemented that can carry out rule-based reasoning rather completely. However, most of them are straight "implementations" of symbolic rule-based reasoning, that is, they carry out symbolic rule-based reasoning *faithfully* in a connectionist framework, serially or in parallel, without any fundamental difference from symbolic systems in terms of logical capabilities or reasoning capacities.

In order to really justify connectionist models in terms of their ability to model various kinds of reasoning, we have to ask the following questions: Can connectionist models do *more and better* in terms of accounting for robust, flexible, and multifaceted human commonsense reasoning, especially in the types of reasoning that are most often dealt with by rule-based paradigms? Can those data (such as in Collins & Michalski, 1990) that are difficult to account for by symbolic rule-based systems be explained by connectionist rule-based reasoning models? There is no way we can answer these questions abstractly from purely cognitive standpoints. Instead we have to answer these questions by building connectionist reasoning systems that can better account for commonsense reasoning. This work develops such a system and shows that connectionist models of reasoning are not just an implementation of their symbolic counterparts; rather, they are better computational models of commonsense reasoning, taking into consideration the approximate, evidential and flexible nature of rule-based reasoning, and similarity-based reasoning (or a limited form of analogy), and also accounting for the spontaneity and parallelism in reasoning processes.

Below we first look into various existing connectionist models of rule-based reasoning. Then we identify some problems that are difficult for them to solve. We move on to develop a new connectionist architecture that can better deal with these problems. Examples are explained in detail to show the working of the system. We will concentrate more on ideas than on technical details.

2. BACKGROUND REVIEWS

Let us look into some previous systems for rule-based reasoning, especially connectionist ones. Symbolic rule-based systems have a long history in artificial intelligence and cognitive science. The early successful work such as those described in Buchanan and Shortliffe (1984) and Hayes-Roth, Waterman, and Lenat (1983) (*e.g.*, MYCIN, PROSPECTOR, and DENDRAL) demonstrated the promise of this overall approach, which adopts a simple representation with modular units called rules composed of a small set of conditions and conclusions. Many elaborate cognitive theories of learning, problem solving, memory, and so on were proposed based on this paradigm. For example, Klahr, Langley, and Neches (1987) contains a large variety of them, including the ACT theory and SOAR. (Nevertheless the paradigm has long been plagued by the *brittleness* problem for large scale systems, as is discussed later.)

Because of this (partial) success, one of the main challenges for connectionism was how to implement rule-based reasoning in a network fashion. This challenge was met by a number of research efforts to build connectionist systems that can perform rule-based reasoning in some way. Touretzky and Hinton (1985) is the first work towards this end. They basically emulate the structure of a symbolic rule-based (production) system, with separate modules for working memory, rules, and facts; an elaborate pull-out network is designed to match working memory data against rules and to decide which matching rule is to fire. Principles of competition and winner-take-all are used for that purpose. The result is the equivalent of a simple sequential symbolic rule-based system (dealing with 3-tuples consisting of one predicate and two arguments).

Barnden (1988; see also chapter 2, this volume) represents another early attack on this problem. In his system, data reside in grid-like networks (called Configuration Matrices), coded with the help of adjacency relations and highlighting techniques. Hardwired rules are used to detect the presence of data that match particular rules, and an "Action Part" module can be used to add a new data structure representing the conclusion from the matched rule. Although there is some parallelism, it is mostly a sequential rule-based system, carrying out symbolic processing.

Besides these early pieces of work, there are also other efforts, for example, Ajjanagadde and Shastri (1989); Dolan and Smolensky (1989); Lange and Dyer (1989); Sun (1989); and Sun and Waltz (1991). They basically have similar functionalities. From these above examples, it is quite clear now that connectionist models are capable of implementing rule-based reasoning in a variety of ways. So now the question is: Can connectionist models account better for *commonsense* reasoning? The evidential, robust, flexible, and multifaceted nature of common-sense reasoning is evident from various studies (such as in Collins, 1978, and Collins & Michalski, 1990) yet they are all absent from these above models. What is really needed for a connectionist model of rule-based reasoning to be able to model commonsense reasoning adequately? We confront the above questions, by analyzing real protocol data and then actually building a new kind of connectionist models as a computational mechanism for commonsense reasoning.

3. COMMON REASONING PATTERNS

Allan Collins collected a number of protocols of commonsense reasoning. He indicated the inadequacy of traditional logic in explaining those reasoning patterns, and argued for the use of different formalisms or frameworks in the study of *common reasoning patterns* found in various commonsense reasoning tasks. Collins and Michalski (1990) did an impressive job in terms of analyzing the data and establishing a unifying framework for explaining them. What is needed is a computational mechanism from which various inference patterns contained in the data can emerge into existence. We believe that the mechanism ought to be analytically simple, structurally unified, and mechanistically sound. Connectionist models in general fit these above descriptions very well, so they might provide such a mechanism.

Let us look at some examples from Collins and Michalski (1990). One protocol is as follows:

Q: Do you think they might grow rice in Florida?

R: Yeah. I guess they could, if there were an adequate fresh water supply, certainly a nice, big, warm, flat area.

In this example, the person answering the question deduced an uncertain conclusion based on partial information, with a piece of crucial information (the presence of fresh water) missing. This example also indicates the need for an additive procedure for accumulating evidence.

Another protocol is as follows:

Q: Is the Chaco the cattle country?

R: It is like western Texas, so in some sense I guess it's cattle country.

Here because there is no known knowledge, an uncertain conclusion is drawn based on similarity with known knowledge.
Yet another protocol is

Q: Are there roses in England?

R: There are a lot of flowers in England. So I guess there are roses.

Here the deduction is based on property inheritance (England HORTICULTURE flower; rose IS flower; so England HORTICULTURE rose), and the conclusion is partially certain and can be drawn only when there is no information to the contrary (i.e., no cancellation). A lot more protocol data similar to these are analyzed, and are presented in Appendix A.

Existing connectionist models, or any computational models for that matter, so far cannot deal very well with these above patterns in a single unified model. (Although some connectionist or non-connectionist systems can deal with *some* of these problems, *e.g*, fuzzy logic, Dempster-Shafer Theory, and Bayesian reasoning, and so on, no one can deal with them *all* very well in a unified framework.)

4. THE BRITTLENESS PROBLEM

Those examples analyzed above are actually manifestations of a general problem that has long plagued symbolic AI for long, namely the brittleness problem.

The brittleness problem can be delineated, for the purpose of this research, as the inability of a system to deal with the following aspects of reasoning in a systematic, unified framework:

• partial information (for example, the first protocol),

• uncertain or fuzzy information,

• lack of matching rules (for example, the second protocol),

• rule interactions, that is, lack of consistency and completeness in a fragmented rule base,

• generalization,

• bottom-up inheritance,

•top-down inheritance (for example, the third protocol),

•learning new rules and modifying existing rules.

Detailed analyses of these aspects show that, while they look like a disparate set of problems, they can all be characterized as reasoning with rules supplemented by similarity-related inferences. We define a measure of *conceptual similarity* (cf. Tversky 1977) as

$$(A \sim B) = \frac{|F_A \cap F_B|}{|F_A|} \in [-1, 1]$$

such that[1]

$$\text{if } ACT_A = a, \text{ then } ACT_B = a *(A \sim B)$$

where F_i is the feature representation of node 'i', and ACT_i is the activation of node 'i'. We define a measure of *knowledge links* (*i.e.*, rules) as

$$(A \rightarrow B) = r \in [-1, 1]$$

such that

$$\text{if } ACT_A = a, \text{ then } ACT_B = a *(A \rightarrow B)$$

where ACT_i is the activation of node 'i', and r is the knowledge link (rule) strength[2] between A and B. Each of these above cases can be analyzed and dealt with utilizing these two concepts, for example, the lack-of-matching-rule situation can be described as:

$$A \sim B$$

$$B \rightarrow C$$

where A is activated ($ACT_A \neq 0$). So we have

---

[1] Suppose there is nothing else affecting ACT_B.

[2] When there are multiple conditions in a rule, this measure becomes a vector, and the multiplication used here is generalized to inner-products of vectors.

$$ACT_C = (B \rightarrow C) * ACT_B$$

$$= (B \rightarrow C) * ACT_A *(A \sim B)$$

Other cases can be described similarly, except learning new rules, which is a separate issue (see Sun & Waltz 1991).

These two mechanisms, conceptual similarity and knowledge links, will be embedded, as explained in the next section, in our new architecture: CONSYDERR (*CONnectionist System with Dual representation for Evidential Robust Reasoning*), so each of these aspects of brittleness can be handled by our system.

5. A SKETCH OF THE MODEL

The CONSYDERR architecture consists of two levels. The first is the CL (CONSYDERR localist level). CL is a connectionist network with localist representation, roughly corresponding to reasoning at the conceptual level (cf. Smolensky 1988). Rules are represented in CL as links between two nodes representing the condition and the conclusion, respectively. The CL uses a FEL (*Fuzzy Evidential Logic*). FEL can handle a superset of Horn clause logic and Shoham's modal logic (or *Causal Theory*; cf. Shoham 1990), so that it can fully accommodate traditional rule-based reasoning and capture commonsense causal knowledge. Moreover, it is capable of approximate and cumulative evidential reasoning and works with partial and uncertain information. Unlike Horn clause logic, it can deal with negative as well as positive evidence. It can handle variable bindings by utilizing the DN/PDN formalism which was introduced in Sun (1989) and Sun (1990). The basic operation of this scheme is simply weighted-sum computations, therefore this scheme can be implemented, with ease, in a connectionist network with weighted-sum node activation functions. Because of the limited space and the need to emphasize the main points in this short presentation, we will not discuss the above points regarding rule representations (see Sun, 1991, for details).

The second level is the CD (CONSYDERR distributed) level. CD is a connectionist network with distributed representation, roughly corresponding to reasoning at the subconceptual level. Concepts and rules are diffusely represented by sets of units overlapping each other. The amount of overlapping of two sets of units representing two different concepts is proportional to the degree of similarity between these two concepts. We call this a *similarity-based representation*, in which units can be features, perceptual primitives, internal goals or affect states. Concepts are "defined" in terms of their similarity to other concepts in these primitive representations. We utilize these primitives only as a substratum for similarity-based representation of higher level concepts.

Now we can link the localist network (CL) with this distributed network (CD), by linking each node in CL representing one concept to all the nodes in CD representing the same concept, and assign them appropriate weights (see Fig. 9.1). Those crosslevel links are moderated by a latch mechanism. The rule links in CL are duplicated (diffusely) in CD. The interactions of the two components are in fixed cycles: first the latch opens to allow the activation of CL nodes to flow into corresponding CD nodes, and then the two parts start settling down on their own simultaneously, and finally the latch opens to allow the activation of nodes in CD to flow back into CL to be combined with the activation of corresponding CL nodes.

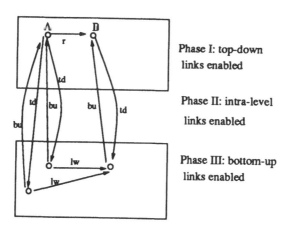

Phase I: top-down
links enabled

Phase II: intra-level
links enabled

Phase III: bottom-up
links enabled

Fig. 9.1. A two-level architecture.

From the above description it is clear that the system is a combination of rule-based and similarity-based components, interwoven together. It implements naturally the functions defined above for knowledge links and conceptual similarity. The synergy of the two types of representation and reasoning helps to deal with the brittleness problem listed above and, therefore, to account for the aforementioned common reasoning patterns.

For example, in order to solve the no-matching-rule situation, we can explore the similarity between the current situation and the rule conditions as represented in the CD part of the system. Consider the following case:

> Cars are for traveling on ground. Airplanes are for traveling in air. Are buses for traveling on ground or in the air?

Buses are closer to cars than to airplanes, based on the similarity as represented with the amount of overlapping in corresponding sets of relevant features[3] in CD. So "traveling on ground" is activated more strongly. CONSYDERR concludes that buses are for traveling on ground.

Another example concerns the problem of inconsistent/incoherent rule bases (rule interaction). We can utilize the rule interactions in CD for the following case:

---

[3] Such as Having-wings, Having-tails, Wheels-on-both-sides, Aerodynamic-shapes, Landing-gears, and so on.

> If carrying cargo, buy utility vehicles. If carrying passengers, buy passenger vehicles. If carrying both cargo and passengers, what shall one buy?

Different types of vehicles are represented as features in CD. When the above two rules are both activated (in response to the question), all features corresponding to both utility and passenger vehicles will be activated in CD. All this information will go up to CL, and the things corresponding to the intersection of utility and passenger vehicles will be activated strongly (because they have all the features). So something like "van" will win.

Other aspects of the brittleness problem can be solved in a similar fashion, including the common patterns identified by Collins and Michalski (1990)[4]. This solution is quite different from Collins and Michalski (see Appendix A for a comparison). Our contention is that this model is conceptually simpler and computationally more efficient (by combining and eliminating many parameters). The learning of new rules can be done through the use of the IARL (or *Incremental Associative Rule Learning*) algorithms, which will be discussed in detail elsewhere (cf. Sun & Waltz, 1991).

For each aspect of the brittleness problem, we performed formal mathematical analyses and arrived at a set of requirements and constraints regarding the parameters (including *td*, *bu*, and *lw*; see Fig. 9.1) of a system that can deal with that particular problem. After analyzing how these requirements and constraints imposed by each of these aspects interact with one another, a synthesis is achieved, so that a unified system is formed with a unique set of parameter settings satisfying all requirements (Sun 1991). Based on that, a large-scale system (named GIRO) consisting of about 200 nodes was built to test, in a realistic setting, how these fragments combine. This system utilizes geographical knowledge extracted from encyclopedias and performs commonsense reasoning based on that knowledge (cf. Sun 1991). The results show that the system performs very reasonably under various circumstances.

6. DETAILED EXAMPLES

6.1. THE PROBLEM

Look at the "Chaco" example (Collins & Michalski, 1990):

> Q: Is the Chaco the cattle country?

> R: It is like Western Texas, so in some sense I guess it's cattle country.

We can put it another way to straighten out the reasoning:

---

[4] We are certainly not implying that we solved the brittleness problem completely. Rather, we are aiming for a simple and elegant model that can deal with some important and predominant aspects of the problem very effectively and efficiently.

Western Texas is cattle country.
Chaco is similar to western Texas (in some relevant aspects).
So Chaco is cattle country.

6.2. AN ANALYSIS

In this example, because there is no known knowledge (or no applicable rules), an uncertain conclusion is drawn based on similarity with known knowledge (rules). Using the formalism we developed, it can be described as:

$$Chaco \sim WesternTexas$$

$$WesternTexas \rightarrow cattlecountry$$

Given "Chaco" with $ACT_{Chaco} = 1$, "cattlecountry" is concluded with $ACT_{cattlecountry}$ calculated as follows:

$$ACT_{cattlecountry} = (WesternTexas \rightarrow cattlecountry)$$

$$* ACT_{Chaco} * (Chaco \sim WesternTexas)$$

where the similarity measure is chosen to facilitate later implementations in the CONSYDERR architecture:

$$Chaco \sim WesternTexas = p * \frac{|F_{Chaco} \cap F_{WesternTexas}|}{|F_{Chaco}|}$$

$p \in [0,1]$ is a parameter used for adjusting the system's behavior, from absolute rigidity to free-floating thinking (see Sun, 1991).

These equations can be readily translated into the CONSYDERR architecture: Links between nodes in both CL and CD represent rule strength measures (the link weights are defined to be the corresponding rule strengths), and similarity measures are implemented with CD representations (we use a set of nodes to represent all features in CD and the amount of overlapping between representations of two concepts expresses the conceptual similarity of these two concepts). See Fig. 9.2.

6.3. THE WORKING OF THE SYSTEM

After starting to receive input data, the CONSYDERR system operates in fixed cycles.
(1) Top-down phase, (2) Settling phase, and (3) Bottom-up phase. This cycle can be repeated to continuously track inputs.

In Top-down phase, the computation is as follows:

$$x_i(t+1) = \max_a ACT_a(t)$$

where a is any node in CL that has $x_i \in CD_a$.

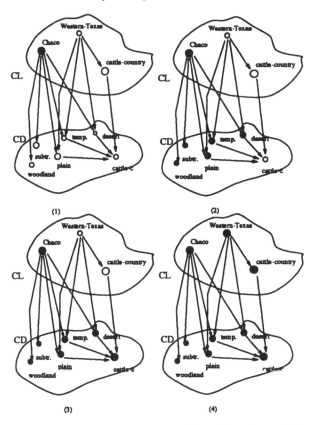

Fig. 9.2. The reasoning process for the Chaco protocol: (1) receiving inputs, (2) top-down, (3) settling (rule application), (4) bottom-up. (To save space, unrelated nodes are not shown here.)

In Settling phase, the computation is as follows:

$$\Delta ACT_a = \alpha \sum W_i I_i(t) - \beta ACT_a(t)$$

and

$$\Delta x_1 = \mu \sum w_1 i_1 (t) - \nu x_1 (t)$$

where W_i, w_i are rule strength (weight) measures, I_i, i_i are the activations of related concepts or features (premises or logical predecessors), and α, β, μ, ν are parameters controlling the network dynamics.

In Bottom-up phase, the computation is as follows:

$$ACT_b (t+1) = \max (ACT_b (t), \sum_{x_1 \in CD_b} \frac{x_1 (t)}{|CD_b|})$$

where b is any node in CL.

Applying this cycle to the example: Top-down phase will activate the CD representation of "Chaco" and activate partially the CD representation of "WesternTexas" based on their similarity; then in Settling phase, rules (links) take effect and this amounts to applying in CD the rule: *WesternTexas is cattle-country*, so the CD representation of "cattle country" is partially activated; finally in Bottom-up phase, the partially activated CD representation of "cattle country" will percolate up to activate the "cattle country" node in CL. The result can be read off from CL. See Fig. 9.2.

6.4. ANOTHER EXAMPLE

Another example is as follows:

> Q: Are there roses in England?

> R: There are a lot of flowers in England. So I guess there are roses.

Here the deduction is based on property inheritance (England HORTICULTURE flower; rose IS flower; so England HORTICULTURE rose), and the conclusion is partially certain and can be drawn only when there is no information to the contrary (i.e., no cancellation).

This inheritance scenario can be expressed as follows[5]:

> England → h-flower

> flower ~ rose

---

[5] Although not shown explicitly in the following formalism, in this case we actually have *flower* ⊃ *rose* and $F_{flower} \subset F_{rose}$.

Given $ACT_{England} = 1$, the activation of "rose" can be calculated with:

$$ACT_{rose} = ACT_{England} * (England \rightarrow h\text{-flower}) * (h\text{-flower} \sim h\text{-rose})$$

Therefore, the same way as before, this can be implemented in CONSYDERR with the two level dual representation and their interaction. Apply the same set of equations as before to this example, utilizing the three phases: the top-down phase will activate the CD representation of "England"; then in the settling phase, rules links take effect and amount to applying in CD the rule: England $\rightarrow$ h-flower, so the CD representation of "h-rose" is partially activated due to similarity with "h-flower"; finally in the bottom-up phase, the partially activated CD representation of "h-rose" will percolate up to activate the "h-rose" node in CL. The result can be read off from CL. See Fig. 9.3.

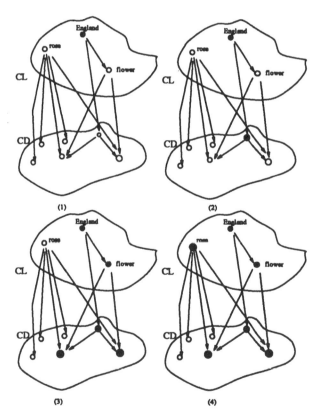

Fig. 9.3. The reasoning process for the England protocol: (1) receiving inputs, (2) top-down, (3) settling (rule application), and (4) bottom-up.

6.5. GIRO: REASONING WITH GEOGRAPHICAL KNOWLEDGE

In our previous discussion of how CONSYDERR accounts for the Collins Protocols, the question of sizes and scalability arises naturally: What if there are a large number of nodes in each level? What if there are a lot of similar concepts, rules and features? In order to show that systems for reasoning in a particular domain can be constructed systematically based on the CONSYDERR architecture and that it will work reasonably despite the existence of interference, distractions, and a large number of related concepts, we construct and study the system GIRO (standing for *a system for Geographical Information Reasoning and Organization*), which stores large amount of knowledge extracted from encyclopedias and reasons about agricultural characterizations of regions.

6.5.1. THE STRUCTURE OF GIRO

The knowledge representation in GIRO utilizes the two level idea in the CONSYDERR architecture by dividing the geographical knowledge represented in the system into two categories: concepts, which include basic geographic areas and regional characterizations (such as "cattle-country"), and features, which include primitive geographical descriptions of areas (such as "highland", "mountainous", and "tropical", etc.). Concepts are represented in CL, and features are represented in CD. Each geographic area represented in CL is connected to its corresponding features in the CD level, and because of the fact that features are shared by similar concepts, the CD representation is similarity-based, that is, two concepts have overlapping CD representations if and only if the two are similar and the amount of overlapping is proportional to the degree of the similarity between them, as alluded to before. Each area is also connected to concepts describing its agricultural products by links, if this knowledge is available to the system. Fig. 9.4 lists concepts for characterizing a geographical area in terms of its agricultural products, such as rice-growing-area, cattle-country, and so on. Fig. 9.5 lists features used in CD.

6.5.2. THE WORKING OF GIRO

GIRO operates this way: once a name of a geographical area is given to GIRO, as imposing a query, GIRO will find out its agricultural characterization, such as "cattle country," "rice-growing area," or "rubber-producing area," through rule application or similarity matching, or a combination of the two. For example, let us choose to reason about "Brazil-north," which is described as "tropical rainforest hilly plateau". We start by giving GIRO a query: What is the main agricultural product of "Brazil-north"? That amounts to activating the node representing "Brazil-north". To answer this question, we let GIRO run to perform its reasoning. The output from GIRO is as follows:

>(consyderr 0)

TITLE: GEOGRAPHY

focusing on context AGRICULTURE : remove feature NIL
setup done
starting running
top down
cl propagating
cd propagating
bottom up

the average activation is 0.1213409896658248
(2, "cattle-country," 0.1249998807907104)
(10, "fruit-veg-growing-area," 0.1249998807907104)
(12, "producing-banana," 0.1249998807907104)
(13, "producing-tropical-fruits," 0.1249998807907104)
(20, "rubber-producing-area," 0.9999990463256836)
(29, "c-Peru," 0.125)
(32, "Bolivia-orient-rainforest," 0.125)
(40, "Guiana-pgs," 0.125)
(41, "Guiana-hilly-country-forest," 0.1666666666666667)
(42, "Guiana-hilly-country-savanna," 0.125)
(45, "Brazil-cw," 0.125)
(50, "Brazil-n," 1)
(60, "Columbia-basin," 0.1666666666666667)
(61, "Ecuador-coast," 0.125)
(66, "Suriname-plateau," 0.125)

"cotton-producing-area"
"coffee-growing-area"
"wine-producing-area"
"potato-growing-area"
"rubber-producing-area"
"goats-area"
"rice-growing-area"
"wheat-growing-area"
"soybean-growing-area"
"rubber-producing-area"
"sheep-country"
"producing-banana"
"producing-tropical-fruits"
"corn-growing-area"
"sugar-producing-area"
"having-roses"
"fruit-veg-growing-area"

Fig. 9.4. Regional characterization included in the GIRO system.

temperate	arctic	woodland	plain	mediterranean
plateau	Mts	coastal-land	lake	tropical
lowland	hill	river-valley-basin	swamp	rainforest
evergreen	deciduous	highland	upland	sparsely-populated
densely-populated	fertile	infertile	flood	prairie
dependable-rainfall	scrub	farming	rugged	subtropical
rainy	savanna	dry arid	grassland	desert

Fig. 9.5. Geographical features included in the GIRO system.

The result shows that it is a rubber-producing area for sure (with confidence value equal to 0.999999), and it is similar, to a small extent, to "Guiana hilly country" and "Bolivia orient rainforest area" etc. (If we want to choose one answer out of many, we can simply use a winner-take-all network on top of this, but this is not an intrinsic part of GIRO and is not needed in this case.) See Fig. 9.6.

Another test is as follows: suppose we want to know about Ecuador coastal area, we give GIRO a query: What is the main agricultural product of Ecuador coast? To answer this question, we let GIRO run to perform its reasoning. The output from GIRO is as follows:

(consyderr 0)

TITLE: GEOGRAPHY
focusing on context AGRICULTURE : remove feature NIL
setup done
starting running
top down
cl propagating
cd propagating
bottom up

the average activation is 0.1433035089856102
(6, "Uruguay-coastal," 0.1666666666666667)
(10, "fruit-veg-growing-area," 0.2499997615814209)
(12, "producing-banana," 0.9999990463256836)
(13, "producing-tropical-fruits," 0.2499997615814209)
(30, "e-Peru," 0.1666666666666667)
(32, "Bolivia-orient-rainforest," 0.1875)
(60, "Columbia-basin," 0.1666666666666667)
(61, "Ecuador-coast," 1)

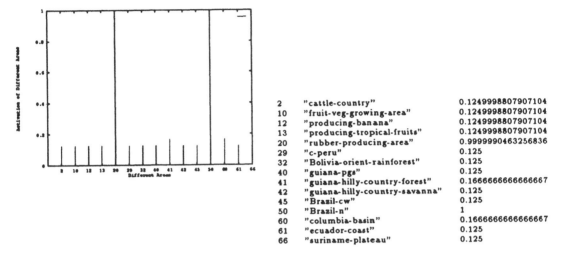

2	"cattle-country"	0.1249998807907104
10	"fruit-veg-growing-area"	0.1249998807907104
12	"producing-banana"	0.1249998807907104
13	"producing-tropical-fruits"	0.1249998807907104
20	"rubber-producing-area"	0.9999990463256836
29	"c-peru"	0.125
32	"Bolivia-orient-rainforest"	0.125
40	"guiana-pgs"	0.125
41	"guiana-hilly-country-forest"	0.16666666666666667
42	"guiana-hilly-country-savanna"	0.125
45	"Brazil-cw"	0.125
50	"Brazil-n"	1
60	"columbia-basin"	0.16666666666666667
61	"ecuador-coast"	0.125
66	"suriname-plateau"	0.125

Fig. 9.6. Output from GIRO: Case 1.

The result indicates that the area is producing banana (with confidence value equal to 0.99999) and is very likely producing tropical fruits and other fruits/vegetables. It is similar, in some way, to "Uruguay-coastal," "eastern-Peru" and "Columbia-Basin." See Fig. 9.7.

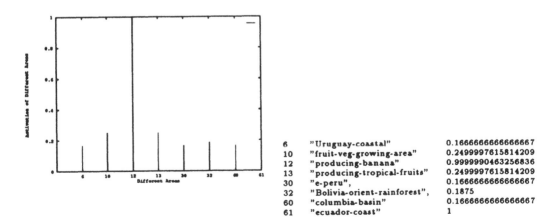

6	"Uruguay-coastal"	0.1666666666666667
10	"fruit-veg-growing-area"	0.2499997615814209
12	"producing-banana"	0.9999990463256836
13	"producing-tropical-fruits"	0.2499997615814209
30	"e-peru",	0.1666666666666667
32	"Bolivia-orient-rainforest",	0.1875
60	"columbia-basin"	0.1666666666666667
61	"ecuador-coast"	1

Fig. 9.7. Output From GIRO: Case 2.

6.6. THE INITIAL SETUP

The question of how we can gather data and set up a large system can be divided into two questions: how do we obtain rule weights and how do we obtain similarity measures?

In GIRO, rules are obtained by going through geography sourcebooks, picking out the relevant information and integrating it into the network with the CFRDN procedure (see Sun, 1991). The rules being put into the system include *WesternTexas is cattlecountry*, etc.[6]

Similarity measures are obtained by an indirect means: we first obtain all the relevant features needed for representing the concepts involved, and then naturally the amount of feature overlap determines the similarity between concepts involved. In order to come up with detailed feature representations for concepts, we pre-establish a set of feature nodes, and we then go through sourcebooks, establishing links (cross-level links) between a concept in CL and its features in CD, based on what we read in the sourcebooks. The features include: altitude, rainfall, vegetation, population, temperature, terrain, and so on, with various ranges.[7]

One thing that needs to be stressed is that everything here is done with a rather mechanical process, and the architecture is modular: new nodes can be added and the existing ones can be deleted at either layers and the effect is localized, without affecting the global structure. Another thing is that similarity is context-sensitive, and mechanisms are needed to focus on relevant features and ignore or discount somehow the irrelevant ones, given the context (or the query, in the above-mentioned cases). This is done by the attention focusing module external to the system, in which a set of "context rules" are used to pick out all relevant features and suppress others (cf. Sun, 1991).

6.7. COMPARISONS

CONSYDERR utilizes parallelism inherent in the data to the maximum extent, especially when compared with Touretzky and Hinton (1985) or Dolan and Smolensky (1989). While most connectionist rule-based systems (Ajjanagadde & Shastri, 1989; Lange & Dyer, 1989, etc.) are functionally comparable to the CL part of CONSYDERR, the CD part is unique in that it provides an efficient way for similarity matching to supplement rule-based reasoning; the CL/CD dual representation scheme constitutes a principled way of accounting for the dichotomy of the conceptual level and the subconceptual (intuitive) level reasoning (Smolensky, 1988; Sun 1991).

---

[6] In general, weights representing rules can be obtained by reading textbooks, instructions, or by using learning algorithms through interactions with the environment. There is no universally applicable way to do this, or in other words, it is domain-specific.

[7] Another possible way of obtaining similarity measures is to conduct a test, asking a group of subjects to rate the similarity of concepts concerned and then construct CD representations based on the collected test scores with the STSIS procedure (see Sun 1991).

More recently Barnden and Srinivas (1990) utilize connectionist rule-based systems to explore similarity in reasoning (i.e., connectionist case-based reasoning); the idea is very similar to ours, but their system requires a complex retrieval/matching process.

The combination of rules and similarity is analogous in a way to a relatively new paradigm of AI — case-based reasoning (CBR), which involves retrieval of relevant cases, similarity matching, and adaptation (cf. Riesbeck & Schank, 1989). In CONSYDERR, the retrieval is accomplished automatically — we consider all existing knowledge at the same time. Similarity matching for finding the best case is done in a truly massively parallel fashion — all cases are matched against the current case at the same time, distributively with simple local computations. Adaptation here is done (somewhat simplistically) with changes in confidence values and rule interactions (see Sun, 1991, for details). However, there are some differences between our approach and that of CBR, for example, integrating rules with cases (i.e., combining rules and similarity matching), uniform representation for cases and rules alike, and massive parallelism (as detailed in Sun, 1991).

7. ADDING VARIABLES TO CONSYDERR

The system described above has only limited expressive power, because of a lack of variable binding. Only a single object can be considered at a time. Consequently if there are multiple objects present at the same time, the representation has to be duplicated several times to accommodate them. This can correspondingly increase the computational complexity several times. Adding variables to CONSYDERR is thus helpful in improving both expressive and reasoning power.[8] (For other reasons why variable binding is important, see Fodor & Pylyshyn, 1988, and Pinker & Prince, 1988)

To add variables to CONSYDERR, one must first answer the question of how to represent variables. Each variable in each fact (predicate) can be handled by one node. The variable can get bound by an application of a relevant rule that has in its right-hand side (RHS) the fact that contains the variable. The binding is done by a numerical value, which represents a particular constant (a binding), being passed along the link (which represents the rule in question) to the node representing the variables, from a node representing a variable having the same name in a fact in the left-hand side (LHS) of the rule applied. For example, suppose we have a rule: "if an area grows something, it is an agricultural area." It can be expressed as follows (where A represents "grow," and B represents "agricultural area"):

$$A(x, y) \rightarrow B(x)$$

and the input is A(a,b) (meaning *area a* grows *b*), where *a* and *b* are constants, for example, *a=Florida* and *b=orange*. The binding *a* is passed to the node representing *x*, and *b* to the one

---

[8] For a more detailed exposition with the DN/PDN formalism, see Sun (1989, 1991) and Sun and Waltz (1991).

representing y in $A(x,y)$. Then by applying the rule, a is further passed from the node representing x in $A(x,y)$ to the node representing x in $B(x)$[9].

Let us look at one level, say CL, to see how this can be done in CONSYDERR. To add variables into CL, the same structure of CL can be kept just as before, but in place of a node now we have an *assembly*, or a collection of nodes interconnected in some way. To serve our purpose of incorporating variables and the variable binding mechanism into the model, an assembly should consist of a certain number of nodes, one of which is for computing and storing confidence values (we call it the C node), exactly the same as before, and the rest are for variables (we call them X nodes). We have to place an upper limit on the number of variables a predicate may have, because we can have only a fixed number of nodes in an assembly (or a network in general). Suppose we are allowed to have k variables, an assembly then contains $k+1$ nodes, each of which except one is for storing and passing along bindings of the variable which it represents. Among all the nodes, the C node of an assembly receives inputs from C nodes in other assemblies which are conditions (LHS) of a rule that use this assembly for its RHS; each variable (X) node receives inputs from variable (X) nodes in the same other assemblies as its corresponding C node, picks up its own binding and passes it on[10]. See Fig. 9.8.

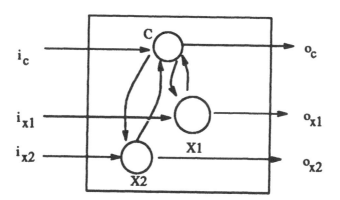

Fig. 9.8. An assembly.

---

[9] However, in order to do this in CONSYDERR, we need to extend the idea of weighted-sum node activation functions to allow the passing and the selection of the numerical values (or symbols) representing bindings in a network. This extension is detailed in Sun (1989, 1991).

[10] Each of the variable nodes in an assembly should communicate with the C node to send its bindings, so that the C node can check consistency (and other things), and should also receive from the C node "instructions", which are to tell a variable node which binding to take in case there are multiple inputs for a variable node. For details see Sun (1991).

Let us look again at the aforementioned example:

$$A(x,y) \rightarrow B(x)$$

and the input is A(a,b), where a and b are constants. We have in CL two assemblies: one for A(x,y) and the other for B(x). The first assembly has three nodes: C, X, and Y. The second assembly has two nodes: C and X. The C node in the first assembly is linked to the C node in the second assembly. The X node in the first assembly is linked also to the X node in the second assembly[11]. See Fig. 9.9. First the C node in the first assembly is activated, and the binding a is passed to the X node in A(x,y), and b to the Y node. Then by applying the rule (i.e., propagating activation along the link), the C node in the second assembly is activated, and a is passed from the X node in A(x,y) to the X node in B(x). Thus a conclusion is reached: B(a).

It should be pointed out that variable nodes do not necessarily contain a particular numerical value or symbol that represents a particular domain object, or in other words, they can be free variables. For example, if we have a rule: $P(x) \rightarrow Q(x)$, given P(z), we can derive Q(z), by representing z with a special symbol in variable nodes of the assemblies for P(x) and Q(x).[12]

The above description regarding CL is readily applicable to CD. From a computational standpoint, CD is exactly the same as CL. The difference is in the representational primitives: instead of concepts and propositions, we have features as basic elements in the CD representation. So whatever works for CL works for CD.

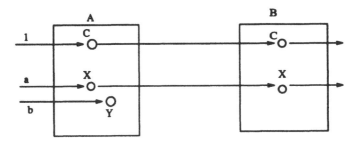

Fig. 9.9. The network for representing the rule: if A(X,Y) then B(X).

---

[11] There should also be some intra-assembly links, which are omitted for simplicity.

[12] The process of setting up a network can be automated by following some fixed steps. For details see Sun & Waltz (1991) and Sun (1991).

One issue we have to look deeper into is the interlevel connections between CL and CD. The main question is how bindings are passed along when top-down activation, or bottom-up activation, is in effect. A simplistic answer is that we can pass appropriate bindings along with activations the same way as in the intra-level case. One problem that arises from this solution is how we deal with the situation, at the bottom-up phase, where different features of the same CL node have different bindings associated with them (see Fig. 9.10). One way to deal with this is to use the majority rule principle, choosing the binding that is associated with more features than any others. A related, but complementary, problem is that, at the top-down phase, how to decide a proper binding when there are more than one bindings received at a CD assembly representing a feature, from different CL assemblies (see Fig. 9.11). This can occur when two assemblies representing two different facts with different arguments and bindings but sharing some features are activated at the same time. This problem can be solved by choosing the binding associated with the assembly that has stronger activation (and hence stronger confidence). The solutions to the above two problems give the system a flavor of competition and winner-take-all[13].

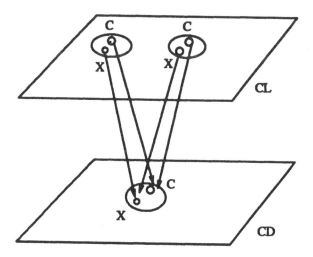

Fig. 9.10. Multiple bindings received during the top-down phase.

---

[13] Obviously, this overall scheme may not work for all cases (see Sun 1991). Nevertheless, it is adequate for dealing with all the interesting cases.

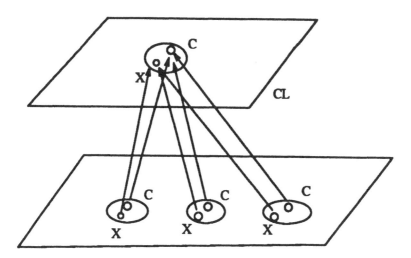

Fig. 9.11. Multiple bindings received during the bottom-up phase.

8. SUMMARY

We analyzed connectionist models for rule-based commonsense reasoning. A connectionist architecture is proposed to account for some common patterns found in commonsense reasoning and to remedy to a certain extent the brittleness problem found in typical symbolic systems. Different from other existing connectionist systems, a dual representational scheme is devised, which has extensional objects (localist representation) as well as intensional objects (distributed representation with features). By using feature-based distributed representation in addition to the localist representation, we are able to explore the synergy resulting from the interaction between these two types of representations and between rule-based reasoning and similarity-based reasoning. This synergy helps to deal with problems such as partial information, no exact matching, property inheritance, rule interaction, and therefore the CONSYDERR system is capable of accounting for many difficult reasoning patterns in one unified system. This architecture also demonstrates that connectionist models equipped with symbolic capabilities are powerful tools for modeling reasoning capacities as well as for constructing efficient practical systems (by utilizing massive parallelism), and they are not mere implementations of their symbolic counterparts.

APPENDIX A. THE COLLINS PROTOCOLS

This appendix presents and briefly examines all the protocols considered, mostly from Collins (1978) and Collins and Michalski (1990). (Some of them were presented before, but are still listed here for completeness.) Our analysis is compared with that of Collins and Michalski.

(1) The first protocol shows uncertain, evidential reasoning:

Q: Do you think they might grow rice in Florida?

R: Yeah. I guess they could, if there were an adequate fresh water supply, certainly a nice, big, warm, flat area.

In this example, the person answering the question deduced an uncertain conclusion based on partial knowledge, with a piece of crucial information (i.e., the presence of fresh water) absent.

(2) The second protocol is as follows:

Q: Is the Chaco the cattle country?

R: It is like western Texas, so in some sense I guess it's cattle country.

Here because there is no known knowledge (in other words, no applicable rules), an uncertain conclusion is drawn based on similarity with known knowledge (or rules).

(3) The third protocol is:

Q: Are there roses in England?

R: There are a lot of flowers in England. So I guess there are roses.

Here the deduction is based on *property inheritance*. Formally, England HORTICULTURE flower; rose IS flower; so England HORTICULTURE rose, to use the jargon of the inheritance theory. The conclusion is only partially certain and is drawn because there is no information to the contrary (i.e., no *cancellation* of properties).

(4) The fourth protocol is:

Q: Is Uruguay in the Andes Mountains?

R: It's a good guess to say that it's in the Andes Mountains because a lot of the countries [of South America] are.

Here there is no rule stating whether Uruguay is in the Andes or not. However, since most South American countries are in the Andes, the *default* is therefore *in the Andes*. Uruguay just "inherits" this default value (although incorrectly).

(5) The fifth protocol is:

Q: Is that [Llanos] where they grow coffee up there?

R: I don't think the savanna is used for growing coffee. The trouble is the savanna has a rainy season and you can't count on rain in general [for growing coffee].

This protocol shows a chain of reasoning: Llanos is a savanna, savannas have rainy season, and rainy seasons do not permit coffee growing.

(6) The sixth protocol is:

Q: Can a goose quack?

R: No. A goose — well, it's like a duck, but it's not a duck. It can honk, but to say it can quack. No. I think its vocal cords are built differently. They have a beak and everything. But no, it can't quack.

Two patterns are present here. One is based on similarity between geese and ducks, independent of knowledge regarding geese, yielding the conclusion that geese may be able to quack. Another pattern is a rule: since geese do not have vocal cords built for quacking, they cannot quack.

(7) The seventh protocol is:

Q: Is Florida moist?

R: The temperature is high there, so the water holding capacity of the air is high too. I think Florida is moist.

In this example the concepts involved are not all-or-nothing, but somehow graded, so the conclusion must be graded, or lower in confidence, corresponding with the confidence values of known facts and rules.

(8) The eighth protocol is:

Q: Will high interest rates cause high inflation rates?

R: No. High interest rates will cause low money supply growth, which in turn causes low inflation rates.

This example shows a chaining of rules: High interest rates will cause low money supply growth, and low money supply growth will cause low inflation rates, so high interest rates will cause low inflation rates.

(9) The ninth protocol is:

Q: What kind of vehicles are you going to buy?

R: For carrying cargo, I have to buy a utility vehicle, but for carrying passengers, I have to buy a passenger vehicle. So I will buy a vehicle that is both a utility and a passenger vehicle. For example, a van.

This example shows the additive interaction of two rules: if carrying cargo, buy a utility vehicle, and if carrying passengers, buy a passenger vehicle. The result is the combination of the two rules: something that is both a utility vehicle and a passenger vehicle.[14]

(10) The tenth protocol is:

Q: Do women living in that [tropical] region have short life expectancy?

R: Men living in tropical regions have short life expectancy, so probably women living in tropical regions have short life expectancy too.

This is another case of using similarity because of the lack of direct knowledge.

(11) The eleventh protocol is:

Q: Are all South American countries in the tropical region?

R: I think South American countries are in the tropical region, because Brazil is in the tropical region, Guyana is in the tropical region, Venezuela is in the tropical region, so on and so forth.

Although the conclusion is incorrect, this example illustrates *bottom-up inheritance* (a form of generalization). Since there is no knowledge directly associated with the superclass "South American countries" as to whether they are in the tropical or not, subclasses are looked at, and a conclusion is drawn based on the knowledge of the subclasses.[15]

---

[14] From this example on, we are no longer using Collins' protocols.

[15] For issues regarding protocol analyses, see Posner (1989).

In Collins and Michalski (1990), these patterns are divided into the following categories:

• Derivation from mutual implication, in which particular values of different entities are related.

• Derivation from mutual dependence, in which functional relationships between two entities are exploited.

• GEN-based transformation, in which what is known about a particular class is generalized to its superclass.

• SPEC-based transformation, in which what is known about a class is specialized to a subclass.

• SIM-based transformation, in which what is known about a class is mapped to another class based on similarity.

• DIS-based transformation, in which what is known about a class is excluded from another class based on dis-similarity.

On the other hand, according to our analysis, there are many fewer categories: the first two categories have little difference and both are dealt with by rule applications; the rest of the categories are similarity related, that is, generalization and specialization are special cases of similarity, and therefore they can be dealt with by similarity matching. Dis-similarity based inference is extremely unreliable: it is generally not the case that, just because the things are different in some particular aspects, they are different in some other aspects. Therefore, this kind of inference is not considered here. Overall, the cases are described and dealt with by rules plus similarity in our analysis.

In the analysis by Collins and Michalski, the confidence of the conclusions reached depends on a number of parameters:

• Conditional likelihood

• Degree of certainty

• Degree of typicality of a subset within a set

• Degree of similarity of one set to another

• Frequency of the referent in the domain of the descriptor

• Dominance of a subset in a set

• Multiplicity of the referent

• Multiplicity of the argument

According to our analysis, however, a smaller set of parameters can be identified: rule weights and similarity. These two parameters can subsume the above parameters used by Collins and Michalski: the first two, conditional likelihood and degrees of certainty, can be easily captured by rule weights; the rest can be accounted for by similarity measures or a combination of rule weights and similarity measures.

ACKNOWLEDGMENTS

I wish to thank Dave Waltz, James Pustejovsky, and Tim Hickey for many helpful discussions.

REFERENCES

Ajjanagadde, V., & Shastri, L. (1989). Efficient inference with multi-place predicates and variables in a connectionist system. In *Proceedings of the Eleventh Annual Conference of the Cognitive Science Society* (pp. 396-403). Hillsdale, NJ: Lawrence Erlbaum Associates.

Barnden, J. E. (1988). The right of free association: relative-position encoding for connectionist data structures. In *Proceedings of the Tenth Annual Conference of the Cognitive Science Society* (pp. 503-509). Hillsdale, NJ: Lawrence Erlbaum Associates.

Barnden, J. E., & Srinivas, K. (1990). Overcoming rule-based rigidity and connectionist limitations through massively parallel case-based reasoning. Tech. Rep. No. MCCS-90--187, Computing Research Laboratory, New Mexico State University, Las Cruces, NM.

Buchanan, B., & Shortliffe, E. W. (1984). *Rule-Based Expert Systems.* Reading, MA: Addison--Wesley.

Collins, A. (1978). Fragments of a theory of human plausible reasoning. In D. Waltz (Ed.), *Theoretical Issues in Natural Language Processing* (pp. 194-201). Urbana, IL: University of Illinois Press.

Collins, A., & Michalski, R. (1990). The logic of plausible reasoning. *Cognitive Science* 13, 1-49.

Dolan, C., & Smolensky, P. (1989). Implementing a connectionist production system using tensor products. In D. Touretzky *et al.* (Eds.), *Proceedings of the 1988 Connectionist Summer School* (pp. 265-272). San Mateo, CA: Morgan Kaufmann

Fodor, J. A., & Pylyshyn, Z. W. (1988). Connectionism and cognitive architecture: A critical analysis. In S. Pinker & J. Mehler (Eds.), *Connections and Symbols* (pp. 3-71). Cambridge, MR: MIT Press,

Hayes-Roth, F., Waterman, D. A., & Lenat, D. B. (Eds.) (1983). *Building Expert Systems.* Reading, MA: Addison-Wesley.

Klahr, J., Langley, P., & Neches, R. (Eds.) (1989). *Production System Models of Learning and Development*. Cambridge, MA: MIT Press.

Lange, T. E., & Dyer, M. L. (1989). Frame selection in a connectionist model. In *Proceedings of the Eleventh Annual Conference of the Cognitive Science Society* (pp. 706-713). Hillsdale, NJ: Lawrence Erlbaum Associates.

Pinker, S., & Prince, A. (1988). On language and connectionism. In S. Pinker & J. Mehler (Eds.), *Connections and Symbols* (pp. 73-192). Cambridge, MA: MIT Press.

Posner, M. (Ed.) (1989). *Foundations of Cognitive Science*. Cambridge, MA: MIT Press.

Riesbeck, C. K., & Schank, R. C. (1989). *Inside Case-based Reasoning*. Hillsdale, NJ: Lawrence Erlbaum Associates.

Shastri, L. (1988). A connectionist approach to knowledge representation and limited inference. *Cognitive Science* 12, 331-392.

Shoham, Y. (1990). Non-monotonic reasoning and causation. *Cognitive Science* 14, 213-252.

Smolensky, P. (1988). On the proper treatment of connectionism. *Behavioral and Brain Sciences* 11, 1-43.

Sun, R. (1989). A discrete neural network model for conceptual representation and reasoning. In *Proceedings of the Eleventh Annual Conference of the Cognitive Science Society* (pp. 916-923). Hillsdale, NJ: Lawrence Erlbaum Associates.

Sun, R. (1990). The discrete neuronal models. In *Proceedings of the INNC-Paris*, pp. 902-907. Dordrecht, Netherlands: Kluwer.

Sun, R. (1991). Integrating rules and connectionism for robust reasoning: An architecture with dual representation. Unpublished doctoral dissertation, Brandeis University.

Sun, R., & Waltz, D. (1991). A neurally inspired massively parallel model of rule-based reasoning. In B. Soucek (Ed.), *Neural and Intelligent System Integration* (pp. 341-382). New York, NY: John Wiley & Sons.

Touretzky, D., & Hinton, G. E. (1985). Symbol among neurons. In *Proceedings of the 9th International Joint Conference on Artificial Intelligence* (pp. 238-243). San Mateo, CA: Morgan Kaufmann.

Tversky, A. (1977). Features of similarity. *Psychological Review* 84, 327-352.

10

Toward Connectionist Representation of Legal Knowledge

Wullianallur "RP" Raghupathi
California State University, Chico

Daniel S. Levine, Raju S. Bapi, and Lawrence L. Schkade
University of Texas at Arlington

In this chapter, we discuss research in connectionism and neurophysiology and examine the potential implications for understanding and representing legal knowledge. Artificial intelligence approaches such as rule-based and case-based while adequate for representing knowledge in the legal function, have proven insufficient for representation of complex, large-scale legal decision making systems that assimilate a variety of inputs. This chapter contributes to three important goals: examination of the legal decision process as a special instance of human decision making, potential use of connectionist approaches to representation of legal knowledge and moving toward comprehensive, unified conceptual frameworks for research.

1. INTRODUCTION

Approaches to understanding and modeling legal decision making have traditionally focused on the symbolic paradigm, represented by the application of artificial intelligence (AI) techniques (Ashley & Rissland, 1988; Gardner, 1987; McCarthy, 1977). Some of the research has also focused on the use of decision analysis techniques and econometric models (Nagel, 1987). While the AI approaches have resulted in design and implementation of simple rule-based or case-based expert systems in specific legal domains, they appear inadequate for representing complex, large-scale legal systems that assimilate the variety of inputs and multiple hypotheses considered in legal decision making (Raghupathi, Schkade, Bapi, & Levine, 1991; Raghupathi & Schkade, 1992a, 1992b). The AI approaches such as rule-based and case-based are generally characterized by axiomatic, relatively closed-world problem solving, and therefore, limit the flexibility and dynamic interaction necessary for successful real-world problem solving.

This chapter discusses research in the nonsymbolic paradigm of connectionism, neurophysiology, and neural processes, and examines the potential and implications of exploring alternative connectionist approaches to the understanding of legal decision making. It focuses on three important issues: examination of the legal decision process as a special instance of human decision making, potential use of connectionist approaches to representation of legal knowledge and moving toward comprehensive, unified conceptual frameworks for research.

Connectionism and neural processes are already being applied to choice in economics, marketing, politics (Leven, 1987), and the application to legal decision making is only a natural extension. It is based on the isomorphic nature of problems and solutions in the other fields. In the long run, results from application of neural processes to the legal domain will not only lead to a deeper understanding of fundamental legal decision processes but also enable study of the normative aspects of legal decision making. This would be a major departure from study of normative aspects from decision analysis, econometrics, and artificial intelligence (Raghupathi et al., 1991).

In the next section, we discuss artificial intelligence applications in legal decision making and identify the limitations of such approaches.

2. ARTIFICIAL INTELLIGENCE AND LEGAL DECISION MAKING

The goal of artificial intelligence in legal decision making has been to automate some aspect of the legal decision making process. The focus has been on the use of methods such as rule-based, case-based, blackboards (Raghupathi & Schkade, 1992a, 1992b) and focusing on specific legal domains. The conceptual approaches to design of AI-based systems include jurisprudential, deep conceptual domain, computer science, and open texture approaches. These focus on the legal domain alone and do not consider general modes of human decision making. Rule-based methods are based on production systems that model human cognition and decision making as applications of sets of IF-THEN rules to problem solving. The application to the legal domain is based on the assumptions that law is a set of rules, that legal experts think in the form of rules, and the expert's reasoning can be captured in the form of IF-THEN rules.

Case-based methods that have been used in information retrieval systems are now being explored as alternatives to rule-based systems. As general models of human reasoning, case-based approaches assume that human decision making involves analogical or precedent-based reasoning. Their application to law involves modeling legal decision as a process of retrieving relevant previous decisions from a database. Riesbeck and Schank (1989) and others argue that human reasoning can be explained in terms of experiences, and suggest that case-based reasoning is the use of such experiences in decision making. They propose it as a more psychologically plausible model of reasoning in an expert. It is suggested by them that experts are willing to tell knowledge engineers the rules used. However, that does not mean experts think in terms of rules. In this sense, rule-based methods appear rationally oriented. On the other hand, case-based reasoning provides very sophisticated case retrievals and solutions to problems that are derived from retrieval of similar cases. While this approach is based on experience, it raises several questions: Are the inputs the same to cases in a specific domain of law? Are cases similar in every respect? Are the goals (e.g., guilty/not guilty) in problem solving the same in every case? How does one account for emotion and affect? Does the set of previous cases capture complexity, interaction between multiple parties, negotiation, due process reasoning, and other qualitative factors that impact the outcome of the case? How does one account for the effects of learning? Additionally, in legal decision making, the same case can be hypothetically interpreted by different parties to support their individual contentions (different motives and goals). What if there is no precise match? How to model multiple hypotheses? These and other questions bring out limitations in case-based methods (Raghupathi et al., 1991).

In an earlier publication (Raghupathi & Schkade, 1992a), we identified several systemic and conceptual differences between the legal function and legal decision making (legal reasoning). The next section discusses the differences.

3. LEGAL FUNCTION VERSUS LEGAL DECISION MAKING

Legal decision making is associated with the general legal decision processes of individuals primarily associated with the law, such as attorneys, judges, legal experts, and others, and the interpretation of the law. It is more normative (prescriptive) and considers issues in an "ideal" world. The outcome of legal decision making is some kind of decision. The legal function comprises the set of activities that involve procedural, routine, repetitive application of the law to meet the operational needs of the organization. The legal function, has emerged rapidly as corporations increasingly perform their legal applications work using new information systems technology and in-house staff. These AI-based legal function systems present representational issues that differ from those of legal decision making systems. For example, these systems typically concern much smaller domains and involve structured applications of law.

In a holistic sense, legal decision making reflects the soft nature of the sociolegal aspects of the law, and considers subjectivity and the value of consequences. Additionally, it involves open system properties (Hewitt, 1985). Openness in representation means the consideration of the flexible and dynamic interaction between multiple inputs, multiple alternatives, due process and opportunistic reasoning, and the complexity that results from interaction among diverse sources of knowledge. Opportunistic reasoning means the decision paths are not specified a priori and the outcome results from negotiation. Due process reasoning refers to the consideration of multiple, often conflicting, goals, beliefs, evidence, and views. Further, ill-structuredness results from uncertainty about goals, and incomplete information. Finally, legal decision making must consider generality — while specific domains may change (e.g., type of legal dispute or law), the process itself is general.

Legal function tasks, on the other hand, are situation and domain specific, fairly procedural and require no urgent consideration of complexity, openness, softness, and generality. Current methods, such as rule-based and case-based, are sufficient to represent the low level, primitive decision processes associated with the legal function. However, more sophisticated approaches that emphasize holism, flexibility, and dynamism are needed to represent the more complex legal decision making processes.

In this regard, many of the AI methods approach legal decision making in an isolated fashion without regard to the internal decision making processes of the individual. They do not differentiate between domain knowledge and the decision making styles of the decision maker. Not everyone concerned with legal decision making processes is an expert in law; individuals fall back on their decision styles to make decisions. Legal expertise in this context refers to possession of domain knowledge alone. Rule-based and case-based methods, while providing explanations for the decisions, do not reflect the actual decision making process per se.

Legal decision making, then, is an integral part of overall human decision making and legal expertise refers to domain knowledge acquired through training and experience. Therefore, models of legal decision making must include models of human decision making, and models, of domain knowledge. Additionally, one must provide for open system properties. In this connection, "legal plasticity" refers to the range of reasoning mechanisms and alternatives possible in problem solving. In a global sense, this includes types of decision styles at the specific individual level, and strategies such as negotiation, plea bargaining, settlement and others at a global level. Further, legal plasticity provides for "satisficing solutions" as opposed to optimal solutions to problems. In contrast, the open-textured nature of law refers to the several possible interpretations of a particular law and is domain specific. The representation of all these features requires adoption of newer, more dynamic approaches. In the next section we discuss research in connectionism and neural processes in the context of legal decision making.

3.1. DESIGN ISSUES IN LEGAL REASONING AND THE LEGAL FUNCTION

Intelligent systems applications development in the field of law has historically been constrained by two factors. First, the representation concept was limited to formal legal decision making based on the rules of law. Second, representations appear to have been technology driven, for nearly all of the early systems are rule-based, wherein rules of law are represented as rules in an AI-based system (or cases in a case-based system). None of the formal legal decision making applications has yet become a functional prototype nor commercially viable (Gruner, 1986; Leith, 1988; Raghupathi & Schkade, 1992a; Susskind, 1986). The limited operational success of these large scale systems is in large part due to the failure to more fully reflect in the representation the diverse systemic features of the legal process. A new approach to representation, for example, a connectionist approach, and more flexible representation methods (neural networks) are needed to produce viable intelligent legal decision making systems (Raghupathi et al., 1991; Raghupathi & Schkade, 1992a, 1992b).

Differences between legal decision making and the legal function can be distinguished in terms of several system concepts. Different design methodologies and representation issues arise due to the systemic differences between legal decision making and legal function systems.

3.2. LEGAL KNOWLEDGE REPRESENTATION AND SYSTEM DESIGN

Despite the domain complexity, most intelligent systems in legal decision making have involved the one-to-one mapping of rules of law onto rules in the system. This type of representational approach does not provide the flexible basis necessary to develop a sociotechnical legal decision making system that affords the openness, softness, complexity and generality to deal with the dynamics of the sociolegal aspects (e.g., jury decisions) of legal decision making.

Rule-based and case-based representation and problem solving are suitable for many legal function applications that often involve narrow, structured, well defined domains. Knowledge representation for legal decision making, however, must include neural networks, objects and combinations of these to adequately represent different levels of knowledge in combination with abstract legal concepts at higher levels and rules of law at lower primitive levels. Combined with the blackboard architecture for complex problem solving, these representational modes enable interaction between multiple sources and levels of legal knowledge and different types of legal decision making.

The use of connectionist models (neural networks) will be a major departure from the current, limited, rule-based and case-based AI approaches to representation.

3.3. SOFTNESS AND OPENNESS

While legal decision making does involve some rigidity in terms of statutes, the application of legal decision making reflects the relatively soft nature of the sociolegal aspects of law. Softness considers subjectivity and value as important considerations in the representation of legal decision making processes. Applications in the legal function, on the other hand, usually involve specific routine, procedural, repetitive tasks. Representation models for the legal function therefore can be more rigid and mechanistic in view of the procedural nature of this applied legal work.

Legal decision making involves open system properties, for, as an integral part of society and organizations, the legal system continually processes inputs and feedback from the environment, including changes in the law, societal values, replacement of legal experts, jury trials, selection of jury members, negotiation, plea bargaining, managerial perspectives and others. The legal system, as a model for social order, exhibits its negentropic nature as legal decision making adapts to changing goals, new evidence, different sources of knowledge, and learning from experience. The legal decision making system must be capable of arriving at similar decisions equifinally by accepting inputs from multiple experts and applying alternate reasoning paths and different approaches to problem solving (Hewitt, 1985).

While the legal literature emphasizes the open-textured nature of the law (Gardner, 1987), openness is a feature of the entire legal system. Openness in the representation of legal knowledge provides for the flexibility to include several interacting domains in legal decision making, accepting inputs from multiple external sources of information and expertise, and accommodating the various reasoning mechanisms (cognitive styles of different participants) that are part of legal decision processes.

In contrast, applications in the legal function are essentially closed system models requiring minimum feedback. Dynamic interaction and flexibility are limited because of the structured nature of legal function tasks (e.g., sentencing guidelines, procedural aspects of a trial and others).

3.4. COMPLEXITY IN LEGAL SYSTEMS

Complexity in legal systems results from interactions internally between subsystems and externally with various systems in the environment, such as the economic and political systems. Within an organizational legal system, there is also interaction and interdependence with the legislative bodies, judiciary, law enforcement, legal experts, managers and the general public. The design of intelligent legal decision making systems must include provisions for the various modes of reasoning and complex interactions between various sources of legal knowledge such as rules of law, judgmental experience of legal experts and managers, customs, legal precedents, common sense knowledge of jurors, and others. Since societal values also impinge on outcomes, holism in representation is essential to deal with sociolegal complexity.

In legal knowledge representation, the tradeoff has historically been between formulating a computer model that is well structured and rigid in specification as opposed to one that provides for flexibility and adaptability. Strictly reductionistic, rationalistic approaches to representation effectively eliminates these essential features. Connectionist models hold considerable promise for assimilating the variety of inputs for complex legal decision making (at a higher level, i.e., human decision making). The legal function emerged because of increased organizational complexity and environmental uncertainty. The growth of the legal function was part of a general pattern of organizational elaboration and differentiation of specialized functions. While legal decision making is complex by nature, the legal function is relatively simplistic, and interaction with the environment is minimal. Because of the procedural nature of most legal function activities, AI-based approaches (such as rule-based and case-based) to knowledge representation are adequate and most often used.

3.5. GENERALITY AND PURPOSE IN LEGAL SYSTEMS

Research in AI has frequently emphasized the need for generality in AI-based problem solving methods (McCarthy, 1987). This is an important issue, for legal decision making applications should be capable of handling a wide range of legal problems.

Current design efforts for AI-based systems in legal decision making, however, tend to be limited to a single domain of law or reasoning (Ashley & Rissland, 1988; Gardner, 1987). Generality in legal decision making suggests that the system cannot be limited to a single domain or a particular type of reasoning mechanism. For purposes of representation, more general problem solving models for the legal decision making domain have to be investigated. Again, the connectionist models possess the characteristic of generality and, being conceptual, can also accommodate features that are unique to particular domains. In contrast, legal function tasks are situation specific and do not require the generality needed by legal decision making systems.

Legal decision making applications are typically designed to arrive at a legal decision. Examples of such systems include CABARET (Trade Secrets Law), CCLIPS (Civil Code), HYPO (Trade Secrets Law), JUDITH (Civil Liability Analysis), MULE (Testing Legal Rules), SENPRO (Formulation of Criminal Sentences), SKADE (corporate "litigate or settle" decisions) and TAXMAN (Classification of Corporate Reorganization for Tax Purposes). Legal decision making culminates in decisions (outcomes) as the result of the interaction between various sources of knowledge and types of reasoning. The goals for legal decision making applications are relatively more vague and ill-defined (changing nature of parties positions, negotiation, new evidence/discovery). Clearly, a holistic and integrative view of representation is needed rather than the current focus on segmentized, disparate approaches that compartmentalize types of legal decision making including jurisprudential, semiotic, conceptual domain, rule based and case based reasoning to name a few (Ashley & Rissland, 1988; Gardner, 1987; Susskind, 1986).

Legal function applications are designed to execute programmed decisions involving narrowly defined legal tasks to achieve specific goals in an organization. Some generic examples of such legal function applications include A-9 (preparation of special documents), ABF (Smart documents), CHOOSE (Tax Planning), CORPTAX (Analysis and Tax Planning), LRS (Organization of Cases and Statutes), PAYE (Tax Calculations), and Tax Advisor (Constructive Ownership Analysis).

3.6. DOMAIN ISSUES

The variety of issues faced by legal decision processes pose significant problems for domain definition in representation. Historically, the boundary identification problem in representation has been addressed by limiting the domain to a particular area of law, type of reasoning or problem solving approach. Such representational limitations have led to the problems with legal decision making systems discussed previously. The representation of legal function applications, while not trivial, is less challenging, for the boundaries of individual systems are limited to specific tasks. It is becoming more common for these tasks to be performed by paralegal and nonlegal personnel who have gained expertise in routine and repetitive tasks in narrow legal domains and who are being increasingly supported by legal function expert systems. Examples of legal function applications include paralegal functions. By and large these are the most readily developed for rule-based expert system applications. Paralegals carry out routine repetitive tasks (Merzon, 1985; Orenstein, 1984) and develop expertise in such domains as drafting of documents, retrieval of documents and cases, translation, verification, executing compliance procedures and therefore provide input for legal decision processes at higher levels. A number of generic applications are currently available to support paralegal tasks. Most of the applications are fairly simple and implemented as rule-based systems. However, they lack the sophistication necessary to support legal decision making tasks.

Examples of legal decision making tasks include the following:

(1) decisions whether to litigate in a particular dispute wherein corporations can drastically reduce the costs of litigation and potential damage awards by evaluating alternatives for out of court settlements by appropriate use of decision analysis (Bodily, 1981), experience and judgement (Raghupathi & Schkade, 1992a);

(2) decide whether to pursue a case in-house or employ outside counsel wherein the decision is based on the evaluation of multiple criteria, cost/benefit analysis, risk analysis and the corporation's available resources to deal with the litigation; and

(3) analyze and evaluate complex legal scenarios with respect to routine activities of the corporations such as acquisitions, mergers, amalgamations, incorporation, monitoring compliance with antitrust laws, and others; and

(4) all types of civil and criminal cases involving interaction between different participants, types of laws, and others.

3.7. OTHER ISSUES

The identification of users and experts in the legal function is straightforward, while deciding whether the attorney is the only user or the expert in legal decision making is not always so clear. Legal decision making involves deeper epistemological and ontological considerations, managerial issues, commonsense reasoning requiring more complex representations, integrated models and implementation architectures. Development time for legal decision making applications is lengthy, cost is very high, design and implementation effort is extensive, risks are considerable, and payoffs uncertain. In contrast, legal function applications involve short development time, low costs and considerably less effort. Legal function applications can be built using available technology such as rule-based expert system building tools and shells. Unlike legal decision making applications, these systems do not require extensive legal knowledge on the part of the knowledge engineer, knowledge acquisition is easier, and application validation is more readily achieved. User acceptance of legal function applications is higher, especially for systems that act as "intelligent assistants" for legal task performance, leading to increased potential for use and commercial viability.

4. CONNECTIONISM, NEURAL PROCESSES AND LEGAL DECISION MAKING

The field of AI in its origin in the 1940s and 1950s, was associated with the effort to model quantitatively the actual neural basis of human psychological functioning. The two fields of AI and neural modeling diverged in the late 1960s but are now again coming closer together in the 1990s (see Levine, 1991, chapter 2, for a historical review).

The type of models that are currently used in both computing applications and neurobiology are called by various names: neural networks, connectionist networks, and parallel distributed processing (PDP) networks. The term *neural networks* has been in use for over 40 years, but neural networks have recently been given a formal definition: "neurally inspired computational tools for modeling neurological and cognitive processes. A neural network is a system of many simple processing elements that usually operate in parallel whose function is determined by network structure, connection strengths, and the processing performed by the computing elements or nodes" (DARPA study, 1988; paraphrased by Parks et al., 1991). The term *connectionism* refers to the fact that the system's cognitive properties are determined by the dynamics of network connections, rather than by imposed rules as in previous AI programs. The term "parallel" refers to the fact that many subsystems of the network are active in parallel, thereby avoiding the constraints of approaches based on serial computer programs. "Distributed" means that representations of complex concepts need not be restricted to single nodes, but may be distributed across large number of nodes. Connectionist approaches suggest nonsymbolic interpretation of processes as the basis for modeling human cognition and perception (Chandrasekharan, Goel, & Allemang, 1988).

Connectionist networks provide more flexibility than rule-based systems and are able to learn a greater variety of cognitive representations. Further, they are holistic in their approach to problem solving and are able to cope with noise (legal plasticity), and degrade gracefully. Connectionist models tend to generalize and exhibit rule like behavior without explicit rules (Raghupathi & Schkade, 1990; Smolensky, 1988). The goal of connectionist approaches has been to model primitive level perceptual processes as well as higher-level processes such as object recognition, planning, problem solving, and language understanding (Smolensky, 1988). Connectionist systems comprise highly interconnected networks of individual processing units and the problem solving occurs as a result of interaction between the individual units.

Connectionist approaches offer tremendous potential for modeling legal decision making by enabling consideration of open system properties such as reflection, parallelism, and due process reasoning. Hewitt (1985) argues that parallelism is fundamental to design and implementation of intelligent systems in many domains. The legal domain is no exception with its need for simultaneous consideration of multiple hypotheses and dynamic reasoning.

Leven (1987) investigated the application of neural processes to a wide range of "choice" problems in economics, marketing, and political decision making. It is argued that existing theories of choice process are inadequate in describing the fundamental problems of valuing, selecting, and acting. Leven draws inspiration from the triune theory of brain to suggest that individuals generally tend to choose habitually; when there is no overpowering habit, one tends to respond emotionally; and finally, when one feels no pressing need for affect, one reasons. However, making choices involves integration of all the three. The triune theory is derived from behavioral studies of MacLean (1970) and others. MacLean hypothesized that the human brain is divided into three "layers" that arrived at different stages of evolution — the deepest layer is the "reptilian brain," responsible for automatic instinctive behavior reflected in some basic maintenance patterns, and some habitual patterns. Above the reptilian brain is the "old mammalian brain" responsible for emotions such as fear, love, and anger, which focus on the needs for individual and species survival. Finally, at the top is the "new mammalian brain," responsible for rational strategies and verbal capacities. The central theme of this view is that in addition to reason and emotion one must consider instinct or habit. Likewise, Mishkin, Malamut, and Bachevalier (1984) show that there are separate systems in the brain for encoding the reinforcement value of events and motor habits. Leven (1987) also suggests that neurophysiological research points to three unique means of transforming, storing, and retrieving events: motoric (instinctive), sensory (affective), and associative (semantic), and these are structured to support both competition and cooperation.

The three-brain theory can provide an appropriate conceptual framework for organizing the work being done on different brain areas. Our choices are made by several competing centers of decision (Grossberg, 1980; Levine, 1986), each asserting a different rule. These rules are conditioned by emotional circumstances and the general amount of excitement in the brain. However, each one of these rules is dominant in different individuals with three different problem solving styles, which Leven (1987) has named after three well known mathematicians: DANTZIG problem solvers typically use direct-solving techniques — tackle one problem at a time; BAYESIAN solvers attempt to find best possible solution; GODEL problem solvers seek meaning, look for causes, and adopt novel approaches. A legal decision making system must provide for all three decision styles. No model of neural process is useful which does not help us explain human behavior, so neither is any model of legal process which ignores fundamentals of human behavior.

Grossberg (e.g., 1980) has built a series of interrelated frameworks for analyzing neural processes. His network includes motivational processes in addition to standard associative learning, and has begun to include habits. They incorporate, among other architectures, the adaptive resonance theory or ART1 (Carpenter & Grossberg, 1987) for classifying spatial patterns; competitive on-center off-surround networks for decisions between stimuli or actions; and gated dipoles for measuring changes in both sensory and motivational data, thereby enhancing novel events. These theories begin to approximate the richness and complexity of human behavior; in Grossberg's networks, system-wide events influence local neural processes, which in turn affect the entire brain environment. Like Grossberg, Changeux (1986) noted variations in brain function between instinctive and associative performance.

Levine and his colleagues (Levine, 1991; Levine, Leven, & Prueitt, 1992) have extended some of Grossberg's architectures to study the integration of the triune brain, the instinctive, emotional, and rational brains (cf. Leven, 1987). Since the integrative function is primarily centered in the frontal lobes (Bapi & Levine, 1990; Pribram, 1973) this work has concentrated on simulating behavioral effects of frontal lobe damage. This includes simulation of perseverative and novelty-seeking behavior of frontal-lobe-damaged human patients and monkeys (Leven & Levine, 1987; Levine & Prueitt, 1989). Efforts are underway to simulate the disruption of sequential plan execution in a goal-directed behavior (Bapi & Levine, 1990). These models of Grossberg, Levine, and others suggest ways that neural networks can be applied to processes in the social sciences. In economics, for example, Heiner (1983, 1985) suggested that traditional models based on rational actors are inadequate to model the choices that determine economic behavior.

This suggestion is amplified by Leven (1987), who discusses why ancient and contemporary theories of the choice process, and hence, mainstream economic theory itself, are not adequate for describing fundamental problems of valuing, selecting, and acting. He argues that a more predictive economic theory must incorporate scientific evidence about how we perceive, process, and recall information, how we make sense of it and act.

Thagard (1989) explains the legal reasoning process in terms of the general theory of explanatory coherence and the ECHO system. He built a connectionist network called ECHO in which nodes represent hypotheses, connected in an excitatory or inhibitory fashion dependent on whether there was an explanatory coherence between them. He applied ECHO both to scientific hypothesis testing (e.g., evolutionary theory) and to legal reasoning (e.g., the Jennifer Levin murder case in New York City). In all these cases, he did simulations which allowed the network to converge to acceptance of one hypothesis and rejection of another (except for another murder case, the Craig Peyer case in California, which resulted in a hung jury in the first trial). One may think of the prosecution and defense as advocating incompatible ways of explaining the evidence resulting in a need to consider interacting, contradictory goals and hypotheses. ECHO addresses these issues through parallelism. ECHO is only a beginning; it does not, its author admits, allow for combination or modification of existing theories. This work is an example of how legal decision making is subsumed by larger, unified theories of human decision making.

In light of various developments in the area of natural neural network modeling, there is a need for integrated approaches to modeling complex human decision making processes, of which legal decision making is an instance. It is similar to application of such integrated approaches to other domains such as economics. For example, in a typical legal decision making situation, different individuals offer competitive-cooperative points of view of the same case, based on individual biases and responsibilities. In a hypothetical situation, the instinctive habitual jury along with the emotional (e.g., advocacy) attorneys offer a dynamic decision challenge for the rational truth-seeking judge. The outcome is the result of interaction among these varied views. An intelligent computational model must simulate to varying degrees these different behaviors in order to provide a balanced view. Rather than focus on rule-based or case-based methods alone, the application of the triune theory as a unified theory captures the richness of the complexities of legal decision making.

4.1. BENEFITS OF CONNECTIONISM IN LEGAL DECISION MAKING

Parallelism: Several aspects of a complex legal problem can be processed simultaneously (e.g., consideration of subhypotheses, partial solutions, different variables). In this regard, a connectionist model is similar to the artificial intelligence blackboard model.

Distribution: Representation of the different types of knowledge is distributed over the network. This leads to a more flexible and dynamic representation enabling consideration of many alternative scenarios in problem solving. The more complex and imprecise relationships can be considered simultaneously.

Coping with noisy data: The connectionist network would tend to generate satisficing solutions (output) in the event of incomplete or noisy data (e.g., consequences of conviction on a lesser charge, plea bargaining, negotiation of sentence when discovery fails to provide all possible information).

Learning: The learning processes in a connectionist network enables discovery of the relevant alternative representations (many possible configurations) of the problem and solution.

Representation: The connectionist approach leads to more flexible and dynamic representation of legal knowledge. Through the use of multitude of layers of neurons and nodes, it is possible to represent and evaluate more hypotheses and alternative solution paths.

Inferencing: The process will be closer to general human decision making. Representation of knowledge is not separated from inferencing (each is available to the other simultaneously). That means, consequences of certain hypotheses being true or a solution generated can be studied immediately. Connectionism uses holistic process to recognize (similar to pattern recognition in humans), perform direct recognition. In the connectionist model, evidence is represented more directly and affects the processing without undergoing any interpretive process.

5. CONCLUSIONS

Theories and models such as the triune theory can be used to explain a variety of decisions and choices that account for habits, emotions, and logic, and provide the means for analyzing qualitative phenomena in the legal domain in their entirety. The application of connectionist approaches and neural processes helps in the move toward open systems, for which current logic-based AI techniques are insufficient.

In this chapter we discussed traditional artificial intelligence approaches to legal decision making and explored the potential of alternative connectionist and neural approaches in a human decision making context.

Further research will focus on analysis of real-world legal cases, design and implementation of computational models based on distributed and connectionist approaches, and the integration of symbolic and nonsymbolic paradigms in legal decision making. For example, within a blackboard framework, one can incorporate connectionist knowledge sources or use neural networks for representation of different aspects of the knowledge (e.g., hypotheses, variables, issues). Domains being currently investigated include settlement decisions and evaluation of product liability and medical malpractice claims.

REFERENCES

Ashley, K. D., & Rissland, E. L. (1988, Fall). A case-based approach to modeling legal expertise. *IEEE Expert*, pp. 70-77.

Bapi, R. S., & Levine, D. S. (1990). Networks modeling the involvement of the frontal lobes in learning and performance of flexible movement sequences. *Proceedings of the Twelfth Annual Conference of the Cognitive Science Society* (pp. 915-922). Hillsdale, NJ: Lawrence Erlbaum Associates.

Bodily, S. E. (1981, May-June). When should you go to court? *Harvard Business Review*, pp. 103-113.

Carpenter, G. A., & Grossberg, S. (1987). A massively parallel architecture for a self-organizing neural pattern recognition machine. *Computer Vision, Graphics, and Image Processing, 37*, 54-115.

Chandrasekharan, B., Goel, A., & Allemang, D. (1988, Winter). Connectionism and Information processing abstractions. *AI Magazine*, pp. 24-34.

Changeux, J. P. (1986). *Neuronal Man*. New York: Oxford University Press.

DARPA Neural Network Study (1988). Fairfax, VA: AFCEA International Press.

Gardner, A. V. (1987). *An Artificial Intelligence Approach to Legal Reasoning*. Cambridge, MA: MIT Press.

Grossberg, S. (1980). How does a brain build a cognitive code? *Psychological Review* 87, 1-51.

Gruner, R. (1986). Thinking like a lawyer: Expert systems for legal analysis. *High Technology Law Journal* 1, 259-328.

Heiner, R. (1983). The origin of predictable behavior. *American Economic Review, 75*, 391-396.

Heiner, R. (1985). Origin of predictable behavior: Further modeling and applications. *American Economic Review 83*, 560-595.

Hewitt, C. E. (1985, April). The challenge of open systems. *BYTE*, Vol. 10, No. 4, pp. 223-242.

Leith, P. (1988). The application of AI to law. *AI and Society, 2*, 31-46.

Leven, S. J. (1987). Choice and Neural Process. Unpublished doctoral dissertation, University of Texas at Arlington.

Leven, S. J., & Levine, D. S. (1987). Effects of reinforcement on knowledge retrieval and evaluation. *Proceedings of the First International Conference on Neural Networks* (Vol. II, pp. 269-279.) San Diego IEEE/ICNN.

Levine, D. S. (1986). A neural network theory of frontal lobe function. *Proceedings of the Eighth Annual Conference of the Cognitive Science Society* (pp. 716-727). Hillsdale, NJ: Lawrence Erlbaum Associates.

Levine, D. S. (1991). *Introduction to Neural and Cognitive Modeling.* Hillsdale, NJ: Lawrence Erlbaum Associates.

Levine, D. S., Leven, S. J., & Prueitt, P. S. (1992). Integration, disintegration, and the frontal lobes. In D. S. Levine & S. J. Leven (Eds), *Motivation, Emotion, and Goal Direction in Neural Networks* (pp. 301-335). Hillsdale, NJ: Lawrence Erlbaum Associates.

Levine, D. S., & Prueitt, P. S. (1989). Modeling some effects of frontal lobe damage — novelty and perseveration. *Neural Networks 2*, 103-116.

McCarthy, J. (1987). Generality in artificial intelligence. *Communications of the ACM 30*, 1030-1035.

McCarthy, T. L. (1977). Reflections on TAXMAN: An experiment in artificial intelligence and legal reasoning. *Harvard Law Review 90*, 837-893.

Merzon, M. S. (1985). Using legal assistants in a corporate setting. *Legal Economics 11*, 49-57.

MacLean, P. D. (1970). The triune brain, emotion, and scientific bias. In F. O. Schmitt (Ed), *The Neurosciences: Second Study Program* (pp. 336-349). New York: Rockefeller University Press.

Mishkin, M., Malamut, B., & Bachevalier, J. (1984). Memories and habits: Two neural systems. In G. Lynch, J. McGaugh, & N. Weinberger (Eds.), *Neurobiology of Learning and Memory* (pp. 65-77). New York: Guilford.

Nagel, S. S. (1987). *Microcomputers as Decision Aids in Law Practice.* New Haven, CT: Quorum Books.

Orenstein, T. P. (1984). Delegating effectively to a paralegal. *Legal Economics 10*, 51-52.

Parks, R. W., Long, D. L., Levine, D. S., Crockett, D. J., Dalton, I. E., Zec, R. F., Siler, G., Nelson, M. E., Bower, J. M., Becker, R. E., McGeer, E. G., & McGeer, P. L. (1991). Parallel distributed processing and neural networks I: Origins and methodology. *International Journal of Neuroscience 60*, 195-214.

Pribram, K. H. (1973). The primate frontal cortex — executive of the brain. In K. H. Pribram & A. R. Luria (Eds.), *Psychophysiology of the Frontal Lobes* (pp. 293-314). New York: Academic.

Raghupathi, W., & Schkade, L. L. (1990). Intelligent systems design: Artificial intelligence versus connectionism. *Proceedings of the 33rd Annual Meeting of the International Society for the Systems Sciences, Portland, Oregon* (pp. 894-922). Pomona, CA: International Society for the Systems Sciences.

Raghupathi, W., Schkade, L. L., Bapi, R. S., & Levine, D. S. (1991). Exploring connectionist approaches to legal decision making. *Behavioral Science* **36**, 133-139.

Raghupathi, W., & Schkade, L. L. (1992a). AI applications in law: A systemic view. *Systems Practice* **5**, 61-78.

Raghupathi, W., & Schkade, L. L. (1992b). The SKADE LITorSET expert system for corporate litigate or settle decisions. *International Journal of Intelligent Systems in Accounting, Finance and Management* **1**, 247-259.

Riesbeck, C. K., & Schank, R. C. (1989). *Inside Case-Based Reasoning.* Hillsdale, NJ: Lawrence Erlbaum Associates.

Smolensky, P. (1988). On the proper treatment of connectionism. *The Behavioral and Brain Sciences* **11**, 1-74.

Susskind, R. E. (1986). Expert systems in law: A jurisprudential approach to artificial intelligence and legal reasoning. Modern Law Review **49**, 169-194.

Thagard, P. (1989). Explanatory coherence. *The Behavioral and Brain Sciences* **12**, 435-502.

11

Markov Random Fields for Text Comprehension

Richard M. Golden
University of Texas at Dallas

David E. Rumelhart
Stanford University

Joseph Strickland and Alice Ting
University of Texas at Dallas

What does it mean to "understand a text?" One popular hypothesis (Schank & Abelson, 1977; Rumelhart, 1977a, 1977b) is that understanding a text involves the construction of some internal representation of the text which is consistent with the reader's world knowledge. The resulting representation may then be used to recall, summarize, or answer questions about the text.

A particular instantiation of this more general theory is the idea that the reader's world knowledge consists of a set of "beliefs" that certain features of the world at the next instant of time will be true given the current state of the world. We will refer to a particular state of the world as a situation which is a collection of binary-valued features each of which can take on the value of "feature absent" or "feature present." Using probability theory as a theory of belief (*e.g.*, Cox, 1946), the reader's world knowledge may then be represented as an assignment of a "degree of belief" or probability to every possible "temporally-ordered sequence of situations" or "trajectory" in situation state space.

A text is considered to be a temporally-ordered sequence of features (*i.e.*, propositions) associated with a partially specified trajectory in situation state space. The first feature in the text is embedded within a situation located at a particular instant in time t. The remaining features of the situation at time t are considered to be unknown and need to be estimated. The second feature in the text is embedded within a situation located at a particular instant in time t' where t' > t. This representation of a text may also be viewed as a set of constraints upon the class of highly probable trajectories in situation state space.

Comprehension is defined as computing the most probable trajectory consistent with the constraints determined by the text. The recall process is modelled by assuming that the end results of the comprehension process (*i.e.*, the most probable trajectory) are combined with the reader's causal knowledge of the world in order to construct a highly probable recall trajectory. A special positive parameter referred to as the retention interval parameter indicates the degree to which the end-results of comprehending a specific text affect the reconstruction of the recall trajectory. If the retention interval parameter is small, then the episodic memory trace formed during the comprehension process is weak in magnitude and the reader must rely upon his or her causal knowledge of the world. If the retention interval parameter is large in magnitude, then the episodic memory trace is strong in magnitude and the trajectory constructed by the reader during recall is almost identical to the trajectory associated with the comprehension process.

For example, Table 11.1 shows how a simple story is translated into a set of abstract propositions or features. Notice that each feature is classified as either an event, a goal, a method, a consequent event, or a consequent state. Note that events, goals, methods, and consequent events are features which become active at certain points in time and then become inactive at later points in time. Consequent states, on the other hand, become active and remain active for all time. Such states may be used by the system to "remember" its past history.

Story	Feature Translation of Story
The grandmother tells the boy to carry the butter to the mother's house.	EVENT: 18. Tell (G, B, Carry(B, Butter, To M))
The boy wants to bring the butter to the mother's house.	GOAL: 19. Desire(B, Bring(B, Butter, To M))
The boy puts the butter on his head.	METHOD: 21. Put(B, Butter, On Head)
The boy carries the butter to his home.	METHOD: 22. Carry(B, Butter, To Home)
The boy arrives at his home.	CONSEQUENT EVENT: 25. Arrive(B, At Home, From G)
The boy was at his mother's house.	CONSEQUENT STATE: 26. At (B, House(M))

Table 11.1. Representing a story as a temporally-ordered feature sequence. B = boy, C = cake, G=grandmother, M=mother.

Table 11.2 shows a partially specified trajectory corresponding to the text in Table 11.1. In particular, if proposition j occurs in position i in the text, then the feature located in row j and column i will be "active" and have the value of one. Note that many of the trajectory features are unobservable and must be estimated. In this example, the six time-dependent features or propositions associated with the text are observable and the remaining thirty time-dependent features must be estimated.

Feature Identification	t=1	t=2	t=3	t=4	t=5	t=6
18. Tell (G, B, Carry(B, Butter, To M))	1	?	?	?	?	?
19. Desire(B, Bring(B, Butter, To M))	?	1	?	?	?	?
21. Put(B, Butter, On Head)	?	?	1	?	?	?
22. Carry(B, Butter, To Home)	?	?	?	1	?	?
25. Arrive(B, At Home, From G)	?	?	?	?	1	?
26. At (B, House(M))	?	?	?	?	?	1

Table 11.2. A partially specified trajectory of length six in a six-dimensional situation state space corresponding to the story described in Table 11.1. The question marks indicate feature values which are unobservable and must be estimated.

Table 11.3 shows a highly plausible (*i.e.*, probable) trajectory which is consistent with the partially specified story trajectory depicted in Table 11.2. The asterisks in Table 11.3 identify the original text whose propositions are temporally-ordered. The plus signs indicate inferences regarding which features have become active as a result of the comprehension process. Notice that multiple features may be active at any given instant in time. Also notice that the "goal" state (feature number 19) becomes active at time t=2 and remains active until time t=5.

1. MOTIVATION FOR THE APPROACH

Experimental evidence supports the hypothesis that the reader's internal "mental model" (*i.e.*, his or her mental representation of the physical world) plays a dominant role in the text comprehension process as opposed to text-based properties such as sentence surface structure or referential coherence (Black & Bern, 1981; Bower & Morrow, 1990; Bransford, Barclay, & Franks, 1972; Glenberg, Meyer, & Lindem, 1987; Keenan, Baillet, & Brown, 1984; Trabasso & VanDenBroek, 1985). It is also known that although memory for the surface structure of a text may be quite good (*e.g.*, Abdi, 1990; Begg, 1971; Bates, Kintsch, Fletcher, & Giuliani, 1980), people usually remember only the meaning of a text (*e.g.*, Bransford & Franks, 1971; Bransford, Barclay, & Franks, 1972). These latter findings are consistent with the hypothesis that a state of the world may be "modelled" as a collection of abstract features.

Feature Identification	t=1	t=2	t=3	t=4	t=5	t=6
18. Tell (G, B, Carry(B, Butter, To M))	*					
19. Desire(B, Bring(B, Butter, To M))		*	+	+	+	
21. Put(B, Butter, On Head)			*			
22. Carry(B, Butter, To Home)				*		
25. Arrive(B, At Home, From G)					*	
26. At (B, House(M))						*

Table 11.3. A trajectory of length six in a six-dimensional situation state space formed as a product of a comprehension process. The asterisks correspond to known active features associated with the text in Table 11.1. The plus signs correspond to features which are "inferred" to be highly probable given the text. B = boy, C = cake, G=grandmother, M=mother.

Mackie (1980) suggested that the reader creates a causal field that is updated as each statement in the story is read. The causal field specifies the circumstances in which the story takes place, and so explicitly identifies states and conditions which may be only implicitly stated in the story. Causal relationships between pairs of events in the causal field are identified using a counterfactual argument. In particular, event A causing event B means that if event A had not occurred in the circumstances, then event B would not have occurred. It also necessary that event A occurs before event B occurs. Evidence that causal chain representations of texts constructed in this manner are psychologically relevant is also available. Events with more causal connections are more likely to be recalled from memory (Trabasso, Secco, & VanDenBroek, 1984; Trabasso & VanDenBroek, 1985; also see Graesser & Clark, 1985), and rated as important (Trabasso & Sperry, 1985; Trabasso & VanDenBroek, 1985). Trabasso, VanDenBroek and Suh (1989) have also begun to study the psychological validity of connecting local causal inferences together to form a causal network.

Furthermore, some researchers (*e.g.*, Cox, 1946) have suggested that human reasoning is more naturally modelled as an inductive rather than deductive logic process. For these reasons, a statistical framework for modelling human knowledge representations and comprehension processes seems appropriate. An additional advantage of a statistical framework is that uncertainties regarding the structure of knowledge in human memory may potentially be dealt with in a more direct manner. Thus, causal relationships among features in situation state space correspond to "local beliefs" regarding the likelihood of occurrence of one feature given another, while the goal of the comprehension process is to find a trajectory which maximizes the "global belief" regarding the likelihood of the entire trajectory in situation state space. The problem is how to relate local beliefs associated with causal relationships to the global belief about which trajectory in situation state space (*i.e.*, which spatiotemporal segment of world knowledge) is most probable given the text.

More formally, let a local belief function be a conditional probability mass function indicating the degree of belief that a story feature is present at time t given the situation associated with time t−1 and the situation associated with time t+1. It is necessary that all such local probability mass functions be derived from a single joint probability distribution which assigns a global probability or degree of belief to every possible trajectory in situation state space. Now if it is assumed that every possible trajectory in situation state space can occur with at least some small positive probability, then the most general approach for assigning probabilities in a consistent manner is to view the collection of random variables associated with the story features as a *Markov random field* (Besag, 1974; Geman & Geman, 1984; Smolensky, 1986). Because of the generality of the Markov random field approach, this is the approach which will be taken in this chapter.

2. OVERVIEW

This chapter is organized into three major sections. In the first section, a method of modelling world knowledge as a statistical environment will be described by introducing the concepts of a situation state space, a dynamical system model of world knowledge, and a graphical temporal-logic notation for specifying complex knowledge structures within a dynamical system framework. A detailed example of a specific story analyzed using this approach is also provided. In the second section, a method for modelling human knowledge representations using Gibbs distributions is proposed, and methods for estimating the parameters of such distributions will be discussed. In the third section, the Gibbs distribution model of human knowledge will be exploited to propose a statistical theory of human comprehension and recall processes. The theory is instantiated using a parallel distributed processing algorithm proposed by Golden (1986; in press) which is an extension of both Anderson's Brain-State-in-a-Box model (Anderson, Silverstein, Ritz, & Jones, 1977) and the back-propagation algorithm (Rumelhart, Hinton, and Williams, 1986). Some simulations of the model to illustrate the basic ideas will also be reviewed.

3. WORLD KNOWLEDGE REPRESENTATION

3.1. SITUATION STATE SPACE

As previously noted, world knowledge is represented as a set of trajectories in a high-dimensional state space. This state space is called *situation state space* (*e.g.*, Golden & Rumelhart, 1991, in press; Rumelhart, 1984). A point in situation state space consists of a collection of d facts or features about the world each of which can be classified as being either "present" or "absent." The reader's current mental state is therefore modelled as a single point in a d-dimensional situation state space. Note that '1' specifies the presence of a feature, while '0' specifies the absence of a feature. At some later point in time, the reader's mental state would be modelled as another point in the same d-dimensional situation state space. It will be convenient, therefore, to order these points according to a time index. Thus, the "unfolding" or "evolution" of the reader's mental state as a function of time, may be represented as an ordered sequence of points or *trajectory* in situation state space.

3.2. STATISTICAL MODEL OF WORLD KNOWLEDGE

Consider a trajectory of length M in a d-dimensional situation state space. This trajectory is formally specified by a collection of dM random variables each of which is constrained to take on the value of either zero or one. This collection of random variables will be referred to as a *random field* which is indexed by the variables i and t. Let $x_i(t)$ indicate a particular value of the random variable associated with the value of the ith feature of the field at time t. A set of d features $x_1(t)$, ..., $x_d(t)$ which have been assigned values of either 0 or 1 specify a *point*, $X(t)$, in a d-dimensional *situation state space*. For example, Table 11.1 may be viewed as a particular realization of the random field where

$$x_{18}(1) = x_{19}(2) = x_{19}(3) = x_{19}(4) = x_{19}(5) = x_{21}(3) = x_{22}(4) = x_{25}(5) = x_{26}(6) = 1$$

and the remaining values of the other random variables in the field are set equal to zero.

A particular realization or sample of the random field is generated by randomly choosing a world knowledge trajectory. More formally, the procedure involves first choosing the point $X(0)$ randomly according to the environmental probability distribution $p_e(X(0))$, and then generating the remainder of the field according to the deterministic (temporal-logic) formula:

$$x_i(t + 1) = \psi_i(X(t)) \tag{1}$$

where the function $\psi_i(X(t))$ is a Boolean algebraic function (Schneeweiss, 1989) which returns the value one if certain logical constraints involving the elements of $X(t)$ are true at time t, and returns the value zero otherwise. The function $\psi_i(X(t))$ may be thought of as a simplified type of production rule which specifies an environmental regularity. Table 11.4 shows some functions which correspond to rules which were used to generate the trajectory in Table 11.1 given appropriate initial conditions. For example, the rule 19 (*the boy wants to bring butter to the mother's house*) is true if the rule 18 (*the grandmother tells the boy to bring butter to the mother's house*) is true, and rule 19 becomes false when the rule 26 (*the boy arrives at the mother's house with the butter*) is true. Formally, these conditions may be expressed as the ψ function:

$$\psi_{19}(X(t)) = x_{18}(t) \cup (x_{19}(t) \cap \neg x_{26}(t))$$

in terms of the proposed feature coding scheme.

An important advantage of modelling world knowledge in the above manner is that "rules" may be incorporated in a straightforward manner into the world knowledge domain, and then the resulting dynamical system may be "run" forward in time with different initial conditions in order to verify that plausible world knowledge trajectories are produced. We sometimes refer to such procedures as "debugging" or "behavioral verification" procedures which guarantee that the "rules" introduced into the system are plausible models of the world which generate trajectories that have the appropriate Markovian properties.

3.3. HMS MACHINE KNOWLEDGE REPRESENTATIONS

A special graphical notation for compactly representing extremely high-dimensional finite-state machines will be used to aid in the construction and evaluation of production rules or function sets. This notation is known as the HMS (Hierarchical Multi-State) machine formalism of Gabrielian and his colleagues (see Gabrielian & Franklin, 1988, 1991, for a review). Suppose that the production rules in Table 11.4 were used to generate the trajectory described in Table 11.3. Fig. 11.3 shows an HMS machine representation of the production rule set in Table 11.4.

Production Rule
$\psi_{18}(X(t)) = 0$
$\psi_{19}(X(t)) = x_{18}(t) \cup (x_{19}(t) \cap \neg x_{26}(t))$
$\psi_{21}(X(t)) = 0$
$\psi_{22}(X(t)) = (x_{21}(t) \cap x_{19}(t) \cap \neg x_{22}(t) \cap \neg x_{2\,5}(t) \cap \neg x_{26}) \cup (x_{25} \cap x_{22})$
$\psi_{25}(X(t)) = x_{22}(t) \cap \neg x_{25}(t)$
$\psi_{26}(X(t)) = x_{25}(t)$

Table 11.4. A set of production rules associated with Fig. 11.3 which define a dynamical system for generating the trajectory in Table 11.3. The dynamical system is defined as: $x_i(t+1) = \psi_i(X(t))$.

Briefly, the HMS machine graphical notation specifies ψ functions or production rules as follows. The heavy arrows in Figs. 11.1-11.3 are called *transitions*, while the lighter arrows are called *controls*. A transition "fires" if all of the controls attached to the transition are attached to states whose values are 1 (*i.e.*, feature present). If a transition is entering a state (*i.e.*, pointing towards a state), then "firing" the transition causes the ψ function associated with that state to return the value 1 (feature present). If a transition is leaving a state (*i.e.*, pointing away from a state), then "firing" the transition causes the ψ function associated with that state to return the value 0 (feature absent). Transitions may be viewed as "pipes" which can be used to pass markers from one state of the HMS machine to another state, while the controls may be viewed as "gates" which prevent markers from entering or leaving states. The heavy horizontal lines in Figs. 11.1-11.3 are called *sources*. Sources may be considered to be states whose truth values are always equal to one (*i.e.*, feature present). Finally, an arrow head which terminates upon a circle is an "inhibitory" connection corresponding to the logical NOT operator.

4. THE GENERIC EPISODE SCHEMA

Although the computational constraint that the causal knowledge representation (*i.e.*, the HMS machine representation) must generate trajectories in situation state space which are psychologically consistent must be satisfied, the class of permissible causal chain representations of even a simple children's story is still rather unconstrained. To attempt to constrain the HMS machine class of representations even further, the "episode" and "try" schema proposed by Rumelhart (1977b) as a problem-solving approach to story understanding were modified so that they would be consistent with the framework we have been developing. In particular, knowledge structures are analyzed by identifying: (i) episodes involving physical causal sequences of events (*e.g.*, the sun's heat is capable of melting butter), and (ii) episodes involving physical attempts by specific protagonists in the story who are trying to achieve specific goals (e.g., a boy trying to take butter to his mother).

Figs. 11.1, 11.2, and 11.3 respectively depict HMS machine representations of generic physical causal schemata, and a generic goal-oriented causal schema. In the physical causal schema, event A becomes active and the activity of A can cause event B to occur. The relationship between events A and B in this physical causal schema is such that B does not occur until event A has ended. Thus, in Fig. 11.1, A might refer to the event that *The roof fell towards the ground*, while event B might refer to the event that *The roof was on the ground* (Fig. 11.1). On the other hand, the physical causal relationship between events C and D is such that as soon as C occurs, then D occurs and event C remains active. Such a situation might arise if C referred to the event *The sun was shining*, while D referred to the event *The butter melted* (Fig. 11.2).

In the generic goal-oriented causal schema (Fig. 11.3), an initiating event activates a goal of the protagonist, this goal is then a precondition for *methods* the protagonist may use to achieve that goal. Notice that additional preconditions emanating from other schemata in the system are allowed to influence the logical conditions for the activation of a particular method. The sequence of methods the protagonist uses to achieve the goal may be best viewed as a type of "script" (*e.g.*, Bower, Black, & Turner, 1979; Schank & Abelson, 1977). As each method is executed, other knowledge features in the system may be turned on or off. These knowledge features are referred to as either *consequent events* or *consequent states*. A consequent event is a special knowledge feature indicating that a consequent state is in the process of becoming active. For example, the method *Put butter on head* might have the consequent event *Butter touches head* and the consequent state *Butter is on head*. For any specific episode schema, one particular consequent event and consequent state pair have a very special status, they are referred to as the *outcome event* and *outcome state* pair for the episode. This pair is special since the outcome state is used to "pop" the protagonist's goal if the protagonist's attempt is successful, and to keep the protagonist's goal active if necessary.

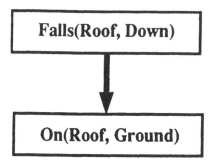

Fig. 11.1. An HMS machine representation for a physical causal schema where the consequent event (On(Roof, Ground)) does not become true until the antecedent event (Falls(Roof,Down)) becomes false.

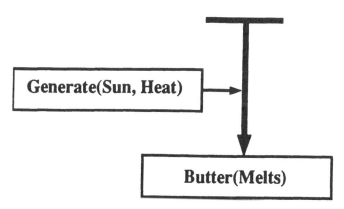

Fig. 11.2. An HMS machine representation for a physical causal schema where the antecedent event (Generate(Sun, Heat)) remains true after it makes the consequent event (Butter(Melts)) become true.

We have found that consequent events and consequent states are useful for coordinating the occurrence of multiple simultaneously occurring episodes since they can be used to place preconditions on either the initiating events in the other episodes or on the methods used by other protagonists in other episodes to achieve specific goals. In fact, we have successfully analyzed four children's stories from Trabasso *et al.* (1984) using these techniques. Table 11.5 and Fig. 11.6 illustrate an analysis of one of these four stories. Nevertheless, the problem of coordinating multiple episodes is a difficult one which we are still currently exploring.

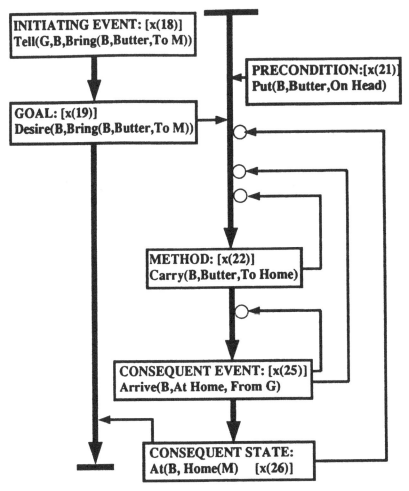

Fig. 11.3. A generic goal-oriented causal schema which describes a protagonist who is attempting to achieve a goal.

5. MODELLING HUMAN KNOWLEDGE REPRESENTATIONS

5.1. THE GIBBS DISTRIBUTION

In this section an approach for modelling human knowledge representations using a "Markov random field" framework is described. One important distinguishing property of a *Markov random field* is that it satisfies what is known as the positivity condition (Besag, 1974). That is, every realization of the field must be assigned a positive (non-zero) probability. In particular, referring to the notation of the previous section consider the probability mass function:

$$p(X(1),...,X(M)) = \frac{1}{Z}\exp[-H(X(1),...,X(M))] \tag{2}$$

where $X(1)$, ..., $X(M)$ is a trajectory (*i.e.*, a realization or sample of the random field), Z is a normalization constant. The function $H(X(1), ..., X(M))$ is an "energy" or self-information function which is a monotonically decreasing function of the likelihood of a trajectory. Probability mass functions with such forms are referred to as Gibbs distributions and clearly satisfy the positivity condition since each of the 2^{Dm} realizations of the field (i.e., each of the trajectories) is automatically assigned a non-zero probability.

Assuming that the probability of the ith feature at time t being active is functionally dependent only upon the situation $X(t-1)$ and the situation $X(t+1)$, and because the random variables are binary, it can be shown (Besag, 1974) that an H function which has the form:

$$H(X(1),...,X(M)) = -\sum_{t=1}^{M} [X(t)^T BX(t-1) + X(t)^T A + \lambda |X(t) - X^0(t)|^2] \tag{3}$$

may be used to construct any arbitrary probability distribution (that satisfies the positivity condition) over the 2^{Dm} realizations of the field by choosing the parameters B, A, and in an appropriate manner.

The parameters of the probability mass function include the elements of the d-dimensional matrix **B** whose ij^{th} coefficient indicates the amount of evidence that the jth feature in the situation at time t-1 provides about the ith feature in the situation at time t. The parameters of the probability mass function also include the elements of the d-dimensional vector **A** whose i^{th} coefficient indicates the amount of evidence for the ith feature in the situation at time t. The constraint parameters are specified by the vectors $X^0(1)$, ..., $X^0(M)$ and the retention interval strength parameter is given by λ.

5.2. PARAMETER ESTIMATION

The goal of the parameter estimation problem is defined as follows: Search for the *most probable* parameter estimates (*i.e.*, maximum a posteriori estimates) with respect to the statistical environment defined by the world knowledge distribution of trajectories (see Eq. 1), the Gibbs distribution (see Eq. 2), and prior distributions upon the parameters. In particular, a uniform prior distribution upon the parameter vector **A**, and a univariate Gaussian distribution on b_{ij} centered at the point b_{ij}^0 are assumed. The variable b_{ij}^0 is derived from human judgment data regarding the degree of belief that feature j causes feature i. The most probable estimates may be shown to be those estimates that minimize the cross-entropy or distance between the Gibbs probability distribution and the world knowledge distribution subject to the constraint that the **B** matrix parameters are close to the human judgment data **B⁰**. Intuitively, the idea is to match the Gibbs distribution to the world knowledge distribution subject to constraints derived from human judgments about the causal relatedness among pairs of features.

There are two technical problems with this approach. First, the normalization constant Z in the Gibbs distribution is not computable in a practical sense since it contains 2^{dM} exponential terms. Second, multiple solutions to the parameter estimation problem are likely because of the extremely large number of free parameters in the proposed Gibbs distribution. The first problem will be referred to as the "decomposition" problem since it is solved by breaking up the global probability mass function into smaller more tractable local probability mass functions whose normalization constants are easy to compute. The second problem will be referred to as the "uniqueness problem". The solution of these two subproblems will allow us to approach the main "parameter estimation" problem.

The decomposition problem. One important advantage of a Markov random field framework is that such a framework facilitates the calculation of local probability mass functions from the global probability mass function. To see how this works, let

$$X = [X(1), ..., X(t), ..., X(M)]$$

be a trajectory (*i.e.*, a realization of the random field) of length M, and let $X_{it,k}$ be the same trajectory with the value of the random variable associated with feature i in situation t set equal to k (note that k may only take on the values of either zero or one). Let $p(X_{it})$ be the trajectory X averaged over both possible values of the random variable associated with feature i in the situation at time t. Applying the basic definition of a conditional probability, noting that $p(X_{it})$ must always be strictly positive by the positivity condition, and exploiting the particular form of the energy function in (3) we have:

$$\frac{p(X)}{p(X_{it,0})} = \frac{\dfrac{p(X)}{p(X_{it})}}{\dfrac{p(X_{it,0})}{p(X_{it})}} = \frac{p(x_i(t)|X(t-1),x(t+1))}{p(x_i(t)=0|X(t-1),X(t+1))} \tag{4}$$

which yields a simple formula for a local probability

$$p_{it} = p(x_i(t) = 1 \mid X(t-1), X(t+1))$$

in terms of the energy function H(X) which is given by:

$$p_{it} = S[- (H(X_{it,1}) - H(X_{it,0}))] \tag{5}$$

where $S[x] = 1 / (1 + \exp(-x))$. Also note that since

$$p(x_i(t) = 0 \mid X(t-1), X(t+1)) = 1 - p_{it}$$

the "local probability mass function" is completely specified.

The uniqueness problem. Because the proposed parametric distribution has many parameters and because the proposed statistical environment must inevitably be a simplified idealized world model, it is reasonable to attempt to introduce meaningful constraints upon the parameter estimation process. The particular constraint which will be imposed will be to minimize the sum squared error between the values of the **B** matrix and a matrix of parameter values **B**$^{\bullet}$ according to the following formula:

$$r(\boldsymbol{B}, \boldsymbol{B^0}) = \frac{\delta}{2} \sum_i \sum_j (b_{ij} - b^0_{ij})^2 \tag{6}$$

where b_{ij} and b_{ij}^0 refer respectively to the elements of the matrices **B** and **B**$^{\bullet}$. The matrix **B**$^{\bullet}$ is a correlation matrix which contains human judgment data regarding what are the relevant correlations between features in situations at neighboring instants of time. For example, consider the question: *Why did the boy want to bring the butter to his mother's house?* If most subjects agree that one answer to this question is that: *The grandmother told the boy to bring the butter to his mother's house*, then the weight in the **B**$^{\bullet}$ matrix which indicates the degree of evidence that the feature: *18. Tell(G, B, Carry(B, Butter, To M))* has upon the feature: *19. Desire(B, Bring(B, Butter, To M))* is set equal to one otherwise the weight is set equal to zero. In this case, the element $b^0(19,18) = 1$. The strength of this constraint is determined by the scalar weight decay parameter δ. Large values of δ indicate a strong influence of the human judgment data, while small values indicate a weak influence.

The parameter estimation problem. The technical setup for the parameter estimation problem is as follows. Let the world knowledge distribution defined by $P_e(X(0))$ (refer to Eq. 1) specify a particular statistical environment from which sample trajectories are drawn. Let $x_i^s(t)$ be the value of the ith feature located at time t in the sth trajectory generated using $P_e(X(0))$ and (1). In the simulations reported here, $P_e(X(0)) = 1$ and the single sample trajectory is known as the *training trajectory*.

The parameter estimation problem is then defined as: Minimize the *learning error function*:

$$e(A,B) = -\sum_{s=1}^{N} \sum_{t=1}^{M} \sum_{i=1}^{d} [x_i^s(t)\ln[p_{it}^s] + (1-x_{i_s}(t))\ln[1-p_{it}^s]] + r(B,B^0) \qquad (7)$$

with respect to the parameter matrix **B** and the parameter vector **A**. The function r(B,B0) is defined as in (6), and p_{it}^s is defined as in (5) and evaluated with the sth trajectory. Actually, the left hand term in (7) is not a "true" likelihood function since it is not technically valid to simply multiply all of the local probabilities within the field together to obtain the joint likelihood function. On the other hand, Besag (1975) shows that as Dm becomes large, that the global minimum of the left hand term in (7) is a consistent estimator and is closely related to traditional maximum likelihood estimation. Accordingly, the left hand term in (7) is sometimes referred to as a "pseudo-likelihood" function (Besag, 1975).

A parallel distributed processing model which can estimate the parameter matrix B and the parameter vector A is derived by constructing a gradient descent algorithm (Duda & Hart, 1973; Rumelhart, Hinton, & Williams, 1986) to minimize the learning error function defined by (7). In particular, the learning algorithm has the following form:

$$\Delta b_{ij} = [x_i(t) - p_{it}] \, x_j(t-1) - \gamma \, (b_{ij} - b^0_{ij})$$

$$\Delta a_i = [x_i(t) - p_{it}]$$

where the notation Δa_i refers to the change in the parameter value a_i, and refers to a positive step constant.

6. MODELLING HUMAN COMPREHENSION AND RECALL PROCESSES

As noted previously, text comprehension is defined as finding the most probable trajectory in situation state space with respect to the Gibbs distribution in (2) given the constraints imposed by the text (see Table 11.2). The constraints in this case are "hard" constraints: Either a feature value is known or a feature value needs to be estimated.

The recall process is modelled in the following manner. First, a story is "comprehended" by the model by computing the most probable trajectory $X^*(1), ..., X^*(M)$. Then the story is "recalled" by the model using the model's "interpretation" of the text $X^*(1), ..., X^*(M)$ as a set of "soft" constraints. In particular, $X^0(t)$ is chosen to be equal to $X^*(t)$ for t=1, ..., M. The magnitude of these "soft" constraints is determined by the parameter (see Eq. 3).

6.1. THE TEXT COMPREHENSION AND RECALL ALGORITHM

Let

$$X^k(1), ..., X^k(t), ..., X^k(M)$$

be the trajectory associated with the kth iteration of the text comprehension/recall algorithm. An algorithm that modifies the trajectory at each iteration so as to increase the probability of the trajectory where the probability of a trajectory is defined according to (2) and (3) is provided in this section. The algorithm is known as the Generalized Brain-State-in-a-Box model (GBSB) model (Golden, in press; also see Golden, 1986).

Step 1: Initialize. The algorithm is initialized. The initial trajectory

$$X^0(1), ..., X^0(t), ..., X^0(M)$$

is a partial specification of the text as in Table 11.2. To use the algorithm to model the comprehension process, all active features are considered to be "known" features and all features in the situation associated with time one are considered to be "known" as well. The remaining features in the initial trajectory are considered as "unknown". The parameter=0. To use the algorithm to model the recall process, the retention interval parameter is positive and the constraint matrix is set equal to the initial trajectory.

Step 2: Update trajectory. Only the features in the trajectory which were classified as "unknown" in Step 1 have their values updated. Feature values are updated according to the following equation:

$$x_i^{k+1}(t) = \sigma[x_i^k(t) + \beta(\sum_{j=1}^{d} b_{ij}x_j(t-1) + \sum_{j=1}^{d} b_{ij}x_j(t+1) + a_i + \lambda(x_i^k(t) - x_i^0(t)))]$$

where $\sigma(x) = 1$ if $x > 1$, $\sigma(x) = 0$ if $x < 0$, and $\sigma(x) = x$ otherwise. The parameter β is a positive step constant of the deterministic update algorithm, and $x^0(t)$ is the ith element of $X^0(t)$. Golden (1986; in press) shows how the parameter β may be chosen so as to guarantee that: (i) at each iteration of the algorithm the probability of the trajectory must either increase or remain the same, and (ii) that the above algorithm will eventually converge to the set of equilibrium points of the algorithm. Note that feature values will "settle" to real numbers between zero and one. In the simulations reported here, $\beta = 0.1$.

Step 3: Check for equilibrium point. If the feature values stop changing or are changing within some small tolerance region, go to Step 4. Otherwise, go to Step 2.

Step 4: Interpret trajectory. The resulting trajectory is interpreted and may be used to summarize and answer questions about the story. Golden and Rumelhart (1991) used the reconstructed recall trajectory to model human recall performance by assuming that the unit with the largest activity value is assumed to refer to the feature (i.e., proposition) that best summarizes that situation.

7. INTERPRETATION OF ALGORITHM AS A PARALLEL DISTRIBUTED PROCESSING MODEL

The above algorithm may be interpreted as a parallel distributed processing model. Fig. 11.4 shows how the model may be "expanded" in time to construct an equivalent multi-layer feedforward network architecture (Rumelhart, Hinton, & Williams, 1986). Notice that the connectivity pattern from one time slice to the next is always exactly the same. The activation of the ith unit in the expanded network at time t is defined as the variable $x_i(t)$. Each unit in this network at each *iteration* of the algorithm sums up a weighted sum of its inputs, a weighted sum of its outputs, its bias, and a special bias weighted by λ which is determined by the retrieval constraint matrix. Fig. 11.5 illustrates the functioning of an individual unit in the system.

This expanded feedforward network is viewed as an approximation to a very complicated recurrent network with complex temporal response properties. The complex recurrent network reconstructs trajectories by cycling forward and backward in time in order to construct a complete trajectory. Intuitively, the model corresponds to "running" the reader's mental model of the world forward and backwards in time in order to reconstruct a fully specified trajectory in situation state space.

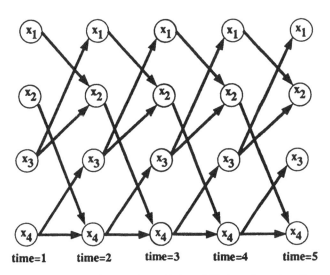

Fig. 11.4. An "expanded" feedforward network consisting of 20 time-dependent feature units which is viewed as an approximation to a complicated recurrent network with only four units. Activation is propagated forward and backwards through the feedforward network until a stable activation pattern is constructed. The notation f_i refers to the ith feature in a situation.

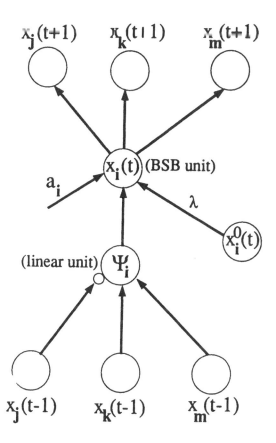

Fig. 11.5. The activation processing details of a particular unit in the feedforward network described in Fig. 11.4. Each unit computes a weighted sum of its inputs, its outputs, a bias, and a special bias associated with the initial trajectory and the retention interval parameter.

8. SIMULATIONS

To illustrate the above ideas, four children stories from Trabasso *et al.* (1984) were analyzed and studied in a series of simulation studies. The results of one such study will be discussed here for purposes of illustration

Step 1: Constructing a Situation State Space

The story is first parsed into event clauses roughly along the lines of Trabasso and his colleagues. Here is the Epaminondas story with event clauses separated by delimiters.

Epaminondas. Once there was a little boy who lived in a hot country./ One day his mother told him to take some cake to his grandmother./She warned him to hold it carefully so it wouldn't break into crumbs./ The little boy put the cake in a leaf under his arm/ and carried it to his grandmother's./ When he got there/ the cake had crumbled into tiny pieces./ His grandmother told him he was a silly boy/ and that he should have carried the cake on top of his head so it wouldn't break./ Then she gave him a pat of butter to take back to his mother's house./ The little boy wanted to be very careful with the butter/ so he put it on top of his head/ and carried it home./ The sun was shining hard/ and when he got home/ the butter had all melted./ His mother told him that he was a silly boy/ and that he should have put the butter in a leaf so that it would have gotten home safe and sound.

In this model, the Epaminondas story is "classified" as a temporally-ordered sequence of event clauses given by:

$$2/5/7/9/10/12/14/15/16/17/18/20/21/22/23/26/27/28/29/30$$

where the above numbers refer to the feature identification numbers in Table 11.4.

Notice that some of the features in Table 11.5 are not explicitly mentioned in the stories. Such features are referred to as "hidden" features and are derived as needed during the process of constructing the HMS machine knowledge representations using the "episode" and "try" schemata. The HMS machine knowledge representations for the Epaminondas story are provided for reference in Fig. 11.6. The numbering of the states refer to the features in Table 11.5.

The model was also tested using a "novel" Epaminondas story despite the fact that all knowledge structures were constructed and derived from the version of the story which was stated above. The novel version of the Epaminondas story corresponds to the following temporally-ordered sequence of event clauses:

$$2/3/4/5/9/11/15/18/21/25/27/30$$

where the above numbers refer to the feature identification numbers in Table 11.5.

Step 2: Estimating Parameters

The network's parameters are estimated using a parallel distributed processing learning algorithm related to the delta rule which minimizes the error function in (7). The network is a simple gradient descent algorithm which uses a fixed step constant. For each story, the network's parameters were estimated using a single training trajectory derived from the HMS machine knowledge representations.

FEATURE IDENTIFICATION	TIME INDEX											
	1	2	3	4	5	6	7	8	9	10	11	12
1. Start Story												
2. Exists (B)	•	+	+	+	+	+	+					
3. B(Little)		•	+	+	+	+	+					
4. Lives(B, In HC)		+	•	+	+	+	+					
5. Tell(M, B, Bring(B, C, To G))				•								
6. Desire(B, Bring(B, C, To G))			+	+	+	+	+	+				
7. Tell(M, B, Hold(B, C, Careful))												
8. Desire(B, Hold(B, C, Careful))				+	+	+	+					
9. Put(B, Under(In(C,Leaf),Arm))				•								
10. Carry(B, C, To G)						+						
11. Breaks(C, Into Crumbs)						•						
12. Arrive(B, At G, From M)							+					
13. At(B, House(G))								+	+			
14. C(Crumbs)							+	+	+	+	+	+
15. Tell(G,B, Is(B, Silly))							•					
16. Tell(G,B, Carry(B,C, OnHead))							+					
17. Told(G,B,Carry(B,C, OnHead))								+	+	+	+	+
18. Tell(G,B,Bring(B,Butter,To M))								•				
19. Desire(B,Bring(B,Butter,To M))									+	+	+	
20. Desire(B, Hold(B, Butter,Careful))									+	+		
21. Put(B,Butter, On Head)									•			
22. Carry(B, Butter, To Home)									+	+		
23. Sun (Shining Hard)		+	+	+	+	+	+	+				
24. Melt(Butter)									+	+		
25. Arrive(B, At Home, From G)										•	+	
26. At(B, House(M))											+	+
27. Butter(Melted)										+	•	+
28. Tell(M, B, Is(B, Silly))											+	
29. Tell(M,B,Put(B, Butter, InLeaf))											+	
30. Told(M,B,Put(B, Butter,InLeaf))												•

Table 11.5. Reconstruction of the novel Epaminondas story trajectory by the model. Note this table also identifies the feature identification numbers in Fig. 11.6.

Human judgment data regarding the causal relatedness of propositions for both stories were provided by a single subject (the first author) in these pilot simulations.

For the Epaminondas story, the following elements of the human judgment data B^0 matrix were set equal to one:

(6,5), (8,7), (9,8), (10,6), (11,9), (12,10), (13,12), (14,11), (15,14), (16,14), (17,16), (19,18), (20,14), (21,17), (22,19), (23,4), (24,23), (25,22), (26,25), (27,24), (28,27), (29,27), (30,29)

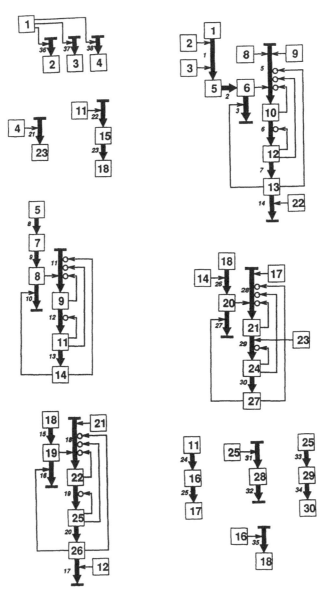

Fig. 11.6. An analysis of the original Epaminondas story using the HMS machine versions of Rumelhart's episode and try schemata. The feature identification numbers (*i.e.*, the numbers in the boxes) refer to the coding scheme described in Table 11.5.

Step 3: Estimating the Most Probable Trajectory

The third step of the simulations involved using the text for each story as an "initial guess" for the comprehension algorithm. In particular, if feature j was located in temporal position i in the story, then the comprehension algorithm did not update trajectory element $x_j(i)$. In addition, trajectory element $x_j(i)$ was set equal to one. Trajectory elements associated with the situation at time slice one were also not updated. The step constant of the algorithm was 0.1.

Figs. 11.7 and 11.8 show the performance of the model for the Epaminondas story after processing the story for 20 and 200 iterations respectively. The three-dimensional mesh plot in the upper-right corner of Figs. 11.7 and 11.8 shows the "training trajectory" which was used in conjunction with the human judgment data to estimate the model's parameters. The three-dimensional mesh plot is interpreted by noting that the height of each point in the mesh-plot corresponds to the activity of a time-dependent feature unit in the system. All points lying on the same horizontal line correspond to the same feature concept (e.g., *19. Desire(B, Bring(B, Butter, To M)))* at different points in time ordered from the top of the graph to the bottom of the graph. All points lying on the same vertical line correspond to the values of all features associated with a situation at a particular instant of time where time is ordered from the left-hand side of the graph to the right-hand side.

In the lower-left corner of Figs. 11.7 and 11.8 is the "story" which is used as a retrieval cue by the system. The upper-left corner of each figure shows the reconstructed trajectory which is quite similar to the original training trajectory despite the fact that a considerably large percentage of the trajectory had to be estimated by the model. The lower-right hand corner of each figure shows that the "energy" (more formally a constant minus the negative logarithm of the likelihood of the trajectory) is a non-increasing function of the number of iterations of the algorithm as shown by Golden (in press; also see Golden, 1986).

Fig. 11.9 shows the performance of the model after 60 iterations on the "novel" Epaminondas story. The performance of the system is quite respectable despite the fact that the novel story "skips" many time steps.

Table 11.5 shows a more detailed look at the Epaminondas trajectory for the novel story. Each column of the table corresponds to a situation located at a particular instant in time, while the rows correspond to the component features of a situation. The asterisks indicate time-dependent active features which are provided by the story. The plus signs indicate time-dependent active features which are reconstructed by the model during the comprehension process. For example, notice that the model correctly infers that feature state: *14. C(Crumbs)* must remain on throughout the trajectory once it is activated, while the goal state *6. Desire(B, Bring(B,C, To G)* turns on and off at approximately the correct times in the story despite the fact that this goal state was never explicitly mentioned in the original text.

9. DISCUSSION AND CONCLUSIONS

In this chapter, a general framework for modelling story comprehension and recall processes has been proposed within a Markov random field setting. It was shown how temporal logic expressions in the form of HMS machines could be used to compactly and intuitively model complicated logical relationships. A quasi-linear parallel distributed processing model was then proposed which could extract useful statistics from the world defined by the HMS machines and combine those statistics with human judgment data about causal relationships to arrive at an "optimal" set of parameters. These parameters were then used to evaluate the ability of the model to reconstruct the trajectories which it had implicitly learned. Despite extremely sparse retrieval cues, the model demonstrated that such trajectories could be adequately reconstructed.

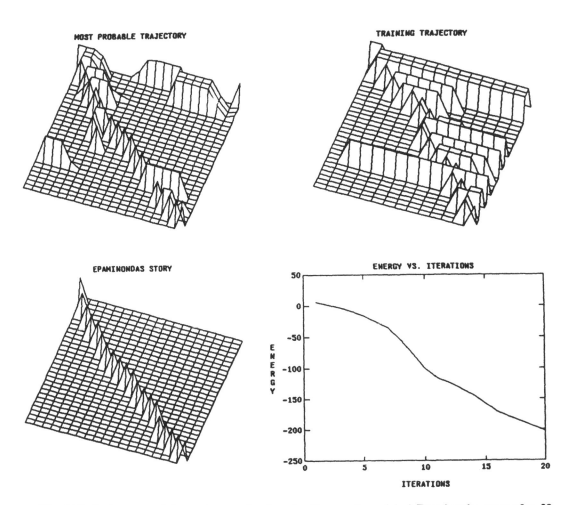

Fig. 11.7. Performance of the text comprehension algorithm on the original Epaminondas story after 20 iterations. See text for additional details.

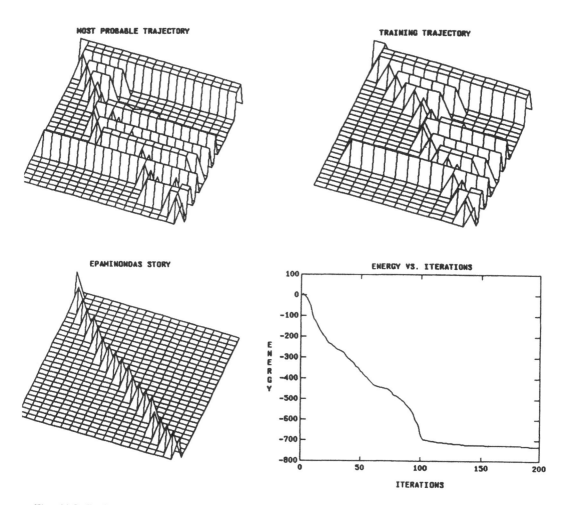

Fig. 11.8 Performance of the text comprehension algorithm on the original Epaminondas story after 200 iterations. See text for additional details.

Although these preliminary simulation results seem promising, they should be viewed with considerable caution. Further research is required to adequately evaluate the computational and psychological adequacy of this approach. In particular, (i) more effective models of world knowledge and human judgment data are required if this model is to be successful at understanding stories, and (ii) improved methods for evaluating the performance of the model are also required. Still, the proposed framework is mathematically tractable, seems to intuitively capture the right properties of the human information processing system, and seems surprisingly effective in these simulation studies.

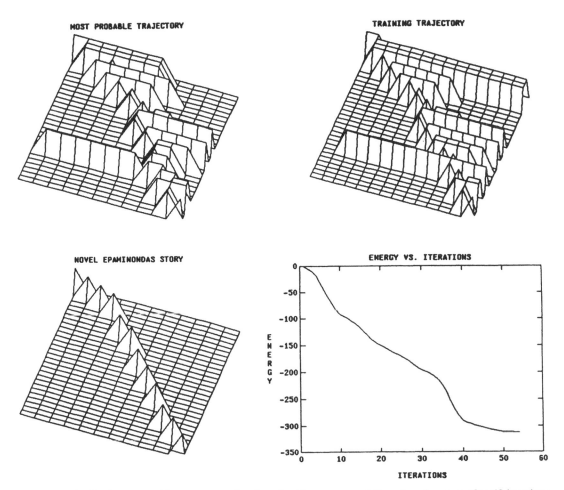

Fig. 11.9. Performance of the text comprehension algorithm on a novel Epaminondas story after 60 iterations. See text for additional details.

ACKNOWLEDGMENT

This research was supported in part by National Institute of Health post-doctoral fellowship HD06943 to the first author while he was at Stanford University, and the Program in Cognition and Neuroscience at the University of Texas at Dallas.

REFERENCES

Abdi, H. (1990). Additive-tree representations of verbatim memory. *CUMFID* **16**, 99-124.

Anderson, J. A., Silverstein, J. W., Ritz, S. A., & Jones, R. S. (1977). Distinctive features, categorical perception, and probability learning: some applications of a neural model. *Psychological Review* **84**, 413-451.

Bates, E., Kintsch, W., Fletcher, C. R., & Giuliani, V. (1980). The role of pronominalization and ellipsis in texts: Some memory experiments. *Journal of Experimental Psychology: Human Learning and Memory* **6**, 676-691.

Begg, I. (1971). Recognition memory for sentence meaning and wording. *Journal of Verbal Learning and Verbal Behavior* **10**, 176-181.

Besag, J. (1974). Spatial interaction and the statistical analysis of lattice systems. *Journal of the Royal Statistical Society, Series B* **36**, 192-236.

Besag, J. (1975). Statistical analysis of non-lattice data. *The Statistician* **24**, 179-195.

Black, J. B., & Bern, H. (1981). Causal coherence and memory for events in narratives. *Journal of Verbal Learning and Verbal Behavior* **20**, 267-275.

Bower, G. H., Black, J. B., & Turner, T. J. (1979). Scripts in memory for text. *Cognitive Psychology* **11**, 177-220.

Bower, G. H., & Morrow, D. G. (1990). Mental models in narrative comprehension. *Science* **247**, 44-48.

Bransford, J. D., Barclay, J. R., & Franks, J. J. (1972). Sentence memory: A constructive versus interpretive approach. *Cognitive Psychology* **3**, 193-209.

Bransford, J. D., & Franks, J. J. (1971). The abstraction of linguistic ideas. *Cognitive Psychology* **2**, 331-350.

Cox, R. T. (1946). Probability, frequency, and reasonable expectation. *American Journal of Physics* **14**, 1-13.

Duda, R. O., & Hart, P. E. (1973). *Pattern Classification and Scene Analysis*. New York: John Wiley and Sons.

Gabrielian, A., & Franklin, M. K. (1988). State-based specification of complex real times systems. In *Proceedings 9th Real-time Systems Symposium, Huntsville, AL* (pp. 2-11).

Gabrielian, A., & Franklin, M. K. (1991). Multi-level specification of real-time systems. *Communications of the ACM* **34**, 50-60.

Geman, S. & Geman, D. (1984). Stochastic relaxation, Gibbs distribution, and the Bayesian restoration of images. *IEEE Transactions on Pattern Analysis and Machine Intelligence* **6**, 721-741.

Glenberg, A. M., Meyer, M., & Lindem, K. (1987). Mental models contribute to foregrounding during text comprehension. *Journal of Memory and Language* **26**, 69-83.

Golden, R. M. (1986). The brain-state-in-a-box model is a gradient descent algorithm. *Journal of Mathematical Psychology* **30**, 73-80.

Golden, R. M. (in press). Stability and optimization analyses of the generalized brain-state-in-a-box neural network model. To appear in *Journal of Mathematical Psychology*.

Golden, R. M., & Rumelhart, D. E. (1991). A distributed representation and model for story comprehension and recall. In *Proceedings of the Thirteenth Annual Conference of the Cognitive Science Society* (pp. 7-12). Hillsdale, NJ: Lawrence Erlbaum Associates.

Golden, R. M. & Rumelhart, D. E. (in press). A parallel distributed processing model of story comprehension. "Discourse Processes".

Graesser, A. C., & Clark, L. F. (1985). *Structures and Procedures of Implicit Knowledge*. Norwood, NJ: Ablex.

Keenan, J. M., Baillet, S. D., & Brown, P. (1984). The effects of causal cohesion on comprehension and memory. *Journal of Verbal Learning and Verbal Behavior* **23**, 115-126.

Mackie, J. L. (1980). *The Cement of the Universe: A Study of Causation*. Oxford: Clarendon Press.

Rumelhart, D. E. (1977a). Toward and interactive model of reading. In S. Dornic (Ed.), *Attention and Performance VI* (pp. 265-303). Hillsdale, NJ: Lawrence Erlbaum Associates.

Rumelhart, D. E. (1977b). Understanding and summarizing brief stories. In D. LaBerge & S. Samuels (Eds.), *Basic Processes in Reading: Perception and Comprehension* (pp. 265-303). Hillsdale, NJ: Lawrence Erlbaum Associates.

Rumelhart, D. E. (1984). Understanding. In J. Flood (Ed.), *Understanding Reading Comprehension* (pp. 1-20). Newark, DE: International Reading Association.

Rumelhart, D. E., Hinton, G. E., & Williams, R. J. (1986). Learning internal representations by error propagation. In D. E. Rumelhart & J. L. McClelland (Eds.), *Parallel Distributed Processing* (Vol. 1, pp. 318-362). Cambridge, MA: MIT Press.

Schank, R. C., & Abelson, R. P. (1977). *Scripts, Plans, Goals, and Understanding*. Hillsdale, NJ: Lawrence Erlbaum Associates.

Schneeweiss, W. G. (1990). *Boolean Functions With Engineering Applications and Computer Programs*. New York, NY: Springer-Verlag.

Smolensky, P. (1986). Harmony theory. In D. E. Rumelhart & J. L. McClelland (Eds.), *Parallel Distributed Processing* (Vol. 1, pp. 194-281). Cambridge, MA: MIT Press.

Trabasso, T., Secco, T., & VanDenBroek, P. (1984). Causal cohesion and story coherence. In H. Mandl, N. L. Stein, & T. Trabasso (Eds.), *Learning and Comprehension of Text* (pp. 83-111). Hillsdale, NJ: Lawrence Erlbaum Associates.

Trabasso, T., & Sperry, L. L. (1985). Causal relatedness and the importance of story events. *Journal of Memory and Language* **24**, 595-611.

Trabasso, T., & VanDenBroek, P. (1985). Causal thinking and the representation of narrative events. *Journal of Memory and Language* **24**, 612-630.

Trabasso, T., VanDenBroek, P., & Suh, S. Y. (1989). Logical necessity and transitivity of causal relations in stories. *Discourse Processes* **12**, 1-25.

12

A Study in Numerical Perversity: Teaching Arithmetic to a Neural Network

James A. Anderson, Kathryn T. Spoehr, and David J. Bennett
Brown University

There are only a few hundred well-defined facts in elementary arithmetic, but humans find them hard to learn and hard to use. One reason for this difficulty is that the structure of elementary arithmetic lends itself to severe associative interference. If a neural network corresponds in any sense to brain-style computation, then we should expect similar difficulties teaching elementary arithmetic to a neural network. We find this observation is correct for a simple network that was taught the multiplication tables. We can enhance learning of arithmetic by forming a hybrid coding for the representation of number that contains a powerful analog or "sensory" component as well as a more abstract component. When the simple network uses a hybrid representation, many of the effects seen in human arithmetic learning are reproduced, including overall error patterns and response time patterns for false products. An extension of the arithmetic network is capable of being flexibly programmed to correctly answer questions involving terms such as "bigger" or "smaller." Problems can be answered correctly, even if the particular comparisons involved had not been learned previously. Such a system is genuinely creative and flexible, though only in a limited domain. It remains to be seen if the computational limitations of this approach are coincident with the limitations of human cognition.

INTRODUCTION

Sometime during the first years of elementary school, students are supposed to learn a few hundred arithmetic facts and a few simple algorithms that use those facts. Many students find the facts and algorithms difficult to learn, and, without constant practice, easy to forget. Simple calculations are prone to errors even at the best of times. But arithmetic learning is a useful and important cognitive skill, is used routinely in daily life and forms the core of more sophisticated mathematical techniques. Considering the impressive cognitive abilities of humans in many domains, why is there so much difficulty with elementary arithmetic?

Neural networks are often said to display "brain style computation." We would like to know if this claim holds for arithmetic learning as well. If it does, we might expect it to be difficult to teach arithmetic to a neural network. We found that it indeed hard for a neural network to learn the multiplication table, though for understandable reasons. When the facts are learned and used, a pattern of errors and response time patterns is displayed that is reminiscent of human behavior. Later in the chapter we address the problem of neural network "programming." Specifically, we show that it is possible to program a simple net to answer questions involving the relation "bigger than."

1. NEURAL NETWORKS

The basic ideas behind neural networks are widely known. A comprehensive review of the basic algorithms was recently published (Hertz, Krogh, & Palmer, 1991) and other introductions are widely available (McClelland & Rumelhart, 1986; Rumelhart & McClelland, 1986; for collections of classic papers in the area see Anderson & Rosenfeld, 1988; Anderson, Pellionisz, & Rosenfeld, 1990).

A neural network is constructed from a great many simple computing elements, whose properties are loosely modeled on the behavior of real neurons. The computing elements are connected together by connections of varying strengths. Elements have activities, a scalar quantity related (perhaps) to something average firing frequency of a real neuron. The most common type of computing element contains an integrator, which adds up contributions from many input units. The integrator is often modeled as the inner product between the connection strengths and the activities of the input units. The resulting quantity is often passed through a nonlinearity to give the final element activity.

A neural network is highly parallel, in that many units are active and computing their outputs at the same time. Because many units are active at once, the state of the system as a whole is called a *state vector*. Given an input state vector, the function of the network is to generate the "appropriate" output state vector as the result of the network computation. *Learning* in a network consists in setting the connection strengths between the units so this occurs, and a number of powerful learning rules are known.

Simple association is one natural form of computation with a neural network. For example, an input pattern can be transformed and modified by the network and the network dynamics made to generate an associated output state vector. Probably the most common practical use of networks at this time is as simple adaptive pattern recognition devices, where an input data vector gives rise to an output state vector corresponding to one of several possible categories. Networks are useful for this class of basically associative operations because of their high degree of parallelism, their claimed good ability to generalize, and their intrinsic noise and damage resistance (see Kohonen, 1989).

2. DATA REPRESENTATION

Although current powerful learning theorems imply that, given very long search times, statistically optimal sets of connection strengths for a particular problem or, more precisely, a particular training set and a particular network architecture, could be found, the network solutions often do not, in fact, generalize well. The resulting systems are sometimes brittle. This should not be surprising. To set up a problem for a network, it is necessary to turn the input data into a pattern of computing element activities, a state vector, for the network. That is, a *representation* of the input data must be formed. There is a folk saying in artificial intelligence that there are three important aspects to any AI system: representation, representation, and representation. Exactly the same is true in neural networks. Unless the initial data representation is of an appropriate type, no network will work well, no matter how clever and powerful the learning rules. If the initial data representation is good even very simple networks will work well.

Working directly with the data representations may give useful insights into the problem, whereas connection strengths set by powerful learning algorithms are often mysterious, and, worse, may reflect more the idiosyncracies of the particular training set used than the desired generalizations (see Geman, Bienenstock & Doursat, 1992). Occasionally, for some problems, letting networks choose their own data representations has been possible and informative. LeCun et al. (1990) use this technique for an application to hand-printed character recognition. Zipser and Andersen (1988) developed an optimal representation in parietal cortex where information about eye and head position must be integrated to compute true spatial position. However, even when the representations developed correspond to known optimal representations such as principal components (Cottrell, Munro, & Zipser, 1988) it is often not clear in what sense the representations found are psychologically meaningful or illuminating.

3. SETTING UP THE PROBLEM

It is appropriate to point out several features of our model of multiplication that illustrate some general principles that we have found useful for psychological modeling.

In focusing on knowledge of the multiplication tables, we fix on a specific capacity that has been carefully studied. There are a wide range of empirical results to constrain the modeling. There is also reason to suspect that the basic kinds of representations and computations employed in multiplication may be common to other psychological capacities.

The behavior exhibited by our network is quite rich. Yet, looked at closely, the network is just generalizing sensibly from its training set. A wide range of interesting behavior emerges robustly from a small number of basic assumptions. To anticipate, we assume that the similarity of the different arithmetic facts is determined by an analog, magnitude code associated with each operand and answer, an assumption supported by a number of experimental results. Given evidence that the heart of the computation is an associative inference, we assume that learning and practice correspond to a strengthening of connections in an associative network. Any one of a number of learning rules for implementing the strengthening might suffice. Finally, we assume that response time corresponds to the time to settle of a network that realizes a dynamical system as it completes an associative inference by reconstructing a previously learned arithmetic fact. Any associative system that conformed to these basic assumptions would very likely exhibit similar qualitative behavior, including, perhaps, a network of real neurons. (For more discussion of representations, including an earlier version of the arithmetic simulations, see Anderson, Rossen, Viscuso, & Sereno, 1990, or Viscuso, Anderson, & Spoehr, 1989).

Let us consider what is involved in learning the multiplication tables. One straightforward way to set up this problem would be as simple association where the two input multiplicands are associated with the proper product. Suppose each of these numbers corresponded to different random activity patterns. The resulting structure is difficult for a network associator to learn, because of severe associative interference. There are a small number of discrete input vectors, each of which is associated with different possible output vectors. For example, an initial seven is associated with ten possible products, "7 times 5 is 35", "7 times 6 is 42", "7 times 7 is 49" and so on. In simple neural network associators using statistically independent codings for each number, this structure gives rise to a pernicious form of destructive interference. The output tends to look like the superposition of the many possible answers associated with each of the two terms. Disambiguation is still possible because the correct answer will be associated with both terms and will be slightly stronger than the incorrect answers. Therefore, it is possible to learn this structure eventually, though with difficulty.

Associative interference does seem to be one reason arithmetic is difficult for humans to learn. Graham (1987) and others have argued from human data that associative effects are the primary mechanisms for both learning and errors. It is worth noting that the "zero's" multiplication tables are easy to learn for both networks and children because there is no associative interference. This is paradoxical, because "zero" is conceptually the trickiest part of elementary mathematics, and was not incorporated into simple arithmetic until the Middle Ages.

4. ANALOG COMPONENT OF REPRESENTATION

It is possible to use representations that are better suited to an associator than uncorrelated patterns. For example, a large body of human experimental data suggests that numbers are considerably more than arbitrary patterns and at least part of their meaning may be represented in an analog manner. One simple demonstration of this involves study of answers to the following types of questions:

Which is greater — 17 or 85?
Which is greater — 74 or 73?

It takes longer to answer the second question than the first. The response time for this and related experiments suggests a *symbolic distance effect*, that is, the larger the difference between the two numbers being compared, the faster the response. Comparison time between two numbers decreases as a function of the absolute difference between them (see Moyer & Landauer, 1967, for early experiments along these lines).

The symbolic distance effect can be very strong. Recent data on two digit number comparisons (Link, 1990) shows that response times can vary from nearly 600 msec for comparisons between numbers close to each other (74 and 73, say) to around 350 msec for comparisons between distant numbers (99 and 11, say). These are huge response time differences. A digital computer could answer these questions by quickly looking at the sign of the difference, showing no relationship at all between the magnitude difference and computation time.

Results from these and other variations of this task, suggest strongly that people have an internal analog representation of number that acts in some respects like a weight or length. In fact, some innovative methods of arithmetic instruction develop this aspect of number explicitly by using, for example, rods of varying length to stand for the different integers. Such techniques would be of little value if quantities were represented and reasoned about as purely abstract entities. Their success appears to contradict the prevailing wisdom that mathematics is the most abstract of the sciences with its practice far removed from the everyday, concrete world. The extremely formal, theorem-proof method used to teach mathematics in college perhaps misleadingly indicates to students that mathematical problem solving is logical in its essence, with discrete steps following one upon the other.

In *The Psychology of Invention in the Mathematical Field* (1945), Jacques Hadamard, a noted mathematician himself, interviewed his peers about how they did mathematics. Most of those he talked to said they did not reason abstractly and discretely, but instead used visualization, or kinesthetic imagery with imagined muscle motions. Language based, and formal, abstract reasoning were conspicuous by their rarity. Einstein was typical when he wrote to Hadamard, "... the words or the language as they are written or spoken do not seem to play any role in my mechanism of thought" (Hadamard, 1945, p. 142). In his *Autobiographical Notes* Einstein (1951) commented that "For me it is not dubious that our thinking goes on for the most part without use of signs (words) ... " (p. 9). (For more examples of the use of nonverbal reasoning in mathematics and physics see Miller, 1984. Further discussion can also be found in Davis & Anderson, 1979.)

How can we make our number representation richer, so as to incorporate some of this analog sensory-like information? One biologically inspired way would be to build a topographic map of number magnitude. A moving 'bar' of activation on a topographic scale formed of individual elements would code the magnitude of the number, just as position on the cortical surface roughly codes visual position or frequency of a sound. This, one might conjecture, is why it is hard to tell which is larger 74, or 73. The two numbers 'weigh' about the same, and so we cannot distinguish them easily based on the analog code. It is unlikely that the nervous system uses exactly this form of representation, but perhaps this representation captures some of the essentials of whatever magnitude code is used.

For our simulations, therefore, we constructed a hybrid code that has both an arbitrary part, a representation of the number name, and a sensory part, a bar that moved from positions on the left of the state vector to positions on the right as number magnitude increased.

5. CODING

The type of coding used for all of the simulations is illustrated in Fig. 12.1. The part of the vector associated with the symbols consisted of random 1s and −1s. For each bar, 5/6 were 1s and 1/6 were −1s (basically 1's with a little noise). The rest of the vector was set to zero. This means that the closeness or similarity of the different facts was determined by the overlap of the bar codes. The spacing of the bars was compressed, with the distance between the beginning of the bar and the symbolic part of the coding growing in a roughly logarithmic fashion with the magnitude of the individual operands and the answers. Most of the simulations were of "qualitative arithmetic," in which the system was asked to produce only a "ballpark estimate" rather than a precise answer.

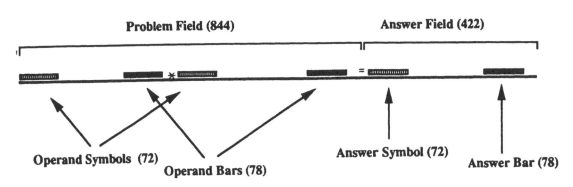

Fig. 12.1. Schematic of the hybrid coding scheme used in the simulations for a 1,266-dimensional system. The hatched bars correspond to quasi-random number "names." The black bars represent activity in the analog region of the representation. As number magnitude increases, the area of activity moves to the right. The numbers in parentheses give the number of vector elements associated with each function.

Many variations of this type of coding were tried — for example, lengthening and shortening the symbol and bar sections, changing the amount of compression, and changing the ratio of the relative amount of space allotted to the operand and answer fields. While changing these parameters does affect performance, the basic lesson of these experiments is that the qualitative behavior illustrated in the simulations we report is robust, surviving wide variations in the values of the parameters.

We also experimented with refinements of the coding scheme designed to scale the performance of the system so that the entire multiplication table could be simulated simultaneously. The goal was to contrive a scheme that kept the heart of the coding qualitative, while at the same time greatly increasing the number of answer bins. We still wanted performance to be driven by the rough magnitude information embodied in the bar codes, thereby preserving the core, psychologically interesting behavior revealed in the simpler, qualitative simulations.

One promising method of scaling the system is simply to add a separate small field with nine new integer symbols, and it is illustrated in Fig. 12.2. (This coding tries to capture hazy intuitions about two digit numbers having a most and a least significant digit.) For all of the simulations discussed, the matrix was trained on a representative sample of 32-34 multiplication facts; with the greater computational resources now at our disposal, we plan to rerun all of the simulations by training the system on the entire multiplication table.

Staggered integers--6 bits per integer

Fig. 12.2. Schematic of the revised hybrid coding scheme; same as the coding shown in Fig. 12.1, with the addition of a 60 bit integer field.

Our hybrid coding has automatic generalization ability built into the representation in that numbers near each other in magnitude will have overlapping magnitude codes. Such topographic codes have also been used for a number of other computational applications, for example, Knapp and Anderson (1984) or Anderson, Gately, Penz, and Collins (1990). Among other things, a hybrid code allows an easy movement from an analog world to a symbolic world, since arbitrary patterns are associated with magnitudes and vice versa. Such a code allows convenient "hooks" to symbol based artificial intelligence, if needed.

6. THE BSB MODEL

The model used for our simulations is a simple nonlinear feedback model called BSB. A number of network modelers have considered feedback systems from the early days of network theory, for example, Amari (1977). More about the BSB model can be found in Anderson, Silverstein, Ritz, and Jones (1977), Anderson and Mozer (1981) and Anderson (in press).

The cognitive computation performed by a simple neural network involves using a stimulus pattern to generate a response pattern. In a feedback system, we can use the well-known pattern completion property of autoassociative nets to regenerate missing parts of learned patterns, or to generate the output portion of a state, given an input. Many feedforward networks have input and output patterns that appear on separate cell layers, but this is not necessary. The anatomy of the model we are using is shown in Fig. 12.3, a single set of neurons projecting to itself by way of a connection matrix, A.

Let us assume we have multiple items stored in the connection matrix A. Let us assume that f is an eigenvector of the connection matrix, A, with eigenvalue λ, that is,

$$Af = \lambda f$$

Suppose a set of units with autoassociative feedback, receiving input from the outside (that is, f) as well as feedback, and adds them together. It can be easily seen that if λ is positive, the magnitude of the pattern grows. Feedback can be used to perform differential weightings of eigenvectors with larger versus smaller magnitude eigenvalues as means of cognitive information processing. In the simplest of the BSB model, the matrix is formed using a Hebbian rule, giving a matrix that is a sum of outer products. In this case the eigenvectors of the connection matrix are essentially the principal components of the training set, producing an optimal basis set for representing the input data, ranked for usefulness by their eigenvalue.

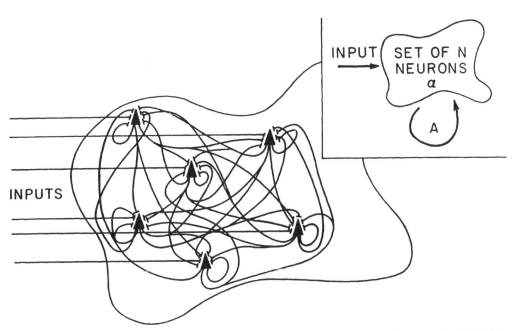

Fig. 12.3. The network architecture for the BSB network used in the simulations. A group of units feeds back and connects to itself. (Reprinted by permission from Anderson et al., 1977. Copyright American Psychological Association.)

Because of the close connection between Hebbian learning and principal component analysis, it is not surprising that principal components have proven to be a useful way to analyze even more modern, multilayer, non-linear neural networks. (See Cottrell, Munro, & Zipser, 1988; Baldi & Hornik, 1989; Linsker, 1988). Although principal component analysis is a linear technique, important problems (i.e., image compression) often do not seem to require in practice more complex nonlinearities, in practice.

Since positive feedback can make the system state vector grow without bounds, one way to contain the state vector is simply to put limits on the allowable firing rate of the elements of the vectors. This is physiologically plausible since neurons have a limited dynamic range. It serves a similar function to the "sigmoid" assumed for the generic neural network neuron and is easier to program and analyze. It has the effect of limiting the state vector to restricted region of state space, hence the name "Brain-State-in-a-Box" or BSB model. The overall system is non-linear, but still functions linearly within the limits of the box.

The activity pattern in a set of neurons feeding back on itself is assumed to be composed of (1) the input to the neurons, (2) the feedback coming back through recurrent connections from past states of the neurons, and (3) the persistence of activity in the state, that is, activity does not drop to zero immediately but decays with some kind of time constant. We assume time is quantized. Suppose x(t) is the state vector at time step t. In general we assume the input is presented only once, at t=0, and then the system "processes" that input. The amount of feedback is given by $\alpha Ax(t)$, where α is a feedback constant. The decay of the previous state is given by a constant, γ, multiplying the previous state, that is $\gamma x(t)$ and A is a connection matrix. Sometimes it is desirable to keep the initial input, f(0), present, perhaps multiplied by a constant δ, which was 1 in the feedback example given above. In the algorithm used, the next state, x(t+1) is given as

$$x(t+1) = LIMIT(\gamma x(t) + \alpha Ax(t) + \delta f(0))$$

The LIMIT operation clips values that exceed upper or lower limits.

For the simulations we report here, we used the vector form of the Widrow-Hoff error correcting technique to form the connection matrix. This algorithm is not so simply connected to principal components, but the eigenvectors may still be interpretable in terms of what the network has learned. The connection matrix is partially connected in that some of the possible connections are set identically to zero.

7. RESPONSE TIMES

To make connection with published experiments we need to consider some aspect of simulation performance that corresponds to response time. Experimental data in many psychological experiments consists of both the result of the task — the answer to an arithmetic problem, for example — and the response time required to produce that answer. If a neural network does the computation and generates an answer, what corresponds to response time? Different classes of network models differ considerably in this respect. In most feedforward neural models (back propagation, for example) an input state vector gives rise to an output state vector in one or two parallel steps. The learning algorithms produce weights so the right input-output relations are produced, but the basic computation is not time dependent without the addition of further mechanisms. On the other hand, some network models have intrinsic behavior in the time domain even when they perform simple computations. Examples are the dynamical system network models such as Hopfield (1982, 1984) networks, resonance models such as ART (Carpenter & Grossberg, 1987), Kosko's BAM model (Kosko, 1988), and the BSB model (Anderson et al., 1977) used for the simulations here.

Hopfield's analysis of network behavior suggested that, qualitatively, activity shown by the brain moves from one relatively long lasting state to another. Network dynamics "computed" the stable states by modifying an input state vector until it reached a final stable state associated with a minimum in a quadratic system energy (Lyapunov) function. In nonlinear systems of this type, state vectors corresponding to the system energy minima are called *attractors*, and the set of all the nearby points in state space that have that attractor are referred to as the *basin of attraction* of that attractor. The BSB model can be shown to be an energy minimizing system, in the sense used by Hopfield (Golden, 1986). Many of the simpler dynamical system neural network models, such as the BSB model used in the simulations in this chapter, have only point attractors. More complex kinds of attractors are also possible, for example, limit cycles (Amit, 1989).

The response time assumption we make here for the dynamical system's behavior is that *simple response time is the time required for an input vector to move to a point attractor.* This approach is similar formally to some classic reaction time models such as the random walk and diffusion models (see Luce, 1986) and is discussed further in Anderson (1991).

8. SIMULATIONS

In the present simulations, the "problem" part of the vector, that is, the two operands, was always clamped, leaving only the answer field free to change without constraint. An activation threshold was also used to keep the zero parts of the vector set to zero, since, especially in the false product simulations (discussed below), these elements would otherwise tend to wander away from zero. There was also a "read out" threshold for the answer field, that is, only activation over this threshold was shown and recorded.

Ever since our first simulations of arithmetic using the hybrid coding, the overall pattern of results of the simulations remained remarkably consistent. Table 12.1 shows a typical recent simulation.

First, there are a number of errors, either wrong answers, or answers where an attractor was not reached in a large number of iterations (60) and was frozen or moving very slightly. Typically, a simulation reconstructs the correct answers about seventy percent of the time.

Second, errors are not random. We find that errors made by the network are close in magnitude to the correct answers. This is also a consistent feature of human error patterns in elementary multiplication (Graham, 1987; Norem & Knight, 1930).

8.1. FALSE PRODUCTS

One way to compare the model to human data is its ability to reject false products. For example, consider the two problems,

Is "8 times 7 = 63" correct?
Is "8 times 7 = 542" correct?

Problem	Correct?	"Response Time" (# Iterations)	Answer Given (if not correct)
2 × 2 = 4	Y	7	--
2 × 4 = 8	Y	27	8 tied with 4
2 × 5 = 10	Y	19	--
3 × 7 = 21	Y	17	--
3 × 8 = 24	Y	24	--
3 × 9 = 27	Y	19	--
4 × 2 = 8	Y	11	--
4 × 5 = 20	Y	21	--
4 × 6 = 24	Y	24	--
4 × 8 = 32	no resp.	60+[1]	
4 × 9 = 36	Y	36	36 tied with 37
5 × 2 = 10	Y	9	--
5 × 7 = 35	no resp.	60+	
5 × 8 = 40	Y	29	--
6 × 3 = 18	no resp.	60+	
6 × 4 = 24	Y	29	--
6 × 5 = 30	Y	33	--
6 × 6 = 36	N	43	46, 48 (tie)
6 × 7 = 42	N	39	48

Table 12.1. Example network performance when tested on trained problems after initial training.

---

[1] "60+" designates a problem on which no solution had been found by the 60th iteration and the simulation was terminated at that point because the system was making no further progress toward a solution.

Problem	Correct?	"Response Time" (# Iterations)	Answer Given (if not correct)
$6 \times 8 = 48$	no resp.	60+	
$7 \times 3 = 21$	Y	29	--
$7 \times 4 = 28$	Y	21	--
$7 \times 5 = 35$	Y	33	--
$7 \times 6 = 42$	Y	23	--
$7 \times 7 = 49$	no resp.	60+	
$7 \times 8 = 56$	no resp.	60+	
$8 \times 3 = 24$	Y	37	--
$8 \times 4 = 32$	N	35	24 tied with 28
$8 \times 6 = 48$	Y	35	48 tied with 42
$8 \times 7 = 56$	Y	33	--
$8 \times 8 = 64$	no resp.	60+	--
$8 \times 9 = 67^2$	Y	41	--

Table 12.1 (Contd.)

When humans do such problems they show a symbolic distance effect: the second answer can be rejected more quickly than the first because the incorrect answer is much further from the correct answer to the presented problem (Stazyk, Ashcraft, & Hamman, 1982). It is easy to simulate such problems with a network. The false product is presented to a trained network. If the network "writes over" the incorrect product part of the state vector then the product is rejected; if it does not, the product is accepted.

The present systematic simulations of false products were done by constructing four false products for those problems that the system answered correctly when simply probed with a problem and a blank answer field. Two of these were "close" false products, for example, 5 x 2 = 20 and 5 x 2 = 30, and two were "far" false products, for example, 5 x 2 = 50 and 5 x 2 = 60. Note that we are asking the system to carry out only qualitative, rather than precise, quantitative, calculations.

---

[2] An incorrect answer was trained on purpose so that this would not be the only problem in the training set with an answer in the 70s.

Fig. 12.4a shows response time data for a representative example and Fig. 12.4b shows data for all of the false products tested using qualitative coding. The system displays a symbolic distance effect similar to that displayed by humans. The error data showed a similar effect: the system accepts six near false products, but no far false products, again, a symbolic distance effect. A simulation with a more precise quantitative coding yielded similar behavior.

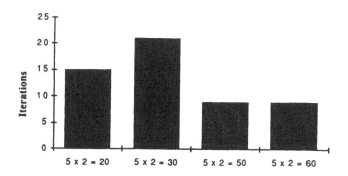

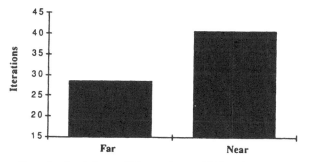

Fig. 12.4. Response times for simulations of false products. (a) Data from one example problem, false products associated with the problem, 5 times 2. (b) Data averaged for near and far examples for all problems. Two near and two far false products were constructed for all the problems in the learning set of arithmetic facts.

8.2. PRACTICE EFFECTS

Humans respond more quickly when offering correct answers to arithmetic problems that they have just practiced, and these priming effects are relatively short-lived (Campbell, 1987; Stazyk et al., 1982).

To test the system for priming effects, it was trained on 32 (qualitative) facts, and then selectively primed on those 24 problems that were initially responded to correctly when probed with the problem before priming. To selectively prime the system, a fact was presented and the weights changed by an amount proportional to the pre- and post- connection activity; that is, an outer product matrix was formed and then multiplied by a small priming constant, and the result added to the overall weight matrix formed during learning. Presumably, more stable changes due to sustained practice correspond to similar changes in the efficacy of connection strengths, though over a longer time course.

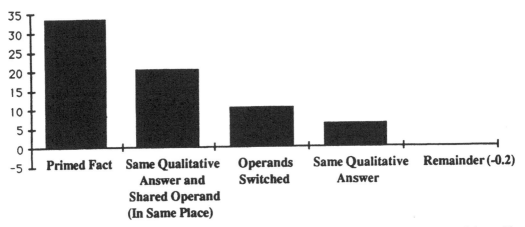

Fig. 12.5. Results of simulated practice effects. Priming affects response time to many aspects of the problem, and can give decreases in response time to problems that share operands and results.

Fig. 12.5 illustrates the basic priming response time data. Not surprisingly, the primed facts exhibited the greatest decrease in response time. The priming generalizes in an interesting way: there is also a substantial, though somewhat less dramatic, decrease in response time in answering problems which share an operand and an answer field with a primed problem. Similarly, there is a somewhat smaller decrease in response time for problems with the operands switched and a small decrease for problems that share only an answer field.

By examining where and how the system changes previous responses to incorrect answers, one can detect a mechanism which produces the correlation between response time and problem error observed in humans. More broadly such an analysis also illuminates the general way in which the strength of competing associations change with priming and practice. There were five problems for which the system failed to give an answer after 79 iterations, but, after a different problem was primed, the system gave an incorrect answer to these problems. In every case the incorrect answers given were in the direction of the prime. Similarly, in seven cases where the previous answer was correct but after the prime was incorrect, all the errors were in the direction of the prime. Moreover, the average response time of the previously correct answers was 44.9

iterations, as compared to the much smaller average response time for all correct responses, 22.8 iterations. Thus the correlation between response time and error rate appears to occur because it is easier to move answers one way or the other when the system has originally been tentative in its responses, that is, has taken a long time to generate its original answer.

8.3. PROBLEM-SIZE EFFECT

One of the most frequently cited aspects of the psychology of simple arithmetic is the general increase of response time with increase of the magnitude of the operands and therefore also the answer. This is referred to in the literature as the *problem size effect*. Correlations of differing magnitudes have also been noted between response time and the smallest or largest operand, as well as with the sum or the squared sum of the operands (Campbell, 1987; Campbell & Graham, 1985; Miller, Perlmutter, & Keating, 1984; Stazyk et al., 1982). Campbell and Graham (1985) propose that the effect results from differing amounts of practice on different problems (i.e., all else equal, the greater the practice, the faster the response times), and the order in which problems are learned (*i.e.*, problems learned first exert proactive interference on problems learned later). They cite some suggestive evidence, taken in part from studies of textbooks, that the smaller problems are learned first and practiced more. Practice and order effects are, of course, easy to model within an associative framework.

Our model suggests additional possible explanations. One possibility is that the effect may result from the pattern of bar codings: especially with the compression, the codings for problems of increasing magnitudes may get successively more "muddled together." A number of our simulations have exhibited a size effect. However, unlike the other effects reported so far it does not appear that the problem size effect resulting solely from the bar code compression is a particularly robust feature of modeling. We plan to explore the issue in more detail by systematically varying the amount of compression of the bar codes in larger simulations.

8.4. OTHER GENERALIZATION EFFECTS

The model also generalizes in interesting ways when presented with completely novel problems. This has been explored in some detail with operand interchanges: The system was trained on one operand order, and then presented with the same problem with the operands reversed. Table 12.2 shows the results of a typical operand interchange simulation. Perhaps somewhat surprisingly, the response is correct 50% of the time, though typically slower (24.2 iterations) than responses to the originally trained operand order (12.6 iterations). Moreover, the two times that the system provided specific incorrect answers, they were close to the correct answer.

Presumably the system makes a reasonable guess based on the similarity of the pattern of bars to a problem that it has been trained on. Such behavior is interesting because the system, in a sense, appears to extract the rule of commutativity, even if imperfectly. It is impossible at present to tell how psychologically plausible this aspect of the system's performance is. One reason is that students typically practice both operand orders when learning a problem, though both orders are not always practiced equally or to equal levels of mastery. There is anecdotal evidence that children do not always generalize well across operand order, and fail to understand commutativity until it is specifically pointed out to them. But the model also has difficulty with commutativity, often generating a reasonable answer, but taking more time to generate correct commutative answers than to generate answers it already knows. Perhaps it is best to think of the rough knowledge of commutativity acquired by the model as constituting an appropriate bias for the system to learn the other operand order more easily. This seems psychologically plausible, though we are not aware of any relevant experimental evidence.

Trained Problem	"Response Time" After Training (#Iterations)	"Response Time" for Switched Operands (# Iterations)	Response Generated with Switched Operands[3]
8 × 9 = 60	9	29	60
2 × 5 = 10	9	11	10
5 × 8 = 40	15	81	*60*
6 × 3 = 20	13	19	20
7 × 3 = 20	19	60+[4]	no response
8 × 3 = 20	13	42	20
4 × 2 = 10	13	60+	no response
7 × 5 = 40	not learned	25	40
3 × 7 = 20	19	27	20
4 × 7 = 30	not learned	60+	no response
5 × 7 = 40	15	27	*30*
3 × 8 = 20	21	60+	no response

Table 12.2. Response time data from a representative operand interchange simulation.

---

[3] Incorrect responses are shown in italics.

[4] See Footnote 1 for explanation of this term.

8.5. NOVEL PROBLEMS

Another test of the trained network model is to present it with completely novel arithmetic facts, which it has not previously encountered in either operand order. In this case the system again often responds reasonably, making "estimates" based on past learning. Table 12.3 gives response time data when the system is presented with 2 x 2 = ?. In the "before" condition, the system had been trained on the qualitative facts, including the 2 x 2 = 10 "fact." In the "after" condition the 2 x 2 = 10 fact had been omitted from the training set. The system still responds correctly in the latter case on all novel problems. Table 12.3 shows response times were nearly the same in the two cases, with those for the untrained condition being only slightly longer.

Novel Problem	Before[5]	After[6]
2 × 2 = 10	7	9
2 × 5 = 10	9	11
3 × 7 = 20	17	21
3 × 8 = 20	19	23
4 × 2 = 10	9	13
5 × 2 = 10	7	9
Mean	10.71	13.57

Table 12.3. "Response Time" results of a representative simulation of responses given to previously untrained (novel) multiplication facts.

---

[5] Response times (# iterations) to selected problems when 2 × 2 = 10, but not the other problems shown, were included in the original set.

[6] Response times (# iterations) to novel problems (not included in the original training set) when 2 × 2 = 10 were *not* included in the original set.

9. PROGRAMMING A NETWORK

We previously justified the use of a hybrid coding and showed that it provided qualitative fits for some experimental phenomena. The representation we used, however, also allows for some flexible control structures to be built into the system as well. We call use of these control structures "programming" following a traditional computer model. We have programming terms (for example, "multiply", "add", "bigger", "smaller") operating on number data. The programming term defines an operation or a relation between two numbers.

As an exercise, let us try to program a network to answer a simple question: "which of two numbers is bigger" or "which of two numbers is smaller." We restrict ourselves to integers. One straightforward, if awkward and inefficient, approach would be to teach the system all the different comparison facts that we want it to know. We can do better by using what we have available to us in our number representation. The symbolic portion of our hybrid representation tells us nothing about relative size, but the analog part of the representation does. This observation suggests a way to do the comparison operation effectively. We want to feed the two state vectors into the network, with a "programming" state vector, "bigger" or "smaller." The network should give an output state vector representing the bigger or smaller number as the answer. Therefore, a schematic diagram of a computation might look like Fig. 12.6.

We have a nonlinear feedback network, BSB, that lets us choose one pattern relative to another, based on their relative amount of feedback, which might correspond to different values for eigenvalues. To choose the larger of two values, therefore, all we have to do is arrange it so that small numbers have smaller feedback weights than large numbers. This is easily accomplished by producing relative inhibition or excitation of different parts of the analog map, and not through detailed synaptic excitation patterns. All that is needed is an excitatory weighting *vector* that is large on one side of the map and small on the other. Therefore, the programming term "bigger" merely has to be associated with this differential vector excitation pattern of the analog portion of the map.

We also observe that it would be quite easy to learn this activation pattern: it is related to differential success rate in the comparison process. With only random pairs of different digits to compare, for example, nine is always bigger than other numbers, one is rarely bigger, and five is bigger half the time. Therefore if the comparison term only corresponded to frequency of success, it would produce the right differential pattern for bigger. We expect that presentation of only a small number of the many possible comparisons allows reasonable estimation of frequency of success. The inverse pattern could be used for programming "smaller."

We can now ask two questions about the model: First, can we get the network to produce the right answers, and, second, do the results agree with the experimental data on response time for "bigger" and "smaller." It was easy to get the network to work. Although we could not directly manipulate the eigenvalues, the structure of the problem is sufficiently regular so that the larger number appeared reliably as the final state of the system.

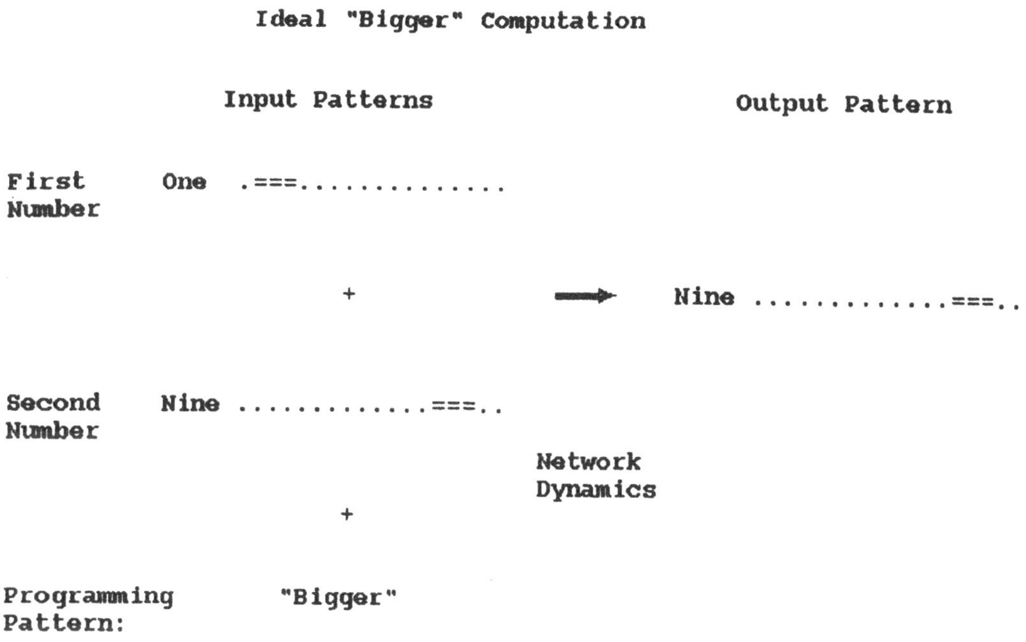

```
                    Ideal "Bigger" Computation


                  Input Patterns                Output Pattern


First       One  .===..............
Number


                         +            ━━▶      Nine ..............===..


Second      Nine ..............===..
Number
                                      Network
                                      Dynamics
                         +


Programming         "Bigger"
Pattern:
```

Fig. 12.6. The way that a flexible neural network computation for a comparison like "bigger" might proceed. Two number representations interact with each other and the programming term "bigger", network dynamics operate, and the correct answer is produced as the output pattern.

Notice that the network actually *constructs* the correct answer in the answer field using network dynamics. The simulations are reliable and show the kinds of qualitative response time patterns we have seen before and that characterize human performance (Banks, Fujii, & Kayra-Stuart, 1976). Errors appeared and response times were long only when the two numbers were close together, as shown in the simulation data of Fig. 12.8.

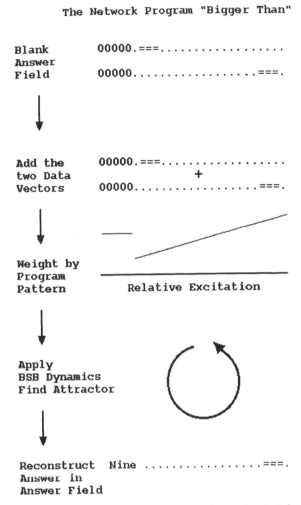

The Network Program "Bigger Than"

Blank   00000.===...................
Answer
Field   00000..................===.

Add the   00000.===..................
two Data   +
Vectors   00000..................===.

Weight by
Program
Pattern   Relative Excitation

Apply
BSB Dynamics
Find Attractor

Reconstruct Nine ....===.
Answer in
Answer Field

Fig. 12.7. A simple neural network program to compare two numbers and output the biggest one. The two data vectors are added together, and weighted by the relative excitation shown. BSB dynamics operate on the vector sum. The final attractor has the correct answer ("nine") in the number field. The correct answer was reconstructed by an estimation and weighting process, based on the bar code part of the representation.

Because the relative excitation results from frequency estimation, we can fortuitously let someone else do part of the work for us for detailed fits of experimental data. Link (1990) proposed a frequency estimation model for two digit number comparison. Link observed that 90s usually were larger when compared to other numbers and teens usually were smaller. He then hooked his frequency estimator up to a random walk response time model. Link's random walk model has many formal similarities to the neural network response model we have been discussing. If neural computation is at all similar to the frequency estimation technique used here, it suggests that the possibilities for easy cognitive computation are limited to a significant extent by physical brain architecture. This is an intriguing and testable suggestion. The discussion of important aspects of language found in Lakoff (1987) is consistent with such an idea, as are the tight constraints on natural concepts that are obviously present and yet very hard to define precisely and logically.

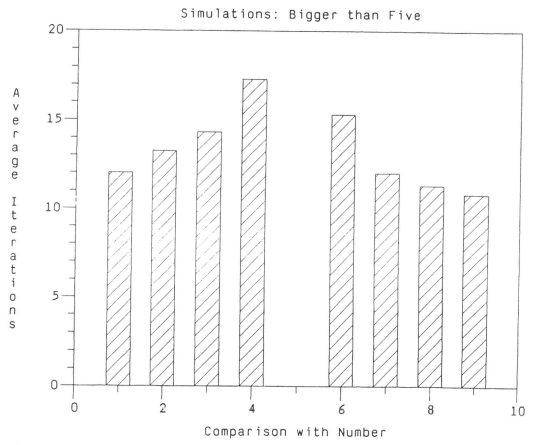

Fig. 12.8. Simulation of the "bigger" program. Iterations measure the time required for the system to reach an attractor. These are all the single digit comparisons with the digit five. Answers were correct in all cases. Note the symbolic distance effect, which is also shown by the experimental data available for this task (see Banks et al., 1976).

10. DISCUSSION

This chapter presents a powerful way of making a neural network model understand and use quantitative information in a human-like way. The key result is that incorporation into the input data representation of a "sensory" or "analog" part along with an abstract part produces a system which acts in simulation much like experimental data from humans. We argued as well that for humans, too, mathematics and the abstract quantities associated with mathematics, are represented in rich and complex ways that often contain a substantial sensory component. Such formally "extraneous" material influences strongly the kinds of errors that humans make. This "extra-symbolic" material gives rise to some of the things that one might call intuition, understanding, insight, or common sense, if humans displayed it, and demonstrate how a large amount of previously learned information can cooperate in order to produce good answers to new problems. This extra-symbolic information and manipulations of it may be responsible for more of the creative aspects of mathematics than formal symbol manipulation. An artificial theorem prover of any complexity should contain such information, if it is to be capable of the insights that humans can sometimes show. It is difficult to make abstract symbolic systems make use of such extraneous information while neural networks can do it if data is properly represented. Thus moving easily between the symbolic and continuous domains may be virtues of neural networks.

There are, however a few drawbacks to the network method. The accuracy of the network computation is often poor because estimation and generalization are at odds with high precision. Use of the analog representations requires huge numbers of computing elements. Luckily, the brain seems to work in a regime where processing elements and connections are cheap, topographic maps are easy to construct, and powerful qualitative computations become possible.

Symbol manipulation as done by humans does not stand alone, and pure symbol manipulation is rarely performed. What seems to be done, if we are to take the leap of assuming the arithmetic simulation is typical of complex high-level cognition, is to form a fascinating hybrid computation: part symbolic and part sensory-based and intuitive, mutually enhancing and supporting each other. Since we live in a world that our sensory systems have evolved to interpret, we expect that the symbol systems we evolve are tightly coupled to our particular universe and are particularly effective in handling it. The psychic distress most normal humans feel when confronted with the internals of computers, that is, when they are not manipulating a computer through a complex interface, is one example of our difficulties when faced with a *real* symbol manipulator.

In artificial systems we have the potential to see how these principles might be implemented, how they work best, and how we can extend them. In the past half century of computer development, we have focused on the development and refinement of aids for formal symbolic methods of computation. Perhaps now we can see a way to develop a different class of artificial systems to help us with mechanical aids for our common sense. We may also be able to better understand our own cognitive abilities.

ACKNOWLEDGMENTS

Support was provided by a grant from the McDonnell-Pew Program in Cognitive Neuroscience to J. A. Some support was also provided by the National Science Foundation under Grants BNS-85-18075, DIR-89-07709, and BNS 90-23283 and by the Digital Equipment Corporation.

REFERENCES

Amari, S.-I. (1977). Neural theory of association and concept formation. *Biological Cybernetics, 26*, 175-185.

Amit, D. J. (1989). *Modelling Brain Function: The World of Attractor Neural Networks.* Cambridge, UK: Cambridge University Press.

Anderson, J. A. (1991), Why, having so many neurons, do we have so few thoughts? In W. Hockley & S. Lewandowsky (Eds.), *From Theory to Data: Essays in Honor of Bennett Murdock* (pp. 477-507). Hillsdale, NJ: Lawrence Erlbaum Associates.

Anderson, J. A. (in press). The BSB model. In M. Hassoun (Ed.), *Neural Network Associators.* Oxford, UK: Oxford University Press.

Anderson, J. A., Gately, M. T., Penz, P. A., & Collins, D. R. (1990), Radar signal categorization using a neural network. *Proceedings of the IEEE 78*, 1646-1657.

Anderson, J. A., & Mozer, M. C. (1981). Categorization and selective neurons. In G. E. Hinton & J. A. Anderson, *Parallel Models of Associative Memory* (pp. 213-236). Hillsdale, NJ: Lawrence Erlbaum Associates.

Anderson, J. A., Pellionisz, A., & Rosenfeld, E. (1990). *Neurocomputing 2: Directions for Research.* Cambridge, MA: MIT Press.

Anderson, J. A., & Rosenfeld, E. (Eds.) (1988). *Neurocomputing: Foundations of Research.* Cambridge, MA: MIT Press.

Anderson, J. A., Rossen, M. L., Viscuso, S. R., & Sereno, M. E. (1990). Experiments with representation in neural networks: Object motion, speech, and arithmetic. In H. Haken & S. Stadler, *Synergetics of Cognition* (pp. 54-69). Berlin: Springer-Verlag.

Anderson, J. A., Silverstein, J. W., Ritz, S. A., & Jones, R. S. (1977). Distinctive features, categorical perception, and probability learning: Some applications of a neural model. *Psychological Review 84*, 413-451.

Baldi, P., & Hornik, K. (1989). Neural networks and principal component analysis: learning from examples without local minima. *Neural Networks 2*, 53-58.

Banks, W. P., Fujii, M., & Kayra-Stuart, F. (1976). Semantic congruity effects in comparative judgements of magnitudes of digits. *Journal of Experimental Psychology: Human Perception and Performance 2*, 435-447.

Campbell, J. I. D. (1987). The role of associative interference in learning and retrieving arithmetic facts. In J. A. Sloboda & D. Rogers (Eds.), *Cognitive Processes in Mathematics* (pp. 107-122). Oxford: Oxford University Press.

Campbell, J. I. D., & Graham, D. J. (1985). Mental multiplication skill: structure, process, and acquisition. *Canadian Journal of Psychology* **39**, 338-366.

Carpenter, G. A.. & Grossberg, S. (1987). ART 2: Self organization of stable category recognition codes for analog input patterns. *Applied Optics* **26**, 4919-4930.

Cottrell, G. W., Munro, P., & Zipser, D. (1988). Image compression by back propagation: An example of extensional programming. In N. E. Sharkey (Ed.), *Advances in Cognitive Science* (Vol. 3, pp. 208-240). Norwood, NJ: Ablex.

Davis, P. J., & Anderson, J. A., (1979). Nonanalytic aspects of mathematics and their implication for research and education. *SIAM Review* **21**, 112-127.

Einstein, A. (1951). Autobiographical notes. In P. A. Schilpp (Ed.), *Albert Einstein: Philosopher-Scientist* (pp. 2-95). New York: Tudor.

Geman, S., Bienenstock, E., & Doursat, R. (1992). Neural networks and the bias/variance dilemma. *Neural Computation* **4**, 1-58.

Golden, R. M. (1986). The "brain-state-in-a-box" neural model is a gradient descent algorithm. *Journal of Mathematical Psychology*, **30**, 73-80.

Graham, D. J. (1987). An associative retrieval model of arithmetic memory: How children learn to multiply. In J. A. Sloboda & D. Rogers (Eds.), *Cognitive Processes in Mathematics* (pp. 123-141). Oxford, UK: Oxford University Press.

Hadamard, J. (1945). *The Psychology of Invention in the Mathematical Field*. Princeton, NJ: Princeton University Press.

Hertz, J., Krogh, A., & Palmer, R. G. (1991). *Introduction to the Theory of Neural Computation*. Reading, MA: Addison-Wesley.

Hopfield, J. J. (1982). Neural networks and physical with emergent collective computational abilities. *Proceedings of the National Academy of Sciences* **79**, 2554-2558.

Hopfield, J. J. (1984), Neurons with graded response have collective computational properties like those of two-state neurons. *Proceedings of the National Academy of Sciences* **81**, 3088-3092.

Knapp, A. G., & Anderson, J. A. (1984). Theory of categorization based on distributed memory storage. *Journal of Experimental Psychology: Learning, Memory and Cognition* **10**, 616-637.

Kohonen, T. (1989). *Self Organization and Associative Memory* (3rd. ed). Berlin: Springer.

Kosko, B. (1988), Bidirectional associative memories, *IEEE Transactions on Systems, Man, and Cybernetics* **18**, 49-60.

Lakoff, G. (1987). *Women, Fire, and Dangerous Things*. New York: Basic Books.

LeCun, Y., Boser, B., Denker, J. S., Henderson, D., Howard, R. E., Hubbard, W. & Jackel, L. D. (1990). Backpropagation applied to handwritten zip code recognition. *Neural Computation* **1**, 541-551.

Link, S. (1990). Modeling imageless thought: The relative judgement theory of numerical comparisons, *Journal of Mathematical Psychology* **34**, 2-41.

Linsker, R. (1988). Self-organization in a perceptual network. *Computer Magazine* **21**, 105-117.

Luce, R. D. (1986). *Response Times*. New York: Oxford University Press.

McClelland, J. L., & Rumelhart, D. E. (Eds.) (1986). *Parallel Distributed Processing* (Vol. 2). Cambridge, MA: MIT Press.

Miller, A. I. (1984). *Imagery in Scientific Thought: Creating 20th Century Physics.* Boston: Birkhauser.

Miller, K., Perlmutter, M., & Keating, D. (1984), Cognitive arithmetic: Comparison of operations. *Journal of Experimental Psychology: Learning, Memory, and Cognition* **10**, 46-60.

Moyer, R. S., & Landauer, T. K. (1967). Time required for judgement of numerical inequality. *Nature* **215**, 1519-1520.

Norem, G. M., & Knight, F. B. (1930). The learning of the one hundred multiplication combinations. In *National Society for the Study of Education: Report on the Society's Committee on Arithmetic*, Vol. 15, NSSE Yearbook 219, 551-567.

Rumelhart, D. E., & McClelland, J. L. (Eds.) (1986). *Parallel Distributed Processing* (Vol. 1). Cambridge, MA: MIT Press.

Stazyk, E. H., Ashcraft, M. H., & Hamman, M. S. (1982). A network approach to mental multiplication. *Journal of Experimental Psychology: Learning, Memory, and Cognition* **8**, 320-335.

Viscuso, S. R., Anderson, J. A., & Spoehr, K. T. (1989). Representing simple arithmetic in neural networks. In G. Tiberghien (Ed.), *Advanced Cognitive Science: Theory and Applications* (pp. 141-164). Cambridge, UK: Horwoods.

Zipser, D., & Andersen, R. A. (1988). A back propagation programmed network that simulates response properties of a subset of posterior parietal neurons. *Nature* **331**, 679-684.

IV

BIOLOGICAL FOUNDATIONS OF KNOWLEDGE

13

Toward a Theory of Learning and Representing Causal Inferences in Neural Networks

George E. Mobus
University of North Texas

1. INTRODUCTION

We perceive the world to operate according to a fundamental principle of causality in spite of the seeming chaotic behavior of nature. The Universe seems to be orderly and we are able to comprehend this order at some very deep level. Some events (states of processes) cause other events, which, in turn, cause still other events. And we find, generally, that certain events tend to be associated with certain other events, which is to say, there is regularity to the Universe. This principle lies at the root of cognition and is the basis for scientific investigation. It can be viewed as the language of nature.

It is useful to view languages as having a syntactic as well as a semantic level of organization. The syntax of causality is a set of rules, the grammar if you will, that describes the temporal and spatial relationships that must exist between two events, say A and B, in order to instantiate an inference of the form A $\Rightarrow$ B (A causes B). At the semantic level, we are provided with the means to reason about the world knowing that A $\Rightarrow$ B. At the very base of this ability is the capacity to predict the future. That is, if A is observed we can infer that B will occur. Furthermore, we infer that B will occur within some specific temporal window. This capacity is fundamental to survival in the natural world. The realization of such a capacity involves several key issues. How is the syntax to be represented? How are these representations to be acquired from experience? And how may they be used semantically to reason from the state of the environment to some future state – how are they accessed and how are they processed?

During the past decade some real progress has been made in understanding how neural systems function (Alkon, 1987, 1989; Getting, 1980; Jaffe & Johnston, 1990; Kandel & Schwartz,

1982; Small, Kandel, & Hawkins, 1989; Starmer, 1987). Additional insights into the details of neural representation, learning and processing have been gained by building formal models of neural networks (Alkon, Blackwell, Barbour, Rigler, & Vogl, 1990; Buonomano, Baxter, & Byrne, 1990; Byrne & Gingrich, 1989; Byrne, Gingrich, & Baxter, 1990; Gelperin, Hopfield, & Tank, 1985; Klopf, 1988; Klopf & Morgan, 1990; Koch & Segev, 1989; Morgan, Patterson, & Klopf, 1990; Rumelhart & McClelland, 1986; Sejnowski, Chattarji, & Stanton, 1989). Here I want to explore an approach to representing and learning causal relations in a formal neural network in which the syntax of causality is the language of neural organization.

1.1. BACKGROUND

To begin understanding how the human mind perceives and reasons about the world, how it captures and uses the regularity of nature, we might ask how it is that causality, or more precisely, causal relations, are encoded in the brain. How does the brain represent causal relations and how are these representations learned? To make the task approachable we note first that all animal life is faced with the same problem of discovering and using regularity in the quest for survival and propagation. Thus by studying primitive (that is phylogenetically simpler) brains we may discern some mechanisms for such encoding which will be found to be invariant across the phylogenetic spectrum.

Specifically, the learning model of conditioning, demonstrable in some very primitive animals, is an operational version of learning and representing a causal relation.[1] The outline of neural and even molecular substrates of conditioned learning has begun to emerge from the laboratories of neuroscience (Alkon, 1987; Kandel & Schwartz, 1982; Small et al., 1989). Connectionist views of classical and operant conditioning, likewise, have provided computational models which may aid in the discovery of these invariants (Carpenter & Grossberg, 1987a, 1987b; Grossberg, 1987; Sutton, 1988; Sutton & Barto, 1987, 1991). Such models, constrained by the wealth of neurophysiological and psychophysical data regarding conditioning, provide valuable insights into the principles of learning and may produce further hypothesis for investigation (Getting, 1980). Additionally, one hopes to find clues that will aid in the construction of machine-based mechanisms with animal-like learning competence (Anderson, Merrill, & Port, 1989; Elman & Zipser, 1988; Morgan et al., 1990; Rumelhart & McClelland, 1986).

In this chapter I introduce a learning mechanism called an Adaptrode (Mobus, 1990; Mobus & Fisher, 1990; Mobus, Cherri, & Fisher, 1993) which solves an important problem in representing temporal information in neurons. A neural network in which Adaptrodes are used to process synaptic efficacy and adaptive thresholds is shown to be competent at the conditioned learning task. The thrust of this chapter, however, is to show how this approach satisfies the

---

[1] Here, of course, I mean subjective causality as opposed to objective causality. The former refers to the "belief" held by the observer that A causes B based on the contiguity and contingency observations that the observer has made. See Dretske (1988), especially chapter 4.

temporal constraints of causality, suggesting that conditioned learning should be considered a basic form of causal relation learning. A number of workers hold that conditioning represents a basic mechanism for more complex learning task (Mackintosh, 1983; Staddon & Zhang, 1991). If this is so, then it constitutes a basis for understanding the more advanced, that is, cognitive, forms of perceiving causal relations that allow us to reason about the world.

1.2. TEMPORAL CONSTRAINTS OF CAUSALITY

Causality imposes several important temporal constraints on the form of any derived inference (Dretske, 1988; Mackintosh, 1983). First, of course, the fact that the event A must precede the event B in order for us to say that A is a cause of B. We rarely say that the breaking window caused the ball to be thrown. More precisely we require that the onset of A precede the onset of B by some $\Delta t > 0$. We can relax this constraint somewhat by requiring (or allowing) that A almost always precedes B, where "almost always" refers to some statistically defined frequency. There may be other causes of B and the occurrence of A may not always result in B. The constraint, however, strongly requires that B never precedes A, at least within some defined latency period, which is to say the temporal relation is one-way.

Another, related but technically different, constraint is that of temporal contiguity. The events must occur within a temporal window of opportunity. This window is defined by the context of events and the memory retention of event A. Thus it is not that B must occur shortly after A, but rather, B must occur after A but before the memory of A fades and no intervening event changes the context established by A. This is a subtle aspect of contiguity not often fully appreciated. Memory plays an important role in inference of causality. If B occurs too long after A has occurred, then the linkage between them is weakened.

A third constraint has to do with computing the correlation of A and B over time (contingency). In probabilistic causality we allow that the occurrence of A may increase the probability of the occurrence of B. The event B can have other, unobserved causes. Thus we infer a causal relation between A and B only if the frequency of co-occurrence is sufficient to the purpose (note this need not be a majority of the times). The temporal constraint, thus imposed, is that a sufficient period has to pass in which multiple occurrences of A and B can be experienced. We note again that memory is involved in keeping a count of the co-occurrences and that memory must persist over the time scale of the "sufficient" observation period.

These constraints, implicit in the prototypical causality rules, underscore the importance of the role of time in learning, representing and processing (reasoning) derived causality rules. Furthermore, we can see from the above discussion that temporal information extends across many time scales. It is not sufficient to deal with just the time scale of the realtime events (A and B). Therefore the nervous system must employ mechanisms which encode temporal information in multiple time domains.

1.3. CONDITIONED LEARNING AS A "SIMPLE" FORM OF CAUSAL REPRESENTATION

One form of learning task that is well documented and embodies causality rules is conditioned learning (Alkon, 1987; Alkon, Vogl, Blackwell, & Tam, 1991; Aparicio, 1988; Dretske, 1988; Gelperin et al., 1985; Grossberg, 1991; Klopf, 1988; Mackintosh, 1983; Pavlov, 1927; Sutton & Barto, 1987, 1991; Tesauro, 1986). In this paradigm (of which there are two flavors) the animal learns to associate an event such as an environmental cue with a behavior (or with a consequence). Though the notion behind conditioning has its origin in laboratory experiments, the general idea of conditioned learning and how it benefits the animal in its natural environment is fairly straightforward. If an environmental event (cue) which is neutral with respect to the animal's survival, is found by experience to precede another event which has direct survival impact, such as the availability of food or pain caused by a wound, then the animal forms a lasting association between those events and can use the prior event to predict the occurrence of the second event. Such predictive ability allows the animal to respond more quickly to the impending meaningful event. This can be seen in the experimental paradigm called classical or Pavlovian conditioning (Pavlov, 1927). The animal learns to associate a conditionable stimulus (CS) with an unconditionable (hard wired) stimulus-response (UCS/UCR). The association results in the UCR being elicited upon presentation of the CS alone. The animal has learned to respond to the CS as if it were the UCS.

The second form of this type of learning involves the stochastic emission of a behavior which reliably produces some beneficial result (for the animal) in the environment. The animal learns to associate the behavior with the beneficial result and can, in principle, emit the behavior by choice in order to elicit the result. This latter form of learning, termed operant (or instrumental) conditioning, depends on a contextual situation, for example a physiological drive, which creates the condition in which the result will be beneficial. In the laboratory setting, animals are kept hungry so that they are "motivated" to press levers or buttons so as to receive a food pellet.

How are these conditioned learning tasks to be viewed as simple causal representations? There is the philosophical side to this question wherein we can speculate over the animal's perceptions and beliefs about cause and effects (Dretske, 1988). However, I am more interested in an operational view in which the animal behaves as if a cause and effect relation has been learned. Whether A (the CS) actually causes B (the UCS) which in turn causes C (the UCR) in an objective sense, or is the perception of the animal is of little concern just now. The point is that the animal responds to A (with C) as if a causal chain had been established. From the standpoint of behavior, there exists the inference of a causal chain.

The balance of this chapter focuses on the way in which neural networks can encode the temporal and associative rules of causality. This is examined at the level of conditioned response learning where it will be shown that a neural architecture can be built in which the prototypical rules, in particular the temporal constraints, of causality can be instantiated in representations of events which are causes (predictors) and events which are effects (consequences or reinforcers). If it is true that conditioned learning is a fundamental basis for higher forms of learning as has been suggested, then this approach may fulfill the promise of directing us toward a theory of causal inference learning and reasoning in higher cognitive processes.

2. REPRESENTING TIME IN NEURAL NETWORKS

As I hope has been established, the role of time in causal inference is central and crucial. In order to meet the temporal constraints of causality we must show how a neural network can encode temporal knowledge, integrated with spatial associative knowledge, such that information processing produces the correct inferential result. In this section I briefly review some methods which have been employed to incorporate temporal representation in neural networks. I then introduce in the next section a novel algorithm for producing adaptive response as the basis for learning in networks. In section 4 I show the results of simulated neural networks based on this algorithm in which conditioned learning is demonstrated.

2.1. PRIMACY OF ASSOCIATIVITY

The vast majority of learning rules that are used in neural network architectures have at their base the assumption of associativity as the driving influence in changing the edge weights associated with processing element inputs. What this means, simply, is that in order for a weight to be modified, there must be some kind of correlation between two or more independent signals in the processing element. These can be, for example, an input correlated with the output of the element such as the Hebb rule (Hebb, 1949; Hertz, Krogh, & Palmer, 1991), input correlated with an error (difference between the output and a desired output or delta rule, Widrow & Hoff, 1960), or two inputs (local interaction rule, Alkon et al., 1990). Such rules can be further modified to take into account the time derivative of the signals (Klopf, 1988; Kosko, 1986) or the error derivative in the case of the generalized delta rule (Rumelhart, Hinton, & Williams, 1985). However, the change in a weight is still dependent on the activity of two or more signals.

This form of associativity is a spatial encoding mechanism. A large number of neural network applications have addressed the issues of pattern learning, classification, and recognition. Their successes have led to what seems to be a general consensus that learning rules must, at their base, be associative. As a result this has led to an interesting problem: How to represent temporal knowledge when the basic rule is associative (Elman, 1990).

2.2. ADDING TEMPORAL REPRESENTATION TO ASSOCIATIVE-BASED NETWORKS

A typical solution to this problem has been an attempt to add temporal representation to an otherwise associative learning scheme. The earliest efforts attempted to construct architectures in which time could be represented by a spatial analogue. For example an avalanche circuit could be used to represent time steps in a sequence (Grossberg, 1982).

Another method for representing temporal information at the level of the network is through recurrent loops and/or time delay units (see Hertz et al., 1991, esp. Section 7.3). In the simplest version a neuron excites itself through a loop with inherent decay. Grossberg (1991 for an excellent review) and others have used this method to instantiate a short-term memory (STM) function at the level of individual neurons. An associative rule is still used to update the weights (called long-term memory — LTM) on the other inputs to the neuron.

Recurrency can be used on a network-wide basis as well. One neuron can excite (through a non-learning connection) another neuron which can, in turn, excite the former directly or through a chain of neurons. This method has been used by a number of workers using the backpropagation learning method. Context units which feed back historical states to earlier layers in the network act as a memory of prior input and processing, thus having an impact on the current processing (Elman, 1990). Systems of this kind have been shown to be able to learn and recognize and/or generate sequences of spatially extended patterns.

2.3. ADDING ASSOCIATIVITY TO TEMPORAL REPRESENTATION — AN ALTERNATIVE

In these systems some form of temporal representation is added to a network architecture based on an associative learning rule. An alternative approach would be to add associative encoding to a temporally based learning rule. I had been interested in the biological phenomenon of adaptive response in which an animal modifies its response to a stimulus based on the time course behavior of that stimulus. This is a fundamentally nonassociative phenomena which can become associative through modulation processes. From this work the outlines of the Adaptrode model emerged and were more recently refined in Paul Fisher's lab at the University of North Texas.

The problem of temporal representation is more complex than simply representing sequences. Perhaps the most important aspect of temporally extended phenomena is that modulation occurs over multiple time scales. The meaning or impact of real time events can be modified by a longer time course activity of those events. A simple example of adaptive response lets us see this. People who decide to go into athletic training experience adaptive response of their muscles. The real time response of the body to athletic demand (performance) changes with time and training. If a rigorous training schedule is maintained the athlete's muscles strengthen and increase in bulk as new tissue is created. This occurs only if the demand schedule is maintained over an extended time period. The muscles come to expect an increase in work load as a result of past experience. They adapt to the expected level of demand. This is a form of learning which is based primarily on activity and time. There are short-term effects, intermediate-term effects and long-term effects that come into play.

Muscle growth however will be constrained, or modulated, by associative factors such as nutrition. Learning takes place if these factors are satisfied. Thus adaptive response is a model of learning in which associative factors act as modulators to an otherwise temporal encoding process.

Could adaptive response be a biologically plausible basis for learning in neural networks? More to the point, could this phenomenon be the basis for efficacy weight updating of synapses, thus bringing temporal representation from the level of a neuron (self-excitation) to the level of the synapse? If so, could the temporal representation meet the criteria of causal inference, which from my prior arguments means conditioned learning?

3. THE ADAPTRODE MODEL

3.1. SIGNALS

The ultimate source of activating signals in a neural network is the real world. The events that trigger these signals are stochastic, episodic and sporadic. It should be noted that the real world also includes the body of an animal (with respect to its brain — the neural network). Signals originating from internal body sources may have similar episodic characteristics, though the episodes may be superposed on periodic carriers.

We represent signals in this model by a train of spikes of constant pulse width and amplitude. A maximum frequency bounds the upper limit of signal strength and information is encoded by frequency modulation within this dynamic range. In reality information can be encoded in multiple temporal domains. The presence or absence of a pulse in a sample window (1 or 0) communicates information in one time domain. But pulses can be grouped in burst patterns with characteristic durations and inter-burst periods. This gives rise to a wide variety of encoding possibilities. For example, within a burst the frequency can be modulated giving rise to a unique integrated burst envelope. Burst lengths may change over a long time scale. The frequency of bursts may change over a long time scale.

What is common to all of these possibilities is the temporal properties of the signal. The Adaptrode is a mechanism for recording the time averaged activity of the signal in multiple time domains with the assumption that these domains are coupled. In this model we attempt to capture the time course behavior of a signal as a prerequisite to associative modulation.

3.2. RESPONSE UNIT

An Adaptrode is comprised of two basic module types. One of these, the weight vector unit, may be present in multiple versions. The other type, the response unit occurs only once per Adaptrode.

The response unit provides the "read-out" of memory in the Adaptrode. The current value of memory is made available on the response line by virtue of current or recent input to the Adaptrode. That is, the response output is a function of input and the memory of the system. Fig. 13.1(a) shows a diagrammatic representation of the response unit. An input signal at $x^0 = 1$, at time step t, regenerates an active memory trace on the response line, r, given by

$$r_{(t)} = [1 - x_{(t)}]r_{(t-1)} + \kappa x^0_{(t)} w^0_{(t-1)} - \delta^R r_{(t-1)} \tag{1}$$

where

κ is a preweighting constant ($-k^{MAX} \leq \kappa \leq k^{MAX}$);
x^0 is the input signal (1,0);
δ^R is a rate constant ($0 \leq \delta^R \leq 1$);
w^0 is a weight variable as described below.

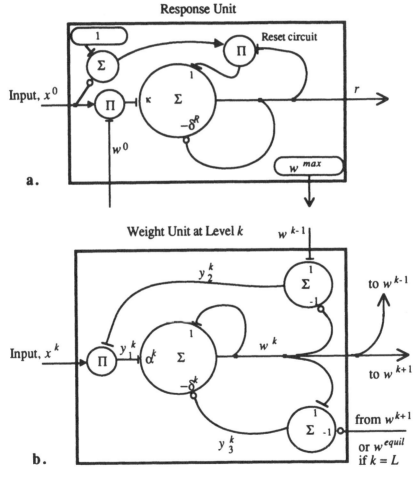

Fig. 13.1. (a) The response unit. From input signals x_0 and w_0 the unit computes a graded response output r. (b) A typical weight unit. An Adaptrode contains 1 to L+1 such units. Weight signals constitute the time domain memory of the system.

Each time the input goes to 1, the response signal is set to the current value of w^0 multiplied by the constant κ. If the latter is negative then the response is negative. In the context of a synapse, this amounts to an inhibitory signal. At all other times (when $x^0 \neq 1$) the response will decay exponentially fast by rate δ^R.

The response unit gives a memory read-out in response to input. The response may last for some period after a transient input goes to zero depending on the rate of decay.

3.3. REPRESENTATION — ENCODING SIGNALS AS TIME AVERAGES IN MULTIPLE TIME DOMAINS

We are interested in the way in which the input signal has varied over multiple time scales. Each of these scales is called a domain and is characterized by set of rate constants which govern the learning and forgetting. Memory will be stored as a form of time average of the signal history from the prior domain. That is, one storage term holds a time average of the real time signal, the next will hold the time average of the first, another holds the average of the second and so on over increasing time domains. Mostly for historical reasons this storage mechanism is called the weight vector (not to be confused with a weight vector of a single neuron) of the Adaptrode.

3.4. THE WEIGHT VECTOR UNIT: POTENTIATION

Each weight in the weight vector should more properly be thought of as a signal that varies over an increasing time scale. The time domains are indexed by $k = \{0, 1, ..., L\}$, where L is the longest time domain. A superscript is used to index weight signals, that is, w^0, w^1,..., w^k, ..., w^L. Each component of the vector is said to occupy a level in the Adaptrode. Higher levels mean longer time domains. The zeroth weight signal is what was used above to compute the response signal. Fig. 13.1(b) shows a typical weight module in which the weight signal, w^k, is computed. The change in any w^k value over time is given by

$$
\begin{aligned}
w^k_{(t)} = w^k_{(t-1)} &+ x^k_{(t)} \alpha^k [w^{k-1}_{(t-1)} - w^k_{(t-1)}] \\
&- \delta^k [w^k_{(t-1)} - w^{k+1}_{(t-1)}]
\end{aligned}
\tag{2}
$$

where

α^k, δ^k are rate constants;
x^k is an input signal at level k;

and

$w^{k-1} = w^{max}$, if $k = 0$, w^{k-1}, otherwise $\qquad$ (3);
$w^{k+1} = w^{equil}$, if $k = L$, w^{k+1}, if $k < L$. $\qquad$ (4).

In the case where $k = 0$, the input signal, x^0, is that which I described above, a pulse coded signal corresponding to neural action potential spike trains. Other input signals, x^k, are described below. The value of w^{k-1} at level 0 is a special case, the constant w^{max}. This constant is generally set to one (1), representing the maximum of some arbitrary scale. It can be shown that for appropriate values of α^0 and δ^0, w^0 encodes a lingering memory trace of the input signal which decays exponentially over time if the signal goes to zero.

A single level Adaptrode does not seem very interesting from the standpoint of memory. The slight lingering trace would soon decay leaving a weight value asymptotically close to zero. However, a multilevel Adaptrode has interesting properties. Each subsequent (higher) level records the time average of the prior level. This in turn decays at a much slower rate. The method by which this takes place is computationally inexpensive but quite effective. It can be seen by Equation (2) that the kth weight is pulled up by the $(k-1)^{th}$ weight by an amount proportional to the distance these two are apart and by the rate constant α^k. Thus, as long as the $(k-1)^{th}$ level is excited (raised above the kth level) there will be pulling force exerted on w^k to raise it. Conversely, the kth weight will be pulled downward by the $(k+1)^{th}$ weight by an amount proportional to their distance apart and the decay constant δ^k.

At any moment then, the kth weight signal is pulled between two opposing forces, which themselves vary over time. The net effect of this process is that the kth level weight is buoyed from below by the $(k+1)^{th}$ weight and bounded from above by the $(k-1)^{th}$ weight[2]. The buoying effect provided by the $(k+1)^{th}$ level weight is the operant condition for multi-term memory. By raising the floor of the kth level weight, likewise the floor of the $(k-1)^{th}$ weight is raised as well. This proceeds all the way back to w^0. And this is, so to speak, the payoff. It is w^0 which is used to compute the read-out or response, r. Thus, if w^0 is maintained for longer periods at a higher value, it means that the response will start from a higher value. In a competitive situation the Adaptrode with the higher starting value is more likely to win. Additionally, in the dynamics of w^0, a higher starting value means that w^0 will respond (grow) a little more quickly on new input. This is because the floor toward which it tends to decay by being raised, exerts a weaker force on the decay side. It thus rises to new heights and does so more rapidly. Fig. 13.2 shows a graph of the behavior of w^0, w^1 and w^2 of a three level Adaptrode with two spaced short bursts of signal at x^0 (all $x^k = 1$) Note how the peak of w^0 on the second burst is higher then on the first.

An Adaptrode can encode the temporal behavior of a signal over as many time domains as there are levels in the unit. The levels are defined recursively so that any number may be used. Selection of the α^ks and δ^ks is quite open; the system is robust to a wide range of choices. However, as a rule one chooses values that cause each $(k+1)^{th}$ level weight to grow and decay much more slowly than the previous level. Long-term memory is differentially transferred from shorter-term memory based on the signal activity history.

---

[2] Mona Cherri, from Texas Women's University, has proven two theorems on the upper and lower bounds of an L-level Adaptrode. See Mobus et al. (1991).

3.5. ASSOCIATIVITY: POTENTIATION GATING AND HURDLING THE GATE

As shown above, the temporal properties of a signal are captured in the Adaptrode at many time scales. The read-out of memory depends on current activity and starts from a base dependent on the history of the signal. Thus far I have only been concerned with the temporal encoding properties of the Adaptrode and have ignored associativity. This will now be rectified.

The additional signals, x^k, where $k > 0$, are the result of another set of processes which establish an associative link between independent Adaptrodes. Such a process is shown in Fig. 13.3. A summing-threshold (Σ-θ) processor receives input signals from the responses of any number of designated Adaptrodes ($\{r_{ab} \mid a \in$ neuron indexes, $b \in$ Adaptrode indexes in neuron a$\}$). If the sum of these inputs exceeds a threshold, which is called a gate, the Σ-θ processor outputs a 1 (one), otherwise it outputs a 0 (zero). Note that some of the Adaptrodes in the set of designated sources may produce negative responses.

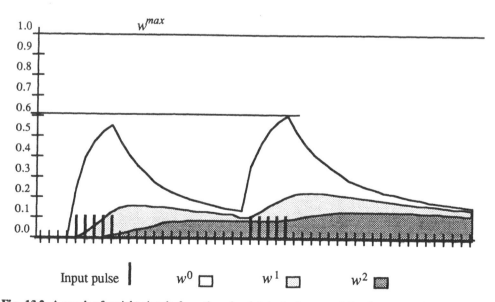

Fig. 13.2. A graph of weight signals for a three-level Adaptrode. α and δ values were chosen to accentuate the behavior for purposes of showing in a graph.

What is the effect of the resulting hurdle signal on the level of the Adaptrode to which it is sent? As can be seen from Equation (2), an input of 0 at x^k results in no increase in the weight value at that level. Subsequently, if w^k is at its equilibrium, no higher level weight value will be increased since increase is dependent on w^k rising. The increase in w^k is blocked by the gate value, the threshold in the Σ-θ processor. Unless the responses of the Adaptrodes in the designated set, called the hurdle set, is sufficient to override the gate, the Adaptrode is prevented from potentiating at the kth level. That is to say, no longer-term memory can be recorded.

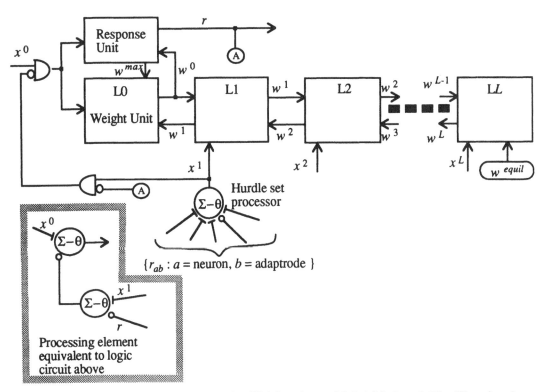

Fig. 13.3. Schematic layout of an Adaptrode. Weight units are labeled L0 through LL. There is only one Response unit per Adaptrode as presently discussed. A hurdle set processor takes as its input, the output from response units of any Adaptrode, including its own. If the sum of these inputs exceeds a set gate threshold, the unit outputs a one (1). A special logic (and equivalent processing element) circuit is shown that enforces the priority in time of the x^0 signal over any x^k.

Hurdling the gate permits potentiation of the kth level in an Adaptrode. The hurdle is determined by response signals from one or more Adaptrodes. No learning can occur in the first Adaptrode unless the hurdle set Adaptrode(s) is sufficiently active. This establishes a correlation requirement which *allows* temporal encoding if met. By selecting the appropriate level in the learning Adaptrode and appropriate source Adaptrodes whose input signals vary over the time scale of interest, one can create short-term to long-term correlation criteria which must be met to obtain learning in the appropriate temporal domain.

One last consideration which establishes the one-way temporal constraint required by causality should be noted. In Fig. 13.3 a logic circuit (and an equivalent processing element circuit) is shown which prevents the x^0 signal from reaching the Adaptrode if a hurdle signal (x^1 in the figure) is already active when r is not active. The purpose of this circuit is to ensure that the Adaptrode has already been stimulated by the x^0 signal prior to the arrival of signals which give rise to the hurdle signal (inputs to other Adaptrodes). This circuit prevents either response or learning from taking place if the hurdle signal arrives *before* the x^0 signal. If x^0 represents a potential causal event (to be learned) and the hurdle signal results from the effect event, then this circuit prevents association of potential cause with the effect since the former did not precede the latter by some Δt. As I show later, this property, along with the temporal encoding scheme described above gives rise to the requisite property of a conditioned learning model that learning goes through a maximum as a function of the interstimulus interval between the onset of the CS (say) and the onset of the UCS.

3.6. MODEL NEURONS AND NEURAL NETWORKS

The conventional formal neuron has a set of input edge weights which are representative of the efficacy of a synapse in contributing to the generation of an action potential by the neuron. Model neurons based on Adaptrodes are not much different except that the single weight (per input) is replaced by an Adaptrode with its internal set of weight signals and its external response. It is the latter which constitutes the input to the spatial integration process leading to an overall activation value for the neuron. Integration is performed once in each time step, the same as the input sample rate, and the resulting activation is compared to a threshold. If the activation exceeds the threshold, then the neuron fires an action potential, otherwise it does not. It is this clocking at the maximum frequency rate which squashes the output signals of neurons to be in the same range as the input signals at the synapses.

Fig. 13.4(b) shows the diagrammatic representation of an Adaptrode-based neuron as compared to Fig. 13.4(a) which shows a "conventional" neuron. The response signals from Adaptrodes, labeled A_1 through A_n, are summed and compared to the threshold, θ, as shown. The output signal, labeled x^0 (where the subscript is used to index neuron signals), will be a 1 (one) if the threshold is exceeded. In Fig. 13.4(b) the output, x^0, serves a second purpose — as input to a special Adaptrode labeled A_0. This Adaptrode may be optionally used for several purposes. One use is to compute a variable threshold based on output signal. This amounts to an activity-dependent learning process at the neuronal level. A second use is to provide a graded response output from the neuron, r_0. This signal may be used to establish cross-neuronal associations as is discussed later.

One major advantage (but also a major problem) gained in constructing neurons with Adaptrodes is the ability to build a wide variety of neuronal types. This is possible because different types of synapses, with different dynamical properties, can be built by designating specific numbers of levels and values of α^k and δ^k for all levels k in that type of Adaptrode. This is an advantage from the standpoint of creating models that emulate real biological neurons. It is problematic from the standpoint of specification. Models that we have built to date have involved no more than three different "types" of neurons and only five different "types" of synapses. Much research is needed to discover a linkage between functional performance and Adaptrode specifications.

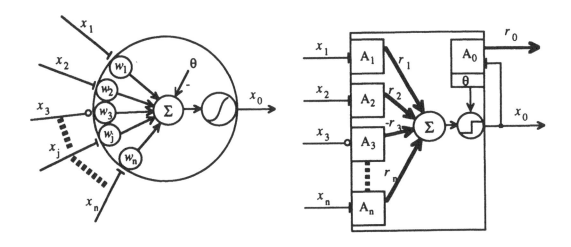

A. Conventional Neural Processor   B. Adaptrode-based Neural Processor

Fig. 13.4. Comparison of conventional formal neuron with Adaptrode-based neuron.

A neural network is constructed from a set of neurons, thus defined, an interconnection specification, a set of input slots and a set of output slots. The last two items hold greyscale values. The slot (called inslots or outslots) values are updated several times per model second — we used a 30Hz sample rate. Inslot data comes from an array representing sensory input, say an image file. Outslot data is recorded each frame in a "response" file. There is no imposed architecture, such as layers or "slabs", in the interconnection matrix, though such architectures can easily be constructed.

Within each sample frame (*e.g.*, the 30Hz rate), the neurons are processed over several iterations (with a 30Hz sample rate and a 300Hz pulse rate, this would be 10 iterations per frame). At the start of each iteration a pulse, or lack thereof, is generated for each inslot based on its greyscale. We have used a negative exponential kernel convolution with a white noise component with good results. The pulse is then available as input to any neuron that has an Adaptrode mapped to that slot. No pulse coding is necessary between neurons, however, the injection of some noise seems useful.

Clearly, explicit timing of external signals is a necessary part of simulations using Adaptrode-based neural networks. Phase relations between sensory signals play an important part in simulating conditioned learning tasks. Data sets cannot consist simply of, say, many images to be exposed to the network for one processing cycle. The time order between parts of an image now become important considerations.

4. CONDITIONED RESPONSE MODEL - BASIC ASSOCIATIVE NETWORK

A very simple neural network comprised of two neurons can be used to demonstrate conditioned learning in this model. Fig. 13.5 shows what I call a Basic Associative Network (BAN) that can learn to associate one (or more) uncommitted input signal (conditionable stimulus) with one of several output signals (unconditioned responses), based on its correlation with a matching input signal (unconditionable stimulus). The system can use the uncommitted signal as a predictor of the onset of the unconditionable stimulus, after learning the association, but only if the former reliably precedes the latter in time.

Before describing the simulation of the BAN, it is necessary to discuss the manner in which one can instantiate instances of classical learning laws by using Adaptrodes. It turns out that one can construct hurdle set definitions and interconnection matrices that allow one to emulate many of the classical learning laws, such as the Hebb rule. As mentioned above, the use of an output Adaptrode (A_0) in neurons provides a graded response signal which is based on the time-averaged frequency of the pulse-coded neuron output. By feeding this signal back to the hurdle set processor of the "learning", input Adaptrodes, one has potentiation in the latter units, based on the correlation between the input signals at those Adaptrodes and the output signal of the neuron (Fig. 13.6).

Some workers have suggested that the Hebb rule need not require actual action potential generation from the neuron (Jaffe & Johnston, 1990). Rather they have used the post-synaptic excitatory potential (EPSP) as representing the post-synaptic activity. Thus sub-threshold membrane potentials can be sufficient cause for learning to occur in the contributing synapses. This can be simulated by using the activation signal produced by the neuron integrator (the Sigma processor) as feedback to the hurdle sets of the learning Adaptrodes (Fig. 13.7).

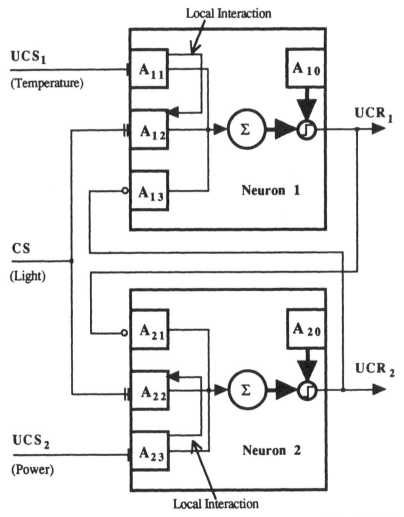

Fig. 13.5. The Basic Associative Network (BAN) is comprised of two neurons which code for different response mechanisms (UCR₁ and UCR₂). External inputs include two unconditionable stimuli (UCS₁ and UCS₂).

Another learning rule which has been explored by Daniel Alkon (1987; Alkon et al., 1991) and his colleagues is the "local interaction" rule, so called because the signal used to gate weight updates comes not from the neuron output (or activation) but from another, nearby, synapse (input). This latter synapse does not learn but simply provides a strong signal that may activate the neuron. If there is a strong correlation between this "flow-through" signal and the input signals to nearby modifiable synapses, then the latter are strengthened accordingly. Alkon et al. (1991) produced a working neural network model they call DYSTAL based on this learning rule. Fig. 13.8 shows an Adaptrode-based neuron using the response of one input Adaptrode as the hurdle source for another group of Adaptrodes to simulate a local interaction rule. The reported simulations below, in fact, rely upon this rule.

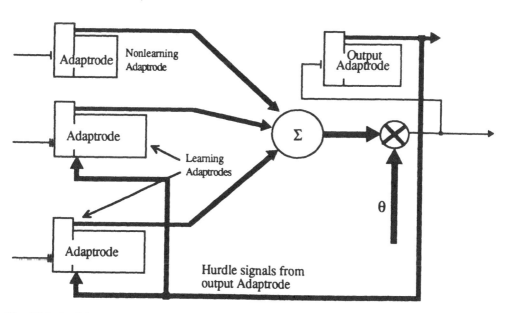

Fig. 13.6. An Adaptrode-based neuron using the Hebb rule for learning.

Compartmental Hebb Rule

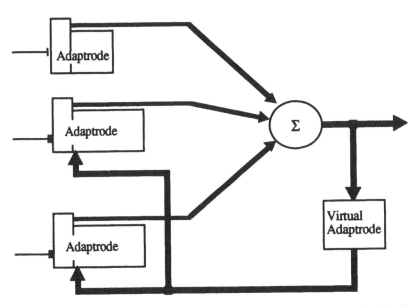

Fig. 13.7. A compartmental Hebb rule. The hurdle sets of the learning Adaptrodes include the output of the summation processor. This provides a learning mechanism that does not depend on the actual firing rate of the neuron.

In spite of the furor over the biological-reality (or lack thereof) of the error backpropagation learning rule (Rumelhart et al., 1985; cf. Crick's comments, 1989), and perhaps more generally of gradient descent processes with their heavy reliance on computational precision, I would not discount the role of error minimization for certain types of learning at a network level in biological systems. With this spirit in mind, I constructed a neural architecture from Adaptrode-based neurons that computes an output error and feeds this signal back to the prior layer of an otherwise feedforward network. Using a form of local interaction rule (as above) and discriminating a Type I (active when it should be quiet) vs. Type II (quiet when it should be active) error one can build a network which fulfills the intent of the delta rule (error minimization-driven learning). By using another neuron to record the time-average values of the total error produced by a single layer in the network, and using the rate of change of this neuron's response, r_0, by using it as a hurdle source for more than one level in the learning Adaptrodes, it is possible to inform a prior layer of its contribution to the overall error. Thereby, the Adaptrodes in this prior layer adjust (potentiate or decay) so as to minimize that contribution. The details are not fully worked out for this architecture, however we simulated small two-layer networks that learn to minimize the error in output (compared with a desired output) in the spirit, though not the method, of backpropagation.

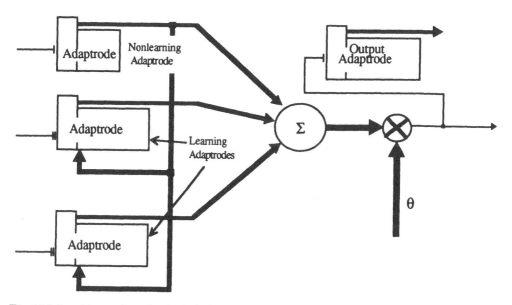

Fig. 13.8. Local interaction rule. A single input Adaptrode acts to hurdle potentiation in a local cluster of input Adaptrodes.

4.1. CLASSICAL CONDITIONING

The two neuron network shown in Fig. 13.5 can be viewed as a simple robot decision controller. The robot, in this case, can sense three environmental conditions, the presence of a power source (i.e., food) at UCS_2, the presence of light at CS, and the presence of high temperature (i.e., pain) at UCS_1. Single flat termini represent non-learning, excitatory inputs, double flat termini represent learning excitatory inputs and circular termini represent non-learning inhibitory inputs. The output of each neuron in the BAN represents an unconditionable response to the corresponding unconditionable input. Thus, a signal at UCS_1 results in an output at UCR_1; values for θ, the threshold, and κ, the preweighting constant, have been selected to assure that an unconditionable input results in an unconditionable output. An input to the conditionable stimulus alone will not, however, produce a response of significance in either of the two neurons even though it is wired to both of them. This is due, in part, to the slower, and weaker response output from the learning Adaptrodes (A_{12} and A_{22}). It is also due to the cross inhibition between neurons. Even if a very strong signal at CS is sustained for a period long enough to drive the w^0 signals in A_{12} and A_{22} high enough to cross their respective thresholds, the cross inhibition between neurons ensures that output from each is inhibited. A signal at CS alone can activate a neuron only if the learning Adaptrode (either A12 or A22) has potentiated to a point that gives w^0 the ability to climb to a value greater than θ.

A priori, there is no reason to associate light with either pleasure or pain. It is a neutral signal. If, however, there is a causal relationship between the presence of light and the presence of one or the other of the unconditionable stimuli, following the constraints of causality discussed above, then the occurrence of light could be used as a predictor of the occurrence of the UCS. Such a prediction could give the robot a "head start" in reacting to the UCS, which, after all means something important. How then can an association be encoded in the BAN, if a causal relationship exists?

Signals presented to the BAN network are stochastic and noisy (about 10% noise). The input signals are modeled after real neural signal bursts after Richmond, Optican, & Spitzer (1990) convolved with a negative exponential probability density function kernel to generate discrete spikes. After as few as three trials with joint presentation at UCS_2 and CS in the mid-range (representing about 120 Hz peak signals for one-half second, on average, of model time) potentiation occurs in A22 as the result of local interaction between A_{21} and A_{22}. This potentiation is sufficient so that Neuron 2 will win the competition as a result of input at CS only. Fig. 13.9 shows the relative levels of w^0 in A_{22} and A_{12} at the third episode of stimulation by CS and UCS_2. Since A_{11} is not active, no potentiation occurs in A_{12}.

We first condition the network with the CS/UCS_2 pairing for one hundred exposures of 30 to 50 time units and a 100 time unit inter-episode interval (Fig. 13.10). This protocol is clearly artificial and deterministic. More realistic protocols, involving stochastic pairing and variable inter-episode intervals have been simulated. These simulations give the same basic results but extend the simulated time period significantly. After conditioning, the robot will reliably and strongly respond with a seeking behavior when stimulated with a mid-range burst of light (CS) alone.

After the network has aged for some period of time without any inputs, Adaptrode A_{22} maintains a residual memory of the association to which it has been exposed (Fig. 13.11). As a consequence of this residual, the network has established a relationship between the associated signals which can be recalled when a signal is injected at CS only. This corresponds to the robot seeing light alone. Because of the potentiation of A_{22}, the input signal at A_{22} will more quickly drive w^0_{22} to a higher value than is achieved in A_{12} at w^0_{12}. In turn, this is enough to drive an output signal at UCR_2 resulting in an inhibitory signal damping the top unit (Fig. 13.12).

In this way, the network has learned to exploit CS, a non-meaningful signal in its own right, as a predictor of some meaningful signal (in this case power availability). The frequency and intensity with which these two signals occurred together in the past determines the reliability of the predicted association in the future. The robot can learn to seek lights (when it is low on power) and enjoy a certain degree of confidence that the association will be valid in the future.

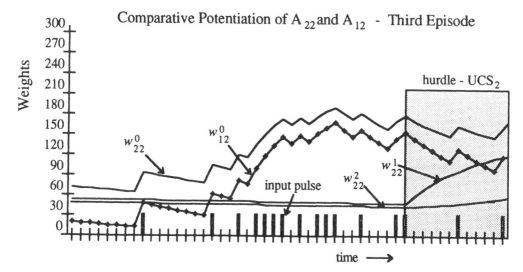

Fig. 13.9. Potentiation comparison between A_{22} and A_{12}. This graph shows the change in w^0_{22}, w^0_{12}, w^1_{22}, and w^2_{22} as a function of the pulsed input and the hurdle signal provided by excitation of UCS_2. w^0_{22} starts the episode (third) with an advantage over w^0_{12}. Toward the end of the episode UCS_2 becomes sufficiently strong so that the response of A_{21} exceeds the gate threshold of w^1_{22}, thus allowing further potentiation of the latter.

1.1.1. CONTIGUITY/CONTINGENCY

Contiguity refers to the nearness in time (and generally in space) of the UCS (sometimes called the reinforcer) to the CS. The closer in time a neutral event is to the occurrence of a meaningful event, the stronger the association between these two. In the Adaptrode, a memory trace continually decays toward its equilibrium value after being stimulated. If a hurdle signal is received within a short time after the original priming, the Adaptrode potentiates, or transfers some of the memory trace to a longer-term memory. If the hurdle signal arrives after too long of a delay, then the original trace has decayed beyond a capacity to pull the longer-term weight signal up.

Basic Associative Network
CS-UCS$_2$ Conditioning

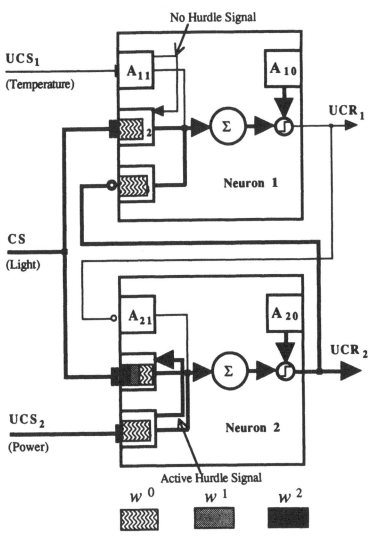

Fig. 13.10. Presentation of CS and UCS$_2$ signals in proper temporal order leads to potentiation of w^2_{22}.

Basic Associative Network

After Conditioning - Residual Memory Trace

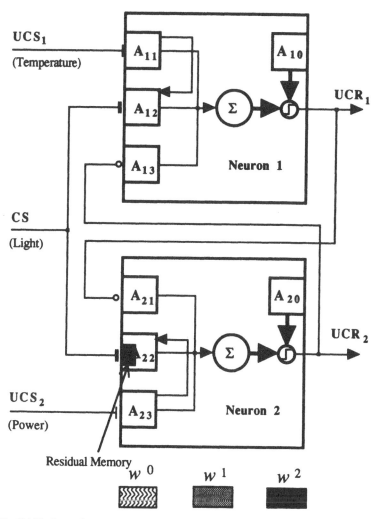

Fig. 13.11. The BAN after aging subsequent to learning an association at A_{22}.

Basic Associative Network
Presentation of CS Only - Association with UCR_2

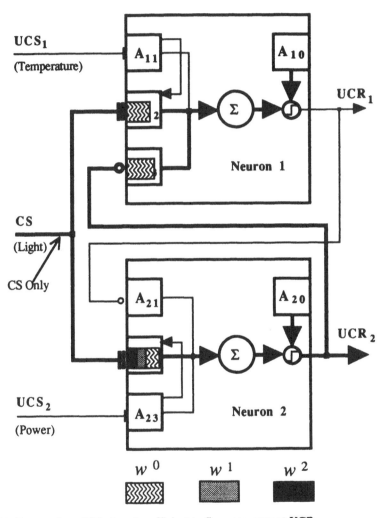

Fig. 13.12. Presentation of CS alone is sufficient to fire a response at UCR_2.

Contingency refers to the correlation between the CS and the UCS. A correlation builds up over time. As was discussed above, if the relative frequency of the co-occurrences of CS with one of the UCSs is higher than that for the other UCS, then an associative encoding between the one with the higher frequency will obtain. In addition, the degree of the correlation depends on the absolute frequency of co-occurrence as opposed to the occurrence of CS alone (without the reinforcer). It should be obvious that the occurrence of the CS alone produces no lasting change in the weight of the Adaptrode.

4.1.2. S-SHAPED ACQUISITION CURVE

One hallmark of conditioned learning is the archetypical rate at which a memory trace is strengthened. Typically, an animal's response rate (the quickness with which it responds to the CS with the UCR) is measured on each trial and this is plotted as a function of number or trials to project a rate of learning curve. The curve is generally shown to be logistic or S-shaped with an initial positively accelerating rate followed by a near-linear period and, finally, a negatively accelerating rate. Such curves have been deemed important evidence of conditioning (Klopf, 1988).

I would generally caution against trying to explain all phenomena with one mechanism and I don't want to be guilty of that here. It seems likely that the logistic rate of memory acquisition may be due to fairly complex network interactions. However, it is intriguing that the encoding rate for the weight signal in the Adaptrode comes closer to approximating a logistic curve as one goes deeper into the structure. Fig. 13.13 shows a graph of the w_2 level weight during a single episode. At this stage of analysis I can only note the interesting way in which a function, which is locally linear, when embedded in a network such as the Adaptrode, gives rise to nonlinear behavior. This is not unexpected due to the recurrent nature of the Adaptrode. But it is worth noting that the specific form of the nonlinearity is that seen in whole-animal models of memory acquisition. It will be the subject of future research.

4.1.3. EXTINCTION

Memories, if not reinforced, fade with time. This is true of nonassociative as well as associative memories, requiring an associated reinforcer. In the classical conditioning model, extinction of a memory arises from the presentation of the CS without the reinforcement generated by a following UCS. Presumably, the CS is no longer acting as a good predictor or has come uncoupled causally from the UCS and so should not be retained in association with the latter. A rather large topic of debate has centered around the exact form which extinction takes. That is, it could be due to simple passive decay (or forgetting), it could be due to active decay selective forgetting — Grossberg, 1991), or as was originally suggested by Pavlov (1927), it could be due to active inhibition. Different opinions on the exact nature of the underlying mechanism abound.

Acquisition of Memory

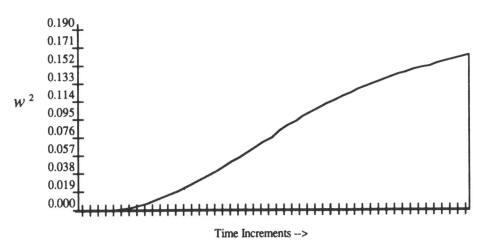

Fig. 13.13. w_2 as a function of time.

As stated above, it is probably dangerous to infer mechanisms from observations of the whole-animal model to the cellular substrates (and neural network models). It would be desirable to correspond performance observations in simple invertebrate systems such as *Aplysia* (Small et al., 1989) or *Hermissenda* (Alkon, 1987) with those in birds and mammals, in order to make such inferences.

In the Adaptrode model, as presented here, the nature of reduction of an effective weight (the response of the Adaptrode) is through passive decay, but one which is proportional to the distance the weight is above equilibrium. However, this is accomplished in a piecewise fashion across multiple time scales. Thus over short time frames, say a series of trials with short inter-episode periods, followed by presentation of the CS only, there would appear to be a rapid decay of the efficacy weight giving the impression of active decay. Over longer time frame protocols, the extinction curve starts to look passive. This is, in fact, what we have seen in simulations. As is discussed below, in the case of learning a new, contrary association, we even see a curve which appears to be due to active decay. These findings suggest that the appearance of passive vs. active decay may be influenced strongly by the temporal nature of the protocol used. This is certainly a testable idea. We have not seen, nor specifically have we looked for, evidence of completely selective forgetting. I suspect that some form of selective forgetting is emergent at the neuronal network level as opposed to the synaptic level of organization.

An interesting aspect of passive decay of long-term memory in the Adaptrode is that the effective weight can decay below the threshold necessary for the single Adaptrode to initiate a neuron output. The memory appears, from the outside to have decayed away. However, because there is a long-term trace remaining, a new series of CS-UCS co-presentations causes reacquisition in a fewer number of trials which is not unlike what occurs in animal models.

4.2. SECONDARY CONDITIONING

Following the protocol given above (statistically significant pairings of CS followed by a UCS) the CS becomes able to initiate the UCR by itself. This is generally referred to as primary conditioning. Secondary conditioning comes from the pairing of a second CS with a following CS that has already been conditioned to predict the UCS (i.e., produce the UCR). Using the compartmental Hebbian rule (Fig. 13.7), we simulated this phenomenon. One compartment, in this model, comprises one UCS input and two or more CS inputs. After training the system on a particular CS-UCS pairing which produced a deep, sustained encoding, we then paired the trained CS, call it CS_1, with another CS input, call it CS_2. The latter successfully became a predictor of the former, and that, in turn remained a predictor of the UCS.

If presentations of the CS signals alone were not occasionally followed by reinforcement from the UCS, then both memory traces extinguished in the reverse order. That is, CS_2 extinguished first followed by CS_1.

4.3. BLOCKING

An interesting phenomenon occurs when a second CS is correlated with the UCS in the same temporal frame as the first CS but for which the first CS has already encoded the association. In this case, the existence of a CS_1-UCR coding blocks the encoding of the second CS, CS_2, from becoming associated with the UCS-UCR. Since a predictor of the UCS already exists, there is presumably no need for a second predictor having the same temporal relation so it is effectively ignored.

It turns out that the same mechanism that gives rise to secondary conditioning is involved in blocking, namely the compartmental Hebbian rule. The actual blocking, however, is due to the gating of input signal to the Adaptrode via the circuit shown in Fig. 13.3. The arrival of a hurdle signal prior to the buildup of a response signal prevents the input signal at x^0 from entering the Adaptrode, thus preventing any growth of w^0 and any run-away effect on potentiation.

4.4. INTERSTIMULUS INTERVAL (ISI) EFFECTS

The window of opportunity for encoding is enforced such that there is an optimum period between the onset of the CS and the onset of the UCS during which the memory strength will be maximum. If the UCS starts too soon after the onset of the CS, then recording will be minimal. If the UCS starts too late after the offset of the CS, then, likewise, recording will be minimum. A plot of recording strength of the memory vs. the interstimulus interval (ISI) shows an inverted U shape as efficacy rises to a maximum then falls off (Grossberg, 1991).

Fig. 13.14 shows a graph of the level of w^2 in an Adaptrode. The time axis shows the number of time increments between the onset of the CS (x^0) and the onset of the UCS (hurdle signal). A short burst of five pulses was used as the CS. The hurdle signal was turned on for 10 pulses. No attempt was made to replicate biological conditions (a typical optimum ISI is 0.5 sec. — Klopf, 1988). The curve as shown is only qualitatively similar to the effect in conditioned learning examples.

The inverted U comes about due to the enforcement of the CS-first rule at the front end (short ISI) and the rapid decay of w^0 and w^1 after the offset of the CS at the tail end (long ISI).

4.5. NON-INTERFERING, MUTUALLY EXCLUSIVE ASSOCIATIONS

Now we address a new and more difficult consideration, one which depends on the multi-time domain encoding capabilities of the Adaptrode.

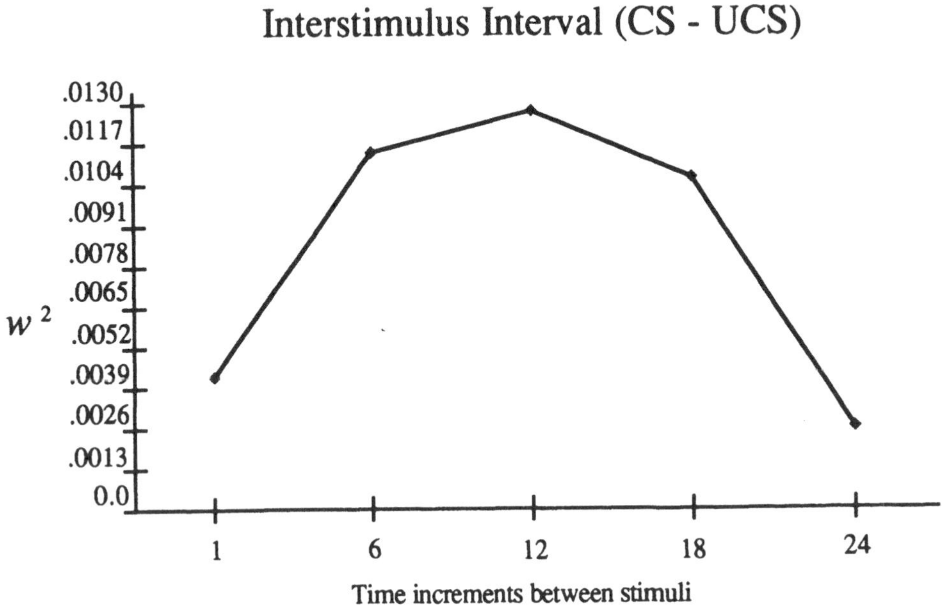

Interstimulus Interval (CS - UCS)

Fig. 13.14. The level of w^2 as a function of ISI.

Suppose that, after primary conditioning as described in Section 4.1, for some short interval of time a contrary relationship exists between UCS_1 and CS as, for example, might happen if a fire were to break out in the robot's environment. First, we would be concerned with the appropriate response — that is, the robot should avoid the fire. Second, we need some means of determining the significance of this contrary condition. Is it just noise or does it represent a more permanent change in the nature of the environment? Third, in the event that this new relationship is temporary (as compared to the duration of the prior conditioning), we certainly don't want the robot to forget the prior association since there is some possibility that the old relationship will again be the norm in the future.

In this experiment the network is exposed to a single high frequency exposure to UCS_1 and CS for 100 time units (Fig. 13.15). This situation is clearly contrary to the system's prior conditioning. The system initially starts to fire the neuron in which the long-term association is encoded as if responding to the availability of power. It takes a small amount of time (approximately 20 time units) for the w^0 value of A_{11} to build to a level sufficient to override, through the inhibitory link at A_{21}, the output of this neuron. However, due to the more rigorous firing of the UCS_1/UCR_1 neuron, the latter wins the competition leading to the appropriate response (avoidance) at UCR_1. Note that, due to the relative lengths of time of exposures to the two different conditions, A_{22} potentiates to w^2 level while A_{12} is potentiated only to w^1.

If the network is now presented with the CS input only (Fig. 13.16), it will, for a short while, respond, if only weakly, with output at UCR_1. The reason is that w^1_{12} has risen to a level just slightly greater than that of w^1_{22}. This will persist until w^1_{12} has decayed to the same level as w^1_{22} at which time the response will be ambiguous. The ambiguity will not last for long. Since the exposure to the contrary condition was short, compared with the "normal" association, and w^2_{12} did not rise significantly, w^1_{12} continues to decay, falling below the level of w^1_{22}. At that time, approximately 300 time units after the contrary conditioning, the network responds with the original UCR_2 response as the older association reemerges as dominant (Fig. 13.17).

This network, then, has the capacity to encode contrary associations which separate in time as opposed to space. The memory traces can be maintained without interference. If the short-term, newly encoded association is actually caused by a new causal alignment in the environment, then it will be reinforced and eventually completely override the former memory. If, on the other hand, the environment returns to the alignment which gave rise to the former encoding, the older memory will reemerge. It will be strengthened (in essentially the manner of reacquisition) by the old reinforcement while the newer trace will decay.

5. CONCLUSIONS AND FUTURE DIRECTIONS

The Adaptrode model has a number of features in common with many of the recurrent models of neural networks. The main difference is that here the recurrent activations, representing memory of prior activations, are brought down to the level of the synapse rather than operating at the level of the network. This allowed us to concentrate on the memory encoding of single channels, capturing the temporal behavior of a signal first. The establishment of associations between signals, both spatial and temporal, is achieved secondarily.

Basic Associative Network
Short-term, Contrary Association

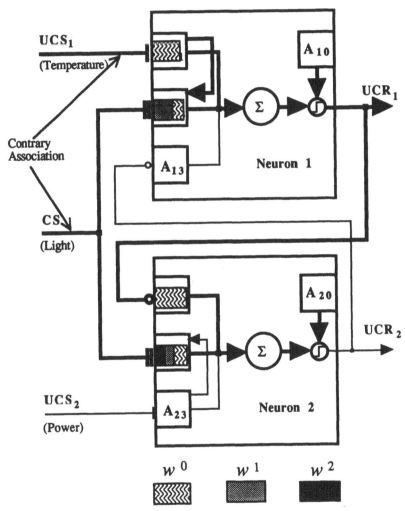

Fig. 13.15. A short but intense, contrary association between UCS_1 and CS leads to some potentiation of w^2 in A_{12}, but little potentiation of w^3. The combined inputs at A_{11} and A_{12} are sufficient to fire neuron 1 and damp out a response from neuron 2.

Basic Associative Network
Short-term Memory Encoded

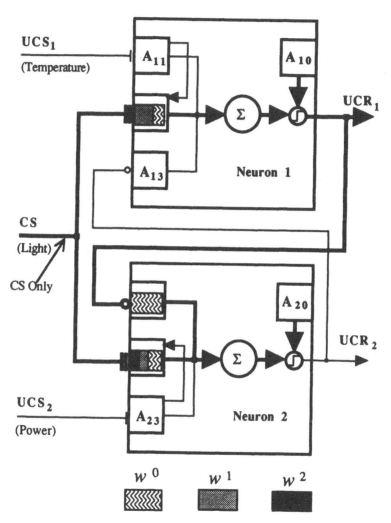

Fig. 13.16. Short-term learning of the contrary association causes output at UCR_1 on presentation of CS alone, shortly after the learning occurred.

Basic Associative Network
Emergence of Long-term Association

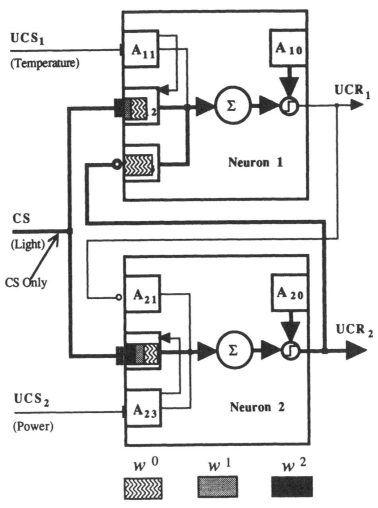

Fig. 13.17. The older association between CS and UCS_2/UCR_2 emerges after potentiation of w^2 at A_{22} decays below the w^3 level of A_{12}.

In this chapter I put forth the notion that neuronal systems that show conditioned learning abilities meet the constraints of causal inference and could thereby be viewed as a fundamental mechanism for higher-level architectures that capture the cognitive flavor of causality. It is not a question of whether the conditionable stimulus causes the unconditionable stimulus (or even that the cause of the former is the cause of the latter). Rather, it is the fact that causal relationships, indeed causal chains, can be inferred from the temporal relationships allowed by conditioned learning. The inference of causality confers an evolutionarily useful ability on its possessor. It allows an animal to predict the future with respect to the occurrence of events that have direct physiological, and/or survival consequences from those that are essentially neutral.

A framework for investigation of higher-level cognitive processes begins to emerge. The synaptic and neuronal substrates of conditioned learning wherein specific temporal constraints on the relationship between two events is being established. The encoded temporal relationship of conditioned learning has the same form as a causal relationship, namely one event, the cause, must precede the other event, the effect, within a temporal window of opportunity. Furthermore, mechanisms such as secondary conditioning may be invoked as a basis for encoding causal chains.

It is a far leap from conditioned learning, say in *Hermissenda crassicornis* (Alkon, 1987), to the cognitive ability, in humans, to infer causality from observations of the environment. The idea that a relatively simple neural mechanism can provide a means for encoding the temporal relationships involved in causality is, however, intriguing. The capacity of the Adaptrode model, to encode the temporal aspects of conditioned learning may provide a useful modeling tool for investigation of higher-order cognitive processes.

Investigations of Adaptrode-based neural networks are just getting underway. We are currently developing neural networks for pattern recognition and categorization as well as models of operant conditioning and adaptive control. A network compiler is being built to allow the construction of very large networks (over 100 neurons and hundreds of thousands of connections). A runtime engine (written in C) is already being used in our lab to run simulations of small network models such as those reported above. Once the compiler is completed we will begin investigating larger-scale learning dynamics.

REFERENCES

Alkon, D. L. (1987). *Memory Traces in the Brain.* New York: Cambridge University Press.

Alkon, D. L. (1989). Memory storage and neural systems. *Scientific American*, July, Vol. 261, No. 1, pp. 42-50.

Alkon, D. L., Blackwell, K. T., Barbour, G. S., Rigler, A. K., & Vogl, T. P. (1990). Pattern-recognition by an artificial network derived from biologic neuronal systems. *Biological Cybernetics 62*, 363-376.

Alkon, D. L., Vogl, T. P., Blackwell, K. T., & Tam, D. (1991). Memory function in neural and artificial networks. In M. L. Commons, S. Grossberg, & J. E. R. Staddon, (Eds.), *Neural Network Models of Conditioning and Action* (pp. 1-11). Hillsdale, NJ: Lawrence Erlbaum Associates.

Anderson, S., Merrill, J. W. L., & Port, R. (1989). Dynamic speech categorization with recurrent networks. In D. Touretzky, G. E. Hinton, & T. J. Sejnowski (Eds.), *Proceedings of the*

1988 Connectionist Models Summer School (Pittsburgh, 1988) (pp. 398-406). San Mateo, CA: Morgan Kaufmann.

Aparicio, M., IV (1988). Neural computations for true Pavlovian conditioning: control of horizontal propagation by conditioned and unconditioned reflexes. Unpublished doctoral dissertation. University of South Florida.

Buonomano, D. V., Baxter, D. A., & Byrne, J. H. (1990). Small networks of empirically derived adaptive elements simulate some higher-order features of classical conditioning. *Neural Networks* **3**, 507-523.

Byrne, J. H., & Gingrich, K. J. (1989). Mathematical model of cellular and molecular processes contributing to associative and nonassociative learning in *Aplysia*. In J. H. Byrne & W. O. Berry (Eds.), *Neural Models of Plasticity* (pp. 58-72). Orlando: Academic Press.

Byrne, J. H., Gingrich, K. J., & Baxter, D. A. (1990). Computational capabilities of single neurons relationship to simple forms of associative and nonassociative learning in Aplysia. In R. D. Hawkins & G. H. Bower (Eds.), *Computational Models of Learning (Vol. 23: Psychology of Learning and Motivation* (pp. 31-63). New York: Academic Press.

Carpenter, G. A., & Grossberg, S. (1987a). A massively parallel architecture for a self-organizing neural pattern recognition machine. *Computer Vision, Graphics, and Image Processing* **37**, 54-115.

Carpenter, G. A., & Grossberg, S. (1987b). ART2: Self-organization of stable category recognition codes for analog input patterns. *Applied Optics* **26**, 4919-4930.

Crick, F. (1989). The recent excitement about neural networks. *Nature* **337**, 129-32.

Dretske, F. I. (1988). *Explaining Behavior: Reasons in a World of Causes*. Cambridge, MA: MIT Press.

Elman, J. L. (1990). Finding structure in time. *Cognitive Science* **14**, 170-211.

Elman, J. L., & Zipser, D. (1988). Discovering the hidden structure of speech. *Journal of the Acoustical Society of America* **83**, 1615-1626.

Gelperin, A., Hopfield, J. J., & Tank, D. W. (1985). The logic of *Limax* learning. In A. I. Selverston (Ed.), *Model Neural Networks and Behavior* (pp. 237-261). New York: Plenum.

Getting, P. A. (1980). Emerging principles governing the operation of neural networks. *Annual Review of Neuroscience* **12**, 185-204.

Grossberg, S. (1982). *Studies of Mind and Brain: Neural Principles of Learning, Perception, Development, Cognition, and Motor Control*. Boston: Reidel Press.

Grossberg, S. (1987). Competitive learning: From interactive activation to adaptive resonance. *Cognitive Science* **11**, 23-63.

Grossberg, S. (1991). A neural network architecture for Pavlovian conditioning: reinforcement, attention, forgetting, timing. In M. L. Commons, S. Grossberg & J. E. R. Staddon, (Eds.), *Neural Network Models of Conditioning and Action* (pp. 1-11). Hillsdale, NJ: Lawrence Erlbaum Associates.

Hebb, D. O. (1949). *The Organization of Behavior*. New York: Wiley .

Hertz, J., Krogh, A., & Palmer, R. G. (1991). *Introduction to the Theory of Neural Computation. Santa Fe Institute Studies in the Sciences of Complexity*. Reading, MA: Addison-Wesley.

Jaffe, D., & Johnston, D. (1990). Induction of long-term potentiation at hippocampal mossy-fiber synapses follows a Hebbian rule. *Journal of Neurophysiology* **64**, 948-960.

Kandel, E. R., & Schwartz, J. H. (1982). Molecular biology of learning: Modulation of transmitter release. *Science* **218**, 433-443.

Klopf, A. H. (1988). A neuronal model of classical conditioning. *Psychobiology*, **16**, 85-125.

Klopf, A. H. & Morgan, J. O. (1990). The role of time in natural intelligence: Implications of classical and instrumental conditioning for neuronal and neural network modeling. In M. Gabriel & J. Moore (Eds.), *Learning and Computational Neuroscience* (pp. 463-495). Cambridge, MA: MIT Press.

Koch, C., & Segev, I. (1989). Introduction. In C. Koch & I. Segev (Eds.), *Methods in Neuronal Modeling: From Synapses to Networks* (pp. 1-8). Cambridge, MA: MIT Press.

Kosko, B. (1986). Differential Hebbian learning. In J. S. Denker (Ed.), *AIP Conference Proceedings 151: Neural Networks for Computing* (pp. 277-282). New York: American Institute of Physics.

Mackintosh, N. J. (1983). *Conditioning and Associative Learning*. Oxford: Oxford University Press.

Mobus, G. E. (1990). The adaptrode learning model: applications in neural network computing. Tech. Rep. No. CRPDC-90-5, Center for Parallel and Distributed Computing, University of North Texas, Denton.

Mobus, G. E., & Fisher, P. S. (1990). An adaptive controller using an adaptrode-based artificial neural network. Tech. Rep. No. CRPDC-90-6, Center for Parallel and Distributed Computing, University of North Texas, Denton.

Mobus, G. E., Cherri, M., & Fisher, P. S. (1993). The Adaptrode: Part I — temporal, nonassociative reinforcement learning in multiple time domains. Manuscript submitted for publication.

Morgan, J. S., Patterson, E. C. & Klopf, A. H. (1990). Drive-reinforcement learning: a self-supervised model for adaptive control. *Network* **1**, 439-448.

Pavlov, I. P. (1927). *Conditioned Reflexes* (V. Anrep, trans.). London: Oxford University Press.

Richmond, B. J., Optican, L. M., & Spitzer, H. (1990). Temporal encoding of two-dimensional patterns by single units in primate primary visual cortex. I. Stimulus-response relations. *Journal of Neurophysiology* **64**, 351-369.

Rumelhart, D. E., Hinton, G. E., & Williams, R. J. (1985). Learning internal representations by error propagation. ICS Report 8506. Institute of Cognitive Science, University of California, San Diego.

Rumelhart, D. E., & McClelland, J. L. (Eds.) (1986). *Parallel Distributed Processing: Explorations in the Microstructure of Cognition*, Vols. 1 & 2. Cambridge, MA: MIT Press.

Sejnowski, T. J., Chattarji, S. & Stanton, P. (1989). Induction of synaptic plasticity by Hebbian covariance in the hippocampus. In R. Durbin, C. Miall, & G. Mitchison (Eds.) *The Computing Neuron* (pp. 105-124). Reading, MA: Addison-Wesley.

Small, S. A., Kandel, E. R., & Hawkins, R. D. (1989). Activity-dependent enhancement of presynaptic inhibition in *Aplysia* sensory neurons. *Science* **243**, 1603-1605.

Staddon, J. E. R., & Zhang, Y. (1991). On the assignment-of-credit problem in operant learning. In M. L. Commons, S. Grossberg, & J. E. R. Staddon (Eds.), *Neural Network Models of Conditioning and Action* (pp. 279-293). Hillsdale, NJ: Lawrence Erlbaum Associates.

Starmer, C. F. (1987). Characterizing synaptic plasticity with an activity dependent model. In M. Caudill & C. Butler (Eds.), *Proceedings of the IEEE First International Conference on Neural Networks* (Vol. IV, pp. 3-10). San Diego: IEEE/ICNN.

Sutton, R. S. (1988). Learning to predict by the methods of temporal differences. *Machine Learning* 3, 9-44.

Sutton, R. S., & Barto, A. G. (1987). A temporal-difference model of classical conditioning. Tech. Rep. No. 87-509.2. Waltham, MA: GTE Laboratories.

Sutton, R. S. & Barto, A. G. (1990). Time derivative models of Pavlovian reinforcement. In M. Gabriel, M. & J. Moore (Eds), *Learning and Computational Neuroscience* (pp. 463-495). Cambridge, MA: MIT Press.

Tesauro, G. (1986). Simple neural models of classical conditioning. *Biological Cybernetics* 55, 187-200.

Widrow, B., & Hoff, M.E. (1960). Adaptive switching circuits. In *1960 IRE WESCON Convention Record* (part 4, pp. 96-104). New York: IRE.

14

Brain and the Structure of Narrative

Karl H. Pribram
Radford University

1. INTRODUCTION

As I was completing the manuscript for a recently published set of lectures (Pribram, 1991), I realized that an especially interesting way to account for the functions of the far frontal cortex of the cerebral hemispheres is in terms of narrative structure. The frontal cortex makes possible effective action based on ordering contextualized events. These, in turn, depend on processes organized by the systems of the limbic forebrain. In this essay, I have therefore excerpted, modified. and extended the material that appears in the earlier text to address the manner in which the frontolimbic forebrain contributes to the structuring of narrative.

Most of my research career has been devoted to distinguishing so-called "associative" functions of the posterior cortical convexity from those of the frontolimbic forebrain. This front-back difference in processing is as pervasive in organizing all mammalian life and mind — and therefore as important — as is the currently popular right-left hemisphere difference for humans. The front-back distinction in processing can be summarized succinctly and formally as follows: The associative systems of the posterior cerebral convexity are committed to extracting invariances from the variety of sensory inputs; the associative systems of the frontolimbic forebrain are engaged in establishing covariations between consequent actions. Posterior processing leads to the identification and classification of objects in space and time. Frontolimbic processing leads to ordering events composed by episodes, and expressing them in coherent narrative. This essay delineates some of the evidence that implicates the frontolimbic forebrain in structuring episodes, events, and narratives.

In order to clarify the role of the several systems composing the frontolimbic forebrain it is necessary to distinguish between episode, event and narrative. These words are often used synonymously. Here *episode* refers to a unit of action that is initiated and terminated by an orienting reaction. An episode provides the context within which contents, text (texture) can be processed.

Event is used in the sense of eventuality, a subset of possible outcomes: for example, the outcome 8 on the throw of dice. Out-come is, in fact, the Saxon equivalent of the Latin event (ex-venire). And, outcome is synonymous with consequence, especially when the event, the outcome is valued, that is, consequential.

Narrative is the act of making known the particulars of the course of events, their consequentiality.

As is detailed below, there is considerable evidence to support the view that the amygdala systems of the forebrain are critically concerned in delineating episodes. In turn, the hippocampal systems are involved in recombining episodes (contexts) to produce novel events. Finally, the far frontal systems of the brain order these contextualized events into narrative structures.

2. THE LIMBIC FOREBRAIN, EPISODES AND EVENTS

2.1. INSTINCT AS SPECIES-SHARED BEHAVIOR

In order to analyze the complex of effects produced by total resection of the temporal lobe, I devised surgical techniques to make possible restricted resections of the medially lying amygdala and hippocampus (reviewed by Pribram 1954, 1958, 1991, Lecture 7). When resections were restricted to the amygdala and adjacent pole of the temporal lobe, the marked taming of the monkeys which had followed resection of the entire temporal lobe, (Klüver & Bucy, 1939; Sanger-Brown & Schaefer, 1888) was reproduced (Pribram & Bagshaw, 1953). Just what might this behavioral change signify?

First it was determined that not only were the monkeys tamed, but they also put everything in their mouths, gained weight, and increased their sexual behavior — all effects that had also followed the total temporal lobectomy. These changes in behavior were summarized under the rubric of the "four Fs": fighting, fleeing, feeding, and sex (Pribram, 1960).

Historically these apparently disparate behaviors were classified together as "instinct" (a term still used to describe the processes underlying such behaviors in the psychoanalytic literature). More recently this concept came into disfavor (see e.g., Beach, 1955) and ethologists substituted the category "species specific" behaviors for instinct because these behaviors can be shown to have a common genetic component. But this substitution loses much of the meaning of the older terminology: Human language is species-specific but not instinctive in the earlier sense. My preference is to retain the concept of instinct as descriptive of the four Fs: What these behaviors have in common is the fact that their patterns are shared by practically all species. What makes the study of geese and other birds so interesting is that we recognize our own behavior patterns in the descriptions provided by ethologists (see e.g., Lorenz, 1969). It is therefore *species-shared behavior-patterns* that are of interest in tracking the effects of amygdalectomy.

2.2. THE BOUNDARIES OF AN EPISODE

The apparently disparate behaviors that characterize the 4 Fs were shown by careful analysis to be influenced by a common process. It is worth summarizing the highlights of this analysis because identifying a common process operating on apparently disparate behaviors is a recurring problem in behavioral neuroscience. In behavioral genetics the same problem entails identifying genotypes from phenotypical behaviors. Thus, qualitative and quantitative determinations were made in each of the four Fs with the following results. In a social hierarchy fighting and fleeing were both diminished provided there was a sufficiently skillful antagonist (Rosvold, Mirsky, & Pribram, 1954). As in the study reported by Sanger-Brown and Schaefer (1888), when a monkey was returned to the social colony after amygdalectomy, he "voluntarily approaches all persons — and fellow monkeys indifferently." Also, having just interacted with his fellow monkey, and perhaps having been trounced, "he will go through the same process, as if he had entirely forgotten his previous experience."

This behavioral change was dramatically demonstrated by displaying a lighted match to such monkeys. They would invariably grab the match, put it into their mouth, dousing the flame, only to repeat the grab when the next lit match was presented. This behavior could be elicited for a hundred consecutive trials unless either the monkey or the experimenter became bored before the session was ended (Fulton, Pribram, Stevenson, & Wall, 1949).

The increases in feeding and sexual behavior that follow amygdalectomy were also shown to be due to a failure in placing limits on actions. For instance, as reported by Sanger-Brown and Schaefer, monkeys with such resections appear to be indiscriminate in what they pick up, put in their mouths, and swallow. But when tests were performed and a record was kept of the order in which the food and nonfood objects were chosen, it turned out that the order of preference was undisturbed by the brain operation; only now the monkeys would continue to pick up additional objects beyond those that they had chosen first (Wilson, 1959). In fact amygdalectomized animals may be a bit slow to start eating but continue eating far past the point when their controls stop eating (Fuller, Rosvold, & Pribram, 1957).

The fact that amygdalectomy impairs the stop — the satiety — mechanism, might suggest that amygdalectomized monkeys are hungrier or have greater appetites. This is not so, however. When deprived of food for from 24 to 72 hours, amygdalectomized monkeys do not eat more rapidly than they did before deprivation whereas, of course, their control subjects do (Weiskrantz, 1956).

Also, after amygdalectomy the effectiveness of food as a reward is diminished. Ordinarily a change in the amount of reward given, changes its effectiveness. After amygdalectomy, changes in amount have much less effect than they do when control subjects are used (Schwartzbaum, 1960).

The disturbances in feeding after amygdalectomy were shown to be due to connections with the satiety mechanism centered in the ventromedial region of the hypothalamus. For instance, a precise relationship was established between the amount of carbachol injected into the amygdala and amount of feeding (or drinking) once these behaviors had been initiated (Russell,

Singer, Flanagan, Stone, & Russell, 1968). Injections into the ventromedial hypothalamic region simply terminate feeding.

Modulation of a stop process was also shown responsible for changes in fighting behavior. Fall in a dominance hierarchy after amygdalectomy, when it occurred, was related to the amount of aggressive interaction between the dominant and submissive animals of the group. After amygdalectomy such interactions were overly prolonged leading to a reorganization of the dominance hierarchy. It was as if the amygdalectomized monkeys approached each interaction as novel. Prior experience, which modulated the behavior of the control subjects, seemed to have little influence after amygdalectomy. This finding characterizes many of the experimental results to be described shortly.

Analyses of the effects of amygdalectomy and electrical stimulations of the amygdala on avoidance (fleeing) behavior brought a similar conclusion. Escape behavior is unaffected and sensitivity to shock is not diminished (Bagshaw & Pribram, 1968). Nor is there a change in the generalization gradient to aversive stimulation (Hearst & Pribram, 1964a, 1964b). What appears to be affected primarily is the memory aspect of avoidance — the expectation based on familiarity with the situation that aversive stimulation will occur. Such expectations are ordinarily referred to as fears that constrain behavior.

The theme recurs when the effects of amygdalectomy on sexual behavior are analyzed. The hypersexuality produced by the resections is found to be due to an increased territory and range of situations over which the behavior is manifest: Ordinarily cats perceive unfamiliar territory as inappropriate for such behavior (see Pribram, 1960, for review). Sexual behavior is limited to familiar situations and situations become familiar as a consequence of rewarding sexual encounters.

The importance of the amygdala in more generally determining the spatial and temporal boundaries of an experience or a behavioral routine — in short, an episode — is attested by the results of another set of experiments. Kesner and DiMattia (1987) presented a series of cues to animals to allow them to become familiar and then paired the initial, intermediate, and final cues of the series with novel cues in a discrimination. When similar tasks are administered to humans, they recall the initial and final cues of the series more readily than they recall the intermediate ones. These are termed the primacy and recency effects. Unoperated monkeys showed both effects in Kessler's experiments. However, after amygdalectomy, monkeys failed to show either a recency or a primacy effect. If the series is taken to be an episode, the effects of amygdalectomy can be considered to impair the demarcation of an episode. As described in the second half of this essay, after resections of the far frontal cortex, ordering within an episode becomes deficient.

2.3. FAMILIARIZATION: EPISODE AS CONTEXT

In this and the next section the evidence is reviewed to show that behavioral habituation serves as an indicator of familiarity and that habituation occurs as a result of visceroautonomic activity. What is oriented to, the novel, depends on the familiar which serves as the context within which an event becomes appreciated as novel.

Habituation is fragile. The process is readily disrupted by head injury or distraction. Some of the factors governing distractibility such as pro- and retroactive interference are well known. Amygdalectomy and resections of forebrain systems related to the amygdala have been shown to increase susceptibility to distraction (Douglas & Pribram, 1969; Grueninger & Pribram, 1969). More on this shortly.

It is, of course, clear from a host of other studies relating brain and behavior reviewed elsewhere (Pribram, 1991), that not all memory storage processes critically depend on the occurrence of visceroautonomic responses. The learning of motor skills, perceptual categorizing, and rote memorization, are examples where the memory storage mechanism operates on the basis of simple repetition. Still, it is equally clear that there are occasions when memory storage is dependent on a "booster" that places a value on the experience and thus leads to a *feeling* of familiarity. It is this booster process in which the amygdala is involved (Pribram, Douglas, & Pribram, 1969).

Familiarity is a feeling regarding a valued experience. In the clinic, patients who have a lesion in the region of the amygdala (and the adjacent horn of the hippocampus) describe experiences that are called *jamais vu* and *déja vu* — the patient enters a place such as his living room and experience a "jamais vu," a feeling of "never having seen," of complete unfamiliarity. Others come into a place they have never been and feel that they have "already seen," are already, *déja*, completely familiar with it.

In the laboratory, familiarity has been shown to be related to reinforcement history. Monkeys were trained to select one of two cues on the basis of a 70% reinforcement schedule: that is, selection of one cue was rewarded on 70% of the trials; selection of the other cue was rewarded on 30% of the trials. Then the cue that had been most rewarded was paired with a novel cue. Control monkeys selected the previously rewarded cue. Monkeys who had their amygdalas removed selected the novel cue. Familiarization by virtue of previous reinforcing experience had little effect on monkeys who lacked the amygdala (Douglas & Pribram, 1966). These monkeys were performing in a "jamais vu mode."

2.4. VALUATION: VISCEROAUTONOMIC PROCESSING

An extensive series of experiments was then undertaken to discover what might be the physiological basis for this deficiency in the familiarization process. The problem was found to center on the fact that ordinarily a novel or a reinforcing event produces a visceroautonomic reaction: A galvanic skin response due to a slight increase in sweating, a brief increase in heart rate, a change in respiratory rate, are some of the readily measurable effects. After amygdalectomy the visceroautonomic reactions to novel or reinforcing events fail to occur (Bagshaw & Benzies, 1968; Bagshaw & Coppock, 1968; Bagshaw, Kimble, & Pribram, 1965; Kimble, Bagshaw, & Pribram, 1965; Koepke & Pribram, 1967a, 1967b; Pribram, Reitz, McNeil, & Spevack, 1979).

These visceroautonomic responses are, in fact, elicited by electrical excitation of the amygdala and the related limbic cortex of the medial portions of the frontal lobe, anterior insula, and temporal pole (Kaada, Pribram, & Epstein, 1949; reviewed by Pribram, 1961). Changes in blood pressure, heart and respiratory rate, gut and pupillary responses, as well as gross eye, head, and body responses are elicited. An entire mediobasal, essentially visceroautonomic, motor system involving the anterior portions of the limbic forebrain has been delineated. As in the case of the classical precentral somatic motor system (see review by Pribram, 1991, Lecture 6) the mediobasal motor process operates by way of a circuit that alters receptors, for example, for adrenaline (McGaugh, 1966), from which signals for processing originate.

In summary, the familiarization process is initiated and terminated by an orienting reaction, a stop to prior ongoing processing, an interrupt that begins and ends a behavioral episode. The episode is thus a demarcated period of stability within which the visceroautonomic effects and hedonic attributes — that is, pain and comfort (see review in Pribram, 1991, Lecture 8) of stimuli are processed. This allows valuation of the episode in terms of its relevance to the organism.

3. THE FORMAL DEFINITION OF EPISODE AS CONTEXT

Familiar episodes provide the context for further processing. Given a formalism describing the neural process coordinate with the perception of images and object-forms (Yasue, Jibu, & Pribram, 1991, Appendices A & B), such a formalism for "context" can be developed. This formalism delineates the conditions under which a system of eigenvectors in Hilbert space forms a complete normalized orthogonal system (CNOS), a mathematical description of a processing context.

With this goal in mind, an abstract geometric formulation of neurodynamics starting from a neural wave function was developed in detail in Yasue et al. (1991). This neural wave function is a complex-valued function of time t and position x in the dendritic network M. The dendritic network M is thought of as a geometric object, that is, a two dimensional compact manifold. Such an object will fall into the composition of well-known geometry of a Hilbert space.

In many other neural network models (e.g., Anderson & Murphy, 1986; Carpenter & Grossberg, 1987; Kohonen, 1984), states of the system are described as finite-dimensional vectors, that is, quantities with a finite number of attributes. A Hilbert space, which is an infinite dimensional vector space with certain additional properties (see, e.g., Halmos, 1957), is a convenient approximation to a finite-dimensional vector space, and is applied frequently to understanding wave phenomena in physics.

For each instant t, the neural wave function is such a complex-valued function $\psi_t = \psi_t(x)$ $= \psi(x,t)$ that the absolute square $|\psi_t|^2$ describes the polarization density and so the integral

$$\int_M |\psi_t(x)|^2 dx \qquad (1)$$

remains finite. Here, dx denotes the invariant volume element of the manifold M. We say in this case that ψ_t is square integrable on M for each t. Let us consider a set of all the square integrable complex-valued functions on the dendritic network M. We denote it by $L^2(M)$ or simply H. From a mathematical point of view, this set of functions manifests a very intuitive geometric structure.

We suppose each element of H a vector. There, the constant multiplication of aψ of a complex number a and a vector ψ is defined to be a vector in H corresponding to a function aψ = (aψ) (x) = aψ(x). The vector sum ψ + φ of two vectors ψ and φ is defined to be a vector in H corresponding to a function ψ + φ = (ψ + φ) (x) = ψ (x) + φ (x).

Orthogonality of two vectors in H can be introduced by defining the inner product of two vectors. The inner product of any two vectors ψ and φ in H is denoted by <ψ,φ> and its value is given by the integral

$$\langle \psi, \varphi \rangle = \int_M \overline{\psi(x)} \, \varphi(x) \, dx \qquad (2),$$

where ——— means to take the complex conjugate. Then ψ and φ are said to be orthogonal with each other if their inner product vanishes, that is,

$$<\psi,\varphi> = 0 \qquad .$$

The inner product may be used to measure the length of a vector. Namely, the length of a vector ψ in H is given by a real number

$$\| \psi \| = \sqrt{\langle \psi, \psi \rangle} \qquad ,$$

which will be called a norm of ψ. This means that the inner product of ψ with itself becomes naturally a square of its length.

Having introduced the notions of vector calculus and norm (i.e., length), we can now measure the distance between two vectors in H. Let ψ and φ by any two vectors in H. Then the vector calculus claims their difference ψ-φ to be another vector in H. This vector ψ-φ indeed represents a balance between ψ and φ. It is therefore natural to call the length $\|\psi$-$\varphi\|$ of this balance vector ψ-φ a distance between two vectors ψ and φ. We denote it by d(ψ,φ). The length of a vector is nothing else but a distance from it to a basis vector O. This basis vector O is called a zero vector, and stands for a unique vector in H with vanishing length. As a function on the dendritic network M, the zero vector O in H corresponds to a constant function with constant value equals to zero.

The totality of all the square integrable complex-valued functions on M thus manifests a geometric structure in which vector calculus with inner product is allowed. Such a geometry is called a Hilbert space geometry in mathematics. It is in this sense, that the set H may be called a Hilbert space.

4. A SYSTEM OF EIGENVECTORS

The neural wave function $\psi_t = \psi_t(x) = \psi(x,t)$ for each instant t may be considered as a vector ψ_t in the Hilbert space of square integrable functions H = L^2(M). As time t passes, an equation of the same form as the wave equation in quantum theory evolves from fundamental neurodynamic considerations as described by (a):

$$\frac{\partial \rho}{\partial t} = -\nu \; div(\rho \, \nabla S) \tag{3},$$

which indicates how the system and control variable couple with each other and (b): the second order partial differential operator, a Laplacian which is nonlinear in the variables ρ and θ.

$$-\frac{\partial S}{\partial t} = \frac{1}{2}|\nu|^2 + U_{ex} - U_{op} - \frac{\nu}{4}\Delta \log\rho \tag{4}.$$

From these fundamental equations a neural wave equation, a variant of the Schroedinger equation, is readily derived:

$$i\nu \; \frac{\partial \psi}{\partial t} = \left(-\frac{\nu^2}{2}\Delta + U_{ex} \right) \psi \tag{5}.$$

In other words, the time-dependent vector ψ_t draws a curve in the Hilbert space H. This curve may be denoted by $\{\psi_t \mid 0 \leq t < \infty\}$.

We are thus working in a geometric framework of Hilbert space H. It seems convenient therefore to rewrite the neural wave equation symbolically as an evolution equation in H. First, let us see the right-hand side of the neural wave equation (3). The Laplacian is a second order linear partial differential operation, and multiplication by a given function U_{ex} is a linear operation. Therefore, we are allowed to think of the object

$$K = -\frac{\nu^2}{2}\Delta + U_{ex}$$

as a linear operator that transforms a vector ψ_t in the Hilbert space H to another vector $K\psi_t$ in H. The term *linear* means that the operation by K to any vector preserves vector calculus. Namely, we have identities

$$K(\psi+\varphi) = K\psi + K\varphi$$
$$K(a\psi) = a(K\psi)$$

where a is a constant, and ψ and φ are two vectors in H. We call this linear operator K a neural wave generator, and rewrite the neural wave equation (5) as

$$iv\frac{d}{dt}\psi_t = K\psi_t \tag{7}.$$

In general, the neural wave equation (5) defines an initial value problem. Given the initial neural wave function ψ_o, it determines the neural wave function ψ_t for all time after. Correspondingly, Eq. (5) may be understood to determine the vector ψ_t for all time after given the initial vector ψ_o in H.

Let $t > O$ be a small time interval. Then

$$\psi_{\Delta t} - \psi_o \approx \frac{d}{dt}\psi_t/_{t=0}\,\Delta t$$

and by Eq. (7) we derive

$$\psi_{\Delta t} \approx \psi_o - \frac{i}{v}K\psi_o\Delta t$$

$$= (1 - \frac{i}{v}K\Delta t)\,\psi_o$$

Successively, we have

$$\psi_{2\Delta t} \approx \left(1 - \frac{i}{v}K\Delta t\right)\psi_{\Delta t}$$

$$\approx \left(1 - \frac{i}{v}K\Delta t\right)^2\psi_o$$

$$\psi_{3\Delta t} \approx \left(1 - \frac{i}{v}K\Delta t\right)\psi_{2\Delta t}$$

$$\approx \left(1 - \frac{i}{v}K\Delta t\right)^3\psi_o$$

and so on. For arbitrary t, we have an identity

$$\psi_t = \psi_{N\psi N}$$

$$\approx \left(1 - \frac{i}{v}K\frac{t}{N}\right)^N\psi_o$$

valid for any integer N. The approximate equality here becomes an exact equality as N passes to infinity. Namely, we obtain

$$\psi_t = \lim_{N \to \infty} \left(1 - \frac{i}{\nu} K \frac{t}{N} \right)^N \psi_o$$

This fact can be understood at least intuitively by the identity

$$\lim_{N \to \infty} \left(1 - \frac{i}{\nu} K \frac{t}{N} \right)^N$$

$$= \lim_{N \to \infty} \left\{ \exp \left(- \frac{i}{\nu} K \frac{t}{N} \right) \right\}^N$$

$$= \lim_{N \to \infty} \exp \left(- \frac{i}{\nu} Kt \right)$$

$$= \exp \left(- \frac{i}{\nu} Kt \right).$$

This symbolic exponential function has the proper meaning of linear operator acting on the Hilbert space H. It is called a *unitary operator* since the transformed vector has the same norm (i.e., length) as the original one.

A solution of the evolution equation (7) can be found by applying the unitary operator $\exp \left(-\frac{i}{\nu} Kt \right)$ to the initial vector ψ_o in H. The curve $\{\psi_t \mid 0 \le t < \infty\}$ representing the time evolution of the neural wave function due to the neural wave equation (5) is given by

$$\left\{ \exp \left(- \frac{i}{\nu} Kt \right) \psi_o \, / 0 \le t < \infty \right\}$$

Although the rewritten neural wave equation (7) is considered as an initial value problem, it can be reduced to a time independent eigenvalue problem. We look for a special solution of Eq. (7) in a form

$$\psi_t = \varphi f(t)$$

where φ is a certain vector in the Hilbert space H and $f(t)$ is a complex-valued function of time t. Then, Eq. (7) can be separated into the following two equations

$$i \nu \frac{df(t)}{dt} = \lambda f(t) \tag{8}$$

$$K\varphi = \lambda\varphi \qquad (9).$$

The former is a simple linear differential equation that admits a special solution.

$$f(t) = e^{i\lambda/vt}$$

where λ is a constant to be determined by the latter equation (9). This constant plays a role of joint coupling the former and latter equations, and called a constant of separation. The latter equation (9) is considered as a typical eigenvalue problem for the linear operator K in the Hilbert space H. A vector ψ in H is said to be a solution if there exists a certain constant λ with which it satisfies Eq. (9). The vector φ is called an *eigenvector*, and constant λ is called an *eigenvalue* of the linear operator K. The linear operator

$$K = -\frac{v^2}{2}\Delta + U_{ex}$$

is known to admit infinitely many solutions of the eigenvalue problem (7) for a wider class of given function U_{ex} (Kato 1966).

Let $\{\varphi_n\}_{n=1}^{\infty}$ be the solutions of Eq. (9) with eigenvalues $\{\lambda_n\}_{n=1}^{\infty}$, namely, each vector φ_n in the Hilbert space H satisfies a linear equation

$$K\varphi_n = \lambda_n\varphi_n$$

Without loss of generality, every eigenvector φ_n can be assumed normalized so that $|\varphi_n|$ = 1. Even if this is not the case, each eigenvector φ_n may be normalized by dividing it by its norm. Suppose each eigenvalue λ_n differs from others. In this case, the eigenvalues of K are said to be nondegenerate. We assume this in what follows for keeping mathematical simplicity. Furthermore, the identity

$$
\begin{aligned}
\lambda_n\langle\varphi_{m,n}\rangle &= \langle\varphi_m, K\varphi_n\rangle \\
&= \int_M \overline{\varphi_m(x)}\left(-\frac{v^2}{2}\Delta + U_{ex}\right)\varphi_n(x)dx \\
&= \int_M \overline{\left\{\left(-\frac{v^2}{2}\Delta + U_{ex}\right)\varphi_m(x)\right\}}\varphi_n(x)dx \\
&= \langle K\varphi_m, \varphi_n\rangle \\
&= \lambda_m\langle\varphi_m, \varphi_n\rangle
\end{aligned}
$$

claims that

$$\langle \varphi_m, \varphi_n \rangle = 0$$

if m ≠ n. This means that the system of eigenvectors $\{\varphi_n\}_{n=1}^{\infty}$ forms a *complete normalized orthogonal system (CNOS)* in the Hilbert space H, and may be considered to define a specific coordinate basis of H. In other words, any vector ψ in the Hilbert space H can be measured by the eigenvectors φ_n of the neural wave generator K, obtaining

$$\psi = \sum_{n=1}^{\infty} \alpha_n \varphi_n$$
$$= \sum_{n=1}^{\infty} \langle \varphi_n, \psi \rangle \varphi_n$$

5. ESTABLISHING EQUI-VALENCE: A CONTEXT TRANSFER MATRIX

When monkeys are trained to select the larger of two circles and then tested to see whether they will select the larger of two squares, unoperated controls select the larger of the squares with no hesitation. After amygdalectomy, transferring the selection to the new pair is severely impaired: Larger is no longer perceived as an independent dimension common to the pair of circles and the pair of squares (Bagshaw & Pribram, 1968). This change in perception is not due to any change in the monkeys' ability to discriminate between cues or between reinforcing events: generalization gradients remain unaltered by amygdalectomy in both a food reinforcement and a footshock deterrence procedure (Hearst & Pribram, 1964a, 1964b). The effect of resection is that larger fails to be perceived as equi-valent, of equal value for the purposes at hand.

The disruption of valuation was demonstrated in another similar experiment. In this experiment the monkeys were trained to select the lighter of two grey square panels embedded in a medium grey background. On test trials, panels of different shades of grey were substituted but the monkeys were still to choose the lighter shade. Control monkeys did just this. The amygdalectomized monkeys, however, hesitated and then selected either of the new panels on a random basis. They perceived the situation as novel, which it was, but failed to perceive it on the basis of the history of reinforcement that placed a value on the relation "lighter of two shades." It is this relation that made the original and substitute panels of equal value, i.e., equi-valent (Schwartzbaum & Pribram, 1960).

Coming back to the general case of dendritic network M and the Hilbert space $H= L^2(M)$, there may exist many different CNOSs. This means that a vector ψ in H (representing a processed sensory input) may have many different coordinate representations. Let $\{\varphi_i\}_{i=1}^{\infty}$ and $\{\xi_j\}_{j=1}^{\infty}$ be two different CNOSs in the Hilbert space H. Then the vector can be decomposed in both CNOSs $\{\varphi_i\}_{i=1}^{\infty}$ and $\{\xi_j\}_{j=1}^{\infty}$, obtaining

$$\psi = \sum_{i=1}^{\infty} \langle \psi, \varphi_i \rangle \, \varphi_i \tag{10},$$

and

$$\psi = \sum_{j=1}^{\infty} \langle \psi, \xi_j \rangle \, \xi_j \tag{11}.$$

The same vector (i.e., neural wave function) ψ can be measured by coordinates ($<\psi,\varphi_1>$, $<\psi,\varphi_2>$,. . .) on the one hand, and ($<\psi,\xi_1>$, $<\psi,\xi_2>$, . . .) on the other. Each CNOS becomes an infinite dimensional orthogonal coordinate system to measure every vector in the Hilbert space H. *The input has become familiarized.*

It is convenient to introduce an intuitive notion of infinite dimensional column vector. If we measure the whole Hilbert space H by the CNOS $\{\varphi_i\}_{i=1}^{\infty}$, each vector ψ in H may be viewed as a column vector

$$\begin{pmatrix} \langle \psi, \varphi_1 \rangle \\ \langle \psi, \varphi_2 \rangle \\ \langle \psi, \varphi_3 \rangle \\ \vdots \\ \vdots \end{pmatrix} \tag{12}.$$

We may equally measure the whole H by the other CNOS $\{\xi_j\}_{j=1}^{\infty}$, and in this case ψ can be seen as

$$\begin{pmatrix} \langle \psi, \xi_1 \rangle \\ \langle \psi, \xi_2 \rangle \\ \langle \psi, \xi_3 \rangle \\ \vdots \\ \vdots \end{pmatrix} \tag{13}.$$

Both column vectors represent the same vector ψ in the Hilbert space H, and so they must be interconnected with each other. Let us decompose a basis vector ξ_j in the CNOS $\{\varphi_i\}_{i=1}^{\infty}$,

$$\xi_j = \sum_{i=1}^{\infty} \langle \xi_j, \varphi_i \rangle \varphi_i$$

Then, we compute an inner product between ψ and ξ_j obtaining

$$\langle \psi, \xi_j \rangle = \sum_{i=1}^{\infty} \langle \xi_j, \varphi_i \rangle \langle \psi, \varphi_i \rangle \qquad (14).$$

This identity shows how the column vectors (12) and (13) are connected with each other. Eq. (14) may be rewritten in an intuitive notion of matrix multiplication. Namely, we have an identity

$$\begin{pmatrix} \langle \psi, \xi_1 \rangle \\ \langle \psi, \xi_2 \rangle \\ \langle \psi, \xi_3 \rangle \\ \vdots \end{pmatrix} = \begin{pmatrix} \langle \xi_1, \varphi_1 \rangle \, \langle \xi_1, \varphi_1 \rangle \cdots \\ \langle \xi_2, \varphi_2 \rangle \, \langle \xi_2, \varphi_2 \rangle \cdots \\ \vdots \qquad \vdots \qquad \cdots \\ \vdots \qquad \vdots \qquad \cdots \end{pmatrix} \begin{pmatrix} \langle \psi, \varphi_1 \rangle \\ \langle \psi, \varphi_2 \rangle \\ \langle \psi, \varphi_3 \rangle \\ \vdots \end{pmatrix} \qquad (15).$$

There, an infinite dimensional matrix with the j–i component given by the inner product $\langle \xi_j, \varphi_i \rangle$ plays an important role. It will be called a *transfer* matrix from the CNOS $\{\varphi_i\}_{i=1}^{\infty}$ to the other CNOS $\{\xi_j\}_{j=1}^{\infty}$.

6. STABILITIES FAR FROM EQUILIBRIUM

An ensemble of CNOS becomes stabilized by virtue of the transfer functions entailed in familiarization. Under conditions in which probabilities play a minor role (such as the recurrent regularities that often characterize physiological states as, for example, those determining hunger and thirst) the stabilities define steady states of equilibrium. When, however, probabilities play a significant role, stabilities occur far from equilibrium and are thus subject to destabilizing influences.

The thermodynamic considerations put forward by Prigogine (1980) regarding stabilities far from equilibrium provide for the formation of such constraints in the form of *attractors* toward which the process tends. Thus the episode, characterized by its temporary stability far from equilibrium, can contain attractors which operate as consequential events. In experimental psychology terms, the attractor is an event which is constructed by cross multiplication among ensembles of CNOS.

Ordinarily habituation of the visceroautonomic components of an orienting reaction occurs within 3 to 10 repetitions of the orienting stimulus. The orienting, distracting stimulus has perturbed a stable organization of redundancies (an organization sometimes referred to as an apperceptive mass), which rapidly restabilizes. After restabilization, there continue to be mild cyclic fluctuations of these components with irregular periods measured in minutes. Originally, we thought these stabilities described states of equilibrium (Piaget, 1970; Pribram, 1958, 1969). The advent of Prigogine's descriptions of stabilities far from equilibrium offered a much richer model: Perturbations of equilibrium states could only lead to a return to equilibrium; perturbations of states far from equilibrium would lead to bifurcations (the shaping of new "hills" or "wells") and provide the potential for achieving novel attractors and therefore new states of stability (McGuinness, Pribram, & Pirnazar, 1990).

The results of the experiments performed in my laboratory, which delineated the effects of amygdalectomy and resections made in related systems, can therefore be conceived as failure to attain temporary stabilities in processing (Pribram 1969, 1980; Pribram et al., 1979). The failure to stabilize was shown to be related to an inability to properly process the structure of redundancy (Pribram 1969, 1987; Pribram, Lim, Poppen & Bagshaw, 1966; Pribram & Tubbs, 1967).

Often the neuropsychological system is actually operating close to equilibrium and perturbation is handled by a return to equilibrium: the distraction of an orienting reaction is either ignored or incorporated into the ongoing process through repetition and familiarization. However if the perturbation is great, a reaction we ordinarily call emotionally upsetting can result in turbulence and a new stability has to be achieved. When, as in the models described here, the process is conceived to be composed of continuous functions, for example, as neurodynamic manifolds described by the Lie algebra, vortices can develop in the turbulent systems. Thus, an often realized possibility is to be "hung up" in the turbulence. But, because this is a chaotic state far from equilibrium, one can deliberately seek constraints in order to anticipate such a change of state and maintain stability.

As noted earlier, destabilization poses the risk that the organism becomes "hung up" in chaotic turbulence. However, in his book *Design for a Brain* (1960), Ashby described an interesting and powerful method for controlling destabilization. His method leads to "catastrophic" and therefore unpredictable restabilizations ("step functions"). In his model, stability was achieved by adding to the computation, numbers taken from a list of random numbers. A similar procedure was found necessary to keep a Hopfield learning network from premature stabilization by falling into a well — an attractor — above optimization. Adding randomicity, "noise" provides maximum possibility (potentiality) for new organizations to develop. As in Prigogine's model one cannot predict just how the system will restabilize because of the randomness injected into the turbulent system. Effective processing is achieved by a heuristic in which the addition of noise is important to preclude premature closure onto a spurious attractor.

The current section discusses the manner in which stabilities far from equilibrium can become perturbed and how destabilization can be controlled and thus provide the ground for innovation.

To this end, let us consider a highly idealized dendrite network, which on the basis of familiarization has become stabilized and isolated electrochemically from other dendrite networks in the system. The dendritic microprocesses of the distribution of the density of the ionic bioplasma as it affects fundamental oscillations of membrane potentials in this isolated dendritic network M can be described by the neural wave equation (5). The neural wave equation (5) may be written as

$$iv \frac{d}{dt} \psi_t = K\psi_t \tag{16}$$

within the realm of Hilbert space geometry. By reducing this equation to a time-independent eigenvalue problem (9), we have found infinitely many stationary solutions of the neural wave equation. They are nothing but the eigenvectors $\{\varphi_n\}_{n=1}^{\infty}$ of the neural wave generator K. In other words, for each eigenvector φ_n and eigenvalue λ_n, a neural wave function

$$\psi(\chi, t) = \varphi_n(\chi) e^{i\lambda_n/vt} \tag{17}$$

solves the neural wave equation (5). As we have seen, the absolute square of a neural wave function represents the density distribution of the ionic bioplasma that manifests the global dynamics of dendritic microprocesses. Thus, each eigenvector φ_n may be understood as a mathematical representative of the typical global dynamics of a dendritic microprocess given by a density distribution of the ionic bioplasma

$$\rho = |\varphi_n|^2 = |\varphi_n(\chi)|^2 = \rho_n(\chi) \tag{18}.$$

Those ionic bioplasma density distributions ρ_n that do not change as the time t passes, manifest temporarily stationary dendritic microprocesses. This means that each eigenvector φ_n represents a set of stable dendritic microprocesses. The fundamental oscillations of dendritic membrane polarizations are synchronized within the dendritic network, and no effective currents of changes in the distribution of the density of the ionic bioplasma exist. In other words, the distribution of ionic bioplasma in the dendritic network is in a temporarily stable state of the dendritic network. The stationary state is stable in the sense that it remains unchanged as long as the dendritic network remains isolated. It is worthwhile to notice here that no other vectors in the Hilbert space different from the eigenvectors φ_n can define the stable dendritic microprocesses.

As detailed earlier, the fact that the isolated dendritic network manifests selectively stable dendritic microprocesses represented by eigenvectors φ_n provides us with the neuronal basis for familiarization. The isolated dendritic network resonates only with selectively limited processes associated with the stationary states φ_n. These tuned resonances are represented by the stationary "familiarized" states of the dendritic network,

$$\varphi_1, \varphi_2, \cdots, \varphi_n, \cdots.$$

Other types of resonance given by a vector φ different from the stationary states φ_n's cannot be realized, as they deform immediately into one of the stationary states by the dispersion effect.

The isolated dendritic network is capable of an infinite variety of stable dendritic microprocesses associated with the familiarized states φ^s, because the neural wave equation (3) admits infinitely many stationary solutions φ^s.

7. INNOVATION

What happens to sensory stimuli to which the organism has become habituated? Do they fail to influence perception and behavior? Many observations and experiments indicate that habituated sensory events, called *S delta* in operant behaviorism and *negative instances* in mathematical psychology, continue to shape the course of learning and, in general, to act as a contextual guide to behavior.

In the process of achieving sensory discriminations, behavior toward the nonreinforced aspects of situation becomes extinguished in steps (see, e.g., review by Pribram, 1986) as these aspects become habituated. Should the situation change, as when another aspect is reinforced, these cues are again noticed (spontaneous recovery). In fact they have been influential throughout the procedure serving as context, the familiar "ground" within which a "figural" content becomes processed.

Whenever a situation changes, an orienting reaction occurs, previously habituated perceptions become dishabituated (Sokolov, 1963). The orienting reaction signals the perception of novelty, the perceived change in the situation. Perceived change can be generated internally — as when an organism becomes hungry. In such instances, "novel events" — restaurant signs begin to populate the landscape — valuing what had become irrelevant. Effort is expended, attention is "paid," and the familiar is experienced innovatively.

There is a great deal of confusion regarding the perception of novelty. In scientific circles, much of this confusion stems from the confounding of novelty with information. Shannon and Weaver (1949) introduced measures on information in terms of bits that reduce the amount of uncertainty in communication. Berlyne (1969) and others then suggested that bits of information and novel events were equivalently arousing, calling them collative variables. However, as is detailed shortly, novelty in the sense used here, neither increases nor reduces the amount of uncertainty; rather novelty is due to a rearrangement of what is familiar, that is, a change in the structure of redundancy. The skill in writing a novel resides not in providing information in the sense of reducing the amount of uncertainty in communication. Rather, the skill lies in portraying familiar events in novel ways, that is in new combinations. If the structure of a novel depended on providing information, *Reader's Digest* would not be in business. Nor is there a reduction in the amount of communicable uncertainty involved in the composition or production of a great piece of music. It is the arrangement and rearrangement of a theme that challenges composer and conductor; the manner in which to structure repetition: "Repetition, ah, there's the rub," exclaimed Leonard Bernstein in his comparison of musical composition to natural language (1976).

A definitive experiment that draws the distinction between a) novelty defined as a change in the structure of redundancy, and b) measures of information (in Shannon's sense) was performed by Smets (1973). Smets used some of the same indicators of arousal as those used in our monkey experiments. He presented human subjects with a panel upon which he flashed displays equated for complexity (difficulty in discrimination), differing either in the number of alternatives (bits) or in the arrangement of analyzable attributes, alternatives (orientations of lines) of a pattern. *Very little visceroautonomic activity was induced by varying the number of alternatives; by contrast changes in arrangement evoked pronounced reactions.*

Innovation depends on an initial step, a process by which the familiar drops into background as current events arouse and habituate. But these earlier events remain available for renewed processing should demand arise. The floor, walls, and doors of a classroom are familiar objects; we are not aware of them. We walk through the door when class is over, failing to notice what we are perceiving while engaged in a discussion following the lecture. But, should an earthquake rearrange things, we become instantly aware of events such as swaying floor and walls and head deliberately for the safety provided by the door's frame.

In the laboratory the process of familiarization is called habituation or, when discrimination is involved extinction, and is demonstrated by a discrimination reversal procedure. Monkeys are trained to select one of two cues by consistently rewarding only one of the cues. After criterion performance (90% or better on 100 consecutive trials) is reached, the reward is shifted to the other cue. Ordinarily monkeys, after a few trials, stop selecting the now nonrewarded cue and proceed to select the now rewarded one. The shift in behavior accelerates as the reversal is repeated. Response to the currently nonrewarded cue has been extinguished, but is rapidly reinstated once the situation demands it (Douglas & Pribram, 1969).

Hippocampectomy (i.e., removal of the entire hippocampal gyrus: hippocampus, and its surrounding subiculum and entorhinal cortex) radically alters this course of behavioral events. The hippocampus, a phylogenetically ancient cortex, is the other major anatomical structure lying within the medial portion of the temporal lobe. As might be expected, extinction (conceived as an extension of habituation) of the response to the now nonreinforced cue remains intact after hippocampectomy.

Not only do the hippocampectomized monkeys show normal extinction, the slope of acquisition of the currently appropriate response does not differ from that of the control monkeys. What does occur is a long series of trials, which intervene between extinction and acquisition, during which the monkeys select cues at random. They receive a reward approximately 50% of the time, which is sufficient to keep them working (Pribram, Douglas, & Pribram, 1969). There is no obvious event that pulls them out of this "period of stationarity"; quite suddenly the hippocampectomized monkeys resume the acquisition of more rewarding behavior. What goes on during the period of stationarity and what prolongs this period for monkeys who have had their hippocampal gyrus resected?

There are currently no techniques for directly assessing what goes on during the period of stationarity. It is clear, however, that rearrangement of the association between cue and reward has occurred and that this rearrangement must be perceived before it can be acted upon. Rearranging must be processed efficiently and appears to take effort (Pribram, 1986b, 1991; Pribram & McGuinness, 1975). A model follows which shows how rearrangement, changing the structure of redundancy, can give rise to novel associations, that is, consequential events.

8. WEAK INTERACTIONS AS POTENTIAL PERTURBATIONS

Each dendritic network of the system is, of course, actually not isolated but connected with other ones. To make the familiarization process of the dendritic network more realistic, we introduce weak dendritic interactions with other networks. This induces multiple transitions between different states of familiarity. Existence of the weak dendritic interaction makes the lifetime of a stability finite. Thus, the dendritic microprocess fluctuates among the temporarily stable states φ^a due to dendritic system weak interactions.

This fact may be well illustrated by means of perturbation theory. Suppose that the dendritic network in question remains isolated until a certain instant, say t^0, and a weak dendritic interaction is turned on at t^0. Time evolution of the dendritic microprocesses is described by the revised neural wave equation (16). However, the neural wave generator K in the right hand side has different forms before and after the onset of a weak dendritic interaction. Let $U = U(t)$ be the additional quasistatic energy due to the weak dendritic interaction. The value of U is relatively small compared with the external static energy U_{ex}. Then, the neural wave equation (16) has the form

$$i v \frac{d}{dt} \psi_t = K \psi_t \tag{19}$$

for $t < t_0$, and

$$i v \frac{d}{dt} = \psi_t = (K + U(t)) \psi_t \tag{20}$$

for $t > t_0$. We call Eq. (19) a non-perturbed neural wave equation and Eq. (20) a perturbed one. We consider onset of a weak dendritic interaction as a perturbation of the neural wave equation.

Suppose that the dendritic microprocess is in one of the isolated, familiarized states, say φ_m, before the onset of perturbation. Then, Eq. (19) claims

$$\psi_t = \varphi_m e^{-i\lambda_m/vt}$$

for $t < t_0$. This suggests that the perturbed neural wave equation (18) may be solved with respect to the initial condition

$$\psi_{t_0} = \varphi_m e^{-i\lambda_m/vt_0} .$$

The perturbed neural wave equation (20) may be solved by the following mathematical procedure.

Let ψ_v be the solution of Eq. (20). We introduce a time-dependent vector $\dot{\psi}$ in the Hilbert space H by

$$\psi_t = exp\left(\frac{i}{v} Kt\right)\psi_t \qquad (21).$$

Then, it solves a reduced perturbed neural wave equation

$$iv\,\frac{d}{dt}\,\psi_t = \hat{U}_t\psi_t \qquad (22)$$

where

$$\hat{U}_t = exp\left(\frac{i}{v}Kt\right)U(t)exp\left(-\frac{i}{v}Kt\right) \qquad (23)$$

is a time-dependent operator in H. The initial condition for ψ_v yields the initial condition

$$\hat{\psi}_{t_0} = \varphi_m$$

for $\hat{\psi}_t$. Equation (22) can be solved immediately by the perturbation series

$$\hat{\psi}_t = \left[1 + \left(\frac{1}{iv}\right)\int_{t_0}^{t}\hat{U}_s ds + \left(\frac{1}{iv}\right)^2\int_{t_0}^{t}\int_{t_0}^{t}\hat{U}_s ds\,\hat{U}_u du + \cdots\cdots\right]\varphi_m \qquad (24).$$

Because the perturbation U is small, the perturbation series (24) can be well approximated by the first two terms, obtaining

$$\hat{\psi}_t = \left[1 + \left(\frac{1}{iv}\int_{t_0}^{t}\hat{U}_s ds\right)\right]\varphi_m \qquad (25).$$

Finally, Eqs. (21) and (25) give a first order approximation to the solution ψ_v of the perturbed neural wave equation (20),

$$\psi_t = exp\left(-\frac{i}{v}Kt\right)\varphi_m$$
$$+ exp\left(-\frac{i}{v}Kt\right)\left(\frac{1}{iv}\right)\int_{t_0}^{t}\hat{U}_s ds\,\varphi_m$$
$$= e^{-i/v\lambda_m t}\varphi_m$$
$$+ exp\left(-\frac{i}{v}Kt\right)\left(\frac{1}{iv}\right)\int_{t_0}^{t}\hat{U}_s ds\,\varphi_m$$

It is convenient to measure the vector ψ_p in the Hilbert space H by means of the specific CNOS $\{\varphi_n\}_{n=1}^{\infty}$ because the perturbation U is so small that ψ_p may not deviate much from the initial state φ_m. Let

$$\psi_t = \sum_{n=1}^{\infty} \alpha_n \varphi_n$$

be the coordinate expansion of ψ_p in terms of the CNOS $\{\varphi_n\}_{n=1}^{\infty}$. Here, the coordinates α_n are given by the inner product

$$
\begin{aligned}
\alpha_n &= \langle \varphi_m, \psi_t \rangle \\
&= e^{-i/v\,\lambda_{mt}} \langle \varphi_n, \varphi_m \rangle \\
&\quad + \left(\frac{1}{iv}\right) \int_{t_0}^{t} \langle e^{i/v\,Ks} \varphi_n, \hat{U}_s \varphi_m \rangle ds \\
&= e^{-i/v\,\lambda_{mt}\delta_{nm}} \\
&\quad + \left(\frac{1}{iv}\right) e^{-i/v\,\lambda t} \int_{t_0}^{t} \langle \varphi_n, e^{i/v\,Ks} U(s) e^{-i/v\,Ks} \varphi_m \rangle ds \\
&= e^{-i/v\,\lambda_{mt}\delta_{nm}} \\
&\quad + \left(\frac{1}{iv}\right) e^{-i/v\,\lambda_{nt}} \int_{t_0}^{t} e^{i/v(\lambda_n-\lambda_m)s} \langle \varphi_m, U(s)\varphi_m \rangle ds
\end{aligned}
$$

Namely, we have

$$\alpha_n = \left(\frac{1}{iv}\right) e^{-i/v\,\lambda_{nt}} \int_{t_0}^{t} e^{i/v(\lambda_n-\lambda_m)s} \langle \varphi_n, U(s)\varphi_m \rangle ds$$

for n $\neq$ m and

$$\alpha_m = \left(1 + \frac{1}{iv} \int_{t_0}^{t} \langle \varphi_m, U(s)\varphi_m \rangle ds \right) e^{-i/v\,\lambda_{mt}}$$

Thus the onset of perturbation causes the change of coordinates from

$$
\begin{pmatrix}
0 \\
0 \\
\vdots \\
0 \\
e^{-i/v\,\lambda_{mt}} \\
0 \\
\vdots \\
0
\end{pmatrix}
\qquad (26)
$$

to

$$
\begin{pmatrix}
\alpha_1 \\
\alpha_2 \\
\vdots \\
\alpha_m \\
\vdots
\end{pmatrix}
\qquad (27).
$$

In other words, the onset of perturbation forces the vector φ_t to deviate from the initial stable, familiarized state φ_m so that it has nonvanishing components along other familiarized states φ_n.

9. NOVEL ASSOCIATIONS: THE ORIGIN OF CONSEQUENTIAL EVENTS

Here, we need a consistent interpretation of the dendritic microprocess associated with the vector ψ_t in H, and coin a new mathematical formulation of association. When the vector ψ_t has the coordinate representation (26) with respect to the CNOS $\{\varphi_n\}_{n=1}^{\infty}$ the dendritic microprocess described by ψ_m remains identical with that of a specific state φ_m. If there is no perturbation, that dendritic network remains isolated and keeps the initial familiarized state ψ_m. Perturbation modifies the vector ψ_t so that its coordinate representation becomes (27).

Let us compute the length of vector ψ_t in terms of the coordinates (27). As the states φ_n form a CNOS in the Hilbert space, we have

$$
|\psi_t|^2 = \sum_{n=1}^{\infty} |\alpha_n|^2
$$

Before the onset of perturbation, $\alpha_n = 0$ except for n = m, and this can be written as

$$
\begin{aligned}
|\psi_t|^2 &= |\alpha_n|^2 \\
&= |e^{-i/v\,\lambda_{mt}}|^2 \\
&= 1
\end{aligned}
$$

After the onset, we have

$$|\psi_t|^2 = \left| 1 + \frac{1}{iv} \int_{t_0}^t \langle \varphi_m, U(s)\varphi_m \rangle ds \right|^2$$
$$+ \sum_{n \neq m} \left| \left(\frac{1}{iv} \right) \int_{t_0}^t e^{i/v(\lambda_n - \lambda_m)s} \langle \varphi_n, U(s)\varphi_m \rangle ds \right|^2$$

It is worthwhile to notice here that the perturbation acts on the vector ψ_0, so that it is no longer parallel to the eigenvector φ_m. It comes to point along many other independent directions of eigenvectors φ_n. For any $t > t_0$ and $n \neq m$,

$$|\alpha_n|^2 = \left(\frac{1}{v} \right)^2 \left| \int_{t_0}^t e^{i/v(\lambda_n - \lambda_m)s} \langle \varphi_n, U(s)\varphi_m \rangle ds \right|^2$$

gives a relative proportion of the vector ψ_t to point along the nth eigenvector φ_n. As the nth eigenvector φ_n is a stable dendritic microprocess, the dendritic microprocess specified by the vector ψ_0, realizes those of the other state φ_n with relative proportion $|\alpha_n|^2$. Thus, the perturbation causes the neural wave function ψ_t to represent typical dendritic microprocesses that resemble those of state φ_n with relative proportion $|\alpha_n|$. Such a neural wave function represents a novel event in which the several independent states are associated on the basis of frequencies given by their relative proportion.

10. THE FAR FRONTAL CORTEX AND NARRATIVE STRUCTURE

10.1. AN EXECUTIVE PROCESSOR

In a continually changing situation where episodic demarcation becomes difficult or when transfer among contexts is blocked other resources must be mobilized. Such situations demand executive intervention if action is to be consequential. This part of the essay addresses the issue of an executive processor, a brain system that directs and allocates the resources of the rest of the brain. Ordinarily, input from sensory or internal receptors preempts allocation (for discussion see, e.g., Miller, Galanter, & Pribram, 1960) by creating a "temporary dominant focus" of activation within one or another brain system (for review, see Pribram, 1971, pp. 78-80). However when extra demands are placed on the routine operations of allocation, coherences among proprieties and priorities must be organized, and practical inference initiated. Proprieties must structure competences, priorities must be ordered and practicalities assessed.

10.2. PROPRIETIES, PRIORITIES AND PRACTICALITIES

The far frontal cortex is surrounded by systems that, when electrically excited, produce movement and visceroautonomic effects. On the lateral surface of the frontal lobe lies the classical precentral motor cortex (for review see Bucy, 1944; Pribram, 1991, Lecture 6). As noted, on the mediobasal surface of the lobe lie the more recently discovered "limbic" motor areas of the orbital, medial frontal and cingulate cortex (Kaada et al., 1949; Pribram, 1961). It is therefore likely that the functions of the far frontal cortex are, in some basic sense, related to these somatomotor and visceroautonomic effects.

At the same time, the far frontal cortex derives an input from the medial portion of the thalamus, the n. medialis dorsalis. This part of the diencephalon shares with those from anterior and midline nuclei (the origins of the input to the limbic cortex) an organization different from that of the projections from the ventrolateral group of nuclei to the cortex of the convexity of the hemisphere. (See Chow & Pribram, 1956; Pribram, 1991 for review).

The close anatomical relationship of the far frontal cortex to the limbic medial forebrain is also shown by comparative anatomical data. In cats and other nonprimates, the gyrus proreus is the homologue of the far frontal cortex of primates. This gyrus receives its projection from the midline magnocellular portion of the n. medialis dorsalis. This projection covers a good share of the anterior portion of the medial frontal cortex; gyrus proreus on the lateral surface is limited to a narrow sliver. There appears to have been a rotation of the medial frontal cortex laterally (just as there appears to have occurred a rotation medially of the occipital cortex — especially between monkey and man) during the evolution of primates.

From these physiological and anatomical considerations it appears likely that the far frontal cortex is concerned with relating the motor functions of the limbic to those of the dorsolateral convexity. This relationship has been expressed by Deecke, Kornhuber, Long, & Schreiber (1985) in terms of the what, when, and how of action.

Deecke et al. (1985) concluded an extensive review of their studies using electrical recordings made in humans that: The orbital cortex becomes involved when the question is what to do; the lateral cortex becomes active when the question is how something is to be done and the dorsal portions of the lobe mediate when to do it. According to the anatomical connections of the far-frontal portions of lobe, described below, "what" can be translated into propriety; "how" into practicality and "when" into priority.

On an anatomical basis, the far frontal systems have been shown to comprise three major divisions (see Pribram, 1987, 1990 for review): One, an orbital, is derived from the same phylogenetic pool as, and is reciprocally connected with, the amygdala (and other parts of the basal ganglia such as the n. accumbens, which have been shown to be involved in limbic processing). As might be predicted from the role of the amygdala in familiarizing, in déja and jamais vu phenomena, this orbital system augments and enhances sensitivities as to what to do, to propriety based on episodic processing (see below).

The second, a dorsal system, is derived from the same root as, and has connections with, the hippocampal system which includes the limbic medial frontal-cingulate cortex. As might be expected from the involvement of the hippocampus in recombinant processing — in innovation — the dorsal far frontal system controls flexibility in when actions are to be engaged, in ordering priorities to ensure effective action.

The third, a laterally located system has strong reciprocal connections with the posterior cerebral convexity. It is this system that involves the far frontal cortex in a variety of sensory-motor modalities when sensory input from the consequences of action incompletely specifies the situation. In such situations practical inference becomes necessary.

10.3. ORGANIZING COHERENCE

In addition to its demarcation by successive orienting reactions, a defining attribute of an episode is that what is being processed coheres — processing must deal with covariation in terms of familiarity, equi-valence and novelty. Covariation can lead to interference, thus resulting in the inability to order the processing of events. Recall that primacy and recency effects were impaired after amygdala and hippocampal damage. With far frontal damage, monkeys show impairment in processing the latter part of the middle of a series. This impairment is attributed to increased pro- and retroactive interference among items in the series (Malmo & Amsel, 1948).

The impairment is also shown by patients with damage to their frontal cortex. These patients fail to remember the place in a sequence in which an item occurs: The patients lose the ability to "temporally tag" events, that is, to place them within the episode. With such patients, Milner (1974, see also Petrides & Milner, 1982) performed a series of experiments demonstrating how the processing impairment affects the middle portions of an episode. In her studies, it is *relative recency*, the *serial position* of covarying experiences, that becomes muddled. Other patients with fronto-limbic damage are described by Kinsbourne and Wood (1975). In keeping with the proposals put forward in this essay, they interpret the impairment in processing serial position as due to a derangement of the context that structures an episode.

Fuster (1988) conceptualized the far frontal processing of context in terms of cross temporal contingencies. Relative recency, for instance, implies that a temporal context exists within which recencies can be relative to one another. However, as indicated by experimental results in which spatial context is manipulated, as in variants of object constancy tasks (Anderson, Hunt, VanderStoep & Pribram, 1976) the contextual influence can be spatiotemporal as well as temporotemporal. In fact, in other experiments (Brody & Pribram, 1978; Pribram, Spinelli, & Kamback, 1967) data were obtained indicating far frontal involvement whenever processing is influenced by two or more distinct sets of covarying contextual contingencies, even when both are spatial.

The computation of this covariation demands that cross temporal, spatiotemporal, and cross spatial contingencies be processed. In classical and operant conditioning, the consequences of behavior are contiguous in time and place with the stimulus conditions that initiate the behavior. Contiguity determines the episode or conditioning "trial." When contiguity is loosened, stimulation that intervenes between initiation and consequence has the potential to distract and thus to prevent the processing of covariation. Processing is destabilized. Perturbation is controlled only if a stable state, established coherence, instructs and directs the process.

10.4. KRONOS, KAIROS, AND PROPRIETY

Covariation has posed special difficulties with respect to an understanding of time. Co-variation must always occur within a defined episode: variation within a context. Our common conception of clock time, based on successions of object-forms in space-time, specifies coherent (correlated) successions within a defined epoch of spacetime and was called "Kronos" by the classical Greeks. However, they recognized another form of time, "Kairos," which concerns the experiencing of an appropriate moment, a decisive moment that may be characterized by an event and its feeling of timelessness or timefullness. The subjective aspects of Kairos were described by Bergson (1922/1965) in terms of *duré* — an experienced duration that is not readily measured in chronological time. In his doctoral dissertation, Ornstein reviewed his own and others' experiments on *The Experience of Duration* (which in its published version was changed by sales minded editors to *The Experience of Time*, 1969).

An analogy attributed to William James was recently developed in a seminar presented to our brain research group by Fred Abraham. The analogy suggests that time is like a string of beads. Kronos, that is, Einsteinian space-time is measured by the *length* of the string. Kairos, as shown by Ornstein, is experienced as a function of the *density* with which the beads (events, episodes) are strung.

But there is yet another, additional, manner of experiencing time: the *order* in which the beads are strung. It is the serial position of events experienced within the context of coherent episodes that gives form to a story, a narrative. The extent and duration of a coherent state in the face of distracting perturbations is ordinarily discussed in terms of limits on processing span.

10.5. MODIFICATION OF PROCESSING SPAN: COMPETENCE NOT CAPACITY

The issue of limited span is usually discussed in terms of a fixed channel capacity. But as reviewed by Pribram and McGuinness (1975, 1982), a considerable volume of work has shown that the central processing span is not fixed. Thus Miller (1956), Garner (1962), and Simon (1974, 1986), among others, have clearly shown that information-processing span can be enhanced by reorganization such as that provided by "chunking." In fact, Broadbent (see review, 1974) showed that with regard to cognitive operations such as attention, limited span is not so much a function of the final common path as it is a function of the central processing mechanisms in the brain.

These data have led to conceptualizing limitations in processing span as limitations in flexible channel competences rather than in channel capacities (Pribram, 1986b; Pribram & McGuinness, 1975), a view also expressed by Maffei (1985). Chunking has been shown, using the asymmetric delayed alternation procedure, to be influenced by resections of the far frontal cortex (Pribram, Plotkin, Anderson & Leong, 1977; Pribram & Tubbs, 1967). In the current section, data are presented demonstrating that electrical excitation of the frontal cortex changes receptive field properties of neurons in the sensory channels of the primary visual cortex. These changes are directly related to the ability to parse or chunk the input. Thus the conception of a limited capacity depending on some fixed channel "exoskeleton" becomes untenable. An increase in processing capability, in competence (in the sense of a deep structure as developed by Chomsky, 1965), becomes possible by way of challenges to a flexible "endoskeleton" of the channel.

Processing span is thus sensitive to structuring as by chunking, a top-down cognitive process. The continuously updated channel structures provide for flexibility in processing with the accumulation of experience, memory-based influences organize the channel structure according to what is momentarily appropriate.

The particular experiments that demonstrate the neurophysiology of top-down processing, processing that implements changes in channel structure, were performed on the receptive field organization of single neurons in the lateral geniculate nucleus of cats and monkeys (Lassonde, Ptito, & Pribram, 1981; Spinelli & Pribram, 1967). Receptive fields were mapped by displaying a small moving dot on a contrasting background. The location and motion of the dot were computer-controlled. Thus the computer could sum (in a matrix of bins representing the range over which the dot was moved) the number of impulses generated by the neuron whose receptive field was being mapped. This was done for each position of the dot because the computer "knew" where the dot was located.

The maps obtained for the lateral geniculate nucleus are usually called Mexican hat functions. The brim of the hat represents the spontaneous background of impulse activity of the neuron. The crown of the hat represents the excitation of the cell by the dot of light shown to the animal when the cell is located at the center of the visual field. Where the crown meets the brim there is a depression indicating that the output of the cell has been inhibited.

The center-surround organization, first described at the optic nerve level by Kuffler (1953) is a cross section of the hat parallel to the brim. The inhibitory surround has been shown (e.g., Creutzfeldt, Kuhnt, & Benevento, 1974, for cortical cells) to be due to hyperpolarizing activity in a lateral network of "local circuit neurons" (Rakic, 1976), which do not generate nerve impulses.

It is this inhibitory surround that can be augmented or diminished by electrical excitation of other parts of the forebrain. Stimulation of the far frontal cortex diminishes the inhibitory surround; stimulation of the posterior intrinsic (association) cortex, specifically in this case, the inferotemporal portion of this cortex produces an augmentation of the inhibitory surround.

Dendritic fields overlap to a considerable extent. Thus when the excitatory portion of the receptive fields become enlarged, the dendritic fields essentially merge into a more or less continuous functional field. By contrast, when the excitatory portion of the receptive fields shrinks, each neuron becomes functionally isolated from its neighbor.

This modifiability of the primary visual system in the direction of greater separation or greater confluence among channels was supported by testing the effects of the same electrical stimulations on the recovery cycles of the system as recorded with small macroelectrodes: Far frontal stimulations produce a slowing of recovery, whereas posterior stimulations result in a more rapid recovery as compared with an unstimulated baseline. Slow recovery indicates that the system is acting in unison; rapid recovery that the system is "multiplexed" — that its channels are separated.

10.6. PROCESSING PRIORITY: SERIAL POSITION EFFECTS

The results of these experiments can be interpreted to indicate that far frontal brain stimulation drives the visual system toward a continuous mode of operation while posterior stimulation drives the system toward a discrete mode. A convolution-correlation model is therefore more appropriate when the focus of brain activity shifts toward the frontal lobes. A matrix model is more appropriate when the focus of brain activity lies more posteriorly. To test this interpretation we need to relate the known behavioral functions of the frontal and posterior portions of the brain to the known advantages of the two types of models.

Convolution-correlation mathematics have been used to model sensory-motor and perceptual-motor learning and skills. Thus Licklider (1951), Uttal (1975), and Reichardt (1978) developed temporal and spatial autocorrelation models to account for their results of experiments on perceptual performances. Cooper (1984) and Kohonen (1972, 1977) used a similar model to describe a variety of properties both perceptual and cognitive. Thus, for example, Cooper developed a model based on the effects of monocular deprivation on the responsiveness of neurons in the visual cortex and made successful predictions of outcomes of experiments inspired by the model. As reviewed elsewhere, our own efforts (Pribram & Carlton, 1986) have used this type of model to tease apart imaging as a function of convolving the various stages of processing in the primary visual system, from object perception, which depends on correlations among patterns in which centers of symmetry are determined by operations performed in the superior colliculus and the visuomotor system.

None of these perceptual and motor skills depend on functions that can be ascribed to the far frontal part of the brain. Nor are they related to the inferotemporal cortex and the posterior intrinsic "association" systems of which the inferotemporal cortex is a part. What is suggested by these successful models is that the convolution-correlation approach is the more appropriate for describing sensory-motor skills leaving the matrix model as more appropriate for cognitive operations such as comprehension (See Pribram, 1991, Lecture 7).

But certain aspects of cognitive processing are better described by a convolutional-correlational approach. The thesis to be presented proposes that such processing entails the computing of inner products of sensory input vectors to establish a coherent context, a processing episode.

Murdock (1979, 1982, 1983, 1985; Murdock & Lewandowsky, 1986) has reviewed the evidence that distinguishes convolution and matrix theories of associative memory. He pointed out that whereas the matrix model (as developed by Anderson, 1970, and Pike, 1984) has the advantage of simplicity in obtaining explicit expressions and to some extent in storage capacity, the convolution-correlation model is more powerful in other respects such as the handling of serial position effects, effects that entail far frontal lobe function.

The convolutional and matrix models differ in that in the convolutional model critical operations are performed on the inner products of its vectors, whereas in the matrix models such operations utilize the outer products of vectors. Murdock (1985) described the difference as follows:

> The basic issue seems to be as follows. I would suggest that an association can be represented as a convolution, information is stored in a common memory vector, and correlation is the retrieval operation. Pike would suggest that an association is the outer product of two vectors, information is stored in a memory matrix or set of matrices, and vector-matrix premultiplication and postmultiplication is the retrieval operation. (p. 132)

Thus the convolutional approach "is not quite ready to be abandoned in favor of a matrix system" (Murdock, 1985, p. 132). But as processing prototypes characterizes the functions of systems of the posterior cerebral convexity (see e.g., Warrington & McCarthy, 1983) the matrix model also is not to be abandoned. This model is clearly viable in the hands of Anderson and his colleagues when applied to learning and performance of discrimination-type tasks (see Anderson, Silverstein, Ritz, & Jones, 1977, for review). Whenever classification is involved, storage as outer products of vectors and retrieval by postmultiplication appears to be more appropriate than storage by association in a common vector produced by convolving inner products.

This line of reasoning leads to the suggestion that reference — that is, in humans, semantic — processing is best represented by a matrix model and that the convolution-correlation model be reserved for episodic processing (see Tulving, 1972, 1985 for review). It is therefore important to find out if indeed the convolution-correlation model more effectively models all aspects of episodic processing.

As noted, a central characteristic of episodic and event processing is its preservation of some sort of place keeping and time tagging: that is, in the perception of serial position within the total processing span. Murdock & Lewandowsky (1986) presented a detailed review of models constructed to account for serial position effects and the evidence upon which they are based. Interference, trace decay, distinctiveness, end-anchoring, dual trace (item and order), and organizational (chunking) factors were assigned critical roles in model building and the convolutional model efficiently handles them all.

How can such models developed to account for remembering serial position effects in the recall of lists of items be relevant to understanding how the brain processes episodic controls? The key to understanding lies in the results of analysis of performance of the delayed response task. Recall that in this task a reward or token is hidden in a particular location chosen from others similar in appearance while the animal is watching — a screen is then interposed between the location and the animal for a short (e.g., 5 seconds) period and then removed, allowing the animal to have access to the reward. After resection of the far frontal cortex, monkeys lose the ability to perform this task. Pro- and retroactive interference effects have been demonstrated to play a role in this impairment (Malmo, 1942; Pribram, 1958; Pribram, Plotkin, Anderson, & Leong, 1977; Stamm & Rosen, 1972; reviewed by Pribram, 1987).

This impairment is almost entirely due to the fact that monkeys with such lesions fail to properly process the initial part of the trial, the hiding of the reward before the screen is interposed. It is the perceptual processing part of the task that is most susceptible to interference, not the memory trace of the initial perceptual experience. Furthermore, items that are identical produce interference in models dependent on trace decay; but as identical items do not interfere with recall of serial position, trace decay cannot account for difficulties experienced after far frontal lobe damage. When items are similar, however, demands on ordering escalate as expected when the convolution-correlation model is used.

To summarize: The effects of (a) amygdalectomy on primacy and recency, (b) the effects of hippocampectomy on primacy, and (c) the effects of far frontal lobe resections on intralist interference (relative recency) stem from inadequate processing at the time of initial exposure to the list of items, the establishment of an episode, the context that stabilizes further processing, and not to effects on the trace of the sensory input. We have all experienced a related phenomenon when we attempt to recite a poem or rehearse a melody: should we be interrupted or fail, for the moment, to be able to continue the recitation or rehearsal we often find it necessary to begin again at the beginning of the entire poem or piece, or at least at the beginning of a major section.

Murdock noted that convolutional and matrix models describe what must be processed but do not address how processing proceeds. There is a class of models, however, that do describe "how" in terms of parallel-distributed processes. The next section reviews the evidence for, and describes extensions of, the convolutional model that indicates how processing proceeds.

10.7. PROCESSING (PRACTICAL) INFERENCE

Scientists interested in perception have been especially intrigued by illusions and pictures in which figures are to some extent hidden by the context in which they appear. Such interest exists because perception is ordinarily experienced as "direct"; thus perceptual processes are difficult to study because, under normal circumstances, they are unavailable to conscious awareness. This is not so when the perceiver is challenged by an ambiguous input.

These perceptual ambiguities are the figural counterparts of the contextually covariant processes discussed so far: injury to the far frontal cortex (and not the systems of the posterior cerebral convexity) dramatically influences the rate of reversal of such figures as Necker cubes, and faces/vases (see e.g., Teuber, 1964). When the injury is severe, reversals may not be experienced at all.

In hidden and reversible figures, ground and potential figures vie for dominance. Figure and ground must be separated out from the ambiguous sensory input. The rate of reversals in reversible figure experiments speeds as the perceiver becomes aware of both figures and this rate can be influenced to some degree by intending to reverse. Rock (1983) has noted that reversals continue after each of the figures has been clearly perceived — indicating that the input continues to provide a processing challenge.

This challenge is met much as the other challenges to order that have been described here: centrally controlled changes are produced in the microprocesses occurring in the input channels. These changes can be conceived to operate much as does a zoom lens. When extended into the telephoto range, good separation between figure and ground occurs. A telephotograph has a very narrow depth of field and enhanced resolution. The same effect is obtained with a large surface hologram; by contrast, cutting such a surface into small areas reduces resolution but enhances depth of field. In the brain, large surface integration of a distributed process is achieved when the boundaries between overlapping receptive fields are attenuated, when the convolutional mode of processing is in force. The evidence presented above indicates that such a mode is placed in operation by virtue of the activities of the frontolimbic forebrain.

Smolensky (1986) extended the convolutional model to cover inference. Smolensky's is a dynamical "harmony" theory in many respects similar to the holonomic brain theory pursued in Pribram (1991). However, instead of relying on Gabor transforms, the transition from harmonic (such as Fourier) analysis to measures on the amount of information being processed is done in terms of electrical circuits (with two resistors in series) that compose a "knowledge atom". The resultant measure on information is statistical.

Optimization is achieved in harmonium by simulated annealing, or, lowering the "computational temperature." This means that randomness of the initial state is "cooled" out: Inference is assumed to be stochastic. By this procedure a completely coherent interpretation can be constructed from an ambiguous input. Similarly, the harmonium model can answer ill-posed problems, those whose answers are replete with interference effects, just as it can answer well-posed problems: "There will be more than one state of highest harmony and the model will choose one of them. It does not stop dead due to insufficient information. Not 'any answer' will do [however]. Harmonium finds the best possible answers to ill posed problems on the basis of rules that have solved well posed problems" (Smolensky, 1986, p. 252).

One such ill-posed problem is the illusion called the *Aubert phenomenon*, a shift in the subjective vertical when a person's body is tilted in the dark. Mittelstaedt (1987) studied the shift of the subjective vertical with great care and has developed a processing model to account for this shift, a model in tune with both the harmony model and the holonomic brain theory. As such, the Mittelstaedt model serves as a precise illustration of this class of models for the resolution of ill-posed problems: When the ordinary context provided by an illuminated situation is absent, internally generated rules provided by previous established contexts attempt to substitute.

Mittelstaedt found "that the apparent orientation of the visual world to the vertical and that of one's own body to the vertical result from two separate computations" (p. 65). The vertical of the visual world, is the resultant of a gravity vector produced by an input from the saccules of the inner ear, and an "idiotropic" vector. Contrary to expectation, this idiotropic vector is not determined by current proprioceptive inputs that influence postural control. What then might be the origin of the idiotropic vector?

Insight into the origin of the idiotropic vector comes from an analysis of the Aubert phenomenon. Aubert (1861) noted that an objectively vertical line of light in an otherwise dark room appeared tilted to 45° when observed with his body tilted to a 90° angle. When the room was lit so that he could see it with all its window frames, walls, and furniture, the line snapped into its true position. When the light was switched off again, the line slowly returned to its apparent — nonobjective — vertical position, that is, it was again seen as 45° rotated from objective verticality.

The frames provided by windows, walls, and so forth, influence to a variable degree the perception of the subjective vertical (see e.g., Stark & Bridgeman, 1983; Witkin & Asch, 1948). Mittelstaedt's experiments show that these frames and the idiotropic vector superimpose to form a new resultant. This resultant is computed by cross multiplication between "circular Fourier components selected from a central nervous system representation of the retinal pattern" and "a central nervous component generator, which is controlled by internal feedback" from the resultant of the cross multiplications.

Neurophysiologically, the extraction of the Fourier components is envisaged by Mittelstaedt to devolve on the orientation selective neurons of the primary visual cortex. "Let the output of all those [neurons] whose preferred orientation falls into the same sector be summed." If a field of parallel lines is used as a panorama, the output of each of the sectorial assemblies can be computed in terms of their Fourier coefficients. By introducing a weighting function, unequal cell densities within sectors and unequal mean amplitudes of the cells' tuning functions can readily be compensated.

In order for Mittelstaedt's model to work, before weighting, "a layer of polarity detectors would be required, that is, cells which peak just once within a full turn of the panorama." Such cells of course do exist: They are cells with receptive fields selective of directionality and orientation as well as the Fourier components specified by spatial and temporal frequency (Pribram, Lassonde, & Ptito, 1981; See review by DeValois & DeValois, 1988).

The Aubert phenomenon is dramatically altered in patients with frontal lesions (Teuber & Mishkin, 1954). This indicates that the far frontal cortex is critically involved in computing the idiotropic vector. In fact, a reasonable speculation would hold that the idiotropic vector is supplied whenever the input from receptors is insufficient to completely specify perceptual context. In such cases, the perceptual system is challenged rather than determined. Percepts gradually drift (e.g., to new orientations) and appear to be no longer "directly" perceived. According to the Mittelstaedt model, in such cases the reciprocal feedback between cross multiplication of the Fourier components representing the sensory input with the central nervous system generator is largely determined by the output from that generator and to a lesser degree by sensory input.

In any generalization of the model to other situations in which the input is ambiguous, conflicting, or demanding of serial position effects, in other words, when the input poses problems that are poorly specified, the output from the central nervous system generator is critical. Due to the storage properties of the frontolimbic systems, the central generator becomes shaped by experience. The process "does not stop dead due to insufficient information." Rather, the process proceeds by constant interaction of the centrally generated component with the results of cross-multiplication of the input vectors, a process that attempts to specify prototypical objects and events. Interaction adds a centrally generated component to enrich each prototype within its boundaries. Inference makes use of this richness, the rules, structures of redundancy, that have been developed on the basis of experience where the input has more completely specified the product of cross multiplication and central generator. The total inference process thus leads to conceiving the best possible fit between prior experience and current input.

11. NEURODYNAMICS AND INFERENCE

The insights gained from Murdoch's, Smolensky's, and Mittlestaedt's models of the inference process can be expressed in terms of neurodynamics as developed in the holonomic brain theory. We noted that external stimuli affect the internal states of dendritic microprocess so that the state vector satisfies the neural wave equation. Time evolution of the state vector is, then, given by a unitary flow in H generated by a unitary operator $\exp\left(-\frac{i}{v}Kt\right)$. For each external stimulus, the neural wave generator K is specified and so is the unitary operator. Then specific state vectors that are invariant under the unitary flow with generator K play important roles to represent stable states of each external stimulus. They can be called "memory" states and specified mathematically as eigenvectors of the operator K. The well-known mathematical fact that those eigenvectors form a CNOS in the Hilbert space H may provide us with a mechanism of *multiple* associations between memory and a specific currently activated process.

11.1. BIAS

We consider the simplest case of a process made up of two dendritic networks, unit A and unit B. Unit A is directly connected to a certain sense organ via nerve fibers and synapses so that it receives a neural signal generated by the effect of the surroundings of the sense organ. As we saw in the preceding sections, the dendritic network manifests limited and temporarily stable dendritic microprocesses. They are represented by stationary neural wave functions, that is, stable states in the Hilbert space H of the unit A. Thus a stable stationary state of the unit A becomes perturbed by the neural stimulus from the sense organ. The perturbation, as we have seen, can trigger a reorganization of the previously stable state.

Suppose that the unit A is excited by a stimulus from a sense organ, causing the dendritic microprocesses of the unit A to resonate. This produces the stationary state of the Hilbert space H_A. If the unit A becomes isolated, it resonates in this fashion "forever." However, because unit A is connected not only with the sense organ but also with unit B, there is a possibility for mutual interaction. Existence of the influence from the unit B makes the lifetime of the resonating stationary state u_A of the unit A shorter.

When unit A is driven both by outputs from the sense organ and from unit B, the output of the unit B plays the role of biasing unit A. The dendritic network of A then resonates to the output of the sense organ with a bias from B. Consequently, the state vector of the unit A becomes a stationary state u_A which is perturbed by the output of the sense organ as biased by the state of the unit B. In other words, the perception of the output of the sense organ depends on the process carried by a state vector u_B of the unit B.

Units A and B can each be considered as an isolated dendritic network as long as the sense organ does not send another input to unit A. This means that the state vectors u_A and u_B of the units A and B are kept unchanged until next series of inputs is generated by the sense organ. Therefore, the synaptic connections between the units A and B become especially tuned to this pair of state vectors u_A and u_B. We call this specific synaptic weighting between the units A and B a neural channel $u_A \otimes u_B$. This highly tuned neural channel $u_A \otimes u_B$ can remain effective even when the next series of outputs of the sense organ again perturbs the state vectors u_A, and u_B. This is the origin of inference. Once a temporary stability becomes established by means of a neural channel $u_A \otimes u_B$, it now acts as the bias contributed by unit B. Thus, the next series of perturbations from the sense organ become biased by the channels established by preceding perturbations. This simple "inference machine" based on dendritic networks A and B provides us with an interesting mathematical model of a more realistic inference process.

Suppose we have a finite number of neural channels between the unit A and B of certain learning processes. We denote them by $(u_A^1 \otimes u_B^1)$, $(u_A^2 \otimes u_B^2)$, $\cdots$, $(u_A^M \otimes u_B^M)$ for M > 0, where u_A^k,s and u_B^j ,s are stationary states of the units A and B, respectively. Each neural channel composes a familiar perception. This strength of susceptibility of each neural channel represents the effectivity of the familiar. Thus, the totality of neural channels between the units A and B specifies the knowledge already obtained. In such a situation, if there happens to be the same output of the sense organ as one of the preceding ones, the bias output of the unit B through the corresponding channel, say $u_A{}^k \times u_B{}^j$, enforces the units A and B to resonate to the stationary states $u_A{}^k$ and $u_B{}^j$, respectively.

On the other hand, suppose we have a previously unexperienced output from the sense organ. The neural channels representing previously experienced perceptions then heavily bias units A and B, and making them keenly sensitive to the stationary states $u_A{}^k$'s and $u_B{}^j$'s, respectively. We investigate this process from the point of view of the Hilbert space geometry.

First, we notice that the finite number of stationary states $\{u_A{}^k\}_{k=1}^M$ span a finite dimensional subspace of the Hilbert space H_A. Similarly, $\{u_B{}^j\}_{j=1}^M$ span also a finite dimensional subspace of H_B. We denote those subspaces by M_A and M_B, respectively. Then, the state vector ψ_A in the Hilbert space H_A can be decomposed into a form

$$
\begin{aligned}
\psi_A &= \sum_{i=1}^{\infty} \alpha_i u_A{}^i \\
&= \sum_{i=1}^{M} \alpha_i u_A{}^i + \sum_{i=M+1}^{\infty} \alpha_i u_A{}^i \\
&= \psi_A' + \psi_A''
\end{aligned}
$$

Here, ψ_A' and ψ_A'' are components of the state vector ψ_A lying in and orthogonal to the finite dimensional subspace M_A. The neural channels between the units A and B biases the unit A so that the component ψ_A' in M_A is easily accomplished but the other one ψ_A'' orthogonal to M_A is not. This is because of the absence of neural channels biasing the state vectors $u_A{}^i$ for $i > M$.

Consequently, this inference process makes the system A and B resonate to the stationary states $\{u_A{}^k\}_{k=1}^M$ and $\{u_B{}^j\}_{j=1}^M$ with probability $|\alpha_k|^2$ for $k = 1,2,\cdots,M$. In other words, the temporary stability in the units A and B of the novel input from the sense organ becomes related to the finite number of stationary states which represent prior experiences. Such a relation to prior experience then drives the neural channel.

11.2. INFERENCE AS THE METHOD OF LEAST SQUARES

It seems surprising that the present mathematical model of the inference process realizes a mechanism of inference similar to that known as method of least-squares in probability theory.

Notice that the state vector ψ_A' is the best estimate of the state vector ψ_A in a sense that ψ_A' is closest to ψ_A within the learned "knowledge" described by the finite dimensional subspace M_A. In the terminology of statistical modeling, the finite dimensional subspace M_A is an estimation space and its orthogonal complement is an error space. The orthogonal projections ψ'_A of the state vector ψ_A onto the estimation space M_A is nothing but a least squares estimator.

Such an inference process takes place when a novel input from the sense organ modifies the state vector of the unit A. However, if this novel input continues for a longer period, the bias effect of the neural channels of the familiarized outputs becomes less dominant and a new neural channel will be made which reflects the orthogonal component ψ''_A. Then, this unfamiliar input from the sense organ comes to be stored in the new neural channel between units A and B. The inference process thus has a procedure for enlarging the scope of inference.

12. TOWARD A MODEL OF NARRATIVE PROCESSING

Whenever values are to be assigned to a process in a quantitative fashion, two attributes must be present: a reference and a unit of incrementation (Pribram, 1960, Sommerhoff, 1974; von Neumann & Morgenstern, 1953). For instance, if we wish to describe the amount of heat in terms of temperature, we need a reference such as that provided by phase changes of water (the freezing and boiling points at appropriate atmospheric pressure), and also a unit of incrementation such as the degree Celsius that divides the range between the freezing and boiling points into 100 equal units (centigrades). For the model of narrative proposed here, an episode within which familiarity is achieved can serve as the reference. The reference is demarcated by a destabilizing interrupt of prior ongoing processing (an orienting reaction) and ends with the next interrupt, which initiates a different processing episode. As reviewed, there is considerable evidence that the amygdala system is integral to this type of processing.

The manner in which the stabilities far from equilibrium are constituted after a destabilizing input has occurred was detailed earlier in the chapter. There, restabilization was achieved by the addition of random "noise". However, another alternative is provided by frontal lobe control over the process: a catastrophic reaction may be circumvented. Control is exercised by using equivocation, the sum of noise and redundancy. This option is provided by redundancies that enhance coherence and therefore constitute "structured" entropy, that is, potential information (Gatlin, 1972; Shannon & Weaver, 1949). The system of eigenvectors in Hilbert space describes the neural nature of this entropic structure.

Under this option, practical inference is exercised to achieve and maintain control over the process. Appropriate orderings of priorities among events, i.e., attractors, is achieved.

The unit of incrementation — the outcome, the event — is computed by cross multiplication of episodes (contexts, ensembles of CNOSs) by the achievement of equi-valence. In terms of neurodynamics, channels made up of a system of eigenvectors describing isovalent junctional polarizations would appear considerably different under the condition "mail a letter" from that mapped under the condition "hungry." Different configurations of values would display different hills and valleys on the polarization contour map. A simpler example would be attending to the color or form of a scene: The pattern of isovalent contours produced by receptive fields responding to color and the pattern of such contours responding to form would be different, much as when one asks all those in a classroom to briefly raise their hands if they are wearing a red sweater and then asking those who are wearing glasses to raise their hands.

Thus, the units of incrementation -- the valuations (weightings) of events -- must be measured in terms of the "distances" between hills — attractors — formed by isovalent contours in each system of eigenvectors. The minimum entropy (Gabor's quantum of information — see Pribram, 1991, Lecture 2) for the bandwidth defined by the isovalent contours serves as the unit of measure on these distances. This results in an entropic domain where the distance between (or density of) attractors delineated by isovalent contours is set in terms of the distances between the minimum uncertainty (wells) attainable in each channel.

Hinton and Sejnowski (1986) developed a "hill climbing learning routine" that moves an element in a stepwise manner over such a contoured terrain. Processing proceeds perpendicular to the contours. In their model, "climbing" is actually down the mountain and is accomplished by random steps to the bottom of the mountain, to a well, when the "elasticity" of the process contracts the "line of climb" into the shortest path. This "moment of truth" may well describe the attainment of familiarity, the consolidation of an episode in memory (McGaugh, 1966; McGaugh & Hertz, 1972).

Hinton and Sejnowski's model can be usefully modified with respect to learning to discriminate alternatives as reviewed in Pribram, 1991, Lecture 7. The process is described as a matter of sharpening generalization gradients until separation between domains is achieved. The "moment of truth" is when the separation occurs. Hill "climbing" is replaced by a stepwise "steepening" of each gradient - by actually changing the shape of each hill, the generalization gradient, until each domain is clearly distinguished and specified.

In Lecture 5 of *Brain and Perception* (1991) it was shown that in the case object-form constancy, specifying the object-form specifies its object centered space and vice-versa. In a similar fashion, specifying separate domains specifies separate events. Thus, in classifying an object-form as a triangle or as a chair, we specify both the domains of triangles or chairs and the events (outcomes) of perceiving a specific triangle or chair. The question remains as to what mathematical group structure most accurately describes such specifications.

When the sensory systems are stimulated by object-forms that can unambiguously be processed as triangles or chairs, only the temporal lobe systems, (posterior inferotemporal cortex and hippocampus — see *Brain and Perception*, Lectures 7 and 9) need be involved. When, however, sensory input fails to completely specify the event and its domain, the systems of the frontal lobe become involved as has been reviewed here. In such instances coherent proprieties, priorities and practicalities become assigned on the basis of inference, that is, on the basis of prior experience. Prior experience, memory, becomes not just a remembrance of the past but a re-membering of a plausible (coherent) future. A story is constructed, a narrative is born: Once upon a time —— and so they lived happily ever after.

ACKNOWLEDGMENT

To Kunio Yasue who contributed all of the mathematical formulations presented here and in *Brain and Perception*, my deepest gratitude.

REFERENCES

Anderson, J. A. (1970). Two models for memory organization using interactive traces. *Mathematical Biosciences* **8**, 137-160.

Anderson, J. A., & Murphy, G. L. (1986). Psychological concepts in a parallel system. *Physica D* **22**, 318-336.

Anderson, J. A., Silverstein, J. W., Ritz, S. A., & Jones, R. S. (1977). Distinctive features, categorical perception, and probability learning: Some applications of a neural model. *Psychological Review* **84**, 413-447.

Anderson, R. M., Hunt, S. C., VanderStoep, A. & Pribram, K. H. (1976). Object permanency and delayed response as spatial context in monkeys with frontal lesions. *Neuropsychologia* **14**, 481-490.

Ashby, W. R. (1960). *Design for a Brain: The Origin of Adaptive Behaviour* (2nd Ed.). New York: Wiley.

Aubert, H. (1861). Über eine scheinbare Drehung von Objekten bei Neigung des Kopfes nach rechts oder links. *Virchow's Archives* **20**, 381-393.

Bagshaw, M. H., & Benzies, S. (1968). Multiple measures of the orienting reaction and their dissociation after amygdalectomy in monkeys. *Experimental Neurology* **20**, 175-187.

Bagshaw, M. H., & Coppock, H. W. (1968). Galvanic skin response conditioning deficit in amygdalectomized monkeys. *Experimental Neurology* **20**, 188-196.

Bagshaw, M. H., Kimble, D. P., & Pribram, K. H. (1965). The GSR of monkeys during orienting and habituation and after ablation of the amygdala, hippocampus and inferotemporal cortex. *Neuropsychologia* **3**, 111-119.

Bagshaw, M. H., & Pribram, K. H. (1968). Effect of amygdalectomy on stimulus threshold of the monkey. *Experimental Neurology* **20**, 197-202.

Beach, F. A. (1955). The descent of instinct. *Psychological Review* **62**, 401-410.

Bergson, H. (1922/1965). *Duration and Simultaneity*. Indianapolis: Bobbs-Merrill.

Berlyne, D. E. (1969). The development of the concept of attention in psychology. In C. R. Evans & T. B. Mulholland (Eds.), Attention in neurophysiology, (pp. 1-26). New York: Appleton-Century-Crofts.

Bernstein, L. (1976). *The Unanswered Question*. Cambridge, MA: Harvard University Press.

Broadbent, D. E. (1974). Divisions of function and integration. *Neurosciences Study Program III*. Cambridge, MA: MIT Press.

Brody, B. A., & Pribram, K. H. (1978). The role of frontal and parietal cortex in cognitive processing: Tests of spatial and sequence functions. *Brain* **101**, 607-633.

Bucy, P. C. (1944). *The Precentral Motor Cortex*. Chicago: University of Illinois Press.

Carpenter, G. A., & Grossberg, S. (1987). A massively parallel architecture for a self-organizing neural pattern recognition machine. *Computer Vision, Graphics, and Image Processing* **37**, 54-115.

Chomsky, N. (1965). *Aspects of the Theory of Syntax*. Cambridge, MA: MIT Press.

Chow, K. L., & Pribram, K. H. (1956). Cortical projection of the thalamic ventrolateral nuclear group in monkeys. *Journal of Comparative Neurology* **104**, 37-75.

Cooper, L. N. (1984). Neuron learning to network organization. In *M. S. Berger (Ed.), J. C. Maxwell, The Sesquicentennial Symposium* (pp. 41-90). Amsterdam: Elsevier North Holland.

Creutzfeldt, O. D., Kuhnt, U., & Benevento, L. A. (1974). An intracellular analysis of visual cortical neurons to moving stimuli: Responses in a cooperative neuronal network. *Experimental Brain Research* **21**, 251-272.

Deecke, L., Kornhuber, H. H., Long, M., & Schreiber, H. (1985). Timing function of the frontal cortex in sequential motor and learning tasks. *Human Neurobiology* **4**, 143-154.

DeValois, R. L., & DeValois, K. K. (1988). *Spatial Vision* (Oxford Psychology Series No. 14). New York: Oxford University Press.

Douglas, R. J., & Pribram, K. H. (1966). Learning and limbic lesions. *Neuropsychologia* **4**, 197-220.

Douglas, R. J., & Pribram, K. H. (1969). Distraction and habituation in monkeys with limbic lesions. *Journal of Comparative and Physiological Psychology* **69**, 473-480.

Fuller, J. L., Rosvold, H. E., & Pribram, K. H. (1957). The effect of affective and cognitive behavior in the dog of lesions of the pyriform-amygdala-hippocampal complex. *Journal of Comparative and Physiological Psychology* **50**, 89-96.

Fulton, J. F., Pribram, K. H., Stevenson, J. A. F., & Wall, P. (1949). Interrelations between orbital gyrus, insula, temporal tip and anterior cingulate gyrus. *Transactions of the American Neurological Association*, 175-179.

Fuster, J. M. (1988). *The Prefrontal Cortex. Anatomy, Physiology and Neuropsychology of the Frontal Lobe* (2nd ed.). New York: Raven.

Garner, W. R. (1962). *Uncertainty and Structure as Psychological Concepts*. New York: Wiley.

Gatlin, L. (1972). *Information Theory and the Living System*. New York, NY: Columbia University Press.

Grueninger, W. E., & Pribram, K. H. (1969). Effects of spatial and nonspatial distractors on performance latency of monkeys with frontal lesions. *Journal of Comparative and Physiological Psychology* **68**, 203-209.

Halmos, P. R. (1957). *Introduction to Hilbert Space*. New York: Chelsea.

Hearst, E., & Pribram, K. H. (1964a). Facilitation of avoidance behavior by unavoidable shocks in normal and amygdalectomized monkeys. *Psychological Reports* **14**, 39-42.

Hearst, E., & Pribram, K. H. (1964b). Appetitive and aversive generalization gradients in amygdalectomized monkeys. *Journal of Comparative and Physiological Psychology* **58**, 296-298.

Hinton, G. E., & Sejnowski, T. J. (1986). Learning and relearning in Boltzmann machines in parallel distributed processing. In D. E. Rumelhart & J. L. McClelland (Eds.), *Parallel Distributed Processing: Explorations in the Microstructure of Cognition. Vol. I: Foundations* (pp. 282-317). Cambridge, MA: MIT Press.

Kaada, B. R., Pribram, K. H., & Epstein, J. A. (1949). Respiratory and vascular responses in monkeys from temporal pole, insular, orbital surface and cingulate gyrus. *Journal of Neurophysiology* **12**, 347-356.

Kesner, R. P., & DiMattia, B. V. (1987). Neurobiology of an attribute model of memory. In A. N. Epstein & A. Morrison (Eds.), *Progress in Psychobiology and Physiological Psychology*. (Vol. 12, pp. 207-277). New York: Academic Press.

Kimble, D. P., Bagshaw, M. H., & Pribram, K. H. (1965). The GSR of monkeys during orienting and habituation after selective partial ablations of cingulate and frontal cortex. *Neuropsychologia* **3**, 121-128.

Kinsbourne, M., & Wood, F. (1975). Short term memory and pathological forgetting. In: J. A. Deutsch (Ed.), *Short Term Memory*. New York: Academic Press.

Klüver, H., & Bucy, P. C. (1939). Preliminary analysis of functions of the temporal lobes in monkeys. *Archives Neurological Psychiatry* **42**, 979-1000.

Koepke, J. E., & Pribram, K. H. (1967a). Habituation of the vasoconstriction response as a function of stimulus duration and anxiety. *Journal of Comparative and Physiological Psychology* **64**, 502-504.

Koepke, J. E., & Pribram, K. H. (1967b). Effect of food reward on the maintenance of sucking behavior during infancy. *Proceedings of 75th Annual Convention, APA*, 111-112.

Kohonen, T. (1972). Correlation matrix memories. *IEEE Transactions: Computers* **21**, 353-359.

Kohonen, T. (1977). *Associative Memory: A System Theoretic Approach*. Berlin: Springer-Verlag.

Kohonen, T. (1984). *Self-organization and Associative Memory*. Berlin: Springer-Verlag. Reprinted in 1988.

Kuffler, S. W. (1953). Discharge patterns and functional organization of mammalian retina. *Journal of Neurophysiology* **16**, 37-69.

Lassonde, M. C., Ptito, M., & Pribram, K. H. (1981). Intracerebral influences on the microstructure of visual cortex. *Experimental Brain Research* **43**, 131-144.

Licklider, J. C. R. (1951). Basic correlates of the auditory stimulus. In S. S. Stevens (Ed.), *Handbook of Experimental Psychology* (pp. 985-1039). New York: Wiley.

Lorenz, K. (1969). Innate bases of learning. In K. H. Pribram (Ed.), *On the Biology of Learning* (pp. 13-94). New York: Harcourt, Brace & World.

Maffei, L. (1985). Complex cells control simple cells. In D. Rose & V. G. Dobson (Eds.), *Models of the Visual Cortex* (pp. 334-340). New York: Wiley.

Malmo, R. B. (1942). Interference factors in delayed response in monkeys after removal of frontal lobes. *Journal of Neurophysiology* **5**, 295-308.

Malmo, R. B., & Amsel, A. (1948). Anxiety-produced interference in serial rote learning with observations on rote learning after partial frontal lobectomy. *Journal of Experimental Psychology* **38**, 440-454.

McGaugh, J. L. (1966). Time-dependent processes in memory storage. *Science* **153**, 1351-1358.

McGaugh, J. L., & Hertz, M. L. (1972). *Memory Consolidation*. San Francisco: Albion Press.

McGuinness, D., Pribram, K. H., & Pirnazar, M. (1990). Upstaging the stage model. In C. N. Alexander & E. Langer (Eds.), *Beyond Formal Operations: Alternative Endpoints to Human Development*. Oxford: Oxford University Press.

Miller, G. A. (1956). The magical number seven, plus or minus two, or some limits on our capacity for processing information. *Psychological Review* **63**, 81-97.

Miller, G. A., Galanter, E. H., & Pribram, K. H. (1960). *Plans and the Structure of Behavior.* New York: Holt, Rinehart & Winston.

Milner, B. (1974). Hemispheric specialization: Scope and limits. *The Neurosciences* **4**, 75-89.

Mittelstaedt, H. (1987). The subjective vertical as a function of visual and extraretinal cues. *Acta Psychologica* **63**, 63-85.

Murdock, B. B. (1979). Convolution and correlation in perception and memory. In L. G. Nilsson, (Ed.), *Perspectives on Memory Research* (pp. 105-119). Hillsdale, NJ: Lawrence Erlbaum Associates.

Murdock, B. B. (1982). A theory for the storage and retrieval of item and associative information. *Psychological Review* **89**, 609-626.

Murdock, B. B. (1983). A distributed memory model for serial-order information. *Psychological Review* **90**, 316-338.

Murdock, B. B. (1985). Convolution and matrix systems: A reply to Pike. *Psychological Review* **92**, 130-132.

Murdock, B. B., & Lewandowsky, S. (1986). Chaining, one hundred years later. In F. Klix & H. Hagendorf (Eds.), *Human Memory and Cognitive Capabilities: Mechanisms and Performances* (pp. 79-96). Amsterdam: Elsevier.

Ornstein, R. E. (1969). *On the Experience of Time.* Hammondsworth, England: Penguin Education.

Petrides, M., & Milner, B. (1982). Deficits on subject-ordered tasks after frontal-and temporal-lobe lesions in man. *Neuropsychologia* **20**, 249-262.

Piaget, J. (1970). *Structuralism.* New York: Basic Books.

Pike, R. (1984). Comparison of convolution and matrix distributed memory systems for associative recall and recognition. *Psychological Review* **91**, 281-294.

Pribram, K. H. (1954). Toward a science of neuropsychology (method and data). In R. A. Patton (Ed.), *Current Trends in Psychology and the Behavioral Sciences* (pp. 115-142). Pittsburgh: University of Pittsburgh Press.

Pribram, K. H. (1958a). Comparative neurology and the evolution of behavior. In G. G. Simpson (Ed.), *Evolution and Behavior* (pp. 140-164). New Haven, CT: Yale University Press.

Pribram, K. H. (1958b). Neocortical functions in behavior. In H. F. Harlow & C. N. Woolsey (Eds.), *Biological and Biochemical Bases of Behavior* (pp. 151-172). Madison, WI: University of Wisconsin Press.

Pribram, K. H. (1960). The intrinsic systems of the forebrain. In J. Field, H. W. Magoun, & V. E. Hall (Eds.), *Handbook on Physiology, Neurophysiology II* (pp. 1323-1344). Washington, DC: American Physiological Society.

Pribram, K. H. (1961). Limbic system. In D. E. Sheer (Ed.), *Electrical Stimulation of the Brain* (pp. 563-574). Austin, TX: University of Texas Press.

Pribram, K. H. (1969). The neurobehavioral analysis of limbic forebrain mechanisms: Revision and progress report. In D. S. Lehrman, R. A. Hinde, & E. Shaw (Eds.), *Advances in the Study of Behavior* (pp. 297-332). New York: Academic Press.

Pribram, K. H. (1971). *Languages of the Brain: Experimental Paradoxes and Principles in Neuropsychology.* Englewood Cliffs, NJ: Prentice-Hall.

Pribram, K. H. (1980). The orienting reaction: Key to brain representational mechanisms. In H. D. Kimmel (Ed.), *The Orienting Reflex in Humans* (pp. 3-20). Hillsdale, NJ: Lawrence Erlbaum Associates.

Pribram, K. H. (1986). The hippocampal system and recombinant processing. In R. Isaacson & K. H. Pribram (Eds.), *The Hippocampus, Vol. 4* (pp. 329-370). New York: Plenum.

Pribram, K. H. (1987). Subdivisions of the frontal cortex revisited. In E. Brown and E. Perecman (Eds.), *The Frontal Lobes Revisited* (pp. 11-39). IRBN Press.

Pribram, K. H. (1990). The frontal cortex - A Luria/Pribram rapprochement. In G. Goldberg (Ed.), *Contemporary Neuropsychology and the Legacy of Luria*. Hillsdale, NJ: Lawrence Erlbaum Associates.

Pribram, K. H. (1991). *Brain and Perception: Holonomy and Structure in Figural Processing*. Hillsdale, NJ: Lawrence Erlbaum Associates.

Pribram, K. H., & Bagshaw, M. H. (1953). Further analysis of the temporal lobe syndrome utilizing frontotemporal ablations in monkeys. *Journal of Comparative Neurology* **99**, 347-375.

Pribram, K. H., & Carlton, E. H. (1986). Holonomic brain theory in imaging and object perception. *Acta Psychologica* **63**, 175-210.

Pribram, K. H., Douglas, R. J., & Pribram, B. J. (1969). The nature of nonlimbic learning. *Journal of Comparative and Physiological Psychology* **69**, 765-772.

Pribram, K. H., Lassonde, M. C., & Ptito, M. (1981). Classification of receptive field properties. *Experimental Brain Research* **43**, 119-130.

Pribram, K. H., Lim, H., Poppen, R., & Bagshaw, M. H. (1966). Limbic lesions and the temporal structure of redundancy. *Journal of Comparative and Physiological Psychology* **61**, 365-373.

Pribram, K. H., & McGuinness, D. (1975). Arousal, activation and effort in the control of attention. *Psychological Review* **82**, 116-149.

Pribram, K. H., & McGuinness, D. (1982). Commentary on Jeffrey Gray's 'The neuropsychology of anxiety: An enquiry into the functions of the septohippocampal system'. *The Behavioral and Brain Sciences* **5**, 496-498.

Pribram, K. H., Plotkin, H. C., Anderson, R. M., & Leong, D. (1977). Information sources in the delayed alternation task for normal and "frontal" monkeys. *Neuropsychologia* **15**, 329-340.

Pribram, K. H., Reitz, S., McNeil, M., & Spevack, A. A. (1979). The effect of amygdalectomy on orienting and classical conditioning in monkeys. *Pavlovian Journal* **14**, 203-217.

Pribram, K. H., Spinelli, D. N., & Kamback, M. C. (1967). Electrocortical correlates of stimulus response and reinforcement. *Science* **157**, 94-96.

Pribram, K. H., & Tubbs, W. E. (1967). Short-term memory, parsing and the primate frontal cortex. *Science* **156**, 1765-1767.

Prigogine, I. (1980). *From Being to Becoming - Time and Complexity in the Physical Sciences*. San Francisco: Freeman.

Rakic, P. (1976). *Local Circuit Neurons*. Cambridge, MA: MIT Press.

Reichardt, W. E. (1978). Cybernetics of the insect optomotor response. In P. Buser (Ed.), *Cerebral Correlates of Conscious Experience*. Amsterdam: North Holland.

Rock, I. (1983). *The Logic of Perception*. Cambridge, MA: MIT Press.

Rosvold, H. E., Mirsky, A. F., & Pribram, K. H. (1954). Influence of amygdalectomy on social interaction in a monkey group. *Journal of Comparative and Physiological Psychology*, **47**, 173-178.

Russell, R. W., Singer, G., Flanagan, F., Stone, M., & Russell, J. W. (1968). Quantitative relations in amygdala modulation of drinking. *Physiology and Behavior* **3**, 871-875.

Sanger-Brown, & Schaefer, E. A. (1888). An investigation into the functions of the occipital and temporal lobes of the monkey's brain. *Philosophical Transactions of the Royal Society of London* **179**, 303-327.

Schwartzbaum, J. S. (1960). Changes in reinforcing properties of stimuli following ablation of the amygdaloid complex in monkeys. *Journal of Comparative and Physiological Psychology* **53**, 388-396.

Schwartzbaum, J. S., & Pribram, K. H. (1960). The effects of amygdalectomy in monkeys on transposition along a brightness continuum. *Journal of Comparative and Physiological Psychology* **53**, 396-399.

Shannon, C. E., & Weaver, W. (1949). *The Mathematical Theory of Communications*. Urbana, IL: The University of Illinois Press.

Simon, H. (1974). How big is a chunk? *Science* **183**, 482-488.

Simon, H. (1986). The parameters of human memory. In F. Klix & H. Hagendorf (Eds.), *Human Memory and Cognitive Capabilities: Mechanisms and Performances* (pp. 299-309). Amsterdam: Elsevier.

Smets, G. (1973). *Aesthetic Judgment and Arousal*. Leuven, Belgium: Leuven University Press.

Smolensky, P. (1986). Information processing in dynamical systems: Foundations of harmony theory. In D. E. Rumelhart, J. L. McClelland, & the PDP Research Group (Eds.), *Parallel Distributed Processing: Explorations in the Microstructure of Cognition. Vol. I: Foundations* (pp. 194-281). Cambridge, MA: MIT Press.

Sokolov, E. N. (1963). *Perception and the Conditioned Reflex*. New York: MacMillan Publishing.

Sommerhoff, G. (1974). *Logic of the Living Brain*. New York: Wiley.

Spinelli, D. N., & Pribram, K. H. (1967). Changes in visual recovery function and unit activity produced by frontal cortex stimulation. *Electroencephalography and Clinical Neurophysiology* **22**, 143-149.

Stamm, J. S., & Rosen, S. C. (1972). Cortical steady potential shifts and anodal polarization during delayed response performance. *Acta Neurobiologiae Experimentalis* **32**, 193-209.

Stark, L., & Bridgeman, B. (1983). Role of corollary discharge in space constancy. *Perception and Psychophysics* **34**, 371-380.

Teuber, H. L. (1964). The riddle of frontal lobe function in man. In J. M. Warren & K. Akert (Eds.), *The Frontal Granular Cortex and Behavior* (pp. 410-444). New York: McGraw-Hill.

Teuber, H. L., & Mishkin, M. (1954). Judgment of visual and postural vertical after brain injury. *Journal of Psychology* **38**, 61-175.

Tulving, E. (1972). Episodic and semantic memory. In E. Tulving & W. Donaldson (Eds.), *Organization of Memory* (pp. 382-403). New York: Academic Press.

Tulving, E. (1985). On the classification problem in learning and memory. In L. G. Nilsson & T. Archer (Eds.), *Perspectives in Learning and Memory* (pp. 67-91). Hillsdale, NJ: Lawrence Erlbaum Associates.

von Neumann, J., & Morgenstern, O. (1953). *Theory of Games and Economic Behavior*. Princeton: Princeton University Press.

Warrington, E. K., & McCarthy, R. (1983). Category specific access dysphasia. *Brain* 106, 859-878.

Weiskrantz, L. (1956). Behavioral changes associated with ablation of the amygdaloid complex in monkeys. *Journal of Comparative and Physiological Psychology* 49, 381-391.

Wilson, W. H. (1959). The role of learning, perception and reward in monkey's choice of food. *American Journal of Psychology* 72, 560-565.

Witkin, H. A., & Asch, S. E. (1948). Studies in space orientation: IV. Further experiments on perception of the upright with displaced visual fields. *Journal of Experimental Psychology* 38, 762-782.

Yasue, K., Jibu, M., & Pribram, K. H. (1991). Appendices: A theory of nonlocal cortical processing in the brain. In K. H. Pribram, *Brain and Perception: Holonomy and Structure in Figural Processing*. Hillsdale, NJ: Lawrence Erlbaum Associates.

15

Neuroelectric Eigenstructures of Mental Representation

William J. Hudspeth
Neuropsychometric Laboratory, Radford, Virginia

1. INTRODUCTION

The mechanisms of the human visual system organize neural representations for several levels of knowledge, ranging from simple sensations to complex conceptual processes. A number of methods have been used to investigate the neural processes involved in knowledge representation. These methods range from studies of single neuron activities to imaging techniques (i.e., CAT, PET, & MRI) that reveal activities in large cerebral systems. Since the activities of single neurons and large brain systems can be driven by sensory, perceptual and conceptual conditions of experiments, there is clearly some uncertainty as to how and where the human nervous system represents knowledge. This state-of-the-art suggests that the activities obtained from different levels of neuronal organization may not have the same meaning, and some effort may be required to discover how each level (i.e., neuron-to-system) participates in the knowledge representation process. This discovery process can be subsumed within a single question: How would one recognize and substantiate *knowledge processes* in the varied activities that can be obtained from the human brain?

1.1. BRAIN AND BEHAVIORAL RELATIONSHIPS

The roles of different levels of neuronal organization in knowledge representation are relatively well defined when considered from the perspective of clinical and experimental neuropsychology (Luria, 1973, 1980). This body of knowledge shows that the systems of the brain are organized in hierarchical manner that reflects the psychological attributes of knowledge representation and usage. Fig. 15.1 presents a schematic diagram of this hierarchical organization (Hudspeth, 1985). This diagram shows that the cortical systems for sensory and motor representation are each composed of a primary (Fig. 15.1: I Systems) core which provides an object-oriented computational space for extracting modality specific *images*. Further, each primary system is enclosed within a secondary (Fig. 15.1: II Systems) layer that, by virtue of learning experiences, images achieve *object constancy* so that objects can be *classified* according to invariant forms and functions (i.e., categories and equivalences). Each of the secondary layers are conjoined by tertiary association structures (Fig. 15.1: III Systems) which assure that sensory specific categories will have equivalent meanings (e.g., reading the word "cat" and hearing the spoken word "cat"). Equally important, the internal core of the limbic system (not shown in Fig. 15.1) provides the organism with basic knowledge of emotions and motives. Thought and behavior are, thus, composed of knowledge of the real world (i.e., from cortical systems I, II & III) and by knowledge of personal emotions/motives (i.e., from the limbic system). The final common strategies for thought and action are coordinated by two well defined compartments of the pre-frontal cortex that have exclusive interconnections with the posterior sensory analyzers (Fig. 15.1: *Fd* System) and the limbic system (Fig. 15.1: *Fo* System), respectively.

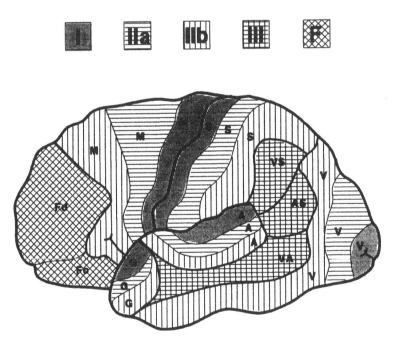

Fig. 15.1. System of cerebral computational compartments which are involved in mental representations. The hierarchical organization is arranged in a top-down manner and designated by the indicated textures for: Frontal (*F*), Tertiary (*III*), Secondary-b (*IIb*), Secondary-a (*IIa*) and Primary (*I*) functions. The primary and secondary functions apply to the sensory and motor processes such as Vision (*V*), Audition (*A*), Gustation (*G*) and the Somatic divisions. The Somatosensory division is partitioned into predominantly Motor (*M*) and Somatosensory (*S*) compartments. Tertiary cross-modal processes are represented by regions within which the principal sensory systems interact: Visuospatial (*VS*), Visuoauditory (*VA*) and Acousticosomatic (*AS*). The frontal executive functions are interconnected to all other systems in a manner that the sensory and motor systems can be regulated by the balance between personal knowledge (*Fd*) and feelings (*Fo*). (From Hudspeth, 1985).

1.2. STRUCTURE OF KNOWLEDGE PROCESSES

Knowledge processes represent an organism's attempt to *interpret* the identity of objects and events that occur in the internal and external world. The ability to extract reliable and invariant interpretations of the dynamic environment is essential for the survival and successful adaptation of the individual organism. This ability depends upon both genetic and experiential factors that begin with conception and are then continually refined over decades of life.

One source of evidence for the structure of knowledge can be found, for example, in the stages of cognitive maturation as described by Jean Piaget (1963), and subsequently extended by several other workers (Case, 1992; Stuss, 1992; Vandermaas & Molenaar, 1992; and van Geert 1991). Several recent studies of brain electrical activities show that the maturation of the regional brain systems, as shown in Fig. 15.1, coincide with the stages of cognitive maturation originally set forth in Piaget's work, and in the aforementioned Neo-Piagetian studies (Hudspeth, 1985, 1987; Hudspeth & Pribram, 1990, 1992; Thatcher, Walker & Guidice, 1987, and Thatcher, 1991). Therefore, it can seen that the study of electrical activities arising from the brain's computational compartments can provide substantial information about the neurobiological organization of knowledge representation in the human brain.

A second source of evidence for the structure of knowledge may be found in detailed investigations of the nature of *mental* representation within the brain's computational systems. In mathematical psychology, for example, mental representations are defined by the quantitative relationships among different categories of experience (Shepard & Chipman, 1970; Shepard, 1975, 1978; Shepard, Kilpatric & Cunningham, 1975). This approach assumes that human experience and knowledge is multidimensional in nature and can be represented by vector subspaces within an n-dimensional geometry. This notion is consistent with a traditional structural definition of human knowledge which is based upon a taxonomy of exemplars, classes, categories, and hierarchies.

1.3. BRAIN ELECTRICAL ACTIVITIES

The human electroencephalogram (EEG) is a record of spontaneous potential (SPs) oscillations that can be readily obtained from a resting subject using scalp electrodes. When external stimuli are presented to attentive subjects, time-locked evoked potentials (EPs) appear in the SP, such that the obtained recordings contain both SP and EP waveshape components.

From 1985 to 1988, my students (Joel Alexander and Chris Ludwig) and I carried out detailed investigations on the structural analysis of the human electroencephalogram, using both SP and EP waveforms. Although the methods we used have been applied by other workers, the approach and design of our experiments were sufficiently unique that it seems likely that we may have discovered a basic principle by which the EEG represents the computational *compartments* of the brain (as in Fig. 15.1) and, as well, the computational *operations* by which those compartments make knowledge representation possible. It will be shown that this basic principle provides nearly perfect *a priori* predictions for the outcome of EEG investigations using either SP or EP waveforms. This primary principle can be stated in the following manner:

Hypothesis: The EEG (SP or EP) waveform is a linear combination of N orthogonal basis waveforms (eigenvectors) which are sufficient in number to span an N-dimensional attribute space composed of K forcing agents (exemplars).

2. FUNCTIONAL ARCHITECTURE OF NEUROELECTRIC POTENTIALS

Neuroanatomists describe the brain's functional compartments and fiber connections by means of exquisitely stained histological sections that reveal an integrated system which is designed to achieve the smooth coordination of functionally distinct activities. By tradition, these neurohistological details are represented on 3 anatomical planes (horizontal (top); sagittal (side) and coronal (front)), so that each perspective can index the relative position of each functional compartment and their interconnections within a 3-dimensional space. It is important to note that highly related functional compartments are connected by means of short-distance horizontal fibers, and conversely, that relatively unrelated functional compartments are integrated by means of long-distance fiber connections. Therefore, it seems likely that the SP waveforms obtained from multichannel EEG recordings from the entire cerebral surface would reflect both the uniqueness of different functional compartments, and as well, their integration by means of short and long distance connections.

To test this proposition, we implemented the primary hypothesis, noted above, in the following way: A.) We defined the number of attribute dimensions as $N=3$, so as to span the cortical surface in a way that would encompass the horizontal, sagittal and coronal boundaries within which all of the computational compartments are confined; and B.) We defined the number of forcing agents as $K=19$, equal to the number of functional compartments, as represented by samples of SP waveforms obtained from 19 recording electrodes (exemplars) on the scalp surface.

We obtained multichannel ($K = 19$) SP waveforms (1 minute recordings) from 25 subjects, with two replications from each subject. We then computed all combinations of similarities and differences (using correlation coefficients) among the $K = 19$ SP waveform recordings to produce a triangular correlation matrix for each subject and replication. The correlation matrices were factored with principal components analysis to obtain 3 eigenvectors (basis waveshapes) and the weighting coefficients required to project each of the $K = 19$ electrodes into a 3-dimensional geometric representation of the cortical surface. On the average, these analyses accounted for 85% of the covariation among the 19 SP waveforms obtained from each subject and replication.

Fig. 15.2 shows the averaged coefficients for 50 SP recordings. As can be seen, the 19 electrodes are positioned in 3-dimensional space at the approximate locations recording electrodes are positioned on the scalp. The contour mappings on the bottom, side and rear panels (e.g., horizontal, sagittal and coronal planes, respectively) reveal functional nonlinearities (i.e., inequalities in electrode distances) that can reliably be manipulated by opening and closing the subject's eyes (Hudspeth, Alexander & Garrett, 1993; Hudspeth, 1993a). These findings show that multichannel SP waveforms can be encompassed by 3 basis waveforms that account for the overall integration of the functional compartments of the cerebral cortex. The findings also reveal that individual electrodes are positioned within this integrated system according to the similarities and differences among the multichannel SP waveforms, in such a way as to index their membership with specific cortical functions. Despite subtle individual differences in SP waveforms, the results obtained with these structural coefficients are virtually predictable across subjects, except in cases of neuropathology.

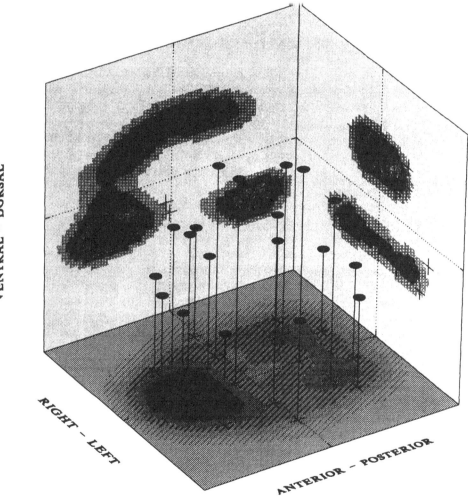

Fig. 15.2. Present a 3-dimensional mapping of the functional architecture of the spontaneous EEG. The distribution of recording electrodes is based upon three basis waveforms extracted from a 19-channel recording of spontaneous EEG activity by means of principal components analysis. The exact position of each electrode is determined by the weighting coefficients for the three PCA components. The gradient mappings on the base, side and rear walls index the density of electrode clustering on the horizontal, sagittal and coronal planes. Individual electrode positions are indicated by plus (+) signs. (From: Hudspeth, 1993a; Hudspeth, Alexander & Garrett, 1993).

Finally, it is clear that a number of analytic methods could be used to compute structural inter-electrode distances (e.g., coefficients) within a 3-dimensional space. However, in one way another, all of these methods converge on a common source - the outcome is based upon similarities and differences in multichannel SP waveforms which can ultimately be reduced to a small and predictable number of basis waveforms. Therefore, our findings with respect to spontaneous (SP) EEG waveforms provide exceptionally robust support for the primary hypothesis advanced above.

3. KNOWLEDGE REPRESENTATION IN NEUROELECTRIC POTENTIALS

The human ability to formulate concepts provides the basic foundation for most forms of cognitive representation. To achieve higher forms of symbolic representation, an individual must learn to suppress impulsive responses to the concrete aspects of reality, and to mentally transform stimuli, signs or symbols into meaningful equivalents for the real or symbolic world. This ability accrues with age and it changes in qualitative character with each stage of cognitive maturation. For Jean Piaget, such transformations constituted the essential core of human intelligence. Therefore, it is important to ask: How does one go about the task of demonstrating conceptual abilities in particular individuals?

If this question was posed to a clinical psychologist, the answer would be quite straightforward: Simply administer any one of a number of intelligence tests that contain a variety of conceptual problems. However, the results of such testing would not lead an understanding of the knowledge representation process. On the other hand, if this question was posed to a mathematical psychologist, the answer could be formulated in a structural manner that allows different perceptual and conceptual (i.e., stimulus) attributes to be related to each other by means of similarities and differences in their meanings. Such formulations are equations by which the elements of knowledge can be represented in classes, categories, and hierarchies. Therefore, the neurophysiological studies in my laboratory have been directed toward this second form of conceptual representation.

Studies of the evoked, or event-related, potential (EP) have been related to all levels of brain function, and several reviews provide substantial evidence for the richness of this method (Regan, 1972; Hillyard, Picton & Regan, 1978; Hillyard & Picton, 1979; John & Schwartz, 1978; Boddy, 1985). These reviews show that there are two general perspectives in the use and interpretation of the EP. These perspectives can be differentiated according to the basic indices extracted from the EP for analysis and inference.

While the EP is a complex waveform of 0.5 to 1.0 sec duration, a number of workers have found that single voltage peaks, confined to specific time-latencies (i.e., the P300), are strongly influenced by general states related to cognitive functions, such as attention, selective attention and certainty-uncertainty. It is important to identify the unit of measurement used in such studies, because the conclusions that can be drawn from these investigations are limited. For example, if a human observer's selective attention covaries with the relative amplitude of the P300 component of the EP waveform, inferences concerning selective attention can only vary along a unidimensional vector. Therefore, it can be seen that single peak components of the EP do not provide inferences concerning classes, categories, or hierarchies that are inherently multidimensional in their structure.

The second perspective is composed of EP studies which are based upon the analysis of complete EP waveforms that can provide a dimensionality of $N > 1$. Of particular interest here, are those studies which show that EPs have similar waveforms when the evoking stimuli have similar interpretations, and conversely, that EPs have dissimilar waveforms when the evoking stimuli have dissimilar interpretations (John, Harrington & Sutton, 1967; John, 1977; Johnston & Chesney, 1974; Begleiter & Porjesz, 1975; Begleiter, Porjesz & Garozzo, 1979; Shelburne, 1970, Duchsbaum, Coppola & Bittker, 1974; Teyler, Roemer, Harrison & Thompson, 1973; Roemer & Teyler, 1977). Such findings imply that mental representations, as reflected in neuroelectric signals, could be accomplished by means of neuroanatomical computations that entail eigenfunctions, as proposed in the primary hypothesis above.

3.1. MODELS OF MENTAL REPRESENTATION

Throughout this chapter, I have carefully applied the terms *similar* (-ities) and *dissimilar* (-ities) because they provide the means with which to develop formal *a priori* predictions concerning the cerebral generation of both SP and EP waveforms. Just as mathematical psychologists use *conjoint* similarities and dissimilarities to describe the structures of mental representation at the behavioral level, it seems likely also that the neurobiological processes of mental representation could be revealed by means of the same strategies. The studies presented below show that the *a priori* prediction of EP waveforms depends upon the application of *conjoint* similarities-differences, both in the selection of stimulus attributes and in the analysis of the resulting EP waveforms.

We implemented this strategy by selecting stimulus attributes in such a way as to construct what we call an *orthogonal stimulus set*, which was then followed by an appropriate analysis that was designed to recover the orthogonalized stimulus attributes within the resulting EP waveforms for each stimulus set, as a whole. In the two examples presented below, each stimulus set contained four stimuli, and each of the four stimuli was composed of two independent attribute dimensions. Figs. 3 and 4 present these examples as a matrix of stimulus attributes (Figs. 15.3A & 15.4A) and in the form of an *a priori* predictor model (Figs. 3B & 4B).

Fig. 15.3A presents a stimulus matrix for a form-color classification (Hudspeth, 1993). As may be seen, the form dimension is composed of two exemplars — circles and triangles. Similarly, the color dimension is composed of two exemplars — red and green. It follows, therefore, that each stimulus is composed as 50%-form and 50%-color. As with any 2x2 matrix of fully nested attributes, the column means (i.e., C1 & C2) are expected to reflect the unitary influence of the color attributes, green and red, respectively. Similarly, the row means (i.e., F1 & F2) are expected to reflect the unitary influence of the form attributes, circle and triangle, respectively. Finally, the grand mean (i.e., CF) is expected to reflect the only common attribute which is shared among the four stimuli, which, by definition, should not contain form or color information. The stimulus matrix can be translated into an *a priori* prediction model by considering the proportion of variance each attribute contributes to each of the cells in the stimulus matrix. As can be seen in Fig. 15.3B, the distribution of attributes among the cells of the stimulus matrix can be represented by the sines and cosines of a unit-circle, and by noting that the squared sines and cosines are proportions. Since the grand mean (i.e., CF) of the stimulus matrix contains none of the form-color attributes, it represents the origin of the unit-circle, set at x = 0, y = 0.

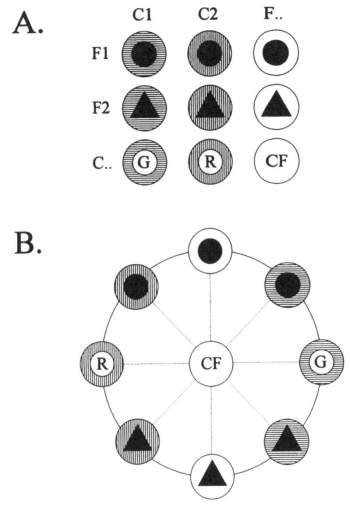

Fig. 15.3. Fig. 15.3A presents the orthogonal stimulus matrix used in the form-color classification experiment. Form attributes are identified with the appropriate form shapes. Color attributes are identified with background hatching, where green colors have horizontal background lines and red colors have vertical background lines. The column and row means are indexed according to the same form and color graphing keys. Fig. 15.3B shows the *a priori* predictor model by which the form and color features of the stimulus set were positioned on the circumference of a unit-circle. A sine-cosine list specifies the position of each stimulus on the X (color) and Y (form) dimensions. The squared sines and cosines can also be used to estimate the proportion of variance each attribute contributes to the stimuli in the set (From: Hudspeth, 1993a, 1993b).

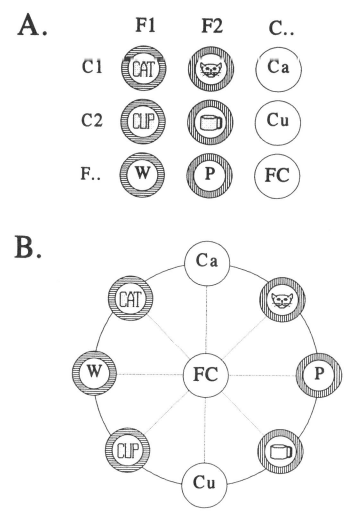

Fig. 15.4. Fig. 15.4A presents the orthogonal stimulus matrix used in the concept-format classification experiment. Concept attributes are identified by the cat and cup stimuli used. Format attributes are identified by the actual word and picture stimuli used. All word stimuli (W) have a horizontal line background and all picture (P) stimuli have a vertical line background. The concepts of cat (Ca) and cup (Cu) are identified by the letter symbols Ca and Cu, respectively. Fig. 15.4B shows the *a priori* predictor model by which the concept and format features of the stimulus set were positioned on the circumference of a unit-circle. In this case the stimuli are numbered: 1 - cat mean, 2 - picture cat, 3 - picture mean, 4 - picture cup, 5 - cup mean, 6 - word cup, 7 - word mean and 8 - word cat. A sine-cosine list specifies the position of each stimulus on the X (format) and Y (concept) dimensions. The squared sines and cosines can also be used to estimate the proportion of variance each attribute contributes to the stimuli in the set (From: Hudspeth, 1993a; Hudspeth & Alexander, 1993).

Fig. 15.4A presents a stimulus matrix for an object concept-symbol format classification (Hudspeth & Alexander, 1993). As may be seen, the object concept dimension is composed of two exemplars — cat and cup. Similarly, the symbol format dimension is composed of two exemplars — word and picture. It follows, therefore, that each stimulus is composed as 50%-object concept and 50%-symbol format. As with any 2×2 matrix of fully nested attributes, the column means (i.e., F1 & F2) are expected to reflect the unitary influence of the format attributes, word and picture, respectively. Similarly, the row means (i.e., C1 & C2) are expected to reflect the unitary influence of the concept attributes, cat and cup, respectively. Finally, the grand mean (i.e., FC) is expected to reflect the only common attribute which is shared among the four stimuli, which, by definition, should not contain format or concept information. This stimulus matrix can be translated into an *a priori* prediction model by means of the same transformations described in the case of the form-color classification above (e.g., Fig. 15.3B).

3.2. ANALYTIC COMPUTATION OF EP BASIS WAVEFORMS

We obtained visual EP waveforms from normal subjects while they were comfortably seated in a quiet darkened room. EP waveform recordings were synchronized with stimulus presentations on a computer CRT monitor so that the EP waveforms would contain information about the evoking stimuli. Two different groups of subjects served in the form-color and concept-format studies (i.e., Figs. 3 & 4), respectively, and the details of our procedure can be found in other works (Hudspeth, 1993). The EP waveforms for each stimulus set were carefully edited by visual inspection to delete data with muscle or movement artifacts from further analysis. Our analyses were focused upon the changes in EP waveforms at each recording location on the scalp so that we could describe the characteristic computations within each cortical compartment. To achieve this end, we constructed data files that contained eight (8) EP waveforms so as to represent each cell of the stimulus matrix (i.e., Figs. 3A & 4A) and position on the unit-circle predictor model (i.e., Figs. 15.3B & 15.4B).

Principal components analysis (PCA) was used to compute and weight N orthogonal basis waveforms for each EP data file. This method allowed us to determine the exact composition of each of the 8 EP waveforms (i.e., representing the stimulus matrix) as a linear combination of the resulting basis waveforms (eigenvectors). The results of PCA analyses for the two experiments provide robust support for the primary hypothesis presented earlier.

Fig. 15.5 presents PCA results from the form-color classification experiment (i.e., green circle, green triangle, red circle, red triangle), consisting of the averaged EP waveforms obtained from the right parietal electrode in eight normal subjects (Hudspeth, 1993). The first column of Fig. 15.5A shows the averaged EP waveforms obtained for each position of the unit-circle (e.g., Clockwise from 0°: CM, GC, GM, GT, TM, RT, RM, RC). These EP waveforms can be decomposed into a linear combination of three basis waveforms (i.e., components 1, 2 & 3). The first basis waveform (Column 2, Component 1), accounts for a common feature in all 8 EP waveforms, which is due to a common forcing agent — the photic energy used to present the stimulus information on a CRT screen. For this reason, Component 1 is frequently called the *exogenous* EP waveform component. It can be seen that Component 1 does not provide information about attributes embedded in the stimulus set (i.e., form or color). The second basis waveshape (Component 2, Column 3) accounts for the *form* forcing agent, such that circle exemplars are composed of basis waveforms having negative weighting coefficients, and triangle exemplars are composed of basis waveforms having positive weighting coefficients. The third basis waveform (Component 3, Column 4) accounts for the *color* forcing agent, such that green exemplars are composed of basis waveforms having negative weighting coefficients, and red exemplars are composed of basis waveforms having positive weighting coefficients. Finally, Column 5 shows that the Residual waveforms contain little if any information (i.e., no more than 0.8%).

Fig. 15.5B sets the stage for a discussion of the cortical computations that are entailed in knowledge or mental representation by summarizing the PCA findings with specific reference to the column and row means of the stimulus matrix (Fig.3A). It will be recalled that we expected the column means (Fig. 15.3A: C1 & C2) would contain only color information, and the row means (Fig. 15.3A: F1 & F2) would contain only form information. Fig 5A verifies these expectations. As can be seen in Fig. 15.5B, circle and triangle EP waveforms vary symmetrically around the exogenous EP waveform component (Column 1), and similarly, green and red EP waveforms vary symmetrically around the exogenous EP waveform (Column 2). Thus, the basis waveforms for form information (Column 3) are simply mirror-images of a single dimensioned waveform vector, and similarly, the basis waveforms for color information (Column 4) are simply mirror-images of an orthogonal waveform vector. All of these findings satisfy the requirements for constructing a *conceptual transfer function*, based upon a unit-circle representation of the EP waveform results obtained from specific stimulus sets.

Fig. 15.7 presents PCA results from the concept-format classification experiment (i.e., word "cat", word "cup", picture cat, picture cup), consisting of the averaged EP waveforms obtained from the right dorso-frontal electrode in a normal subject (Hudspeth & Alexander, 1993). It should be noted here that, when using complex visual stimuli, individual differences in EP waveforms were sufficiently large that signal averaging should not be used. However, once the basis waveshapes and weighting coefficients have been computed, group averages can be obtained as before. The first column of Fig. 15.7A shows the averaged EP waveforms obtained for each position of the unit-circle (e.g., Clockwise from 0°: AM, PA, PM, PU, UM, WU, WM, WA). These EP waveforms can be decomposed into a linear combination of three basis waveforms (i.e., components 1, 2 & 3). The first basis waveform (Column 2, Component 1), accounts for a common feature in all 8 EP waveforms, which is due to the *exogenous* EP waveform component. As before, Component 1 does not provide information about attributes embedded in the stimulus set (i.e., concept or format). The second basis waveshape (Component 2, Column 3) accounts for the *concept* forcing agent, such that cat exemplars are composed of basis waveforms having negative weighting coefficients, and cup exemplars are composed of basis waveforms having positive weighting coefficients. The third basis waveform (Component 3, Column 4) accounts for the *format* forcing agent, such that picture exemplars are composed of basis waveforms having negative weighting coefficients, and word exemplars are composed of basis waveforms having positive weighting coefficients. Finally, Column 5 shows that the Residual waveforms contain a small and insignificant amount of systematic information (i.e., no more than 6.3%).

Fig. 15.7B sets the stage for a discussion of the cortical computations that are entailed in knowledge or mental representation by summarizing the PCA findings with specific reference to the column and row means of the stimulus matrix (Fig.4A). It will be recalled that we expected the column means (Fig. 15.4A: F1 & F2) would contain only format information, and that the row means (Fig. 15.3A: F1 & F2) would contain only concept information. Fig 6A verifies these expectations. As can be seen in Fig. 15.7B, cat and cup EP waveforms vary symmetrically around the exogenous EP waveform component (Column 1), and similarly, picture and word EP waveforms vary symmetrically around the exogenous EP waveform (Column 2). Thus, the basis waveforms for concept information (Column 3) are simply mirror-images of a single dimensioned waveform vector, and similarly, the basis waveforms for format information (Column 4) are simply mirror-images of an orthogonal waveform vector. All of these findings satisfy the requirements for constructing a *conceptual transfer function*, based upon a unit-circle representation of the EP waveform results obtained from specific stimulus sets.

3.3. CORTICAL COMPUTATION OF BASIS WAVEFORMS

In an effort to avoid any form of analytic solipsism, we have analyzed our data sets with many different methods. Our preferred analysis, PCA, is only one among a number of analytic methods that could be used to decompose an 8-EP waveform data set into its constituent basis waveforms. However, it will be shown here that the brain appears to use very elegant processes to orthogonalize stimulus attributes in a way that accomplishes conceptual classifications, and that these outcomes (i.e., transfer functions) can be demonstrated with no more analytic power than *addition, subtraction and division*. The key to this analytic power arises from the design of the orthogonal stimulus set and the expected allocation of attribute variances within a stimulus matrix (e.g., Figs. 3A & 4A).

The expected allocation of attribute variance are stated above with respect to the composition of EP waveform averages for the columns and rows of the stimulus matrix. According to the analytic results from PCA, each column of the stimulus matrix is represented by a single EP basis waveform which is simply sign-reversed to reflect the two exemplars on the column dimension. Similarly, each row of the stimulus matrix is represented by an orthogonal basis waveform, which is sign-reversed to reflect the two exemplars on the row dimension. Therefore, it follows that if the EP waveforms for the column and row attributes are averaged (i.e., addition, division) into their respective marginal cells, and the grand mean (e.g., exogenous EP waveform) of the stimulus matrix is removed (i.e., addition, division, subtraction) from the remaining EP waveforms, then the column and row marginal deviation EP (ΔEP) waveforms should reproduce the basis waveforms obtained from the considerably more complex PCA procedure.

Fig. 15.5. Fig. 15.5A presents the results of a principal components analysis (PCA) for the right parietal (P4) electrode in the form-color classification experiment. Column 1 presents the ORIGINAL EP waveforms for the 8 stimulus positions on the unit-circle model: CM - circle mean, GC - green circle, GM - green mean, GT - green triangle, TM - triangle mean, RT - red triangle, RM - red mean and RC - red circle. Column 2 presents Component 1, the exogenous basis waveform for each stimulus position. Column 3 presents Component 2, the form basis waveform for each stimulus position. Column 4 presents Component 3, the color basis waveform, for each stimulus position. Column 5 presents the RESIDUAL waveform which obtains after removal of the first three basis waveforms. Weighting coefficient are presented to the left of each basis and residual waveform

A: MN P4

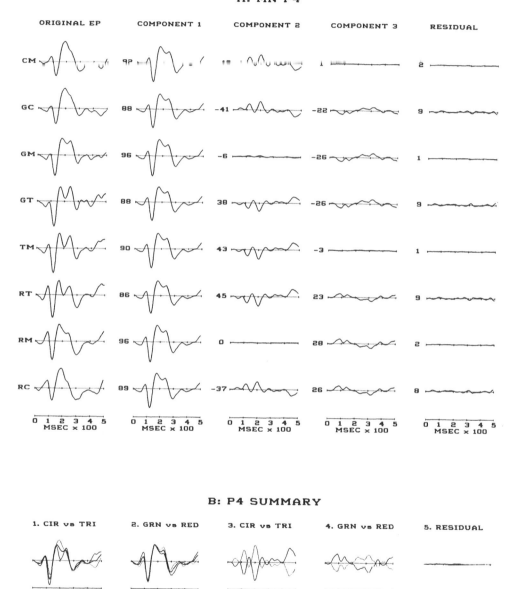

B: P4 SUMMARY

to index the magnitude of the specific basis waveform. The coefficients should be read as C/100 as they were scaled for printing. A 500 millisecond time index is placed under each of the five waveform columns. Fig. 15.5B present a SUMMARY of the PCA findings for the P4 electrode that is formatted for direct comparisons with the calculations shown in Fig. 15.6. The text describes these comparisons. (From Hudspeth, 1993a).

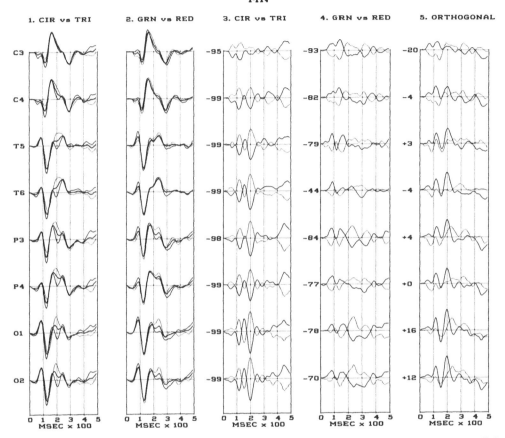

Fig. 15.6. Presents the EP and ΔEP waveforms obtained for the form-color classification experiment. Columns 1 presents the EP waveforms for the circle and triangle means. Note that, at each electrode location, these waveforms deviate symmetrically around the local exogenous EP waveform (shown as a thick line). Similarly, Columns 2 presents the EP waveforms for the green and red means. Note that, at each electrode location, these waveforms also deviate symmetrically around the local exogenous EP waveform (shown as a thick line). When the local exogenous EP waveform was removed, ΔEP waveform-pairs for the form axis and the color axis were nearly identical and sign-inverted. In contrast, ΔEP waveform-pairs for the orthogonal axes were effectively uncorrelated. The sign and magnitude of the squared correlation coefficients (r^2) for each pair of ΔEP waveform is presented to the left of the tracings for each recording location and axis comparison (form, color and orthogonal). *Data Tracings:* Each waveform-pair is composed of dotted and solid line tracings that identify primary features named in each Figure heading. In all cases, the first named feature is the dotted line, and the second named feature is the solid line. *Scaling Factors:* The epoch length of each waveshape was 500 msec, using 100 points with 5 msec/point resolution. The amplitude of all EP waveforms was equated by transformation to a Z-Score scale with a Mean = 0, and σ = 1.0. Please note that the scaling for ΔEP waveforms is twice that of EP waveforms.

We tested this hypothesis with data sets obtained from the form-color classification experiments (Hudspeth, 1993). Fig. 15.6 presents the results of these calculations for the 8 electrode locations from which we obtained data. These findings are presented in the same format as those shown in the Summary of PCA results presented in Fig. 15.5B. For a direct comparison, note the electrode identified as 'P4' in Fig. 15.6. It can be seen that the EP waveforms for circle and triangle in Fig. 15.6 (Column 1) vary symmetrically around the exogenous EP waveshape computed for the CF cell of the stimulus matrix. Similarly, the EP waveforms for green and red in Fig. 15.6 (Column 2) also vary symmetrically around the exogenous EP waveshape. While the EP waveforms for each stimulus are obviously the same as those depicted in Fig. 15.6B, note that the exogenous EP waveform in Fig. 15.6: (CF average) is identical to the exogenous basis waveform (Component 1) obtained from the PCA method. Similarly, the ΔEP waveform-pairs for circle and triangle in Fig. 15.6 (Column 3) are identical in shape and polarity to the second basis waveform (Component 2) obtained from the PCA method (Fig. 15.5B). Finally, the ΔEP waveform-pairs for green and red in Fig. 15.8 (Column 4) are nearly identical in shape and polarity to the third basis waveform (Component 3) obtained from the PCA method (Fig. 15.5B).

Fig. 15.6 shows that the ΔEP waveforms (Columns 3, 4, 5) obtained from all recording locations provide direct evidence that brain systems compute orthogonal eigenfunctions to represent the attribute dimensions and exemplars embodied within an orthogonal stimulus set. Fig. 15.6 presents squared correlation coefficients (i.e., % predictability) printed next to each ΔEP waveform-pair to index the strength of the experimental effects. Column 3 shows that the form dimension contained nearly perfect basis waveform-pairs, with predictabilities of no less than 95%. Column 4 shows that the color dimension contained less well determined basis waveform-pairs, with an average predictability of 75%. Finally, Column 5 presents the averaged ΔEP waveform-pairs for the form and color dimensions which show that the brain orthogonalized the basis waveforms with an average error of 7.3%.

We repeated the same procedures with data sets obtained from the concept-format classification experiments (Hudspeth & Alexander, 1993). Fig. 15.8 presents the results of these calculations for 16 electrode locations. These findings are presented in the same format as those shown in the Summary of PCA results presented in Fig. 15.7B. For a direct comparison, note the electrode identified as "F4" in Fig. 15.7. It can be seen that the EP waveforms for cat and cup in Fig. 15.8 (Column 1) vary symmetrically around the exogenous EP waveshape computed for the FC cell of the stimulus matrix. Similarly, the EP waveforms for picture and word in Fig. 15.8 (Column 2) also vary symmetrically around the exogenous EP waveshape. While the EP waveforms for each stimulus are the same as those depicted in Fig. 15.7B, note that the exogenous EP waveform in Fig. 15.8: (FC average) is identical to the exogenous basis waveform (Component 1) obtained from the PCA method (Fig. 15.7B). Similarly, the ΔEP waveform-pairs for cat and cup in Fig. 15.8 (Column 3) are identical in shape and polarity to the second basis waveform (Component 2) obtained from the PCA method (Fig. 15.7B). Finally, the ΔEP waveform-pairs for picture and word in Fig. 15.8 (Column 4) are identical in shape and polarity to the third basis waveform (Component 3) obtained from the PCA method (Fig. 15.7B).

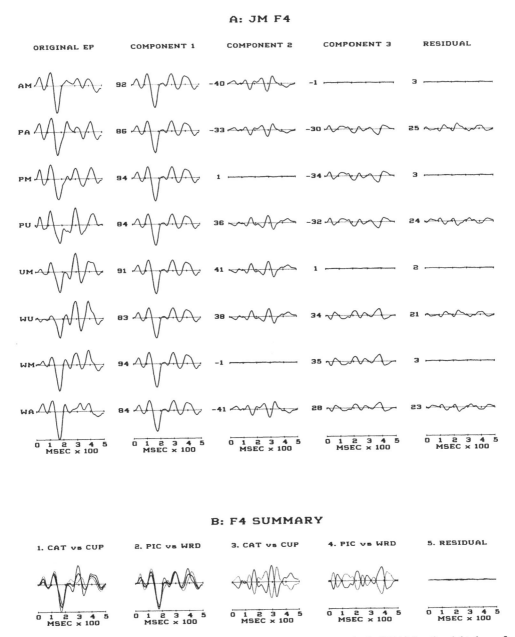

A: JM F4

ORIGINAL EP   COMPONENT 1   COMPONENT 2   COMPONENT 3   RESIDUAL

B: F4 SUMMARY

1. CAT vs CUP   2. PIC vs WRD   3. CAT vs CUP   4. PIC vs WRD   5. RESIDUAL

Fig. 15.7. Fig. 15.7A presents the results of a principal components analysis (PCA) for the right dorso-frontal (F4) electrode in the concept-format classification experiment. Column 1 presents the ORIGINAL EP waveforms for the 8 stimulus positions on the unit-circle model: AM — cat mean, AP — picture cat, PM — picture mean, PU — picture cup, UM — cup mean, UW — word cup, WM — word mean and AW — cat word. Column 2 presents Component 1, the exogenous basis waveform for each stimulus position. Column

Fig. 15.8 shows that the ΔEP waveform-pairs (Columns 3, 4, 5) obtained from all recording locations provide direct evidence that brain systems compute orthogonal eigenfunctions to represent the attribute dimensions and exemplars embodied within an orthogonal stimulus set. Fig. 15.8 presents squared correlation coefficients (i.e., % predictability) printed next to each ΔEP waveform-pair to index the strength and direction of the experimental effects. Column 3 shows that the concept dimension contained nearly perfect basis waveform-pairs, with predictabilities of no less than 90%. Column 4 shows that the format dimension contained slightly less well determined basis waveform-pairs, with an average predictability of 86.6%. Finally, Column 5 presents the averaged basis waveform-pairs for the concept and format dimensions which show that the brain orthogonalized the basis waveforms with an average error of 7.7%.

3.4. NEUROELECTRIC TRANSFER FUNCTIONS FOR CONCEPTUAL CLASSI-FICATIONS

It will be recalled that we modeled these experiments on the methods of mathematical psychology, in which mental representation is defined as the ability of human subjects to co-relate stimulus attributes according to meaningful dimensions embedded within a set of stimuli. Further, the fact that different subjects provide the same behavioral interpretations for a configuration of stimulus attributes can be taken as evidence that the subjects share a common set of meanings which are based upon each subject's mental representations. In much the same manner, we intended to intrude into subject interpretations well before behavioral action was required, so that we could determine whether the brain's neuroelectric behaviors would provide similar interpretations for the configuration of stimulus attributes embodied in the orthogonal stimulus sets we used. Therefore, our experiments can be interpreted in the same manner as behavioral studies of mental representation, with the exception that, in our experiments, the observed interpretations arise from cortical computations. We reasoned that a conceptual transfer function could be defined by the agreement between the *a priori* predictor model (i.e., Figs. 15.3B & 15.4B) and the configuration of the 8 ΔEP basis waveforms that represent an orthogonal stimulus set, as exemplified in the form-color and concept-format experiments.

We computed transfer functions for each recording electrode, based upon the 8 deviation (ΔEP) waveforms used to represent a stimulus matrix. To avoid individual differences in ΔEP waveforms, the transfer functions were determined for each individual subject before estimating group statistics. Again, we used PCA to compute the conjoint similarities and dissimilarities among the 8 ΔEP waveforms to obtain the weighting coefficients needed to project each of the waveforms onto the circumference of a unit-circle. The results of these calculations allowed us

---

3 presents Component 2, the concept basis waveform for each stimulus position. Column 4 presents Component 3, the format basis waveform, for each stimulus position. Column 5 presents the RESIDUAL waveform which obtains after removal of the first three the basis waveforms. Weighting coefficient are presented to the left of each basis and residual waveform to index the magnitude of the specific basis waveform. The coefficients should be read as: C/100 as they were scaled for printing. A 500 millisecond time index is placed under each of the five waveform columns. Fig. 15.5B present a SUMMARY of the PCA findings for the F4 electrode that is formatted for direct comparisons with the calculations shown in Fig. 15.8. The text describes these comparisons. (From: Hudspeth, 1993a; Hudspeth & Alexander, 1993).

to make direct comparisons between the *a priori* model and the observed conceptual transfer functions.

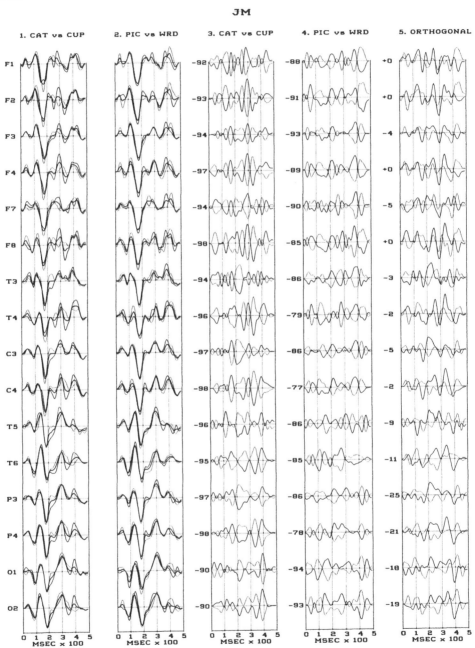

Fig. 15.8. Presents the EP and ΔEP waveforms obtained for the concept-format classification experiment. Columns 1 presents the EP waveforms for the cat and cup means. Note that, at each electrode location, these waveforms deviate symmetrically around the local exogenous EP waveform (shown as a thick line). Similarly,

Fig. 15.9A presents the averaged (N = 8 subjects) transfer functions for the eight recording electrodes used in the form-color classification studies (Hudspeth, 1993). The PCA analyses accounted for more than 83% of the covariance within all of the transfer functions. Fig. 15.9B presents scatter-plots for the observed transfer functions (Y) and the predictive model (X), measured as the angular position (degrees of arc) of each ordered pair (X, Y) on the circumference of a unit-circle. The nonparametric correlations between the predictive model and the observed transfer functions were equal to 1.0 at all electrode positions. We also computed the distribution of angular errors of the observed vectors around their expected angular positions on the unit-circle, and in general, color attributes had a weaker influence on the transfer functions than did the form attributes. These findings also provide robust support for the primary hypothesis with respect to intra-compartmental computations which are based upon EP waveforms.

Fig. 15.10 presents the averaged (N = 12 right handed subjects) transfer functions for the 16 recording electrodes used in the concept-format classification studies (Hudspeth & Alexander, 1993). The PCA analyses accounted for an average of better than 80% of the covariance within each transfer function, and the texture gradients shown in Fig. 15.10 describe the averaged regional differences in the observed cumulative eigenvalues. The nonparametric correlations between the predictive model and the observed transfer functions were equal to 1.0 at all electrode positions. These findings also provide robust support for the primary hypothesis with respect to intra-compartmental computations which are based upon EP waveforms.

4. DISCUSSION

4.1. SURVEY OF FINDINGS

This review of investigations from our laboratory has shown that spontaneous (SP) and evoked (EP) neuroelectric signals can be used to address a number of issues in cognitive neuroscience. For example, this review has shown that the age-dependent changes in SP waveforms obtained from different computational systems are highly correlated with a general

---

Columns 2 presents the EP waveforms for the picture and word means. Note that, at each electrode location, these waveforms also deviate symmetrically around the local exogenous EP waveform (shown as a thick line). When the local exogenous EP waveform was removed, ΔEP waveform-pairs for the concept axis and the format axis were nearly identical and sign-inverted. In contrast, ΔEP waveform-pairs for the orthogonal axes were effectively uncorrelated. The sign and magnitude of the squared correlation coefficients (r^2) for each pair of ΔEP waveform is presented to the left of the tracings for each recording location and axis comparison (concept, format and orthogonal). *Data Tracings:* Each waveform-pair is composed of dotted and solid line tracings that identify primary features named in each Figure heading. In all cases, the first named feature is the dotted line, and the second named feature is the solid line. *Scaling Factors:* The epoch length of each waveshape was 500 msec, using 100 points with 5 msec/point resolution. The amplitude of all EP waveforms was equated by transformation to a Z-Score scale with a Mean = 0, and σ = 1.0. Please note that the scaling for ΔEP waveforms is twice that of EP waveforms. (From: Hudspeth, 1993a; Hudspeth & Alexander, 1993).

model of cognitive maturation. Further, this review has shown that the functional integration of different computational systems can be reliably predicted from the organization of neuroanatomical systems by means of 3-basis waveform vectors extracted from multichannel SP waveforms. Finally, this review has shown that EP waveforms provide transfer functions for perceptual and conceptual classifications by means of orthogonal basis waveforms which arise within different computational systems.

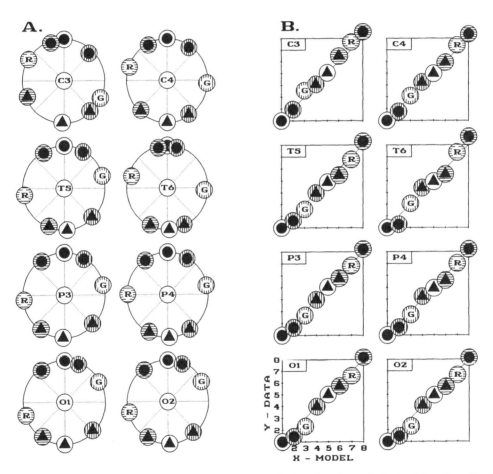

Fig. 15.9. Presents a graphic analysis of the form-color transfer functions for each electrode location. Fig. 15.8A presents the observed output transfer functions for each electrode location. These results show how well the observed ΔEP data sets reproduce the unit-circle classification. Fig. 15.8B presents scattergrams based upon the *a priori* model (MODEL - X axis) and the averaged transfer functions (DATA = Y axis). *Symbol Key:* circle, triangle, green and red features are represented by the same graphic coding scheme as shown in Fig. 15.3. (From Hudspeth, 1993b).

Taken as a whole, the findings reported here imply that, in a well designed investigation, using a representative set of SP and EP measures, it would be possible to examine a subject's specific cognitive abilities (EP classifications), determine the origin and integration of the computational systems that generate these signals (SP structures), and as well, provide an estimate of the subject's level of cognitive maturation. While we are some distance from this goal, most of the work in my laboratory is directed toward this outcome. What seems most important, is that this approach seems to result in a high level of theoretical and empirical integration as it pertains to the study of neuroelectric signals and functional neuroscience.

4.2. IN SEARCH OF A PROCESS

Of particular interest here are the investigations which were designed to explore the primary hypothesis concerning the generation of neuroelectric basis waveforms that: a.) reveal the global integration of computational systems and b.) provide transfer functions for mental representations within computational systems. Our findings show that the integration of computational systems (SP waveforms) are determined by 3 basis waveforms which account for approximately 85% of the covariation within a multichannel SP recording. While we have intensified our search for additional basis waveforms (or noise), it is nonetheless true that the complexities of a multichannel SP recording are completely (i.e., 85%) reducible to 3-dimensions which have exquisite neuroanatomical accuracy in the horizontal, sagittal and coronal planes, respectively. Therefore, it is reasonable to entertain the hypothesis that the functional systems of the brain comprise a closed (i.e., finite-dimensioned) Hilbert space, which is based upon a finite number of interconnected neuronal generator systems.

Moreover, it is also the case that each neuronal generator system provides, in EP waveforms, the exact number of signed basis waveforms (i.e., is completely reducible) needed to account for the dimensions and exemplars embodied in perceptual and conceptual classifications. Again, I am inclined toward the same hypothesis: first, that mental representations are constructed by means of waveform eigenstructures within a unitary Hilbert space (i.e., neuroanatomical system), and second, that these observed behaviors suggest that major brain systems are *computational* compartments. (For a discussion of Hilbert spaces, see: Hamermesh, 1989; pp. 68-114).

For those who are more comfortable with intracerebral recordings from single and multiple neuron(s), Young and Yamane (1992) have recently shown that macaque anterior inferotemporal cells are able to classify human faces (i.e., photographs) by means of two attribute dimensions that coexist (i.e., a linear combination) in cell discharge patterns, and which are sufficient to uniquely identify 27 different faces. If we concur with traditional mechanisms for generating action potentials, then the underlying slower dendritic potentials may likely behave according to the principles of a Hilbert space.

4.3. IN SEARCH OF A MECHANISM: SAND, LIGHT AND NEURON

It is not entirely satisfying to propose a fairly accurate process by means of which computational systems could accomplish mental representations without some discussion (even speculation) of the neurohistological fabric that might mediate such computations. This discussion is also relevant for efforts to construct realistic neural networks; i.e., able to perform conceptual transformations.

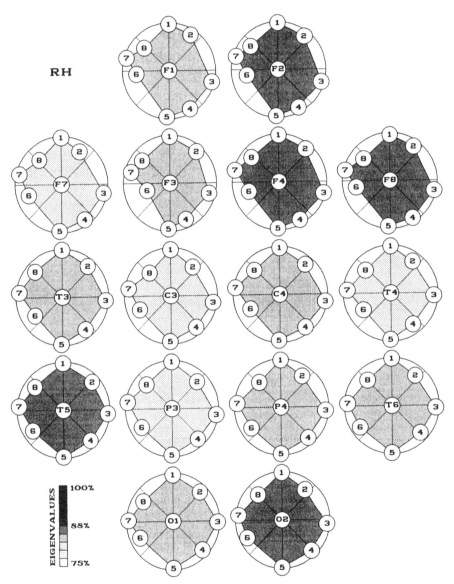

Fig. 15.10. Presents a graphic analysis of the concept-format transfer functions for each electrode location, based upon averages from 12 right handed subjects. The cumulative eigenvalues for each electrode is scale between 75%-100%, and the texture plotted within each of the 16 drawings provides an index for each electrode. *Symbol Key:* cat, cup, picture and word features are represented by the same graphic coding scheme as shown in Fig. 15.4.

Slightly more than fifty years after the psychological sciences were founded, several workers began to recognize fundamental flaws in theories of how the brain represents direct experience and memories of direct experience. Those concerns centered on both the processes and structures needed to accomplish such representations. On one hand, specific experiences and their memories might reside in specific cortical regions. But then, were the storage locations infinite or finite? That could be a problem. On the other hand, specific experiences and their memories could be etched into selective synaptic pathways known as traces. But then, could new traces overwrite older traces? That could be a problem too. With these problems in mind, some workers proposed dynamic (i.e., re-writable) traces (Köhler, 1923). Unfortunately, dynamic traces still posed a serious threat to older traces.

Wheeler and Perkins (1932) were the first workers to implement *interference patterns*, a dynamic non-trace model, for mental representation and memory reconstruction. Further, they assumed that cognitive complexity was based upon brain maturation and differentiation, such that the representational skill of brain systems naturally expanded to encompass new experiences and memories. They employed a mechanical analogy, called Chladni's plate, upon the surface of which a layer of vibrating sand could be made to partition itself according to perturbations with additional vibratory stimuli.

Eighteen years later, Lashley (1950) reported on his 30 year series of experiments in which he removed varying amounts, in varying locations, of the rodent cerebrum, so that he could localize and characterize memory processes. He was conclusive about the fact that, as he removed larger areas of the cortex, memory deficits increased. However, he was unable to find any particular cortical region that was required in memory processes. He concluded that experience and memory might be based upon neuroelectric interference patterns that were widely distributed across the cerebrum, such that memories could be retained in the presence of large cortical lesions. It should be clear that the lissencephalic structure of the rodent cerebrum is not a proper model for the structures and functions of the human brain, and that Lashley's principles may not apply. However, I would want to retain his conclusions regarding neuroelectric interference patterns.

It was not until Gabor's (1946) discovery of the optical hologram that a number of workers recognized a very realistic and life-like instantiation of the interference pattern (Westlake, 1967; Willshaw, Buneman, & Longuet-Higgins, 1969; Van Heerden, 1970; Pribram, 1971, 1991; Hudspeth & Jones, 1975, 1977). The holographic model was appealing because images and memories of images could be distributed across the entire surface of a representational system, and a complete image, albeit of low resolution, could be reconstructed from a small fragment of the representational system and, thus, could sustain the types of lesions Lashley applied to the rodent brain. However, there are substantial difficulties in the neural holographic model. First, an optical hologram *requires* both a linear reconstruction surface and, as well, linear reference and object signals. Neither of these conditions obtain within the computational systems of the brain. Moreover, there are perceptual demonstrations which clearly obviate the existence of neural holograms. First, nearly all introductory psychology textbooks provide a demonstration for locating the eyes' blind-spots, the retinal location from which the optic nerve leaves the eye, and at which, there are no photic receptors. By using monocular vision, the blind-spot can be located at about 7° beyond the point of fixation in the temporal visual field, and nothing can be seen within the region of this very small hole. Similarly, individuals with punctate lesions of the primary striate cortex have a deficit called central blindness, in which the portion of the visual field which is mapped by the injured cortex is experienced as an empty hole. Neither of these exceptions should occur if neural holograms provided the means for mental representation.

While the brain's computational systems are not linear, these surfaces can provide undistorted transformations of sensory input (i.e. images) by means of the neurohistological geometries of cortical mapping surfaces. For example, Schwartz (1980) has provided a detailed description for the geometry of the primary visual cortex. The significant components of this geometry are composed of the striate boundaries and the spatial density of vertical columns and hypercolumns confined within those boundaries. Schwartz characterized the boundaries of the striate system in several mammalian species, and according to his calculations the striate system can, in general, be considered a *simply connected domain*, in which retinal information is preserved by means of conformal transformation. Conformal transformation is significant for cognitive neuroscience because it is a means by which perceptual constancies (invariance with dilation, rotation & translation) can be preserved within a computational domain.

Further, Schwartz estimated the spatial distribution of receptive fields within the striate system. This distribution could be described by a range of receptive field sizes and proximities which are small and dense in the striate representation of the fovea and which increased logarithmically in the striate representation of eccentricity in the peripheral field. This logarithmic function constitutes a gradient of magnification which plays an important role in forming a unitary computational space in which the eigenfunctions of mental representation can obtain. The adjacency of vertically oriented columns and hypercolumns within the striate system provides the means for interactions among the dendritic potentials arising from constituent columnar structures. However, the term "interaction" is far too vague for my intent or comfort. I would rather specify that these interactions are composed of the conjoint similarities-dissimilarities in the dendritic potentials arising from constituent columnar structures. My formulation implies that computational systems have internal correlation and eigenfunction processors, a notion for which there is no immediate evidence.

There may be a more satisfactory and simple solution to this problem. It is well know that columnar structures have unique tuning characteristics (eye, color, spatial frequency, orientation), and it might be expected that their dendritic potentials would reflect this selective characteristic. Dendritic potentials in adjacent columns can be expected to have a partial coherence which is preserved in the algebraic sum of the two potentials. It can be seen that the algebraic sum of similar potentials will preserve the coherent feature, and conversely, the algebraic sum of dissimilar potentials fails to provide a coherent feature. Thus, at any moment in time, the striate mapping system is primarily composed of coherent dendritic potentials that reflect only a selected set of tuning features. However, when a subject's fovea is fixed on a stimulus, the cortical magnification factor (i.e., logarithmic gradient) provides an amplification of coherent dendritic potentials which is proportional to the eccentric position in the visual field. In the region of foveal representation, all of the coherent dendritic potentials are effectively multiplied by means of the algebraic sum of numerous and densely packed receptive fields. This magnification is achieved in much the same manner as the summation of a Fibonacci series, except that here, the distance between elements (i.e., receptive fields) is logarithmic. The complete global mapping of the striate system should now contain a field of magnified coherent dendritic potentials that are based upon a selected set of receptive fields which are driven by the stimulus attributes viewed by the subject. There are two generalizations that follow from this analysis. The first deals with the interpretation of the coherent waveforms and the second deals with the visual image embedded within the mapping function.

If coherent dendritic potentials reflect only the common attribute sources in the visual field, then I am tempted to suggest that these potentials are the basis waveforms from which perceptual and conceptual representations are constructed. In effect, this mapping represents the common cross-products of uniquely tuned features, which is simply a different way to say that the striate system constructed eigenfunctions by means of selective summation and amplification of coherent dendritic waveforms. The EP studies reported in this chapter suggest that this notion could be sound.

Finally, Schwartz (1980) suggests that the visual image is enfolded within the forward Radon transformation of the conformal mapping function, and that the image could be instantiated (i.e., extracted) with an inverse Radon transformation. It is reasonable to believe that these analytic methods could provide valuable information about image formation in the striate system. However, as with other efforts to endow cortical tissues with sophisticated analytic prowess (FFTs, hologram), there is the potential for falling into analytic solipsism. Could these principles be demonstrated in convergent measurements or procedures? Preferably, such measurements need to be made in such a way as to: a.) bridge the distinctions between cells and systems; and b.) apply to the most complex perceptual or conceptual task possible.

REFERENCES

Begleiter, H., & Porjesz, B. (1975). Evoked brain potentials as indicators of decision making. *Science* **187**, 754-755.

Begleiter, H., Porjesz, B., & Garozzo, R. (1979). Visual evoked potentials and affective ratings of semantic stimuli. In H. Begleiter (Ed.), *Evoked Brain Potentials and Behavior*. New York: Plenum Press.

Boddy, J. (1985). Brain event-related potentials in the investigation of language processing. In: D. Papakostopoulos, S. Buttler, & I. Martin (Eds.), *Clinical and Experimental Neuropsychophysiology*. London: Croom Helm.

Buchsbaum, M., Coppola, R., & Bittker, T. E. (1974). Differential effects of congruence, stimulus meaning and information on early and late components of the averaged evoked response. *Neuropsychologia* **12**, 533-545.

Case, R. (1992). Role of the frontal lobes in the regulation of cognitive development. *Brain and Cognition* **20**, 51-73.

Gabor, D. (1946). Theory of communication. *Journal of the Institute of Electrical Engineers* **93**, 429-441.

Hamermesh, M. (1989). *Group Theory and It's Applications to Physical Problems*. New York: Dover.

Hillyard, S. A., Picton, T. W., & Regan, D. (1978). Sensation, perception and attention: Analysis using ERPs. In E. Callaway, P. Tueting, & S. H. Koslow (Eds.), *Event-related Brain Potentials in Man*. New York: Academic Press.

Hillyard, S. A., & Picton, T. W. (1979). Event-related brain potentials and selective information processing in man. In J. E. Desmedt (Ed.), *Progress in Clinical Neurophysiology, Vol. 6, Cognitive Components in Cerebral Event-related Potentials and selective Attention,* J. E. Desmedt (Ed.) Basel: Karger.

Hudspeth, W. J. (1985). Developmental neuropsychology: Functional implications of quantitative EEG maturation [Abs]. *Journal of Clinical and Experimental Neuropsychology* 7, 606.

Hudspeth, W. J. (1987). Symposium on functional neuroscience: Neurophysiological correlates of Piagetian maturation. Meeting of Western Psychological Association, Long Beach, CA.

Hudspeth, W. J. (1990, July). VEPs and dimensions of visual perception. *Proceedings of the Fifth International Congress of Psychophysiology, [abs],* 132.

Hudspeth, W. J. (1993a). Neurocybernetic devices. U. S. Patent and Trademark Office,Washington, DC: Pending.

Hudspeth, W. J. (1993b). Neuroelectric concepts: Form-color classification. *Brain and Cognition* 21, 226-246.

Hudspeth, W. J., & Alexander, J. E. (1993). Neuroelectric concepts: Word-picture classification. Submitted for publication.

Hudspeth, W. J., Alexander, J. E., & Garrett, A. S. (1993). Functional architecture of the human electroencephalogram. Unpublished manuscript.

Hudspeth, W. J., & Jones, G. B. (1975). Stability of neural interference patterns. *Holography in Medicine.* Guilford, England: I.P.C. Science and Technology Press.

Hudspeth, W. J., & Jones, G. B. (1977). Neural models for short-term memory. *Neuropsychologia* 16, 201-212.

Hudspeth, W. J., & Pribram, K. H. (1990). Stages of brain and cognitive maturation. *Journal of Educational Psychology* 82, 880-883.

Hudspeth, W. J. & Pribram, K. H. (1992). Psychophysiological indices of cerebral maturation. *International Journal of Psychophysiology* 12, 19-29.

John, E. R., Harrington, R. N., & Sutton, S. (1967). Effects of visual form on the evoked response. *Science* 155, 1439-1442.

John, E. R. (1977). *Functional Neuroscience (Vol.2): Neurometrics: Clinical Applications of Quantitative Neurophysiology.* Hillsdale, NJ: Lawrence Erlbaum Associates.

John, E. R., & Schwartz, E. L. (1978). The neurophysiology of information processing and cognition. *Annual Review of Psychology* 29, 1-29.

Johnston, V. L., & Chesney, G. L. (1974). Electrophysiological correlates of meaning. *Science* 186, 944-946.

Kohler, W. (1923). Zur theorie des Sukzessivvergleichs und der Zeitfehler. *Psychologie Forschungen* 4, 115-175.

Lashley, K. S. (1950). In search of the engram. *Symposium of the Society of Experimental Biology.* Cambridge, England: Cambridge University Press.

Luria, A. R. (1973). *The Working Brain: Introduction to Neuropsychology.* New York: Basic Books.

Luria, A. R. (1980). *Higher Cortical Functions in Man.* New York: Basic Books.

Piaget, J. (1963). *The Origins of Intelligence in Children.* New York: W. W. Norton & Company.

Pribram, K. H. (1971). *Languages of the Brain: Experimental Paradoxes and Principles in Neuropsychology.* Englewood Cliffs, NJ: Prentice-Hall.

Pribram, K. H. (1991). *Brain and Perception: Holonomy and Structure in Figural Processing.* Hillsdale, NJ: Lawrence Erlbaum Associates.

Regan, D. (1972). *Evoked Potentials in Psychology, Sensory Physiology and Clinical Medicine.* New York: Wiley-Interscience.

Roemer, R. A., & Teyler, T. J. (1977). Auditory evoked potential asymmetries related to word meaning. In J. Desmedt (Ed.), *Progress in Clinical Neurophysiology, Vol. 3. Language and Hemispheric Specialization in Man: Cerebral Event-Related Potentials.* Basel: Karger.

Schwartz, E. L. (1980). Computational anatomy and functional architecture of striate cortex: A spatial mapping approach to perceptual coding. *Vision Research* **20**, 645-669.

Shelburne, S. A., Jr. (1973). Visual evoked response to language stimuli in children With reading disabilities. *Electroencephalography and Clinical Neurophysiology, 34*: 135-143.

Shepard, R. N. & Chipman, S. (1970). Second-order isomorphism of internal representations: Shapes of states. *Cognitive Psychology* **1**, 1-17.

Shepard, R. N. (1975). Form, formation and transformation of internal representations. In: R. Solso (Ed.), *Information Processing and Cognition: The Loyola Symposium.* Hillsdale, NJ: Lawrence Erlbaum Associates.

Shepard, R. N. (1978). The mental image. *American Psychologist* **33**, 125-137.

Shepard, R. N., Kilpatric, D. W., & Cunningham, J. P. (1975). The internal representation of numbers. *Cognitive Psychology* **7**, 82-138.

Stuss, D. T. (1992). Biological and psychological development of executive functions. *Brain and Cognition* **20**, 8-23.

Teyler, T. J., Roemer, R. A., Harrison, T. F., & Thompson, R. F. (1973). Human scalp-recorded evoked-potential correlates of linguistic stimuli. *Bulletin of the Psychonomic Society* **1**, 333-334.

Thatcher, R. W., Walker, R. A., & Guidice, S. (1987). Human cerebral hemispheres develop at different rates and ages. *Science* **236**, 1110-1113.

Thatcher, R. W. (1991). Are rhythms of human cerebral development traveling waves? *Behavioral and Brain Sciences* **14**, 575.

Vandermaas, H. L. J., & Molenaar, P. C. M. (1992). Stage-wise cognitive development: An application of catastrophe theory. *Psychological Review* **99**, 395-417.

van Geert, P. (1991). A dynamic systems model of cognitive and language growth. *Psychological Review* **98**, 3-53.

van Heerden, P. J. (1970). Models of the brain. *Nature* **225**, 177-178.

Westlake, P. R. (1967). Towards a theory of brain functioning: The possibilities of a neural holographic process. *20th Annual Conference on Engineering in Medicine and Biology,* Boston.

Willshaw, D. J., Buneman, O. P., & Longuet-Higgins, H. O. (1969). Nonholographic associative memory. *Nature* **222**, 960-962.

Wheeler, R. H., & Perkins, F. T. (1932). *Principles of Mental Development.* New York: T. Y. Crowell.

Young, M. P., & Yamane, S. (1992). Sparse population coding of faces in the inferotemporal cortex. *Science 256,* 1327-1331.

16

Automatic Versus Controlled Processing in Variable Temporal Context and Stimulus-Response Mapping

Jean Paul Banquet
Boston University and CNRS Paris

Saad El Ouardirhi and Antoine Spinakis
Université Pierre et Marie Curie

Mark J. Smith
Hôpital de la Salpêtrière, Paris

Wilfried Günther
Nervenklinik Bamberg

Automatic versus controlled processing was explored in an experimental situation including a *stimulus-response* (S-R) mapping *reversal* after practice of a *constant mapping* (CM) condition. Then, this control-inducing process was compared to the control required by first learning the task, and also by an increase in the *processing load*.

The purpose of the investigation was not a strict individualization of automatic versus controlled tasks, as in most experiments on this subject. We claim that the level of the task is inappropriate for such an individualization. We rather used the methodology of *event-related potentials* in an attempt
— to tease apart automatic versus controlled *processing stages* inside a task;
— to evaluate the effects of attention-control modulation on these different processing stages.

1. INTRODUCTION

Since Shiffrin and Schneider's experimental characterization of automatic and controlled processes in cognitive tasks (1977), these psychological constructs have encountered diverse fortunes. Automatic processing is supposed to be fast, parallel, capacity free, insensitive to intentionality and inaccessible to consciousness. Conversely, controlled processing is slow, serial, capacity limited, intentionally modulated and can be consciously accessed. Several experimentally testable criteria of control have even been advanced, among them the task dependence on limited resource capacities or on intentionality. Most of the tasks which were first characterized as automatic on the basis of these or similar criteria, such as target visual search in a consistent mapping (CM) condition, the Stroop interference task, semantic priming, and frequency judgment tasks, failed to pass the test of these criteria under more stringent conditions, mostly during interfering dual tasks (Hoffman, 1990).

In spite of an elusive, fuzzy, and possibly ever changing border between these two processing modes, the distinction may still retain some heuristic, operational, and (hopefully) theoretical value. But we must perhaps first acknowledge that a cognitive task is neither fully automatic nor fully controlled, but somewhere in between, on a continuum bounded by these two ideal categories (Banquet, Smith, & Renault, 1990). Furthermore, the task entity could well constitute an inappropriately complex level for the assessment of automaticity or control. Assuming that any task results from several parallel or serial processing stages, it could be that stages become automated, but others remain controlled (Jonides, Naveh-Benjamin, & Palmer, 1985).

The data which founded the conclusions of Schneider and Shiffrin (1976) and Shiffrin and Schneider (1977) resulted from a paradigm using a multiple frame visual search task. The items simultaneously presented on a CRT screen served either as distractors or probes for a variable size memory set, presented before each trial (consisting of 20 successive frames). Automatic processing characteristics typically occurred when subjects had to detect memory set items that were never distractors, that is, in consistent mapping condition (CM). Controlled processing characteristics appeared in situations when memory set items and distractors were interchanged from trial to trial, namely in variable mapping (VM) situations.

Shiffrin and Schneider assume two qualitatively different mechanisms to account for VM and CM results. In VM search, serial comparisons are performed: a given memory item is compared to all displayed items before a switch to the next memory item can occur. Conversely, CM allows a fast automatic encoding of familiar behavioral units. In such a way, controlled processing can then reorganize these units into new chunks or unitized elements. Shiffrin and Schneider further claim that "a mapping of stimuli to an internal detection or attention response can be learned in LTM, during CM search... Thus in LTM an automatic attention response to each target will be learned: the subject can simply wait for the occurrence of one of the learned attention responses... the target is always matched or compared first, before any distractor." They further suggest that unknown and unexpected events are originally matched feature by feature. As automatic processes take over, after repeated presentations, events become eventually matched as new unitary entities or chunks. Several arguments support their view:

1- Automatic search can be learned, but not (or at least not to such an extent) controlled search in VM.

2- The interchange of memory set and distractor set produces substantial negative transfer. This negative transfer is attributed to the learning of an automatic attention response which carries over its effects even after the memory set items are used as distractors.

An alternative, more mechanistic and unified interpretation of the same results is given by Grossberg (1978) in the framework of its theory of STM and LTM. While agreeing on the unitization process during learning, Grossberg emphasizes that the "automatic attention response" in CM condition should not result from a qualitatively different mechanism from the mechanisms operating in VM conditions. The differences are not between serial and parallel processing, which are both present anyway during any information processing. The difference comes from different levels of parallel processing.

Consider VM search: Unfamiliar memory set items are filtered by lower order codes that are available. And eventually a new code or category is created for a new item. Conversely, suppose that the memory set items are familiar. Then, as they are "read-in" from the screen, they are automatically recoded by their *sequential auditory* codes. Here the process of adaptive coding corresponds to the heuristic notion of unitization in terms of Shiffrin and Schneider. Note that in an unfamiliar sequence of familiar items, familiar items are encoded by the old, previously learned visual category codes. Yet, the sequence by itself will generate a new spatial pattern of activity across the STM buffer of sequential auditory codes. This pattern specifically codes serial order in STM. Then, a nonspecific *rehearsal* wave can read the items out of the STM buffer, but one at a time. As such, serial processing mode obtains here. Any given item, once read out of the auditory buffer and translated into its visual code forms a visual *subliminal expectation*. Then, the items of a visual frame can be sampled until a match occurs. A resonant burst of activity from the visual code terminates the search and elicits the behavioral response. If no match occurs, a new rehearsal wave can read out the next item according to either a *primacy*, or *recency* gradient (or both). Readout by nonspecific arousal, even from a serial buffer, is a parallel operation. Nonetheless, this is a VM controlled search, which according to Shiffrin and Schneider (1977) uses only serial processing.

In CM search, repeated use of the same memory set gradually generates a chunk or higher order auditory code. During the read-in, this code can sample the visual codes for all the items over successive trials. When this higher auditory code is activated, in the readout mode, the previously sampled visual codes of *all* memory set items are subliminally activated. Matching with any one of these codes generates a resonant burst. This step can be said to be more parallel than the corresponding step in VM search, where the priming of visual codes occurs serially. In this interpretation, the activated auditory to visual codes and templates differ in VM and CM searches, but the underlying mechanisms are otherwise similar.

Previous experiments (Banquet & Grossberg, 1987; Banquet, Günther, & Smith, 1987; Banquet, Smith, & Günther, 1992) used cognitive learning paradigms involving combined behavioral and electrophysiological indices to monitor: - the progressive automatization of a task, or the emergence of an expectancy as a result of inference processes; - sharp transitions between automatic and controlled modes as a result of mismatch or novel situations. In the experiment reported here, the issue of automaticity, voluntary control and processing load was addressed, using the same methodology but more exhaustive data analysis, with the goal of determining specific structures or at least event related potentials (ERPs) relevant to the different processing modes.

The paradigm presented here can be said to be homologous to the paradigm of Shiffrin and Schneider, but with memory, test and distractor sets all equal to one. We emphasized exploring the attentional control modulation of cognitive processes involved in a discrimination task with a post-learning reversal of target and non-target (or distractor) items, in an otherwise constant mapping condition. Unfortunately, simple global behavioral indices, such as reaction time (RT), are not very illuminating about the individualization of single processing stages or specific modulatory attentional processes. They can only very indirectly account for each step. Conversely, ERPs allow for a natural, even though not always easy, temporospatial segmentation of the processing window in component stages, corresponding to the ERP components. Furthermore different components can be related to different aspects of attention. In such a way, the phasic automatically triggered *orienting reaction* is reflected by a component named N2b. The tonic focal or *selective attention* is expressed by the Processing Negativity component (Näätänen, Simpson, & Loveless, 1982). The more complex incentive-motivational aspect of attention sustaining anticipation-preparation could be related to Contingent Negative Variation (CNV) as suggested by Grossberg (1982b, 1984). In this way it should be possible: — to contrast automatic versus controlled stages combined in a same task, and — to tease apart the respective contributions of the different modes of attention involved in control processes. Thus, the concepts of automaticity and control should not apply to global tasks, but rather be restricted to specific processing stages reflected by specific components.

2. METHODS

2.1. PARADIGM

The failure to individualize fully automatic or controlled tasks (as strictly defined by Schneider & Shiffrin, 1976; Shiffrin, 1988; Shiffrin & Schneider 1977) could result from testing cognitive processes at an inappropriate level. Such an entity as an automatic task could very well have no existence. Conversely, a segmentation of the task into its component stages, could allow the individualization of automatic or controlled stages. Therefore, the paradigm proposed here did not attempt at a strict characterization of automatic versus controlled tasks. Yet, it used the criteria of consistent mapping (CM) and variable mapping (VM) or rather mapping reversal to define experimental conditions in which either automatic or controlled processing modes dominated, compared to the preceding conditions. Multielectrode ERP recordings were used to help segment the task into component processes.

A dual task paradigm comprised an explicit controlled primary task (counting a certain type of stimuli) and a noninterfering implicit secondary task (stimulus sequence probability evaluation), which was not requested by the instructions for the performance of the task. Most of the authors view stimulus probability as an automatically encoded characteristic of the (intermediate term memory) trace (Hasher & Zacks, 1979). Furthermore, the resulting subjective probability seems to affect processing automatically (Banquet & Grossberg, 1987; Banquet et al., 1992; Duncan-Johnson & Donchin, 1977; Johnson, 1988; Johnson & Donchin, 1982). Yet, as for most of the prototypical automatic processes, some experimental evidence suggests that the capacity (Naveh-Benjamin, 1986) and intentionality (Greene, 1984) criteria of automaticity and control are not fully satisfied. But the strict characterization of the processing modality of the task is not crucial here. Only the characterization of some of the experimental conditions as involving a supplementary factor of control compared to others matters. Two noninterfering subtasks, one dominantly controlled, the other dominantly automatic, were independently manipulated as follows.

Low versus high pitch auditory stimuli were delivered binaurally, in three Bernoulli sequences of 150 stimuli each. The subjects' task was to count one or both of the stimuli.

1- During each of the three (150 stimuli) sequence event probability was shifted about every 50 stimuli from .2/.8 to .5/.5 to .8/.2 (or reverse order), while S-R mapping was kept constant for the duration of the sequence.

2- At the onset of the second (150 stimuli) sequence the probability condition was kept the same as it was at the end of the previous sequence. But the S-R mapping reversed such that the previously counted stimulus became uncounted and conversely. While the automatic task was kept constant, a factor of control was introduced in the task by changing the previously practiced S-R relationship. As in the first sequence, the probability shift took place after ~50 and 100 stimuli.

3- At the onset of the third (150 stimuli) sequence, while the probability condition was kept the same as at the end of the previous sequence, subjects were instructed to count both types of stimuli separately. This greatly increased the processing load and difficulty of the task.

4- *Targetness factor* (count versus no-count) was assessed by separate evaluation of counted and uncounted events.

3. DATA

3.1. DATA TYPE

The bulk of experimental data was provided by electrophysiological indices of brain activity named event related potentials (ERPs). These indices are scalp-recorded by noninvasive techniques in humans. Only the endogenous ERPs related to cognitive and motor responses to the above described stimuli were considered.

ERP variations in amplitude, latency and topography were analyzed as a function of the experimental factors. These parametric variations reflect much more accurately than the simple behavioral indices the different information processing stages: encoding, identification, categorization, context updating, inference, preparation, as well as the different modalities of attention. These electrical indices are profitably associated to and correlated with behavioral indices such as reaction time (RT) (Kutas, McCarthy, & Donchin, 1977). Since their discovery (Sutton, Braren, Zubin, & John, 1965), the number of components has continually increased and they have been endowed with diverse functional significances (cf. Banquet et al., 1992, for a survey; Donchin et al., 1978).

The drawbacks of this approach are at least threefold:

1- The amplitude ratio between background spontaneous activity and ERPs is unfavorable to the latter. Fortunately, ERP frequency is in the low range, below the frequency of dominant alpha and ERP onset is time locked to the stimulus onset. Therefore, the two techniques of filtering and averaging were implemented in this work, in order to increase the signal to noise ratio.

2- The amount of information collected, even with a few electrodes, defies the capacities of direct analysis. To cope with this, different methods of data compression and representation have been used. As a first step, we used multidimensional analysis methods that constitute powerful tools for data compression, correlation and classification.

3- Spatiotemporal overlap between the different ERP components makes their individualization difficult. Factorial analysis is also one of the most powerful ways for teasing apart the components originating from different generators.

3.2. DATA COLLECTION AND RECORDING

Fourteen normal subjects (age 25-42) were recorded and twelve of the records were submitted to multidimensional analysis. Each of these records resulted in 18 experimental conditions: 3 probabilities × 2 stimuli × 3 tasks.

ERPs were recorded from 14 electrodes disposed according to a cruciform montage (fronto-occipital longitudinal midline and bitemporal transversal line) complying with international standards and using linked earlobes as reference. Supra and suborbital electrodes located around the right eye monitored ocular movement potentials. This montage allows one to explore anterior and posterior brain poles, as well as the two hemispheres.

The amplified electrical signal was digitized in real time (250 Hz). The signal in the nominal bandpass of the system (.7-150 Hz) was further digitally filtered in the band 0-30 Hz. Trials contaminated by electro-oculogram artifacts were rejected from the analysis.

3.3. DATA ANALYSIS

Different methods of multidimensional analysis have been implemented on the totality of the records. A global correlation between variables (amplitude as a function of time), between items (experimental conditions × electrode locations × subjects), and finally between items and variables was thus possible. The projections of the items and/or variables were performed in a reduced factorial space, making the interpretation of the data more tractable.

Factorial analysis, mostly multidimensional scaling (or Correspondence Analysis (CA)) and Principal Components Analysis (PCA) have been combined with Ascending Hierarchical Classification (AHC), mostly to individualize the ERP components. The common denominator to all these methods is their linearity. Yet, the use of CA on variables suitably partitioned in different modalities, according to their distribution curves, induces a "delinearization" of the problem (Benzécri, 1973). The extensive use of CA in the analysis of these data justifies some elaboration on its peculiarities.

Theoretical foundations of CA can be traced back to R. A. Fisher. Most of the theoretical and practical developments are due to Benzécri (1973) and his group (Lebart & Fénelon, 1973). Hill contributed to the diffusion of the method (1974). CA can be viewed as a particular case of PCA performed on contingency or binary data tables. The chi-square distance, the actual metric of this type of analysis, defines the similarities between either item-profiles or parameter-profiles." It is the only metric which is in agreement with the universal principle of distributional equivalence, based on the symmetry relations that may exist in the data" (Benzécri, 1973). As with other factorial methods, the goal of CA is to define a reduced reference system generated by the eigenvectors derived from the diagonalization of the contingency matrices, in particular. The resulting factorial axes derive from rotation of the original coordinate system into an orientation corresponding to the direction of maximal variance. The reduction in the dimension of the new reference system is gained through taking into account the only factorial axes accounting for a "significant" part of the total variance.

There are several advantages to be gained from CA, compared to more usual factorial methods such as PCA.

1- The analysis of inhomogeneous data sets is made possible after binary codification.

2- Transition formulae allow a rigorous simultaneous scatter configuration, in the same subspace, of statistical items and variables affected of weights which are their conditional frequencies. In this space, the proximity between item points and parameter points has real meaning. Graphs can be interpreted: i- from the viewpoint of items looking for their clustering as a result of similar characteristics; ii- from the viewpoint of the parameters, strongly correlated if close to each other on the graph; this aspect is particularly important in the present analysis since it is one of the bases of the individualization of the ERP components; iii- lastly, by considering the relative position between item- and parameter-points: the item-points with scores important for a given parameter will project, on the factorial plane, in the neighborhood of this parameter point and vice versa. This property allows for an easy characterization of clusters.

3- Even though the method by itself is linear, nonlinear relations between parameters or items can be evidenced due to the segmentation of each variable in different modalities.

4- The components of "supplementary" parameters or items, not participating in the determination of the factorial axes, can be easily computed by using transition formulae. In this respect, factorial axes can be compared to discriminant functions established on a set of data, and later tested on a new set.

5- An advantage of CA specific to this type of ERP data made of positive and negative polarity components results from the transformation of the original continuous variables into discrete modalities. Thus, negative maxima fall into the lower end modalities, while positive maxima fall into the upper end modalities of the variable interval. Combining this information with the known latency of the components, it becomes usually easy to identify a cluster as corresponding to either a positive or negative component. Conversely, this information on the polarity of the components is entirely hidden in a type of analysis such as a PCA performed on covariance or correlation matrices.

For these reasons, and also because multidimensional analysis is particularly suited to untangle the main trends structuring this huge corpus of data, this type of analysis and data compression were performed prior to any attempt to cast the results into more conventional forms such as spatiotemporal maps or graphs.

Yet, another type of ERP information that could even be more relevant to constrain neural network models of cognitive processing is discarded from this work. Provided a sufficient electrode coverage of the scalp, the Laplacian (spatial second derivative) of these electrical potentials computes electrical fields which are reference independent. By solving the inverse problem, these electrical fields can be used for the determination of the most plausible configuration of the electrical generators (modeled as dipoles) of the different ERP components. Specific configurations of brain, skull and other conductive milieux given by brain imaging techniques can be expected to make the configuration even more accurate. These two approaches are complementary. Functional and structural information could in principle cooperate to put constraints on neural network models of the circuits involved in a task. Once more, the importance of the concept of level of analysis in the neurosciences and the complementarity between different levels are emphasized.

4. RESULTS

We do not analyze independently the different factors of the CA analysis. It suffices to say that the first factors, related to the larger eigenvalues, picked up most of the variance related to the different experimental factors. We rather analyze the *factorial planes* in terms of the *clusters* formed by the different temporal variables which are, in most cases, easily related to their corresponding ERP components that have known latency boundaries. We first present general results concerning the organization and the relations between the different components in the window of analysis. Then more specific information will concern the latency, duration, location, and functional significance of the different variable clusters, and therefore corresponding ERP components. The individualization of these clusters resulted from the intersection of the geometrical clusters of CA with the classes of an Ascending Hierarchical Classification (AHC) using the same chi-square distance, thus making more stable and stronger classes.

4.1. GENERAL RESULTS

The first characteristic common to positive and negative ERP components is "*energetic*" in nature. The time-amplitude variables were spread throughout the (first) factorial plane according to a *spiral* centered at the origin of the plane, where the earliest instants of the time window were located. From there it diverged to the periphery of the plane where the latest instants of the time window were located. This organization of the data results from the increase in amplitude and variance of the ERPs as the processing stages proceed from the instant zero of stimulus delivery to the end of the interstimulus interval (ISI). More degrees of freedom become available as information and processing become more complex.

The second general characteristic has to do with *temporal dynamics* of the ERP components. Periods of stability of the ERP activities were manifested as phases where the variables tightly clustered at one single location of the factorial plane, and therefore corresponded to a functionally homogeneous component of the ERP, insofar as factorial axes have a precise functional significance. In this way, it was mathematically possible to disentangle the between-components spatiotemporal overlap, that takes place in a conventional representation of the ERP components. Between these clustering phases of stability, large short-lasting "functional" jumps took place on the factorial planes, corresponding to what could be called *phase transitions* between two functionally stable and different types of activity. It is surprising that these ERP data which are indeed evoked potentials, present the same alternation of stability and transition phases as spectral and coherence data analyzed by the same type of multidimensional techniques, but concerning the spontaneous EEG activity during sleep-waking cycle, in particular during the REM-slow wave sleep phases (Banquet, 1981). There is no way to discard these results as simple artefacts of the method of analysis. These facts could be related to the notions of fixed points and phase transitions in dynamical systems. Certainly, the concept of stability in dynamical systems is not specifically related to slow dynamics. Grossberg (1973) treats STM as going to stable attractors, as a short-time approximation. Yet, at the physiological level a distinction should be made between stable attractors of LTM dynamics and stable attractors of STM dynamics such as the ones captured by ERP components. Alternatively, could these transient stabilities mean unstable attractor points?

4.2. SPECIFIC COMPONENT-RELATED RESULTS

Considering the preponderance of tardive components over the earlier ones, it was necessary to perform both a global analysis (over the entire 1250 msec window of analysis), and a partial analysis limited to the first 650 msecs, in order to get rid of the size effect on the first factor, due to late ERP preponderant amplitude. As mentioned earlier, the analysis was focused on the exploration of the ERP components based on their latency, topography and polarity, rather than on the interpretation of the factors that would be more appealing to an applied mathematician. This interpretation of the ERPs is motivated by the issue of controlled versus automatic processes. The intersection of the clusters of AHC and of CA associates the robustness of the classification derived from AHC (which takes into account all the dimensions of the variable space), with the geometrical characteristics of the clustering derived from the projection of variables and items on the factorial planes (which takes at most three factorial dimensions simultaneously into account). Because of the preponderant contribution of the late components to the variance of the data, they are analyzed first. That does not mean that their functional significance is more important. But they certainly correspond to more complex processes. Positive and negative components will be analysed concomitantly. As a general approximation, negative components predominate at the beginning and the end of the window of analysis, and positive components in between.

A terminal negative cluster C1 during the last 300 msec (912-1250) of the window of analysis could be sorted into tonic C11 and phasic C12 subclusters. C11 included time-variables occurring at the beginning and end of the interval, but probably spanned the entire period, being masked in the middle by the phasic activity. The diffuse localization of this activity on both hemispheres, but more centroparietal than frontal, suggests a semiautomatic (or semicontrolled) process. Its temporal occurrence just before the forthcoming stimulus, suggests a terminal component similar to Contingent Negative Variation (CNV: Tecce, 1972; Walter, Cooper, Aldridge, McCallum, & Winter, 1964) which is related to the process of anticipation-preparation, rather than to the continued processing of the preceding stimulus. Finally, the associated experimental conditions characterizing these variables (non-target stimuli delivered in the second sequence, immediately after the first shift in S-R mapping) suggest these activities be interpreted as reflecting, during anticipation-preparation, an inhibition process of the S-R mapping previously learned and automatized during the preceding stimuli sequence. C12 time-amplitude variables corresponded to a shorter (960-1152 msec), dominantly frontotemporal activity, superimposed on the previous one. C12 points were associated to experimental conditions of frequent target stimuli delivered at the beginning of the second sequence, immediately after the first change in S-R mapping. The dominant frontal location of the activity combined with the targetness of the stimuli suggest a highly controlled process related to preparation or priming of a new response. Thus, a combined interpretation of the two clusters indicates a diffuse process of semi-automatic inhibition, overridden by a phasic more local, controlled activation. It is well known from Posner type paradigms (where a warning stimulus probabilistically predicts the handedness of a response to an imperative stimulus) that preparation, and in this particular case, motor preparation, involves a nonspecific plus a specific component. It is also now well established that terminal-CNV includes, beyond simple motor preparation, perceptual, and cognitive anticipation (Damen & Brunia, 1987). In particular terminal CNV is still present when the post imperative task has no motor component whatsoever (Ruchkin, Sutton, Mahaffey, & Glaser, 1986). The presence of inhibition-activation processes at this preparatory level of information processing, quite similar to those we encounter in the earlier ERP activities, suggests that the processes of psychomotor preparation are a kind of anticipated repetition or priming of the forthcoming cognitive and motor processes. As such, they are modulated like the actual (after stimulus delivery) cognitive and motor processes themselves, by the biases and automatisms induced by previous learning.

A C2 cluster was composed of negative as well as positive simultaneous activities at 784-880 msecs, frontally located for the negative components and central for the positive part. This bipolarity replicates the structure of the preceding C3 cluster corresponding to a P600 component. The related experimental condition for the negative part corresponds to the rare target (counted) stimuli in the first subsequence. In this experimental condition, an attended controlled process is called for, for at least three reasons: 1- first subsequence of the experiment corresponding to a novel experimental condition; 2- rare stimuli inducing a dishabituation and orienting response; 3- targetness of the stimulus, requiring the activation of a cognitive response. But in this case there is no factor of inhibition, since no previous S-R mapping has been learned. The positive counterpart of the activity is not so easy to interpret, but corresponds to equiprobable target stimuli, a condition combining a difficulty in the probability evaluation (equiprobable events) as well as a demanding controlled counting task. We do not dwell on the description of these components, because they range in a still largely uncharted temporal window of the ERP components.

With the C3 cluster we enter in the latency range of the positive complex, made of three components: P600, P3b and P3a. The C3 cluster corresponding to P600, was also made of negative and positive components. The negative anterior component extended between 592-672 msecs, with maximal activity on centro-frontal areas and some leaking into temporal cortical areas. The related experimental conditions were rare, target or non-target events of the first sequence, events of the third sequence (all targets) and non-target events of the second sequence, after the shift in S-R mapping. There is therefore a similarity with the functional significance of the C2 negative cluster. Yet, the functional scope of the C3 seems to be broader. It includes in fact most of the conditions presenting a *cognitive difficulty*: - rare events in the first sequence; - non-targets in the second sequence requiring an inhibition of previously learned S-R mapping; - events in the third sequence requiring a double count. It seems that earlier component generators were managing most of the difficult experimental conditions, whereas a more strict specialization took place for later activities. This cluster certainly does correspond to the negative component of the P600 or slow wave. Therefore, the functional significance of the P600 component can be transferred to this cluster, in particular its being related to events that need further processing due to perceptual or more cognitive difficulties or equivocations (Ruchkin & Sutton, 1983; Ruchkin, Sutton, Kietzman, & Silver, 1980a; Ruchkin, Sutton, & Stega, 1980b). As already mentioned, the difficulty of the task is exemplified here by the presence of rare events of the third sequence that requires the separate counting of both type of stimuli. The inhibitory activity implied by the experimental condition of non-target rare events in the second sequence (after shift in the S-R mapping), is certainly related to the inhibition of an actual previously learned cognitive response (and not to the inhibition of an outdated preparatory set as for the inhibitory activity encountered in the C1 cluster), because its latency lies in the time range of the cognitive counting response. The positive counterpart of the cluster (512-656 msecs) was made of activities maximal at the posterior cerebral pole and at centro-temporal areas. It corresponded very precisely and uniquely to experimental conditions of target equiprobable events in the second sequence, after the shift in S-R mapping. Therefore, these events repeatedly require an activation of a new response pattern combined with an inhibition of previously learned S-R relations, if inhibition of a no-go response makes sense. This appears to be an interesting contribution to the functional individuality of positive and negative components of P600.

The next positive cluster C4 was composed of two subclusters (307-380 and 400-480 msecs) both of them with temporo-parietal maxima that were related, because of this localization of their peak activities and of their latencies, to the P3b ERP component. This interpretation is also in agreement with the eliciting experimental conditions: equiprobable or rare, target or non-target events, whatever their sequence of occurrence. The important determining factor here is the *probability* of the events. If a control factor is involved, it has nothing to do with the inhibition-activation pattern, but corresponds to reactive attention shift triggered by a rare event. The robustness of the process, and its nonsensitivity to other factors such as variation in S-R mapping, or processing load seem to be the hallmark of a fully routinized process learned early during its ontogeny, and that does not need further learning to become fully operational. Yet, probability processing is not the only determining factor of P300 amplitude. P300 is elicited during the performance of a cognitive task in general, and more specific factors, controlled or not, such as stimulus meaning, targetness and information transmission, also affect its amplitude (Johnson, 1986).

The last cluster that was related to the positive complex, C5 (224-290 msecs) is notable because of its positive polarity and its frontocentral maximum. Most of the positive components are posterior or central or at best diffusely located. The P3a component is an exception, having a frontocentral maximum. That makes easy the identification of C5 with P3a, granted that the latency ranges are also congruent. P3a paired with the preceding negative component N2b is classically interpreted as a reflection of a cortical orienting reaction. In our results (Banquet & Grossberg, 1987; Banquet et al., 1992), P3a also reflects local probability or better temporal order of the events, while it does not reflect global prior probability of the sequence of events. These two interpretations are not contradictory, but the last one has a more cognitive connotation.

Immediately preceding the positive complex, a pair of overlapping negative components could be called, by symmetry, the negative complex. It was made of two subcomponents, N2a (Mismatch Negativity, MMN) and N2b. The corresponding negative clusters were also split into two subgroups: C61 between 176-208 msecs was located in an extended area of the cortex: fronto-centro-parietal. The correlated experimental conditions were rare, target or non-target events, whatever their sequence. The location and the latency of the components of this cluster corresponded to the mismatch negativity. This component reflects the process of automatic stimulus identification by stimulus-template comparison or match. This function is also congruent with the experimental conditions characterizing the cluster, since rare stimuli entail a mismatch condition that induces a maximum amplitude of the MMN. The twin cluster C62 corresponded to latencies 240-272 msecs. Its topography presented a centro-parietal maximum. These spatiotemporal characteristics correspond to N2b component (Näätänen & Gaillard, 1983; Renault & Lesèvre, 1978), which is thought to reflect an orienting process triggered by the previous mismatch, and predominate when the stimulus is attended, or at least salient enough to capture attention.

Finally, the last group of clusters corresponds to the earliest components. The earliest positive cluster C7 between 160-200 msecs presented a maximal activity at centro-parietal sites. It was associated to experimental conditions of rare target or non-target events, whatever their sequence. Because of its location, its eliciting experimental conditions similar to that of the P3b, and also its maximum activity on the same factorial axes as P3b, this early positivity is interpreted as an early reset, occurring in the "top-down" priming-expectancy condition, after learning. In a previous experiment (Banquet & Grossberg, 1987; Banquet et al., 1992) this component was found either at 120 msecs (after one session learning) or 160 msecs (after overlearning, in a second session). We related it to similar components found in comparable conditions but interpreted differently by Desmedt, Huy, and Bourguet (1983), or to the first component of the P160-N2b-P3a complex individualized by Näätänen and Picton (1986), as overriding the MMN, in an attended channel.

The earliest negative cluster, C8, was subdivided into two subgroups: C81 at 64-112 msecs, with a frontal maximum, was characterized by non-target equiprobable events in the second sequence, after alteration of the S-R mapping. These events are supposed to require a maximal inhibition of the previously learned S-R relation. C82 at 128-160 msecs, with posterior maxima, was related to target equiprobable events in the second sequence, after S-R mapping alteration. Therefore, these events require a combination of inhibition of the previously learned S-R relation, plus an activation of a new pattern of response. These early negative activities correspond, by their latency and localization to non-specific and specific components of the Processing Negativity (PN; Näätänen, Simpson, & Loveless, 1982; Näätänen, Gaillard, & Mantysalo, 1978) that occurs in attended channels, with an amplitude proportional to the degree of match between stimulus and template. It is a controlled, attended component. Because of that and of the temporal proximity with the preceding anticipation-preparation (CNV) activity, there is no surprise that the same determinants of controlled inhibition-activation are found for both types of activity.

5. DISCUSSION

Obviously, the type of analysis presented here must be complemented by a display of the rough electrical traces of the average activities corresponding to the different experimental conditions. Nevertheless, this analysis is interesting in its own right. Beyond allowing a better separation between negative and positive components, and a suppression of the overlap between components of the same polarity, it gives a different, more global perspective on the ERP data analysis, emphasizing the functional relations and continuity between successive components, at no detriment to the individuality and specificity of each of them. It must also be emphasized that all the individualized clusters, with the exception of one, were easily related to known preexisting ERP components, on the basis of three congruent criteria: latency, topography, and functional significance.

5.1. INHIBITION — ACTIVATION PATTERN

It has been possible to trace back three different phases of the cognitive process where a consistent pattern of attended control, made of inhibition-activation occurred. This inhibition-activation pattern was essentially invoked by the early events of the second sequence, immediately after the alteration (by instruction) of the S-R mapping. Each time that a simple *inhibition* was required, it corresponded to a frontal and negative activity, while an *activation* pattern corresponded to dominantly centro-posterior activity, positive for the middle latencies (P600) but negative at the very beginning and very end of the window (PN and CNV). Each of these similar control patterns can be interpreted differently, because of their different timing.

In their normal order of occurrence, and taking the stimulus delivery as time zero, this inhibition-activation pattern occurred first for the PN. In our interpretation of the PN, this pattern reflected the *actual* inhibition-activation required by the very early processing of a *primed* event. In a previous experiment, including a learning paradigm (Banquet & Grossberg, 1987; Banquet et al., 1992), it has been shown that this priming effect can occur as a result of probability context learning, and has two very different outcomes, according to the match or mismatch between the primed and the actually delivered stimulus. In this paradigm, the inclusion of changes in S-R mapping has endowed the attended-controlled process reflected by the PN with a particular significance of inhibition-activation.

The next inhibition-activation pattern can be traced back later at the level of the P600 or slow wave, another well documented stage of controlled processing. As earlier mentioned, this component was related to events that require, for perceptual or cognitive reasons, a supplement of processing to disambiguate an equivocation, or perform a difficult processing task (Ruchkin et al., 1980a, 1980b). P600 presents the peculiarity of being simultaneously bipolar, negative frontally, and positive posteriorly. Therefore we have the peculiarity of a frontal negative inhibition pattern, and of a parietal positive activation. In this experiment, there is no particular perceptual difficulty. There does exist a cognitive difficulty in the third session, when the subject has to keep a separate count of the two stimuli. This difficulty is reflected in the amplitude of the P600 component. But also, the plasticity of the system allows its adaptation to the specific requirements of the task. For this reason, the stimuli of the second sequence that require control because of the alteration in S-R mapping, also become correlated with P600. It is suggested that this inhibition-activation pattern, consecutive to S-R mapping alteration, corresponds to the casual *bottom-up* processing of an unprimed event that tends to elicit, at an automatic level, an outdated, previously automatized S-R pattern. Nevertheless, this pattern fails to match the currently active pattern in executive memory, thereby inducing an inhibition-suppression of the incorrect response. It must be noted that the next cluster, C2, is also bipolar and does not correspond to any yet chartered ERP component. Yet, C2 does not correspond to an inhibition-activation pattern but to the control required by learning the first S-R relation when the events are presented for the first time in the first subsequence. Is the difficulty related to the first confrontation with the cognitive task tackled by the same generators as the ones confronting the shift in S-R mapping, but at a later latency? Or does this component correspond to a new generator?

The last phase of occurrence of the inhibition-activation pattern is more of a surprise. Because of its timing, at the very end of the ISI window, it cannot reasonably be attributed to an ongoing processing of the preceding stimulus. The fixed ISI, this timing, the location and the negative polarity of the activity, all are in favor of an *anticipation-preparation* activity akin to a late CNV component. Thus, we are confronted to the interpretation of an inhibition-activation, even before the actual processing initiated by the stimulus delivery takes place. Thus the spurious activation of the outdated S-R relationship occurs even at the preparation stage of processing, and the subject can correct the irrelevant preparatory set, because even if he or she does not still know the targetness (count/no-count) of the forthcoming stimulus, he or she does know, by instruction recorded in *executive memory*, that a new S-R relationship obtains, in the second sequence.

It can be noted that these data support both the proponents of early selection and late selection theories, since controlled processes can be traced very early after stimulus delivery, or later at the level of P600. But it must be emphasized that the two types of attended control seem to be waged in totally different manners. Late control (P600) seems to result from casual bottom-up processing of a non-primed, non-expected stimulus that tends to elicit an irrelevant response, due to previous training. Conversely, early control, such as reflected by PN seems to result from top-down priming processes either endogenously triggered due to (probability or linguistic) context processing, or consecutive to an instruction to selectively attend a channel. Finally, the inhibition-activation pattern present in CNV-like activity affects a preparatory set, suggesting that spurious activation of a previously automatized but now outdated S-R pattern can also occur and be inhibited at a preparatory stage of the task. Whatever their time of occurrence, all these inhibition-activation patterns reflect what Schneider and Shiffrin (1976) and Shiffrin and Schneider (1977) call *negative transfer*. This negative transfer is attributed to learning of an automatic response which carries over its effects even after change of the S-R mapping rule.

5.2. ENDOGENOUS VERSUS REACTIVE CONTROL

Beyond this pattern of inhibition-activation, there is a stretch of activity, mostly between 150 and 570 msecs where the components are not sensitive to the inhibition-activation pattern. In this window are found MMN, N2b, P3a, P3b. This does not mean that all these components reflect automatic processing. MMN does, but N2b requires or calls the phasic orienting reaction. P300 is an ambiguous and complex wave, with more than one component. In this experiment, it demonstrates its capacity to monitor stimulus probability changes in the sequence. On the factorial planes, P300 is mostly characterized by rare events whatever the sequence, since rare events elicit the largest amplitudes. It could be hastily concluded that this component reflects automatic processing. Yet, in a remarkable series of dual task experiments, Donchin's coworkers have been able to establish P300 amplitude as a reliable index of controlled processing, and at the same time to prove the relevance of the *multiple resource* theory (Donchin et al., 1984; Wickens, 1984). If, and only if, a primary and a secondary task draw on the same resource pool, fewer resources are allocated to the secondary task (as evidenced by a decrease of the corresponding P300 amplitude) as the difficulty of the primary task increases, requiring additional resources to keep a constant performance. Whenever the measure of the P300 to the primary task is possible, its amplitude is then shown to increase. Are these results contradictory with the results of this study? It is rather plausible that there are different modalities of controlled processes, corresponding to different modalities of attention. The control process witnessed in the inhibition-activation pattern is endogenously generated as result of a mismatch between a automatically generated outdated response pattern that is not congruent with the new relevant S-R mapping. The control process in the dual task experiments is reminiscent of a focal attention triggered by an external stimulus, either the continuously tracked target of the primary task or the discrete stimuli of the secondary task. In the implicit task of our experiment P300 elicitation by rare events seems to be dependent on an *orienting reaction* triggered by the mismatch between stimulus and template.

It must be emphasized that this paradigm was mostly developed to demonstrate a high level attended control process and the transition from automatic to control processing. Indeed, the control concerned the final outcome of the task, here a cognitive response. It can be argued that the cortical orienting reaction, as reflected by the N2b component corresponds also to the instantiation of some kind of control, due to the violation of an expectancy. From what has been previously mentioned, it can be inferred that these two types of control are different. The timing of the corresponding components and their topography differ. The N2b is dominantly central, the inhibition components are mostly frontal, and the activation activities are mostly posterior. There is an obvious difference in antecedents, N2b is triggered by an automatic mismatch process, while the activation-inhibition pattern is initiated either voluntarily or by a mismatch between an outdated and automatically activated S-R pattern and a controlled, relevant S-R pattern. It has been seen in the results, how this N2b is part of a more complex pattern, including P160 (interpreted as a reset component, similar to P3b), and P3a, with orienting and possibly temporal context updating functions. But our tools of investigation are not, as yet, sophisticated enough to eliminate any collusion between the two types of attended processing. The sole fact that a dominantly right hemispheric frontal generator has been found for MMN (Giard, Perrin, Pernier, & Peronnet, 1989) must inspire caution. Indeed, the frontal lobes are supposed to be the location of voluntary executive control. And MMN is the prototypic component reflecting automatic processes. This would make of the *cortical orienting reaction*, triggered by MMN and reflected by the consecutive N2b component, an hybrid process bridging the gap between automatic and controlled processing modes. Besides this classical cortical orienting response there is an even more specific pattern of attention-catching, when the event delivered is not only rare, but entirely new in the midst of an ongoing sequence. Then a particular frontal positive wave is elicited, that tends to become more posterior with repetition of the event (Courchesne, 1978; Courchesne, Hillyard, & Galambos, 1975).

The transition from more or less control to full automatization of a task is not analysed by this paradigm. This problem has been documented in different experiments. Automatization is at the phenomenological level reflected in particular by a floor effect on the behavioral response such as RT. In a discrimination task embedded in a learning paradigm (Banquet & Grossberg, 1987; Banquet et al., 1987, 1992), this automatization criterion at the behavioral level was associated with an opposite evolution for the negative (MMN) and positive (P300 complex) ERPs. A pattern of *habituation* obtains for the negative component, with decrease in baseline level and amplitude of the negative component. Also the amplitude difference between response to match and mismatch decreases. Positive components follow an inverse, or better mixed pattern. Their baseline amplitude increases, while their amplitude difference in response to rare and frequent events decreases. More importantly, significant spatial variations tend to line up both frontal and parietal components on a common central location, suggesting migration of the corresponding generators.

5.3. AUTOMATICITY, CONTROL AND UNDERLYING STRUCTURES

The data interpreted here were not analyzed in the perspective of differentiating right and left hemisphere functions, even though the relevant information is present in the data, due to the transverse montage of electrodes. But the theory that interprets the right hemisphere as related to the processing of novel information and the left hemisphere as more selectively concerned with the processing of routinized information (Goldberg & Costa, 1981) has strong neuropsychological and neurochemical foundations and seems a promising orientation to investigate. This interpretation of the hemispheric functions is in any case relevant to the automatic versus controlled dilemma. Relating the two problems could provide sound structural and anatomical basis to a question that, until now, has resorted largely, if not uniquely, to functional psychophysiology. This supposed *transversal gradient* of control (between right and left hemisphere) must be compared to the more classical anterior-posterior *polar gradient* that makes the frontal lobe the locus of executive control (Baddeley, 1986; Levine, 1986). This last hypothesis is largely supported by these results whereby most of the controlled ERPs have a nonspecific frontal component, in this case mostly related to inhibition. Conversely, when activation is required by the experimental condition, the maximal activity becomes posterior. Making the right hemisphere the support of *reactive control*, in response to an external event, and the frontal pole the support of a *voluntarily waged* control would reconcile the two hypotheses.

Some theories relate right hemisphere dysfunction to depression and left hemisphere dysfunction to schizophrenia. The fact that a voluntary control, under the form of inhibition with or without activation, interfered at three different stages with the ongoing processing, emphasizes how much either an overbearing (schizophrenia) or a weak (depression) control could hinder a normal flow of cognitive processes.

5.4. AUTOMATICITY, CONTROL AND THEORIES IN NEUROSCIENCE

The notions of automaticity and control evoke resonances with different neuroscience theories or paradigms.

Let us set apart the two dominant paradigms, Connectionism and Artificial Intelligence, that purport to model brain-mind activity and put different emphasis on automatic and controlled processes. In a more specific way, this automatic-controlled distinction is relevant to the stability-plasticity dilemma that confronts the adaptive-brain (Grossberg, 1975, 1976a, 1976b, 1978, 1980, 1982a, 1982b). The automatic mode of functioning is an indication that some stability has been reached by practice or learning. Conversely, attentional control triggered by orienting to unexpected or novel stimuli opens the way to plasticity, that is, memory reset and incorporation of new information into already existing or newly created codes. It can certainly be argued that plasticity does not need attended control. Furthermore, voluntary control does not need novelty and can be "endogenously" instantiated. In the same theoretical framework, some of the characteristics of the automatic-controlled distinction are conveyed by the notions of bottom-up and top-down processes, even though the overlap between the two types of concepts is only partial (Banquet et al., 1990).

Most modern theories of long-term memory (LTM), on the basis of neuropsychological research, and with different terminologies, make a clear distinction between *declarative*, explicit processes (knowing what) and *procedural*, implicit operations (knowing how). But most of the time no clear stance is taken on the existence of unique or dual underlying structures. Is it legitimate to compare LTM registers or structures such as declarative and procedural memory and automatic-controlled working memory (WM) modes? The answer is yes in so far as LTM and WM modes are functionally related, that is, most of the automatic processing is recorded into procedural memory, while most of the attended controlled processing is stored in explicit memory. But there is crosstalk or leakage between the two stores. Some of the previously most controlled processing (e.g., motor learning) may at some point be recorded in and recalled from procedural memory, and conversely some of the most automatized processing can, for some (e.g., contextual) reasons, be brought under explicit control. A partial answer to the question on the unity or duality of structures underlying explicit and implicit memory and automatic versus controlled processing modes could come from the previously mentioned developments in the debate on interhemispheric functional specialization. A new interpretation of an important part of the results on interhemispheric functional differences suggests that the right hemisphere is bound to the processing of novel, attention calling information, while the left hemisphere is devoted to routinized processing. The left hemisphere would be dedicated to using multiple, fully developed, and domain-specific descriptive systems. Conversely, the right hemisphere would be more adapted to processing new information that has no straightforward coding in the preexisting descriptive systems. Integration within modality specific areas would be emphasized in the left hemisphere. Intermodal integration by associative areas would rather take place in the right hemisphere (Goldberg & Costa, 1981).

Abrupt shifts or progressive alterations in operating mode appear to be essential to the normal functioning of the brain engaged in cognitive processes. Indeed, part of the cognitive deficits encountered in major mental perturbations seem to be rooted in the incapacity of the mind to readily alternate its operating modes. A possible defect in task automatization is documented in schizophrenia as an abnormally lasting dominance of frontal lobe activity during practice of a motor task (Günther, Breitling, Banquet, Marcie, & Rondot, 1985). Similar imbalance in favor of the voluntary controlled mode of functioning has been found in anhedonic subjects (Pierson, Ragot, Ripoche, & Lesèvre, 1987). Depressed subjects not only present difficulty at task automatization. Moreover, they seem to present a perturbation of the transfer of automatically collected information to an attended controlled processor. This, in turn, induces a disruption of the top-down processes of expectancy-priming, anticipation, and psychomotor preparation. Some of these operations lie at the very base of *inference* which is the foundation of the highest and most humane cognition (Banquet et al., 1992). Nonetheless, these patients present little deficit in general or specific preparation when the preparatory set is induced by an external warning stimulus (Smith, 1991).

6. CONCLUSION

This analysis of controlled and automatic modes of processing is relevant to both normal and pathological functions of the brain. In a normal subject, automatization of a process, whenever possible, is the end result of learning. This functioning mode addresses the stable side of the stability-plasticity dilemma (Grossberg, 1976a, 1976b, 1980, 1982a, 1982b). It affords the brain to deal with routine situations at little expense of processing resources. Yet, without the ability of automatic attention switching or orienting, the panoply of processing tools would be incomplete. It would be difficult to address unexpected or novel situations. This functioning mode concerns the plastic side of the dilemma. It allows the brain, possibly at the expense of larger processing resources, to cope with the continuous change and evolution of the environment. At the highest step of evolution, the attended control mode of processing can even become waged independently of any external event. An internal voluntary decision can engage the highest functioning mode at will. In this way the individual is given a lever to interact with his or her own evolution.

All the cognitive studies of psychopathological processes indicate that most of the basic perceptual, motor, and even cognitive processes are robust. They require anatomical or serious functional lesions to be disrupted. Conversely, high-level sophisticated processes, such as inference, which do not necessarily hinder the performance of classical psychological or other tests of cognitive processing, seem to be affected. The subtle dynamics at the basis of the transitions between attended control and automaticity, in either direction, seem to pertain to these easily disrupted processes.

Two results seem to be particular to this research: There are different types of control processes, somehow related to the different varieties of attention. These different types of control are reflected by different components of the ERPs strongly suggesting different generators. Conversely, the same pattern of control, here the inhibition-activation pattern, if it is sufficiently salient because of the requirements of the task, can be grafted on different components occurring at different steps of the cognitive process. Furthermore, these results suggest that the strict separation between automaticity and control is properly impossible at the level of a task. Even at the level of the ERP components, it is not an easy task. Besides the very early precortical components, not analyzed here, which seem to be dominantly automatic (but not so obviously inaccessible to some type of controlled modulation), the only ERP component fully meeting the criteria of automaticity is so far the MMN. Most of the others require some type of control to be elicited or at best reflect a mixture of controlled and automatic processes.

ACKNOWLEDGMENTS

We gratefully acknowledge the comments of S. Grossberg, D. Levine, and D. Bullock. This work was supported in part by a NATO grant and DGA grant # 9114470/A000/DRET/DS/SR to J. P. Banquet and by INSERM.

REFERENCES

Baddeley, A. D. (1986). *Working Memory*. Oxford: Oxford University Press.

Banquet, J. P. (1981). Organisation spatio-temporelle de l'EEG des stades de sommeil, *Electroencéphalographie et Neurophysiologie Clinique* 11, 75-81.

Banquet, J. P. & Grossberg, S. (1987). Probing cognitive processes through the structure of event-related potentials during learning: an experimental and theoretical analysis. *Applied Optics* 26, 4931-4946.

Banquet, J. P., Günther, W., & Smith, M. J. (1987). Probability processing in depressed patients. In R. Johnson, Jr., R. Parasuraman and J. W. Rohrbaugh (Eds.), *Current Trends in*

Event-Related Potential Research. Electroencéphalographie et Neurophysiologie Clinique Supplement 40, 645-650.

Banquet, J. P., Smith, M. J., & Günther, W. (1992). Top-down processes, attention, and motivation in cognitive tasks. In D. S. Levine & S. J. Leven (Eds.), *Motivation, Emotion, and Goal Direction in Neural Networks* (pp. 169-208). Hillsdale, NJ: Lawrence Erlbaum Associates.

Banquet, J. P., Smith, M. J., & Renault, B. (1990). Bottom-up versus top-down: An alternative to the automatic-attended dilemma? *The Behavioral and Brain Sciences* 13, 241-248.

Benzécri, J. P. (1973). *L'Analyse des Données*, Vol. 2. Paris: Dunod.

Courchesne, E. (1978). Changes in P3 waves with event repetition: Long-term effects on scalp distribution and amplitude. *Electroencéphalographie et Neurophysiologie Clinique* 45, 754-766.

Courchesne, E., Hillyard, S. A., & Galambos, R. (1975). Stimulus novelty, task relevance, and the visual evoked potential in man. *Electroencéphalographie et Neurophysiologie Clinique* 39, 131-143.

Damen, E. P. J., & Brunia, C. H. M. (1987). Changes in heart rate and slow brain potentials related to motor preparation and stimulus anticipation in a time estimation task. *Psychophysiology* 24, 700-713.

Desmedt, J. E., Huy, N. T., & Bourguet, M. (1983). The cognitive P40, N60, and P100 components of somato-sensory evoked potentials and the earliest electrical signs of sensory processing in man. *Electroencephalography and Clinical Neurophysiology* 56, 272-285.

Donchin, E., Heffley, E., Hillyard, S., Loveless, N. E., Maltzman, C., Ökman, A., Rösler, F., Ruchkin, D., & Siddle, D. (1984). The orienting reflex and P300. In R. Karrer, J. Cohen, & P. Tueting (Eds.), *Brain and Information: Event-Related Potentials*. New York: New York Academy of Sciences 425, 39-57.

Donchin, E., Ritter, W., & McCallum, W. C. (1978). Cognitive psychophysiology: the endogenous components of the ERPs. In E. Callaway, P. Tueting, and S. Koslov (Eds.), *Event-Related Brain Potentials in Man* (pp. 349-441). New York: Academic Press.

Duncan-Johnson, C. C., & Donchin, E. (1977). On quantifying surprise: the variation in event-related potentials with subjective probability. *Psychophysiology* 14, 456-467.

Giard, M. H., Perrin, F., Pernier, J., & Peronnet, F. (1988). Several attention-related waveforms in auditory areas: A topographic study. *Electroencephalography and Clinical Neurophysiology* 69, 371-384.

Goldberg, E., & Costa, L. D. (1981). Hemisphere differences in the acquisition and use of descriptive systems. *Brain and Language* 14, 144-173.

Greene, R. L. (1984). Incidental learning of event frequency. *Memory and Cognition* 12, 90-95.

Grossberg, S. (1973). Contour enhancement, short term memory, and constancies in reverberating neural networks. *Studies in Applied Mathematics* 52, 213-257.

Grossberg, S. (1975). A neural model of attention, reinforcement and discrimination learning. *International Review of Neurobiology* 18, 263-327.

Grossberg, S. (1976a). Adaptive pattern classification and universal recoding. I: Parallel development and coding of neural feature detectors. *Biological Cybernetics* 23, 121-134.

Grossberg, S. (1976b). Adaptive pattern classification and universal recoding. II: Feedback, expectation, olfaction and illusion. *Biological Cybernetics* 23, 187-202.

Grossberg, S. (1978). A theory of human memory: Self-organization and performance of sensory-motor codes, maps, and plans. In R. Rosen & F. Snell (Eds.), *Progress in Theoretical Biology* (Vol. V, pp. 233-374). New York: Academic Press.

Grossberg, S. (1980). How does a brain build a cognitive code? *Psychological Review* 87, 1-51.

Grossberg, S. (1982a). *Studies of Mind and Brain: Neural principles of learning, perception, development, cognition, and motor control.* Dordrecht: Reidel.

Grossberg, S. (1982b). Processing of expected and unexpected events during conditioning and attention: A psychophysiological theory. *Psychological Review* 89, 529-572.

Grossberg, S. (1984). Some psychological and pharmacological correlates of a developmental, cognitive and motivational theory. In R. Karrer, J. Cohen, & P. Tueting (Eds.), *Brain and Information: Event-Related Potentials.* New York: New York Academy of Sciences.

Günther, W., Breitling, D., Banquet, J. P., Marcie, P., & Rondot, P. (1985). EEG mapping of left hemisphere dysfunction during motor performance in schizophrenia. *Biological Psychiatry* 13, 249-262.

Hasher, I. & Zacks, J. T. (1979). Automatic and effortful processes in memory. *Journal of Experimental Psychology: General* 108, 356-388.

Hill, M. O. (1974). Correspondence analysis: a neglected multivariate method. *Applied Statistics* 23, 340-354.

Hoffman, J. E. (1990). Event-related potentials and automatic and controlled processes. In J. Rohrbaugh, R. Parasuraman & R. Johnson, Jr. (Eds.), *Event-Related Brain Potentials, Basic Issues and Applications* (pp. 145-157). New York: Oxford University Press.

Johnson, R., Jr., & Donchin, E. (1982). Sequential expectancies and decision making in a changing environment: an electrophysiological approach. *Psychophysiology* 19, 183-199.

Johnson, R., Jr. (1986). Triarchic model of P300 amplitude. *Psychophysiology* 23, 367-384.

Johnson, R., Jr. (1988). The amplitude of the P300 component of the event-related potentials: Review and Synthesis. In P. K. Ackles, J. H. Jennings & M. G. H. Coles (Eds), *Advances in Psychophysiology*, 1988, Vol. III. Greenwich, CT: JAI Press.

Jonides, J., Naveh-Benjamin, M., & Palmer, J. (1985). Assessing automaticity. *Acta Psychologica* 60, 157-171.

Kutas, M., McCarthy, G., & Donchin, E. (1977). Augmenting mental chronometry: the P300 as a measure of stimulus evaluation time. *Science* 197, 792-795.

Lebart, I., & Fénelon, J. P. (1973). *Statistique et Informatique Appliquées.* Paris: Dunod.

Levine, D. S. (1986). A neural network theory of frontal lobe function. *Program of the Eighth Annual Conference of the Cognitive Science Society* (pp. 716-727). Hillsdale, NJ: Lawrence Erlbaum Associates.

Näätänen, R., & Gaillard, A. W. (1983). The orienting reflex and the N2 deflection of the ERPs, In A. W. Gaillard & W. Ritter (Eds.), *Tutorials in Event-Related Potential Research: Endogenous Components* (pp. 119-142). Amsterdam: North-Holland.

Näätänen, R., Gaillard, A. W., & Mantysalo, S. (1978). Early selective attention effect on evoked potentials reinterpreted. *Acta Psychologica* 42, 313-329.

Näätänen, R., & Picton, T. W. (1986). N2 and automatic versus controlled processes, In W. C. McCallum, R. Zappoli, & F. Denoth (Eds.), *Cerebral Psychophysiology: Studies in Event-Related Potentials*. EEG supplement 38. Amsterdam: Elsevier, pp. 169-186.

Näätänen, R., Simpson, M., & Loveless, N. E. (1982). Stimulus deviance and evoked potentials. *Biological Psychology* 14, 53-98.

Naveh-Benjamin, M., & Jonides, J. (1986). On the automaticity of frequency coding: Effects of competing task load, encoding strategy, and intention. *Journal of experimental Psychology: Learning, Memory, and Cognition* 12, 378-386.

Pierson, A., Ragot, R., Ripoche, A., & Lesèvre, N. (1987). Electrophysiological changes elicited by auditory stimuli given a positive or negative value: a study comparing anhedonic with hedonic subjects. *International Journal of Physiology* 5, 107-123.

Renault, B., & Lesèvre, N. (1978). Topographical study of the emitted potential obtained after the omission of an expected visual stimulus. In D. Otto (Ed.), *Multidisciplinary Perspectives in Event-Related Brain Potential Research* (pp. 202-208). Washington, DC: U. S. Government Printing Office.

Ruchkin, D. S., & Sutton, S. (1983). Positive slow wave and P300: Association and dissociation. In A. W. Gaillard & W. Ritter (Eds.), *Tutorials in ERP Research-Endogenous Components* (pp. 233-250). Amsterdam: North-Holland.

Ruchkin, D. S., Sutton, S., Kietzman, M. L., & Silver, K. (1980a). Slow wave and P300 in signal detection. *Electroencephalography and Clinical Neurophysiology* 50, 35-47.

Ruchkin, D. S., Sutton, S., Mahaffey, D., & Glaser, J. (1986). Terminal CNV in the absence of a motor response. *Electroencephalography and Clinical Neurophysiology* 63, 445-463.

Ruchkin, D. S., Sutton, S., & Stega, M. (1980b). Emitted P300 and slow wave event-related potentials in guessing and detection tasks. *Electroencephalography and Clinical Neurophysiology* 49, 1-14.

Schneider, W., & Shiffrin, R. M. (1976). In D. LaBerge & S. J. Samuels (Eds.), *Basic Processes in Reading: Perception and Comprehension*. Hillsdale, NJ: Lawrence Erlbaum Associates.

Shiffrin, R. M. (1988). Attention. In R. C. Atkinson, R. J. Herrnstein, G. Lindzey, & R. D. Luce, (Eds.). *Stevens' Handbook of Experimental Psychology* (2nd Ed.) New York, Wiley.

Shiffrin, R. M., & Schneider, W. (1977). Controlled and automatic human information processing: II. Perceptual learning, automatic attending, and a general theory. *Psychological Review* 84, 127-190.

Smith, M. J. (1991). Pathophysiologie cognitive du ralentissement dépressif: description clinique, analyse, mesure. Unpublished doctoral dissertation, Université Pierre et Marie Curie, Paris.

Sutton, S., Braren, M., Zubin, J., & John, E. R. (1965). Evoked potentials correlates of stimulus uncertainty. *Science* 15, 1187-1188.

Tecce, J. J. (1972). Contingent negative variation (CNV) and psychological processes in man, *Psychological Bulletin* 77, 73-108.

Walter, W. G., Cooper, R., Aldridge, V. J., McCallum, W. C., & Winter, A. (1964). Contingent negative variation: An electric sign of sensory-motor association of expectancy in the human brain. *Nature* **203**, 380-384.

Wickens, C. D. (1984). Processing resources in attention. In R. Parasuraman & D. R. Davies (Eds.), *Varieties of Attention* (pp. 63-102). New York: Academic Press.

Author Index

(Italics denote pages on which complete references appear)

Subject Index